No. 10

DOWNING STREET

No. 10

DOWNING STREET

A House in History

R. J. Minney

WITH ILLUSTRATIONS

LITTLE, BROWN AND COMPANY *Boston Toronto*

For
ARTHUR BRYANT

Preface

THIS is the history of a house. No. 10 Downing Street, though few are aware of it, consists in fact of three houses that were joined together nearly two and a half centuries ago. The oldest of these houses, of which the Cabinet room forms a part, is three centuries old. Before it took its present form King Charles the First lived in it as a child, then his sister Elizabeth, grandmother of George the First, and later on, Cromwell and his wife. It was reconstructed for Charles the Second's illegitimate daughter, the Countess of Lichfield, before it was joined with the other two houses, both on Downing Street, for Sir Robert Walpole, the first Prime Minister in Britain, in 1735. It was No. 5 at first and was changed to No. 10 just over a century ago, but I have kept throughout to the present numbering of the houses in order to be consistent. I have also, for the same reason, viewed the floors of No. 10 as they appear from Downing Street; it should be remembered, however, that the ground floor at that end is the first floor on the garden side, because of the slope of the ground.

I have tried to tell here of its construction by Sir George Downing, of its many vicissitudes through the years, of the people who lived in it – not all of them were Prime Ministers – of the deliberations and decisions, some of them magnificently impressive, others ill-judged and obstinate, which affected the destiny of Great Britain, leading to the acquisition of a vast Empire, the loss of America, the building up of another and vaster Empire and the emergence of the Commonwealth. There has been repeated rioting in the street, the windows of the house have been smashed, Prime Ministers have been set upon by the mob on their way to Parliament and suffragettes have chained themselves to the railings at No. 10.

The book is not, however, a history of England, but the trend of events is traced so that the narrative may the more easily be followed and one may be able to assess how much of the country's remarkable history still lurks in every shadow.

It may help readers not familiar with British Parliamentary conventions to know that the sons of peers, even when they bear a courtesy title, are in fact commoners and are eligible for election to the House of Commons until their succession. Scottish peers, not being peers of the United Kingdom of Great Britain, are without seats in the Upper House, but select sixteen of their number to represent them there. Irish peers used also to elect representatives to the Lords; all others were and still are eligible for election to the House of Commons, whereas Scottish peers are not.

Each Minister has at least four secretaries – a Parliamentary Secretary, who can be a Member of either House and is a junior Minister and the Minister's deputy in office; a Personal Parliamentary Secretary, who is a Member of Parliament; a Permanent Secretary, who is a member of the Civil Service in the department of State under the control of the Minister; and one or more personal secretaries, the chief of whom is also a Civil Servant, the others being in the personal employ of the Minister.

It would have been impossible to write this book without the help of a great many people. Chief of these have been the officials of the Ministry of Works responsible for the care of No. 10 Downing Street, of whom I must name Mr. John Charlton, Inspector of Ancient Monuments in London, Mr. A. E. Coules and Mr. L. W. Johnson. With the consent of the Prime Minister, I was allowed to look over the house before the recent very elaborate reconstruction was begun; and on its completion I was most generously helped by Mr. Raymond Erith, the architect responsible, who personally took me round to see the changes that had to be made. The Public Record Office has placed at my disposal the many documents relating to the house, telling of the alterations and repairs it underwent through the centuries.

I must also express my deepest gratitude to those who have lived in the house and have given unsparingly of their time to tell of their own experiences in it, supplying photographs and plans to guide and assist me. These cover the years from the time when Asquith became Prime Minister in 1908 up to the present day: they include Lady Violet Bonham Carter and her brother the Hon. Anthony Asquith; Lady Megan Lloyd George and her sister Lady Olwen Carey Evans; Bonar Law's son Lord Coleraine and his two daughters Lady Sykes and Lady Archibald; Ramsay MacDonald's daughter Mrs. Ishbel Peterkin; Mrs Neville Chamberlain and Miss Marjorie Leaf, who was her secretary; Mrs. Kathleen Hill, Sir Winston Churchill's personal secretary, and Mrs. G. E. Landemare, Lady Churchill's cook; Earl Attlee; the Countess of Avon; Lady Dorothy Macmillan; and Mr. J. R. Colville, who served as secretary to three Prime Ministers – Mr. Neville Chamberlain, Sir Winston Churchill and Lord Attlee. In addition I have been greatly helped by Miss M. E. Stenhouse and Miss Gwen Davies, both of whom have been associated with the house from 1919 until, in the former's case, her retirement in 1960.

Photographs and plans of No. 10 Downing Street were very kindly supplied by the Ministry of Works, the Public Record Office and the London County Council. For other photographs I have to thank Viscount Astor, Mrs. Ishbel Peterkin and the British Museum; for cartoons reproduced here, Sir David Low, Vicky, Mrs. Strube; and others credited in the List of Illustrations.

R. J. M.

CONTENTS

1	Before Downing Street	1
2	George Downing	7
3	Downing Street	18
4	Number 10	23
5	Early Residents	30
6	Sir Robert Walpole	36
7	Walpole at No. 10	49
8	His Immediate Successors	61
9	Sir Francis Dashwood	66
10	Revolt of the American Colonies	72
11	Lord North and the War of Independence	88
12	The Younger Pitt	113
13	The Napoleonic War	130
14	The Doctor Moves in . . .	140
15	The Return of Pitt	147
16	His Two Unworthy Successors	156
17	Spencer Perceval	163
18	The Unremembered Chancellor	172
19	'Prosperity Robinson'	180
20	Canning's Short Reign	186
21	Wellington Moves in	194
22	Grey and the Reform Bill	214
23	Melbourne, then Peel	233

CONTENTS

24	Used only for Offices	251
25	Palmerston's Finest Hours	258
26	Disraeli and Gladstone	266
27	'Jingoism'	279
28	Gladstone's Unhappy Return	290
29	The Home Rule Battle	301
30	W. H. Smith Moves in	308
31	The Boer War	319
32	The Great Liberal Years	328
33	Battle with the Lords	335
34	The Prime Minister's Lodgings	343
35	Lloyd George and the First World War	352
36	The Fall of Lloyd George	360
37	First Labour Government	365
38	The Return of Baldwin	378
39	The National Government	385
40	Baldwin and the Abdication	392
41	Second World War and Churchill	398
42	Attlee's Six Years	413
43	Eden and Suez	419
44	The New No. 10	429
	Prime Ministers and Others who have Lived at No. 10	441
	Bibliography and Sources	445
	Index	453

ILLUSTRATIONS

following page

Sir Robert Walpole, the first Prime Minister
(*RTHPL**)   62

Maria Skerrett, Walpole's mistress and later his
second wife (*By courtesy of the Marquess of Cholmondeley*)   62

William Pitt, first Earl of Chatham (*RTHPL*)   62

Lord North (*RTHPL*)   62

The Younger Pitt (*RTHPL*)   62

Lady Hester Stanhope, niece of the younger Pitt
(*RTHPL*)   62

The Duke of Wellington (*RTHPL*)   142

Benjamin Disraeli, first Earl of Beaconsfield
(*RTHPL*)   142

William Ewart Gladstone (*RTHPL*)   142

Margot Asquith, later the Countess of Oxford and
Asquith (*RTHPL*)   174

David Lloyd George with Clemenceau and President Wilson (*RTHPL*)   174

Bonar Law with Poincaré, Mussolini, and M.
Theunis (*Central Press Photos Ltd.*)   174

* *RTHPL – Radio Times Hulton Picture Library.*
*Crown Copyright material is reproduced by permission of the Controller, H.M. Stationery
Office.*

Ramsay MacDonald with his daughter Ishbel, his
son Malcolm and younger daughter Joan (*RTHPL*)   174

Sir Winston Churchill (*Toni Frissell*)   174

Plan of the older section of No. 10 Downing Street,
designed by Sir Christopher Wren in 1677 (*Crown
Copyright*)   206

Sir Christopher Wren's note on the plan of 10
Downing Street (*Crown Copyright*)   206

Ground plan of 10 Downing Street as reconstructed
by William Kent in 1735 (*Crown Copyright*)   206

The 'house at the back' *circa* 1677 (*By kind
permission of Viscount Astor*)   238

No. 10 Downing Street from St. James's Park in
1827 (*London County Council*)   238

The Downing Street cul-de-sac in 1827 (*Crown
Copyright*)   238

The famous front door of No. 10 Downing Street
(*Crown Copyright*)   238

The entrance hall of No. 10 (*Crown Copyright*)   238

The main stone staircase (*Crown Copyright*)   270

The ante-room, just outside the Cabinet Room
(*Crown Copyright*)   270

The Cabinet Room (*Crown Copyright*)   270

The Prime Minister's section of the Cabinet table
(*Crown Copyright*)   270

The first of a row of three drawing-rooms on the
first floor (*By courtesy of Mrs Ishbel Peterkin*)   270

The middle drawing-room (*Crown Copyright*)   270

The large State Drawing Room (*Crown Copyright*)   270

Soane's State Dining Room (*Crown Copyright*)   270

The walled garden of No. 10 Downing Street
(*Crown Copyright*)   302

Cartoon of John Wilkes by Hogarth   302

Gillray's cartoon 'Britannia between Death and the
Doctors'   382

John Doyle's cartoon 'Reading The Times'   382

A cartoon from *The Gladstone ABC* (*RTHPL*)   382

Sir David Low's cartoon 'The Wolf at the Door'
(*London Express News and Feature Services*)   382

Strube's cartoon 'The Old Champ' (*London Express News and Feature Services*)   382

Vicky's cartoon 'Labour troubles!' (*London Express News and Feature Services*)   382

MAPS AND PLANS

page

Before Downing Street; Westminster in 1658 (*London Topographical Society and the Guildhall Library*)   xx

Westminster in 1955 (*Crown Copyright: Reproduced by permission of the Director-General, Ordnance Survey*)   435

No. 10 Downing Street: Floor plans before the 1960 reconstruction (*Crown Copyright: Reproduced by permission of the Controller, H.M. Stationery Office*)

Ground Floor, Nos. 10, 11 and 12   438

First Floor, Nos. 10, 11 and 12   439

Second Floor, Nos. 10 and 11   440

No. 10
DOWNING STREET

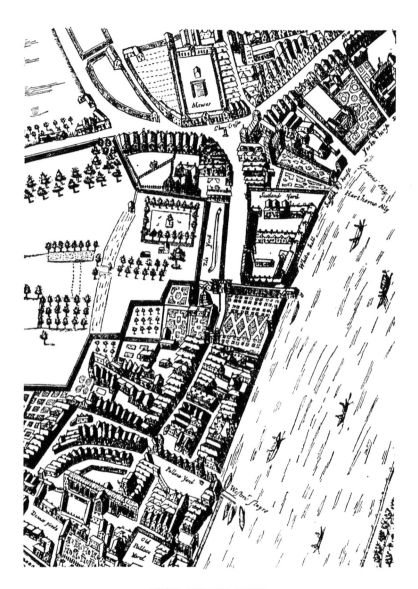

BEFORE DOWNING STREET

The map, by William Faithorne, taken from his *An Exact Delineation of the Cities of London and Westminster and the Suburbs* of 1658, shows Whitehall, as it was at that time, running from Charing Cross (which stood where the statue of Charles the First is now) to the Holbein Gate alongside the Tilt Yard, now the Horse Guards. The narrow street from the Holbein Gate to the other, New Gate, was called 'le Kingstreete'. By the New Gate, running to the west, Downing Street was built. The old Cockpit is the octagonal building by the Holbein Gate. Westminster Abbey is easily identifiable to the left of Old Palace Yard.

(*See also page 435.*)

CHAPTER 1
Before Downing Street

It would be best to begin by trying to visualize what the setting was like before Downing built his street. Was there an expanse of open country, or were there streets and houses between Charing Cross and Westminster?

There is no need to go back farther than the sixteenth century. A highway, called The Street, and sometimes written 'le Kingstreete', about a third the present width of Whitehall, ran along what is now the middle of that roadway. There were houses on both sides.

To the east, the side nearer the river, there was the large and substantial York Place, the London residence of the Archbishop of York, with a number of smaller houses behind and beside it for his retinue and his household staff, as well as a chapel, a counting house, palatial accommodation for the King and Queen when they came to stay, and vast gardens sweeping down to the river.

From here, along the river front, stretched the town houses of the nobility and of certain bishops, forming a continuous line of imposing town mansions as far as St. Paul's and the City.

On the main highway linking Charing Cross with Westminster stood the massive gateway of York Place. When Wolsey was elevated to the archbishopric of York, he moved into this residence and began at once to enlarge and extend it. He absorbed the cottages and gardens and tenements on both flanks, taking in, on the north, land that once belonged to the Kings of Scotland, known then, as now, as Scotland Yard. He redecorated and embellished the main residence and built a great new hall where were held banquets 'set with masks and mummeries',[5]* to which the young King Henry the Eighth came by water from his Palace at Greenwich, alighting, at times masked, at the Privy Steps, together with other masked men and women who gave themselves out to be strangers coming 'as ambassadors from some foreign prince', a scene which has been vividly depicted by Shakespeare in *Henry VIII*.

On the other, or Downing Street side of the highway, the dwellings were for the most part humble cottages with small gardens opening on to narrow lanes, and scattered groups of tenements separated from each other by alleys. There was also a large manor house called the Mote, which stood in sixty acres of arable and pasture land. Most of the land on this side belonged to Westminster Abbey, or more correctly to the Abbey of St. Peter's, Westminster, which was at one time a collegiate monastery; some of the land was owned by Eton College, part no doubt of the endowment assigned when Henry the Sixth established the college for poor scholars in 1445. Near to the Mote, whose exact position has not been determined, was a large brewhouse called the Axe, on the site of and beside which Downing Street was eventually built. The land on which this brewhouse stood had once belonged to the Abbot of Abingdon, from whom the Crown acquired it.

There were a great many trees, so that the whole of this section appeared to be almost rural; in the spring and summer the gardens were filled with snowdrops and daffodils, honeysuckle and roses. But the smell from the open sewers overwhelmed the scent of the gardens, and the lanes became soggy when it rained.

Fronting the main highway on this side were two or three residential inns, such as the Bell and the Rose, all with gardens. There was also a

---

* Numbered references are to the Bibliography, p. 445.

line of small shops. The main road was full of ruts and travellers in coaches or seated on heaped wagons were jolted uncomfortably. Most of the gentlemen and ladies rode on horseback, wearing capes over their smart ruffs, and were greeted deferentially by the ill-dressed and dirty pedestrians, many of whom begged for money or a crust of bread.

A ditch separated this conglomeration of cottages and tenements from an extensive field which is now St. James's Park. From the Abbey and its adjacent church of St. Margaret's Westminster, there rambled all the way down to the river the buildings of the old Royal Palace of Westminster, the principal residence of the Sovereign since the time of Edward the Confessor, who built the Abbey. Here the principal offices of the Government, such as the Parliament, the Exchequer, and the Courts of Law, had special buildings assigned to them. In the past, as though forming part of his baggage, these departments of State went with the King as he moved from one residence to another, allowing each vacated palace to be aired for a time since sanitation was woefully inadequate, but they had by now become fixed in the Palace of Westminster. The House of Commons, meeting originally in the Chapter House of the Abbey, had lately been moved to St. Stephen's Chapel, the upper floor of a two-storied chapel,* running from the western entrance of Westminster Hall to the river. The Speaker's Chair was placed on the altar steps and the Members ranged themselves on either side, the Government facing the Opposition, not yet grouped rigidly in parties, but so set merely through the accident of architecture. Across a wide courtyard to the right as one faced the river, was the House of Lords.

In 1512 a fire destroyed some of the Palace buildings, but enough was left of the halls, built of white Kentish rag, for much of the business of State still to be carried on in the original chambers. Westminster Hall survived undamaged and here the Courts of Law continued to hold their sessions, with a fairground of stalls within the hall where stationers, booksellers and general traders served the litigants, offering them books and shirts and kerchiefs while they waited to attend the Courts of Chancery, Common Causes or the King's Bench. Henry the Eighth,

---

* On the lower floor was the chapel of St. Mary.

but recently come to the throne and now twenty-one years of age, declined to live amid the charred ruins and moved his court to the Palace at Greenwich, from where he used to come in his barge to visit his Lord Chancellor and Chief Minister, the massive, heavy jowled, puffy-eyed Wolsey, robed always in red 'satin, taffety, damask or caffe'.[5]

This proud prelate, the son of an Ipswich butcher who was fined for selling bad meat and for letting his house to doubtful characters for illegal purposes, had acquired by his energy and his brilliance, a predominant influence in the affairs of State, and had adopted a way of life that far outshone the King's. His retinue numbered many hundreds and when he set forth as Lord Chancellor for the Courts at Westminster Hall, he was preceded by men on horseback carrying two enormous silver crosses and was supported by a great procession, among whom, with a show of humility, he alone rode on a mule. In fact his hauteur and his arrogance knew no bounds. He forced his servants to serve him on their knees, caused bishops to tie his shoe latchets, and dukes to hold the basins when he washed. For the nobles and for Parliament he had but scant regard. His morals were lax, his house was filled always with beautiful, loose women and his many illegitimate children – an example that the young King was not slow to adopt.

In 1529 when Wolsey was stripped of all authority and Henry the Eighth became absolute ruler, the King made him vacate his princely residence and moved into it himself. Improving on its already dazzling magnificence, Henry converted it into the Palace of Whitehall. The style of architecture introduced earlier by Wolsey at Hampton Court was retained and the grounds were enormously extended. Between the new Palace and the Houses of Parliament stretched the vast Privy Garden, up to the very verge of Palace Yard. On the other side of the highway, the King acquired the Mote and many of the cottages and tenements, inns and shops, which were demolished to provide land for His Majesty's recreational needs. Four tennis courts were laid out, one of them a vast open court, two of the others covered. There were also bowling alleys, a coney yard and a pheasant court; a Cockpit was constructed for cock fighting – an octagonal building adorned at the top with the figure of a lion; next to it was a tilt-yard for jousting, on the site of the present Horse Guards. A 'sumptuous gallery' was built

4

beside the tilt-yard for 'the Princes with their nobility . . . to stand or to sit, and at Windowes to behold all the triumphant Iustings, and other military exercises.'⁶ The tilt-yard was also used for bear baiting. The gallery continued westward to a stairway leading down to the fields beyond, soon to be transformed into St. James's Park. A second gallery led to the Cockpit, with handsome lodgings alongside, one of them for the Keeper of the Palace.

Two enormous gates were built across King Street, with arches through which the traffic passed and overhead galleries as a means of access from the Palace to the recreation grounds. There were also lodgings above and beside both gates for members or friends of the Royal family and for officials. The Holbein Gate (which, though it bore his name, seems not to have been connected with Holbein unless he happened to have designed some of the mural decorations) linked the northern end of the Privy Garden with the tilt-yard. The other, known as the New Gate, stood nearer the Abbey at the corner of what later became Downing Street.

On moving into his new Palace the King was appalled to find that the main highway, skirting the Palace buildings, was used by the public for funeral processions. Past the windows of the gilded reception rooms, gay with music and laughter, the royal revellers saw sorrowing mourners go by with coffins, weeping, lamenting and chanting dirges. This had to be stopped, but since there was no other road by which the families living around Charing Cross could take their dead to St. Margaret's, Westminster, a separate cemetery was constructed for their use at St. Martin-in-the-Fields.

His Majesty further found most displeasing, both to eye and nose, the ditch separating his new recreation grounds from the great spread of fields to the westward, known as St. James's Fields after the hospital in their midst where fourteen 'maidens that were leprous' resided. He acquired the land, which like the hospital was owned by Eton College, and had the whole of it enclosed by a wall of brick. A park was laid out and the hospital was replaced by St. James's Palace. Thus a sweep of Royal Parks and residences stretched from the river to where Buckingham Palace now stands, but at that time only an open space with a road beyond leading to Kensington. The first house on the site of Buckingham Palace, Goring House, was not built until the following century.

The King's arbitrary indulgence of his whims went unchallenged by a people grateful and relieved at seeing an end to many years of misery and anguish in the civil warfare known as the Wars of the Roses, with the two contending factions united now in the person of Henry the Eighth, heir of both claimants to the Crown. A century later royal arbitrariness was no longer tolerable and Charles the First, on becoming the centre of a further civil war, was made to pay for it with his life.

The revelry Wolsey had brought to this setting was maintained by Henry the Eighth and after a short intermission was resumed by his daughter, the pale, indomitable Queen Elizabeth, who had inherited also her father's acquiline nose and red-gold hair. The coming of the Stuarts brought a number of changes. Following a fire at the Palace of Whitehall, James the First had Wolsey's Banqueting Hall rebuilt by Inigo Jones: it still stands. The plans drawn up by Inigo Jones for the rebuilding of the rest of the damaged Palace were only partially carried out: hereafter the Sovereign lived chiefly at St. James's Palace and at Greenwich.

Across the highway, though untouched by the fire, the changes were more considerable. The Cockpit ceased to be used for cock-fighting in 1607 and was converted into a handsome new theatre, which still bore the same name; and much of the recreation ground, including some of the tennis courts, made way for new houses in which courtiers, friends and relatives of the King took up their residence.

CHAPTER 2
George Downing

GEORGE DOWNING was born in 1623 of a well-to-do East Anglian family. His grandfather was a teacher at Ipswich Grammar School with an interest in education so intense that on the birth of his son shortly after the founding of Emmanuel College at Cambridge, he christened the child Emmanuel. George's mother – Emmanuel's second wife – was Lucy Winthrop, also of East Anglia. The two families knew each other well. Her brother John Winthrop, like her husband Emmanuel, was a barrister attached to the Inner Temple; they were all staunchly Puritan and vehemently resentful of the odious restrictions constantly imposed on the Puritans by King Charles the First's High Anglican clerics.

In March 1629, when George was six, his father, writing from London to his brother-in-law, informed him of the King's high-handed dissolution of Parliament because of its blunt protest against these restrictions. Winthrop, finding that life in England was becoming intolerable, decided to leave it. He wrote to his wife: 'I am veryly persuaded, God will bringe some heavye Affliction upon this lande, and that speedylye'; and again a few weeks later: 'But where we shall spende the rest of o^r short tyme I know not . . . my comfort is that thou Art willinge to be my companion in what place or conditio soevere, in weale or in woe.'[7]

In all this he received the wholehearted support of Emmanuel Downing. Winthrop acted promptly. On 26th August 1629, at a meeting at Cambridge, he and eight others, all men of substance, drew up an 'Agreement' and undertook to emigrate to New England with their families 'Provided always, that . . . the whole Government, together with the patent of the said Plantation, be first, by an order of Court, legally transferred and established to remain with us and others who shall inhabit upon the said plantation.' It is clear from this that the community decided to be self-governing and not, like the other settlements there, come under the control of the Government in London.

Shortly afterwards John Winthrop was elected the First Governor of Massachusetts and on 22nd March of the following year (1630) he set sail from Southampton,* together with James Downing, Emmanuel's son by his first marriage. They were to have been accompanied by ten ships, taking in all 700 passengers, 240 cows and 60 horses, but there was a delay and only three of the ships actually left with the Winthrops, the others following. All the settlers were prepared to work with their hands, build their own houses, and face the hazards of wolves and Indians.

The journey across the Atlantic took ten weeks. Emmanuel Downing, who had helped his brother-in-law to embark on this adventure, which was of such tremendous consequence in the founding of a new nation, planned to follow with his wife and young children. 'I shall desire to hasten over soe soone as the Lord shall open me the way, which I hope will be ere long,' he wrote on 8th October 1630. In the following April he wrote to say that they would be sailing 'next Spring'; but his wife feared that the dangers of the journey and the hardships to be faced in the settlement might be too much for the children, and so their departure was postponed. On 1st March 1635/6†, he

---

* Winthrop set out ten years after the sailing of *Mayflower* with the Pilgrim Fathers.
† Until 1752 the legal new year in Britain began on 25th March, though New Year's Day was popularly reckoned as 1st January. It was customary to put for all dates between 1st January and 25th March the two years involved: e.g. 1st March 1635/6, that is 1635 legally but popularly and actually 1636.

wrote to his nephew, also John Winthrop and later Governor of Connecticut, saying of his wife: 'She feareth much hardshipp there, and that we shall spend all, ere wee be setled in a course to subsist even for foode and rayment', and urged that his nephew should write and encourage her to come over.

It was not until March 1637 that Lucy Downing revealed what was really deterring her. She had set her heart on giving her son George a university education and had decided to send him to Cambridge. 'I am bould to present this sollissitous suit of myne', she wrote to her brother, 'with all earnestnes to you and my nephew Winthrop, that you will not condecend to his goeinge over till he hath either attayned to perfection in the arts hear, or that theer be sufficient means for to perfect him theerin with you, wich I should be moste glad to hear of: it would make me goe far nimbler to New Eng.'

The colony, as it happened, had already decided that a college should be established at a new town, which was to be named Cambridge, as about seventy of the leading men in the colony had been educated at Cambridge. Finance for this was provided 'through the noble benefaction of John Harvard', a Puritan minister and graduate of Emmanuel College, who had bequeathed for the purpose half his estate and his entire library of three hundred books, and it was after him that the new college was to be named.

The Downings, on learning of this, at last crossed the Atlantic. The population of the colony had grown in its eight years to over ten thousand persons. The Downings set up their home at Salem and were ardent members of the Puritan church there. George, not quite sixteen, was among the first students at Harvard and graduated in 1642. Shortly afterwards he took a job at £4 a year as a teacher of 'the Junior pupils' at Harvard.

He was not content to continue for long on that small salary. His mother noticed his restlessness. 'I am troubled concerning my sonne Georg,' she wrote to her brother the Governor. 'I perceive he is strongly inclined to travill. Eng. is I fear unpeaceable' – the Civil War had already broken out – 'and other countryes perilous in point of religion and maners. Besides we have not wearwith to accomodate him for such an ocasion: and to goe a servant I think might not be very fit for him neither, in divers respects.'

9

Massachusetts was soon hit by an economic crisis, brought on by the Civil War in England. Trade languished and there was acute distress. George decided to leave and sailed for the West Indies as an instructor to the seamen – it is believed in spiritual matters.

He visited a number of islands – the Barbados, Antigua, Nevis, St. Christopher and Santa Cruce. His letters home show that his aim was fixed mainly on the opportunities for making money. Writing to his cousin, the younger John Winthrop, after a visit to the Barbados, he says: 'I believe they have bought this year no less than a thousand Negroes, and the more they buie, the better able they are to buye, for in a yeare and a half they will earne (with God's blessing) as much as they cost.' This is indicative of the aspiration that was to guide George Downing's actions to the end of his life.

After a year of roving in and around the Caribbean, Downing, on learning that the Puritans at home had won many resounding victories against the King and that a number of settlers had in consequence begun to return to the homeland, set sail himself for England, where he arrived in the summer of 1646. Cromwell's forces had already won the battles of Marston Moor and Naseby.

Downing became a Puritan preacher and toured the country delivering sermons. A letter from Maidstone in Kent, written by Mrs. Lydia Bankes to a friend in New England on 28th August 1646 and more ill-spelt than others of that period, states: 'Pray let my Inderred respect be presented to your wife as all so to Mrs. Downind and her hosband desiring them to rejoyce with me for that the lord is ples to make her sone a Instrument of praise In the hartes of tose that regoyce to hear the Sperrit of god poured forth apon our young men according to his word let her know that he prech In our town of maidston a day or to befor this letter was wrot to the great soport of our Sperites.'

Before long he was attached as a preacher to Colonel Okey's regiment, which formed part of Fairfax's army. It is important to bear this appointment in mind in view of Downing's behaviour some years later when he betrayed Colonel Okey and brought him to the scaffold.

How Downing manœuvred himself out of his spiritual role and became Chief of the Intelligence Staff to Cromwell's forces in the North, is far from clear. All we know is that he attached himself to a Republican Member of Parliament, Sir Arthur Haselrig, on the latter taking up his appointment in March 1648 as Governor of Newcastle, in which area Fairfax's army was operating. The Civil War was by now practically over and the King was a prisoner in the Isle of Wight.

But during that summer fresh Royalist risings occurred and Cromwell travelled to the North to suppress them. After routing the Scots at Preston, Cromwell went on to Edinburgh, attended by Haselrig and apparently also Downing. That Cromwell came in personal contact with Downing at this time is certain, for a year later, in November 1649, Downing was singled out to take on the role of Chief of the Intelligence Staff, which at that time bore the title of Scoutmaster-General and had the equivalent rank to Major-General.

Downing was by now only twenty-six years old. It was his function to survey and control 'le service des espions et des correspondences secrètes', as Pontalis described it.[8] He received a salary of £365 a year and an expense allowance of £4 a day, out of which he was expected to pay his agents or spies. That he contrived to retain a great deal of this money for himself is indicated in a letter from his mother, who quotes her brother as saying that 'Georg is the only thriveing man of our generation. Mr. Winsloe tould him he is a purchaser', by which was meant a purchaser of land, as is corroborated by George's father, who wrote: 'I heare by divers, of his purchase of 2 or 300l. per annum.' Hugh Peter, the Puritan divine, estimated that George Downing's investment in property was bringing him in as much as £500 a year. Nevertheless he did his work well. 'One of the causes of the success of Fairfax and Cromwell was the efficiency of their intelligence staff.'[12] No records survive of what Downing actually did. This may be due to his precaution that no record should be kept of his activities; or, as is equally possible, Downing took care, after the return of King Charles the Second, to destroy all evidence of the part he had played against the King's father.

The Calendars of State Papers Domestic cast a light on some of Downing's activities. On 24th July 1650 the Council of State required 'Mr. Downing to take care that daily notice be given to the Council of what passes in the army, and to speak to Mr. Attorney, that the posts may be ready to carry the letters'; on 10th August 1651, 'The letter read to be sent to the Lord Mayor, with a copy of the letter from Scoutmaster-General Downing to be published at Paul's this afternoon' – this letter described the progress of the Scottish campaign; on 14th October 1651 Downing had to attend a Committee of Parliament to confer with the Deputies from Scotland. In June of the following year (1652) Downing was authorized by the Council of State 'to obtain gunpowder and round shot for which need is urgent', and he was given 'power to impress wagons, etc., for its carriage. All Mayors and Sheriffs to co-operate.' In October 1653 Downing together with others was ordered to sort the Scottish records in the Tower and report to Cromwell, the Protector; on 5th December of that year he was appointed by the Council of State to inquire into certain 'discoveries' and 'to examine' witnesses.

It is obvious from these entries that the work Downing was engaged on was of importance and that it brought him in constant contact with the highest authorities. His reports include a vivid eyewitness account of the battle of Worcester in 1651.[13] How much the secret intelligence he supplied contributed to this and other of Cromwell's victories is not known. The outbreak of war with the Dutch in 1652 led to Downing having to continue his secret service activities until that war ended two years later.

In 1654 he made a most advantageous marriage. His bride, the daughter of Sir William Howard and sister of the first Earl of Carlisle, was not only well connected, but young, beautiful and rich. In that same year Downing was elected a Member of Parliament for Edinburgh and sat in the first House of Commons of the Protectorate.

Cromwell obviously thought highly of him, for he sent Downing abroad on important missions. In 1655, appalled by the massacre of the Protestant Vaudois by the Duke of Savoy's troops, he dispatched Downing to convey his indignation not only to the Duke, but to Louis the Fourteenth in Paris. Downing called on Cardinal Mazarin, at the time the most powerful man in Europe. Reporting to Thurloe, the Secretary of State, Downing states that he was received with 'great civility'. Later that evening, he adds, Mazarin 'send me his owne supper with this complement, that it being too late to provide anything, he had sent what was made ready for himselfe, and would seek a supper himselfe; he also send his owne plate and servants to wayte, and the Captain of his guard.'[16]

A year later Downing was sent by Cromwell to the Hague as

Ambassador on a salary of £1,000 a year and a liberal allowance for expenses.

While in England Downing was an active interventionist in the debates in Parliament. As a rule his line was moderate and he quoted constantly from the Bible. Once, when the House found itself without a minister to read the prayers, Downing was told 'that he was a Minister, and he would have him to perform the work. Mr. Downing acknowledged that he was once a Minister', but declined to undertake it and the House began its session without prayers.[14]

He was a devoted supporter of Cromwell and in January 1657 he was the prime mover in the House of Commons to get Cromwell crowned King. But Cromwell, aware that the very word King was hateful to his soldiers, by whose support he ruled, declined after some hesitation.

The Dutch, at the time of Downing's arrival as Ambassador, were Britain's greatest rivals both as a trading nation and as a naval power. But they were Protestants and Cromwell's main interest was to further the cause of Protestantism. Into the alliance between the Dutch and the Swedes, both Protestant nations, Downing was instrumental in inserting Britain. It was Cromwell's purpose to establish a powerful Protestant League against the Catholic alliance formed by the Pope, the Holy Roman Empire and the King of Spain.

Downing's activities included a considerable amount of spying, for at the Hague lived the sister of Britain's exiled 'King', Charles the Second. She had married, at the age of ten, William, Prince of Orange, who had been working ceaselessly for the restoration of his brother-in-law to the English throne. A week after the death of the Prince of Orange in 1650 his wife, by then nineteen, gave birth to his heir, who later became William the Third of England. Charles often came to see her and the plotting for his return continued. Of this Cromwell was well aware and instructions were sent to Downing to be ceaselessly vigilant. The Secretary of State Thurloe ordered him to develop a secret intelligence service in order to keep the Protector fully informed of all such moves in Holland and elsewhere on the Continent.

With his ample experience, Downing set to work with speed and skill. At the merest whisper that Charles or his brothers, the Duke of York (later James the Second) or the Duke of Gloucester, were planning a visit to the Hague, Downing instantly intervened. A protest to the

Dutch Council of State led to the Princes being barred. He also obtained an order to stop English ministers in Holland from praying for the exiled King. In consequence he was thoroughly detested by Charles and his court, composed chiefly of men brought to ruin through their loyalty and ever plotting to regain what had been lost. A letter from John Lane at the Hague to his friend Sir Edward Nicholas in England says of Downing: 'He is a fearful gentleman. The day after the Princess came to town he set 2 of his footmen to stand sentry the whole day, one on the top of the stairs before the door, the other at the corner of the house, to watch the back gate, but there has been none since. He has hired another house. I hope the next remove of him and the rest of his comrades will be to the gallows, where they may have their due reward.'[15]

More than one attempt was made on Downing's life. 'Indeede they are very angry at mee,' he informed Thurloe after one such attempt when a Dutchman seen leaving his house was set upon by mistake, 'for that I have by little and little extremely disturbed and spoyled their kingdome here; and exceeding angry they are at this last action of mine, in obteyning, that Charles Stuart should be noe more prayed for heere.'[16] The letter is undated, but the internal evidence shows that it must have been written late in July or early in August 1658.

Downing contrived by wile and cunning to get one of Charles's more trusted courtiers, Sir John Marlow, into his pay and service, and before long he drew in still another, an even more important member of the exiled court, Tom Howard, brother of the Earl of Suffolk. Proudly he revealed to Thurloe that he had got Howard into his clutches through blackmail. Howard, Downing states, 'had a whoor in this country, with which he trusted his secrets and papers: these two afterwards falling out, a person in this town got all the papers from her.' This gave Downing his chance. 'But if it should be known,' he adds, 'that I have given you this account he would endeavour to have me killed.' Downing had with him at the Hague his wife and the two children, a boy and a girl, born so far of the marriage. The thought doubtless crossed his mind that their lives too might now be imperilled.

All the papers that came into Downing's possession were copied and sent on to Thurloe. After Cromwell's death on 3rd September 1658, he was careful to pass on only some of the information he received, for Downing was by now uncertain whether the Protectorate would endure or the Royalists would succeed in bringing back the King. A like uncertainty prevailed in England. Cromwell had named his son Richard as his successor. But there were signs of trouble from the outset. It gathered momentum until in May 1659, after only a few months in the saddle, Richard was forced to abdicate. Generals in command of sections of Cromwell's vast army had already begun to manœuvre in the hope of attaining the chief position for themselves. A fresh civil war seemed imminent.

Meanwhile Thurloe, concerned as to what moves were being made across the Channel by Charles, sent Downing on 27th May specific instructions to forward all information he was able to gather through his network of spies of a possible Royalist thrust. Downing, however, felt it prudent to provide himself with a possible line of escape. He got in touch with Tom Howard and, learning that Charles was planning to come to the Hague to see his sister, informed Howard that he would not on this occasion prevent the visit.

While there Charles had an unexpected call from an 'old reverend-like man with a long beard and ordinary grey clothes.'* The old man fell on his knees, pulled off his beard and revealed that he was Downing. He begged His Majesty to leave at once, lest he be seized by the States General and handed over to the authorities in England.

This was one step towards safeguarding his future. He took another by crossing over to England at the end of 1659 to see for himself how events were drifting. It had been Downing's aim in life to acquire as many offices as possible provided each brought him an income; and he was fortunate, before coming to the Hague as Ambassador, to obtain the lucrative post as one of the Tellers of the Exchequer, which brought him in a further £500 a year. The rooms assigned him for this work were in Whitehall and he had as his personal clerk there the diarist Samuel Pepys, whose references to Downing are far from flattering. The diary describes Downing as 'so stingy a fellow I care not to see him'.

During his brief stay in London in that vital winter of 1659, Downing

---

* From 'a transcript from the handwriting of the famous Mr. Lockhart', who was the nephew of Downing's contemporary and friend Sir William Lockhart, the English Ambassador in Paris.

sent for Pepys one morning 'and at his bedside he told me, that he had a kindness for me, and that he thought that he had done me one; and that was, that he had got me to be one of the Clerks of the Council; at which I was a little stumbled, and could not tell what to do, whether to thank him or no; but by and by I did; but not very heartily, for I feared that his doing of it was but only to ease himself of the salary which he gives me.'³ Pepys' salary was only £50, one tenth of the sum Downing was receiving while Pepys did his work as a Teller and also ran errands for him.

Downing returned to The Hague in March 1660, a very few weeks before the Restoration. But even now he was by no means certain how things might develop. He wrote to Thurloe: 'I should be infinitely obliged to you, that you would a little let me know what things are likely to come to.'¹⁶

Soon a glimmer of light began to illumine the trend of events. General Monk, who had served Charles the First and later became one of Cromwell's leading generals, had so far remained silent but watchful. Even when he marched with his army from Scotland to London in February, it was by no means clear which side he would take. The rival generals waited in anxious uncertainty. But it was to Monk that the gentry turned, begging him to maintain peace. On the day before Monk reached London there was a battle in the Strand between the cavalry and the infantry, and the fleet sailed up the Thames to deal with the disaffected soldiers. Monk protested his adherence to republican principles, but a few days later he secretly got in touch with the exiled King.

On learning of these portentous developments, Downing lost no time in seeing Tom Howard again and begged him to inform the King that his sole intention was to serve His Majesty. Writing of the interview to the Marquis of Ormonde, Howard stated that Downing was 'alleging to be engaged in a contrary party by his father who was banished into *New England*, where he was brought up and had sucked in principles that since his reason had made him see were erroneous, and that he never was in arms but since the King's death, nor had never taken oath or engagement of any kind' – almost all of which, as the records show, was untrue.

Downing also showed Howard a confidential letter sent him in cypher by Thurloe. If the King, Downing added, would pardon him and accept his services, he was ready to work secretly on the Army in England, with which he had considerable influence.

In need at this juncture of all the help he could get, the King agreed. Howard was asked to tell Downing that His Majesty would not look back on past 'deviations', but would accept 'the overtures he makes of returning to his duty'. He also assured Downing that all he did to help would be kept secret.

It is impossible now to discover what exactly Downing did to assist the Restoration, so skilfully did he contrive to conceal his moves. What is known, however, is that in no time at all Thurloe himself was brought in as a supporter of the King; and on 21st May, a week before returning to England, Charles the Second rewarded Downing by knighting him at Breda. Pepys, who had crossed the Channel with the fleet, travelling with his cousin Admiral Montagu, later the Earl of Sandwich, records that Downing 'called me to him . . . to tell me that I must write him Sir G. Downing.'[3]

CHAPTER 3
Downing Street

I⊤ was prior to this, while Downing was still in Cromwell's service and before he left to take up his post at The Hague, that he acquired an interest in the land that bears his name. It seemed a simple transaction, but did not prove to be so.

The land was Crown property and, as the sale was made by Cromwell's Parliamentary Commissioners after its confiscation, the sale was cancelled at the Restoration and the land was restored to the Crown.

But Downing was determined to get it back if he could. The land had first been sold in June 1651, two years after Charles the First's execution, to Robert Thrope and William Proctor, and Downing had bought it on the death of the survivor in November 1654. It was, however, too early, so soon after the Restoration, for him to attempt an adjustment. He had made his peace with the King, but he had still to discover what the King's true attitude was towards him.

Downing returned to England with his wife and children in May 1660, a day or two after the King, and hung around Whitehall to seize any chance that offered. He bustled about, called on the new Ministers and offered to help in any way he could. His experience in negotiating trade treaties in Holland was readily recognized and he was called into consultation by the newly formed Council of Trade, the precursor of the Board of Trade.

In all Downing spent a year in London. He succeeded in making some headway, but gained no favour from the King other than the return of his old job. In June 1661 he was back at the Hague as Ambassador.

He had now to prove himself anew and soon saw his opportunity for doing so. It was the King's resolve to punish those who had been responsible for his father's death. Some of the regicides were seized in England, but others had fled to the Continent and it became Downing's purpose to round these up, even if his agents had to search all Europe for them. It was, he felt, an effective way to earn the King's gratitude and to obtain further favours.

Downing discussed this with Lord Clarendon, the Lord High Chancellor and in effect chief Minister, before returning to the Hague, and on arriving there he received a letter from Clarendon's son, stating specifically: 'My father is very much troubled to heare of so great a concourse of disaffected people into those parts, but he desires you will still have an eye upon what persons doe come over thither'; and again a few days later: 'I am sure I did tell you in one of my letters that you were to doe all you could *to lay hands upon the rogues.*'*

As a first step, Downing saw De Witt, the head of the Dutch Government, and persuaded him to insert an additional clause in the treaty of alliance under negotiation, to provide for the surrender of any regicides found in the country. One of these he knew was at Rotterdam; others, including Colonel Okey, in whose regiment Downing had served as chaplain, were at Strasburg. His next move was to try somehow to inveigle these others to Holland. He worked through his network of spies, still spread across Europe, and eventually found a Dutch businessman named Abraham Kicke, who knew some of the fugitives. Downing promised to pay Kicke £200 for every man he was able to hand over, and threatened to ruin him if he failed.

* The italicized words were written in cypher. The letters are quoted from MSS at the British Museum.

The Dutchman set out at once. By the following March he succeeded in decoying to Holland three of the fugitives – Okey, Barkstead and Corbet. The ruse he used was revealed by Downing himself in a letter to Secretary Nicholas dated 17/24th March, 1661/2. The deluded men told their friends in Delft that they had come 'to that place at that time to lay out ten thousand pound sterling there for ye setting up of severall manufactures for ye imployment of ye poor.'[17]

On learning of their arrival, Downing at once obtained from De Witt a warrant for their arrest. Then, arming his servants, he went after them himself. Downing has described what occurred. 'Knocking at ye doore one of ye house came to see who it was and ye doore being open, the under Scout and ye whole company rushed immediately into ye house, and into ye roome where they were sitting by a fyere side with a pipe of tobacco and a cup of beere, immediately they started up to have gott out at a back Doore but it was too late, ye Roome was in a moment fulle. They made many excuses, ye one to have gott liberty to have fetch^t his coate and another to goe to privy but all in vayne.'

A contemporary pamphlet, describing the incident in considerable detail, states that Colonel Okey had been assured earlier by Downing that he would be safe if he came to Holland. 'This Generous and Plain-hearted Colonel,' the pamphlet goes on, '. . . did without the least Hesitation repose a great deal of Trust and confidence in one whom he had been instrumental to raise from the dust: little thinking that his New-England Tottered Chaplain whom he Cloathed and Fed at his table, and who dipped with him in his own dish, should prove like the Devil among the twelve to his Lord and Master.'[18]

Pepys states that 'the Dutch were a good while before they could be persuaded to let them go'. But in the end Downing prevailed on them and the three men were taken on board *Blackmore* at dead of night and sent across to England. After a brief imprisonment in the Tower, they were sentenced on 16th April 1662 and executed at Tyburn on the 19th. Of the shameful part Downing played in this, Pepys wrote on 12th March: 'Sir G. Downing (like a perfidious rogue, though the action is good and of service to the King, yet he cannot with any good conscience do it)'; and again, on 19th April: '. . . all the world takes notice of him for a most ungrateful villain for his pains.'[3]

Evelyn, Pepys' contemporary diarist, dismissed Downing as 'a pedagogue and fanatic preacher not worth a grote' who 'insinuated' himself into the King's favour and 'became excessive rich'.

Charles the Second, however, as Downing had expected, was grateful. His father's execution was to him a martyrdom, and so it seemed, not so much vengeance, but a just retribution that he should punish those who had sinned. His gratification was shared by Lord Clarendon and by the Secretary of State, Sir William Morice. The latter wrote to Downing on behalf of the Government: 'We doe heere al magnify your diligente and prudente conduct in the seisinge and conveyinge over of the regicides, and we thinke few others would have used such dexterity, or would have compassed so difficult a business.'*

The King rewarded Downing with a baronetcy. It was a good moment, Downing felt, to raise the question of the land he had been forced to give up. He wrote to His Majesty explaining that the land had come to him in settlement of a debt. He would not, he said, have entered into the transaction otherwise, but had been forced to do so because of some money that had been owing to him. This is not supported by such other evidence as is available. He further reminded the King of a promise His Majesty had made in Holland that he 'would have a care' of Downing's estate.

The King granted his plea. On 23rd February 1663/4, Downing was given a lease of the site and the buildings standing on it – 'all that messuage or house in Westminster, with all the courts, gardens and orchards thereto, situate between a certain house or mansion called the Peacock in part and the common sewer in part on the South side and a gate leading to King Street called the New Gate in part, and an old passage leading to a court called Pheasant Court in part, and an old passage leading from the great garden to St. James's Park in part, on the North side, and abutting on King Street on the East side and upon the wall of St. James's Park on the West side.'

The land was 'to be held by said Downing for 99 years, including the unexpired portion of the 60 years' term granted in the premises to Sir Thomas Knevett by King James I'; of this, fourteen years had by now expired. The rent was to be '£20 per an. payable to the Crown, and £4 per an. payable to the Keeper of Whitehall during the said

---

* British Museum MSS., 22, 919.

60 years, and £4 per an. increase during the remainder of said term of 99 years.'

Downing was given 'liberty to build thereon subject to the supervision of the Surveyor General of Crown Lands and with proviso not to build further than the West part of the house called the Cockpit was then built' – which means no closer to the Park than where No. 10 now stands.

On this site, together with the Peacock, an inn to the south which Downing also acquired, he eventually built the street of houses that bears his name.

CHAPTER 4
Number 10

No. 10 Downing Street consists in the main of two houses. The one at the back, older and nearly twice as large, was built in 1673 on the site of the Cockpit 'lodgings', which adjoined Henry the Eighth's famous Cockpit and 'le Tennys Courte'. On the west its garden skirted St. James's Park; on the south lay Hampden House with its out-buildings and garden – it was the lease of this latter house that Downing had acquired.

The Cockpit lodgings, a group of buildings,* formed the residence of the Keeper of the Palace of Whitehall and must have been built by 1530, for in March of that year Thomas Alvard, the first Keeper of the Palace, went to live there.

In Elizabeth's reign, Thomas Knyvet, on becoming Keeper, moved in and it was here, in the reign of her successor James the First, that Knyvet received a call as Justice of the Peace for Westminster, 'about midnight' of 4th/5th November 1605, 'to come with proper

---

* As the Cockpit was a distinctive building all the houses or 'lodgings' around it bore its name.

attendants' to search the vaults of the House of Lords. Setting out with an armed guard and attendants carrying lanterns, he found Guy Fawkes (who came of a good Yorkshire family and was not a ruffian) busily at work laying faggots and gunpowder. Knyvet seized him and ordered the guards to take him away. As a reward Knyvet, already a knight, was made a Privy Councillor and was raised to the peerage, thus having the right to use the Upper House himself, which he did regularly. Brought to justice, Fawkes expressed 'his utmost regret' that he had been prevented from blowing up the place, with the Lords, the Ministers and the King in it. He was hanged together with three of his accomplices in Old Palace Yard in front of the Parliament buildings.

A few months earlier Knyvet vacated the largest (the No. 10 part) of his Cockpit lodgings which was required for the King's son, Prince Charles, later King Charles the First, who was then only four years old. As compensation the King gave Knyvet £20 a year for life.

The Prince, however, left the house shortly afterwards and it was got ready for his sister, Princess Elizabeth. To accommodate the household of the young Princess, who was eight at the time, the Little Close Tennis Court alongside was built upon to provide a kitchen and living quarters for her domestic staff.

The Princess married the Elector Palatine in 1613, when she was seventeen, and thus became the grandmother of King George the First. The house then reverted to the use of the Keeper of the Palace, who at that time was Lord Rochester, later the Earl of Somerset. But his wife did not like the place 'there being many doors and few keys'.[19] Later, the Earl of Pembroke, on becoming Keeper, moved in and continued to live there through the dark and desperate years of the Civil Wars; and it was through a window of this house in January 1649 that he saw King Charles the First, whose home it had been for a time, being led past to his execution outside the Banqueting Hall in Whitehall. Pembroke died in the house exactly a year later.

Oliver Cromwell then moved in and lived there for four years, leaving it in 1654 to go to the main Palace of Whitehall, where he is said to have changed his bedroom every night through fear of assassination. There had been numberless plots against him, for, though he had raised the status of the country to unprecedented heights in the esteem of the world, his rule was undisguisedly a military dictatorship, which more and more of the people were learning to loathe. After his death in September 1658, his widow returned to the house and remained there until the Restoration.

On the day of King Charles the Second's stirring entry into London, 29th May 1660, General Monk, now created the Duke of Albemarle, was given this as well as some of the adjoining houses, together with two large and lovely enclosed gardens, as his London residence and stayed there throughout the harrowing months of the Great Plague, although almost all the courtiers and the bulk of London's population thought it more prudent to flee to the country.

Albemarle died in this house in January 1670/1 and that part of it nearest to St. James's Park was then largely rebuilt for the Duke of Buckingham. The accounts for March 1670/1 list the charges for 'pulling downe and Altering severall Roomes at ye Cockepitt for his Grace the Duke of Buckingham'. A party wall apparently separated the house from the Cockpit theatre, used in Cromwell's time only for concerts of 'rare music', but plays were once again presented there after the Restoration. The records show that by 1673 the workmen took down sixty feet of boarded partition in the upper gallery and the boxes of the theatre, put up a boarded partition in a lower room next to the pit, and took down the roof and ceiling floor of the gallery between the playhouse and the outer lodgings next to the park, which implies that a part at least of the theatre was incorporated in the house.

The house as altered for Buckingham was large and spacious. It ran from north to south, parallel with Whitehall, with the garden on the east side, the further side from the Park. Its size and outer shape has not since been changed and can still be discerned in the rear section of No. 10 Downing Street, though the interior has been very greatly altered.

On the southern flank, where Downing Street now runs, there stood at that time, as it had for a century and a half earlier, an old half-timbered house, which had once been a brewhouse called the Axe. Together with its outhouses, cottages and garden, it occupied almost the entire length of Downing Street, running from the New Gate on King Street to St. James's Park. The ground had belonged at one time to the Abbot of Abingdon, who leased it to Nicholas Palle and later to his widow Elizabeth Palle. This was never incorporated in the Palace, but the land appears to have been acquired by the Crown during the reign of Henry the Eighth, for we find that the Axe was confined by now only to that portion of the premises adjoining New Gate on King Street.

The rest of the premises were let to Everard Everard, a goldsmith, who both lived and worked here, and afterwards to John Baptist Castilain, a gentleman of the Privy Chamber, who lived here until 1593. Queen Elizabeth, who was greatly attached to Thomas Knyvet, made a gift to him of these premises for life, without rent 'in consideration of the expenditure he had incurred on the repairs of the house',[1] James the First extended the lease, making it run for a term of sixty years after Knyvet's death, so that his heirs might benefit. As far as is known, Knyvet never himself lived in this section of No. 10 Downing Street, though as we have seen he did live in the back section for some years as Keeper of the Palace.

On his death in 1622 the premises went to his widow, who died a few months later. She in turn left it to her niece Mrs. Hampden, who took in the Axe and adapted and converted the whole of it into a residence for herself, set in an attractive garden. It thus came to be known as Hampden House.

Mrs. Hampden was the mother of John Hampden, who won his place in history by refusing to pay 'ship money' to Charles the First, and the aunt of Oliver Cromwell as well as of Colonel Edward Whalley, one of the prime movers in the King's execution. She was left undisturbed at the Restoration and continued to live in Hampden House until her death two years later. The lease still had twenty years to run and she left the property to her four grandsons – Richard Hampden, Sir Robert Pye, Sir John Hobart and Sir John Trevor.

It was a lease of the land on which this house stood that was granted by Charles the Second to Downing in 1663. Having obtained permission to build, it was his intention to pull down Hampden House and use the entire site for the building of a row of houses stretching from Whitehall to the Park. But Mrs. Hampden's grandsons were not prepared to surrender what remained of their lease and Downing's endeavours to get possession failed, despite his complaint to the authorities that 'the houseing . . . are in great decay and Will hardly continue to be habitable to the end'. He had in consequence to wait until the lease ran out in 1682 before he could build his street.

Downing had amassed considerable wealth, by what means is not known. In January 1661, just before going to Holland as King Charles's Ambassador, he bought the manor house of East Hatley in Cambridgeshire, twelve miles from Hitchin, and kept on adding to his estates until he became the largest landowner in that county.

He had, while Scoutmaster-General, obtained for his father the position of Clerk of the Council of State in Edinburgh. The old man was glad to be back from Massachusetts and carried on the work until his death on the eve of the Restoration. Downing's widowed mother went shortly afterwards to live at East Hatley, where she looked after her two small grandchildren during Downing's absence with his wife on his fresh term as Ambassador at the Hague. Writing to one of her daughters, Mrs. Downing, now nearing seventy, often complained of the hardships she had to endure. Ten years later we find her struggling on an allowance from her son of only £23 a year – 'more your brother Georg will not hear of for me; and that it is onely covetousnes that maks me aske for more. He last sumer bought another town, near Hatley, called Clappam cost him 13 or 14 thousand pound,* and I really beleeve one of us 2 are indeed covetous.'

Downing stayed at the Hague until the summer of 1665. Not long after his return he was appointed Secretary to the Treasury and lived, while in London, in his town house at Stephen's Court, New Palace Yard, opposite the House of Commons, of which he had remained a Member all the time he was abroad. He was also near enough to keep an eye on such other building alterations as were going on near the land he had acquired off Whitehall.

An interruption came when the King sent him again to The Hague in 1671. Warned that Downing was hated by the Dutch and that 'the rabble will tear him to pieces', the King smiled wryly and said: 'Well, I will venture him.' The forecast proved to be correct, for three months later, fearing the mounting fury of the mob, Downing suddenly left the Hague. On arriving in London he was arrested for leaving his post without leave and was sent to the Tower. He was imprisoned there for six weeks, then released.

The alterations to the Cockpit lodgings at the back of Hampden

---

* It is thought that this figure may be exaggerated.

27

House were by now in progress and before long Downing saw the Duke of Buckingham move in. In 1674, when Buckingham fell from favour, the house underwent still further and very considerable alterations. It was being prepared as a suitable residence for Lady Charlotte Fitzroy, the King's illegitimate daughter by Barbara Villiers, Duchess of Cleveland, who moved in on her marriage to the Earl of Lichfield. Another storey was added, so that there were now five floors, counting basement and attic. Still large and square and with a great many windows on which the tax was specially remitted,* the house stood in a much enlarged garden and looked out onto St. James's Park, where deer grazed upon the grass, the trees were tall, the flowering shrubs abundant and the criss-crossing paths were decorated with sculpture.

Seeing these extensive alterations around the Cockpit, Downing, with the lease of Hampden House now running out, applied for permission to build further towards the Park, beyond the limit imposed earlier which forbade him to build farther west than the Cockpit. 'He therefore prays', the appeal stated, 'to have his term made up again to 99 years at the old and increased rent and with liberty now and at all times hereafter to build upon any part of the premises: he intending to erect none that shall have a prospect towards the Park but such as shall be fit for persons of good quality to inhabit in and be graceful and ornamental to the said Park.'

After an inspection of the site by Sir Christopher Wren, as Surveyor-General of the Works, this permission was granted on 25th January 1681/2. The Royal Warrant to the Attorney or Solicitor-General granted 'Sir George Downing Bart. authority to build new and more houses further westward on the grounds granted him by the patent of 1663/4 Feb. 23.' It added: 'The present grant is by reason that the said Cockpit or the greater part thereof is since demolished; but is to be subject to the proviso that it be not built any nearer than 14 feet of the wall of the said Park at the West end thereof. But with liberty also to him to build vaults or cellars from the said buildings to the wall of the said Park & to make a walk thereupon, and also with liberty to him to cope the wall of the said Park (so far as the same does abutt on the

---

* The window tax was first levied in 1696. All houses not paying Church and poor rates were assessed for a special rate according to the number of windows in the house. The tax was repealed in July 1851.

28

premises) with free stone and set flower pots or statues thereupon for the beautifying and ornament of the said buildings.'

All grants of leases included a clause 'for reassumption by the Crown upon payment to the lessees of what shall be by them . . . expended in building.'

The Hampden House lease ended in 1682 and Downing was able at last to build his row of houses. Fifteen were erected with astonishing speed. Of these the largest stretched back towards the Countess of Lichfield's home. Together these two, when eventually joined, though that was not to be for another fifty years, formed the No. 10 Downing Street we know.

CHAPTER 5
Early Residents

THE early residents of the two houses must inevitably be dealt with separately.

The very first resident, living in the house at the back as first substantially altered and having the shape and outline it has now, was, as has been noted, the Duke of Buckingham. He was the second Duke, heir of the tall, handsome, unscrupulous George Villiers, who was a favourite of James the First and with whom young Prince Charles rode in disguise all the way to Spain in the hope of making the Infanta Dona Maria eventual Queen of England. But she threatened to become a nun if forced to marry a heretic and the Prince of Wales returned without a bride.

The younger Buckingham was brought up with King Charles's children and fought for the King during the Civil War. In 1648, when only twenty years of age, his estates were sequestered by the Cromwellians and he fled to Holland; but he returned three years later and took part in the battle of Worcester.

Buckingham managed to escape again to the Continent, but to

Cromwell's great indignation returned to England in 1657 and married Mary, only daughter of Lord Fairfax. Cromwell had him arrested and sent to the Tower. On the return of Charles the Second he was given many offices of importance and, after the fall of Clarendon in 1667, became one of the most influential men in England.

It seems probable[1] that, before its conversion, this house was occupied for a few months by the young Prince of Orange (later King William the Third) when he came on a visit to his uncle King Charles the Second in October 1670,[1] for Albemarle had but recently died and the reference to the Prince of Orange living in a house with the brick wall 'next ye parke' as well as other identifying allusions appear to confirm this. The Prince would thus appear to have been the last occupant of the house before its conversion.

Buckingham lived here for three years, from July 1673 to March or April 1676, when, following his fall from favour, he retired to the country.

The King's daughter and son-in-law, the Earl and Countess of Lichfield, were the next residents. She was only twelve years old when they moved in, her husband not yet twenty-one. She is described as having been 'celebrated for her "blameless" beauty and her numerous issue'.[177] She had eighteen children.

It is puzzling why this house, so recently adapted and decorated for Buckingham, should within three years have had to be largely rebuilt for the Lichfields. There is no record of a fire, but the soil in this neighbourhood is very treacherous and, since houses were not at that time built on deep foundations, as was to be shown recurrently in the case of No. 10 Downing Street, this may have been a cause. The garden of the house appears to have been considerably widened, for it is now described as a 'great garden'.

When Downing began to build his row of houses in 1682, the Lichfields were gravely disturbed by their nearness. The Countess promptly wrote to her father about the loss of privacy. The King replied: 'I think it a very reasonable thing that other houses should not look into your house without your permission, and this note will be sufficient for Mr. Surveyor to build up your wall as high as you please, the only caution I give you is not to prejudice the corner house, which you know your sister Sussex is to have, and the building up the wall there will signify nothing to you, only inconvenience her.'

'Your sister Sussex' was the King's elder daughter Anne, also by Barbara Villiers. Older by two years than her sister Charlotte, she had married Lord Dacre, later the Earl of Sussex. The 'corner house' in which the Sussexes were to live was apparently the large house on the site of the present No. 12 Downing Street.

A near neighbour of the Lichfields on the other side, by the old Cockpit, was Princess Anne, the King's niece. She lived here from 1684 until 26th November 1688. Her father, the Duke of York, who ascended the throne in 1685 as James the Second, was faced by ever increasing hostility because of his ardent support of Catholicism and his endeavours to resume the arbitrary powers of which an angry nation had stripped his father. Anne, aware that her husband, Prince George of Denmark, did not approve of the King's resolve, had a secret back staircase built off her bedroom, and on her husband coming out openly against her father, she made her escape by night down this stairway. Later that year, after her father had fled the country, she returned to the house and it was here that the new King, William the Third, who was married to her sister Mary, called to see her.

The Lichfields left their house at about the same time, for they were closely attached to the fugitive King James the Second, whom the Earl had been serving as Master of the Horse.

Some months later, Lady Lichfield sold the remainder of her lease 'to Mr. d'Auverquerque', one of the Dutch courtiers of the new King. D'Auverquerque, a younger son of the Count of Nassau, came to England with William the Third and replaced Lichfield as Master of the Horse. On becoming naturalized, he received an English peerage and anglicized his name to Lord Overkirk. He and his wife, Frances D'Arson de Sommerdick, who was naturalized some years later, lived together in this house for eighteen years until his death in 1708. The house was referred in that year as being 'situate in Downing S$^{tr.}$ Westminster',[25] which strictly speaking it was not.

Lady Overkirk stayed on until her own death in January 1720, when the house was 'resumed' by the Crown and an order was given 'for repairing and fitting it up in the best and most substantiall manner' at a cost of £2,522.

Even before the repairs and decorations were completed a new tenant moved in. The house was now assigned to Count Bothmar, a German nobleman,who had come to England ten years earlier as the accredited representative of the Elector of Hanover, the heir presumptive to the English throne. By that date, 1710, all Queen Anne's children having died, it was clear that the Elector, descended from Princess Elizabeth, sister of King Charles the First, would be her successor. As has already been noted both the Princess and her brother Charles had once lived in this house.

During the last four years of Queen Anne's reign Bothmar was regarded by many as 'the virtual ruler'[26] of England, and he maintained his supremacy as the most influential of the new King's advisers when the Elector, who knew hardly any English, ascended the throne as King George the First.

To Bothmar the house was a constant source of irritation, for he complained ceaselessly of 'the ruinous Condition of the Premises'. He had 'a Double Wall' built 'to form an Entry to the said House from the North side', that is to say where the Horse Guards Parade is now, and a double stairway, which still stands, was provided to lead from the terrace to the garden on the Park side; a french window opens onto the terrace from the Cabinet room. In July 1730 still further repairs were undertaken, but since these cost only £280, it would seem that the house was not as dilapidated as Bothmar made out.

Bothmar died here in 1732 and the ratebook shows that Sir Robert Walpole, who had been Prime Minister for eleven years – six of them to George the First and five to his son George the Second – took the house over. But he did not move in until three years later, for the alterations he required were extensive. He called in William Kent, who had been working on his magnificent country house at Houghton in Norfolk, and got him to reconstruct the interior and to design a set of handsome new rooms and a new staircase. At the same time, in order to enlarge the place, Walpole told him to take in the adjacent house in Downing Street, the lease of which was obtained for him by the King. The entrance to the big house from the Park was closed and a fresh entrance was provided on Downing Street, almost as it is today. The two houses have been one ever since.

The house in Downing Street had, until now, few distinguished residents. For a short time (1688 to 1689) the Countess of Yarmouth lived there, Lord Lansdowne for four years from 1692 to 1696, and the Earl of Grantham from 1699 to 1703.

In 1720 Downing Street was described as 'a pretty open Place, especially at the upper End, where are four or five very large and well-built Houses, fit for Persons of Honour and Quality; each House having a pleasant Prospect into St. James's Park, with a Tarras Walk.'[6]

From time to time a number of Downing's houses remained untenanted, for an advertisement in *The Daily Courant*, dated 26th February 1722, announced: 'To be Lett together or apart, by Lease, from Lady Day next – Four large Houses, with Coach-houses and Stables, at the upper end of Downing Street, Westminster, the Back fronts to St. James's Park, with a large Tarras Walk before them next the Park. Enquire of Charles Downing, Esq., Red-Lyon Square.' In the ratebook for 1731, No. 10 and the small house alongside are shown as being in the occupation of John Scroop and Mr. Chicken respectively. Four years later Walpole, wanting to extend the house as far as the passage on the east (now known as the Treasury Passage) which led to the stables and coach houses at the back, persuaded Chicken to move to another of Downing's houses a few doors nearer Whitehall, and this small house was added to the other two, thus making No. 10 three houses in one.

Beyond these, towards the Park, the row of Downing's houses continued, ending in the corner house, once occupied by King Charles the Second's daughter Anne, Countess of Sussex. In front of it, against the Park wall and jutting out towards the present Foreign Office building, was the fifteenth of Downing's houses, which formed the end of the cul-de-sac: the open space in front of it was known at the time as Downing Square.

Downing, as far as can be ascertained, never lived in this street himself, for he died in July 1684, not long after it was completed. He had eight children, three sons and five daughters. His eldest son, also named George, married Lady Katherine Cecil, daughter of the Earl of Salisbury. By his will, dated 20th August 1683, Downing left the Downing Street portion of his estate in trust for his youngest son Charles. As trustees he nominated his son-in-law Sir Henry Pickering,

Bart., and Lord Morpeth.* The Charles Downing referred to in the *Daily Courant* advertisement was Downing's grandson. His elder brother, Sir George Downing, the third baronet, left no heir and used a part of his inheritance to found and endow Downing College at Cambridge, the university to which old Emmanuel Downing and his wife Lucy had been so greatly attached.

---

* Downing's nephew. Viscount Morpeth was the heir of Lady Downing's brother, the Earl of Carlisle.

CHAPTER 6
Sir Robert Walpole

WALPOLE was the son of a well-to-do Norfolk farmer. One of nineteen children, he was born in 1676 and was thus nine years old at the death of Charles the Second. The family was able to trace its descent in a direct line from an ancestor who came over with William the Conqueror. Edward Walpole, grandfather of Sir Robert, sat in the Parliament of 1660 and voted for the restoration of the monarchy. His convivial son Robert, in Parliament until his death in 1700, played an active part in politics as a Whig, and, despite his addiction to ale, won a high reputation for his prudence and his skilful handling of money, a talent which his famous son was fortunate enough to inherit.

Unexpectedly, following the death of his two elder brothers, young Robert Walpole, who had been brought up to manage the farms and attend the cattle markets, became heir to the family fortune, which provided him with an income of £2,000 a year. This he greatly enlarged by a fortunate marriage to Catherine Shorter, the grand-daughter of a former Lord Mayor of London. Not many months after this, in January 1701, Walpole, not yet twenty-five, entered Parliament, representing Castle Rising, the constituency vacated by his father's death; but a year later, for the General Election, he went to King's Lynn, a much more important borough, where the Walpoles also had influence, and remained its Member until he went to the House of Lords forty years later as the Earl of Orford.

It was not until he was almost sixty* and had been Prime Minister for fourteen years that Walpole moved into No. 10 Downing Street. His climb began early and was quite rapid. This was all the more remarkable at a time when political power was controlled by wealth and birth, for he had not much wealth and, belonging merely to the country gentry, no family connections of any consequence to assist his advancement, but had to rely on his exceptional ability and his untiring capacity for work. In London he joined the right clubs so as to meet influential people and went out of his way to cultivate those who could be useful. Abandoning his father's rigid frugality, he borrowed money and spent it lavishly. Soon he was heavily in debt, but his geniality and his eager participation in the social round brought him considerable attention, and his skill as a debater in the House of Commons led even his opponents to admit that he was as good as half his party put together.[29]

The party system began to take shape early in the reign of Charles the Second. The political grouping was based broadly on the religious division prevailing in the country, the Tories being for the King and the established church, the Whigs for Parliamentary supremacy, freedom of conscience and religious toleration for the Dissenters: in consequence the Tories came to be regarded as the reactionary party, the Whigs as progressive. Even at the end of Queen Anne's reign, when the two parties had been in existence for half a century, they were by no means organized and disciplined as political parties came to be later; each consisted of little groups often divided one from the other: only an identity of aim and interest led to some of these groups working together. The Tories in general had supported King James the Second, the Whigs had been responsible for his replacement by William the Third. Similarly in the closing years of Anne's reign it

---

* Kent's alterations took three years.

was the Whigs who were intent on the Protestant succession by bringing in King George the First from Hanover, while the Tories still favoured the legitimate line of the Stuarts. Both parties had at their head wealthy and influential families who had acquired a vast number of pocket boroughs, one of which, Old Sarum, had not a single house in which to lodge a voter. The distribution of Parliamentary seats was startlingly uneven: as many as 142 Members, almost a quarter of the total in the House, came from the five counties in the south-west corner of England, stretching from Cornwall to Wiltshire. Many of the boroughs could be bought and sold, and often were just before an election. Cromwell introduced a measure of reform by redistributing some of these seats and enfranchising growing towns like Manchester and Leeds, which had been completely without any Parliamentary representation; but Charles the Second cancelled all his changes. The Duke of Newcastle, with immense estates in thirteen counties, owned or controlled a large number of the Whig family boroughs, others were under the influence of such powerful Whigs as the Devonshires, the Townshends and the Bedfords. By intermarriage, by entering into business and other alliances with the more powerful merchants and bankers, by securing the support of the Crown and by exercising Parliamentary control for so many years, the Whigs had established themselves in an almost impregnable position.

During the reign of George the Second the Crown too acquired a great many boroughs, to which George the Third was to add many more. Thus in the hands of the King and his chosen Ministers lay almost complete control of the House of Commons. The counties, returning two members each, also came under this influence, for their representatives were drawn generally from the families of the largest landlords in the area. A few boroughs such as Westminster, Coventry and Preston, and of the counties Middlesex, had an independent electorate, and it was these seats, together with the boroughs owned by wealthy merchants lately returned from India, or by West Indian planters and rich slave traders, that led from time to time to an unpredictable variation in the votes in the House. The life of a Parliament was limited to three years: there were thus frequent elections. It should be remembered too that the population of England and Scotland, joined by the Act of Union in 1707, totalled barely eight millions, less than a sixth of what it is now; but only an infinitesimal proportion, a hundred families or so, formed the effective ruling class by controlling or influencing the elections.

After the flight of James the Second the Whigs, having been responsible for it, inevitably came into power. But the pattern changed when Queen Anne came to the throne. Like her father and her uncle Charles the Second, she insisted on exercising the Sovereign's right to select Ministers and dismiss them whether they had the support of Parliament or not. She even attended all Cabinet meetings and the more important discussions in the House of Lords. While he enjoyed the Queen's friendship and support, Marlborough, a Tory by disposition, was able to play a leading part in politics, but the hostility of that party to the continuation of the war with France after his triumph at Blenheim, caused him to turn away from them and to support the Whigs, retaining in the Government through his overwhelming influence, only such moderate Tories as Harley and St. John.

Walpole established himself as the leader of the younger Whigs in his very first years in the Commons. His consistent support of Marlborough and the war led to his displacing St. John in the important office of Secretary at War early in 1708. It was a notable triumph, as St. John had been his keenest rival at Eton, where Walpole had gone on a grant after his tight-fisted father had falsified his age. Lord Godolphin, whose heir married Marlborough's daughter, replaced Harley as Lord Treasurer, as the head of the Government was then called.*

Walpole rose magnificently to his opportunity. He worked untiringly for the army, kept in constant touch with Marlborough, the Commander-in-Chief in the field, and, though not himself in the Cabinet, was brought into the very hub of events. The Government, however, was doomed to a brief existence. The Queen, weary of the ill-tempered, domineering Duchess of Marlborough, resolved to get rid of the Duke and was greatly aided by the country's revulsion at the terrible slaughter at Malplaquet. St. John, harnessing the bitter irony of Swift, reviled Marlborough, who was accused of greed, cruelty and corruption in a succession of pamphlets which the public read avidly.

* In time the Lord Treasurer became the First Lord of the Treasury.

Squires and tradesmen resented the ever-mounting taxation; the poor blamed the bad harvests on the war; and on 5th November of that year (1709), a notable anniversary observed annually because of the deliverance of James the First and his Ministers from the gunpowder plot and because it marked also the happy arrival of William the Third in the country, Dr. Henry Sacheverell, an outspoken and fiery preacher, used the occasion for delivering a violent sermon at St. Paul's, deeply critical of the Government. The references to Godolphin, only thinly veiled, were offensive, and the Government decided on Sacheverell's impeachment, a course which neither Marlborough nor Walpole favoured. The trial stirred the country to intense anger. Cheering crowds followed Sacheverell down the Strand to the court at Westminster Hall. Though found guilty, his sentence was light: he was merely prevented from preaching for three years and his sermon was publicly burnt. Nevertheless the country rejoiced. Bonfires were lighted everywhere. So great was the unpopularity of the Whigs that at the General Election, too dangerously near, the voters, egged on by the clergy, confirmed the Queen's dismissal of the Whigs. The Tories were triumphant and Harley came back to office as Lord Treasurer.

Strenuous efforts were made by Harley to retain Walpole, though a Whig, in the new Government, but Walpole refused to serve. The tables were thereupon viciously turned upon him. Walpole was sent to the Tower, accused of corruptly receiving £1,000 on a contract for forage while he was Secretary at War. It was eventually established that he had not received a penny of this money. Meanwhile, he was expelled from Parliament, was re-elected by the voters and was once again expelled. His prison cell became the meeting place of the aristocratic Whigs. His praise was sung in ballads in the street. In the end he was completely exonerated and on his release resumed his place in the House with his reputation very greatly enhanced.

The closing year of Queen Anne's reign, bringing acutely to the forefront the question of the succession, was marked by a widespread intrigue for the restoration of her Catholic brother the Pretender, calling himself King James the Third, an absurd, paralytic figure dressed generally in a velvet greatcoat, a cocked hat and the Garter, who had his exiled court at Saint-Germain just outside Paris. The tension both in England and Scotland was extremely acute. Plans

were in hand for open rebellion, in which many Tories were implicated. Risings in support of the Pretender were organized to take place
in London and elsewhere. Civil War was expected. Meanwhile Marlborough, who had taken refuge in Holland after his fall, was trying
with the full support of the Whigs to persuade the Dutch to send over
ships and troops to assist the cause of the Hanoverians. The aged and
ailing Queen's sympathies were clearly with her brother, but she died
half way through the year and speedily James the First's great-grand-
son was brought over from Hanover and placed on the English throne
as King George the First.*

The new King, fat, stupid and fifty-four, arrived with a retinue of
more than three hundred Germans, among them a Lutheran clergyman,
a score of physicians, surgeons and apothecaries, cooks, housemaids,
and trumpeters, and in addition, three Turkish servants. In selecting
his Government, not unnaturally, he turned exclusively to the Whigs,
and before long Walpole became Chancellor of the Exchequer and
in effect head of the Government, with his brother-in-law, Lord
Townshend,† as Secretary of State. The country was not wholly prepared to accept the new King. Rioting occurred in some places. In many
churches there was outspoken opposition to the new monarch. But
the Whigs took the strongest precautions to prevent their opponents
bringing in French assistance in support of the Pretender. Louis the
Fourteenth being now old and his country impoverished by war, they
got none. The crisis passed and the new dynasty was established, though
in the succeeding thirty years recurrent efforts were made to unseat it.

The first of these assaults was made in the following year, 1715.
There was a rising in Scotland on behalf of the Pretender and an army
marched south to restore the Stuarts to the throne. But not three
hundred men in England were prepared to assist them and they
surrendered when they got as far as Preston. Among their supporters
were many highly placed Tories and with these Walpole decided to
deal with the utmost severity. Normally a man of moderate temper,
he exercised his clemency only towards the rank and file. The pleas

---

* Had Anne died two months earlier, her successor would have been George the First's
mother, the Electress Sophia.
† Lord Townshend, a neighbour in Norfolk and a close friend of the family, married
Walpole's sister Dorothy in 1713.

of the rebel Tory peers he dismissed without mercy. He had been offered, he revealed to the House of Commons, as much as £60,000 to spare the life of the Earl of Derwentwater, but contemptuously he rejected the offer.

George the First, delighted though he was at his elevation from a modest German principality to the throne of one of the most important kingdoms in Europe, was distressed at discovering that he possessed far less authority than he had in Hanover. He knew hardly any English, and despite the regular flow of reports from Count Bothmar, he was unfamiliar with political procedure and public feeling in England and was wholly dependent on his Whig Ministers. He had brought with him his two old and ugly mistresses and a swarm of avaricious German courtiers, all eager to secure as their rightful spoils the most highly paid sinecures. Walpole's resolve to resist this brought upon him their united hostility. The intrigues against him were led by Bothmar, who was then still in residence in the house that was to form a substantial part of No. 10 Downing Street. The mistresses whispered maliciously in the King's ear. One of them, the Countess of Schulenberg, now transformed into the Duchess of Kendal, Walpole was convinced would readily have sold the King's honour for a shilling advance on the highest bidder.[29] The intriguers were joined by a group of covetous Whigs, and together they prevailed on the King. Walpole left the Government in disgust.

He was not out of office for very long. The brilliance he had displayed in disentangling the complexities of the nation's financial problems led to his return in 1720. Harley, who had succeeded him at the Exchequer, had striven to ease the burden of debt left by the war by arranging for a private trading concern, the South Sea Company, to take over £30 million of the National Debt, in return for a complete monopoly of the trade with South America. The opportunities seemed so vastly promising that there was a rush to purchase the Company's shares. Not only speculators but men and women of slender means joined in avidly. Walpole, when the proposal was initially debated in the House of Commons, pointed out the 'dangerous lure for decoying the unwary to their ruin by a false prospect of gain'. The House nevertheless approved it. Having given his warning, Walpole retired to Houghton, his home in Norfolk.

For some months the Company's shares rose rapidly. 'South Sea is all the talk and fashion; the ladys sell their jewells to buye.'* Then quite suddenly the shares began to fall. When the crash came panic set in. In the calamity the Government were directly implicated and every eye turned now to Walpole. He returned in triumph. A grateful Sovereign rewarded him eventually with the Garter.

Walpole's rise to the supreme office followed not long afterwards, in April 1721. That he was able to achieve this by the time he was forty-five despite his modest beginnings and while he was still heavily burdened by debt was due to his unique qualities – his intense application to work, his unflagging energy, and above all to his understanding and skill in handling people, both in Parliament and outside it. His manipulation of the finances of the country amounted almost to wizardry and brought immense benefits to the traders and lasting prosperity to the nation. The factions that divided the Whigs were resolved by his shrewdness or by death's fortunate intervention; and he was well set for his long term as Prime Minister,† which spanned more than twenty uninterrupted years and is the longest in the history of the country. But it was impossible to foresee this when it began. Walpole knew that the King did not like him: the whispers of his German courtiers still buzzed faintly in his ears; and Walpole knew too that when the King's son succeeded (and His Majesty was already in his sixty-seventh year), his dismissal must follow; for the son hated his father and had gathered about him the chief opponents of his father's Government, all of them Walpole's bitterest enemies. The hatred was generated by his father's vile treatment of his mother, who had been incarcerated in a desolate castle in Hanover and left to die there: and for this Walpole realized he and his Government would soon have to pay.

The death of George the First occurred in June 1727. He died in a carriage on his way to Hanover. Walpole, on learning the news, drove to Richmond Lodge and aroused the new King from his afternoon nap. 'I have the honour,' Walpole began, 'to announce to your Majesty, that your royal father, King George the First, died at Osnaburgh on Saturday the 10th instant.' His Majesty, dishevelled and not

* Mrs. James Windham.
† Walpole was the first to be referred to as 'Prime Minister'.

quite awake, became angry and roared inexplicably: 'Dat is one big lie!'

Walpole awaited his dismissal, but it did not come. Boorish and ill-tempered though George the Second was, he was only too well aware of his limitations and relied almost entirely on his wife Queen Caroline to guide him. She was intelligent and, liking gossip and gaiety was drawn to Walpole because of his sparkle and vivacity; not only was he allowed to remain as Prime Minister, but soon his friends became friends of the King and Queen.

Walpole directed his energy to providing stability. He was aided in the latter by the abolition of the three-year Parliament, introduced in the reign of William the Third, and the lengthening of its term to seven years by the Septennial Act of 1716. This removed the fluctuations and constant upheavals caused by too frequent elections. Having secured, with the help of the Duke of Newcastle and other powerful manipulators of the ballot, the majority he needed in the Commons, and with the use also of the boroughs in the control of the Crown, he was assured of support for long enough to carry out his plans. That he succeeded in maintaining his control of the House for twenty-one consecutive years is generally attributed to the adroit use of bribery. It would be more exact to describe it as a calculated and adept distribution of patronage, for there were an enormous number of archaic offices, many of them mere sinecures, as well as exorbitant pensions, all of them in the gift of the Crown, which the chief Minister was in a position to confer in exchange for support in the House by the grateful recipients or their relatives. In many instances such public money was paid without requiring any service in return, as in the case of the Sweeper of the Mall or the Clerk of the Pipe; in others which carried certain duties a humble clerk was often employed at a small fee to fulfil them, as had happened in the case of Pepys and Downing. That such a wide distribution of emoluments would be regarded by present standards as corruption is undeniable. But it is at the same time arguable that Walpole did not so much corrupt the age as that he was forced to operate in an age already corrupt. Convinced that the measures he wanted to get through the House were advantageous to the nation, he found himself unable to attain this end by any other course. What he aimed at was to avoid getting entangled in war, to set the finances of the country on a sound footing, and to ensure conditions in which trade could flourish. All this he achieved. He also strove to ensure that the Government of the country should not be at the mercy of a monarch's whim, but should be made independent of him, in short that in future the House of Commons and the Cabinet should govern the country. He was able to attain this through the detachment, often the indifference, of the King who, like his father, was absent in Hanover for long periods, leaving England in the care of Walpole and the Whigs. Thus the royal prerogative in the selection of Ministers was in the course of time reduced to the formal fiction that endures to this day.

Until he moved into No. 10 Downing Street in 1735, Walpole lived in St. James's Square, going at weekends to Richmond where he hunted with the harriers and to his estate at Houghton, in Norfolk, for Christmas and the long summer recess – Parliament met for only four months or so in the year. At each of these places he entertained munificently but was inclined to be parsimonious over little things: he insisted, for example, on getting twopence back on every empty bottle and, though Chancellor of the Exchequer as well as First Lord of the Treasury, he was not above employing a smuggler, as many others did at that time, to evade the excise and customs duties. The annual salary from his two offices, totalling £7,400, together with certain perquisites, made it possible not only for him to pay off his enormous debts, but provide himself with estates of great magnificence. It was an age of luxurious country houses and extensive parks, beautified by lakes, Grecian temples and mock ruins, with occasionally a hired hermit to give it colour. Every nobleman, every merchant as he acquired wealth, built grandly and spent prodigious sums on furniture and pictures, combing the Continent for its treasures. Walpole began to emulate them while his means were still slender. On moving in 1714 into a little house behind Chelsea Hospital, he set about its embellishment and called in the aid of John Vanbrugh. A terrace was built with an octagonal summer house; then an orangery; then an aviary filled with rare singing birds. He loved the house and it was here that some of his Cabinet meetings were held until he moved to No. 10. He next turned his attention to the rebuilding and decoration of Houghton, calling in William Kent to evolve

the improvements and fill it with elegant furniture, while his ambassadors scoured the capitals of Europe for pictures.

Before moving into Downing Street he sent Kent to look over the
old Cockpit lodgings, once occupied by King Charles the Second's
daughter, the Countess of Lichfield, and more recently by Count
Bothmar. The house was Crown property and King George the
Second, appreciative of all Walpole had done for the Hanoverian
dynasty and the country, offered it to him as a personal gift. But
Walpole declined it, saying that 'he would only accept it for his Office
of the First Lord of the Treasury, to which post he got it annexed for
ever.'* The King also acquired the lease of the two houses in Downing
Street to which it was joined, as well as some stables alongside, and
Kent, engaged then in building the Treasury on the site of the Cockpit
and adjacent to one of Henry the Eighth's tennis courts, effected the
fusion with admirable skill. The work was extensive. Part of the interior was gutted. The houses were linked by a long room on the
Whitehall side with corresponding rooms above. The remainder of
the space between the two main houses was left as an open courtyard.
Drawings of what was done are preserved in a scrapbook in the Metro-
politan Museum of Art in New York. The numerous staircases that
cluttered the three houses were ripped out and a handsome new stone
staircase was inserted, rising from the garden floor (joined now to the
basement on the Downing Street end) to the first floor: its iron balus-
trade was embellished with a lovely scroll design and a mahogany
handrail. This staircase still stands. The house at the back, left with
three floors as before, had its central section surmounted with a pediment. A portion of the Horse Guards Parade had been enclosed with
a wall in Bothmar's time, with a gate opening onto the Parade. But
it was not converted into a garden until Walpole moved in. It was
then laid out and developed at the expense of the State. Letters patent
issued by the Lords of the Treasury on 16th April 1736,† state that 'a
piece of garden ground scituate in his Majesty's park of St. James's,
& belonging & adjoining to the house now inhabited by the Right
Honourable the Chancellor of His Majestys Exchequer, hath been
lately made & fitted up at the Charge . . . of the Crown', and that the

---

* Horace Walpole, *Aedes Walpolianae*.
† Public Record Office.

said house and garden were 'meant to be annexed & united to the Office of his Majesty's Treasury & to be & to remain for the Use & Habitation of the first Commissioner of his Majesty's Treasury for the time being.' As it was necessary 'that some Skilfull person should be appointed to look after . . . the said piece of ground', they selected Samuel Milward for the post at a salary of £40 a year.[1]

Kent's sketches show the interior elevations of seven main rooms on the ground floor and the first floor all facing the garden or the park: these he decorated sumptuously – the sketches indicate the pictures hanging on the walls together with the names of the artists. Many of the marble mantelpieces he put in still survive. But the pictures on the walls were Walpole's personal property and were taken away by him when he left.

The largest room on the ground floor (at the back in the Cockpit section of the house)* was made into a levee room and study for Walpole (it measures forty feet by twenty), and it was here that the Cabinet met and still meets. It was made magnificently impressive, with enormous windows looking out onto the garden and the Horse Guards Parade beyond, and opening through a french window onto Bothmar's terrace, from which a double flight of stairs leads down to the garden. Alongside it was Walpole's dressing-room and beside it the Parlour.

The bedrooms were on the floor above. Lady Walpole's was on the Whitehall side with a dining-room beside it. The corner room, overlooking both St. James's Park and the Horse Guards Parade, was the drawing-room. The walls of these rooms were covered with brocade, as at Walpole's house at Houghton.

Money had been spent lavishly. The work was well done. A delightful home, spacious and decorated with taste, had been provided for the King's first minister. But neither Kent nor Downing had given much thought to the foundations: both adhered to the practice of their time. The foundations, at a depth of no more than six feet in certain parts, rested on timber sills or beams laid loosely on the treacherous soil, into which the river's silt oozed at intervals, even as far in as this. It was inevitable that the timber would rot and that the house should be in need of constant and costly attention.

---

* The first floor if looked at from the garden side.

But it still stands – a part of it nearly three centuries old. That part, the old house in which King Charles the First had lived as a child and Cromwell after him, had lost its identity: it was no longer a noble edifice on St. James's Park, but a house in a narrow cul-de-sac called Downing Street. It gazed onto a similar row of houses, not built by Downing, standing where the Foreign Office is now. Most of these houses took in lodgers: M.P.s from the provinces and especially Scotland used to stay here for the Parliamentary session. The writer Tobias Smollet had rooms in one of them when he practised as a surgeon; Boswell, Johnson's biographer, rented rooms in another almost facing No. 10. At the Whitehall corner, on that side, stood an inn, called the Rose and Crown, from which, as the placards announced, 'Louis Barbay, successor to the late Mrs. Maria Wickstead, Being the only Person that has possession of her Secret for Curing Sore Throats and Wens, though of ever so large a Size', sold lozenges and powders, together with 'Directions how to take them'.

But despite all this the rear section of No. 10 has lost neither its character nor its atmosphere, for it is that part of the house that all who have lived in it love best and it is there that in every shadow there seems to lurk something of the country's great history.

CHAPTER 7
Walpole at No. 10

WALPOLE was sixty when he moved into No. 10. For some years he and his wife had been living separate, independent lives, but they kept up the fiction of still being together and she moved into the house with him. At first, after their marriage, their attachment was warm and passionate, as his letters to her show. She had a child, or a miscarriage, almost every year. He indulged her every whim, and, though his financial difficulties in those years were crippling, he pandered to her extravagance and his own by getting deeper and deeper into debt. She was restless and sought continual distraction in social gaiety – the opera, costly dresses, jewels, even the card-table. It was whispered that she was wanton, but of this there is no reliable evidence, though the birth of her youngest son, the famous letter writer Horace Walpole, after a gap of eleven years, gave some substance to these rumours, for Walpole was scarcely ever with her at the time of the conception. Nevertheless he acknowledged the child, but left him completely to his mother. She was rarely at No. 10 and hardly ever accompanied Walpole on his visits to Houghton, but lived mainly by herself in their home in Chelsea, went to Bath for the season and did not bother to visit her husband even when he was ill, as he often was, at times gravely ill.

Short in stature, of great bulk and with a multiplicity of chins, he was far from attractive physically. Yet in every gathering he was the centre of interest even before he attained the heights. Boisterously hearty, he danced, drank and hunted, as untiring in his play as at his work. In manner he was courteous, but his conversation was often coarse and he was apt to forget that ladies were present, a forgetfulness at times apparent even in the presence of the Queen. Though calm and unruffled as a rule, when he did lose his temper, he would rise abruptly from the Cabinet table and break up the meeting, saying 'nobody was fit for business once they had lost control'. It was his conviction that difficulties should be avoided not provoked: 'Let sleeping dogs lie', he would say. No detail escaped his attention. Every letter was written in his own hand, instead of being dictated to a clerk, and he wrote thousands of letters in the course of his official business. He even transcribed personally the letters he received, jotted down extracts from dispatches and added to each his own memoranda.

The historic beginning of the Prime Minister's move into his official residence was recorded in the London *Daily Post* of 23rd September 1735 in a single brief sentence: 'Yesterday the Right Hon. Sir Robert Walpole, with his Lady and Family, removed from their House in St. James's Square, to his new House, adjoining to the Treasury in St. James's Park.'

A week later his first important reception in this house, a breakfast party, was announced in the same newspaper: 'This morning about 9, the Queen, the Duke, and the Princesses, attended by the Principal Officers and Ladies of the Court, intend to come from Kensington and Breakfast with Sir Robert Walpole, at his new House near the Treasury in St. James's Park. Some choice Fruits, Sweetmeats and Wines, with Tea, Chocolate, etc., have been sent in for the Entertainment of the Royal and Illustrious Company. Sir Robert Walpole continues to Lodge at his House at Chelsea, till the Meeting of Parliament, when he will, with his family move to that in St. James's Park.'

And two days later: 'When her Majesty Breakfasted with Sir Robert Walpole on Wednesday last, at his House in St. James's Park, the Right

Hon. the Lord Walpole,⋆ Edward Walpole, Esq., and Horace Walpole, Esq., Sir Robert's three Sons, waited at Table on her Majesty and the Royal Family. The Earl of Grantham, by her Majesty's Order, left a handsome Sum to be distributed among the Servants.'

Walpole sought solace for his domestic infelicity from a number of mistresses. Because he acted with the utmost discretion in an age when discretion was disregarded, it was thought that his earlier affairs at any rate were casual and unimportant, though one of these mistresses presented him with a daughter named Catherine Daye. But in 1725 when Maria Skerrett came into his life, all discretion was abandoned. They had met at the house of Lady Mary Wortley Montagu at Twickenham and the wooing is said to have taken him a full year. They began to go about together quite openly and she often stayed with him at No. 10 Downing Street, even when his children were there; of these his eldest, Lord Walpole, was in his thirties, whereas Horace had just left Eton and was about to go on to King's College, Cambridge. Maria's portraits show her to have been a tall, thin and rather plain young woman: her contemporaries do not speak of her as being attractive in appearance. But her wit, charm and her uncommon commonsense came in for a great deal of praise. Walpole was certainly deeply in love and his devotion lasted until the end of her life. Some months after the death of his wife in 1737 (she was buried at Westminster Abbey with an eulogistic epitaph composed by her son Horace) Walpole married Maria – or Molly, as he called her. The marriage took place in March 1738.

Walpole's younger brother Horatio, writing of this to a friend, said: 'My brother brought home this lady on Sunday last; who is indeed a very sensible, well behaved modest woman, appears not at all elated with her new situation and I daresay will be generally esteemed.' Another caller at No. 10, Sir Thomas Robinson, later Lord Grantham, wrote of her to Lord Carlisle: 'All the well wishers to Sir Robert Walpole have been to wish him and his lady joy. I did it to both with great sincerity. Everybody gives her a very good character, both as to her understanding and good nature.'

Most distressingly, their happiness ended a few weeks later. On 6th

---

⋆ Sir Robert Walpole's eldest son was made a peer in 1723.

June the new Lady Walpole died through a miscarriage. Horatio wrote of his 'inexpressible concern for poor Lady Walpole's death on her own account, but more particularly by reason of the deplorable and comfortless condition in which it has flung my brother, who had his happiness, and indeed very deservedly, wrapt up in her.'

By her Walpole had two illegitimate daughters, of whom only one, Mary, survived. She later married Colonel Charles Churchill, an illegitimate son of General Charles Churchill and Anne Oldfield. For many years she was a housekeeper at Windsor Castle and lived on until the beginning of the nineteenth century.

Walpole had been at pains to make ample provision in case Maria Skerrett should survive him, and characteristically (since he had already done the same for his children) all the provision was made out of public funds. He began these arrangements even before their marriage, by which time she was already assured £400 a year for life. To this he added £200 a year from the office of Inspector and Examiner of Books of Patent. She was next assigned £500 a year from the office of the Comptroller-General of Accounts of His Majesty's Customs – in all a total of £1,100 a year.

Though inconsolable, Walpole found fresh solace less than a year later. Lord Egmont noted in his diary on 11th April 1739: 'Sir Robert Walpole being a widower has youth enough about him, notwithstanding the age of 64, to take a new mistress, the sister of Mr. Glenn, the new Governor of Carolina, which Mr. Glenn married a natural daughter of my Lord Wilmington.'

Walpole was greatly attached to his brother Horatio and did all he could to further his career. He began as a lawyer but became a diplomatist in 1706 and was appointed by Walpole as secretary to General James Stanhope at Barcelona. He was already a Member of Parliament and, despite his many ambassadorial missions abroad, remained in Parliament for an unbroken period of fifty-four years. When Walpole became First Lord of the Treasury Horatio was made Secretary to the Treasury. As early as 1717 Walpole appointed him for life Surveyor and Auditor-General of the Plantation (American) Revenues of the Crown. This brought Horatio a substantial income as well as an office almost alongside No. 10 Downing Street. Here he took up his residence in 1723. The house, which adjoined the old Cockpit, had once belonged to Lord Clarendon. Horatio soon found he required more space for the ledgers dealing with the revenues from America, and petitioned for the lease of premises abutting on one side on to the houses in Downing Street and on the other on to the stables of Count Bothmar, at that time in residence in the back section of No. 10. He asked for a lease of fifty years to be granted to him personally. This was agreed to. He also purchased a portion of the Downing Estate for the small sum of £185 and annexed it to these premises. Thus for some years the brothers were next door neighbours and Horatio and his wife came constantly to No. 10. Walpole's other visitors did not take at all kindly to them. Horatio was coarse-featured, his speech was marked by a Norfolk accent and his clothes were far from elegant, indeed they were often dirty. Lord Hervey has left an unflattering picture of him and his wife. Horatio he describes as 'a very disagreeable man in company, noisy, overbearing, affecting to be always jocose . . . as unbred in his dialect as in his apparel, and as ill bred in his discourse as in his behaviour; with no more the look than the habits of a gentleman.' Of his wife 'Pug', he is still more unkind: 'A tailor's daughter whom he had married for interest, with a form scarce human, as offensive to the nose as to the eye.'[23] But Walpole was fond of them both and had them always with him.

Young Horace Walpole often stayed at No. 10 and had a stream of his own visitors. Amongst his closer friends was Thomas Gray, the poet, who had been at Eton with him, and later they set out together on a long Continental tour. Walpole himself, being fond of company, also did a great deal of entertaining here. He used to hold a levee in the drawing-room on the first floor to which his political admirers, as well as his opponents, came. One can visualize the throng of bewigged gentlemen in their long velvet coats, some of bright scarlet, others of cerulean blue, trimmed with gold or silver lace, mounting the stone stairs in their buckled shoes. The most prominent men in his Government would have come constantly and the younger men, destined one day themselves to be prominent, would have regarded it as a privilege to be of the company. Of these the most famous was certainly William Pitt the elder, later Lord Chatham. Born in 1708, he was singled out early as a politician of outstanding quality. From his letters, written in 1734 when he was in his twenties, one gets the impression that he was

53

a supporter of Walpole's. But two years later, after Pitt was elected to Parliament, a certain petulance became noticeable in Walpole's manner towards him and in Pitt there developed a fierce hostility. Among other notable men who came to No. 10 were the great Lord Chesterfield, the essayists Addison and Steele, the Duke of Newcastle, most powerful Whig of the day, the Earl of Halifax and even Lord Bolingbroke. Dr. Johnson, a year younger than Pitt, always held Walpole in high esteem. 'He was the best minister this country ever had,' Johnson said of him some years later, 'for if we would have let him be, he would have kept it in perpetual peace.'

That Walpole had been able to maintain peace for a whole generation was not achieved without difficulty and the exercise of constant vigilance. To begin with he had to reverse the earlier policy of the Whigs, who had ardently supported Marlborough's wars and had readily placed all the resources of England at his disposal. The adjustment was by no means easy and it took time. Europe was in a continuous ferment because of the dynastic ambitions, the incessant plots and counterplots of its more unscrupulous rulers. From these it was not always possible to remain detached, since the plots, affecting as they did the flow of trade, threatened the prosperity of England. Only with ingenuity and tact was Walpole able to avoid embroilment in Europe's wars and to keep open the vital channels of trade. The King's Hanoverian dominions, affected as they constantly were by the ambitious designs of others, made it essential for Walpole to placate His Majesty and also, by a judicious distribution of patronage and preferment, ensure the support of his own plans in the House of Commons. By delaying tactics, by last-minute compromises and by skilful adjustments through his brother and his other agents, he succeeded in evading involvement for a whole generation. He was faced from time to time with having to explain to the King why British troops could not be used in his German quarrels. One morning, not many months before moving into No. 10 Downing Street, he said to the Queen with considerable satisfaction: 'Madam, there are fifty thousand men slain this year in Europe, and not one Englishman.'

His difficulties had begun to multiply before he moved into Downing Street. While he was still poring over Kent's plans for reconstruction, examining designs for his new furniture, and going through the costs which as Chancellor of the Exchequer he would have to authorize the Treasury to meet, trouble arose over his plan to introduce fresh excise duties. Taxation he had consistently reduced: it was his intention now to reduce the land tax and counterbalance it by extending the existing duties on tea, coffee and chocolate to tobacco and wine. That it would have been of advantage to the country was undisputed, but a clamour was raised against it in 1733 and Walpole gave way. True he still had control of the Commons, and in the Lords the Whig majority was maintained by a careful selection of Bishops.* Nevertheless discontent, prompted by ambition, was discernible even among his followers, especially among the younger men of whom William Pitt, still in his twenties, was one of the most active and outspoken. When Walpole yielded to their assault on the home front they quickly switched the attack to foreign affairs, for the situation had become much more critical on the Continent. But Walpole was still able to show that he had lost none of his old flair. He had to apply persuasion and pressure in turn on the Holy Roman Emperor, on Cardinal Fleury of France, on the Queen of Spain, and, when these failed, he had to offer bribes in the form of territorial or dynastic concessions which one or other of them coveted. His opponents, attributing his achievements to luck and eager themselves for office after twenty years of waiting, gathered in force to get him out. He was ageing. Ministers he had sacked, reluctant before to defy him, showed signs now of doing so. There were clashes with Newcastle, a powerful and much younger Minister, who began to turn his thoughts to his own future. With him were other members of the Cabinet – Lords Hardwicke and Harrington. They did not find it easy. As Pope, an intimate of Walpole's most formidable enemies Bolingbroke (formerly St. John) and Swift, expressed it:

> Seen him I have; but in his happier hour
> Of social pleasure ill-exchanged for power:
> Seen him uncumbered with the venal tribe,
> Smile without effort and win without a bribe.

* Catholics were still excluded from both Houses and were to remain so for many more years.

After Queen Caroline's death his position became weaker. The King's heir, Frederick, Prince of Wales, having quarrelled with his father, set up a separate court in a rented house in Leicester Square and gathered about him a rival Government that was ready to take over: it was the second time this had happened during Walpole's long rule.

In 1738, shortly after his marriage to Maria Skerrett and her untimely death, he faced his most turbulent storm. France's prestige and power, so low a generation before, had increased greatly, largely because of Walpole's detachment from Europe. An alliance formed between that country and Spain was regarded with the utmost suspicion by the great commercial organizations in England, who felt that their own opportunities of trading with the Spanish countries across the Atlantic would be gravely endangered. They worked themselves into a frenzy and were supported by Walpole's opponents, who saw in this an opportunity of driving him out of office, since it was quite unlikely that he would go to war. Pitt, in a rousing speech, proclaimed: 'When trade is at stake it is your last retrenchment: you must defend it or perish.' Half-forgotten atrocities committed some years before by Spain against British buccaneers were recalled and the entire country clamoured for a war of vengeance. They were backed by Parliament and even by some of Walpole's colleagues in the Cabinet. Known now as the Patriots, they took as their symbol Captain Jenkins' ear, cut off as long as seven years before. Jenkins was called to the bar of the House, made to produce the severed ear and to describe how it had been sliced off to an accompaniment of jeers at the English King. National pride was roused, mingled with which was the hope of increased commercial gain in the South American trade routes controlled by Spain.

Walpole assured the nation that redress for past outrages as well as security for the future could much more easily be obtained by peaceable negotiation. To make war on a nation whose trade routes were of vital importance to Britain, would, he argued, do more harm than good. But the country would not be soothed. The Spanish, it was insisted, must abandon their right to search British ships. This the Spaniards refused to concede, nor after nine years of war were they compelled to concede it.

The war, forced on Walpole in 1739, was received by the public with frenzied enthusiasm. Walpole said: 'They now ring the bells, but they

56

will soon wring their hands.' He immediately offered his resignation, but the King refused to accept it. Pressed further, he still refused. 'Will you desert me in my greatest difficulties?' cried His Majesty pitifully.

In the Cabinet of six, most of them peers, dissension, already acute, became critical. On not more than three of his colleagues could Walpole any longer rely. The King's efforts to draw them together were without avail. Violent altercations took place every day. In 1740 when Walpole decided to make Lord Hervey the new Lord Privy Seal, the Duke of Newcastle put forward the name of Carteret, to whom he had secretly offered it. 'Oh,' exclaimed Walpole, 'I always suspected that you had been dabbling there, and now I know it. But if you make such bargains, I don't think myself obliged to keep them.' The office was thereupon given to Hervey.

Hervey did not stand by Walpole in his hour of crisis. He described later another clash in the Cabinet room between Walpole and the Duke of Newcastle:

'Just as Sir Robert Walpole was upon his legs to go away, the Duke of Newcastle said, "If you please, I would speak one word to you before you go"; to which Sir Robert Walpole replied, "I do not please, my Lord: but if you will, you must." – "Sir, I shall not trouble you long." – "Well, my lord, that's something; but I had rather not be troubled at all. Won't it keep cold till tomorrow?" – "Perhaps not, sir." – "Well, come then, let's have it"; upon which they retired to a corner of the room, where his Grace whispered very softly, and Sir Robert answered nothing but aloud, and said nothing aloud but every now and then, "Pooh! Pshaw! O Lord! O Lord! pray be quiet. My God, can't you see it is over?" '

The most critical attacks upon Walpole in Parliament were based on the accusation that during his years of office he had usurped the sole power of directing all public affairs, of making appointments to all public posts, recommending all honours – in fact of doing everything that the Prime Minister does today.

Samuel Sandys, who was to succeed Walpole as Chancellor of the Exchequer and to move into No. 10, led the attack in the House of Commons, declaring that 'According to our constitution we can have no sole and prime minister: we ought always to have several prime ministers or officers of state; every such officer has his own proper department; and no officer ought to meddle in the affairs belonging to the department of another.'

The attack, made and supported in both Houses, was defeated in both Houses. But a minority in the Lords insisted: 'We are persuaded that a sole, or even a First Minister, is an officer unknown to the law of Britain, inconsistent with the constitution of this country, and destructive of liberty in any government whatsoever.'

Neither Walpole not his supporters denied this principle, they merely rejected the facts. Walpole, insisting that he had never usurped the authority of First Minister, said: 'As one of His Majesty's council I have only one voice.'

Despite his disclaimer, Walpole was in fact Prime Minister and was the first to be called that. There had generally been a 'prime' Minister: in Queen Elizabeth the First's time the custom was to call him 'Mr. Secretary' since the Sovereign had the ultimate authority and her Secretary did no more than act on her dictation: the word survives to this day in 'Secretary of State'. Later, when more Ministers were needed, the Sovereign remained the prime selector and arbiter and each Minister was responsible only to the Crown. With the coming of the Hanoverians it was inevitable that one of these Ministers should exercize this authority in the name of the King. He and his colleagues were still liable to be brought to account separately by impeachment, since the Crown was above the law. The acceptance later of collective responsibility by the Cabinet freed the Prime Minister and his colleagues from being blamed individually for measures agreed by them all, then approved by Parliament, and ultimately endorsed by the King.

At the General Election in the summer of 1741 great exertions were made to defeat Walpole. It was argued that, since he never wanted the war, he could hardly be more than half-hearted in conducting it. In Scotland only six of the forty-five constituencies were for his party; the twenty-one boroughs of Cornwall were almost all opposed to him. None the less Walpole's friends were confident of having a majority of at least forty in the new House.

At this anxious time Walpole must have paced his bedroom at No. 10 restlessly through the night. His son Horace, who was then living in the house, noted on 19th October 1741: 'He who was asleep as soon as his head touched the pillow, for I have frequently known him snore ere they had drawn his curtains, now never sleeps above an hour without waking; and he, who at dinner always forgot he was minister, and was more gay and thoughtless than all his company, now sits without speaking, and with his eyes fixed for an hour together.'[32]

The battles in the House went on day after day. There were endless divisions. Over the election of the Chairman of Committees Walpole's opponents threw out his nominee by a majority of four. At this a great shout went up, loud, exultant and sustained. In the succeeding days Walpole managed to scrape through with narrow majorities. The debates went on through the night, and night after night, in order to tax and wear down his strength. He was forced on one occasion to wait until four in the morning before being allowed to rise and speak. His opponents even insisted on the House sitting on Saturdays, so as to keep him from having his customary relaxation with the harriers at Richmond. His sons begged him to give it up, arguing that after gaining one success with a worthwhile majority, he should retire. Leaning across the supper table, Walpole laughed at the suggestion. Though now sixty-five, he informed them proudly that he was younger than any of them. And certainly his vigour, his endurance and his spirits seemed undimmed.

Horace, however, realized that the end could not now be very far. On 17th December he wrote: 'Trust me, if we fall, all the grandeur, all the envied grandeur of our house, will not cost me a sigh: it has given me no pleasure while we have it, and will give me no pain when we part with it. My liberty, my ease, and choice of my own friends and company, will sufficiently counterbalance the crowds of Downing-street. I am so sick of it all, that if we are victorious or not, I propose leaving England in the Spring.'

After the Christmas recess the battles became even fiercer. The sick and the bedridden, the lame and even the blind were dragged or carried to the House to record their vote. Walpole's eldest son who, as auditor of the Exchequer, had a residence that communicated with the House, arranged that some of the invalids supporting his father should wait in comfort in his quarters until the division. The Opposition learned of this and stuffed the keyhole with dirt and sand; thus when the division was called it took too long to unlock the door and they were prevented from voting.

No fewer than 503 Members, the greatest number known, took part in the division. Walpole secured a majority, but it was no more than three and it was evident, even to him now, that he would have to go.

A few days after this, on the evening of 2nd February 1742, in a still further division, Walpole was defeated by sixteen votes and he walked out of the chamber for the last time, after having dominated it for forty years. At St. James's Palace the King, deeply moved, fell on his neck, wept and kissed him, and begged Walpole to come and see him frequently.*

Walpole accepted a peerage and went to the House of Lords as the Earl of Orford. He continued to live at No. 10 for some months. On 30th June Horace, changing his mind about their Downing Street residence, wrote: 'I am willing to enjoy this sweet corner while I may, for we are soon to quit it.' His father, he added, was moving 'into a small house of his own in Arlington Street, opposite to where we formerly lived. He is for my living with him; but then I shall be cooped.'

For some days a London mob carried Walpole's effigy in procession through the streets, making their way each day to the Tower. Horace ran after them to look at the other effigy they bore and found it to be of a female attended by three footmen and labelled 'Lady Mary'. It was meant to represent Walpole's illegitimate daughter by Maria Skerrett, born before their marriage, but given by the King the status of an Earl's daughter. The mob eventually tired of it and a year after his fall, in the coffee-houses and the clubs of London, men began to raise their glasses to drink Walpole's health and to demand that he should be asked to go back to the Treasury, where he had rendered such admirable service for so long. His advice was constantly sought by his successors. But his health had begun to fail and in March 1745 he died.

* Horace Walpole's letter to Horace Mann, 4th February 1742.[82]

CHAPTER 8
His Immediate Successors

WALPOLE was succeeded as First Lord of the Treasury by the Earl of Wilmington. As one of the leading members of the political group around George the Second when he was Prince of Wales, Wilmington, then Sir Spencer Compton, was expected to become Prime Minister the moment George the First died. That he did not was ascribed by contemporary gossips to an incident a few days after the new King's accession. Queen Caroline, concerned as to what allowance she would receive if she survived her husband, was told by Spencer Compton: 'As much, Madam, as any Queen of England ever had, which is £50,000 a year.' Hearing of this, Walpole astutely doubled the figure. He informed one of the Queen's courtiers that if Her Majesty had 'referred the matter to him he should have named £100,000'. This, it is said, won him the support of Queen Caroline, who remained staunchly loyal to him through the years.* Whatever the basis of this gossip, Walpole did something that was operative

---

* As it turned out the Queen died in 1737, twenty-three years before the King.

immediately. With the Civil List and control of the Commons still in his hands until a new Government displaced him, he set the Queen down for an allowance of £100,000 a year for life, the payments to begin at once. It may well have been contributory to his remaining on as Prime Minister while Compton, Speaker of the House of Commons at the time, was compensated with a peerage and became Lord Wilmington, but had to wait fifteen years for the chief ministerial office. By then he was in his seventieth year.

Horace Walpole described Wilmington as a 'solemn debauchee'; Lord Hervey said he was fond only of money and of eating. Most Members of Parliament referred to him as 'The Old Woman' – 'the most honourable title I have heard given him,' said Walpole in a letter to the Duke of Dorset. Lord Rosebery, calling him the favourite nonentity of King George the Second, added that his choice as Prime Minister had its advantages, 'for, always incapable, he was now moribund. ... So Wilmington reigned, and Carteret governed for a while in Walpole's stead.'⁴⁴

Having a fine town house of his own at the corner of St. James's Square and Pall Mall, Wilmington preferred not to live at No. 10 himself, but passed it on to the Chancellor of the Exchequer, who presumably, as second Lord at the Treasury, had the next claim. The Chancellor was Samuel Sandys – Walpole's most consistent opponent. Of his abilities also his contemporaries had an unflattering opinion. Writing of this unexpected tenant at Downing Street, Horace Walpole said: 'Mrs. Sandys came yesterday [29th June 1742] to give us warning; Lord Wilmington has lent it to them.' The Walpoles were forced to move out in a hurry for, writing of it again some years later,* Horace Walpole added: 'Four years ago I was mightily at my ease in Downing Street, and then the good woman, Sandys, took my lodgings over my head, and was in such a great hurry to junket her neighbours, that I had scarce time allowed me to wrap up my old china in a little hay.'

It was not only Horace Walpole's china that was moved. Everything was taken out. All the furniture, the pictures, the crockery, the linen, the silver, the cutlery, every vase, every ornament, the carpets and curtains, being the personal property of Walpole, were removed. The next occupant, like his successors for a century and a half afterwards,

* In 1745.

Sir Robert Walpole, the first Prime Minister, who by joining three houses together created No. 10 Downing Street. The portrait, painted by J. van Loo in 1740, hangs above the mantelpiece in the Cabinet Room.

Maria Skerrett, Walpole's mistress and later his second wife. She lived with him at No. 10.

William Pitt, first Earl of Chatham, from a painting by Brampton. Though not Prime Minister at the time, his vigorous leadership during the Seven Years War won Britain a vast Empire. He never lived at No. 10.

Lord North, from a painting by Nathaniel Dance. His twelve years at No. 10 Downing Street as Prime Minister (1770–82) were shadowed by the stress and anxieties of the American War of Independence.

The Younger Pitt, Chatham's second son, Prime Minister for a total of twenty years. From a painting by J. Hoppner.

Lady Hester Stanhope, niece of the younger Pitt and for a time his hostess at No. 10 Downing Street. The portrait, from a lithograph by R. J. Hamerton, shows her in the dress she wore while living with the Druses on Mount Lebanon in Syria for nearly thirty years.

came to a completely empty house, which he had to furnish and equip himself. The State provided nothing, save the tables and chairs for the offices.

The Sandys, who had ten children, the eldest not yet twenty, must have been faced with some discomfort in accommodating so large a family as well as a host of servants in a house by no means big and where rooms had also to be found for secretaries' offices and for waiting Ministers and callers. At any rate they insisted that there were 'several Repairs necessary',* and these were carried out while they still lived there. Sandys, however, did not enjoy the tenancy for long, for in December of the following year (1743) he ceased to be Chancellor of the Exchequer and was given a peerage; but, though expected to vacate the premises, appears to have been in less of a hurry than when he came in and stayed on at No. 10 for some months until 1744.

His successor at the Exchequer, Henry Pelham, who had become First Lord of the Treasury on Wilmington's death in July 1743, preferred, like Wilmington, to live in his own house and lent No. 10, not to another member of his Government, but to his elder daughter, Catherine, for her to live in after her marriage to his nephew the Earl of Lincoln. The young couple were in their early twenties and Lincoln was not even remotely interested in politics. Thus in less than ten years No. 10 ceased to be the official residence of the Prime Minister and became the private home of his relatives. Lincoln's only known excursion into politics occurred when he acted as mediator, possibly at No. 10, between his two uncles Henry Pelham, the placid Prime Minister, and his blustering, bad tempered elder brother, the powerful Duke of Newcastle, who had married a granddaughter of the great Duke of Marlborough and had been in the Government as a Secretary of State for twenty years.

The quarrel between the brothers had produced a crisis. Pelham had viewed with alarm the possibility of a coalition between Pitt and Newcastle. Lincoln stepped in to heal the breach and drew up a treaty of peace, which he persuaded the brothers to sign.

The Lincolns lived at No. 10 for eight years (until 1753) and, when they left, Pelham lent the house to another of his daughters, who had

---

* Public Record Office: note dated 3rd August 1742.

just married Lewis Watson. So once again it was the home of another young bride, but this time not for long, for the Prime Minister died in the following year, 1754, and his younger daughter and her husband were asked to leave by the new Prime Minister, their uncle the Duke of Newcastle.

In the ratebook for that year Watson's name was crossed out and a new name was entered. It was put down as 'Henry Legg', but, more accurately, it should have been Henry Bilson-Legge. He was a younger son of the Earl of Dartmouth and knew the house well, for he had lived there for some years while private secretary to Walpole. Now, at the age of forty-six, he returned in the exalted position of Chancellor of the Exchequer. The Duke of Newcastle preferred to remain in his own house, which was far more luxurious, and possibly also because he did not wish to face the upheaval of moving his furniture and his pictures.

Legge had learned much from Walpole and had already won a great reputation as a financier. His chief's opinion of him was that he had 'very little rubbish in his head'; but later, angered by his 'endeavouring to steal'* his daughter Maria, Walpole refused to accept him as a son-in-law and told Legge to leave No. 10. In his twenties at the time and well connected, Legge decided to take up a political career. He was elected to Parliament in 1740 and within eight years, with Pitt as his patron, rose to be a Lord of the Admiralty and a Lord of the Treasury. He was then sent as Envoy-Extraordinary to Frederick the Great, a first cousin of King George the Second. The King felt he mishandled the mission and ever afterwards referred to Legge as a fool. It was only with difficulty that he was persuaded now to accept him as Chancellor of the Exchequer, but imposed the strict condition that Legge 'should never enter his closet'. Horace Walpole, who had lived at No. 10 with him, described him as having 'a creepy, underhand nature', a mean appearance and an uncouth dialect, adding that he 'aspired to the lion's share by the manœuvre of the mole'. Though inclined to be deferential, Legge was undoubtedly artful.

In 1755 he further angered the King by refusing to sign the Treasury warrants to pay mercenaries for defending the King's Hanoverian possessions. 'We ought to have done buying up every man's quarrel

---

* Horace Walpole.

on the Continent,' Legge said. For this he was dismissed, after holding the office of Chancellor of the Exchequer for little more than a year, but he stayed on at No. 10, which was as well, for he was reappointed Chancellor after a brief interval and remained in that office as well as at No. 10 until 1761.

The Seven Years War (1756–1763), in which Britain fought on the side of Frederick the Great chiefly against France, led, through the victories of Clive in India and of Wolfe in Canada, to the acquisition of a vast Empire. Soon after its outbreak the Duke of Devonshire succeeded Newcastle as Prime Minister, but Newcastle resumed the chief office a few months later. Nevertheless it was Pitt who, having begun life as a soldier and served for some years in the 1st Dragoon Guards, now as Secretary of State inspired and roused the nation. Though not in fact Prime Minister, he was at the helm through these memorable and triumphant years, fulfilling what he had asserted at the outset: 'I know that I can save the country and that I alone can.' Pitt's background was not aristocratic, nor did he belong to the landed gentry. His grandfather Thomas Pitt was a merchant who made a great fortune by fighting the monopoly of the East India Company and filching their trade. Pitt had in consequence an understanding of the aspirations and needs of the great commercial organizations and saw the immense advantage these brought to the country. Hence the aggressiveness of his policy (the reverse of Walpole's) to neglect no opportunity, even if it involved war, of seizing the trade routes and centres and protecting them by establishing supremacy at sea. Newcastle, content to have the conduct of domestic policy, allowed him to dominate the Cabinet, to stir the country with the passion of his oratory, to attend to the prosecution of the war, to plan the campaigns and to choose the commanders.

Pitt never lived at No. 10 Downing Street, nor did either of the two Dukes. Thus the memorable events, the anxious planning and the critical study of the stirring activities half across the world, were neither considered nor debated in this house, as it is by no means certain that Cabinet meetings continued to be held there. For most of those historic years Legge was resident here and in the final months, while peace was being discussed, there was at No. 10 quite the most preposterous man ever to occupy the high office of Chancellor of the Exchequer or to live at No. 10 Downing Street.

CHAPTER 9
Sir Francis Dashwood

IN 1760 George the Second died at the age of seventy-seven, after a reign of thirty-three years. The Hanoverian dynasty had ruled for close on half a century. There followed now a grandson, George the Third, who was only just twenty-one. His father, Frederick Prince of Wales, had died nine years earlier, in 1751, and the education of his heir, then aged twelve, was left to his mother and the courtiers around her. With the immense advantage of having been born an Englishman, who could speak English fluently and was able to identify himself with the people, he had been brought up to assert himself and recover the traditional rights of the Sovereign, usurped by the Ministers in the two preceding reigns.

As always the Opposition had cast hopeful eyes towards the heir. They had been disappointed when George the Second succeeded and were cheated of their hopes at the death of Frederick Prince of Wales. Were they to be ignored again now by his son? They soon saw that they were not. Their time had come at last, for George the Third lost no time in asserting himself. When Newcastle, greatest and most powerful of the Whigs, called at St. James's Palace as Prime Minister, with a draft of the new King's Speech,* he was told to see a Tory member of the Household, the Earl of Bute. Newcastle was astounded, but nevertheless he did as he was told.

Bute was a Scot and his coming into English political life caused both surprise and annoyance. He was completely unknown in politics: he had indeed been engaged for the bulk of his life in agricultural and botanical pursuits in Scotland. A chance downpour of rain, it is said, was responsible for his emergence from obscurity. While in England shortly after the Jacobite rising of 1745, he had gone to a race meeting at Egham, where the Prince of Wales, prevented by the rain from leaving, asked him to join in a game of whist. Out of this casual meeting there developed a friendship and Bute was appointed a Lord of the Prince's Bedchamber. He was tall, handsome, ambitious, but vain and shallow. His intimacy with the Princess after the Prince's death led to a scandal which was given wide circulation in scurrilous lampoons. But he remained in the Household and his influence grew. He became the companion and confidant of young Prince George and it was not surprising that on ascending the throne the new King turned to him instead of the rightful Ministers. Within two days of the King's accession Bute was made a Privy Councillor. Five months later he entered the Cabinet as a Secretary of State. There he intrigued incessantly. In May 1761 he was elected to the House of Lords as a Scottish representative peer, and early the following year he replaced Newcastle as Prime Minister.

This marked a break in the long run of Whig influence which had lasted for close on half a century. Not since the closing years of Queen Anne's reign had any Tory been given office. Regarded as the enemies of the reigning house, the Tories had been excluded from all lists of new peerages. None of them was even made a baronet, a Deputy Lieutenant or a Justice of the Peace: for not until the final defeat of the Young Pretender, James the Second's grandson, in the rising of 1745 had the House of Hanover felt secure. Now, fifteen years later, with Bute, a Tory and a Scot, they returned to power.

Their attitude to the Seven Years War with its magnificent conquests

---

* Though read by the Sovereign, the Speech is prepared by the Prime Minister and sets out the Government's policy for the coming session.

across the Atlantic and in India, was precisely what the Tory attitude was to Marlborough's war. They wanted it brought to an end at all costs, and in this they were supported by the young King, who had a contempt for Hanover and its Continental entanglements and spoke of his ancestral heritage as 'that horrid Electorate which has always lived upon the very vitals of this poor country'. The war was by no means unpopular with the merchants and traders who were acquiring brisk fortunes. Nevertheless peace negotiations were begun. The treaty obligations with Frederick the Great, the uncle of George the Third, were shamelessly abandoned. Pitt, who had warned that Spain was about to enter the war in support of France, was treated with indifference and resigned in disgust. As he drove through the streets of London, his carriage was stopped by cheering crowds, who clung to the wheels of his coach, hugged his footmen and kissed his horses. 'This is worth two victories to us,' declared the French on learning of his departure. Spain came into the war, as Pitt had warned. Peace was eventually attained in 1763. Britain gave up a number of her conquests but retained her gains in India and Canada.

The hostility towards Bute was widespread and overwhelming. The great Whig families hated him because of his harsh measures against them: he stripped many of them of their Lord-Lieutenancies and had even inflicted his hostility on their retainers, such as housekeepers and messengers, who were hounded out of their jobs. He was hated also because he was a Scot, for the Scots were generally regarded as disloyal and treacherous because they had twice in thirty years, in 1715 and in 1745, risen to support the cause of the Stuarts. But Bute's crowning offence in the eyes of the people was his responsibility for the resignation of Pitt, the idol of the nation, and Bute soon found it impossible to appear in the streets without a bodyguard of prize-fighters to protect him from the fury of the mob. His coach was smashed while he was driving to the Guildhall. At the banquet itself he was treated with coldness.

In May 1762 he made the astonishing choice of Sir Francis Dashwood as his Chancellor of the Exchequer. Dashwood, born to wealth and a baronetcy, was fifty-four at the time he moved into No. 10. Most of his life had been spent in profligacy. During the customary Grand Tour on the Continent, he had called on the Young Pretender at his exiled court in the Muti Palace in Florence, and for some years afterwards Dashwood's favourite toast was 'The King over the water!' On entering Parliament, he attached himself to the feather-brained and immoral Frederick Prince of Wales. He thus became a member of the circle to which Bute belonged and they got on extremely well together: on no other grounds can his selection for the exalted office of Chancellor of the Exchequer be explained, for he could not undertake even a simple addition in arithmetic. Of far more absorbing interest to him was lechery. He formed exotic clubs such as the Divan, where he and his rakish friends dressed in Turkish robes of green and crimson, wore pale blue turbans and drank toasts to 'The Harem!' and the infamous brotherhood of Franciscans (which derived its name from his) who met as members of the 'Hell Fire Club' in the ruins of the Cistercian Abbey at Medmenham near Dashwood's home in Buckinghamshire 'for all the purposes of lasciviousness and profanity', according to a contemporary observer.

The 'friars' were twelve in number. The walls of the room in which they performed their horrid rites were painted with gross indecencies. Dashwood, the most profane, we are told, of that blasphemous crew, 'acted as a sort of high priest, and used a communion cup to pour out libations to heathen deities'. In their burlesquing of hallowed religious rites they even went so far as to bring in a baboon to partake of the Sacrament.

This orgiastic club was started in 1745 and Dashwood was still a member of it when he became Chancellor of the Exchequer. His heavy face, his voluptuous lips, the dull vacant look in his eyes bore the imprints of a life spent in heavy drinking and sensual dissipation. No desire of his appetite was ever denied the fullest indulgence. His appointment as Chancellor was met with guffaws of laughter. Ridicule was heaped upon him by the wits of the day, for all who knew him were aware that in mind and behaviour he was no more than an adolescent.

During the eleven months he spent at No. 10 Downing Street, the house was not much affected by his mania for fanciful and extravagant redecoration. On his country house he had spent a fortune on new Palladian façades, on building temples buried in groves, on cascades, thickets, wooded knolls and a profusion of sculpture displaying nymphs and satyrs in libidinous or obscene poses. He doubtless required a greater spaciousness than No. 10 afforded, nor was he there long enough to leave his mark. The house was, of course, filled with beaux and rakes. There was much noisy drinking and a certain amount of lecherous indulgence, save possibly when his wife Sarah, 'a poor forlorn Presbyterian prude', as Horace Walpole called her, happened to be there.

Few frolics of ingenuousness could have surpassed the folly of appointing Dashwood to the Exchequer at such a critical juncture. The Seven Years War was still in progress and, even though Bute was striving to bring it to an end, its heavy cost had to be met.

In 1763, shortly after the treaty of peace was signed, Sir Francis Dashwood introduced his first Budget to a scoffing House of Commons. Such of his depraved friends as were in the Government, like the Earl of Sandwich who was First Lord of the Admiralty, listened with patience. But others, even those who had participated in the unholy rites at Medmenham, such as John Wilkes and the poet Charles Churchill, greeted his attempts at handling the finances of the nation with the utmost contempt. 'His Budget speech', states William Lecky, 'was so confused and incapable that it was received with shouts of laughter.' Among the taxes he imposed, was, surprisingly from one who drank so heavily, one on cider and perry, which led to a great deal of rioting in the fruit-growing counties, for the public regarded it as an extension of the detested system of excise and an infringement of popular liberties.

In the public gallery on that day was James Boswell, Dr. Johnson's biographer. He listened to Dashwood, but does not even refer to him in describing his visit.[50] Boswell happened to be a neighbour of Dashwood's in Downing Street at the time. Since Downing had built his row of houses eighty years had elapsed. In one of the row of houses facing it, indeed in the house exactly opposite No. 10, Boswell had rented some rooms for the period of his stay in London. His rooms were up two flights of stairs and he had, he tells us, 'the use of a handsome parlour in the forenoon' and was able to dine with the landlord and his family 'at a shilling a time'. To him Downing Street appeared to be 'genteel'. But with many of the houses letting rooms to lodgers, there is no doubt that it had lost some of the gloss it had in Downing's day.

Bute, obtuse and stubborn, declined to be influenced by the general contempt for Dashwood; the latter, however, in time came to realize that he was being pointed at in the street as the worst Chancellor of the Exchequer in the history of England. He might indeed have remained in this office and at No. 10 had Bute not lost his position as Prime Minister. This occurred shortly after Dashwood's deplorable Budget speech. An attack on Bute by Wilkes in the *North Briton* led to Bute's sudden resignation on 8th April 1763 and equally abruptly Dashwood had to move.

He had used the house not so much for political gatherings and discussions as for convivial carousing with his disreputable friends. Dashwood was rewarded for his incapacity with a peerage. The title he took, Lord Le Despencer, was an old one once held by a kinsman. Revived now, it made him the premier Baron of England.

Boswell also moved, shortly after Dashwood. He found his Downing Street landlord 'a very rude, unmannerly fellow, in whose house no gentleman could be safe in staying', and went to other lodgings in the Temple.

CHAPTER 10
Revolt of the American Colonies

BUTE was glad to go. Though covetous of power and adroit in his intrigue to obtain it, he confessed that 'fifty pounds a year and bread and water were luxury compared with what I suffer.'

He advised the King to appoint George Grenville as his successor, despite the fact that Grenville was a Whig. Grenville, Pitt's brother-in-law, had been in Newcastle's Government when Bute joined it as Secretary of State. Finding that they worked well together, Bute kept him on when he took over the office of Prime Minister and also made him Leader of the House of Commons. Bute had always regarded Grenville as able and ambitious but easy to manage, and it was his intention now to use Grenville as a cloak while he himself continued to govern from behind.

Grenville, who was fifty, became both First Lord of the Treasury and Chancellor of the Exchequer. The rate book records that in the summer of 1763 'the Honble George Grenwell' moved into No. 10 Downing Street. The spelling of the name is of course inaccurate, but with his move into No. 10 the house became once again the residence of the

Prime Minister after a gap of twenty-one years; Grenville was in fact the second Prime Minister to live here.

With him unfortunately there emanated from this house the first of the high-handed and obstinate impositions that led eventually to the loss of the American colonies. Grenville and his successors, in the course of the next two decades, contrived by their folly to enrage and rouse the colonists until war finally severed the link with the mother country.

Grenville belonged to a rich family which had intermarried with the even richer Temples. Together they mustered a number of peerages and exercised a considerable influence. His first year in the House of Commons coincided with Walpole's last and, in combination with his cousins and their more brilliant friends at Eton, the Lyttletons and the Pitts, they formed the group of 'Boy Patriots' who were in relentless opposition to Walpole. After Walpole fell Grenville received office, first at the Board of Admiralty, then in 1747 as Junior Lord of the Treasury. Thus, quite early in life, he became a constant visitor to No. 10. Pitt and he, together in Newcastle's Government in 1754, worked in the closest co-operation. Their harmonious relationship was drawn even closer after Pitt's marriage to his sister, Lady Hester Grenville, but degenerated, under Bute's recent baleful influence, to a bitter hostility.

On discovering that Bute intended, after his resignation, to use him as a cloak, Grenville made it clear at once that he had no intention of undertaking such a role and insisted on not allowing anyone to come between him and the King. He pointed out that Bute had resigned because of his unpopularity, and it was his resolve for that very reason not to consult him. The King demurred. To get rid of Grenville, Bute tried to persuade Pitt to take on the supreme office. But the attempt failed and Grenville, secure now in the saddle, induced His Majesty not only to deny Bute access to the Court, but to debar him from even living in any part of London.

Grenville was regarded by his contemporaries as an 'industrious, careful and capable official', but, soon after moving into No. 10, he earned the less flattering reputation of being 'arrogant, didactic and tiresome'. It was said that he had an overweening self-esteem, that he was crippled by his stubborn hatreds. Horace Walpole, waspish yet often penetrating in his judgement, says of him: 'Scarce any man ever wore in his face such outward and visible marks of the hollow, cruel and rotten heart within.' He nevertheless conceded that Grenville had great abilities.

In appearance Grenville was thin and colourless, in manner finicky and tedious. He had married in 1749 the sister of the Earl of Egremont – 'a strong-minded and ambitious woman' who 'was believed to exercise great influence over her husband's conduct'.* They had a large family of young children when they moved into No. 10, the eldest of them only just thirteen. A younger son, William, only three at the time, was destined to return to the house as Prime Minister forty years later. The second son George eventually became the Marquess of Buckingham. Grenville's domestic life was extremely correct. No liaisons were ever imputed to him. He was uninterested even in harmless diversions and was seen neither at White's nor at Newmarket races. His entire time was spent on work. 'He took public business', states Burke, 'not as a duty which he was to fulfil, but as a pleasure he was to enjoy.'⁶⁰ As a consequence, living detached and aloof, it could hardly be expected that he was popular. It was agreed, however, that he was scrupulously honest, which is doubtless why, when Leader of the Commons under Bute, he left the bribing of its Members to Bute, who opened an office for the purpose in Westminster and is said to have paid as much as £25,000 in a single morning out of the secret service funds in order to secure a majority in support of one of his measures.

In the two years Grenville was at No. 10 he did much that was harmful. The Seven Years War had saddled England with a heavy debt, and it was Grenville's resolve that, as the American colonies had to be defended during the war, a part at least of the burden should be borne by them. Indeed they had benefited greatly from the outcome. The French had been driven out of both Canada and Louisiana, and the line of forts between those two regions, set up arrogantly to assert that all the land westward as far as the Pacific was French, had been seized and destroyed. The largest of them, Fort Duquesne, had been renamed Pittsburg after the architect of the conquest. Thus not only security but immense opportunities for expansion had been given to the British settlers in America. Accordingly in Grenville's very first

* Lord Russell.

Budget, on 9th March 1764, he imposed taxes on imports into North America which the colonists as well as many in England regarded as severe.

Forty years earlier Walpole had set an example that was much more intelligent and fair. He repealed the duties on all timber and hemp sent to England from the American colonies and allowed the colony of Carolina to carry its rice direct (provided a British ship was used) to any port south of Cape Finisterre without landing first in England as had previously been required. This concession Walpole extended later to Georgia. 'The consequences of both which well-judged laws has been that our own plantation rice has been preferred to the rice of Verona and Egypt.'[62] It was regarded as a far-reaching change in Britain's policy and as the beginning of the emancipation of the colonies from commercial subservience to the mother country.

Grenville unfortunately did not avail himself of this admirable example. His policy indeed went entirely the other way. His Sugar Act, imposed in 1764, was intended to regulate the import by America of foreign molasses, the staple ingredient required for the manufacture of rum. There was an outcry in the colonies against this. The aid of the Navy was required to enforce it and garrisons of regular troops, numbering several thousand, were stationed in various parts of the country in case they should be needed to suppress disorder. Next Grenville's Currency Act denied to the colonists the right to issue their own bills of credit. But the most fiercely resented of all his measures was the infamous Stamp Act: it was to prove the starting point of the American War of Independence. This Act imposed on 22nd March 1765, extended the British system of Stamp duties to the colonies. Stamps were required on every deed, licence, newspaper and advertisement. It was expected to raise £100,000, a third of the cost of the troops stationed in America. Introducing it in the House of Commons, Grenville referred to the Americans as 'children of our own, planted by our care, nourished by our indulgence'. To which the intrepid Colonel Isaac Barré, who had fought with Wolfe in Canada, retorted: 'Children planted by your care? No! Your oppression planted them in America. They fled from your tyranny.... They grew by your neglect of them.... They have nobly taken up arms in your defence' – in the recent war when the colonists fought the French in

North America. 'The same spirit', he added, 'which actuated that people at first, will continue with them still.'

Apart from this rebuke there was, it must be confessed, hardly a murmur in Parliament against the Stamp Act. Opposition to it in America, however, was vigorously voiced the moment news of it reached that country. It was apparent to the colonists that, together with the Sugar Act and other earlier duties, this was a still further assertion of the British Parliament's resolve to impose taxation without even a pretence of representation. Never before in the century and a half of American colonial history had this been so emphatically asserted – and the colonists decided to resist it. Protests were made in some of the local legislatures and recorded in angry resolutions. At the prompting of Massachusetts, where Downing had spent so many of his growing years, a Congress assembled in New York and was attended by delegates from nine of the colonies. Violent demonstrations occurred in that city. The newly formed Sons of Liberty, supported by a furious mob, broke into the Lieutenant-Governor's house: he managed, however, to escape and took refuge in Fort George behind an augmented garrison. The mob thereupon burned him in effigy, set fire to his coach and threatened to storm the fort. There was a skirmish with the English soldiers, resulting in the death of one colonist and the wounding of several others: this was the first blood shed in the struggle for American Independence. In Boston too there were scenes of mob violence. The house of the Chief Justice was wrecked and the Stamp Distributor was forced to resign. Similar disturbances occurred in other States, stamps were burned, revenue officers were tarred and feathered. Trade between the colonies and England was seriously interrupted. Many firms in England, especially in Liverpool and Bristol, were faced with bankruptcy, and unemployment spread all over the country. Rioting seemed imminent in Britain too, and there was the further risk that the French and the Spaniards, having but recently lost most of their overseas possessions, would seize the opportunity of embarrassing the British by aiding the colonists, in the hope of recovering something in the process. By the following March the Stamp Act had raised a mere £4,000 instead of the expected £100,000.

Earlier, soon after he became Prime Minister, Grenville was involved in another struggle, no less important in its consequences, for it led to the gaining of a series of liberties, including eventually the freedom of the Press. These flowed from his prosecution of John Wilkes, whose attacks in the *North Briton* had brought about the fall of Bute. Wilkes was not of heroic stature, but events singled him out for that role. The son of a well-to-do London distiller, whose ambition was that his son should be a gentleman, young Wilkes was given a good education and sent to Leyden University in Holland, where he acquired polish and manners and formed friendships with young Englishmen in a position to get him into society. He developed into a brilliant talker and seemed not to be unduly handicapped by his hideous, lop-sided face and disfiguring squint. 'It takes me only half an hour to talk my face away,' he used to say. For many years his closest companion was Thomas Potter, the son of the Archbishop of Canterbury, who drew him into a dissolute life and was responsible for his becoming one of Dashwood's fraternity at the Hell Fire Club at Medmenham. Potter befriended him more advantageously by giving up his Parliamentary seat at Aylesbury. By paying £7,000 for it, Wilkes was able to get into the House of Commons in 1757 at the age of thirty. Potter also introduced him to the influential Grenville family, with the head of which, Lord Temple, Wilkes early established a close relationship. It was Temple who helped Wilkes in June 1762 to launch the *North Briton*, which carried on week after week a relentless attack on Lord Bute. 'Every person', Wilkes wrote, 'brought in by the Whigs has lost his post – except the King.' Temple's connection with the publication did not deter his brother George Grenville★ from prosecuting Wilkes, for the persistence of the attacks, the most virulent of which appeared in the famous No. 45 of 23rd April 1763, made it clear that, despite the change in Government, Grenville was not going to be spared. Indeed Wilkes stated quite bluntly that Grenville's Ministry was nothing more than the shadow of Lord Bute.

In spite of their decision, Grenville and his Cabinet were uneasy about arresting Wilkes. After a week's hesitation and discussion, they finally decided to issue not a specific but a general warrant against 'the authors, printers, and publishers of the *North Briton* No. 45.' Wilkes

★ Lord Temple inherited his title through his mother.

was not named. As many as forty-eight persons were seized (some of them were dragged out of their beds) before any move was made against Wilkes. When they arrived at last to take him, Wilkes asked why the warrant should be served on him rather than on the Lord Chancellor, or on Bute, 'or my next door neighbour'. They came back, however, in considerable force, seized him and took him off to the Tower. A writ of *habeas corpus*, which he had taken the precaution to apply for, led to his immediate release.

Wilkes thus won the first round and there were celebrations at his release. By his action he had rendered a lasting benefit to every citizen, for no general warrants have been issued since. All the others arrested under this warrant were also freed and a total of some thousands of pounds was paid to them in compensation.

It was not, however, the end of the affair. The Government, with the King most vigorously behind Grenville, were determined to deal with Wilkes. But they decided to move cautiously. The issue of a general warrant had been condemned, but the attack in the *North Briton* could still be dealt with. First the House of Commons was induced to denounce the paper as a 'false, scandalous, and seditious libel', then Wilkes was expelled from the House. This deprived him of his Parliamentary privilege, behind which he had until now been shelter-ing. Next, by a despicable trick, with the aid of spies and the adminis-tration of bribes, they contrived to get hold of some sheets of an indecent poem called 'An Essay on Woman', which had been printed for Wilkes but not published. It was obvious that it was never Wilkes' intention to publish it, since only thirteen copies had been printed, apparently only for private circulation among friends. The evidence indeed suggests that the poem was not written by him but by Potter, who was by now dead.

Two of Wilkes' earlier Hell Fire friends, the Earl of Sandwich, now a Secretary of State, and Sir Francis Dashwood, now Lord Le Despencer, took an active and eager part in the moves against him. For his services Dashwood was soon rewarded by Grenville. He removed his brother Lord Temple from the Lord Lieutenancy of Buckinghamshire and conferred that honour on Dashwood. Against Sandwich, Wilkes was able to make a neat and witty thrust. 'Pon my soul, Wilkes,' Sandwich had said, 'I don't know whether you'll die upon the gallows or of the pox'; to which Wilkes replied: 'That depends, my Lord, whether I first embrace your lordship's principles or your lordship's mistress.'

Sandwich was responsible for bringing the 'Essay on Woman' before the House of Lords. Wilkes' prosecution was ordered by both Houses and he was found guilty in the King's Bench on both charges. He had in the meantime been challenged to a duel by a fellow M.P. named Samuel Martin and was severely wounded. He left for Paris and, on failing to return for the court's sentence, he was outlawed.

Grenville, flushed by his triumph, instantly issued two hundred injunctions against various journals. This, as well as the arbitrary action of the two Houses against Wilkes, roused the indignation of the country. There were cries of 'Wilkes and Liberty' in every street. That the Press should have the right to criticize the decisions and actions of Ministers, and of the Sovereign himself if need be, was asserted and in time won.

The King, though in complete sympathy with Grenville's ill-judged and harsh handling of both the American and the Wilkes crises, had developed a strong personal dislike of him. Because of his own large family (there were eventually as many as fifteen children) the King had moved from St. James's Palace to the more spacious Buckingham House, and had asked Grenville to buy some fields to the west so that the gardens might be made worthy of a royal palace. But Grenville, as frugal with public money as with his own, refused to spend the few thousand pounds this would involve. 'In consequence of this refusal,' Macaulay records, 'the fields were soon covered with buildings, and the King and Queen were overlooked in their most private walks by the upper windows of a hundred houses.' His Majesty was also weary of Grenville's arrogant, dogmatic and patronizing attitude and declared that he would much rather give an audience to the devil than to the Prime Minister. Grenville lectured His Majesty interminably. The King complained: 'When Mr. Grenville has wearied me for two hours, he looks at his watch to see if he may tire me for an hour more.' Secretly His Majesty tried again and again to replace Grenville and even approached Pitt, whom he did not like either, but Pitt refused to serve unless he was given a free hand in the selection of his Ministers.

Grenville had begun to weary the House too, loyal and supine though it was in his support. During one of the debates on the unpopular cider tax introduced by Sir Francis Dashwood when he was Chancellor of the Exchequer, Grenville in a long, rambling speech kept asking where else they could get the money. 'Tell me where?' he repeated several times. Pitt, who was seated opposite, delighted the House, but infuriated his brother-in-law, by humming the well-known tune of 'Gentle Shepherd, tell me where'. For the rest of his life Grenville was known as 'The Gentle Shepherd'.

It is arguable that the first symptoms of George the Third's madness were produced by the constant irritations he suffered from Grenville. Often the King was seen to be choking with rage while the Prime Minister went on with one of his prolonged harangues. His Majesty kept gesturing to indicate that he wanted to be left alone, but Grenville could not be stopped. The King fell seriously ill early in 1765 after enduring two years of this. Arrangements were made for the appointment of a Regent, and His Majesty was greatly offended when he found that his mother was not to be on the Council. This was too much for him. He instantly dismissed Grenville. To the end of his life, which was not to be for a further fifty-five years, whenever the King's mind was disturbed, his thoughts went back to his agonizing interviews with Grenville. They haunted him to the end.

Realizing that Pitt could not be persuaded to succeed, the King turned in despair to the Marquess of Rockingham, a man of honour, dignity and great ability. He was at this time only thirty-five years old, but had the supreme advantage of belonging to one of the wealthiest Whig families, with vast estates in Yorkshire. His father, Mr. Thomas Watson-Wentworth, ever greedy for honours, had risen rapidly first to be a Knight of the Bath, then a baron, next an earl and then a marquess; and it was said of him by Sir Robert Walpole: 'I suppose we shall soon see our friend Malton* in Opposition, for he has had no promotion in the peerage for the last fortnight.' His son, when only fifteen, had fought with the Duke of Cumberland's forces against the Young Pretender in 1745. He succeeded to the title at the age of twenty and shortly afterwards was appointed a Lord of the Bedchamber to the King, but when Bute began his persecution of the Whigs and the Duke of Devonshire was removed from the Privy Council, young

---

* He was Lord Malton at the time.

Rockingham had the courage to resign his office at Court. That occurred as recently as three years before his selection by the King to be Prime Minister.

Those three years were spent in Opposition to Bute and to Grenville. The Whigs were by now divided. They had been greatly weakened by the death of the Duke of Devonshire, the senility of the Duke of Newcastle and the immaturity of the Duke of Portland. In June 1765 the Old Whigs section elected Rockingham as their leader and, though the King felt he 'had not two men in my bedchamber of less parts than Lord Rockingham,' he had no alternative now but to give him the chief office. Rockingham tried to induce Pitt and Lord Shelburne to join his Government, but both refused. Rockingham's ministry was all the weaker for this and lasted only a year and a few days. He did not himself move into No. 10; the house was once again occupied by the Chancellor of the Exchequer, William Dowdeswell.

Dowdeswell, some years older than the Prime Minister, was just forty-four. He had been at Leyden with Wilkes and had got into Parliament as the Member for the family borough of Tewkesbury. Though in the House of Commons for nearly twenty years, he had in no way distinguished himself. According to Horace Walpole he was 'heavy, slow, methodical without clearness, a butt for ridicule, and a stranger to men and courts', but Walpole conceded that he was 'esteemed by the few to whom he was personally known'.

He was in straitened circumstances and had a 'numerous family', which had somehow to be crammed into the restricted space at No. 10 for apart from the kitchen with its quarters for the menservants and the second floor (as seen from the Downing Street end) which was for the housemaids who also occupied the tiny attic floor of six rooms above it, the family had only the ground floor, half of which at that time was taken up by offices and the one floor above that, both looking on to an enclosed courtyard.

Not much entertaining appears to have been done here during Dowdeswell's stay, but among the regular visitors to the house was Edmund Burke, the brilliant young Irishman, who was Rockingham's private secretary. Burke was elected to Parliament later that year (1765) and his very first speech in the House, in January 1766, marked him out as a man of remarkable eloquence.

Burke stoutly defended the ministerial policy towards the American colonies. Nevertheless Dowdeswell, a sound financier, in his only Budget repealed the odious Stamp Act which had so incensed the Americans. He was not content, however, with just righting a wrong. In order that his action should not be regarded by the colonists as a weakness, he introduced at the same time a Bill insisting on England's right to tax her colonies and asserting in the most vehement terms that 'all votes, resolutions or orders, which had been passed by any of the general assemblies in America, by which they assumed to themselves the sole and exclusive right of taxing his Majesty's subjects in the colonies, were annulled and declared contrary to law, derogatory to the legislative authority of Parliament, and inconsistent with their dependency upon the Crown.'*

Insistence on this principle was Dowdeswell's contribution to the worsening of Britain's relations with America. When the repeal of the Stamp Act was debated Pitt fought strenuously against the inclusion of these insulting clauses. Ill though he was, he made the long and exhausting journey from Bath, where he had been taking the waters, and spoke with outraged ardour in the House against the assertion of a principle which he recognized would greatly incense the Americans. 'It is not repealing a piece of parchment that can restore America,' he said, 'you must repeal her fears and her resentments.' He applauded the resistance of Massachusetts and Virginia. The British Parliament, he declared, had no right to tax the colonies. It was Pitt's last speech in the House of Commons. Grenville, in defence of the imposition, for which he had been responsible the year before, rose angrily and denounced the colonists as traitors, adding that those who defended them were no better. On Pitt's side were ranged the commercial and manufacturing interests of the country.

On the night of the final debate the public gallery, the lobby, even the staircases were crowded with anxious men, most of them merchants. Others waited in the street all night to learn the outcome of the vote. The repeal was finally agreed to by an immense majority. When the doors of the House were thrown open, the Members, making their way to their chairs through the dim February dawn, heard a

* Annual Register for 1766.

great roar of cheering and saw hats flung into the air as the crowd learned the news. Grenville was greeted with a storm of hissing.

The general feeling throughout the country was that Pitt should be asked to take over the Government. Pitt was ill, yet he responded to this further appeal from the King. His aim was to bring together all parties. Rockingham refused to serve under him, but most of the Cabinet agreed to stay on. To these he added his own close supporters. Minor offices were given to some of the gentlemen at Court, which greatly pleased the King. It was regarded as being all in all a makeshift administration, consisting of 'patriots, courtiers, King's friends and republicans',★ but hopes nevertheless rose high. Declining the office of First Lord of the Treasury, Pitt took for himself the Privy Seal. Constantly indisposed, a chronic victim to gout since he was at Eton, he felt he could not take on the burden of leading the House of Commons and accepted a peerage. He thus moved out of the scene which he had so long dominated as 'The Great Commoner' and became the Earl of Chatham. The Duke of Grafton, a descendant of King Charles the Second from one of his mistresses, was appointed First Lord of the Treasury. But neither he nor Pitt moved into No. 10. The house was occupied instead by the new Chancellor of the Exchequer, Charles Townshend, who had a link with Sir Robert Walpole through his grandfather Viscount Townshend's subsequent marriage to Walpole's sister Dorothy.

Before moving in he pointed out that the house was in a dreadfully dilapidated state and needed a great deal of repair. Ten days later, on 12th August 1766, the Treasury was informed that at the 'desire of the Rt. Honourable the Chancellor of the Exchequer, we have caused the House in Downing Street belonging to the Treasury to be surveyed, & find the Walls of the old part of the said House next the street to be much decayed, the Floors & Chimneys much sunk from the levell & no party Wall between the House adjoyning on the Westside. We are of Opinion that to repair the present Walls, Chimneys & Floors next the street will not be for His Majesty's service: We have therefore made a plan & Estimate for taking down the Front next the street & also the East Flank Wall of the Hall, to build a party Wall on the Westside to

★ Burke.

83

prevent the danger of Fire, to repair the remaining part of the Old Building & to Erect an additional Building adjoyning thereto. All which Works besides employing such of the Old Materials that are sound & good will Amount to the sum of Nine hundred & Fifty pounds.'

As only thirty years had passed since the three houses forming No. 10 were completely reconstructed and lavishly redecorated for Sir Robert Walpole, it is surprising that such extensive repairs, and even reconstruction, should have been required again so soon. The reconstruction, it will be noticed, was to be done to the house in front, that is to say the house built by Downing, which was by this time over eighty years old. It was now that the present Downing Street façade was provided – a modest brick frontage with a small six-panelled oak door, adorned with an attractive semicircular fanlight and a double swirl of ironwork which holds up an iron lamp surmounted by a crown. The entrance hall with its black-and-white marble squares, still in use, was also put in then. The work was carried out by the architect Kenton Couse, who also added the large bow front to the small house on the Whitehall side, incorporated in Walpole's time.

How long the work took is not clear, but the Townshends seem to have moved in and must have suffered considerable discomfort from dust and noise as they tried to sleep and eat and entertain in the unshrouded sections of the house. It is possible that the work was spread out over some years, in which case Lord North, who moved in with his family eight months after the Townshends, would have had to put up with it too.

Townshend was a younger son of the third Viscount Townshend. He has been described by Macaulay as 'the most versatile of mankind' and indeed had many gifts. Burke called him a 'prodigy'. His sparkling wit dazzled every company. But he had also unfortunately a great many failings: he was neither sincere nor reliable, but veered in his opinions like a weathercock. Tall and handsome, with a loud voice and a louder laugh, he too had been at Leyden with Wilkes, whom he alternately defended and criticized in the House. Dowdeswell, his predecessor as Chancellor of the Exchequer, was often the butt of his vehemence. In Parliament since he was twenty-two, Townshend had served in a number of administrations. By his marriage to Caroline, the wealthy daughter of the Duke of Argyll and widow of the Earl of Dalkeith, he became the stepfather and guardian of the young Duke of Buccleuch, and a cousin by marriage to Lord Bute. This and his own personal connections helped greatly in his advancement, but his light-hearted flippancy even on the most serious subjects came in for much criticism. According to Horace Walpole he did not care whether he or others were in the right: his only object in speaking was to show how well he could adorn a bad cause or demolish a good one.

His hauteur and arrogance estranged many. He treated his colleagues in the recent Rockingham administration (in which he was Paymaster-General) with undisguised contempt and described that Government, although a member of it, as a 'lute string administration fit only for summer wear'. Ostentatiously he abstained from defending its measures.[40]

Pitt had at first a high opinion of Townshend and was particularly impressed by his skill as a debater. As early as 1758 he declared that Townshend's abilities were such as had not appeared since the House was a House. But in the succeeding years he modified this opinion and was only with reluctance persuaded now by Grafton to make him Chancellor of the Exchequer.

Learning of this in advance, Townshend informed Lord Rockingham privately that nothing would induce him to accept it. For one thing his salary as Paymaster-General was £7,000 a year, whereas the Chancellor of the Exchequer got only £2,700. But when Pitt's offer was made Townshend asked for time to think it over. Pitt gave him twelve hours to make up his mind. Townshend sat up all night in his nightshirt with a group of friends, seeking their advice. He also wrote to the Duke of Grafton, and kept running to the window every time a coach passed in case it brought the Duke's answer. In the morning, before it reached him, he had to deal with Pitt's offer. He accepted, but a moment later regretted his decision and begged Pitt to be allowed to change his mind. Pitt agreed; then two days later Townshend changed his mind again. Pitt was furious. Grafton pleaded with Pitt and the appointment was gazetted before Townshend could change his mind again. It is recorded that on this being settled he hurried off to Sir Joshua Reynolds to have his portrait painted in his robes of office.

Now a member of Pitt's Cabinet, he lost no time in running down his new colleagues and speaking disparagingly even of Pitt. His personality was so assertive that, during Pitt's many absences from the Cabinet through illness, Townshend did not find it difficult to dominate over the rest, most of whom were in fact at loggerheads. Again and again Townshend unblushingly adopted a line of action that was completely contrary to the policy laid down by Pitt. This proved particularly disastrous in his handling of American taxation. In his Budget of 1767, when the normal English land tax of four shillings in the pound was cut down to three shillings by his opponents Grenville and Dowdeswell, Townshend promptly announced that, in order to make up the deficiency, duties would be levied at the port of arrival in America on all imported tea, paper, glass and other articles. This astonished his colleagues in the Cabinet, for as a member of the previous Government, Townshend had supported the repeal of the Stamp Act.

At the time Pitt was completely incapacitated; by May he was kept from having any communication with his Cabinet and had even to decline a visit from the King. Grafton, nominally in charge, tried to restrain Townshend, but was unsuccessful. Writing of this later Grafton said: 'No one in the ministry had sufficient authority in the absence of Chatham to advise the dismissal of Townshend.' He, and others of the same mind in the Cabinet, foresaw that these new impositions, estimated to produce a mere £40,000 in all, would not merely enrage the Americans, but would inevitably lead to the loss of the colonies. Yet they were imposed. Immediately the news reached America anti-importation associations were formed. There was rioting. Townshend replied by suspending the legislative functions of the New York assembly and set up special boards of commissioners to collect the dues.

A few weeks after these calamitous developments, Townshend fell ill with 'a putrid fever', as it was called, and died at No. 10 Downing Street on 4th September 1767. But the damage had been done and England before long had to face the consequences.

There were three children of his marriage, a girl and two boys, the eldest only ten when the family moved into No. 10. Not much entertaining seems to have been done there, for Townshend appears to have been very much in demand as a guest by his men friends. Horace

Walpole tells us of a supper party at General Conway's at which Townshend with his bubbling wit 'kept the table at a roar until two o'clock in the morning'.

His funeral took place from No. 10. 'Tomorrow,' recorded the *London Chronicle* for 5th/8th September, 'the remains of the Rt. Hon. Charles Townshend, Esq., will be carried from his house in Downing Street, Westminster, in order to be interred in the family vault at Raynham in Norfolk.'

CHAPTER 11
Lord North and the War of Independence

It fell to Townshend's successor, Lord North, the fourth in this dismal sequence, all of them residents at No. 10, to accomplish the complete severance of Britain's link with the American colonies. He was appointed Chancellor of the Exchequer in October 1767.

Townshend foresaw that North would be his successor, for shortly before he died, Townshend said, pointing to North: 'See that great heavy, booby-looking, seeming changeling; you may believe me, when I assure you as a fact, that if anything should happen to me, he will succeed in my place, and very shortly after come to be First Commissioner of the Treasury.'

The choice was the King's, who persisted in selecting his own Ministers. He thus departed from the practice Walpole had introduced and had for so long exercised in the two preceding reigns. In the brief span of seven years since he ascended the throne, George the Third had adroitly gained this advantage and maintained it by the expenditure of vast sums of money on buying pocket boroughs and by the skilful use of the royal patronage to ensure a comfortable majority in the House of Commons.

His selection of North led to much speculation and gossip. The striking physical likeness between him and the King caused many to believe that he was the King's illegitimate half-brother. Indeed Frederick Prince of Wales, whose Christian name North bore, used often to chaff North's father, Lord Guilford, a Lord of the Bedchamber in the Prince's household, and say that 'the world would think one of their wives had played her husband false',[38] for both North and the King had large protuberant eyes which 'rolled about to no purpose', a wide mouth, thick lips, an inflated visage and 'the air of a blind trumpeter'.*

A few weeks after his appointment, North moved into No. 10 Downing Street. He was thirty-five years old, half a dozen years the King's senior. In Parliament since the age of twenty-one, he had applied himself diligently to the business of the House and was found to possess both ability and an admirably controlled temper. He was also an able debater and his popularity with his fellow members was high.

These not inconsiderable advantages were marred, however, by a disability which the King's grandfather, George the Second, had been quick to notice. Seeing North with all the 'boobies and fools and madmen' around his son Frederick Prince of Wales, the old King observed: 'There is my Lord North, a very good poor creature, but a very weak man.' The Prince of Wales had often used him as a messenger to carry letters to his father and mother at Hampton Court. The lackeying of those early years was maintained even after North attained high office. Whatever order the King gave was carried out with unhesitating alacrity. Nor was it only to the King that he was subservient. Throughout his life he was dominated also by his father.

Though the Earl of Guilford was exceedingly rich, he allowed his son no more than £300 a year. North, in consequence, found it a desperate struggle to make ends meet. He was expected to acquire his own fortune through marriage, as his father had done no fewer than three times. When at last at the age of thirty-four North married a

---

* Horace Walpole.

girl of sixteen, he was assured that she was 'a lady of great fortune . . .
the Somersetshire heiress of more than four thousand a year'. But these
expectations were never fulfilled. Anne Speke, of Dillington in
Somerset, had a sweet and placid disposition, but little more. Many
were unkind about 'poor Anne's face', which was described as 'pud-
dingy', but the portrait of her by Reynolds does not support this. That
she had great charm is clearly apparent and North remained a devoted
husband. No scandal ever touched their lives. He used, however, to
jest about her appearance as well as his own and, drawing in their very
plain eldest daughter, it was his habit to say: 'We are considered to be
three of the ugliest people in London.' Their poverty North's father
refused to ease, doubtless feeling that his son should have chosen more
wisely. Lady North's expectations were centred on a rich relative, Sir
William Pynsent, who also lived in Somerset. Infuriated that Anne's
husband should have supported the cider tax imposed by Dashwood
and Grenville, Pynsent left his entire fortune to Chatham, whose
ridicule of Grenville during that debate with snatches of 'Gentle
Shepherd, tell me where', had pleased him immensely. The will was
contested by the Norths, but without success.

Their domestic felicity, rare until then at No. 10, won from their
daughter Charlotte this recorded comment: 'I never saw an unkind
look or heard an unkind word passed between them. His affectionate
attachment to her was unabated as her love and admiration of him.'[63]

For No. 10 Downing Street, North developed a great affection. He
was there for fifteen years, from 1767 to 1783 – eight more than
Walpole. Most of all he appears to have become attached to the large,
handsome and impressive Cabinet room, from which some of his most
disastrous orders were issued, and for the bedroom in which he must
have passed many nights of sleepless anxiety.

His life here was chiefly a round of domestic quiet. He often spent
the evenings alone with his wife playing chess or quadrille. Of his
political visitors the most frequent were the two Ministers who sat
beside him on the Treasury bench, where, Gibbon says, North often
slumbered, 'supported by the majestic sense of Thurlow on the one
side, and the skilful eloquence of Wedderburn on the other'. Wedderburn was the Solicitor-General. Thurlow later became Lord Chancellor.

Because of his unflagging industry and the endless hours he spent on documents and reports, often sitting up until the small hours of the morning, ready allowance was made for this tendency to fall asleep on the Front Bench. But it was obvious to many that North often feigned sleep as an effective commentary on a tedious debate. He never used it more effectively than against the wearisome George Grenville. Once when Grenville rose to speak, North, aware that he would embark on a long historical disquisition, asked a neighbour to wake him when Grenville began to deal with current affairs. On being roused, he heard Grenville rambling on about the reign of King William the Third, and convulsed the House by exclaiming quite audibly: 'Zounds, Sir, you have woken me up a century too soon.' On another occasion, on being chided by a speaker for not listening to the debate, North stirred in his seat and muttered: 'I was not asleep, but I wish to God I had been.'

While he was able to keep critics at bay with his ready wit and his playful banter, on the more serious plane he cut a very different figure. He had an unattractive presence, his gestures were ungainly, and his speech was often indistinct.

Chatham was nominally still the head of the Government, though he had not been in touch with his Ministers or had any part in the conduct of affairs for more than two years. During that time measures known to be in conflict with his pronounced views were passed, such as Townshend's import duty on tea. His policy was either ignored or abandoned. His friends Amherst and Shelburne were dismissed. In October 1768 Pitt finally sent in his resignation in a letter in his wife's hand, and the Duke of Grafton, who had deputized ineffectively in his absence, was appointed his unhappy successor.

Early the following year North decided, as Chancellor of the Exchequer, on repealing all but one of the duties imposed on the American colonists by Townshend. The reason for the repeal was the ruinous effect on British manufacturers of the trade boycott in America, which had brought unemployment to Great Britain and a great deal of distress. The one duty North proposed to retain was the duty on tea. The proposal was discussed at great length by the Cabinet at No. 10 and on 1st May, 1769, it was eventually agreed to by a majority of only one.

The Governors of the various American colonies were informed in a circular letter that it was not the British Government's intention to impose any further taxes on America for the purpose of raising revenue. Why then was the duty on tea, amounting to threepence a pound and expected to bring in only £300 a year, retained? It was because North, and the King, regarded its retention as vital if Britain was not to lose all her rights over the colonies. Once again it was an assertion of authority. North had argued in the Cabinet that every concession had been regarded by the colonists as a weakness. He declared that he was not prepared to capitulate to the extremists. The imperial link had to be maintained. But the solitary vote on which its retention was based destroyed that link, for to the colonists it was a symbol of their state of dependence and that they resented.

North was unable to see that the Americans had any cause to be aggrieved. He was granting relief, he said. The duty on tea in England was a shilling a pound, in America it was only threepence, so they got their tea cheaper, much cheaper.

Immediate action was taken in America to prevent the tea being landed. At every port men were enrolled for this purpose. Of all the ports Boston was at the time quite the most flourishing. Its ships were engaged in a brisk and expanding trade, not only with the other American colonies and the West Indies, but also with Europe, with Guinea and as far afield as Madagascar. Its merchants were immensely prosperous. It had insisted on making its own laws ever since Downing's uncle, John Winthrop, was elected the first Governor of Massachusetts nearly a century and a half before. In 1765 it had taken the lead in opposing the Stamp Act. Its violent resistance now led to British troops being quartered in the town. On 5th March 1770 a street brawl, accompanied by the baiting of a British sentry, caused the soldiers ill-advisedly to open fire. Five in the crowd were killed. It was referred to afterwards as the 'Boston Massacre'. This was only the beginning, worse was to follow.

Meanwhile the Duke of Grafton had found it impossible to maintain his position as Prime Minister. Apart from his manifest difficulty in controlling a ministry which contained almost as great a diversity of opinions as there were members, he had now to face a new and more vituperative critic in print than Wilkes had ever been. The onslaughts on the Government, which took the form of open letters published in the *Publick Advertiser*, were signed 'Junius', a name that was and still is believed to conceal the identity of Sir Philip Francis, but this has never been conclusively established. He attacked Grafton savagely and in time went so far as to warn the King that what had been acquired by one revolution 'may be lost by another'. At this time too, Chatham, now on the way to recovery, walked unexpectedly into the King's levee and expressed in the strongest terms his disapproval of the Government's recent measures. Then, appearing in the House of Lords leaning heavily on a crutch, his gouty foot swathed in an enormous bandage, he informed their lordships that for three years he had hung his head in shame and went on to denounce the Government's senseless actions against America. Soon he found still another stick with which to belabonr the Government. This was providentially provided by Wilkes, who, risking arrest, had returned from his exile earlier in that year 1769 in order to take part in the General Election. Amid delirious scenes of enthusiasm and rioting, he was elected by the County of Middlesex with a sweeping majority. Thereupon, as a Member of Parliament, he surrendered himself to the authorities. But the Government, feeling it wiser to evade the issue, declined to arrest him. Wilkes, however, was not to be cheated. In a coach drawn by a cheering mob, he took himself to jail.

He proved to be much more formidable behind the walls of the King's Bench prison. Riots occurred at the prison gates and Scottish troops (a tactless choice), firing to disperse the mob, shot and killed six people and wounded many more. The Government congratulated the Scottish regiment, but Wilkes, referring to it as the 'Massacre of St. George's Fields', made capital of it in his petition to the House claiming Parliamentary privilege. The Government promptly rescinded the outlawry, but on the original conviction for libel, Wilkes was fined £1,000 and sent to prison for twenty-two months.

There remained the question of his membership of Parliament. The King, having acquired a vast number of seats in the House through purchase and influence, insisted in a letter to Grafton: 'The expulsion of Mr. Wilkes appears to be very essential and must be effected.' But the Prime Minister preferred not to adopt so drastic a course. He sent a message privately to Wilkes to suggest that each should leave the other alone. He was prepared, he said, to release Wilkes and allow him to take his seat in the House if Wilkes refrained from referring to the legality of his past treatment. This offer Wilkes rejected with scorn. In consequence the whole of the succeeding Parliamentary session was occupied chiefly with the Wilkes affair. While privately prepared to forgive, the Government now publicly insisted that Wilkes' expulsion was necessary to satisfy the honour of Parliament.

After a long and angry debate, at three o'clock in the morning of 3rd February 1769, the House expelled Wilkes. The voters of Middlesex promptly re-elected him, whereupon the House expelled him for a second time, and Middlesex elected him for a third time. The Government then declared the election null and void. The defeated candidate, Colonel Luttrell, who had polled only 296 votes to Wilkes' 1,143, was accepted by the House as the true Member on the ground that only his votes were valid.* Triumphantly North, the most active of Grafton Ministers, exclaimed, in tones similar to those he used against the American colonists: 'Tame submission ever produces insult. It is vain to look for respect if you do not dare to assert your rights.'

Chatham, although he had seen some merit in Wilkes in his early years, had recently come to regard him as a 'worthless profligate'. Nevertheless he did not approve of the way Wilkes had been treated. To adopt Luttrell as the rightful Member for Middlesex when Wilkes had been repeatedly elected by the populace seemed to Chatham quite monstrous and he launched a devastating attack against both the Government and the House of Commons for their action. In May he presented a Bill in the House of Lords demanding a reversal of the Commons decision. The Bill was rejected, but Grafton, increasingly unhappy, felt he could go on no longer and resigned the Premiership in January 1770.

The King had already decided on making North his successor and had in fact written to offer him the position four days before Grafton resigned. North thus attained the chief office three months short of his thirty-eighth birthday. But he had in fact been mainly responsible for the conduct of affairs and had played the dominating role in the Wilkes' affair as well as in the accentuation of the crisis in America.

* An earlier parallel to this is the expulsion of Sir Robert Walpole and his re-election by King's Lynn in 1712, as has already been described.

Both were to demand his further anxious attention during the succeeding years.

Another matter, seemingly of small importance though the Opposition made much of it, involving North before he became Prime Minister, was the seizure by the French of the island of Corsica. It was pointed out that this would provide France with an additional naval base in the Mediterranean, but North, declaring that it was but a trifling compensation for France's vast losses to Britain during the recent war, added: 'If we were to attack France wherever she went, we should indeed be the bullies of Europe, and like bullies we should come off with a bloody nose.' He refused to take any action, but it is worthy of reflection that, had he intervened and taken Corsica, Napoleon, born later in that same year 1769, would have been a British subject.

The transition to the chief office made no change whatever in North's mode of life. He continued to live at No. 10 Downing Street. He submitted, as always, to the direction of the King and still referred all problems, private as well as public, to his father. Some ascribed this to his extreme conscientiousness. Others, with more accuracy, attributed it to his innate irresolution. He had no Party of his own. In his Government he had the survivors of two wrecks – the ministry of Chatham and the ministry of Grafton. Denying that he was either a Whig or a Tory, though his policy, which was the King's, and his speeches in support of that policy betrayed that he was essentially a Tory, he kept on such Whigs as were prepared to remain in his Government (these were of the group around the Duke of Bedford) and would gladly have included others, such as those around Chatham and Rockingham, had they agreed to serve. Chatham indeed was girding himself for a more spirited attack and was engaged in uniting his followers with those around Rockingham in order to make the Opposition more formidable. Nevertheless in the Commons North still enjoyed the majority secured by the astute application of money and patronage by the King. Well-placed relatives provided North with some further influence. His mother's brother was the Earl of Halifax, who had been President of the Board of Trade for ten years. Through his father's second marriage, he had as stepbrother the Earl of Dorchester, whose brother Henry Bilson-Legge had already been Chancellor of the Exchequer.

In the minds of many, including Chatham, North was regarded as the puppet of Bute, who was still believed to be lurking at the King's side, whereas, broken now in health, Bute was in fact in Italy. But the belief persisted and brought North much odium. At times the attacks on him in the House were fierce. Most brilliant and vehement of his critics was Charles James Fox, then only twenty-one. Corpulent, swarthy, somewhat saturnine, bright-eyed and black-haired, he was descended through his mother from King Charles the Second. His father, Lord Holland, had acquired a considerable fortune while Paymaster-General in the Seven Years War. Astutely North detached young Fox from this hostile group by inducing him to become a Junior Lord of the Treasury. The strain thereupon lessened and North was seen to be in fine spirits when he visited his eldest son at Eton and again later when he left with his wife and family of five children to spend the recess near her home in Somerset.

The relief was, however, transient. North was soon engulfed in fresh difficulties. They came in an unending sequence. There was trouble when Spain seized the Falkland Islands. The Opposition rose in wrath at North's impassivity. Chatham in a speech of immense power in the House of Lords insisted that 'the first great acknowledged object of natural defence in this country is to maintain such a superior naval force at home that even the united fleets of France and Spain may never be masters of the Channel.' North, despite his desire to avoid war, thought it necessary now to examine Britain's ability to engage in it should it prove unavoidable. The Navy was found to be in a deplorable state and immediate steps had to be taken to build new warships. The naval dockyards began to buzz with activity. Press gangs got busy in the back alleys and stews. The policy of retrenchment was halted. The land tax was raised by a shilling to its former wartime level. Stocks began to fall. North described the situation as being one of 'precarious peace, of too probable war'. After a time the crisis passed and the islands were restored to Britain without a shot being fired.

Then came a still further brush with Wilkes. His term of imprisonment ended in April 1770. Still a member of the House of Commons but with Luttrell occupying his seat, he was elected now an alderman in the City of London. In area a mere square mile, the City was proud of its hard-won rights and fought stoutly to preserve them. They could have secured no more active watch-dog than Wilkes and were ready to render him their fullest support in his battles. The centre of the country's commercial activity and in command of immense wealth and influence, it was nevertheless, despite such noble and historic buildings as the Guildhall and the Mansion House, anything but elegant in appearance. The streets were unlit and unpaved and cluttered with garbage, foul and revolting to the nostrils. Carts and coaches churned up the mud when it rained and gentlemen preferred always to ride in a sedan chair with perfumed handkerchiefs held to their noses. From assault and robbery there was little protection. Pickpockets abounded. Drunkenness was common. Abuse was shouted at passers-by, especially if they were foreigners. Indecent songs were sung in the streets and there was a persistent lampooning of prominent personages.

It was not over these, however, but over the publication of Parliamentary debates that trouble arose not long after Wilkes' election as alderman. The objection to publishing any reports of Parliamentary proceedings was explicitly expressed some years before by William Pulteney, one of Sir Robert Walpole's most severe critics. 'To print or publish the speeches of Gentlemen,' he said, 'looks very much like making them accountable without doors for what they say within.' Garbled reports of debates in the House had been published since the time of Queen Anne. They appeared at first in pamphlets and later in a monthly publication called *The Political State*, but gave no more than brief indications of what was said by the speakers. A bolder line was taken some years afterwards in the *Gentleman's Magazine*. Its editor Edward Cave together with some friends sat in relays in 1732 in the public gallery and surreptitiously made notes, which were later elaborated and published in the magazine in defiance of the strict Parliamentary prohibition. As a precaution the actual names of the speakers were withheld and fictitious names, capable of being deciphered, were used. Parliament's indifference to these early, restrained endeavours at reporting their proceedings encouraged Cave to come out after a time with the actual names of the speakers. Instantly a standing order was passed, describing it as 'a breach of privilege . . . to presume to give, in written or printed newspapers any account or minute of the debates' and 'that upon discovery of the author, printers or publishers of any such newspaper this House will proceed against the offenders with the greatest severity.'

Cave had no alternative now but to resort again to subterfuge. Describing them as 'Reports of the Debates of the Senate of Lilliput', he continued the practice under this thin disguise, avoiding names now, and in 1737 engaged Samuel Johnson, at that time twenty-seven and not yet famous or honoured with a doctorate, to take it on. On the very meagre notes supplied him, Johnson used his powers of invention and the reports were often not only distorted but inaccurate. Only the essence of what was said was retained. A Tory, not from rational conviction, but because in his childhood he had heard much talk about the villainies of the Whigs, Johnson admitted that he took care that 'the Whig dogs should not have the best of it' in the reports.

With the passing years this practice was adopted by a number of other printers. In London and the other big towns the sale of newspapers had expanded greatly. There was an apparent hunger for political news and some printers had taken the liberty of printing parliamentary reports without any attempt at disguise or subterfuge.

Angered by this, the Government in 1771, some months after the release of Wilkes, decided to take action. Six printers were summoned to attend at the Bar of the House. Some appeared and were admonished, but others, who had been arrested in the City, were taken before Wilkes and another alderman named Oliver, and were dismissed on the ground that the Speaker's Writ did not run within the City bounds. Oliver, as a Member of Parliament, was ordered to attend in his place in the House; Wilkes was summoned to the Bar as an ordinary member of the public, but declined to appear unless allowed to take his seat as the Member for Middlesex. North, having played right into his hand, decided not to take the matter any further in so far as it concerned Wilkes. But Oliver, as well as the Lord Mayor of London, Brass Crosby, who was also a Member of Parliament, were dealt with by the House.

On the morning the Lord Mayor was to appear, all the approaches to Parliament were blocked by angry mobs. The moment they caught sight of North's coach, taking him the short distance from No. 10 to St. Stephen's, they attacked it and reduced it to matchwood. A burly man thrust his staff into North's face and the crowd quickly closed in, ready to lynch the Prime Minister. But a Member of Parliament, though opposed to North's policies, came to his rescue and dragged him, shaken, dishevelled and cut about the face, into the safety of the House.

North had not quite recovered when he rose to address the House. Tears were seen to gather in his eyes and he finished lamely by apologizing for his life and work. Once again, and it was in time to become wearisome, for he never missed an opportunity of repeating it, North informed the Members: 'I certainly did not come into office at my own desire. Had I my own wish I would have quitted it a hundred times. . . . There are but two ways I can get out now – by the will of my Sovereign, which I shall be ready to obey, or the pleasure of the gentlemen now at our doors, when they shall be able to do a little more than they have done this day.'

Both the Lord Mayor and Oliver were sent to the Tower. The printers were not discouraged by this but went on publishing Parliamentary reports, to which they now boldly attached the full names of the Members. North, aware that Johnson was a Tory, had been in touch with him of late and asked him now to issue an explanatory statement on behalf of the Government. To this Wilkes replied in a spirited 'Letter to Samuel Johnson LL.D.' 'Junius' rushed to Wilkes' support, with the City dignitaries wholeheartedly behind him, as well as the Opposition in the House of Commons. Soon the entire country appeared to be for Wilkes. His portrait was hung in shop windows, tacked on to trinkets and displayed prominently in the ale houses. At about this time he won a further triumph by gaining a verdict against the Earl of Halifax in the oft-postponed case he had brought some years before for illegal arrest on a 'general warrant'. The Earl was ordered by the courts to pay Wilkes £4,000 in damages. It was a further rebuff to North, as Halifax was his uncle, but he thought it more prudent to look the other way.

At the end of the Parliamentary session Crosby and Oliver were released from the Tower. This was marked by an outbreak of joyous rioting in the course of which No. 10 Downing Street was attacked and the windows and lamps were smashed. It was the only form of popular protest in an age when neither the Press nor Parliamentary elections could provide an adequate outlet for public feeling. In the General

Election of 1774, Wilkes, on being re-elected to the House of Commons, was allowed to take his seat without further fuss.

The ban against Parliamentary reports was now tacitly dropped. Indeed North actually supplied Dr. Johnson from time to time with a précis of what was said in the House, leaving it to Johnson to expand them into speeches. Told by a friend once that Chatham's speech was the best he had ever read, Dr. Johnson replied curtly: 'That speech I wrote in a garret in Exeter Street.' When North was Chancellor of the University of Oxford he was responsible for the degree of Doctor in Civil Law being conferred on Johnson; he wrote to Convocation from 'Downing Street, March 3, 1775' to make the proposal.

Johnson was often at No. 10 and was looked at askance not only by the other visitors but even by the footmen, for he was awkward in his movements, growling and grunting as he walked in, always dressed in untidy, filthy garments, his shoes caked with mud and looking like a scarecrow. He used to drop in also to see the great Lord Chesterfield in the same shabby clothes, but after a time he was politely told by the servants that his lordship was not in.

Hansard, only twenty-two then and a friend of Dr. Johnson, began publishing his 'Journals of the House of Commons' as early as 1774, but it was not until 1803 that his printing house, using shorthand for the purpose, started issuing its famous record of 'Parliamentary Debates', which still bear his name.

Walpole had made a habit of going away for weekends to his house at Richmond. North had no house near enough to London, but the King, by granting him the reversion of the Rangership of Bushey Park, which was held by the Earl of Halifax, provided a like opportunity on 7th June 1771. As it happened the Earl died on the very next day and North was able, until the end of his term as Prime Minister more than ten years later, to leave Downing Street with his family on a Friday and return on Monday, save when crises kept him in town.

He did not indulge in much entertaining. By temperament he was little attracted to the diversions of the time. He was not a gambler and when whist was played at No. 10 the stakes were always small. This would have excluded a large number of those who were in his Government. Charles James Fox, for example, used to play through the night at his club in St. James's, often losing thousands of pounds in the course of an evening. Nor did North share the adulterous tendencies of his First Lord of the Admiralty, the Earl of Sandwich. He had neither the figure nor the means to dress as elegantly as many of the fops who came to No. 10 in their richly embroidered velvet jackets with quizzing glasses raised to peer at the ladies pacing out a leisurely minuet. Nor can one see him participating in the ill-mannered pranks in which the beaux often indulged for a bet, as when some years earlier the effeminate Mr. Nugent (later Lord Nugent) undertook for a wager to spit in the Earl of Bristol's hat. Passing Lord Bristol as he stood in the doorway, richly dressed, with his hat held under his arm, 'the inside uppermost; Mr. Nugent, turning round to spit, and affecting not to perceive Lord Bristol, performed the act in his Hat.'[38]

Pretending the utmost distress, Nugent tendered a thousand apologies. Lord Bristol assured him that it was of no importance, took out his handkerchief, and wiped the hat. Nugent had won his wager, but early the next morning he received a challenge to a duel, out of which he tried but found it difficult to wriggle. It was finally settled by both Nugent and Lord Temple, who had made the wager, apologizing publicly to Bristol in the main club-room at White's.

For some years a frequent visitor at No. 10 was Lord Clive of Plassey. The East India Company, through Clive, had acquired vast territorial possessions in India. The trading company thus attained the status of a ruling power. Detachments of the English armed forces had always been employed for the protection of its fortified trading stations in Madras, Calcutta and elsewhere, but by now the number of troops in the company's service ran to 15,000 men, counting horse and artillery and local levies of sepoys. Its right to administer these territories and to control the destinies of many millions of Indians was challenged in Parliament by Chatham and by Clive himself, who on his homecoming had used a part of his wealth for acquiring seats in the House of Commons for himself and his nominees. Both insisted that Britain should take over these administrative duties. Others, however, regarded the adoption of such a course as an outrageous infringement of the rights of a private trading corporation, guaranteed by a charter – a view that North was disposed to support, for, while he saw the advantage of the Crown taking control, he also foresaw long drawn out and bitter disagreements, the result of which could not be foretold.

The East India Company, despite its extensive acquisitions, was almost bankrupt. Its employees, on the other hand, its merchants and factors, by trading on the side, by breaking every rule and pocketing the gains, had returned home with great wealth, had bought large country houses, often from men ruined by gambling, and were living like Nabobs. In 1761, Clive, though by now broken in health, had returned to India at the express wish of the company, to put a stop to the rapacity of the English merchants. The Augean stable was cleansed, but the moment his back was turned avarice was once more given full rein. His victims meanwhile had hurried home and, vowing vengeance, had bought seats in Parliament and even on the Board of the East India Company.

North had many talks with Clive and with others who had served in India. Affluent, sun-bronzed men drove up to No. 10 in their magnificent coaches or were carried there in sedan chairs. It was not an easy tangle for North to unravel. His predecessor at the Exchequer, Charles Townshend, had arranged for an annual payment by the company of £400,000 to the Treasury. North insisted on its continuance, since it formed a substantial contribution to the Government's total Budget of £8,000,000. He also decided that a Governor-General should be appointed and, on Clive's recommendation, Warren Hastings, who had served with Clive in India, was selected for this post in 1773. Dowdeswell, a predecessor of North's at No. 10, described these arrangements as 'a medly of inconsistencies dictated by tyranny, yet bearing throughout each link the mark of ignorance.' The Select Committee, on whose recommendations the adjustments were based, seeking a scapegoat, eventually turned on Clive, himself a member of the committee. Since Clive was one of the first to bring home a large fortune, he was sternly criticized for setting a bad example. In view of his close and friendly relations with Clive, both in the House of Commons and at No. 10, North was uncomfortable at the turn the discussions had taken. But the committee, and especially its chairman John Burgoyne, were relentless. Clive – the 'Heaven-born General', as Chatham had called him – was censured, and only as an afterthought was it added that 'Lord Clive did at the same time render great and meritorious services to his country.'

It was not many months after this that events in America took a critical turn and North, who had boasted that 'our dominions are at least as extensive as we could wish; and their improvement, not their extension, should be our chief aim', found that, through his folly and his obstinacy, quite the most important part of these dominions was soon to be lopped off.

On 18th December 1773, angry inhabitants of Boston, dressed up as Indians, unloaded all the tea brought in by the East Indiaman *Dartmouth*, amounting in all to 300 chests, and flung it into the sea. In England those who had lulled themselves into the belief that the troubles in these colonies had died down, were startled when this news reached them six weeks later. Nothing in fact had died down. Resentment was still smouldering. It was at its fiercest in Massachusetts, where the Puritan ideas had undergone little or no modification since the days of the Winthrops and the Downings, who had left Britain to escape domination by English legislators. The unhappy memories they brought with them were handed down to successive generations and were passed on to the expanding population in this and other States, thirteen in all at the time, with a total population of three million, who, despite their diversity and many inter-State jealousies, were united in their opposition to this and their other grievances. They resented, for example, the presence of a large standing army, which, they insisted, was no longer required since the French had been driven out of Canada and the South. The assurance that the army was there in order to protect them from the Red Indians who roved the hills and plains just beyond the fort-lined frontier of Pennsylvania, Maryland and Virginia, was dismissed with contempt. They resented equally the hordes of appointments made by Whitehall of Governors and other officials down to the humblest tide-waiter. 'Most of the places in the gift of the Crown', it was complained, 'have been filled with broken Members of Parliament, Valets de Chambre, electioneering scoundrels, and even liveried servants.' Many also felt that they were looked down on as 'Colonials'. There was little knowledge among Ministers in London as to how the American colonists lived and thought. The only relationship they could visualize was that of mother and child. George the Third often talked of the obedience which a colony owed to its Mother Country.

The Stamp Act, which introduced direct internal taxation for the first time, had been stoutly defended by North and its repeal was as vigorously opposed by him. He was obviously not the right Minister to meet the gathering crisis with understanding and sympathy, nor did the orders of the King assist him to do so. On hearing of the 'Boston Tea Party' His Majesty wrote to North of the need 'of compelling Boston to submit'. On these instructions North acted. If the Boston outrage, he told the House, had occurred in any foreign port there would have been a stern demand for satisfaction. In this instance, he said, satisfaction was not enough, there must also be security for the future. A series of fresh coercive Acts was thereupon introduced. The charter of Massachusetts was revised. The Governor was given power to appoint all officials, to nominate all members of the Council and to curb the freedom of local assemblies. The port of Boston was closed to all trade and was to remain closed until full compensation, estimated at £15,000, was paid to the East India Company for the tea dumped into the sea. The Governor was further ordered to arrest all those who had taken any part in the incident and to send them to England for trial. To enforce these measures four battalions of infantry were sent out from England, and General Gage, the British Commander-in-Chief in America, was appointed the new Governor of Massachusetts. 'We are now to establish our authority,' North declared, 'or give it up entirely.' The King, in an exhilarated note, wrote: 'The die is cast. The colonies must either triumph or submit.'

War now became inevitable. All the States rallied round Boston when these dire tidings reached America, brought by a strange irony in a ship named *Harmony*. The cry of 'Slavery' went up in all thirteen States, and the colonists, convinced that neither their pockets nor their consciences were safe, girt themselves to resist. Muskets were brought out and cleaned and men turned out to drill on village greens and in market squares. Cannon and munitions arrived for the colonists from France and other countries in Europe, and everywhere in America the name of North was 'cursed from morn till noon and from noon till morn'.[64] The King declared 'Blows must decide' and the four British battalions were increased to 20,000 soldiers – 'regulars, German huntsmen, picked Canadians and three or four regiments of light horse'.[65]

Even before the first clash at Lexington on 19th April 1775, the already numerous critics in England of North's policy were persistently vocal, both inside and outside Parliament. In the Commons Charles James Fox, until recently a member of North's Government, as well as Edmund Burke and Colonel Isaac Barré, the Irish-born son of a French refugee with a scar across his cheek to remind one of the capture of Quebec, raged ceaselessly against him. Chatham in the Lords was no less fierce in his denunciations. All over Britain money was collected for the relief of the widows, orphans and aged parents 'of our beloved American subjects inhumanly murdered at or near Lexington'. But the Government, having a majority in the House, would not be deflected from their perverse course.

During the six and a half years the war lasted, a steady decline was noticeable in the appearance and demeanour of Lord North. He moved between Downing Street and the House of Commons, a poor, pathetic, bewildered figure. In the Cabinet room at No. 10, he was incapable, he confessed, of choosing between the clashing opinions of his colleagues and was unable to make any decisions of his own, which was scarcely surprising, seeing that from childhood he had learned to rely on the influence and judgement of others. Each Minister ran his own department without bothering to consult the Prime Minister and went above his head direct to the King. They not only ignored North, but plotted and intrigued against him as well as against each other. Lord George Sackville, who had changed his name to Germain because of an inheritance, had recently been appointed Secretary of State for the Colonies and therefore had the war largely under his direction, though he had not long before been cashiered from the army because of cowardice and had been debarred from ever holding army rank again. Yet, through their friendship, North had given him this exalted authority as well as a place in the Cabinet. But far from showing any gratitude, Germain had for North nothing but contempt, and when he gave a ball in London to which everyone of note was invited, North and his wife were the only two excluded: Lady North thought this rather 'odd'.

Another minister, Richard Rigby, who was Paymaster-General but not in the Cabinet, expressed his contempt by declining to sit on the Government benches. North lacked both the ability and the driving force required to direct a war. His distress was acute and obvious. Very rarely now was he able to escape with his family to Bushey for a snatched weekend and even more rarely to the more remote peace of Somerset.

When not required in the House for questioning and debate, he spent almost all his time in Downing Street.

When he complained of his vexations and his distress of mind, his opponents, even his colleagues, jeered at him for not resigning. They attributed this to his chronic need of money. In *The Duenna*, a play by Israel Pottinger presented in London in 1776, North, depicted as Boreas, is made to sing:

> 'Tis true I'd dispense with the post that I hold
> If with it I should not dispense with my gold,
> But avarice seconds ambition so well,
> That I'd follow my old Master *Walpole* to hell.

In fact North kept trying to resign. Pitifully he pleaded with the King to release him. Describing himself as unworthy and incapable, he declared that his memory had gone, his strength was exhausted, his capacity worn to a shred. But His Majesty begged him not to desert him in this time of trial, to which, quite bluntly, North replied that 'the almost certain consequences of His Majesty's resolution will be the ruin of his affairs'.

The pressure of North's debts was overwhelming. His personal expenses greatly exceeded his income and, since his father was still alive, no inheritance had yet become available. His annual deficit was estimated at £1,500, and, as John Robinson, his secretary at the Treasury, has noted in his papers, North's recurrent moods of despondency were due more to his private financial worries than to the adverse drift of the war across the Atlantic. In September 1777, when the war had been in progress for two years, the King, concerned at the harassed state of North's mind, wrote privately to Robinson. The reply he received stated: 'Mr. Robinson thinks he perceives what oftentimes adds to Lord North's distress of mind when the weight of public business oppresses him, but that Mr. Robinson durst not on any account presume to mention to His Majesty without His Majesty's special command.' The command having been given, Robinson indicated a variety of causes – the smallness of North's income, the expenses of his growing family, the heavy expenditure required to maintain his position. He added that, though much money had to be borrowed and a mortgage of £6,000 had been effected, there were still many debts outstanding to tradesmen.

'The thought of this situation frequently distresses his mind and makes him very unhappy.'

The King thereupon wrote direct to North: 'You have at times dropped to me that you had been in debt ever since your first settling in life and that you had never been able to get out of that difficulty. I therefore must insist you will now state to me whether 12, or £15,000 will not set your affairs in order, if it will, nay if £20,000 is necessary I am resolved you shall have no other person concerned in freeing them but myself.' He added the hope that 'some of the Employments for life will in time become vacant that I may reward your family'.[45] Ten years earlier, North, having not long held the office of Chancellor of the Exchequer, had rendered the King a similar service. After a fierce tussle with the Opposition, he had got the Commons to agree to pay the King the sum of £500,000 to meet his personal debts. North was shortly afterwards rewarded with the Garter.

In addition to his private anxieties North had to sustain the unending strain of national problems, such as unbalanced war budgets, an inadequate Navy unable to prevent war supplies pouring into the American colonies from Europe, and serious deficiencies in recruiting, for Englishmen were unwilling to go out and fight their fellow-countrymen with whose aspirations they were greatly in sympathy. So North hired mercenaries from Germany. 'I wish much for an assistance of foreigners', he wrote to the Secretary at War Lord Barrington, 'and shall think your Lordship does an effective service to the Country if you can bring us a considerable supply, either by private recruits or by corps.' What roused the greatest fury on both sides of the Atlantic was that Red Indians should have been used to fight the colonists. By such a desperate, and as many felt despicable, expedient was the army expanded.

The American States, having set up in 1774 a central Congress in Philadelphia to represent them all, had also appointed a commander-in-chief to lead their joint forces. To George Washington, a tobacco planter, this supreme responsibility was assigned. He was of precisely the same age as Lord North, both being forty-three at the outbreak of war. John Wesley, writing to North, warned him that the colonists were 'terribly united' and would dispute every inch of the ground.

The first serious reverse suffered by Britain was at Saratoga in the autumn of 1777. New York had by now been taken by British troops and Philadelphia was occupied after the American defeat at Brandy-wine. All seemed to be going well and the news of the rout at Saratoga brought consternation to the Cabinet room at No. 10. North burst into tears. Lord George Germain was like a man stunned; William Eden, his Under-Secretary, learned of it later and felt he was having a hideous dream. Ministers upbraided each other. In the House there was an outburst of anger against the Government. Fox, still in his twenties, remembering Germain's cowardice at Minden, threatened him with another trial. North turned to him gratefully and whispered: 'Charles, I am glad you did not fall on me today, for you was in full feather.'

In the Lords, Chatham, emerging once more from his retirement, spoke with the utmost vehemence and passion against 'the monstrous measures that have heaped disgrace and misfortune against us – that have brought ruin to our doors. . . . I love and honour the English troops: I know their virtues and their valour: I know they can achieve anything except impossibilities; and I know that the conquest of English America is *an impossibility*. You cannot, I venture to say it – *you cannot* conquer America. . . . You may swell every expense and every effort still more extravagantly; pile and accumulate every assistance you can buy or borrow; traffic and barter with every little pitiful German prince, that sells and sends his subjects to the shambles of a foreign prince: your efforts are for ever vain and impotent – doubly so from this mercenary aid on which you rely; for it irritates, to an incurable resentment, the minds of your enemies – to overrun them with the mercenary sons of rapine and plunder; devoting them and their pos-sessions to the rapacity of hireling cruelty! If I were an American, as I am an Englishman, while a foreign troop was landed in my country, I would never lay down my arms – never – never – never.' Who, he demanded with intense anger, is the man who 'has dared to authorize and associate to our arms the tomohawk and the scalping-knife of the savage, to call into civilized alliance the wild and inhuman savage of the woods, to delegate to the merciless Indian the defence of disputed rights, and to wage the horrors of his barbarous war against our bretheren?'[67]

Soon the situation became far more grave. For two years the French had been sending munitions and fighting men to the colonists: they had also, on America's Declaration of Independence on 4th July 1776, accorded it immediate recognition. Now, encouraged by Saratoga, they were preparing to assist more substantially by joining actively in the war. The consequences of this were clearly apparent to the distracted and despondent Cabinet. No longer would the fighting be confined to the continent of America, but it would spread to India, the West Indies and possibly even to Ireland. There would be naval actions on the high seas, and there was the further risk that before long Spain would follow France's example, since Spain too was still smarting from the losses she suffered in the Seven Years War. The Dutch were another likely enemy; they had also been sending help to the Americans. The chance had come to all of them for revenge.

To prevent these alarming developments, North felt that peace should immediately be made with the colonists. He realized that, in view of their hostility towards him, his own resignation was essential. He put this to the King and suggested that Chatham should be appointed his successor. But the King, while prepared now to accept North's resignation, would not hear of Chatham becoming Prime Minister. A member of the Cabinet possibly, but he would not have Chatham in the chief role. On this he was adamant. Chatham, now in his seventieth year, had not much longer to live. He appeared in the Lords for the last time in April 1778. Already infirm, he limped to his seat with the aid of a crutch and was supported on one side by his son William, on the other by his son-in-law Lord Mahon. The peers rose to make way for him. They noticed that both his legs were swathed in flannel and that his wig, too large for his emaciated head, almost obscured his features. But in his eyes there was still the old fire. After a rambling speech he said: 'My Lords, if we are to fall, let us fall like men.' Then he raised his hand to his breast and collapsed. He was caught as he fell and was carried into one of the lesser houses in Downing Street, where he lingered for a few days until he was able to be moved to his home at Hayes, where he died a few weeks later. There seemed now to be no one to replace North.

The outbreak of war with France, the traditional enemy, later in the year, rallied the nation behind the Government. Recruiting became brisk. In time Spain, and eventually Holland too, came in on the other side. Though repeatedly warned that it would be infinitely more difficult now to conquer America, North resolutely refused to recognize the Declaration of Independence. The anxieties that followed reduced him to a nervous wreck. He became short-tempered, petulant, uncivil even to his friends. For hours he sat inactively in his room at No. 10, neglecting affairs of State, not even troubling to read the dispatches from America, leaving vacancies in important offices of Government unfilled. He sank into an indolent apathy which caused the King the greatest concern. Writing to Robinson, His Majesty suggested that the Prime Minister should pull himself together and treat his colleagues with more civility. This note, left deliberately on his stricken master's desk, had its effect, but only for a time. Crowds began to boo North in the street on his short drive to the House, and all through one sleepless night an angry mob in Downing Street attacked No. 10. The loss of the American markets was bringing ruin to the merchants and ever-increasing unemployment to the workers. With the combined French and Spanish fleets outnumbering the British in the Channel, there was a constant fear of invasion. At the coffee houses men waited anxiously for news. The Prime Minister, renowned for his imperturbability in public, was seen to dissolve into tears in the House.

The war was not his only anxiety. The easing of some of the lesser restrictions which had for so long oppressed the Roman Catholics, driving many to France, just as earlier the Puritans were driven across the Atlantic, brought down on North the wrath of many agitated Protestants. Lord George Gordon, President of the newly formed Protestant Association, after dispatching an angry letter to him in January 1780, called at No. 10 to see North and demanded the repeal of the concessions. North refused. In June, rioting broke out all over London and went on for many days. On the evening of 7th June, while North was entertaining some friends to dinner at No. 10, the riotous mob surged into Downing Street. One of the guests, Sir John Macpherson, later Governor-General of India, has described what happened:[38]

'We sat down at table, and dinner had scarcely been removed, when Downing Square, through which there is no outlet, became thronged with people, who manifested a disposition, or rather a determination, to proceed to acts of outrage. . . . Mr. Brummell, North's private secretary, who lived in the same street, was in attendance, but did not make one of the company.' Brummell was the father of Beau Brummell, whose second birthday it was that day.

Lord North, inquiring what was being done to defend No. 10, was told that there were 'twenty or more grenadiers, well armed, stationed above stairs . . . ready on the first order to fire upon the mob.' He ordered that two or three persons should be sent out to inform the crowd of this in order to prevent bloodshed.

'The populace,' Macpherson goes on, 'continued to fill the little square, and became very noisy, but they never attempted to force the front door. . . . By degrees, as the evening advanced, the people . . . began to cool and afterwards gradually to disperse without further effort. We then sat down again quietly at the table and finished our wine.

'Night was coming on, and the capital presenting a scene of tumult or conflagration in many quarters, Lord North, accompanied by us all, mounted to the top of the house, where we beheld London blazing in seven places, and could hear the platoons firing regularly in various directions.'

In October of the following year 1781 the American war moved to a speedy conclusion after the surrender of Lord Cornwallis's forces at Yorktown. This shattering news was brought to Lord George Germain's house in Pall Mall on 25th November and he hurried that Sunday afternoon, between one and two o'clock, to convey it to the Prime Minister at No. 10 Downing Street. Asked afterwards how North received it, Germain said: 'As he would have taken a ball in his breast.' He 'opened his arms, exclaiming wildly, as he paced up and down the apartment during a few minutes, "O God! It is all over" ', and repeated the words 'many times under emotions of the deepest consternation and distress'.

It was obvious that North could remain in office no longer. Attacks were made on him from all sides, many of them abusive. The King begged North not to deliver him into the hands of his enemies, by which he meant the Opposition, who had all along supported America. A frantic endeavour was made to form a coalition. But this failed. After the Christmas recess, motions of censure against the Government came in rapid succession. Blistering speeches were made by Fox and others. Shaken by his narrow majority of only ten, North saw the King again on 15th March 1782 and begged to be released. A still further vote of censure, to be made five days later, North strove to anticipate by resigning, but he was unsuccessful.

On 20th March a crowded and excited House awaited the Prime Minister. He arrived at a quarter-past four in the afternoon. He had come on after a further visit to the King and was in full dress with the blue ribbon of the Garter. On reaching his seat he turned to address the Chair, but the Earl of Surrey, who was to move the vote of censure, rose at the same time to begin his attack. Each refused to give way and there was an uproar in the House. North eventually managed, during a fleeting lull, to get out the words that any motion the Opposition intended to make was unnecessary because the Government had that day ceased to exist.

Startled by this announcement, the House quietened and the Prime Minister was able to speak. He told them that they would presently have another leader. 'Having for so many years held a public situation and being entrusted with the management of public affairs, I am perfectly conscious I am responsible for my conduct, and whenever my country shall call upon me to answer, it is my indispensable duty to answer for every part of that conduct.'

He then drove off in his coach through the snow to dine with some friends at No. 10 Downing Street. We learn that the atmosphere at the dinner table was calm and the conversation cheerful.[66] The strain and torment of his fifteen years of office gave place to a sense of immense relief.

CHAPTER 12
The Younger Pitt

NORTH continued to live at No. 10 for some months after his resignation. His successor as First Lord of the Treasury was the Marquess of Rockingham, a Whig and one of his sternest critics, who had held the chief office before in 1765, though only for a year. Once again he chose not to live at the official residence of the Prime Minister, but stayed on in his own house in Grosvenor Square.

It is believed, but it is by no means certain, that his Chancellor of the Exchequer, Lord John Cavendish, took over a part of No. 10, the rest presumably being occupied still by Lord North and his family, for they were certainly in residence until the younger Pitt moved in as Chancellor of the Exchequer later that year.

Lord John Cavendish, now fifty, was a younger son of the Duke of Devonshire. For a member of such an exalted family, he was personally undistinguished in appearance. With him in Rockingham's Government were Charles James Fox and Lord Shelburne as the two Secretaries of State, Burke, who had once been Rockingham's private secretary, and the promising young playwright and politician Richard Brinsley Sheridan. It was a Government of Whigs.

This ministry of Rockingham's lasted even a shorter time than his first. After being sixteen years in opposition he was Prime Minister again for less than four months. He died and was succeeded by the Earl of Shelburne, the great landowner and later the first Marquess of Lansdowne. It was the King's choice. Fox, feeling that he should have been selected, promptly resigned and was followed by both Burke and Sheridan. Cavendish, a close friend of Burke's, left too, and young William Pitt, only twenty-three at the time, was appointed Chancellor of the Exchequer in his place and also Leader of the House of Commons.

Writing to his mother two weeks after his appointment, Pitt stated: 'Lord North will, I hope, in a very little time make room for me in Downing Street, which is the best summer town house possible.' But North, who had lived there continuously for fifteen years, was reluctant to leave, and at the end of the month Pitt, writing again to her, said: 'I expect to be comfortably settled in the course of this week in a *part* of my vast, awkward house.' Did North vacate only a part of it, one wonders, as he had possibly done for Lord John Cavendish?

Until now Pitt, having trained for the law, had been living in chambers in Lincoln's Inn on an allowance of £300 a year. Chatham's means, despite his handsome inheritance from Sir William Pynsent, had been scant. The State had paid his debts, amounting to £20,000, and had also endowed the earldom with an annuity of £4,000, to enable his heir to sustain the peerage. His younger son William had by his precocious brilliance been marked out from childhood for the noble destiny he was to assume so early in life. In health he was frail. Tall, slender, often ill, he had been advised at the age of fourteen to drink port in order to build up a more robust physique. He reacted miraculously to it, but even so was not considered strong enough to face the rigours of the normal routine at Eton, where his father and brother had been, but was educated at home by tutors. The education he thus acquired was remarkable. His brain was able to absorb the intricacies of mathematics as well as the complexities of the classics. In both he attained heights far beyond the range of other men. He was also trained by his father, whom he so greatly admired, to develop his eloquence and his declamatory skill, which, added to the natural melodious cadence of his voice, caused the House of Commons to listen always with rapt attention and wonder.

He was elected to Parliament in 1780 at the age of twenty-one. Chatham had by now been dead for two years and England was at war not only with the American colonies, but also with France and Spain and Holland. With his very first speech young Pitt made a remarkable impression. Burke, a great orator himself, was moved to tears and exclaimed: 'It is not a chip of the old block; it is the old block itself.' Fox, eleven years Pitt's senior, recognized for years as an outstanding debater and destined to be Pitt's fiercest opponent, on hearing the enthusiastic acclaim and the remark that Pitt was likely to be one of the foremost men in Parliament, replied very quietly: 'He is so already.' Less than two years afterwards, on North's fall, Pitt was invited to join Rockingham's Government, together with Fox and Burke. He was offered one of the most highly paid offices, carrying a salary of £5,000 a year,* but this he haughtily declined, stating that he would not accept any post that did not give him a seat in the Cabinet. Such arrogance, such astonishing self-confidence were weighed against the young man's resolve to go on living on a mere £300 a year rather than be inveigled into office by a sum nearly twenty times as large. Here was a man who could not be bought, it was said. A few months later he became Chancellor of the Exchequer.

There were three main parties at the time in the House of Commons – the Whigs who had served under Chatham and were now led by Shelburne, to which group Pitt belonged; a second group of Whigs, by far the larger, was under the leadership of Fox, to which Burke and Sheridan were attached; and North's party which consisted chiefly of Tories. None of these three was large enough to stand alone against the other two and it was obvious that a hostile combination, however ill-assorted, could easily bring Shelburne's Government down. That soon happened. Bitter resentment led Fox to form a coalition with North. It was an astonishing conjunction, for Fox had but recently denounced North as 'void of every principle of honour and honesty' and had threatened him with impeachment. He declared now: 'It is not in my nature to bear malice or live in ill-will.' Peace negotiations with France and America had been begun by the Rockingham Government and quarrels had occurred between Fox and Shelburne over the terms. The

---

* The Vice-Treasureship of Ireland, an office once held by Chatham himself.

treaty, about to be signed, accepted the independence of the American colonies; to France and Spain very little of what had been won in the widespread and devastating war waged by Pitt's father was to be returned. Nevertheless Fox and North most vigorously criticized the terms and censured the Government. Their combined vote brought down the Government and Pitt ceased to be Chancellor of the Exchequer after holding that office for only nine months. He was asked by the King to take on the Premiership, but refused it. He preferred to bide his time until Fox and North, who were certain to be invited next to form a Government, were given the opportunity of displaying their joint incapacity to the bewildered country.

Neither Fox nor North in fact became Prime Minister in the new and fantastic coalition. For some weeks there were arguments, then the Duke of Portland was adopted as the head of this 'ill-omened and unnatural marriage', as Pitt called the most unscrupulous coalition known to history.[67] The Peace Treaty they had insisted on rejecting was in the end accepted unaltered.

The Duke of Portland chose to live at No. 10 Downing Street. Born William Cavendish-Bentinck, the Duke was now fifty-five. He was tall, fresh complexioned, full of dignity and benevolence, but 'a convenient cipher'. Fox and North were appointed his two Secretaries of State; thus at the Cabinet table where North had presided for so many years, he now had a lesser place and was under another's guidance, a not unfamiliar role for him.

Portland, it seems clear, had the whole of No. 10 Downing Street to himself. By May he and his family had established themselves in the house and had already begun to entertain on an elaborate scale. The *Morning Herald* of 29th May 1783 reported: 'Yesterday the Duke of Portland gave a grand dinner to several foreigners of distinction, and to the ministers of state, at his house in Downing Street, Westminster.'

During the very few months he was there, the Duke made the most of his stay, socially at any rate. The *Morning Herald* of 1st August 1783 tells us: 'His Grace the Duke of Portland yesterday gave a grand turtle-feast to several of the Nobility, at his house in Downing Street.' Before the end of that month the Duke had to leave, not because he was driven from office, that came in December, but because the house was in need of still further attention. Only seventeen years had elapsed since the very substantial alterations had been begun for the Townshends, but it had been left uncompleted, for a note from North, dated 30th September 1774, asks that the work on the front of the house, 'which was begun by a Warrant from the Treasury dated August 9th, 1766', should be finished.

This new need of attention became apparent in 1781. In March of the following year a committee consisting of North and others, after inspecting the condition of the house, found that the money spent so far was insufficient and considered a statement from the Board of Works, declaring that 'the Repairs, Alterations & Additions at the Chancellor of the Exchequer's House will amount to the sum of £5,580, exclusive of the sum for which they already have His Majesty's Warrant. And praying a Warrant for the said sum of £5,580 – and also praying an Imprest of that sum to enable them to pay the Workmen.' This was just before Pitt moved in as Chancellor of the Exchequer.

The work was apparently still in progress when Pitt took up his residence, which may explain Pitt's use of the words 'settled . . . in *part* of my vast, awkward house' in a letter to his mother. It seems not to have been satisfactorily completed by the time Portland moved in, for on 15th April 1783, a very few weeks before his first big dinner, it is recorded: 'Mr. Couse reported that having been directed to go over the House in Downing Street he had caused an Estimate to be made for sundry Works desired to be done by the Dutchess of Portland.' But it was not until after the turtle-feast in August that the work was begun. On the 8th August 'Sir William Chambers Rec^d a Letter from Mr. Beirne, private Sec^ty to the Duke of Portland, relative to Painting, &c, the House in Downing Street'*; and later that month it was announced in the Press that 'The Duke of Portland is removed to Burlington House, where his Grace will reside while his house in Downing Street is repairing.' Portland never returned, for before the work was completed he fell from power.

In addition to the repairs required, elaborate alterations were undertaken – the Cabinet room, for example, was extended. This was achieved by removing the east wall and rebuilding it several feet inside the adjoining secretaries' room, which thus became smaller and its

---

* Public Record Office, Works 4/16.

fireplace was thrown out of centre. At the new entrance to the Cabinet room a screen of coupled Corinthian columns (four in all) was erected. They supported a moulded entablature, which is continued round the room. Similarly the large drawing-room on the floor above – the corner room adjoining Kent's Treasury and looking out on to the Horse Guards Parade – was enlarged by the removal of the wall on the south side and its replacement by a screen of two Ionic columns. At the same time the pediment on the Horse Guards front was removed* and a plain parapet was erected. The architect to whom this work was entrusted, Robert Taylor, a man in his sixties with wide experience, was knighted on its completion.

Pitt's comments on No. 10 are quoted in Cleland's *Memoirs of Pitt*.[180] On 17th June 1783, that is shortly after moving out for Portland, he referred to 'the expense of repairing the house in Downing Street, in which he had the honour to be lodged for a few months. The repairs of that house only, had, he said, but a year or two before he came into office, cost the public 10,000*l.* and upwards; and for the seven years preceding that repair, the annual expenses had been little less than 500*l.* The alterations that had cost 10,000*l.* he stated to consist of a new kitchen and offices, extremely convenient, with several comfortable lodging-rooms; and he observed, that a great part of the cost, he had understood, was occasioned by the foundations of the house proving bad.' Four days later, on 21st June, the *Morning Herald* commented: '£500 p.a. preceding the Great Repair, and £11,000 the Great Repair itself! So much has this extraordinary edifice cost the country – for one moiety of which sum a much better dwelling might have been purchased.' The sums mentioned were very large indeed for those days when money had many times its present value. Pitt undoubtedly liked staying there: he was there in all for twenty years; Walpole, who had built the house towards the end of his premiership, was there for less than seven.

After leaving it in April 1783 Pitt, as the Leader of the Opposition, busied himself mainly with Parliamentary reform, which his father, facing the realities of Britain's industrial expansion, had foreseen was inevitable. Of the country's eight million inhabitants only 160,000 had

---

* The pediment was replaced in 1937.

the right to vote. Pitt's father had represented the rotten borough of Old Sarum, which consisted only of ruins, yet returned two Members, and Pitt had himself got into Parliament, on the nomination of one of the ruling families, for a pocket borough. With frankness and courage he had earlier denounced this system, asking if it was true representation to enter the House 'under the control of the Treasury or at the bidding of some great Lord or Commoner, the owner of the soil?' As Leader of the Opposition he returned to the attack. He proposed the abolition of these corrupt boroughs and suggested that in their place there should be added a hundred county members, and that London should be given a much fuller representation – reforms that would have anticipated in some measure those that were to be fought for so acrimoniously and so violently fifty years later. But the House rejected the plan by a majority of almost two to one, since it would have affected the seats of hundreds of Members. Astonishingly both Fox and Burke, though in principle dedicated to the cause of reform, voted with North against the motion.*
The following month Pitt introduced another Bill. Having already attacked 'the corrupt influence of the Crown', he now demanded the reduction of sinecures and pensions to a total not exceeding £90,000 a year. This was aimed at ending the King's control of Parliament. It was agreed to. During the recess, Pitt went to Paris on a brief visit. As the son of Chatham he was lionized. Among others he met was Talleyrand, a meeting Talleyrand often recalled. It was the only time Pitt left England. He was accompanied by William Wilberforce, who later worked for the abolition of the slave trade: they were together at Cambridge, met again as Members of Parliament and remained lifelong friends – one of the very few Pitt admitted into his circle of intimacy.

When Portland's Government fell in December Pitt, now twenty-four, was asked again by the King to form a Government. He accepted this time and returned to No. 10 Downing Street as Prime Minister. 'The Boy', as he was called, took on also the Office of Chancellor of the Exchequer. When the House of Commons learned of his appointment as Chief Minister there was an outburst of loud and prolonged laughter. But Pitt was unaffected by their derision. Fox prophesied that 'The Boy' could not survive as Prime Minister for a month. In fact he

* Burke said: 'I look with filial reverence on the Constitution of my Country.'

retained that office for nearly eighteen years and after a brief break returned to it for a further two years.

At the outset, however, he was faced with insurmountable difficulties. Few were prepared to serve in his Government. His cousin the second Earl Temple declined his offer of appointment as a Secretary of State. Pitt was thus forced to take the best of those who were ready to join.

On the evening of 23rd December 1783, when the appointments were finally made, a swarm of Members were seen hurrying along Downing Street through the bleak, wintry weather. They made their way into No. 10 in small groups. Of Pitt's first Cabinet of seven all except himself were members of the House of Lords. In those days, and indeed until the present century, every new Minister had to seek re-election and it was to avoid this, with the risk of their defeat at the polls, that Pitt, like others before him, preferred to appoint peers.

He had no illusions about the difficulties ahead. Unsupported in the Commons by any of his Cabinet, he faced on the benches opposite the most powerful debaters of the day – North and Fox, Burke and Sheridan. Also ranged against him was North's formidable following. The heart of any seasoned Prime Minister might well have been daunted by such adverse odds, but Pitt faced them with his unquenchable confidence and with an air of contempt. They opposed him at every turn. Division after division brought defeat. He was defeated sixteen times in twelve weeks, overwhelmingly defeated, but he remained calm and resolute.

Outside the House support for him was assured. The people soon made it quite clear that they were wholeheartedly behind their young Prime Minister. They gathered round and cheered him in the streets. When he went to the City of London to receive the Freedom, all the shops along the Strand and Fleet Street were illuminated in his honour. This had its effect on the House, for the majority against him soon began to dwindle. The followers of both Fox and North, never happy about their alliance, showed signs of mutiny. Pitt's nights, passed in solitude in his bedroom at No. 10, were no longer anxious. He decided to dissolve Parliament and on 24th March 1784 sought the verdict of the country. The result justified his expectations. No fewer than 160 of North's and Fox's supporters were defeated. Pitt was now secure.

He was resolved to make England great again, as it was when his father was at the helm. It would take time, he realized, and to achieve it he needed stability and continuity in office. His immediate attention was directed to the economic recovery of the country. The protracted war with the American colonists and its vast extension by three European enemies had played havoc with the nation's budget. Only two years had elapsed since its termination, while five years ahead (though it could not be foreseen) lay the French Revolution, destined to involve Britain in an even more prolonged and devastating war. Pitt used these years well. The financial rehabilitation of England was accomplished with remarkable speed. Never before, not even in Walpole's long years of uninterrupted peace, had the country known such immense prosperity. The industrial revolution, accelerated by Crompton's invention of the spinning 'mule' in 1779 and given a further fillip by Watts' steam-engine, had an ever widening effect on the life of the people. New towns, haphazardly built and with a deplorable disregard of the welfare of the worker, had begun to spring up everywhere. The scene was changing rapidly. Though in Westminster and Mayfair men still went about in periwigs and buckled shoes and women dressed their hair so loftily that they found it difficult to sit upright in their coaches and sedan chairs, a profound change was soon to be imposed by the French Revolution and the war that followed, a change from which men's fashions at any rate have not yet recovered.

'The Boy', secure now with a majority in the House, was faced still with the relentless hostility of Fox, not only in Parliament but outside it. In his very first months as Prime Minister, while Pitt was driving past Brooks's in St. James's Street, his carriage was attacked by a gang of ruffians. Members of the club rushed out but only to egg on the rioters. The doors of Pitt's carriage were smashed and it was with difficulty that he escaped injury by taking refuge in White's. Unhesitatingly the finger of accusation was pointed at Fox, who was said to have planned the outrage in order to incapacitate the young Prime Minister. Fox, however, vehemently denied the charge. He had an alibi, he said. 'I was in bed with Mrs. Armistead, who is ready to substantiate the fact on oath.'*

Fox had a powerful ally in the Prince of Wales, who maintained the

---

* Fox married her secretly some years later.

121

tradition of the Georges by not speaking to his father. Thus, in still another reign, though in a far more embittered form now, was the royal quarrel dragged into the political arena, George the Third backing Pitt, the Prince ranging himself beside Fox. It was, however, not so much politics as a community of taste and outlook that drew Fox and the young Prince together. Both found wine, women and the gaming tables irresistible. Both were burdened heavily with debt and often the worse for liquor. Fox, moreover, had rendered the Prince an inestimable service by relieving him of his mistress, Mrs. Mary Robinson, the beautiful but extravagant actress famed for her rendering of the role of Perdita in *The Winter's Tale*. The liaison had begun when the Prince was sixteen and she some years older. In time he tired of her and, having transferred his affections to Mrs. Fitzherbert, was anxious to have his adolescent liability taken off his hands. In May 1783 Fox, using his authority as Secretary of State in the Coalition Government formed with North, urged Parliament to give the Prince the enormous income of £100,000 a year. Even North was staggered. It was cut down, on the King's insistence, to half that sum, and in addition a cash payment of £60,000 was made from the Civil List.

Fox was completely discredited. His unscrupulous exercise of bias, his insincerity and appetite for office, which had led to principles being thrown into the discard, utterly disgusted the country and especially the powerful men in the City. It rebounded tremendously to Pitt's advantage.

One of Pitt's earlier dilemmas arose on the return of Warren Hastings from India in the spring of 1785. Hastings had served in that country for thirty years and on Clive's recommendation had been appointed the first Governor-General. Though in temperament as well as appearance he and Clive were quite dissimilar, this slight, gentle, dapper intellectual, with deep reflective eyes, had like Clive made enemies of those he had found it necessary to reprimand or dismiss, and, returning home ahead of him, they had without scruple launched the wildest and vilest accusations against him. Of these enemies his fellow councillor in Calcutta, Sir Philip Francis, suspected of being the author of the 'Junius' letters, was the most prominent, numbering among his closer friends Burke and, through Burke, Fox and Sheridan. Pitt, conscious of their determination to impeach Hastings, was reluctant to receive him with any mark of favour lest he should be charged with shielding a criminal; he was careful at the same time not to side with the critics, lest he should appear to be abandoning to the wolves a public servant who had undoubtedly rendered great service during his term of office. Declaring that he was neither the friend nor the foe of Hastings, Pitt decided to wait, and by his inactivity left himself open to the charge of weakness if not cowardice. Burke insisted on an impeachment. Pitt, preoccupied by developments in Europe which seemed likely to involve the country in war, nevertheless gave a great deal of his time to studying the papers on the case and to discussing them with Wilberforce, Dundas and others, often over breakfast at No. 10. His father had backed Clive with pride and would undoubtedly have stood by Hastings. But Pitt, still in his twenties and feeling his feet, was more cautious. In the House he rebutted all the strictures levelled against Hastings, but to the surprise of all he suddenly swung the other way and censured Hastings on one solitary count.

Warren Hastings' trial began in 1788 and went on for seven years. In the end the Lords found him not guilty on all charges. But the cost of the long trial brought financial ruin to Hastings, who was by no means a rich man. His appeal to Pitt to meet his costs was rejected. The East India Company, however, came to his rescue. They granted him £90,000 in cash and an adequate annuity. This was an unattractive and unworthy episode in Pitt's long and distinguished tenure of the office of Prime Minister.

Another crisis, involving this time the Prince of Wales, confronted the Prime Minister in 1788 when the King, driving through Windsor Park, suddenly stopped his carriage, alighted and shook hands with a low-hanging bough of an oak tree, which he mistook for the King of Prussia. On learning of this the Government decided that a Regency would have to be set up. As the Prince of Wales was the obvious and inescapable choice, the hopes of the Opposition rose high. Fox returned hurriedly from Italy. Pitt's Government, it was generally felt, could no longer survive. Sympathizers in the City, in expectation of Pitt's fall, speedily subscribed the sum of £100,000 and offered it to him as a gift. But, despite his great need of money, Pitt refused it. In the House, though Fox fought vigorously, Pitt insisted on imposing restrictions to prevent the Prince from granting pensions, conferring peerages, or disposing of Crown property. This withheld from him all power to reward his friends. But before the Act could come into operation the King unexpectedly recovered. The crisis passed, but the danger that the malady would recur was ever present.

It was during these still peaceful years that Pitt, stirred by Wilberforce's horrifying description of the traffic in slaves, promised his wholehearted support for its abolition. He was revolted by the conditions during the transit of human cargo in ships from Africa to America – huddled below decks, chained to each other, suffering constantly the acutest agony, to which a great many succumbed. Some months later in the autumn of 1788, Pitt personally introduced the motion in the House. He described the trade as 'shocking to humanity, abominable to be carried on by any country, and which reflected the greatest dishonour on the British Senate and on the British nation.' A Bill was passed in the first instance to regulate the slave trade. In the following May Pitt gave his full support to a further motion brought in by Wilberforce for its total abolition and found himself in the same lobby as Fox and Burke. But the slave merchants, with vested interests in Parliament, were too powerful and too numerous, and the motion was lost. Year after year it was raised in the House. In April 1792 a motion for its gradual abolition was carried in the Commons but postponed by the Lords. With the outbreak of the long and devastating war with France shortly afterwards, no further action was taken for many years. Similarly Pitt's endeavours to reform the electorate were baulked and had to be deferred. He realized that he would have to move cautiously if he was to accomplish what had to be done. Like Walpole, he found it necessary to use both influence and patronage in order to secure the support he required in Parliament. Fortunately he had the backing of the King, who was grateful to Pitt for his deliverance from the bondage he had suffered under the Coalition. Noticing that the Whig majority in the Lords was no longer compliant, His Majesty expressed his readiness to create more peers. The Upper House was small at the time. The peers numbered in all only 240, of whom fifteen, being Roman Catholics, were not allowed to sit. Pitt added 140 to their number. By this means, by granting places and pensions, bishoprics, judgeships and receiverships in excise or customs, he made both Houses pliable – and was thus assured of the triumph of his policy.

Despite his masterly handling of the finances of the nation, Pitt's personal finances were completely beyond his control. He lived extravagantly. The bills kept mounting and he was dunned ceaselessly for payment. Tradesmen waited on the doorstep of No. 10 to waylay him as he went in and out. Unmarried, he invited his sister, Lady Harriet Pitt, to come and live at No. 10 and take charge of the household and the bills. For two years, until her marriage in 1785, she kept the tradesmen at bay and his affairs in reasonable order. After she left chaos descended again.*

His kinsman Lord Rosebery, himself Prime Minister more than a century later, says of Pitt: 'Throughout his life, from the cradle to the grave, he may be said to have known no wider existence' than the House of Commons provided. 'It was his mistress, his dice-box, his game preserve; it was his ambition, his library, his creed.' Yet one gets glimpses of his playful ease with children. One evening two Cabinet Ministers, arriving at No. 10 for an interview, found the Prime Minister on all fours on the floor, his face blackened with burnt cork, and children romping around him.† Pitt asked the Ministers to wait while he went and washed his face. When he returned the children noticed an astonishing change in his bearing. His manner became lofty, his talk formal. After the Ministers left he blackened his face again and rejoined the children.

Though solitary by choice and detached in bearing, Pitt did go in for entertaining, and he did so on a reckless scale with no thought whatsoever of cost. His dinner parties at No. 10 Downing Street were wildly lavish. The bills he ignored. Sir Nathaniel Wraxall records: 'It was commonly asserted that the Collectors of Taxes found more difficulty in levying them from the Chancellor of the Exchequer, than from almost any other Inhabitant of Westminster. Even Tradesmen's Bills, particularly those of Coachmakers, were said to be frequently paid, not in Money, but by ordering new Articles, and thus augmenting the Pressure of the Evil itself.'

To escape the stress of office (for his debts seemed to cause him scarcely

* Lord North, who lived at No. 10 for fifteen years, was also in great financial difficulties, but it was never as acute as this – partly because he was not so extravagant, largely because he worried, whereas Pitt didn't.
† One of these was the daughter of his sister Harriet, who had died a year after her marriage to Edward Eliot.

any uneasiness) Pitt, a few months after becoming Prime Minister, took the lease of a house on Putney Heath, which had for him the advantage of being near Wilberforce's house at Wimbledon. A year later, however, he decided to move. He bought a site at Holwood Hill, near Bromley, about ten miles from Downing Street and at that time in the heart of the country. He described it as 'a most beautiful spot, wanting nothing but a house fit to live in'. Its building imposed a further severe strain upon his finances. Nevertheless it was here that he found such relaxation and happiness as his temperament would allow.

The governing of the country he kept almost wholly in his own hands. Not content with being Prime Minister as well as Chancellor of the Exchequer, he also took on the chief duties of the Secretary of State nominally responsible for foreign affairs. The arranging of all alliances in Europe, the handling of all correspondence with Ambassadors, Kings and Emperors, he always conducted himself. Thus in a Cabinet still limited to approximately half a dozen members, Pitt undertook quite half the work and subjected the rest to his own personal direction. The other Ministers were in consequence no more than ciphers.

England's prestige when Pitt took control was at its lowest ebb because of the disasters suffered in the American War of Independence. Europe treated her with indifference if not contempt, a humiliating decline from the high esteem to which Pitt's father had raised the country less than a generation before. Pitt realized that no heed whatsoever would be paid to what England said or felt until England was strong again, and it was to this that he gave his consistent attention. Since it was on the sea that England relied both for her security and her trade, Pitt made the reconstruction of the Navy his most urgent task. Many of Britain's battleships at the end of the American war were barely able to crawl home across the Atlantic. Some indeed were not even able to do that, but foundered through the rottenness of their hulls. 'There was not one ship', stated Admiral Byam Martin, 'in a condition to be placed in the return as fit for service without repair.' Nor were the naval dockyards in a position to undertake such work. The inefficiency and waste were found by Sir Charles Middleton, the Comptroller, to be utterly appalling. Pitt selected Admiral Howe to be First Lord of the Admiralty. Howe during the American war had command of the North American station, while his brother commanded the British land forces. The Admiral had held this office before with great credit and now, despite sharp differences with the Navy Board, he not only redressed abuses but got more work and far longer hours of work from the Admiralty dockyards than ever before, and gave out further contracts to private yards for the building of still more warships. In his Budgets Pitt allocated vast sums to meet these greatly enhanced costs and by 1785, when he had been in office for less than two years, he was greatly reassured to learn that ninety sail-of-the-line and as many frigates were nearing completion.

The effect of this on foreign affairs was as Pitt had expected. He was able at last to play his part in the adroit balancing of power in Europe, with a particularly watchful eye on the shifting events in Belgium and Holland which lay all too near the English shores. As always the dynastic ambitions of European rulers were at work. The Emperor of Austria, Joseph II, evolved an ingenious scheme for the exchange of Bavaria, which he wanted, for Belgium, which was then under his control and had brought him endless friction with France. Pitt foresaw that such an exchange would be disadvantageous to Britain. He had already tried to improve relations between England and France. He had arranged a commercial treaty which provided favourable terms of trade and granted the citizens of both countries free entry without passports. But he was only too well aware of French designs on Belgium and of the continuing French intrigues in Holland. Prussia, at the same time, was strongly opposed to Austria acquiring Bavaria and thus dominating southern Germany. Conducting the negotiations personally and in secret, Pitt promptly formed an alliance with Prussia. Frederick the Great had died recently and his successor, Frederick William of Prussia, in September 1787 moved his troops to the Dutch frontier, as had been arranged, while Pitt sent the British fleet off the Dutch coast. The Prussians then marched into Holland and found whole companies of French soldiers dressed in Dutch uniforms. The French, caught red-handed, gave way. A triple alliance was then signed for mutual security between Great Britain, Prussia and Holland. It was England's first diplomatic success for a generation.

Pitt had begun to play the role his father had once played. The tough, aggressive attitude Chatham had inherited from his grandfather, the merchant interloper, which had made him stretch out and seize trade routes and trading stations for Britain, young Pitt adopted now. Only in a measure was he successful, for by temperament and disposition he was more fitted for raising the nation to greatness by pursuing a policy of peace.

Nevertheless for a time he maintained the aggressive role. After a year, in 1789, there was trouble with Spain. The large island of Vancouver, off the west coast of Canada and today an integral part of Canada, was the bone of contention. The Spaniards claimed the whole of the Pacific coast of America and Canada, as far north as Alaska, which at that time was Russian. British ships were seized by Spain at Nootka Sound, in Vancouver, an admirable natural harbour, and Pitt instantly demanded, not only the return of the ships and full reparation, but also a renunciation of Spain's fantastic claims. To support this Parliament voted a million pounds for the further strengthening of the British fleet. In all two and a quarter millions were spent in naval preparations. Spain climbed down and Britain's mastery of the seas was restored.

In his third thrust Pitt was not so successful. Catherine the Great of Russia, with designs on Turkey, had seized the fortified port of Oczakoff, on the Black Sea. Encouraged by his two brinkmanship triumphs and regarding Russia's action as a possible threat to British interests in the Mediterranean, Pitt insisted that the Russians must withdraw. He was given a substantial vote in the House, but within twenty-four hours, aware that Catherine was not likely to be intimidated, Pitt cancelled his instructions. This time it was he who climbed down, for war was the last thing he wanted, since he realized that it would undo all he had so far achieved; nor would the country be prepared, he felt, to shed blood for an obscure, swampy port, of which no one had ever heard. Not all in the Cabinet agreed with him on this. There were endless quarrels. Many were eager to force a showdown. Pitt's wise and courageous decision led to the resignation of his Foreign Secretary Lord Carmarthen, later the Duke of Leeds; and Pitt's personal reputation suffered too, both abroad and at home. But he foresaw only too clearly that his earlier rash attitude, had it led to war, would have wrecked the entire financial edifice he had so patiently been erecting, and would have postponed, possibly for years, the many schemes for reform he still planned to put into operation.

Even after the outbreak of the French Revolution, Pitt adhered resolutely to his resolve to avoid war at almost all costs. No one could have regarded the Revolution with greater detachment. In introducing his Budget for 1790, a few months after the fall of the Bastille, Pitt spoke with the greatest optimism of Britain's future. Even as late as 1792 he said: 'Unquestionably there never was a time in the history of this country, when, from the situation of Europe, we might more reasonably expect fifteen years of peace than at the present moment.'

War came within ten months.

CHAPTER 13
The Napoleonic War

BEHIND Pitt's detached attitude to what he called 'the present convulsions in France', there lurked a certain sympathy with the aspirations of the revolutionaries, which before long he went so far as to express quite openly. It may be that he saw in the upheaval a weakening of his country's implacable enemy. It can, however, be said with certainty that he shared neither Fox's glowing conviction that 'it is the greatest event that has ever happened in the world', nor that of Burke, now completely estranged from Fox, who described the French as the ablest architects of their own ruin. By the spring of 1790, still feeling that Britain would in no way be involved, Pitt realized that 'the restoration of tranquillity' would be distant, but added that 'whenever her system shall become restored, if it should prove freedom rightly understood, freedom resulting from good order and good government, France would stand forward as one of the most brilliant powers in Europe', enjoying the kind of liberty which Englishmen venerated.

In the House, having triumphed in his second General Election, Pitt's position was even more assured by the disarray of the Opposition.

The Whigs, led by Fox and once closely united, had been split by the French Revolution into two irreconcilable factions. Fox and a handful of others were wholeheartedly for the Revolution. They toured the Radical clubs in the country and made inflammatory speeches in support of the revolutionaries. Fox's exhortations were fanned by Tom Paine's cheaply priced book *Rights of Man*, of which many hundred thousand copies were sold. There was a continuous flow of deputations across the Channel from this Foxite group. They were received by the French National Convention with rapture and were fortified with the assurance that England's own day of deliverance was near at hand, to achieve which every possible assistance was offered.

Burke, on the other hand, was equally energetic in denouncing the rebels. In speech and in pamphlet he attacked the Revolution with fiercest passion. It was indeed in answer to his *Reflections on the French Revolution* that Tom Paine published his *Rights of Man*. There were clashes in the House between Burke and Fox. When Fox remarked amid an uproar that there was surely no loss of friendship between them, Burke shouted back angrily: 'Yes – yes – there is a loss of friends. I know the price of my conduct. I have done my duty at the price of my friend. Our friendship is at an end.' All who felt as strongly as Burke, and he had many supporters, clamoured for war. But Pitt (at whom Burke had sneered in his *Reflections*, crying 'The age of chivalry is gone') kept calmly on his intermediate course, unswayed even by the King's anger at what was happening in France.

When the Emperor Leopold of Austria, understandably deeply concerned about his sister, the lovely and feckless Marie Antoinette, talked of going to war and went so far as to sign a pact for this purpose with the King of Prussia and the Elector of Saxony, Pitt refused to be drawn in. He merely expressed his regret that the King of Prussia, as an ally of Britain, should have joined in the pact. Burke, entirely on the side of the Kings, talked to the fleeing aristocrats as they arrived in England in boatloads, offered them encouragement and hope, and sent his son to spur on those who had escaped over the frontier to Germany. Make war, he urged, for he felt that unless the Revolution was ruthlessly stamped out, its principles would endanger every State.

Europe's crowned heads, having assembled 80,000 men under the Duke of Brunswick, began their march on France in August 1792. The

Revolutionary army was routed. Panic spread and the panic brought in a reign of terror in France. The mob in Paris broke into the Tuileries and the King was moved to the Temple as a prisoner. A month later there was a massacre of aristocrats in the jails.

In command of the Hanoverian troops serving under the Duke of Brunswick was George the Third's son, Ernest Duke of Cumberland, who was in his early twenties. Brunswick's initial success did not last. At Jemappes the tide turned against him and the whole of the Netherlands lay open to the Revolutionaries. Flushed by their victory, the French offered to send their troops to help people everywhere to rise against their rulers. 'All Governments are our enemies,' declared the President of the Convention, 'all peoples are our allies.' An immediate attack on Holland was ordered.

This made it impossible for England to stand aloof any longer. It was through Pitt's influence that Holland had refrained from joining the coalition against France. His plan had been to confine the war so that hostilities would end quickly. In a desperate endeavour to preserve peace he was even prepared to recognize the French Republic. During most of that dismal, rainy autumn, so great was Pitt's distraction that he was unable to concentrate on anything. He was often away from No. 10 and wrote scarcely any letters. The moves made now by the French forced his hand. He was not prepared to tolerate the presence of the French fleet at Antwerp or to desert his Dutch allies, faced as they were by French aggression. One final bid for peace was made by him in December 1792. He offered to help Austria acquire Bavaria if Austria made peace with France. He also informed France that he would stand aside so long as Holland was not invaded.

In January 1793 news reached England of the execution of Louis the Sixteenth; Marie Antoinette was left to linger at the Conciergerie for a further nine months. A shudder of horror swept the country. All the theatres were closed and the nation went into mourning. George the Third was deeply moved and the crowds showed their sympathy by gathering round his carriage and shouting for an immediate declaration of war. But Pitt even now refused to act. The French, however, attributing his forbearance to fear, declared war on England on 1st February 1793.

Fortunately Britain's Navy, so recently strengthened, was powerful.

But her army had been sadly neglected. In his efforts to keep his Budgets balanced, Pitt had been reducing the land forces and had lopped off not long before a further 17,000 men. He had felt it would be enough for Britain to rely upon her Navy and to leave the campaigns on land to the immense armies of her Continental allies. He was to find that these allies could not be relied upon to serve any but their own interests.

At home, as an immediate precaution in view of the mischief being stirred up by Fox and his followers, Pitt brought in a series of stern measures. His Aliens Act imposed a close watch on the activities of all foreigners. He suspended Habeas Corpus. A special proclamation was issued against all seditious publications, and with the sales of Tom Paine's book still soaring, a prosecution of Paine was ordered. Many were in sympathy with Paine and substituted for the National Anthem 'God Save the Rights of Man' at public functions. At a meeting in Surrey, called especially to hear this proclamation, Paine suddenly appeared and began distributing copies of his book. He appeared also at a meeting in London, called by the Friends of Liberty, but was advised by the poet William Blake: 'You must not go home, or you are a dead man.' His friends hurried him to Dover and put him on a pacquet for France, where on his arrival the jubilant Revolutionaries elected him to the Convention.

Pitt received a great accession of strength by the coming over to his side of the Old Whigs, led by the Duke of Portland. His friend Wilberforce, however, took a pacifist line and for a time the two were estranged. Though opposed to war, Pitt was far from dejected. He entered the conflict with the firm conviction that it would prove of short duration. France, he knew, was bankrupt and its affairs in appalling disorder. He proved, however, to be wrong. The war lasted for eight years and the Peace of Amiens in 1802 provided only a brief respite, after which the war was resumed and went on for a further fourteen years.

In those first eight years he was faced with overwhelming difficulties. Not only were his allies unreliable, but neither they nor the British produced a single general of any distinction, until, much later, General Suvarov took the field at the head of the Russian armies, whereas the French had Napoleon Bonaparte, an outstanding general of that or any other age. At sea, however, the British fleet, commanded by men of great brilliance, gained victory after victory. Howe, Jervis and Hood were joined before long by young Horatio Nelson, who in 1798, after winning the Battle of the Nile, bottled up Napoleon and his army in Egypt. These successes still further extended Britain's already vast Empire. The remaining colonies of France, as well as the Dutch settlements at the Cape of Good Hope, in Ceylon and elsewhere, were seized once Holland came under French control. But these triumphs were not without their shadows. There was the constant fear of invasion and Britain had to see to her coastal defences. Small parties of French troops did manage to land at remote, isolated coves in England and in Ireland, but they were soon ejected and many prisoners were taken. There was also an unfortunate series of Naval mutinies – at Portsmouth, at Sheerness, and at the Cape of Good Hope.

Pitt's greatest anxiety during these trying and strenuous years was the raising of money to carry on the war. He had to find vast sums to pay out in subsidies to the Prussians and the Austrians for the maintenance of their armies in the field. The demands of Britain's Navy were also great, and Pitt realized that unless trade was sustained his task would be wellnigh impossible. To begin with a great part of the money was raised by loans. This he supplemented by appealing for voluntary contributions, and, despite his own pressing debts and the demands made on his purse by his mother and his elder brother, Lord Chatham, he himself subscribed £2,000. At that moment the bailiffs were actually on their way to seize his furniture at No. 10 Downing Street. Friends tried to keep him solvent. The King considerately appointed him Warden of the Cinque Ports, which provided him with an income of £3,000 a year, but Pitt promptly gave away £1,000 of this to launch the Dover Volunteer Corps, one of the first to be formed in the country. It was found later that his own extravagance was not alone responsible for his insolvency. He was swindled systematically by tradesmen (the bill from his hatter alone for just the one year 1793 was for £600) and also by his household staff at Downing Street, where his expenses were at times higher when he was away than when he was in residence.

In addition to loans and voluntary contributions, it became inescapable as the war dragged on that taxes, which he had been trying to keep down, should be raised. It was now that income tax was introduced in England for the first time. Although the levy was small, a mere twopence in the pound on incomes of £60 to £65 (incomes below £60 were exempt) and scaled up to two shillings in the pound on incomes of £200 a year or more, it caused an uproar. The ruin of the country was predicted. Pitt was booed and jeered at in the streets. His carriage had to be guarded by a squadron of horse. But he refused to give way, and trade, far from suffering, improved despite this.

Among the angriest critics of income tax in the House of Commons were Sheridan and George Tierney. The latter, an irritable and extremely prickly Irishman, had been attacking Pitt persistently on a wide range of issues. In a debate on the activities of the pressgang his criticism of Pitt drew a terse rejoinder from the Prime Minister on Tierney's repeated attempts at obstructing the work of national defence. Pitt's rebuke was sharp. The strain of the war had begun to tell on his nerves and it had been noticed for some time that he was becoming irritable. His manner at Cabinet meetings had led to angry quarrels. Protesting in the House against Pitt's rebuke, Tierney demanded an immediate apology. But this Pitt firmly refused to give. The moment the House rose Tierney sent the Prime Minister a challenge to a duel. Without hesitation Pitt accepted it.

On the following Sunday, 26th May 1798, Pitt, having made his will, left No. 10 Downing Street early in the afternoon and walked down to St. James's Park. From Birdcage Walk he climbed the steps to Queen Street and got into a chaise for Wimbledon Common. Pitt, Tierney and their seconds met on Putney Heath at three that afternoon. The Speaker of the House of Commons, Dr. Addington, who had tried repeatedly to prevent the duel, rode to the scene on horseback, but drew up before he reached it and climbed a small hill from which to observe the outcome. He dismounted by a gibbet on which a felon had recently been hanged.

He saw the seconds arguing with the contestants. They were trying to persuade both Pitt and Tierney to abandon the project, but neither would agree to do so. The pistols were then handed to them. The twelve paces were measured. Both fired, but the shots went wide. The seconds tried once again to dissuade them, but without avail. A second pair of pistols were then handed out and again Pitt and Tierney faced each other. Pitt was seen to fire his into the air and Tierney missed for a second time. Urged now to regard their honour as having been fully satisfied, they agreed at last to shake hands. Addington then came down and joined the group. 'You must dine with me,' he said to Pitt and the two returned to London together.

For a dozen years, ever since the marriage of his sister Harriet to his friend Edward Eliot, Pitt had been living alone at No. 10. Harriet's daughter often came round to see him and he enjoyed the gay diversion of spending a little time with her and other children. But all knew that his private life was lonely and empty. At weekends when he was at Holwood he often saw Lord Auckland, who was his neighbour there and Postmaster-General in his Government. Auckland's daughter, Eleanor Eden, he had known since her childhood. She was twenty now, very lovely and vivacious. She had for the Prime Minister a deep admiration and affection which made her delight in his company, and in his turn Pitt, though at thirty-eight almost twice her age, was attracted by her gentleness and her striking beauty. Before long it became obvious that they were both very much in love. That they would marry was never doubted. But Pitt, after many weeks of anguished reflection, felt that it would not be fair, heavily burdened as he was by debt, which already amounted to £30,000, to ask her to share his problems and his plight. Forced by a fresh pressure upon his purse to take out a second mortgage of £7,000 on Holwood, he decided that he could no longer leave the girl's expectations in doubt. So early in the year 1797, the year before his duel, he sent Lord Auckland a 'most private' letter explaining the position. He stated that 'whoever may have the good fortune to be united to her is destined to more than his share of human happiness', but his own 'obstacles' were decisive and insurmountable.[53]

Auckland was deeply distressed on reading it. He called to see Pitt and offered to help in every way he could, even financially. But Pitt did not feel it would be right to allow himself to be persuaded. He was resolute, and in fact he never married. Later Eleanor accepted a proposal from Lord Hobart and, on his succeeding his father, became the Countess of Buckinghamshire. Pitt gave her husband a place in his Government and they were both frequent visitors at No. 10. But Auckland never fully forgave Pitt.

Pitt strove ceaselessly to bring the war to an end, provided, of course, this could be achieved with honour. Repeatedly, and sometimes at intervals of only a few months, he tried to open negotiations with the

French, but again and again he was rebuffed. So it dragged on. As each coalition of European powers collapsed, Pitt by offering increased bribes of money, formed still another coalition. At times Britain found herself alone, without a single ally, ready to negotiate, but never to surrender.

In his endeavours for peace Pitt was supported wholeheartedly by the new Under-Secretary for Foreign Affairs, George Canning, a brilliant young man of only twenty-seven, who was one day himself to move into No. 10 Downing Street as Prime Minister. The Foreign Secretary was Pitt's cousin, Lord Grenville, son of the 'Gentle Shepherd' George Grenville, who as Prime Minister had been responsible for imposing the Stamp Act on America. Lord Grenville did not support Pitt's view, or his own Under-Secretary's. Like the King, he felt there should be no compromise until the Bourbon heir was restored to the French throne. What was at stake for Britain, Pitt was only too well aware. Challenged in the House by Tierney to state in one sentence 'without ifs and buts' the object of the war and why it was being pursued, Pitt replied: 'I know not whether I can do it in one sentence, but in one word I can tell him that it is security; security against a danger the greatest that ever threatened the world; . . . against a danger that has been resisted by all the nations of Europe, and resisted by none with so much success as by this nation, because by none has it been resisted so uniformly and with so much energy.'

In 1798 his difficulties were accentuated by the outbreak of a rebellion in Ireland. A French invasion was timed to coincide with it, but the Irish were routed at Vinegar Hill before the French forces could land. The Irish problem had for centuries bedevilled the life of every Government in England. Attempts to solve it has been made by Queen Elizabeth, by Cromwell and by William the Third, but the brutal methods adopted – the dispatch of armies, the sacking of towns, the burning of villages and the destruction of crops to starve the people into submission – brought quiescence for a time, but not pacification. After an interval rioting, arson and murder broke out anew and was followed by a new cycle of coercion. When Ulster was subdued after the flight of the Earls of Tyrone and Tyrconnel in the reign of James the First, from whom, because of his Catholic mother Mary Queen of Scots, the Irish had expected so much, the six northern counties were parcelled out among English and Scottish colonists, with only small sections of the least productive land reserved for the Irish. The site of the sacked town of Derry was adopted by London and renamed Londonderry. The relationship with the Irish was one of conquerors and conquered and it bred bitter resentment which no clemency in the succeeding years could eradicate. The Irish Catholic gentry were severely penalized; their land was taken over by the new Protestant aristocracy who numbered less than a sixth of the total population: among them were a few Catholic proselytes who had agreed to conform only to preserve their property. There was a continuous exodus. Men left to enlist in foreign armies, serving Spain or France or the Holy Roman Empire. Thousands went to settle in the West Indies and in America. Ireland's population, once equal to half that of England, dwindled to little more than three million. The country was wholly agricultural and when the crops, largely potatoes, failed there was famine and a heavy death roll through starvation. The flourishing wool industry had been deliberately destroyed, in fact all industrial enterprises were banned to prevent competition with England's manufacturers and traders. The vast numbers of unemployed took to smuggling, which came to be a major activity in the country; its furtive practise developed criminal instincts which found a wider outlet in every political upheaval. There was a Parliament, with both a House of Commons and a House of Lords, but only Protestant freeholders were permitted to vote. Of the 300 M.P.s only fifty-two were really elected. The remaining seats were owned by Whig potentates or were obtained for their nominees by bribery.

The large numbers of Irish who had migrated to America took with them an undying hatred of England and eagerly aided the colonists in their War of Independence. Many returned later to Ireland resolved on winning a similar freedom for their country by the use of similar tactics. In 1793, a few weeks after France declared war, Pitt granted Irish Roman Catholics a substantial measure of relief. Though still debarred from sitting in Parliament, they were given the right to vote, to bear arms, to hold commissions in the Army below the rank of Major-General, to serve in grand juries, to become members of corporations and to receive university degrees – all these had been denied them before. Pitt began to feel that the best solution would be to unite the two countries on the lines that England and Scotland were united a hundred years before. Ireland would thus, like Scotland, be given the right to send Members to the British Parliament in London. This union was effected on 1st January 1801.

Pitt wanted at the same time to remove all the civil disabilities imposed on Roman Catholics so that they should in future enjoy the same rights as Protestants. He wanted also to help the Roman Catholic clergy. The Established Church in Ireland was Protestant and the Catholic peasantry had to pay taxes for its support, while no aid whatsoever was given to the Catholic church, which in fact served the vast majority of the population. To such measures there was considerable opposition in the Cabinet. Of the dozen Ministers who now sat round the table at No. 10, no fewer than a third – the Lord Chancellor Lord Loughborough, the Duke of Portland, Lord Liverpool and Lord Westmorland – were vigorously opposed to the granting of these further concessions. There were heated arguments and the Lord Chancellor was indiscreet enough to speak of Pitt's plan to the King, who declared hotly: 'I shall reckon any man my personal enemy who proposes any such measure.' His Majesty's attitude, like that of the four rebellious Ministers, was based on the strong anti-Catholic feeling in England at that time. There was a great fear that if the Catholics were granted equal rights Ireland would be lost just as America had been lost. Many were convinced that the security of Britain was entirely dependent on keeping Ireland and its ports under British control.

When Pitt informed the King that he proposed to substitute a political oath for the existing sacramental test so that Catholics should be able to take their seats in the House of Commons in London, the King became furious. In his Coronation oath, he said, he had sworn to uphold the Protestant faith and not to accept the 'superstitious and idolatrous . . . sacrifice of the Mass.' He refused to yield. Pressed further, His Majesty told Pitt never to mention the subject again. Thereupon Pitt handed in his resignation.

CHAPTER 14
The Doctor Moves in...

ANTICIPATING that Pitt would be intractable, the King had been secretly trying for some days to sound Dr. Addington, the Speaker of the House of Commons, to see if he would take on the office of Prime Minister. Despite his personal affection for Pitt, His Majesty was tired of his 'authoritative manner' and had indeed been trying to find a successor since August 1799, nearly eighteen months before. His earlier efforts to induce Lord Malmesbury* and William Windham† to accept the office failed through their loyalty to Pitt.

Addington, though even more closely attached to Pitt, for his father had been Chatham's doctor and the two sons had known each other

---

* Formerly Sir James Harris. Thirteen years older than Pitt, he had been at Oxford with Fox. Was Ambassador at St. Petersburg and later at The Hague, where he helped to further Pitt's policy. His wealth gave him a prominent place in society, where his handsome presence and lively conversation won him wide popularity.
† A Whig Member of Parliament since 1784, one of the very few to be elected as a supporter of the Fox–North Coalition. He went over to Pitt after the outbreak of the French Revolution, was made Secretary at War by Pitt in 1794 and given a seat in the Cabinet.

since childhood, nevertheless informed the King of his readiness to serve. He did not, however, find it easy to form a Cabinet and His Majesty had to ask Pitt if he would be prepared to carry on until Addington was ready. Placing the needs of the country above any personal feeling, Pitt agreed at once. He even went so far as to plead with his recent colleagues in the Cabinet and his friends to join the new administration. Most of them, including Lord Grenville, Windham, Cornwallis and Castlereagh refused, but Pitt was able to induce his brother Chatham, as well as Lord Hawkesbury (later the Earl of Liverpool) and the Duke of Portland, who had opposed him on the Catholic question, to support Addington.

In February 1801, with the new Prime Minister not yet ready to take over, Pitt introduced the Budget. The King meanwhile had begun again to show signs of acute distress and anxiety. He assembled his family and read his Coronation oath out to them, saying that if he broke it by agreeing to any relaxation of the restrictions on Catholics, he would be compelled to abdicate and let the Crown pass to another. Shortly afterwards the King's madness returned. Pitt was on the point of setting up the Regency and of imposing the same restraints on the Prince of Wales as he had planned in 1789, when the King showed signs of recovering. From his sick bed, His Majesty sent a message to Pitt, blaming him for the return of his malady. Touched by this and in order to assist his recovery, Pitt assured the King that he would not again raise the question of Catholic emancipation during the King's lifetime: to this assurance he remained tied for the rest of his life.

When at last Addington's Cabinet was complete – it consisted chiefly of men who, as Macaulay states, could hardly be considered even second-rate – and the news got out that Pitt was no longer Prime Minister, it struck the country like a thunderclap. There was widespread consternation. The general feeling may best be expressed in the words of Lord Minto,* at that time Britain's Ambassador in Vienna: 'I have long looked on him as the Atlas of our reeling globe.' Yet to Pitt no alternative to his resignation seemed possible. To have put it to a vote in Parliament, or worse still to have appealed to the country,

---

* Formerly Sir Gilbert Elliot. Educated in Paris where he became an intimate friend of Mirabeau. Entered Parliament in 1776 as an independent Whig and later became an ally of Burke. Was envoy-extraordinary to Vienna from 1799 to 1801.

seemed to him a dangerous procedure in time of war, since it would doubtless have set a large section of the people against the King.

Pitt vacated No. 10 for Addington, who moved in almost at once. They were almost of an age, Addington at forty-four being two years Pitt's senior. It was through Pitt that Addington, who had been trained for the law, first came into politics, and through Pitt's influence that he was elected Speaker. He was not entitled to the prefix of 'Doctor': it was first used in derision and it stuck. A tall, heavily built man, he was mild and conciliatory in manner, and not particularly prepossessing. He succeeded Pitt now as First Lord of the Treasury and Chancellor of the Exchequer, but it soon became obvious that he was not able to undertake either of these tasks. A mere plodder, most of his political life had been devoted to working on committees. As a debater he was a complete failure. His only asset was that he had the confidence and support of the King, due to his father having also been the King's doctor. Thus it was to his parent that he owed his astonishing and quite unmerited rise to the chief office of State.

He knew No. 10 Downing Street well of course, for he had frequently been Pitt's guest there. It is recorded of an occasion there when Addington was with a small party which included Grenville and Burke, that Pitt, speaking of the French Revolution, declared that England would not be much affected by it, but would 'go on as we are until the day of judgement.' Burke retorted: 'Very likely, sir. It is the day of no judgement that I am afraid of.'[68]

Addington's position was insecure throughout the two and a half years he was Prime Minister. Pitt's continued support of him, both in the House and out of it, especially on financial matters where the need was greatest, led eventually to a breach with Grenville and Canning, both of whom were vehemently hostile to Addington. Their attacks on him often became attacks on Pitt too. Canning accused Pitt of 'deserting' and contrasted the two men in the memorable jingle: 'Pitt is to Addington as London is to Paddington'. Fox described the substitution of Addington as no more than a 'juggle', implying that Pitt was still ruling from behind the scenes, while others, like Malmesbury and Auckland, called it a strategic prelude to a triumphant return by Pitt, which in fact it proved to be, though there is no evidence to support the view that Pitt had any such design in mind when he

The Duke of Wellington, Prime Minister for nearly three years. He lived for only part of that time at No. 10. From a portrait by Thomas Phillips and S. Freeman.

Benjamin Disraeli, first Earl of Beaconsfield. He was twice Prime Minister. From a photograph taken late in life.

William Ewart Gladstone, Disraeli's opponent and four times Prime Minister. From a photograph during his first term as Prime Minister.

resigned. His official statement in the House on 25th March 1801 dealt with his resignation in calm and measured terms, but it was soon apparent to his friends that he was extremely sorry to go. 'There were painful workings in his mind, plainly discernible; most of the time tears in his eyes, and much agitated,' wrote George Rose, a Member of Parliament, a Secretary of the Treasury and one of the few in Pitt's intimate circle.

Addington lost no time in securing peace with France. This was, of course, what Pitt himself had been trying to achieve all along. Addington was greatly helped by the dramatic change that had just taken place in France. Napoleon, whom Pitt described as 'this last adventurer in the lottery of revolutions', had seized power as First Consul and needed a breathing space. At sea the war was still going triumphantly for Britain, thanks to Nelson's victories at Copenhagen, in the Straits of Gibraltar, and elsewhere. Yet in his negotiations for peace, Addington was prepared to accept terms that were far from advantageous. The French were allowed to keep their vast conquests on the Continent, including both Belgium and Holland, the occupation of which had led to the war. She was also given back all the colonies Britain had seized. Spain and Holland benefited similarly, save for Trinidad and certain Dutch posts in Ceylon, which Britain was permitted to retain. Malta had to be given up and went back to the Knights of St. John, Egypt was handed over to the Sultan of Turkey, and the Cape of Good Hope to the Dutch.

Parliament was outraged. Grenville called the terms disgraceful and ruinous. This view was shared by many. But Pitt urged their acceptance, although he described them as perhaps less than adequate. He had himself, he said, been unsuccessfully striving for peace for at least six years, but not until now was there a stable enough Government in France with which they could come to any agreement. England was weary of the long-drawn-out war, and the House of Commons eventually accepted the terms in March 1802.

Peace secured – 'a peace which everybody is glad of and nobody is proud of', said a critic – Addington appealed at once to the country and won a sweeping victory at the elections. It did not, however, secure his position for long. The popular assumption that peace would endure was shattered when Napoleon resumed his aggressions and sent forth his victorious armies to make still further conquests.They overran Switzerland in October of that same year (1802), seized Elba and, across the Atlantic, occupied Louisiana* and the two Floridas. Under these conditions peace was clearly more dangerous than war, and war with France broke out again in May 1803.

With this Addington's tenure of No. 10 Downing Street was doomed. The country wanted Pitt back. The first sign of this was given on his entry into the House after a long absence, when he was greeted with shouts of 'Pitt! Pitt!' His speech, which lasted nearly two hours, was one of the most memorable he ever made. 'Never, to be sure, was there such an exhibition,' wrote young Thomas Creevey, who entered Parliament for the first time in the preceding year and kept a fascinating record of events in his journal.[75] 'He exhorted, or rather commanded, Ministers to lose no time in establishing measures of finance suited to our situation.' He roused the members to so high a pitch of enthusiasm, that there were cries of 'Hear, Hear!' thrice repeated, equivalent, it was said, to three cheers. Even Fox, Pitt's bitterest and his worthiest foe, was moved to say that, had Demosthenes been present, he would have admitted, and even envied, the oration.

But Pitt, still true to his loyalty, refrained from making any attack on Addington. The hopes of his supporters which had risen high, were acutely disappointed. They remonstrated with him, but Pitt refused to yield. Canning commented dejectedly: 'P. has thrown all away. Us, the Country, and Himself, in consideration of which last we must forgive the other two.' In his later speeches Pitt confined himself to exhortation, to indicating the lines along which action should be taken, such as the erection of field-works to cover London in case of invasion, the strengthening of the Navy, the provision of a coast flotilla, and the raising of a general levy for defence – for Napoleon had an army of 100,000 men waiting at Boulogne and more than a thousand boats to bring them across the Channel.

A like loyalty was not, however, shown in return by Addington. His brother, John Hiley Addington, had obtained editorial privileges from *The Times* and used 'often a column or more' of that newspaper

---

* It was taken over from Spain. A month later, in order to raise money, Napoleon sold Louisiana to the United States of America.

for winning support for the Government. It is recorded in *The History of The Times*[57] that 'in spite of the assistance Pitt rendered the Administration by abstaining from giving or provoking overt opposition, the tone of these articles was at first unfriendly to him, then strongly critical, and at last personally offensive.' George Rose described one of the articles as 'detestable in all its parts.'

After the resumption of war Addington realized that it was no longer possible to carry on without Pitt. Repeated efforts were made to bring Pitt into his Government. He even suggested that the two should serve as Secretaries of State under another Prime Minister, but Pitt declined. By now the two friends no longer visited each other and in the rare letters they exchanged the tone was entirely formal, beginning always with 'Dear Sir'. In January 1804 Grenville, who had meanwhile entered into an alliance with Fox, urged Pitt to join them against Addington's 'manifestly incapable' administration. Though only too well aware of the feebleness of the Government, which Creevey described as 'such pitiful, squirting politicians as this accursed Apothecary and his family and friends', Pitt still held aloof. Some weeks later, however, he revealed the only condition on which he would be prepared to return. 'I do not see how, under any circumstances, I can creditably or usefully consent to take part in any Government without being at the head of it.'*

With this view large numbers of people, both in the House and outside it, were in complete agreement. Canning, despite his anger on Pitt's resignation, had already expressed this thought in verse:

> And O! if again the rude whirlwind should rise,
> The dawning of peace should fresh darkness deform,
> The regrets of the good and the fears of the wise
> Shall return to the pilot that weathered the storm.

He took up the theme actively now and urged that 'the administration of the Government be placed in the hands of Mr Pitt.' The King's son, the Duke of York, reinforced this, stating: 'Mr. Pitt must come in . . . it is impossible he should not; the public call for him; they will force Mr. Addington to give way.' The King, on discovering what

---

* In a letter to his friend and former colleague Henry Dundas, later Viscount Melville.[5]

was afoot, became enraged and once more his mind showed signs of becoming unhinged.

Shortly after Easter 1804 Pitt decided that it was time to take effective action. Rising in the House on 25th April, he delivered a shattering attack on the Government. This sealed Addington's fate. His majority reduced to a mere thirty-seven, he offered his resignation, and the way was open for Pitt's return.

But the King, still troubled by fears regarding the removal of Catholic disabilities, would have none of it. For some days he refused to see Pitt. But eventually he gave in. It was their first meeting for three years. For three hours His Majesty argued, laying down all sorts of conditions. Pitt wanted a truly national Government in which all factions should be included. But the King refused firmly and absolutely to have Fox. The discussion grew very heated and, fearing for His Majesty's mind, Pitt finally agreed to leave Fox out. His own health was failing, for on taking office again Pitt said: 'I think my health such that it may cost me my life.'[47]

A few days later Addington left No. 10 Downing Street with his wife and family – they had one son and four daughters – and all his furniture. With the return of Pitt the house once more became a bachelor establishment, but with a difference.

CHAPTER 15
The Return of Pitt

PITT did not return to No. 10 alone. He had been living at
Walmer Castle as Warden of the Cinque Ports, drilling the local
volunteers in his uniform as their Colonel-in-Chief, and training his
telescope towards Boulogne where Napoleon's formidable army
waited to invade Britain. At the castle his young niece Lady Hester
Stanhope had kept house for him. It cannot be said that she was able to
impose the efficiency in the management of his servants and his
accounts that Pitt's sister Harriet had displayed during her short stay
at No. 10 when he first became Prime Minister. But she wrought
nevertheless a considerable change in the setting and atmosphere. Now
twenty-seven, she was lively and diverting and brought a brightness
into his life which it had sadly lacked; and he was glad to have her
accompany him to Downing Street.

Hester was the daughter of the Lord Mahon, who together with
Pitt had escorted Chatham when he entered the House of Lords to
make his last speech on the American war. Mahon had been a warm
supporter of his brother-in-law in the Commons, but not long after

succeeding his father as Earl Stanhope, his sympathies swung suddenly towards the French Revolutionaries. He abandoned his title, called himself Citizen Stanhope, took down the tapestries from his walls, describing them as 'too damned aristocratic', and erased the armorial bearings from his plate. Hester was at that time an impressionable girl of fourteen, but despite the republican influences in her home the aristocrat in her was little affected. In appearance she resembled her uncle Pitt. She was tall, held her head proudly poised, her nose uplifted. But in temperament there was much of her grandfather Chatham in her – a violent temper and an unflinching courage. Her vivacity, her radiance and her magnetism supplied a compelling attractiveness, which was lit by her deep blue eyes and the brilliant colouring of her skin and hair. She rode well and fearlessly, talked without cessation, was blunt and often tactless – a strange wild creature, romantically interested in men and at times outrageously unconventional in her behaviour.

Her mother had died when she was very young and, after enduring for some years the tyranny of her eccentric father, she went to live in Somerset with her grandmother, old Lady Chatham. Also living there was her young cousin Harriet, the only child of Pitt's sister Harriet. From time to time she had visited Pitt at Walmer and after Lady Chatham's death was taken completely under his care. 'How amiable it is of Pitt,' wrote Lord Mulgrave to Major-General Phipps, 'to take compassion on poor Lady Hester Stanhope, and that in a way which must break in upon his habits of life. He is as good as he is great.' But Pitt enjoyed having her with him, though occasionally, after his return to Downing Street, he had to chide her to curb her unbridled tongue, for she could not sit silent and listen to the conversation of her uncle and his distinguished friends, but would assert her own opinions, which were not always well-informed.

The atmosphere at No. 10 changed entirely with her coming. She sat opposite him at the other end of the table, the hostess from the start. She was intolerant and mocking, was rude to the Prince of Wales, mimicked the affected lisp of the great Whig ladies of Devonshire House, yawned when she was bored by the chatter of the wives of Cabinet Ministers, and once scoffingly, when Addington flaunted his Garter in the drawing-room, humbled him by asking if he needed it to

148

tie up his injured leg. Many thought her eccentric. Such unconventional behaviour brought on her, as well as on Pitt, a great deal of ridicule. For the most part the great Whig ladies kept aloof. But Hester preferred to invite her own friends to No. 10. Her uncle found their company congenial. The house was often crowded. Entertaining was done once again on a lavish scale and the expenses reached even greater heights of extravagance.

The King's insistence on the exclusion of Fox from the Government deprived Pitt of the support of some of his closest and ablest supporters, for not only did his cousin Grenville refuse to come in without Fox, but he persuaded others too to keep out. Pitt had accordingly to form a Government out of the available remnants, some of whom had served under Addington. They were weak and lacking in talent, and the new administration was sneeringly described as consisting of 'William and Pitt'. Yet, though they seemed at the time to be insignificant, no fewer than six of them, if we include Pitt, had the qualities required for the office of Prime Minister and indeed all but one of them attained that office, while the sixth declined twice to accept it.* The entire Cabinet, save only for himself and Lord Castlereagh, was in the Lords. Arrayed against Pitt in the Commons, again as when he first took office, were men of formidable debating skill who missed no opportunity of trying to embarrass him. But though tired and ailing and now forty-five years old, he grappled with them with resolution and resource.

On the day Pitt took his seat in the House for the second time as Prime Minister, 18th May 1804, Napoleon was proclaimed Emperor of the French. Shortly afterwards the American Ambassador in Paris crossed over to London with an offer of peace, which he took to No. 10 Downing Street, accompanied by Fox. The offer was too vague for Pitt to be impressed by it. Aware that Napoleon's army was still at Boulogne waiting to cross to England, Pitt was not prepared to relax any efforts to meet and repel the invasion if it came. During the recess, he still went down to the coast to drill his men and to see to the defences. Tirelessly he urged the country to face the danger with that

* The future Prime Ministers were: Spencer Perceval, the Earl of Liverpool, George Canning and Viscount Goderich – some were junior Ministers at this stage; the one who twice refused was Lord Castlereagh, heir to the Marquess of Londonderry.

'just confidence, which neither despises nor dreads the enemy' and to bear in mind what was at stake, 'what it is we have to contend for. It is for our property, it is for our liberty, it is for our independence, nay for our existence as a nation; it is for our character, it is for our very name as Englishmen, it is for everything dear and valuable to man on this side of the grave.'[52]

Later that year Spain re-entered the war against Britain and Pitt's Budget had to provide for greatly increased outgoings. The death duties were raised. A new loan of twenty million pounds was floated and a million a year had to be set aside to pay the interest on it.

The estrangement between Pitt and Addington was brought to an end during the summer. Pitt conferred a peerage on him, making him Viscount Sidmouth, and invited him to join the Cabinet as President of the Council. At the same time Pitt brought in the Earl of Buckinghamshire, who had married Eleanor Eden, Lord Auckland's daughter: she was thus a frequent visitor in the house of which she might have been the chatelaine.

These Cabinet changes were soon followed by a blow which darkened for some weeks the discussions round the famous table. One of the Ministers, Viscount Melville, formerly Henry Dundas, one of Pitt's closer friends, his associate from the earliest years, and now First Lord of the Admiralty, was accused by a Commission of Naval Inquiry of having misapplied public funds while Treasurer of the Navy in Pitt's former administration. Pitt's enemies were jubilant. Thomas Creevey, whose journals have delighted successive generations, recorded with glee: 'We have had indeed most famous sport with Lord Melville. You can form no notion of his [Pitt's] fallen crest in the House of Commons, of his dolorous, distracted air. . . . His own ruin must come next, and that, I think, at no great distance.' Creevey was wrong. Melville had not used the money for his own profit, but had merely been negligent in not preventing his deputy from engaging in private speculations with these sums. Pitt was determined to do what he could to help his colleague and was fully supported by the Cabinet when he demanded the appointment of a special Parliamentary Committee for further investigation.

The debate on this in the House went on all through the night.

Pitt, Canning and Castlereagh rebutted the savage attacks of the Opposition, but it came as a shock to Pitt, when at four o'clock in the morning, his closest friend Wilberforce rose and joined in the censure. The House, however, was equally divided and the Speaker, his face ashen, had to cast the decisive vote. He gave it against the Government.

There followed an astonishing and memorable scene, such as the House has rarely seen. There were shouts of jubilation from Pitt's enemies, but his friends, seeing him in a state bordering on collapse as he pressed his hat down on his head, formed a protective group round him and escorted him from the House all the way to Downing Street.

It has been averred that this was the most shattering blow in Pitt's life, a blow which he took far more badly than any of Napoleon's victories. Not normally prone to showing any emotion, he was now often seen to be near to tears. In consequence of the vote Melville was impeached, but he was acquitted on every count. He nevertheless resigned. When in October 1805 the news of the battle of Trafalgar reached Pitt, he wrote to Melville to congratulate him, adding that it was his energy at the Admiralty that had contributed much to this victory.

Not long after Melville, Addington (now Sidmouth) resigned too. This was inevitable after the persistent attack by Addington's friends on Pitt during his terrible ordeal over Melville. Next Buckinghamshire left. Though shaken, Pitt remained indomitable. His war policy was slowly bringing the country away from the defensive line Addington had for so long pursued and was setting in motion forces that were eventually to bring victory.

In reconstructing his Government Pitt once more sought permission from the King to bring in Fox, for he realized it would also bring in Fox's followers as well as Grenville, and would strengthen his Government considerably. But his long journey to Weymouth proved fruitless. His Majesty remained adamant. Pitt, enfeebled in health and with not long to live, was thus left to carry the great weight of the war alone, fighting not only the enemy across the Channel, but the formidable array of opponents in both Houses. Lord Rosebery held the view that, if the King had yielded, he might have saved Pitt's life. Pitt may have had the same thought in mind when he said: 'I wish the

King may not live to repent – and sooner than he thinks – the rejection of the advice which I pressed on him at Weymouth.'

Pitt's predominant purpose in the months that remained to him was to bring Napoleon's triumphant armies to a halt and to prevent the invasion of England. Napoleon repeatedly declared that all he needed was command of the Channel for just twelve hours in order to cross with his vast army from Boulogne, but those twelve hours proved elusive and were denied him for ever after Nelson's resounding victory at Trafalgar.

Pitt, unable to send a large enough force to the Continent, had already embarked on a fresh gigantic alliance. At a great cost in subsidies and with the promise of the fullest possible support with ships and men, he succeeded in forming his great Third Coalition, comprising Britain, Russia, Austria, and a somewhat wavering Prussia. And it was to deal with the menace this offered that Napoleon had begun to move his army from Boulogne, even before Trafalgar, for it had become increasingly clear, after Villeneuve's flight from Nelson and his retreat to Cadiz, that the French fleet would never be able to provide the cover he required. In his very first clash with the new Coalition he won a resounding victory. On 19th October 1805 his army inflicted a crushing defeat on the Austrians at Ulm, taking 30,000 prisoners. News of this did not reach Pitt until 3rd November. A Dutch newspaper was brought to him at No. 10 Downing Street. Unable to read it and with no one there to translate, he drove in his carriage up Whitehall to Lord Malmesbury's house in Spring Gardens, accompanied by Lord Mulgrave. Malmesbury recorded in his diary: 'They came to me to translate it which I did as best I could; and I observed but too clearly the effect it had on Pitt, though he did his utmost to conceal it. . . . His manner and his looks were not his own.' Promptly and unflinchingly he sent a dispatch to Vienna, urging the Austrians to rally and make a fresh effort. To the Prussians in Berlin he sent Lord Harrowby to stress the urgency for immediate action and offered to send 60,000 men to augment their forces.

Each day, Hester Stanhope has recorded, 'Pitt would be up at eight in the morning, with people enough to see for a week, obliged to talk all the time he was at breakfast, and receiving first one, then another; until four o'clock; then eating a mutton chop, hurrying off to the

House, and there badgered and compelled to speak and waste his lungs until two or three in the morning! – who could stand it? . . . and having eaten nothing, in a manner of speaking, all day, he would sup . . . and then go to bed to get three or four hours' sleep, and to renew the same thing next day, and the next, and the next . . . – it was murder.' Often indeed the brief respite in bed was disturbed by the arrival of an urgent rider clattering along Downing Street with dispatches, bearing, more often than not, fresh disastrous tidings. Once roused, Pitt found it impossible to regain his rest, but would sit musing, planning, sending down for more port. His two bottles a day, maintained rigorously since the doctor had prescribed it so beneficially in his boyhood, had been supplemented in recent years by a third bottle, then a fourth. At times his friends begged him not to drink any more, especially when he had to go back to the House to speak. But it had become a necessity by now, and few had ever seen him the worse for it. Addington recalls but one occasion when Pitt, called unexpectedly from the table at No. 10 to answer an attack in the House, appeared to be under the influence of drink. It happened that one of the clerks of the House that night had fallen ill and was complaining of a severe headache. 'An excellent arrangement,' Pitt murmured wryly, 'I have the wine, and he has the headache.' Occasionally he was seen to take a solitary walk in St. James's Park in the morning; or he would ride to Wimbledon and Cox Heath to review the troops and inspect the new 'military carriages'.

His dedication to the service of his country was unremitting and selfless. Again and again the King pressed him to accept the Garter, but he repeatedly refused. He wanted nothing – neither honours, titles, nor financial rewards. On his way to the Lord Mayor's banquet that year, 1805, he was again rousingly cheered as his coach came in sight. The crowd rushed forward, unyoked the horses and dragged the coach all the way to the Guildhall. There he was toasted with the wildest acclamation as the saviour of Europe. Pitt replied very briefly. 'I return you many thanks,' he said, 'for the honour you have done me. But Europe is not to be saved by any single man. England has saved herself by her exertions, and will, I trust, save Europe by her example.' It was the last speech he ever made. It was also his last appearance in public.

A month later, while at Bath where he had gone to take the waters, news was brought of Napoleon's scattering of the armies of Russia and Austria at Austerlitz. The Coalition was now completely shattered, and once again Britain was left to fight on alone. 'Heavy news,' Pitt said and called for more brandy. Then he asked for a map and said he wanted to be left alone.

He decided to leave Bath and return to London at once. Because of his extreme weakness the journey of a hundred miles took as long as three days. In every town, in every village, the crowds flocked to catch a glimpse of him. On reaching Putney, he felt he could go no farther and said he would like to rest there for a few days and stayed in a rented house before undertaking the final stage of the journey to Downing Street. Each morning he declared he was better. The doctors assured his niece Hester that there was no cause for alarm. But his emaciated frame shocked and disturbed her. Two days later, on 14th January 1806, while Pitt, propped up with pillows, sat talking to his friend Lord Wellesley, a former Governor-General of India and brother of Wellington, he fainted. Wellesley hurried back to London to warn Pitt's cousin Lord Grenville that death was now very near. He found Grenville drafting a resolution of censure and planning a fresh attack upon the dying Prime Minister. After listening to Wellesley Grenville broke down.

Before leaving for Bath, Pitt had arranged to give a dinner at No. 10 Downing Street on 19th January in honour of the Queen's birthday. Aware now that he could not attend it, he insisted nevertheless that it should be held and sent his niece to make his apologies and see to the arrangements. It was a very mournful meal.

Pitt knew he was dying. He kept asking if there was news from Harrowby, whom he had sent to talk to the Prussians in Berlin. 'How is the wind?' he inquired. 'East? That will do. That will bring him quick.' In the early hours of the morning of 23rd January 1806 Pitt gasped and, crying out in a clear voice: 'O my country! How I leave my country!' he died.

Lady Hester records that 'the carriages had been waiting at the door, ready for a long time' to take him to Downing Street. Her brother James hurried on to No. 10, where he 'sealed up everything'.

The nation grieved. A State funeral was arranged and Pitt was laid in Westminster Abbey beside his father. Later the House of Commons voted the sum of £40,000 to pay his debts. 'Never in my life,' said Fox, his life-long opponent, 'did I give a vote with more satisfaction.'

CHAPTER 16
His Two Unworthy Successors

THE moment Pitt died the Government collapsed. The King sought in vain for a new head for this headless body. He appealed to Hawkesbury (later the Earl of Liverpool), who felt he was not prepared at this stage to accept the supreme responsibility; Castlereagh said he was not equal to it; so in the end the King decided on forming a coalition – a 'Ministry of all the Talents', it was called. Even Fox, whom His Majesty had consistently refused to have in the Government, was invited to join. Addington returned too and, with Fox in, Grenville no longer stood out. These were the men who had hounded Pitt to his death. The principles on which they had opposed him, chief of which was the emancipation of the Catholics, for which they felt Pitt had not fought hard enough, they put to one side on taking office. Their prime concern, they declared, was to proceed with the war, which indeed had been Pitt's concern all along.

A head had still to be found for this assorted collection of Ministers, consisting of aristocratic Whigs under Lord Grenville, of more progressive Whigs under Fox, and of Tories under Addington (now Lord Sidmouth). For this role Grenville was at last selected.

He insisted on moving into No. 10 at once. On 14th February 1806, a week before Pitt was buried, the *Morning Herald* reported: 'Lord and Lady Grenville visited yesterday Mr. Pitt's late house, in Downing Street. His Lordship gave orders that everything might be ready for the reception of his family by next Monday week.' But the Grenvilles had to wait 'owing to the bad state of repair of the House.' Once again the Office of Works had to send in builders and carpenters. The repairs, which took some weeks to complete, cost £2,200. It was not until the spring that the impatient new Prime Minister was able to move in.

Grenville knew the house well of course. His father had been Prime Minister in 1763 – forty-three years before. Grenville, the youngest of his sons, was only three years old then: his stay on that occasion lasted barely eighteen months, it was not to be for as long now. In the intervening years he had repeatedly visited the house, both as a guest, mounting the handsome staircase to the first floor drawing-room, and as a member of the Government, for he had held various offices under Pitt, the first time as Lord-Lieutenant of Ireland in 1782 and later as Foreign Secretary, with Canning as his assistant: the Cabinet room had in fact been for him a familiar setting for close on twenty years.

George the Third was not happy at having him as Prime Minister. His father, Chatham's 'Gentle Shepherd', had wearied the King with his interminable speeches and even after forty years His Majesty was still haunted by that agonizing memory. Like his father, Lord Grenville was both lacking in tact and extremely stubborn. Though blessed with an unremitting zest for work, and not without ability, he had not, as Lady Hester Stanhope observed, the talent to lead. 'Some can only do well', she wrote, 'when under the guidance of another person's star. What was Lord Grenville without Mr. Pitt? With him to guide him he did pretty well; but as soon as Mr. Pitt was dead, he sank into obscurity.' He had nevertheless an exalted opinion of his own capabilities and regarded himself as Pitt's superior, just as his father had thought himself superior to Chatham. The Grenvilles were extremely wealthy and most powerfully connected. Three of his uncles had been Ministers – Lord Temple, Lord Cobham (also a Temple) and Chatham. There were interlocking links with the Pitts, to which he added still another by marrying Anne Pitt, a daughter of Chatham's nephew, Lord Camelford. Of this marriage, which took place in 1792, and the change it had brought in Lord Grenville's life, Lord Mornington (later Lord Wellesley) said in a letter to him: 'I cannot tell you with how much pleasure I saw your *ménage*. I told Pitt that matrimony had made three very important changes in you which could not but affect your friends – (1) a brown lapelled coat instead of the eternal blue single breasted, (2) strings in your shoes, (3) very good perfume in your hair powder.'[179]

It will be seen from this that men's fashions had undergone a considerable change since Pitt's first Administration. In these brief years wigs had gone completely out of use, save in the law courts, where they still survive. Men now powdered their own hair (as Pitt did latterly) and Lord Grenville, who was almost bald, appeared in consequence to belong more to the late nineteenth century than to the eighteenth, though in fact he had reached middle age by the time the eighteenth century ended. Men's clothes had changed too. The elaborate brocaded coats were replaced by jackets that were simpler and far less picturesque. The contrast between Grenville's portrait and his father's would suggest that more than a hundred years separated them.

Despite his overweening self-confidence, Lord Grenville was aware that he lacked certain essential attributes. In a letter to his brother, the Duke of Buckingham,* he confessed: 'I am not competent to the management of men.' This, though accurate, was an understatement. His shortcomings were far greater. The Ministry of all the Talents was found to be a complete misnomer. Fox, one of its principal members, described it in these words: 'We are three in a bed.' Sheridan, also in the administration, said of Grenville: 'I have known many men knock their heads against a wall, but I never before heard of a man collecting bricks and building a wall for the express purpose of knocking out his own brains against it.'

The one memorable achievement of Grenville's brief year as Prime Minister (his father is remembered for having imposed the Stamp Act on the American colonists) was the further limitation of the Slave Trade. This Act was passed in February 1807. In the following month

---

* Not to be confused with the Earl of Buckinghamshire.

he was dismissed from office by the King, for taking up the precise line which had led to Pitt's dismissal six years earlier, namely the emancipation of the Catholics. Once again the old King firmly refused to have it even mentioned in his presence.

The Ministry, however, was already in decline. Fox had died in the preceding autumn: he outlived Pitt by only a few months. On 7th May, 1807, the *Morning Chronicle* announced: 'Lord Grenville will remove today from Downing-Street to his house at Dropmore.' He was glad to go. He wrote to his brother Buckingham of 'the infinite pleasure I derive from my emancipation.'

Not yet forty-eight, he was exactly the same age as Pitt, but his political career was already over. He spent his remaining years at his magnificent country house in Buckinghamshire, tending his garden, writing books, collecting pictures and china. He was devoted to his wife Anne, but there were no children. In the country, as at Downing Street, he entertained sumptuously.

His successor as First Lord of the Treasury was the aged Duke of Portland, now in his seventieth year, who had been Prime Minister before for a few months in 1783, just before Pitt's first term. At that time Portland headed, as a 'convenient cipher', the notorious coalition which included both Fox and North. He had been dismissed ignominiously then, but it did not deter him from writing to the King while Lord Grenville was still Prime Minister, to offer himself again for the chief office. 'If your Majesty should suppose', he wrote, 'that in forming such an Administration, I can offer your Majesty any services, I am devoted to your Majesty's commands; but while I say this I feel conscious that my time of life, my infirmities, and my want of abilities, are not calculated for so high a trust.'[77]

He came this time as the head of a Tory Government. His furniture was taken back into No. 10 on 21st July, ten weeks after Grenville vacated the house. Spencer Perceval was appointed Chancellor of the Exchequer, George Canning became Foreign Secretary, both destined to live in that house as Prime Ministers.

Portland was not blessed with much intellect. As a speaker he was poor and hardly ever spoke in the Lords, even after he became Prime Minister. He had been in and out of office at intervals, owing his inclusion wholly to his powerful connections. At the early age of twenty-eight, for example, he was appointed Lord Chamberlain in the Marquess of Rockingham's short-lived Government; in Pitt's first Ministry he was given the Home Office and held it for six years. When Addington took over he remained in the Cabinet as Lord President of the Council, and on Pitt's return was kept on as Minister without Portfolio. His political influence was immense. He kept pouring out money to get his followers into the House of Commons, without ever calculating the cost. Horace Walpole records that Portland once took £30,000 with him to meet the expenses of an election at Carlisle 'and it is all gone already'.

Earlier in life he was expected to marry Sir Robert Walpole's granddaughter, Lady Waldegrave, one of the most beautiful women of the time. But nothing came of it and he married instead Lady Dorothy Cavendish, the only daughter of the Duke of Devonshire. Not particularly well off then, Portland decided to go and live at Burlington House in Piccadilly, the London home of the Devonshires. Some years later he inherited a considerable sum of money on the death of his mother, the granddaughter and heiress of the famous Duke of Newcastle. His wife died some years before his second term as Prime Minister and he came alone now to No. 10 Downing Street.

No sooner had he succeeded Grenville than doubts of his own capacity began to assail him. 'My fears', he stated, 'are not that the attempt to perform this duty will shorten my life, but that I shall neither bodily nor mentally perform it as I ought.' His chief Ministers, Canning, Liverpool, Perceval and Castlereagh, acted quite independently of him, each managing his own department without any reference whatsoever to the Duke. Of others in the Government, Sir Arthur Wellesley (later the Duke of Wellington), home from his brilliant victories in India, was Chief Secretary for Ireland, and Lord Palmerston Civil Lord of the Admiralty: both of them were later Prime Ministers.

Portland left No. 10 Downing Street in October 1807, less than three months after moving in, and Spencer Perceval, the Chancellor of the Exchequer, moved in. Portland returned to the far greater comfort of Burlington House, from where he continued to exercise such supervisory control as he could enforce over his unruly team. He was listless, worried and often ill. The war with Napoleon dragged endlessly on, its conduct chiefly in the hands of the Secretary for War

Lord Castlereagh. Pitt had said with astonishing foresight as he lay dying that nothing but a war of patriotism, a national war, could now save Europe, 'and that war', he added, 'should begin in Spain'.

An opportunity for the fulfilment of this prophesy was provided unwittingly by Napoleon himself towards the close of 1807, the year following Pitt's death. A French army under the command of General Junot was sent into Lisbon. The Portuguese royal family fled to Brazil, where they established their kingdom in exile. On the way the French troops took possession of Spain. In both countries there arose the fiercest resentment against the invaders.

To stir up a war of patriotism, Sir Arthur Wellesley, given leave from his ministerial office, was sent in the summer of 1808 to Portugal in command of a division of British troops. The young general was at the time only thirty-nine, precisely the same age as Napoleon. Foolishly Castlereagh allowed him to be superseded after his initial victory at Vimeiro and Wellesley resumed his ministerial duties in London. In Portugal Sir John Moore, senior to Arthur Wellesley and regarded by many as the greatest soldier of the day,[84] having missed the chance of following up Wellesley's success, was forced to retreat in mid-winter to the beaches of Corunna, from which the British troops had to be evacuated to England – as more than a century later they were evacuated from Dunkirk. The burial of Sir John Moore, mortally wounded at Corunna, is commemorated in Charles Wolfe's famous poem beginning 'Not a drum was heard, not a funeral note. . . .'

There followed a series of rows in the Cabinet. Canning, the Foreign Secretary, said: 'It makes one sick with shame to think of it', and threatened to resign unless Castlereagh was dismissed. The rows reached their climax in a duel fought by the two Ministers in the late summer of 1809. John Wilson Croker, Secretary of the Admiralty and closely associated with many of the senior members of the Government, recorded in his journal: 'The duel took place on the 21st September (Thursday), on Putney Heath. Lord Yarmouth, Castlereagh's first cousin and second, told me afterwards that Charles Ellis, who was Canning's second, was so nervous for his friend's safety that he could not load his pistols, and that Lord Yarmouth either loaded Mr. Canning's pistols for Mr. Ellis, or lent him one of his own, I forget which but I think the latter.' Both missed the first time. When they fired again, a button was shot off Castlereagh's coat, Canning was wounded in the thigh, severely but not dangerously. Both then returned to London and both resigned from the Government. The Foreign Office was taken over by Lord Wellesley (Arthur Wellesley's brother), while Lord Liverpool went to the War Office. Some months later Arthur Wellesley was restored to his command in Portugal.

Portland, ill and often in excruciating pain, had a paralytic stroke in August 1809. He resigned in October and died a few weeks later. The Chancellor of the Exchequer, Spencer Perceval, who had already been living at No. 10 since Portland vacated it two years before, succeeded him as Prime Minister.

CHAPTER 17
Spencer Perceval

THE Hon. Spencer Perceval was the younger son of the Earl of Egmont. Through his mother he was closely connected with the Earl of Wilmington, who had succeeded Walpole as the second Prime Minister of Britain. His family was extremely wealthy, but he himself, as a younger son, was left with only £200 a year and had to rely on making a living at the Bar.

In appearance he was not particularly prepossessing: singularly small and slender, with pale, pinched features redeemed only by his lively eyes. He was lacking too in some of the social graces. Sir Samuel Romilly describes him as a man 'with very little reading, of a conversation barren of instruction and with strong invincible prejudices on many subjects, yet by his excellent temper, his engaging manners and his sprightly conversation he was the delight of all who knew him'.[85]

He fell in love with Sir James Wilson's remarkably beautiful daughter, whose sister had married Perceval's brother Lord Arden, but, lacking his brother's great wealth, Perceval was not considered eligible by her family and there was considerable opposition to their union. Nevertheless perseverance and devotion secured her as his bride when he was twenty-seven: she arrived for the wedding, it is recorded, dressed 'only in her riding habit'.[85] The young couple lived for a time in modest lodgings over a carpet shop in Bedford Row; later they were able to move to a more comfortable house in Lincoln's Inn Fields, bought with some money inherited by his wife, but with the arrival of a fresh child each year their resources became increasingly strained. The pressure of work thus went on unrelieved. Often the position was desperate and, though weary through scurrying from one brief to another, he had to sit at his desk far into the night, writing articles for the *British Critic* or pamphlets because another child was on the way.

A turn in his fortunes came in 1790 when he published a political pamphlet on the constitutional issues involved in the impeachment of Warren Hastings, which was then in progress. Pitt was impressed by it, a meeting was arranged – they had supper together – and Perceval was drawn eventually into a political career. But in the meantime he was engaged by Pitt as counsel for the Crown in some notable trials, including the prosecution of Tom Paine.

When Perceval was elected to Parliament in 1796, Pitt offered him the post of Chief Secretary for Ireland, but he declined it, stating that he could not afford to accept it because of his growing family: at the time there were five children. 'Even if you were prepared', he added, 'to offer me such terms as I should think sufficient to answer the claims of my family upon me, I would not accept them, because I should feel they would be so much too great for any service I could render to the Public.'

So greatly was Pitt impressed by this and by Perceval's outstanding ability that two years later, when Pitt was about to fight his duel with Tierney, on being asked whom he regarded as a likely successor if the duel proved fatal, Pitt after some reflection replied: 'Perceval,' because, he added, he was the most competent person and 'the most equal to cope with Mr. Fox'.[73]

Although he consistently supported Pitt's Government, Perceval was in fact a staunch Tory: he would have had far less in common with Chatham than he had with Pitt, who by the suspension of his programme of reforms after the outbreak of war and by his adoption of strong repressive measures for the security of the State had drawn the Tories to his support, and had come to be regarded by most Whigs as the head of a Tory Administration.

Perceval was not invited again to join the Government until Addington succeeded Pitt in 1801, when he was appointed Solicitor-General and a year later Attorney-General. On Pitt's return to Downing Street in 1804 Perceval was asked to stay on in the Government, but he imposed conditions: he insisted that Fox should not be included, that Addington's administration should not be censured, and that the question of Catholic emancipation, to which he was strongly opposed, should not be raised. These were exacting conditions, but Pitt accepted them, partly because he wanted Perceval, but chiefly because the conditions had already been imposed by the King.

After Pitt's death Perceval left because of his violent opposition to Lord Grenville's Whig outlook, and became the Leader of the Opposition in the Commons. Nothing the Whigs did was ever right in his view. He even went so far as to make a stand against the Prince of Wales because of his friendship with Fox and incurred the Prince's further enmity by siding against him in the two *causes célèbres* – over the guardianship of Miss Minnie Seymour, the adopted daughter of Mrs. Fitzherbert whom the Prince had married, and in the case for adultery brought by the Prince in 1806 against the Princess of Wales, whom he had bigamously married for the purpose of providing an heir. Perceval championed the Princess's cause and helped to establish her innocence. He was applauded for his daring, but many regarded it as sheer folly, for in the event of a Regency his political prospects would undoubtedly suffer irreparably. In 1807, with the Regency still three years away, he served in the Duke of Portland's Government as Chancellor of the Exchequer and continued to hold that office when at the age of forty-seven he became First Lord of the Treasury.

By the time Mr. and Mrs. Perceval moved into No. 10 Downing Street in 1807 they already had six children, and six more were born to them while they lived in the house. It must have been extremely uncomfortable for a household of that size in that rambling old place, with secretaries and offices on the ground floor, official reception rooms and some of the main bedrooms on the floor above, nurseries on the floor above that, and accommodation to be found in the basement and attic for cooks, tweenies, parlourmaids, chambermaids, governesses and a housekeeper. At the back, alongside and above the stables, the grooms and coachmen slept, most of them doubtless rolled up in blankets on the floor. The noise until the children were put to bed must have been incessantly distracting. Those not in close contact with it admired the atmosphere of domesticity at No. 10, but others declared that it would have been better for the country if Perceval had deceived his wife, whipped his children, and spent more time in getting on with the war.

Arthur Wellesley, back in the Peninsula since April 1809, drove the French out of Oporto in May and won the battle of Talavera in July; for these victories he was rewarded with a peerage and became Viscount Wellington. But not even these remarkable successes caused Perceval to be liked either in the House or in the country. Again and again he was defeated in divisions, the people grumbled ceaselessly at the high taxation (in addition to the cost of the British forces in Spain, the Spanish army had to be subsidized and they insisted on being paid in gold); it was indeed touch and go whether the Government would endure. But Perceval plodded on tirelessly, working late into the night, often exhausted by the strain and anxiety. What he lacked was the ability to grapple with the many problems that confronted him, and his slight nervous stutter did not help his efforts to explain them to the House. The great promise of his early years, the semblance of strength when Portland was too weak a Prime Minister and Perceval took charge of the helm, gradually dissipated and, as the mists cleared, his own inadequacy was starkly revealed. It was remembered that when he was invited to be Chancellor of the Exchequer, he hesitated because the salary was too small and he had also to be given the Duchy of Lancaster to supplement it. It was also remembered that it was part of the bargain that he should move into No. 10 as Chancellor so that a home should be provided rent free. Thus set up, he bought himself a house at Ealing (now the public library) and used to ride there from Downing Street for a breath of fresh air, as Ealing was in the country then, and doubtless his family followed or went on ahead.

Then quite unexpectedly, while he was still Chancellor of the Exchequer, but responsible for the conduct of Portland's Administration, Perceval was confronted early in 1809 with a critical development in the affairs of the Duke of York. The Duke, a tall, fair-haired man in his forties and the favourite son of the King, had been trained in Germany as a soldier and had served, though not effectively, in some of the battles on the Continent against the Revolutionary forces of France. More recently, appointed Commander-in-Chief of the British Army, he had formed an illicit alliance with Mrs. Mary Anne Clarke, a frail beauty with dazzling dark eyes, and had moved her into his London house. Always promiscuous with her favours, she directed her attention to acquiring as much money as possible, since the Duke was by no means generous. From young officers in the Army eager for promotion, she extracted large sums on the promise that she would influence the Commander-in-Chief in their advancement. This emerged when Colonel Wardle, a member of the Opposition, asked in the House for a committee to investigate the conduct of the Duke of York in his capacity of Commander-in-Chief. The Government decided to defend the Duke and Perceval as Leader of the House took on the task. The inquiry lasted seven weeks and was given the greatest possible publicity. It was proved that Mrs. Clarke had in fact taken money with a view to influencing promotions, but it was not established that the Duke received any part of it or that he was influenced by her to make the promotions, though some that had been paid for were in fact made. When the vote was taken 196 Members of Parliament thought the Duke guilty, but, though exonerated of complicity by a majority of eighty-two, he nevertheless resigned at once. The Prince of Wales could have influenced the votes, for the Opposition consisted largely of his followers, but he stood aside, saying: 'I have been no party to my brother's irregularities. I have never been connected with the woman with whom my brother has been connected. Indeed I dislike such society.'

All this was doubtless a greater ordeal for Perceval than for the Duke, who took it with astonishing calm. In addition Perceval had the heavy strain of producing Budgets for what was the crucial phase of the Napoleonic war when almost all Europe was closed to British trade.

'We want gold,' he stated in a memorandum to Croker shortly after becoming Prime Minister. 'Our warehouses are clogged with merchandise which the Continent would be most glad to purchase, but their tyrant will not let them.'

Then at the close of the year 1810 the question of setting up a Regency cropped up again. Following the death of his beloved daughter Princess Amelia, the King lost his reason, this time permanently. It was quite clear to Perceval that he would have to go. For the Whigs it was a Heaven-sent opportunity. They had been out of office for twenty-seven years, save for the brief interlude under Lord Grenville on the death of Pitt. The Prince too rejoiced; for the time had come at last for him to reward the many faithful friends who had stood by him. But Perceval was resolved not to let him have things entirely his own way. Restrictions, identical with those earlier imposed by Pitt, were inserted in the Regency Bill, denying the Prince the right to create peers, to confer sinecures or grant pensions, and excluding from his control the whole of the King's personal property. None of this was palatable. Not only the Prince of Wales, but his brothers too protested most vehemently against it.

Perceval defied the Princes and refused to give way. While the Bill was going through the House, the Regent-to-be angrily denounced the Government to his friends. 'By God,' he said, 'they shall not remain an hour.' But a week later, when the Act was passed, the Regent decided to accept it and retained the Government, despite the pressing advice of Sheridan and other Whigs who had called to urge Perceval's dismissal. Sheridan informed Creevey later that evening at Brooks's that the Regent had expressed his regret at 'being compelled to continue a Government not possessing his confidence', but added that, should the King's condition not improve 'after a certain time', the Government would have to go.[75]

Creevey was even more angry when some weeks later, while walking past No. 10 Downing Street, he peered through the area railings and saw through the basement windows 'four man cooks and twice as many maids preparing dinner for the Prince of Wales and Regent.' Writing to his wife, Creevey poured out his disgust. 'He whose wife Perceval set up against him in open battle – who at the age of 50, could not be trusted by the sd. Perceval with the unrestrained government of these realms during his father's incapacity – he, who, on his last birthday at Brighton, declared to his numerous guests that it was his glory to have bred up his daughter [Princess Charlotte] in the principles of Mr. Fox – he who, in this very year, declared by letter to the said

Mr. Perceval, and afterwards had the letter published as an apology for his conduct, that he took him as his father's Minister, but that his own heart was in another quarter – by God! This is too much.'

Though the King lingered in madness until his death nearly ten years later, the Regent throughout that time made no change in the Government, and Perceval continued in office until his own life was ended. The dinner to which Creevey refers doubtless passed pleasantly. The Regent came to recognize Perceval's many fine qualities and, because of his courageous stand against the Prince, Perceval rose greatly in stature with the public. He was no longer spoken of sneeringly as 'Little P.' Some even went so far as to say that he was treading in the footsteps of the immortal Pitt. His manner as a speaker and as a debater had improved and he often took a strong, independent line, at times liberal in spirit, as when he refused to prosecute members of the early trade unions at the insistence of the employers and also when he supported Wilberforce's efforts to remedy the abuses of the slave trade.

Napoleon had prophesied that 'if the Prince of Wales is put at the head of affairs, Wellington's army will be recalled' from the Peninsula. But the prophecy proved to be false. Wellington continued to harass the French troops. There was, however, a feeling among some members of the Cabinet that Wellington's army was not being adequately supported by the Government. Wellington himself did not share this view but his brother, Lord Wellesley, who was Foreign Secretary, resigned on this and other counts, and, though the rest of the Cabinet still held together, there was undoubtedly great dissension among them.

Soon there came a turn in the war which greatly worsened Britain's position. As a retaliation to Napoleon's closing of the Continent to British trade, Perceval stopped all supplies reaching France from across the seas. Neutral ships were most rigorously searched and before long a quarrel developed with America. There had been tension between the two countries because French privateers had been allowed to use American harbours for refitting and, despite repeated British protests, the Americans still persisted in rendering them this service. When the British took to searching American ships, not only for supplies to France but for press-ganged sailors who had deserted from the Navy and were only too readily protected with American citizenship, things came to a head. America complained that her trade was suffering and promptly stopped the sale to Britain of raw cotton from the Southern States. By June 1812 Britain and America were once again at war.

In the midst of the crisis that led to this war, the Prime Minister, while on his way from Downing Street to the House of Commons on the afternoon of 11th May 1812, was stopped in the street by a Member of Parliament and asked to hurry to an urgent debate. Perceval, who had always been interested in prophecies and had written a pamphlet and some articles on the subject, appears to have had a premonition that his death was near, for he had made his will and gave it to his wife, mumbling something about his 'impending fate'. Some days before this, a Cornishman named John Williams had dreamed – three times, he said – that he was in the lobby of the House of Commons and saw someone 'dressed in a snuff-coloured coat and yellow metal buttons, take a pistol from under his coat' and fire it at 'a small man, dressed in a blue coat and white waistcoat'.[73] He saw in his dream that 'the ball entered under the left breast of the person at whom it was directed'.

On that afternoon of 11th May, Perceval, small in stature, was dressed, like the man seen in the dream, in a white waistcoat and a blue coat. He entered the lobby of the House at a quarter past five. A man, who, according to *The Times* 'had a short time previously placed himself in the recess of the doorway within the Lobby, drew out a small pistol and shot Mr. Perceval in the lower part of the left breast.' Perceval staggered a pace or two and fell into the arms of Members who had rushed forward. He said just the one word 'Murder', and some minutes later he died.

The man who shot him, John Bellingham, was dressed as in the dream. When seized, he said 'I am an unhappy man', and explained that he had at one time been doing business as a merchant in Russia, had gone bankrupt, but was arrested for fraud and sent to prison in Archangel for five years. Since his release and return to England he had been seeking redress and had approached many Members of Parliament and had even written to the Prime Minister. Not receiving a satisfactory reply he had decided to shoot the Prime Minister.

The body of Perceval was taken back to No. 10 Downing Street, where it was kept for five days until the funeral on 16th May. His grieving widow and children had the sympathy of a shocked nation, in whose eyes Perceval through his unflagging devotion to duty had begun to assume the stature of greatness.

CHAPTER 18
The Unremembered Chancellor

THE new Prime Minister was the Earl of Liverpool, who in Perceval's Government was Secretary of State for War and the Colonies, which at that time were combined. He belonged to a Tory family. His father, Charles Jenkinson, had been secretary to Lord Bute and had later served as Secretary at War under Lord North; he was raised by Pitt to be President of the Board of Trade and held the post for many years during Pitt's long reign. He was in consequence a constant visitor at No. 10.

His son Robert, now Prime Minister, was elected to Parliament, no doubt through his influence, at the early age of nineteen. He already knew Pitt and won that great man's commendation with his maiden speech. Chance provided him with an unforgettable experience: he happened to be in Paris on 14th July 1789 and actually saw the storming of the Bastille.

Office was given to him early, but it was not until Addington succeeded Pitt that he entered the Cabinet as Foreign Secretary. He was then thirty years old, and played an important part in the conclusion of a treaty of peace with France – the short-lived peace of 1802. His father had in the meantime been made the first Earl of Liverpool.

On Pitt's death in 1806 he succeeded him as Lord Warden of the Cinque Ports and the King also offered him the Premiership, but Liverpool (Lord Hawkesbury at the time) refused. Two years later he succeeded his father as the second Earl. It was by the choice of his Cabinet colleagues and the Regent that he was now appointed First Lord of the Treasury at the age of forty-two.

Like so many of his predecessors, he preferred not to live at No. 10. He had already moved into his father's fine town house in Whitehall – Fife House – and No. 10 was assigned to his Chancellor of the Exchequer, Mr. Nicholas Vansittart. In order not to hasten unduly the departure of Perceval's widow and her large family, Vansittart waited until their home in Ealing was got ready to receive them. Thus it was not until the following year, 1813, that he finally took possession of No. 10.

Vansittart was the son of a wealthy merchant in the East India service, Henry Vansittart, who adjusted the spelling of the family name, which had been van Sittart, after the town of Sittard in Limburg. His father and grandfather had made their fortunes as directors of the Russia Company; and Henry Vansittart, moving to India, succeeded Clive as Governor of Bengal in February 1760.* Nicholas was not born until six years later and so was forty-six when he became Chancellor of the Exchequer. He had married Isabelle, the sister of Eleanor Eden, with whom Pitt had been in love, but their life together was all too brief for she died a very few years afterwards. There were no children and he never married again. No. 10 must have seemed strangely quiet after the departure of the Perceval family.

Nicholas Vansittart knew the house well, for he had been joint Secretary of the Treasury for three years in Addington's Administration, the other secretary being Addington's brother John Hiley Addington, whose hostility to Pitt was expressed so consistently in *The Times*. Pitt appointed Vansittart Secretary for Ireland in 1805, but Perceval put him back in the Treasury and later offered him the Chancellorship of the Exchequer, which he refused at the time. Now

* Lord Liverpool's maternal grandfather, Mr. William Watts, had also been Governor of Bengal.

he was to occupy that office and live at No. 10 for more than ten years.

America declared war on England on 18th June 1812, ten days after Liverpool formed his Administration. Four days later Napoleon began his ill-fated march on Moscow. The Cabinet doubtless continued to meet at No. 10 while Mrs. Perceval was still in residence. Few changes were made in the Government. Lord Castlereagh had returned to the Foreign Office some months earlier and was now also Leader of the House of Commons. Eldon, that ageing reactionary, remained Lord Chancellor. Sidmouth (formerly Addington) moved over to the Home Office, Palmerston stayed on as Secretary at War, a position he had already occupied for three years and was to retain for a further sixteen. Canning was invited to come in but the old hostility that had led to his duel with Castlereagh still separated them.

As late as July 1812, three weeks after the chief ministries had been filled, attempts were still being made to bring in Canning. Replying to Charles Arbuthnot, a junior Minister, on the 18th July, Canning said: 'The price to be paid on coming in would cost me a bitter pang – not from any personal feeling towards C. upon my honour, but from a sense of humiliation – hard to endure, & I *think* unnecessary to be proposed to me. I have not demanded the lead [the Leadership of the House of Commons] for myself. It is not my fault that such a thing as lead has been known or named in these discussions. I should be contented if it could be put in abeyance as between C. and me – as it would be if continuing nominally with the Chancp. of the Ex. in a third hand – even in Van's. Why not? He can live in the house – write the letters – give the dinner & read the speech – and C. and I could assist in the House, doing the business of our respective Departments.'

Canning wanted equality, Castlereagh insisted on having preeminence, and as a result Canning, by far the more brilliant of the two, had to wait ten years until Castlereagh's suicide before returning as Foreign Secretary.

Vansittart, in the office and the house that Sir Francis Dashwood had once occupied, could not have been much comforted by the thought that his father and two of his uncles had once been friends of Dashwood and members of the disreputable fraternity of Franciscans at the Hell Fire Club at Medmenham. It was indeed one of these uncles, Robert Vansittart, who had brought in the baboon to receive the Sacrament

Margot Asquith, later the Countess of Oxford and Asquith. The photograph shows her as an oriental snake-charmer at a fancy dress ball at Devonshire House in July 1897.

David Lloyd George (right) with Clemenceau, the French Premier, and President Wilson, both of whom visited the British Prime Minister at No. 10 Downing Street at the end of the First World War.

Bonar Law (second from left) with the French Premier Raymond Poincaré (on his right), Signor Mussolini, and M. Theunis, the Belgian Premier, in the State Drawing Room at No. 10 in December 1922.

Ramsay MacDonald with his daughter Ishbel (standing), who was his hostess at No. 10 at the age of twenty, his son Malcolm and his younger daughter Joan.

Sir Winston Churchill, three times Prime Minister.

during their blasphemous rites. In time Robert reformed and became Professor of Civil Law at Oxford and Recorder at Windsor. Nicholas' father settled down too as Governor of Bengal, but he did not long survive the birth of Nicholas, the youngest of his five sons. When the boy was only four years old, the father set out on an important mission to India, but was lost with the ship at sea.

The new Chancellor of the Exchequer was quite unlike either his father or his uncles. After a very brief spell of gaiety in the fashionable world, he turned away from it, became home-loving, diligent and pious, and was described by many as 'mouldy'. He had been called to the Bar, but on getting into Parliament devoted a number of years to writing pamphlets, most of them on finance. They gave the impression that he had quite a flair for economics. But many criticized his schemes as being unsound, and some indeed were found later to be unworkable.

His first Budget, presented within a few days of taking office, must largely have been prepared by his predecessor Perceval. In view of the pressing need for more money, the existing taxes were raised, a heavier levy was imposed on male servants, carriages, horses and dogs. But even these were soon found not to be enough. With Wellington's campaign proceeding in the Peninsula, bringing most heartening victories, with the war against America to be sustained and a vast Navy to be kept supplied, still further burdens had to be heaped year after year upon a people who had already endured close on twenty years of war. And even now few felt that the end was in sight. Not until news reached England of Napoleon's retreat from Moscow in the autumn of 1812, did hopes begin to rise. But they soon faded. With a fresh force of young conscripts Napoleon inflicted a telling defeat on the Prussians and the Russians in Saxony. Wellington had to withdraw his troops from Burgos and return to Portugal. But in May 1813 the tide finally turned. Napoleon's brother Joseph, appointed King of Spain, was routed by Wellington at Vittoria and scurried back to France. In October British troops, wading across the Bidassoa estuary, invaded France. Napoleon himself was defeated a few days later at Leipzig by the combined forces of Russia, Prussia, Austria and Sweden, and five months later the Allied forces marched into Paris. Napoleon abdicated and was sent to Elba.

The sense of relief in the Cabinet room was not one of undiluted jubilation, for the war against America still continued. The British troops from the Peninsula were sent across the Atlantic to bring the American war to a speedy conclusion, and once again large numbers of Englishmen were engaged in hostilities against those who but a generation before had been their countrymen. The consistent British successes on land were counterbalanced by some notable American naval victories, especially on Lakes Erie and Champlain. In August 1814 a British expedition descended on Washington and set fire to the White House. Not long after that, in December 1814, the war ended, with a give and take on both sides in the terms of settlement.

It provided but a brief respite, for Napoleon's escape from Elba early in 1815 brought a renewal of the war. Still heavier taxes had to be introduced, and it was not until after the final victory at Waterloo that Vansittart was able, in his Budget in February 1816, to adjust the financial policy to a peace basis. A large decrease in taxation was expected. It was felt that now at last the property tax would be abolished. But Vansittart merely reduced it. Its retention was met with a howl of angry protests in the House of Commons. Members insisted that it was purely a war measure; to continue it in peacetime was a breach of faith. When a vote was taken its abolition was carried. Vansittart was forced also to remit the extra tax on malt, and had to make up the deficiency from other sources. He increased the soap tax very considerably and got the rest by borrowing. His financial policy was subjected to consistent attack throughout his ten years at the Exchequer. Fiercest of his critics was George Tierney, whose quarrel with Pitt had led to a duel. In each Budget Vansittart introduced 'a new plan'. Some of these plans were quite fantastic. One, for instance, was for handing over the payment of naval and military pensions to contractors, who would be given a fixed sum annually for forty-five years, but he could find no one to take on such a contract. It was patent that he lacked the talent to deal with the finances of the country at this most critical juncture. His name could hardly be mentioned in any circle without expressions of loathing. Even on his own side of the House, little regard was shown him, yet he was kept on in office for six years after Waterloo.

Meanwhile, following Napoleon's abdication and before his escape from Elba, the great powers had met at the Congress of Vienna to dispose of the many countries in Europe Napoleon had annexed. Metternich acted as host at the magnificent but impoverished Austrian court, and Talleyrand, after serving Napoleon, now represented the returned Bourbon King of France, Louis the Eighteenth, who had been living in exile in England in a mansion near Aylesbury. Castlereagh, mistrustful of Russia, concerned himself solely with ensuring the Balance of Power in Europe, a policy that Britain strove at all times to maintain. In consequence the disposal of the liberated territories was effected with no regard whatsoever to the wishes of the inhabitants or to the national yearnings for independence which had contributed so vitally to Napoleon's downfall. After a call at No. 10 Downing Street by Henry Brougham, the young Whig who later became famous as Lord Chancellor, Vansittart wrote a memorandum which Lord Liver-pool sent on to Castlereagh in Vienna: it was to plead for the re-unification and independence of Poland, which had been carved up by her neighbours in a series of ruthless partitions during the preceding century. But it was unsuccessful. The Congress hurriedly dispersed when the startling news reached Vienna of Napoleon's escape from Elba and of the assembling of a large new army.

One of Vansittart's closer friends was the Duke of Cumberland, a younger son of George the Third and quite the most unpopular member of the Royal family. He was with the Hanoverian troops at the battle of Leipzig in 1813 and thereafter lived abroad for sixteen years. On his visits to London it was his practice to call on No. 10 Downing Street to see Vansittart. Among others who came to the house were those who had served in India and had links with Vansittart's father. Another frequent visitor was Nathan Rothschild, a Jewish banker, who had come over from Frankfurt in 1797, when only twenty, to establish a branch in England for the family firm of bankers, already represented in the key capitals of Europe by his father and his four brothers. Despite the troubled and confused state of communications during the long war, this family was able to keep money in circulation even across hostile frontiers and were able, for example, to transport gold to Wellington throughout his campaign in Spain. For some of the talks his brother James Rothschild managed, despite the war, to come to London from Paris and saw both Vansittart and the Prime Minister, Lord Liverpool, at No. 10. 'His Lordship's reason for wishing to see

Mr. J. Rothschild', wrote Mr. John Herries, the Commissary-in-Chief, who had been Spencer Perceval's secretary at No. 10 and now conducted the correspondence on behalf of the Chancellor of the Exchequer, 'is to receive from him the general information which he is enabled to give respecting the state of Paris.'* The meeting took place at eleven o'clock on the morning of 29th January 1814.

The Rothschilds had a network of agents all over Europe and used carrier pigeons to convey their information, finding this a much speedier method than dispatch by couriers on horseback. It was partly by this means that news of the victory at Waterloo was brought to England – a day ahead of the official dispatches. Wellington had just taken Castlereagh's place at the Congress of Vienna when the news of Napoleon's escape reached that exalted gathering. The four great powers, England, Russia, Prussia and Austria, immediately undertook to send an army of 150,000 men each and Wellington, on Britain's behalf, guaranteed to give the Allies in addition a subsidy of five million pounds. He then left Vienna to command the British forces against Napoleon.

An agent of the house of Rothschild at Ostend, the moment he learned of the victory at Waterloo, crossed the Channel and the news was brought by Nathan Rothschild himself from his office in St. Swithin's Lane to Vansittart at No. 10.

For years after the war had ended, the austerity continued. The country was saddled with a vast national debt and heavy taxation was unavoidable. Trade, which had been expected to revive with the removal of barriers, in fact declined. Unemployment was widespread. Many thousands were reduced to starvation and had to scavenge in the gutters for food. Even the heroes home from Waterloo and the Peninsula suffered the most agonizing privation. In the large towns, born of the Industrial Revolution, the conditions were indescribable. In Birmingham more than half the population lived in cellars. Out of such desperation came ugly scenes of rioting. The Prince Regent was stoned as he drove through the streets of London. Vansittart, attending divine service at the Millbank Penitentiary, was pelted with stale bread by the women prisoners. The Government, diagnosing this as an out-

---

* These letters are preserved in the archives of Rothschild's Bank.

crop of the French Revolution, were resolved on preventing its spread and resorted to the use of force. Troops were sent out to quell the angry mobs. Rioters were hanged or transported overseas – to Botany Bay now that America was no longer available to receive them.

In 1820 George the Third died. During his long reign America had been lost and two vast new empires had been won – one of these in the Seven Years War, concluded shortly after he came to the throne, the other in the recent war against France. Twice he had been served by both father and son as Prime Ministers – Chatham and Pitt, George Grenville and Lord Grenville. His heir, who had ruled as Prince Regent for ten years, now ascended the throne as George the Fourth. The new King's heir, Princess Charlotte, an only child, had died three years before. His niece the future Queen Victoria, was then only eight months old. There was an ugly scene at the King's Coronation at Westminster Abbey in July 1821: when Queen Caroline arrived the doors were shut and she was barred from entering. Canning, who had joined the Cabinet after the war, immediately resigned in protest.

Vansittart was removed from the Exchequer in December 1822, was given a peerage and became Lord Bexley; but Lord Liverpool kept him on in the Cabinet as Chancellor of the Duchy of Lancaster. He had, however, to vacate No. 10 for the new Chancellor, Frederick John Robinson.

'Van is to be crowned with a coronet!' exclaimed Canning.* 'Laugh if you will, but it is a most serious relief to me.'

---

* In a letter to Charles Bagot.

179

CHAPTER 19
'Prosperity Robinson'

FREDERICK ROBINSON, later Viscount Goderich and later still the first Earl of Ripon, was a young man, just turned forty. He came of a family with powerful political connections. His grandfather had been a Secretary of State under the famous Duke of Newcastle and, despite the ridicule heaped upon him by Chatham, was rewarded with a peerage and became the first Lord Grantham. Robinson's father, the second Lord Grantham, was Foreign Secretary under Shelburne; his uncle was Lord Malmesbury; his mother was the daughter of the second Earl of Hardwicke. He was thus surrounded by overwhelming influence. Later he married Lady Sarah Hobart, the only child of the fourth Earl of Buckinghamshire: her stepmother was Pitt's Eleanor Eden.

Young Robinson was at Harrow with Palmerston and got into the House of Commons at the General Election of 1806 while in his early twenties. A moderate Tory, he held office under Portland and, having become a close friend of Castlereagh, resigned when the latter left the

Government after his duel with Canning. Such early and rapid advancement would suggest that he was not without ability, but his contemporaries were of the opinion that he had hardly any. George the Fourth, when Robinson was appointed to the Exchequer, felt that the appointment was 'very likely to give great satisfaction to the country gentlemen',[77] but a few years later decided that he was a 'blubbering fool'.

An early blunder was committed by him on 1st March 1815, when the country was suffering the acutest privation. Robinson, then Treasurer of the Navy, brought in a Bill to prevent the import of wheat into the country until the average price in England was eighty shillings a quarter, with a similar ban to exclude other grain. The Bill passed both Houses, but caused much rioting. Robinson's house in Old Burlington Street was attacked, most of his furniture and some very valuable pictures were destroyed. What was left he brought with him now to furnish No. 10. He married towards the end of the war and by the time he came to Downing Street he had only one child, a daughter aged eight.

His face was round and pudgy, his complexion bright. In manner he was nervous and vague. Croker states[74] that he had 'an absent enthusiastic way of telling stories which were often very much *mal à propos*'. An instance of this was his frequent narration of the old jest with which Lord North used to regale his friends about the ugliness of his wife and daughter. One evening Robinson told the story to a woman seated beside him at a party and found that it was not received with much relish. The woman turned out to be North's daughter. Like his grandfather, Robinson was the genial butt of everybody, and was often referred to as the 'Duke of Fuss and Bustle'.

He astonished his contemporaries by earning a considerable reputation as Chancellor of the Exchequer. The years of austerity had been maintained too long by Vansittart and Robinson decided that the time had come for substantial reductions in taxation. In his very first Budget, introduced a month after he moved into No. 10, he made a wide series of cuts, reducing among other things the long standing window tax, which he cut by half. This was greeted in the House by loud and hearty applause such as had not been heard for a generation or more at a

Budget statement.* Further reductions followed: in 1824 he reduced the duties on rum, on raw silk and on foreign wool. In 1825 he reduced the duties on iron, hemp, coffee, sugar, wine, spirits and cider. A succession of fine harvests and a steady improvement in the country's trade brought great prosperity and earned him the nickname of 'Prosperity Robinson'.

Despite the many tributes paid him, in his own mind he was uneasy, for it had begun to leak out that his knowledge of finance was only superficial and that his Budgets were worked out for him by William Huskisson, the President of the Board of Trade, a man of outstanding ability, very closely associated with Canning. Robinson had also the help of John Herries, who had rendered Vansittart such great assistance in his dealings with Nathan Rothschild. Robinson's biographer admits: 'He had the faculty of using the brains of his subordinates.'[86]

With his own fine collection of furniture and pictures so recently destroyed, he strove to provide the nation with worthy centres where a taste similar to his own could be indulged. In May 1823, only a few months after becoming Chancellor of the Exchequer, he obtained a grant towards the new building for the British Museum; and in the following year he allocated the sum of £57,000 for the purchase of the Angerstein collection of pictures with which the National Gallery was started, and as a trustee was concerned too with the acceptance of the design for the building in Trafalgar Square which houses the pictures.

He next turned his attention to the house in which he lived. No. 10 Downing Street, with its rambling passages and warren of rooms, some of them offices, others bedrooms, though constantly repaired, often at great cost, had not been elaborately redecorated since Kent merged the three houses together for Walpole ninety years before. Robinson now called in John Soane, the eminent architect, to examine the building with a view to effecting improvements. Soane, in his seventy-third year, was architect to the Bank of England and was also responsible for much of the rebuilding in Whitehall. He designed for No. 10 a new and very handsome dining-room, panelled in oak with reeded mouldings. It stands on the first floor, but its lofty ceiling is raised right through the next floor, so that it actually occupies two floors. He also provided an

---

* Annual Register for 1823.

ante-room alongside, similarly panelled and decorated: it served
as a smaller dining-room and is now known as the breakfast-room.
He further inserted some new cubicles and, as the record states,
'the Passage of communication therewith'. The cost of all this
was approximately £2,000.* The work was done while the Robinsons still lived in the house. In 1829, after its completion, the Office
of Works, in its report on the house, stated: 'This is a large old
Building which has been altered, and added to, at many different
periods, and tho' in a substantial condition requires very frequent
repairs.'

While the work was in progress fate dealt a cruel blow to the
Robinsons. Their daughter, now in her twelfth year, died after a short
illness. The effect was shattering. His wife went down with a severe
illness and Robinson wrote to the Prime Minister to ask if he could be
sent to the Upper House so that he might be relieved of the heavy
work he had to undertake in the Commons as Chancellor of the Exchequer. But, with the country going through a severe economic
crisis, Lord Liverpool replied that 'such a change would be quite
impracticable.' The general prosperity, due to the expansion of trade,
especially with the South American colonies now struggling for freedom from Spanish rule, collapsed suddenly and there was once again
widespread unemployment, as in the years after Waterloo. There
followed the most reckless speculation, which the banks did nothing to
check; indeed the Bank of England encouraged it by advancing money
freely.[103] A run on the banks followed and there was panic. Many
London banks and eighty country banks failed. Mills and workshops
closed down. Wages fell rapidly. Thousands of the workless lived on
the edge of starvation and begged in the streets for food. There was
rioting and scenes of the wildest disorder. Units of the armed forces,
since there was no organized police, were sent into the big towns to
quell the mobs, and once again there was a spreading fear of revolution. Sir Robert Peel, the Home Secretary, connived at the use of
agents provocateurs and spies by the military authorities.

Lord Liverpool, in rejecting Robinson's plea, added: 'This is the first
session you will have had of real financial difficulty, and I do not think

* Public Record Office.

it would be for your credit that you should appear to shrink from it. . . . Your voluntarily quitting the office of Chancellor of the Exchequer at the present moment would infallibly bring on the crisis which must lead to the dissolution of the Government.'[76]

So Robinson had to remain in office and grapple with the difficulties. In January his wife was pregnant again and on 24th October a son was born to them who later became Viceroy and Governor-General of India and Marquess of Ripon.

Lord Liverpool had himself been very ill when he refused Robinson's request, and six weeks later he was found lying on the floor of his bedroom 'in a violent apoplectic fit, quite senseless', wrote Lord Eldon, the Lord Chancellor. For two years Liverpool had been harassed by intrigues in the Cabinet, and the strain had worn him down. A few weeks later he resigned: he died in the following year. Though undistinguished by his own achievements, he managed to remain Prime Minister for fifteen years, the longest term anyone has held the office other than Walpole and Pitt.

There were in the Government men of marked talent – Canning, who had succeeded his arch-enemy Castlereagh at the Foreign Office when the latter, having but recently become the Marquess of Londonderry, cut his throat with a knife; Robert Peel at the Home Office; Palmerston Secretary at War; Lord Wellesley as Lord-Lieutenant of Ireland; and his brother the Duke of Wellington, who had joined the Cabinet in 1818 as Master-General of the Ordnance. Of these Wellington, surprisingly, was expected to be the new Prime Minister. A stir was caused when it was learned that the King had sent for Canning, who was lying ill at Brighton as a result of a severe chill he had caught at the Duke of York's funeral.

Canning drove up to London for the interview. The question of Catholic emancipation had come again to the fore in recent weeks and Canning was strongly in favour of it; Wellington in the House of Lords and Peel in the Commons were its most violent opponents. In the hope of obtaining a balanced Government, the King suggested that Canning should remain in office, but that a peer 'of anti-Catholic opinions' should be Prime Minister. It was at once clear whom His Majesty had in mind, and Canning refused to agree to it. Whether he stayed at the Foreign Office or went to the Treasury, he said, he must have, and be known to have, the 'substantive power of First Minister'; failing this, it was his firm decision to resign.

After two weeks of royal hesitation, and considerable intrigue behind the scenes, the King sent for him again, and Canning was appointed Prime Minister.

CHAPTER 20
Canning's Short Reign

GEORGE CANNING was born in Londonderry and regarded himself as an Irishman because his ancestors, though of English origin, had lived in that country for a century and a half. His father, disowned by his family, had struggled to make a living by writing and had married a poor but beautiful Irish girl. On his death in 1771, exactly a year after his son's birth, his wife and only child were left destitute. She tried to make a living on the stage and eventually married a dissolute actor. At this point her brother-in-law, Stratford Canning, a prosperous London banker, fearing the evil influence of this union on his nephew, offered to take charge of him. He settled £200 a year on the boy, sent him to Eton, where he rose to be head of the school, and then to Christ Church, Oxford.

At the home of his uncle, a staunch Whig, Canning met Fox and Sheridan and later got to know Burke extremely well; at Oxford he became a close friend of Lord Liverpool, then Robert Jenkinson, and of Pitt's cousin Lord Grenville. He was introduced to that centre of Grand Whiggery, Devonshire House, and attended the impressive supper parties where rank and wealth and beauty mingled.

But his admiration was focused on Pitt, who, having been brought up a Whig, had during the war drifted closer to the Tories. Canning decided on a political career and, like Burke, broke with the Whigs after the outbreak of the French Revolution and joined the Tories. He had just emerged from his teens, but he was sufficiently prominent to be lampooned by Fox's friend Colonel Fitzpatrick in the lines:

> The turning of coats so common is grown
> That no one would wish to attack it,
> But no case until now was so flagrantly known
> Of a schoolboy turning his jacket.

At twenty-two he wrote to ask Pitt for an interview and was received at No. 10 Downing Street on 15th August 1792. Writing of it to a friend at Oxford, he described how he 'was ushered into that study in which so many great statesmen and great scoundrels have at different times planned their country's ruin and the advancement of their own futures'. Pitt was obviously impressed by the brilliance of the young man, for he took immediate steps to find him a seat in Parliament. Canning made his mark quickly as a speaker of wit and vigour, and within three years was appointed by Pitt Under Secretary of State for Foreign Affairs. One of the first things he did now was to settle an allowance of £500 a year for life on his mother and stepsisters.

His chief at the Foreign Office was Lord Grenville. Canning disliked his staunch adherence to Whig principles and his cold, unbending aristocratic air, but nevertheless remained in the Government until Pitt resigned in 1801. A little before this, in July 1800, his marriage to Joan Scott, sister-in-law of the Duke of Portland's heir, brought him a dowry of £100,000, a very considerable sum in those days, which made him both rich and independent. Thus by the time he was thirty his fortunes had changed from the dire poverty of childhood to extreme affluence.

His strong attachment to Pitt and his contempt for Addington caused him to launch a series of most bitter attacks on Addington and his Cabinet. In addition to his quip 'Pitt is to Addington as London is to Paddington', he was more pointedly offensive, when, on the proposal that the Thames estuary should be defended by the erection of block-houses, he perpetrated the rhyme:

> If blocks can the nation deliver,
> Two places are safe from the French;
> The first is the mouth of the river,
> The second the Treasury Bench.

These attacks, though often quoted with chortling approval, redounded in the end to Canning's disadvantage. The more earnest Members of the House disapproved of his levity, and it was believed that it was because of this that Pitt, on returning to No. 10 in May 1804, offered him the subordinate post of Treasurer of the Navy, which Canning nevertheless accepted. It was not until the Duke of Portland moved into No. 10 in 1807, that Canning was given an opportunity worthy of his talent and became Secretary of State for Foreign Affairs. He used it with striking effect. Napoleon had just forced Tsar Alexander the First of Russia to make a separate peace and to co-operate in excluding all British trade from the Continent. Sweden, Britain's only remaining ally, had been induced to renounce the alliance and the Russian and Swedish fleets were about to seize the Danish fleet when Canning by a bold move foiled them. With secrecy and speed, he dispatched British warships to Elsinore in July 1807. The immediate surrender of the Danish fleet was demanded by Britain with the promise of its return at the end of the war. The demand was refused. Copenhagen was thereupon bombarded and the entire Danish fleet was seized, together with a great mass of naval stores, and taken to British ports. Canning thus added the finishing stroke to Nelson's resounding victory at Trafalgar less than two years before.

In October Napoleon arranged that Portugal should be divided between France and Spain. But a few months later he deposed the Spanish King and placed his own brother Joseph Bonaparte on the throne. Canning instantly decided that British forces should be sent to support the enraged Spaniards, who were eager to drive the occupying French forces from their country.

Following his quarrel with Castlereagh, he was for some years out of office, and even after his return in the subordinate post of President of the Board of Control (forerunner of the India Office), his support of Queen Caroline in the divorce proceedings brought by King George the Fourth in 1820, led to a further term in exile. He agreed two years later, with no apparent hope of office, to go out to India as Governor-General. It meant his retirement from political affairs in England for a number of years. On the eve of his departure Castlereagh's suicide completely changed the pattern of his life. Liverpool invited him to return to the Foreign Office. Canning, however, insisted on having Castlereagh's 'whole inheritance' – not only the Foreign Office but the Leadership of the House of Commons as well. This was agreed to, and for the next five years Canning exercised an influence that was far-reaching and momentous. It is on his statemanship in these years that his fame rests.

He completely reversed Castlereagh's foreign policy. Ever since the Congress of Vienna, which Castlereagh attended, and his close support of Metternich, Castlereagh had come to be regarded as a friend of despots and dictators. He was associated with the European alliances formed to 'preserve the peace' and suppress all insurrections prompted by the desire for national freedom. Canning, on the other hand, returned to the earlier progressive policy of Pitt and gave his sympathy, and later even encouragement, to national movements in various parts of the world – in Europe to the liberation of the Greeks from the Turks (in which Lord Byron died) and to the defence of Portugal from Spanish intervention; in South America and Mexico to the revolt of the Spanish colonies and their recognition as independent states. 'I called the New World into existence,' Canning said, 'to redress the balance of the Old.'

By thus extending the influence of Britain and raising its status in international affairs, Canning became the most popular statesman in the country. The King, overlooking his attitude in the divorce case, held him now in very high esteem. There were nevertheless undoubted difficulties when the succession to Liverpool arose. Canning, though a Tory, was far more enlightened and progressive than the majority of his colleagues in Liverpool's Government. Most bitterly opposed to him was the Duke of Wellington, who detested not only his foreign policy but also his championship of Catholic emancipation. It was certain that if the King selected Canning as Prime Minister, quite a number of his colleagues in the Cabinet would resign. This would mean the break up of the Tory Party, which had been in office (save for Lord Grenville's short term of twelve months) ever since 1783. That was undoubtedly why his Majesty proposed to make 'a peer of anti-Catholic opinions' the new Prime Minister. Canning's refusal to accept this was based on the certainty that he would have the backing of the Whigs, since they approved of his progressive outlook. There were a few waverers among the Whig peers. Earl Grey, for example, asserted that 'the son of an actress' was 'de facto incapacitated from being Premier of England'.[81] But they were eventually won round. A coalition between the progressive Tories and the Whigs seemed a possible solution and among those who advocated it was Lord John Russell: *The Times* also hinted at it in an inspired leading article.

When, after two weeks of hesitation, the King finally asked Canning to form a Government, the Duke of Wellington resigned instantly and even gave up his position as Commander-in-Chief of the Army. Another to leave was Robert Peel, a brilliant young Tory, who, though not yet forty, had been seriously regarded by many as the rightful successor to Lord Liverpool. He was a member of the new middle-class thrown up by the Industrial Revolution and had been especially trained for a political career by his father, a prosperous textile baronet. Elected to Parliament on coming of age, he had within a year been given a junior ministerial post by Spencer Perceval, and in 1812 was appointed Chief Secretary for Ireland by Lord Liverpool. He remained in office throughout Liverpool's long reign and succeeded Addington (Lord Sidmouth) as Home Secretary in 1822, an office which he now relinquished. Canning was sorry to see him go. The Lord Chancellor, Lord Eldon, a reactionary Tory, also resigned and was followed by three other peers. Lord Londonderry, Castlereagh's brother, at the same time resigned his position as Gentleman of the Bed-chamber, refusing to serve the King because of his selection of 'that man'.

Canning lost no time in moving into No. 10. In his Government he had two former residents of that house – Nicholas Vansittart, now Lord Bexley, and Frederick Robinson, now Lord Goderich. Viscount Palmerston, who had been Secretary at War in the previous Government, retained that position and was now given a seat in the Cabinet; the Duke of Portland, son of a previous Prime Minister and Canning's brother-in-law, was also found a place in the Cabinet as Lord Privy Seal. Canning himself, like others before him who were not in the

Lords, took on the office of Chancellor of the Exchequer as well as First Lord of the Treasury. His Government was in fact a coalition. It included George Tierney, a Whig and Pitt's sternest critic, and Lord Lansdowne,* also a Whig, who went to the Home Office.

The country went wild with excitement on learning that Canning had become Prime Minister. Such enthusiasm had not been seen since the days of the Pitts. Even the King, generally disliked, enjoyed some of the reflected popularity for having made the choice. The Press too gave it their fullest support. No premiership could have had a more auspicious beginning.

When Canning moved into No. 10 he was crippled by rheumatism, and still had hanging about him the cold he had caught at the Duke of York's funeral. He was in fact ill for most of the four months that remained of his life. He was now fifty-seven. His devoted wife Joan, his constant companion for twenty-seven years, nursed him with solicitude and care and sought to alleviate in so far as she could the greatly increased strain he had now to endure. Of their three sons, the eldest, George, to whom the Princess of Wales had been godmother, had died in 1820, the second, William Pitt Canning, was a captain in the Royal Navy and was to meet his death by drowning off Madeira a few months after the death of his father. Only two of the children, Charles, aged fourteen, who was to be Governor-General of India at the time of the Mutiny and to be rewarded with an earldom, and Harriet, slightly older, who was to marry the first Marquess of Clanricarde and to be the ancestress of the Earls of Harewood, were young enough to live at No. 10 Downing Street with their parents.

Canning's earlier arrogance and pugnacity had softened with the years. He was far more conciliatory in his manner. Nevertheless the hostility against him in Parliament was sustained and unrelenting. Foremost amongst his critics were his former friends and colleagues. He had indeed to meet attacks from the extreme wings of both parties. In the House of Lords he was subjected to a ceaseless onslaught from Earl Grey for the Whigs and the Duke of Wellington for the 'high Tories'. This so enraged Canning that he thought seriously of taking a peerage in order to deal with them since Lord Goderich ('Prosperity Robinson')

---

* Lansdowne's father was Lord Shelburne, the Prime Minister under whom the younger Pitt served as Chancellor of the Exchequer in 1782.

could not. His wife declared later that it was Grey's attacks in particular that shortened her husband's life.

With his working majority in the Commons, Canning was able to put through such measures as he felt were necessary and urgent. He had set aside, however, all thought of Parliamentary reform, once so dear to his master Pitt. He had even to modify his plan for amending the Corn Law of 1815, which excluded the import of all foreign wheat, for as Cobden had declared, the duty was maintained exclusively in the landed interest and the opposition in both Houses to any interference with it was overwhelming.

Among Canning's closer friends were his young secretary Augustus Stapleton, with whom he spent many happy hours at No. 10, and Sir Walter Scott, the novelist, who never had the opportunity of visiting him in Downing Street, but spent a joyous summer with him by Lake Windermere in 1825, when in company with Wordsworth and Southey they rode through the woods by day, paddled in the lake by moonlight, and engaged in 'high discourse', as Scott's biographer Lockhart records, 'mingled with as gay flashings of courtly wit as ever Canning displayed'.

Canning was a man of fine commanding appearance. With wigs no longer worn, his baldness gave him a wide, but distinguished forehead. His nose was almost as hooked as Wellington's. He liked the company of beautiful women, gambled hardly at all and never drank to excess. As an orator many of his contemporaries ranked him with the Pitts. His voice was resonant, his delivery, his choice of words, his imagery and the clarity of his reasoning, while magnificently impressive, were regarded by some as theatrical. It was said of him that he spoke with his head and not his heart.

On 1st June 1827 he presented his only Budget to the House. His handling of the intricacies of finance was considered quite astounding. Three weeks later, speaking on the Corn Amendment Bill, he made what was to be his last speech. In the gallery on that occasion was young Benjamin Disraeli, then twenty-three years old. Later he said of it: 'I can recall the lightning flash of that eye and the tumult of that ethereal brow. Still lingers in my ear the melody of that voice.' The Bill was passed by the House of Commons but was thrown out by the Lords because of the Duke of Wellington's vigorous opposition.

Parliament rose at the beginning of July. With the cold still lingering and suffering also from gout, Canning decided to see his doctors. They found his constitution strong, with 'stamina for several years to come'. He had in fact barely four weeks to live. Huskisson, President of the Board of Trade and one of his closer friends, saw him later that month. Canning, on being told that he looked ill, denied that there was anything wrong with him and talked of going abroad. On the 20th he went to stay with the Duke of Devonshire at his house in Chiswick. As Fox had died there twenty-one years before, Devonshire was careful not to give Canning the same room. 'I had a great foreboding when he came here, and would not allow of his being in the room below where Fox had died,' he said. From Chiswick he went to see the King on the 29th. His Majesty asked anxiously after his health. Canning said he did not know what the matter was, but felt 'ill all over'. He suffered the acutest agony for about a week and died in the early hours of 8th August.

His body was taken back to No. 10. *The Times* described him as being 'frightfully attenuated . . . so greatly changed that those who were most intimately acquainted with his person would not now recognize it'.

A strictly private funeral was insisted on by his widow. Only relatives and his doctors were invited 'to attend in Downing Street' and to go 'from thence in procession to the Abbey'. His body was buried at the feet of the younger Pitt.

He was the last of five Prime Ministers to die in harness within one generation. The others were Pitt, the old Duke of Portland, Spencer Perceval and Lord Liverpool.

Wellington was not prepared even now to say one kind or generous word of him, but was brutal enough to describe Canning's death as a 'great public advantage'.

CHAPTER 21
Wellington Moves in

THE King lost no time in selecting his successor. He sent for Lord Goderich ('Prosperity Robinson'), who was in Canning's Government as Secretary for War and the Colonies and Leader of the House of Lords. This was Goderich's first and only term as Prime Minister.

The choice was not generally approved. A fellow peer described Goderich as not fit to manage even a poultry yard.[88] But it was the King's desire to provide a continuity of Government without any upheaval or interruption, and he felt this would be achieved by moving Goderich up.

He had been given a viscountcy by Canning to deal with the fierce and persistent attacks in the Lords. But Goderich just looked on helplessly while the Government was defeated again and again. He returned now to No. 10 after an absence of only four months and his stay this time was to be for exactly four months – a tedious moving of furniture, carpets, curtains and pictures in and out of the house.

Though he had the status of Prime Minister, he was too limp to exercise the authority. Being in the Lords, he could not take on the office of Chancellor of the Exchequer as well: that was given, on the King's insistence, to J. C. Herries who had greatly helped Goderich when he was Chancellor. The disgust of his Whig colleagues at his yielding to the King on this brought upon him unforeseen difficulties. There were incessant quarrels between Herries and Huskisson, the President of the Board of Trade. It spread and soon involved others in the Cabinet. There were 'perpetual brawls and disagreements'.[74] Goderich was quite unable to keep the peace, and the continuing dissension made it impossible for him to remain in office. He went to see the King early in January 1828 and begged to be allowed to resign. He then burst into tears and the King, offering him his pocket handkerchief to dry his eyes, agreed to let him go. He was the only Prime Minister who never met Parliament while holding that office.

This was the Duke of Wellington's opportunity, and he got it. He had expected to succeed Lord Liverpool, but had been passed over twice. Nevertheless the total loss of time involved was no more than eight months.

The Duke, it was thought, did not really want the office. Indeed, after his quarrel with Canning, which many put down to pique at having been passed over, he had affirmed quite flatly in the House of Lords: 'To be appointed to a station, to the duties of which I was unaccustomed, in which I was not wished, and for which I was not qualified. . . . My Lords I should have been worse than mad if I had thought of such a thing.'[88]

It surprised many that the King should have sent for him, for the King was exceedingly angry when Wellington resigned his position as Commander-in-Chief on Canning's appointment and resumed it on Canning's death. Nor was he the King's first choice now. Others were interviewed, but they were either unwilling or unable to form a stable Government.

Sent for at last, Wellington rode to Windsor and found the King lying ill in bed. His Majesty was 'dressed in a dirty silk jacket and a turban nightcap, one as greasy as the other'.[68] From the bedclothes he announced 'Arthur, the Cabinet is defunct', and proceeded to mimic the words and actions of the retiring Ministers.

Wellington asked for time to think it over. He wanted to consult his friends, he said, and asked if His Majesty had any preferences and prejudices as to who should be included in the Government. His Majesty said he had no objections except to Lord Grey.

Wellington informed his friend General Sir Colin Campbell: 'If people think I like this station they are mistaken. The nation has rewarded, and over-rewarded me. My line is to command the army, but if I think I can do any good by being Minister, I am willing to sacrifice my time and habits and do what I can.'

Lord Grey wrote to Wellington's ardent supporter Creevey: 'To me it seems that the Beau, as you call him, is placing himself in a situation of dreadful responsibility and danger. His taking the office of Minister, after all that passed on that subject last year, to say nothing of other objections, would, in my opinion, be a most fatal mistake, and I still hope there may be time and that he may find friends to advise him to avoid it.'[75]

Not all, however, shared this view. Many, like General Sir Charles Napier, who happened to be a close friend of Wellington's, were delighted; Napier said: 'The best chance for England is having the greatest man of Europe for her ruler.'

Wellington was now in his fifty-ninth year. In forming his Government he retained six of those who had served under Goderich – four of them had also been in Canning's Government, of which Wellington had been such a severe critic. Peel, who had associated himself with that criticism, was appointed Home Secretary and Leader of the House of Commons, but foresaw trouble. 'If we are to make a point of honour of taking in everyone who went out with us' – at the time of Canning's appointment – 'there are not offices enough. . . . The Duke and I thought at first that some of our old friends might be disposed to retire from age and a desire to relieve the Government from embarrassment. I fear this is not the case, and that all expect to come in.'

Among those who were left out was Lord Eldon, Lord Chancellor in Liverpool's Government. He had stood by the Duke during his quarrel with Canning and was intensely angry at being excluded. He lost no time in rallying the more extreme Tories and became one of the bitterest opponents of the Duke.

But this does not appear to have disturbed Wellington. The country as a whole seemed to be in favour of the appointment. The magic of his name, the memory of his great victories over Napoleon and especially the battle of Waterloo, won only a dozen years before, his blunt and decisive manner, his intolerance of any nonsense or interference, made him a formidable figure in the eyes of the people and even of Europe. It was felt that 'he had never failed'. The country needed a strong and stable Government and it was hoped that he would provide this for a generation at least.

His surname should by right have been Colley, but an ancestor changed it to Wesley following an inheritance: the family was related to John and Charles Wesley, the evangelists. A still further change was effected in 1798 when the Duke was still a young man, the Wesley was then extended to Wellesley. For more than two centuries the family had lived in Dublin. Wellington's father, the Earl of Mornington, was a Professor of Music at Trinity College, Dublin; in time four of his five sons were peers, Wellington himself attaining the greatest distinction of them all with a dukedom.

At school, both at Chelsea and later at Eton, Arthur Wellesley was regarded as unsociable, combative and far from scholarly. After his father's death, inability to meet his school bills led to his being withdrawn from Eton. His mother took him to Brussels, where his love of music caused him to learn to play the fiddle, a diversion he contined to enjoy in maturity. She regarded him as the least intelligent of her sons. He was also the ugly one – 'fit food for powder', which was why he was sent to a military academy at Angers, despite the fact that his constitution was not robust enough for such rigorous training. He was not, however, sent to join his regiment after being gazetted a Lieutenant in the 73rd in 1787, but was appointed A.D.C. to the Lord-Lieutenant of Ireland and participated in the far less arduous social round in Dublin. But with his private income only £125 a year, he found it necessary to take lodgings with a Dublin bootmaker, and often had to borrow money from him. It was during this period, while still an A.D.C., that he was elected to the Irish Parliament. He made his first speech in 1793, the year the war with France began. At about this time too Wellington, still Arthur Wesley, fell in love with the Hon. Catherine Pakenham, the daughter of Lord Longford. But her family considered him too poor to be accepted as a possible suitor; it was not until his return from India, after eight years of distinguished military service, that he was regarded as eligible. The marriage was fruitful: there were two sons; but it was not a happy one. His roving eye sought fresh romantic conquests. In 1814, after Napoleon was exiled to Elba and the Duke was appointed British Ambassador in Paris, he met and fell in love with Harriet Arbuthnot, the attractive young wife of one of the Embassy staff. There had been earlier attachments but this one was to endure. The Arbuthnots and the Duke became inseparable. Harriet began to dominate Wellington's life; she vetted every invitation he received and, if she was not also asked, refused to allow him to go. She was known to his friends as the Tyrant, he as the Slave.

In 1806 he entered the English House of Commons as the Member for Rye, joined Lord Liverpool's Cabinet in 1819 as Master-General of the Ordnance, resigning, as has been noted, on Canning's accession.

It was impossible for him as Prime Minister to retain his position as Commander-in-Chief and he resigned once again, this time with reluctance and regret.

The Duke did not move into No. 10 Downing Street at once. He already had in Apsley House, at the corner of Piccadilly and Hyde Park, a magnificent residence bought from his brother, the Marquess Wellesley, with money presented to him by a grateful nation after Waterloo; and it was not until August, seven months after he became Prime Minister, that he decided to move in, and then only because Apsley House was to undergo alterations. *The Times* of 5th August 1828, reported: 'Part of the furniture of the Duke of Wellington's residence in Piccadilly was begun to be removed to the house in Downing-street belonging to His Grace as First Lord of the Treasury, which His Grace, it is expected, will occupy during the time that Apsley-house is undergoing repair'; and again a week later, on the 12th: 'The Duke of Wellington has left Apsley House . . . for his official residence in Downing-street.' As the alterations at Apsley House were on an elaborate scale, with a view to making it an even more majestic residence, Wellington had to stay at No. 10 for eighteen months.

He knew the house well, of course. He had visited Pitt there: his brother Wellesley was a close friend of Pitt's and a constant visitor. Wellington himself described* an encounter in another house in Downing Street which was being used at the time as the Colonial

* To Croker.[74]

Office.* He had called to see Lord Castlereagh, the Secretary for War and the Colonies, and was shown into 'the little waiting-room on the right hand'. He found there another visitor, also waiting to see Castlereagh, and recognized him 'from the likeness to his pictures and the loss of an arm' to be Nelson. It has been generally believed that these two great figures of the Napoleonic war, meeting here for the only time in their lives, did not recognize each other or exchange a word even by way of greeting. Wellington states that Nelson 'entered at once into conversation with me, if I can call it conversation, for it was almost all on his side and all about himself, and in, really, a style so vain and so silly as to surprise and almost disgust me'.

Nelson, who had not long to live, for it was September 1805, a very few weeks before the battle of Trafalgar, was wearing an excess of stars and ribbons and looked, as Sir John Moore wrote in his diary of his own meeting with the Admiral, 'more like the Prince of an Opera than the Conqueror of the Nile'.

After a while Nelson got up suddenly and left the room. He had apparently gone out to establish the identity of the other visitor and returned in a few minutes to the waiting-room, his manner completely changed. All that Wellington 'had thought a charlatan style had vanished, and he talked of the state of this country and of the aspect and probabilities of affairs on the Continent with a good sense, and a knowledge of subjects both at home and abroad, that surprised me equally and more agreeably than the first part of our interview had done; in fact, he talked like an officer and a statesman. . . . I don't know that I ever had a conversation that interested me more. If the Secretary of State had been punctual, and admitted Lord Nelson in the first quarter of an hour, I should have had the same impression of a light and trivial character that other people have had, but luckily I saw enough to be satisfied that he was really a very superior man; but certainly a more sudden and complete metamorphosis I never saw'.[74]

Before moving into Downing Street Wellington had to face a serious Cabinet crisis. When he constructed it, aware that half the Tories, especially the more extreme members of the Party, were against his Government, he had taken in four Canningites – Huskisson, Lord

---

* This house stood at the end of the cul-de-sac, where the steps now lead down to St. James's Park.

Dudley, Charles Grant and Lord Palmerston. But within four months an incident, neither serious nor unprecedented, led to a series of events the consequences of which were far-reaching. A Bill was brought in by Lord John Russell, a Whig and a member of the Opposition, to disfranchise the grossly corrupt borough of East Retford in the county of Nottingham. The Government agreed to accept this. The Whigs insisted that the two seats thus released should be given to Birmingham, which was not represented in the House at all. Peel would not agree to it: the Government, he said, wanted the two seats to remain in Nottingham. On this issue Huskisson, though a member of the Government, voted with the Whigs and felt that in the circumstances it was right for him to offer the Duke his resignation. To him this seemed to be no more than a necessary formality and he fully expected the Duke to ask him to stay. This was explained to the Duke but he declined to see it in that light. The resignation was offered, he said, and he accepted it. Many felt that the Duke, not liking Huskisson, was glad to see him go. But not only did Huskisson leave, with him went the three other Canningites, Palmerston, Grant and Dudley, who instantly resigned too. The Duke was not sorry. In the Cabinet they had provoked ceaseless arguments. They differed from the rest 'upon almost every question', Lord Ellenborough has recorded,[104] 'meeting to debate and dispute, and separating without deciding'.

Their replacement caused further consternation, for the Duke brought into the Government two military men: General Sir George Murray, who had served with him in the Peninsular War, took Huskisson's place as Colonial Secretary, and Sir Henry Hardinge, the Duke's liaison officer at Waterloo, succeeded Palmerston as Secretary at War. The Duke's Irish friend, Lord William Vesey Fitzgerald, went to the Board of Trade in Grant's place. Harriet's husband, Charles Arbuthnot, was given the Duchy of Lancaster. Much was said by the Opposition about these changes. It was pointed out that, being accustomed to instant obedience in the army, Wellington could not brook men about him who questioned his commands.

Much more was to follow. The appointment of Vesey Fitzgerald, who sat for the Irish constituency of Clare, necessitated his having to seek re-election. Fortunately, though a Protestant and a large landowner in Ireland, he was in favour of the Catholics having full equality and was in consequence extremely popular in his constituency. But the Catholic Association decided to put Daniel O'Connell up as his opponent. O'Connell was a man of spirit and intelligence as well as a Catholic, and behind him stood the entire Roman Catholic hierarchy. He had been intended for the priesthood, but took up law and rose as high as it was possible for a Catholic to rise. Tall, red-headed, with a typically Irish face, he had a voice of tremendous power and melody. His abhorrence of bloodshed was sincere: he always urged his followers to avoid violence. It was obvious that he would prove a formidable opponent. It was obvious too that if elected he would not be able, as a Catholic, to take his seat in the House. The challenge in fact was not only a protest, but an attempt to prove that the democratic franchise was no more than a mockery.

The whole countryside rallied to O'Connell's support. Mass meetings were held. Rousing speeches stirred the populace. Flags and banners were borne through the streets. Many thousands camped out in various parts of the constituency. Always perfect order prevailed. Catholic priests led their flocks in regimented groups to the polling booths. Peel, who was Home Secretary and therefore responsible for the preservation of peace even in Ireland, wrote to Sir Walter Scott, the novelist: 'I wish you had been present, for no pen but yours could have done justice to that peaceful exhibition of sobered and desperate enthusiasm.'[105]

O'Connell was elected; Vesey Fitzgerald, the new President of the Board of Trade, lost his seat. All Ireland was roused. 'In this country,' wrote Sir Maurice Fitzgerald, M.P. for Kerry, 'the danger is appalling and it is rapidly progressive.' It became clear to Wellington and Peel, both strongly opposed to Catholic emancipation, that it was no longer the cry of just a small section of Irish agitators, but had the support of the entire country. The alternatives they faced were concession or revolution. Force, Peel saw, would provide no solution – 'the question would remain precisely what it was, but with all animosities doubly infuriated'. Many nevertheless expected Wellington to deal with the situation with the firmness he had always exercised against rebellion. But, as he said afterwards in the House of Lords, he viewed it as 'a question entirely of expediency'; as in war, on finding a position untenable, he had always found it necessary to retreat. He informed the Lords that he would lay down his life to avoid one month of civil war, and it was realized that the Catholics were at last going to get their way. The question now was how would the Tories take it, for the Duke had formed his Government on the strict undertaking that 'the Roman Catholic question should be considered as one not to be brought forward by the Cabinet'. And how would the King take it? Would he be as difficult as his father George the Third?

Wellington had first to deal with Peel, his chief and most able lieutenant, on whom he had to rely for the handling of the House of Commons. Peel, an uncompromising Protestant, was not prepared to make concessions; and, even when ultimately persuaded, warned the Duke 'that it would not conduce to the satisfactory adjustment of the question, that the charge of it in the House of Commons should be committed to my hand'. It was his intention, he said, to announce his conversion to the necessity for adopting such a course, and then resign. The Duke succeeded in persuading Peel to remain at the helm.

Nothing of this was revealed either to the public – Wellington never believed in taking the people into his confidence – or even to his colleagues in the Cabinet. Early in the new year, 1829, he went to see the King. His manner with His Majesty, he has himself summarized in these words: 'I make it a rule,' he said, 'never to interrupt him, and when in this way he tries to get rid of a subject in the way of business which he does not like, I let him talk himself out, and then quietly put before him the matter in question, so that he cannot escape it.'

To begin with, hints were given both to the King and the public. There was a reference in the King's speech at the opening of Parliament on the 5th February that the whole Catholic question would be 'considered' and 'reviewed'. This so enraged the King's brother, the Duke of Cumberland, that he immediately left Hanover and drove for ten nights through deep snow to the coast, then crossed the turbulent Channel.

When he arrived at No. 10 Downing Street he was told that the Cabinet was sitting. His Royal Highness decided to wait. After some time Wellington emerged and suggested that he should stay to dinner. 'Duke,' said Cumberland, 'I do not like to dine with you, not thinking it right to dine with a man whose measures I shall probably feel it my duty to oppose most strenuously in a very few days.' He was nevertheless persuaded to stay, but, still indignant at the end of the dinner, went on to Windsor and exercised his pressure on the King.

The next move was for Wellington to take the Cabinet into his confidence. He was not prepared to stand any nonsense from them. Asked bluntly by Croker if he had told them that unless they supported him they must resign, the Duke replied: 'There are people who, if you allow them any loophole, will indulge their own vanity or prejudices to any extent, and if I were not to show a determined resolution where should I be? If those in my rear have any excuse for slipping away, how can I meet the enemy in front? Besides how am I to bring down my *household troops* if there is any wavering amongst a class of my official men?'[74]

The one danger point now was the King, for the Duke of Cumberland had worked on him successfully. In March, together with Peel and Lord Lyndhurst, the Lord Chancellor, the Duke went to see His Majesty at Windsor. The King, very fat and ailing, had been drinking brandy and water. The audience was most painful. The King talked for six hours, pausing only to take further sips of brandy. He referred to his Coronation oath. He talked of abdicating. Since garrulity had marked his father's madness the Duke was convinced that the King was mad. Had not His Majesty's delusions led him to believe that he had fought in Spain and also at Waterloo? Wellington tried to interrupt him, but could do no more than interject an occasional word. At length he managed to say that the only course left was for the entire Government to resign. With that the three Ministers rose. His Majesty accepted their resignations and they left. Shortly after their return to London, where they joined the rest of the Cabinet at dinner, Wellington received a letter from the King. It conveyed the royal consent. The postscript added: 'God knows what pain it costs me to write these words. G.R.'

The House of Lords proved to be much more difficult to handle than the Commons. Not only were most of the Tory peers against it, but the Whigs, taking advantage of Wellington's change of front, jeered unsparingly. One of them said derisively that the Duke's manœuvre could best be expressed in the words: 'My Lords! Attention! Right about face! Quick march!' Criticism was fired at him from both sides. It was a new experience for the Duke, and he did not like it at all. Most persistent of his critics was Lord Winchilsea, an unyielding, loud-voiced peer, who did not confine his attacks to the House of Lords, but sent a letter to the Press, accusing the Duke of having resorted to a mean subterfuge in order that he 'might the more effectively, under the cloak of some outward show of zeal for the Protestant religion, carry on his more insiduous designs, for the infringement of our liberties, and the introduction of Popery into every department of the State'. This incensed Wellington. Any reflection on his honesty and his inflexible integrity was more than he could brook. He promptly challenged Winchilsea to a duel, although duelling had always been most rigorously forbidden in the Army by the Duke himself. It was, he had said, an unnecessary risk for his officers to take over a private quarrel. That risk he was himself resolved to take now. He demanded of Winchilsea 'that satisfaction . . . which a gentleman has a right to require, and which a gentleman never refuses to give'.

Wellington entrusted the staff work to the Secretary at War, General Sir Henry Hardinge. It was arranged that the duel should take place in Battersea Fields early on the morning of 21st March 1829. Hardinge asked the Duke's physician, Dr. Hume, to go there but did not reveal who the duellists were to be. The doctor drove along the King's Road, Chelsea, to Battersea Bridge: the Duke and Hardinge mounted their horses in Downing Street and rode to Battersea. A soldier, recognizing the Duke as he went by, said afterwards: 'I saw that there was mischief in his eye, so I followed and saw what happened.'[106]

The doctor was the first to arrive. He got out of his carriage and waited. A moment later he saw the two horsemen approaching and was flabbergasted. The Duke rode up laughing and said: 'Well, I daresay you little expected it was I who wanted you to be here.' Hardinge and the Duke then rode to the top of the hill to see if Winchilsea and his second, Lord Falmouth, were in sight. Presently they returned, dismounted and told the doctor to take the pistols out of the case and bring them along. This the doctor did, concealing the pistols under a cloak thrown over his arm. Together they proceeded to a clearing where they were joined by Winchilsea and his second.

'Now then, Hardinge,' the Duke said brusquely. 'Look sharp and step out the ground. I have no time to waste. Damn it! Don't stick him up so near the ditch. If I hit him, he will tumble in.'

Falmouth was in a very agitated state and 'could hardly perform his task'. The pistols were loaded. The ground was measured out. The Duke and Winchilsea took up their positions. Before they were allowed to shoot, Hardinge stepped forward and drawing a paper out of his pocket, read a strongly worded protest, reminding Lords Winchilsea and Falmouth that they alone would be answerable for the consequences.

The Duke had been wondering all morning whether to shoot his opponent. If he killed him it would undoubtedly mean prison, at any rate until the trial. So he decided to shoot him in the leg.

On the order to fire 'the Duke raised his pistol and presented it instantly', but 'observing that Lord Winchilsea did not immediately present at him, he seemed to hesitate for a moment, and then fired without effect'.[88]

Winchilsea thereupon raised his arm above his head and fired into the air. Then, approaching Hardinge, he declared that, having received the Duke's fire, he now felt he was at liberty to give the Duke the reparation he desired.

Hardinge said: 'The Duke expects an ample apology, and a complete and full acknowledgement from Lord Winchilsea of his error in having published the accusation against him.'

Falmouth, producing a paper from his pocket, read out Winchilsea's admission of his error. This seemed to end the matter. But the Duke was not prepared to accept it. 'This won't do,' he said. 'It is no apology.'

'I assure you what I have written was meant as an apology . . .' Falmouth began. But the Duke insisted that unless the word 'apology' was inserted, the duel would have to be resumed.

Winchilsea and Falmouth eventually gave in. Hardinge then rebuked them for 'bringing this man (pointing to the Duke) into the field, where, during the whole course of a long military life, he never was before on an occasion of this nature'.

The Duke meanwhile had remounted and, touching the brim of his hat with two fingers, said 'Good morning, my Lord Winchilsea; good morning, my Lord Falmouth,' and rode off. He went straight away to see Harriet Arbuthnot and found her at breakfast. She said afterwards that, had she known of it beforehand, she would have 'died of fright'.

Not only had the Duke's honour been satisfied, but he had made an

example of Winchilsea and the House of Lords listened more atten-
tively and respectfully thereafter to what the Duke had to say about
Catholic emancipation. He succeeded where Pitt had failed. The Bill
was passed. Thus, as a result of the avalanche caused by Huskisson voting against the Government over East Retford and the Duke's acceptance of his resignation, the Catholics were at last granted equal rights.
'Well, I said I would do it,' observed Wellington, 'and I have done it
handsomely, have I not?' It was the one measure that distinguished
Wellington's tenure of office as Prime Minister. George the Fourth
remarked with a growl. 'Arthur is King of England, O'Connell King
of Ireland, and myself Canon of Windsor.'

Catholic peers, including the Duke of Norfolk, so long debarred from
taking their seats in the House of Lords, were now admitted. Daniel
O'Connell came over from Ireland to take his rightful place in the
House of Commons. But allowing equal rights to the Jews was quite
another matter. The following spring a Jews' Relief Bill was opposed
by the Duke. 'This Christian community', he wrote, 'will not much
like to have Jewish magistrates and rulers. . . . It besides gives a false
colouring, and throws ridicule upon the great measures of 1828 and
1829, which it resembles only in name.'[104]

Wellington was not as tall a man as is generally supposed. He was in
fact only five feet nine inches in height, not very much taller than
Napoleon. As his pictures show, a sharp aquiline nose separated two
penetrating grey eyes. In build he was spare but muscular, and he
walked with a resolute, springy step. He was always most attentive to
his clothes, which earned him the nickname of 'Dandy' as a young man
and 'Beau' later. His endurance, both physical and mental, was astonishing. He worked prodigiously. Every letter he received was read and
answered personally. This took up a considerable amount of his time.
Hours were spent over them in his study at No. 10 as well as at Apsley
House in the evenings. He was a tartar for detail. Nothing was overlooked.

It could not be said that he had a great intellect. His mind in fact was
simple and direct. He always went straight to the heart of things. Nor
was he a good speaker. His articulation was indistinct, his delivery
over-emphatic and vehement, and what he said was littered with
superlatives, far too many superlatives. In gesture he was sparing. He

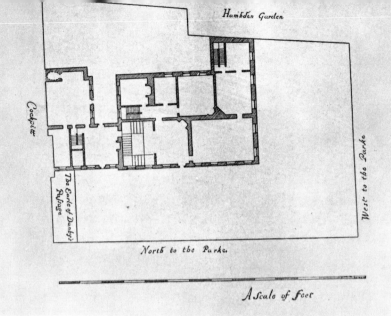

The older section of No. 10 Downing Street, designed by Sir Christopher Wren in 1677 when he was Surveyor General to King Charles the Second. It shows the garden as it is to this day. The large room at the corner of the house, flanked by the garden on two sides, later became the Cabinet Room. Downing Street, built five years later, ran along 'Hambden Garden' at the top of the sketch.

A Mapp of the Grounds & Buildings thereon being part of St James Parke granted by his Maj:ty to Sr Walter St John & others: Bounded Eastward wth the Beuildings of the Cockpitt, southward wth the wall of Hamden Garden, Northward 140, foote in Length to the Parke, westward 85 foote in Length to the Parke.

Chr: Wren

S: G:

Aprill 10:th

1677

Sir Christopher Wren's note, written in his own hand, refers to the plan shown above.

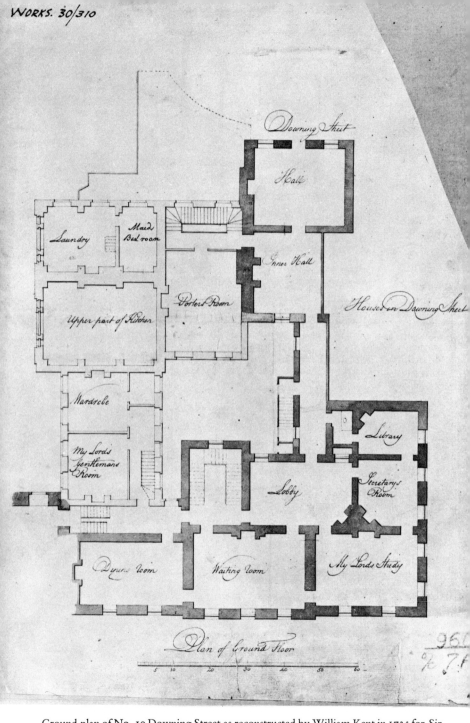

Downing Street

Hall

Inner Hall

Laundry

Maids Bed room

Porters Room

Houses in Downing Street

Upper part of Kitchen

Wardrobe

Library

My Lords Gentlemans Room

Secretarys Room

Lobby

Dining room

Waiting room

My Lords Study

Plan of Ground Floor

5 10 20 30 40 50 60

Ground plan of No. 10 Downing Street as reconstructed by William Kent in 1735 for Sir Robert Walpole. 'My Lords Study', at the bottom of the sketch, is the Cabinet Room. The Downing Street house, to which it was joined by a corridor, is at the top of the sketch. The area space between the two main houses is clearly visible.

spoke as a rule standing bolt upright, with his arms folded across his chest. Though priding himself on his imperturbability, he was in fact quick-tempered and unwilling ever to admit that he had been in the wrong.

In January 1829, like the younger Pitt and Lord Liverpool, he was appointed Lord Warden of the Cinque Ports and often went down at the end of the Parliamentary session to spend a little time in Walmer Castle, away from London. His trim, frock-coated figure and full head of snow-white hair, so familiar in Downing Street during his many years in Liverpool's Cabinet and now as Prime Minister, could be seen along the Channel coast where Pitt had once drilled his volunteers. In the autumn Wellington made the round of the famous country houses, with Harriet Arbuthnot generally a guest too, accompanied always by her husband for the sake of propriety. Wellington's wife rarely went with him. Though they still lived under the same roof, both at Downing Street and at Apsley House, the estrangement was irreparable. Her devotion to him, however, remained unimpaired and it was pitiful (as Peel and others have recorded in their letters and diaries) to see her eyes fixed upon him with adoration, while he completely ignored her.

All through 1829 the King's health declined steadily. His mind was going and Wellington found him increasingly difficult to talk to. His Majesty busied himself with alterations to the Guards' uniform; and though the Duke boasted that 'nobody can manage him but me', he often complained bitterly.[88] 'If I had known in January 1828 one tithe of what I do now, and of what I discovered in one month after I was in office, I should have never been the King's minister, and should have avoided loads of misery! However, I trust that God Almighty will soon determine that I had been sufficiently punished for my sins, and will relieve me from the unhappy lot which has befallen me! I believe there never was a man suffered so much; and for so little purpose!' But he was not to be relieved yet: he was to remain in office for still another year.

In January 1830, Apsley House being ready for his return, he vacated No. 10 Downing Street but retained the Cabinet room as his office, and lent the house to his old friend Earl Bathurst, who was in the Government as Lord President of the Council. Thus, after having been occupied for some years by Chancellors of the Exchequer and Prime

Ministers, No. 10 once again passed into the occupation of one who was neither.

Bathurst, who was seven years older than Wellington, was to live here for a whole year. He was not marked by any ability. Charles Greville, whose diary throws such a vivid light on people and events of his time, was in his youth Bathurst's private secretary and describes him as 'a very amiable man though his talents were far from brilliant . . . a bad speaker, greatly averse to changes, but unwillingly acquiescing in many . . . nervous, reserved, with a good deal of humour, and habitually a jester. . . . His conversation was generally a series of jokes, and he rarely discussed any subject but in a ludicrous vein'.

Because of his friendship with Pitt, Bathurst was given office in 1783, when he was only twenty-one, and had been kept on by Pitt's successors – Portland, Spencer Perceval, Liverpool, and now Wellington. In addition to these important offices, Bathurst contrived to secure a number of lucrative sinecures and achieved further the distinction of the Garter. He was very attached to the Duke and resigned with him when Canning became Prime Minister. Married in 1789, he had four sons and two daughters, all of them now grown to maturity – his eldest son was forty by the time he moved into No. 10.

Greville indicates that, for all his joviality, two men had reason to dislike Bathurst. One of these was Napoleon. Bathurst was Secretary for War and the Colonies from 1812 to 1827 and 'his conduct to Napoleon', Greville states, 'justly incurred odium, for although he was only one of many, he was the Minister through whom the orders of Government passed, and he suffered the principal share of the reproach which was thrown upon the Cabinet for their rude and barbarous treatment of the Emperor at St. Helena. He had not a lively imagination, and his feelings were not excited by the contemplation of such a striking example of fallen greatness.'[79]

The other with a grievance against Bathurst was Greville himself. 'So far from feeling any obligation to him,' he writes, 'I always consider his mistaken kindness in giving me that post as the source of all my misfortunes and the cause of my present condition. He never thought fit to employ me, never associated me with the interests and the business of his office, and consequently abandoned me at the age of eighteen to that life of idleness and dissipation from which I might have been saved had he felt that my future prospects in life, my character and talents, depended in great measure upon the direction which was at that moment given to my mind.'

Greville in fact did not do at all badly. The grandson of the Duke of Portland who had twice been Prime Minister, and connected also with most of the ruling families, including the Cannings, he was given early in life the sinecure office of Secretary of the island of Jamaica and when he was twenty-seven was appointed Clerk of the Privy Council. The latter brought him in constant touch with all the leading statesmen over a period of nearly forty years. His diary, a perceptive record of his impressions, has been a source on which history has fruitfully drawn.

From the beginning of 1830, the King's health was seen to be failing fast. In June he died. Wellington did not view with any satisfaction the prospect of serving under his successor William the Fourth. He feared that the new King's outlook would be too liberal and that His Majesty would press for the inclusion of Lord Grey in the Government. But his fears were unfounded. The King proved to be reasonable and tractable and the Duke confessed that he could do more business with him in ten minutes than with his predecessor in ten days.

King William was if anything inclined to be too matey. At short notice, allowing the Duke's household only twelve hours for the necessary preparations, His Majesty arrived at Apsley House for dinner with the King and Queen of Württemberg. After dinner William delivered a long and wearying speech, to which the Duke replied very briefly.

The death of George the Fourth necessitated a General Election. Wellington, aware of his weakness in the House of Commons, sought to strengthen it. He approached Lord Melbourne, who as William Lamb had served in Canning's Government. But, as an avowed Canningite, who had resigned from Wellington's Government with Huskisson and the others, Melbourne refused to serve unless Huskisson was brought back too and, what was far more difficult for the Duke to swallow, unless Lord Grey was also included in the Government. Wellington declined even to listen to such a proposition.

While the election was in progress a fresh revolution broke out in France. Once again there were barricades in the streets of Paris. Troops were called out, but were found to be helpless against the mob. There was a possibility that Britain might be drawn into a war and that many of the European monarchs would gladly once again take up arms against the revolutionaries. But Wellington did not want another war. He wrote to his Foreign Secretary Lord Aberdeen: 'There are some bitter pills to swallow. . . . However, the last chance of peace is to swallow them all!'

In that year of revolutions there were risings in a number of countries on the Continent, including the Netherlands, where crowds rioted in the streets of Brussels, insisting that the artificial link with Holland, set up by Wellington in 1815, should be severed. This goal was achieved by the end of September (1830) when Belgium became an independent kingdom. There was trouble in England too. As early as April the Earl of Sefton was writing to Creevey: 'The Beau's troubles are not over yet. The distress in the country is frightful. Millions are starving, and I defy him to do anything to relieve them.'[75]

During the General Election a cry that had not been heard for many years – though there had been murmurs and resolutions had been passed from time to time at Radical meetings – spread suddenly throughout the country. It was the cry for Parliamentary Reform. In their distress the suffering masses, the unemployed and hungry, had come to believe that once they had the vote all could be set right, for the remedy would then be in their own hands. That was the dream born of their desperation, whenever a fresh industrial depression drove them to rioting and crime. For the acute distress that began just before Wellington came to power, no alleviation had yet been found. But a check upon crime had been imposed by the formation of the police force by Peel, by whose Christian name of Bobby a policeman is still colloquially known. The protracted misery of the workless had been aggravated by the displacement of more and more handloom weavers through the adoption of spinning jennies and of agricultural labourers by the introduction of threshing machines. Trade unions had been formed, secretly at first – some were even known as 'secret societies' – but the protection they afforded was not yet adequate. So more than ever Parliamentary Reform seemed to be the panacea. The political agitation spread and for the first time it was being effectively organized. At Birmingham a Political Union of the Lower and Middle Classes was started with a programme which included manhood suffrage. Similar unions were formed elsewhere. The people of England had been greatly encouraged by O'Connell's success in Ireland and, later in the year, by the new revolution in France; and they were determined at all costs to obtain the vote. More than half a century before, Chatham had said that Parliament would have to 'reform itself from within, or be reformed with a vengeance from without'. The public were no longer prepared to wait. The Whigs, inactive and in disarray during their long spell out of office and deterred by the Napoleonic wars from agitating earlier, now closed their ranks and took up the popular cause. Lord Althorp, heir to Earl Spencer, had just been elected Leader of their Party in the House of Commons. In the Lords Earl Grey was at the helm. With them, as vocal in the cry for Parliamentary Reform, stood Lord John Russell, who had already made an effort to disfranchise corrupt boroughs. Ardent support was given to them by Henry Brougham, a brilliant young Whig destined to be a future Lord Chancellor, as well as by Lord Lansdowne and Lord Holland, a nephew of Charles James Fox.

Wellington was as strongly opposed to Parliamentary Reform as he had been to Catholic emancipation: more so, for it involved tampering with the constitution, and that he regarded as most dangerous. The time was scarcely propitious, he felt, for constitutional experiments, with revolution again astir in many parts of Europe.

Wellington lost a large number of seats in the General Election. Two of Peel's brothers and his brother-in-law were defeated. The Government was greatly weakened. But the Duke remained unperturbed. He was prepared to fight it out, since principles were at stake.

When the House met, the country awaited a declaration of policy from the Government – on the relief of distress and also on the burning question of Parliamentary Reform. The Duke lost little time in declaring in the House of Lords that he was not prepared to bring forward any measure of reform, but that he should 'always feel it his duty to resist such measures when proposed by others'. To a colleague he wrote: 'I have no leisure to discuss Parliamentary Reform either in writing or in conversation. I confess that I doubt whether it will be carried in Parliament. If it should be carried it must occasion a total change in the whole system of that society called the British Empire; and I don't see how I could be a party to such changes, entertaining the opinions that I do. . . . I foresee nothing but a series of misfortunes for the country in all its interests, and even affecting its safety. I cannot be a party in inflicting those misfortunes.'[88]

There were ugly developments in various parts of England, most marked in the new industrial towns of the North. Wellington decided to meet this with force. He provisioned his various garrisons and warned the officers to avoid the narrow streets. Repeatedly news reached him of plots against his life. The great hero of Waterloo, cheered once to the echo, was now booed and hissed wherever he went and stones were hurled by angry mobs through the windows of Apsley House. He ignored these demonstrations and insisted on going to the most troubled region in the North for the opening of the railway between Manchester and Liverpool. Not that he attached much importance to this novel mode of locomotion. He thought it quite unpractical and shared the view that no good could come of the invention because stage coaches already travelled at the rate of eight and sometimes ten miles an hour. The idea of accelerating the pace to twenty miles an hour was to him a matter for derision: even at twelve miles an hour the speed would be impossible to control, he said. Nevertheless he went to the opening, with his Spanish cloak over his shoulders. His train had an immense canopy which had to be lowered as it puffed through the tunnels. He saw at the ceremony the local Member of Parliament, his hated former colleague Huskisson. They shook hands and had hardly finished talking when an oncoming locomotive struck Huskisson, who through lameness was unable to get away quickly enough. He died a few hours later.

Despite the hostility expressed before his visit, Wellington was received with enthusiasm by the crowds, and returned to London more determined than ever to fight against Parliamentary Reform. He made a spirited speech in the House of Lords in November which, Creevey records, 'at once destroyed what little popularity the Duke had left and lowered him in public estimation so much that when he does go out of office, as most assuredly he must, he will leave it without any of the dignity and credit which might have accompanied his retirement'.

The feeling in the country was very strong. All classes appeared to be against him. He was extremely unpopular even among the merchants in the City, for his speech in the Lords had 'brought about an alarming fall in the Funds', states Princess Lieven. 'He is followed in the streets, hooted, and almost attacked by the mob.' As a precaution he cancelled the visit he was to make with the King and Queen to dine with the Lord Mayor on the 9th November. His eldest brother, Lord Wellesley, described this as 'the boldest act of cowardice he had ever heard of'.[95] The Duke also arranged for the defence of his home, Apsley House.

A few days later, on 15th November 1830, the Duke's Government fell – not on the question of reform, but on a simple vote on the Civil List. The Opposition was out for his blood and it did not matter what the issue was, they were determined to get him out – and they did.

The Duke was at dinner at Apsley House when the vote was taken in the Commons. An excited gentleman brought him the news. All Wellington said was 'Do not tell the women.' The next day he resigned.

CHAPTER 22
Grey and the Reform Bill

THE King sent for Lord Grey, the Leader of the Whigs. This marked their return to power after forty-eight years of eclipse, save for Grenville's brief ministry. Grey moved almost at once into No. 10 Downing Street.

He was by no means a young man: he was nearly sixty-seven. His father, a general and later the first Earl Grey had served in the American War of Independence against the rebellious colonists. Young Grey, having witnessed the rout of the Whigs by Pitt in the General Election of 1784, became one of Pitt's most vigorous opponents. He joined Fox's circle, an association that worked greatly to his disadvantage. Like Fox he was out of office for most of his life, serving for only a few months as First Lord of the Admiralty, then as Foreign Secretary, during Grenville's short term as Prime Minister. It was on Fox's death that Grey became Leader of the Whigs. In the following year 1807, after being in the House of Commons for nearly twenty years, he succeeded his father as the second earl: the earldom in fact was given to the General while his son was in the Grenville Government.

Throughout his political life Grey had been interested in Parliamentary Reform. Indeed his first Reform Bill had been introduced as long ago as 1797. It was defeated by 165 votes in a House of Commons of 350 members. As he loved living in the country and spent a great deal of his time at Howick, his home in Northumberland, many expected him to give up politics. He hovered on the brink of doing so for some years. Writing to his wife in 1804, he said: 'I feel more and more convinced of my unfitness for a pursuit which I detest, which interferes with my private comfort, and which I only sigh for an opportunity of abandoning decidedly and for ever. Do not think this is the language of momentary low spirits; it really is the settled conviction of my mind.'

Very tall and strikingly handsome, he was often looked upon as the most attractive man in Europe. His charm won him the friendship of many of the great Whig ladies, in particular of the beautiful Duchess of Devonshire, with whom, though she was many years his senior, he was believed to have been very much in love as a young man. But, despite his charm, his manner was inclined to be lofty and somewhat severe, at times even unsympathetic. This led to many estrangements. George the Fourth, who was prepared to like him because of Fox, was appalled by the stand he took over Mrs. Fitzherbert and later by his refusal to countenance the divorce of Queen Caroline; after that the King would not agree to Grey being admitted into any Government. It was only after the King's death in 1830 that he got his chance of becoming Prime Minister. Thus at the advanced age of almost sixty-seven, with a total of barely twelve months' experience in office, he found himself faced with forming a Government, composed inevitably of men who were equally new and untried. He selected them with care and they formed an admirable group. Lord Althorp, the heir to Earl Spencer, was appointed Chancellor of the Exchequer and Leader of the House of Commons. Lord John Russell was entrusted with the task of Parliamentary Reform, to which Russell was as dedicated as Grey himself. Palmerston, Melbourne and Brougham were also given office. Many of the minor ministries were filled by Grey's relatives, for he adhered closely to the Whig tradition that the family had a right to such appointments. A place was also found for his old friend Thomas Creevey, the diarist and gossip, who had been struggling on a private income of £200 a year: he was appointed Treasurer of the Ordnance with an office in the Tower of London and a salary of £1,200 a year. Creevey, now sixty-two, showed a boyish delight in the minute details of the Ordnance survey maps which were then being engraved for the first time.

In a letter to his stepdaughter Miss Elizabeth Ord on 31st January 1831, when Grey had been in office only a few weeks, Creevey said: 'I dined in Downing Street with Lady Grey. . . . After dinner the private secretary to the Prime Minister and myself being alone, I ascertained that, altho' Lord Grey was gone to Brighton ostensibly to prick for Sheriffs for the year, his great object was to put his *plan of reform* before the King,* previous (if he approves) to its being proposed to the House of Commons. A ticklish operation, this! to propose to a Sovereign a plan for reducing his own power and patronage. However, there is the plan all cut and dry, and the Cabinet unanimous upon the subject. . . .' Billy† has been in perfect ecstasies with his Government ever since they arrested O'Connell.‡ Wood§ says if the King gives his Government his real support upon this Reform question, without the slightest appearance of a jib, Grey is determined to fight it out to a dissolution of Parliament, if his plan is beat in the Commons. My eye, what a crisis!'[75]

Grey was married at the age of thirty to Elizabeth Ponsonby, the daughter of William, later the first Lord Ponsonby. Though constantly beset by women and himself attracted to them, he appears to have enjoyed marital felicity: at any rate his wife presented him with nine sons and five daughters; of these fourteen, the eldest was thirty-three, the youngest only eleven, and all but those who had already established themselves in separate homes moved into No. 10 Downing Street with him. Grey's young grandchildren often came to stay too. It was eighteen years since the house had held so large and lively a family; it must have known an unechoing quiet after Mrs. Spencer Perceval vacated it with her twelve children.

---

* William the Fourth was living at the time in the ornate oriental Pavilion built by his brother, the Prince Regent, when Prince of Wales.
† The King.
‡ Daniel O'Connell, the Irish M.P. who defeated Vesey Fitzgerald at County Clare, was arrested for defying a Government order.
§ Grey's private secretary.

Fortunately the King was well disposed towards Parliamentary Reform; he realized that it was the will of the people. Creevey, writing after Grey's return from Brighton, states: 'Grey says the King's conduct was *perfect*. . . . He bestowed much time and thought in going over every part of the plan, examined its bearings, asked most sensible questions, and, being quite satisfied, with everything Grey urged in its support, pledged himself irrevocably to do the same. . . . Grey said, too, the Queen was evidently *better* with him. It seems that her manners to him at first were distant and reserved, so that he could not avoid concluding that the change of Government was a subject of regret to her. . . . But he satisfied himself that she has no influence with the King, and that, in fact, he never even mentions politicks to her, much less consults her – that her influence over him and to his *manners* has been very great and highly beneficial, but there it stops.'

The Queen, whom King William had married late in life, setting aside for dynastic reasons the coarse Mrs Jordan, who already had many children by different fathers and had presented him with ten more of his own, was Princess Adelaide of Saxe-Coburg-Meiningen: she was only half his age. Surprisingly he settled down to a virtuous married life. The Queen was never popular. But he, though regarded as eccentric, was well liked. After a long spell of service in the Navy, where he met Nelson and was best man at his ill-fated marriage, Prince William spent some time in New York, the only Royal Prince to visit the American colonies while they were still colonies. This visit occurred during the War of Independence and the rebels, with encouragement from George Washington, planned his capture, but the Prince managed to escape. Later he decided to stand for election to the House of Commons as M.P. for Totnes in Devonshire, but George the Third (his father) muttering: 'I well know that it is another vote added to the Opposition,' circumvented it by creating him the Duke of Clarence.

Grey, despite the many distractions over the preparation of the Reform Bill, did a great deal of entertaining at No. 10. Among the most frequent guests were the great Talleyrand, Napoleon's famous Foreign Minister and now French Ambassador in London, and the Duchess de Dino, who, though married to his nephew, was Talleyrand's mistress.

Created a Prince by Napoleon, Talleyrand was seventy-seven and suffered from many physical infirmities. Short, his ankles weak, his feet deformed, he tottered about 'like a fuddled village schoolmaster', states Croker. But his mind was quite unimpaired. He had played a multitude of eventful parts, serving both Napoleon and the Bourbons. After the Revolution of 1830 he urged the Duke of Orleans to accept the throne of France as Louis Philippe. The grateful King offered him the Foreign Ministry, but he preferred to come to England as Ambassador. His life had still a further eight years to run. His wide experience, his remarkable memory, his great wit, and his immense wealth, for he had enriched himself through the years, won him many admirers and friends, notably Lord Brougham, whom Grey presently appointed Lord Chancellor. For his niece he obtained the status of Ambassadress: Talleyrand described her as 'the cleverest *man* or *woman* he ever knew'. In England, where he was denounced and hated during the war, not everyone was prepared to receive him. Creevey records how Lord Sefton heard 'the Dino' entreating Lady Grey at No. 10 Downing Street 'to use her influence with Lady Durham [Lady Grey's daughter] to let her boy, and I believe a little girl, to come to a child's ball at the Dino's on Monday next. So when Lord Grey was handing the Dino to her carriage, Sefton and Lady Grey being left alone, the latter said to him: "Was there ever anything like the absurdities of Lambton?* He not only won't be introduced to Mons. Talleyrand and Madame de Dino, but he chooses to be as rude as possible to them whenever he meets them. . . ." Just as Lady Grey was finishing, Grey returned, and she said: "I was telling Lord Sefton of Lambton's nonsense;" and then they both joined in abusing him, as well they might. . . . However, I hope he will go on offending Lord and Lady Grey, and be himself out of [*illegible*].'

Lady Grey was 'at home' one evening a week at No. 10. Creevey records on 19th February 1831: 'Lady Sefton, her three eldest daughters and myself went after dinner last night to Lady Grey's weekly. . . . Our Vaux† was there with his daughter. I had some very good laugh-

* Should be Lord Durham. Charles Lambton is Durham's elder son and grandson of Lord and Lady Grey. The boy was the subject of Sir Thomas Lawrence's celebrated picture, 'Master Lambton'.
† Lord Brougham and Vaux, the Lord Chancellor.

ing with him, and he was in his accustomed overflowing glee. We had some very pretty amusement with Viscount Melbourne,* who is very agreeable. . . . Grey was very loud to me in praise of Edward Stanley.'†

Among the regular visitors at No. 10 was Viscount Palmerston, Foreign Secretary for the first time, and Lord John Russell,‡ who was Paymaster-General in the Government. A younger son of the Duke of Bedford, he was at the time thirty-eight years old, 'a little fellow not weighing above 8 stone', Creevey writes. Wellington described him as 'a host in himself'. Though others worked on the Reform Bill with him, the credit for it was unstintingly given to Russell – 'who,' Creevey states, 'without taking law or anything else, creates in fact a perfectly new House of Commons. . . . What a coup it is! It is its *boldness* that makes its success so certain. . . . A week or ten days must elapse before the Bill is printed and ready for a 2nd reading; by that time the country will be a flame from one end to the other in favor of the measure.'§

The country was, but the House of Commons was less enthusiastic. It was passed at four o'clock in the morning by the narrow majority of one vote. The street outside was thronged with people waiting for the news. Macaulay, as he got into a cab, was asked by the driver: 'Is the Bill carried, sir?' 'Yes, by one,' he replied. 'Thank God for it, sir,' said the driver.[107]

Grey decided on an instant dissolution of Parliament. The Lords, to prevent this, prepared an address to the Crown, protesting against a dissolution. Grey and Brougham, on hearing of this, promptly left a Cabinet meeting and hurried from Downing Street to St. James's Palace to urge the King to come and prorogue Parliament before the Lords could pass their resolution.

They arrived at the Palace at half-past eleven in the morning. The King was angry that the Lords should dare to interfere with his prerogative. There was no time, he realized, for adopting the usual ceremonial for proceeding to the House and he was prepared to waive this

---

* Melbourne was Home Secretary in Grey's Government.
† Later the Earl of Derby and a future Prime Minister. He was in Grey's Government as Chief Secretary for Ireland.
‡ Lord John, himself Prime Minister later, was the grandfather of Bertrand Russell.
§ 3rd March 1831.[75]

in the emergency, declaring that he was ready to go in a hackney carriage if necessary. But Brougham had already sent for the escort.

The Lord Chancellor hurried to Parliament to put on his State robes. The Lords with equal haste were trying to get their resolution through. The argument got so fierce that many were about to come to blows. In the midst of this uproar Brougham entered. He was greeted by jeers and hoots. Then suddenly the booming salute of guns could be heard, announcing that the King was on his way.

The doors were thrown open by the attendants and His Majesty bustled in, his crown a little askew. The Commons, in the middle of an equally stormy debate, with Peel angry and out of control, were summoned in by Black Rod.

The dissolution was announced: Lord Sidmouth, as Addington a former Prime Minister, said to Grey: 'I hope God will forgive you for this Bill, for I cannot.'

Three nights later Lady Grey had her usual 'weekly' at No. 10. Creevey describes it[75]: 'I wish you could have been with me when I entered our Premier's drawing-room last night. I was rather early, and he was standing alone with his back to a fire – the best dressed, the handsomest, and apparently the happiest man in all his royal master's dominions. . . . Lady Grey was as proud of my lord's speech as she ought to be, and *she*, too, looked as handsome and happy as ever she could be. . . . She said at least 3 times – "Come and sit here, Mr. Creveey." You see the course of this uniform kindness of Lady Grey to myself is her recollection that I was all for Lord Grey when many of his present worshippers were doing all they could against him. . . . Upon one of the duets between Lord Grey and me last night, who should be announced but Sir James Scarlett.* He graciously put out a hand for each of us, but my lord received him so coldly, that he was off in an instant, and Grey said to me – "What an extraordinary thing *his* coming here! the more so, as I don't believe he was invited. . . ." Lady Grey said to me – "I really could not be such a hypocrite as to put out my hand to Sir James Scarlett".'

Grey's cheerfulness, based on his conviction that the country would support him, proved to be fully justified when the election results were

---

* A former Whig Attorney-General, who had just resigned from the Party because of his violent opposition to the Reform Bill.

declared. The new House of Commons passed the second reading of the Reform Bill with a majority of 136. Months of debate followed before it eventually left the Lower House for the Lords, where it fell to Grey to introduce it. Their lordships were by no means disposed to accept it. Wellington, who had been in very low spirits for some time, was as hostile as ever to the measure and determined to defeat it, co-vinced still that it would 'destroy the country' and seriously affect 'the property of every individual in the country'. He had discovered as Prime Minister that party discipline differed greatly from discipline as enforced in the Army. His authority as Leader of the Opposition, he found now, was even more tenuous. 'Nobody does anything but what he likes, excepting myself,' he complained. 'We are all commanders, and there are no troops. Nobody obeys or ever listens to advice but myself.' Even Peel, once his staunch lieutenant and now referred to as 'that fellow in the House of Commons', had been proving difficult. 'One can't go on without him,' the Duke said, 'but he is so vacillating and crotchetty that there is no getting on with him. . . . I can't manage him now at all.' Grey he had never liked but felt that it was his duty to co-operate with the King's chief Minister on all matters affecting the foreign policy of the country and he often called at No. 10 Down-ing Street for that purpose. But help him with the Reform Bill – that the Duke absolutely refused to do. The Tory peers rallied behind him. Even the Earl of Winchilsea, but recently his opponent in the duel, offered his support and the Duke, in amiable reciprocation, went out to inspect his yeomanry. The Bill had to be defeated – and it was. For all Grey's urgent pleading it was rejected by the House of Lords by 41 votes.

Many expected Grey to resign. But Brougham advised him to adopt the course followed earlier by Pitt, which it was obvious at once would prove effective. His proposal was that the King should be asked to create a sufficient number of new peers to outvote the Opposi-tion. This stratagem was not at all in keeping with Grey's aristocratic attitude: he thought it quite unconstitutional and flatly refused to adopt it. Many members of the Cabinet were, however, in favour. The pro-posal was debated by the Cabinet for hours at a time all through the month of September 1831. In the end, with the majority against him, Grey gave way. A fresh Reform Bill, only slightly modified, was then

prepared and presented to the Commons, who passed the second reading in December by a majority of 162. On New Year's Day 1832 the
Cabinet decided that the King should be informed without further
delay of the need to create additional peers.

Grey went down to Brighton where the King often stayed in the
winter. He found His Majesty far from favourably disposed to the
idea and was told bluntly that he hoped such a course would not be
necessary.

Meanwhile, with mounting public anger at the delay, there had
been alarming incidents in various parts of the country. In Derby the
jail had been stormed. In Bristol there had been fierce rioting for
three days: five hundred people had been killed and fires raged in the
streets of the city. Nottingham Castle, belonging to the Duke of Newcastle, and other famous houses had been burned down. Lords travelling in their carriages to their country seats were attacked by mobs.
The violence was described as 'unparalleled since the Civil War'. The
country appeared to be on the verge of revolution.

Wellington wrote to the King, urging the need for strong immediate action, and even hinted that he was prepared to take charge once
again and rescue His Majesty from the present Government. The
Duke drove through London with an armed servant on the box and
a brace of double-barrelled pistols at his side.

The King had already 'pronounced himself for Reform', and
Wellington, though convinced that this would mean the end of the
monarchy, was nevertheless not prepared to desert His Majesty. He
began, however, to feel that it was not longer possible 'to govern in his
name without Reform. But the more gentle and gradual the reform,
the better for the country,' he said. This view began to spread in the
Upper House and waverers were found among the ultra-Tories. Grey
was greatly relieved at this, for the whole thing had got out of hand.
'Damn Reform,' he said. 'I wish I had never touched it.' Melbourne
and Palmerston shared his caution, but others in the Cabinet, notably
Brougham, Althorp and Durham, did not. The King was relieved too
and more hopeful of the Bill getting through without the creation of
additional peers.

The debates in the House of Lords were long and wearisome. The
arguments went on night after night and were so exhausting that the

Duke of Cumberland had to be carried out of the Chamber on one occasion. The second reading was eventually passed by a majority of nine. But, in the Committee stage after the Easter recess, a motion was brought in by Lord Lyndhurst, Wellington's Lord Chancellor, that the most vital clause of the Bill, namely the disfranchising of the rotten boroughs, on which the Tories mainly depended for their support, should be postponed, and the Government was defeated by 35 votes. This brought the crisis to a head.

Once again Grey went to see the King. His Majesty was at Windsor. The Prime Minister arrived together with the Lord Chancellor, Lord Brougham, and suggested that 'sixty, or perhaps even eighty' peers would have to be created. The King was startled by the number and said he would like a little time to think it over. Grey was prepared to wait until the morning, but stated that the entire Government would resign if the King did not agree.

They did not return to London until eleven o'clock that night. Creevey states: 'The King had not even preserved his usual civility. . . . He did not even offer the poor fellows any victuals, and they were obliged to put into port at the George posting-house at Hounslow, and so get some mutton chops.'

In the morning a royal messenger arrived at No. 10 with a letter stating that His Majesty had accepted Grey's resignation. Grey had for some years been carrying on a regular, one might even say an intimate correspondence with the Princess Lieven, the wife of the Russian Ambassador. He wrote at once to inform her that 'our resignations have been accepted', adding in a further letter on the next day: 'Personally, what has happened is no cause of regret to me; and were it not for my fear of what the consequences of it may be to the King and to the country, I should look forward with real pleasure to the season when I may return to Howick.' Meanwhile he stayed on at No. 10 and waited.

The King lost no time in sending for Wellington. He asked the Duke to form a Tory administration to pass the Reform Bill. About that the King was quite firm, since it was obvious that the country was determined to have it. The Duke, despite his own opposition to Reform, which had in no way changed, was 'perfectly ready to do whatever His Majesty may command me. . . . No private consideration shall prevent me from making every effort to serve the King'.[88] He told his supporters that 'the efforts of all ought to be directed to render that Bill as little noxious as possible'. Peel was asked for his assistance but refused to give it. He had given way on Catholic emancipation, but was not prepared to make a second recantation. For five days the arguments went on. A large number of Tories were interviewed, but none of them was ready to serve under Wellington, except his two military supporters, Generals Murray and Hardinge. Meanwhile the country got restive and began to prepare for further action. Private houses hung out cards stating: 'No taxes paid Here until the Reform Bill is passed.' A run on the Bank of England was planned: placards declared: 'To stop the Duke – go for gold.' Soon the run actually began. London was in a ferment. The King's carriage was attacked on Constitution Hill. Abuse was shouted at the Queen. *The Times* in a leading article went so far as to urge the people to revolt. A number of soldiers deserted and joined those who were preparing for violence. Grey was in a curious dilemma, for, with the Government no longer in existence, if a revolution had broken out there were 'no really responsible Ministers to suppress it or to negotiate with its chiefs'.[96]

The King was at a loss to know what to do. He did not want to give in to Grey; and Wellington was unable to form an Administration. Even the Speaker of the House of Commons was approached, for after all Addington had been Speaker of the House before becoming Prime Minister. In despair His Majesty turned again to Grey and begged him to moderate his demands and water down the Reforms. But Grey was adamant. He and the Cabinet insisted on 'The Bill, the whole Bill, and nothing but the Bill.' Finally the King gave in. He asked Grey to resume office and gave him this pledge in writing: 'His Majesty authorizes Earl Grey, if any obstacle should arise during the further progress of the Bill, to submit to him a creation of Peers to such extent as shall be necessary to enable him to carry the Bill.'

Thus the battle was won and after eight days the Whigs were back in office. Wellington retreated. He and his followers stayed away from the House of Lords when the vote was taken – 'skulked in clubs and country houses'. The measure was passed by a majority of 84 on 4th

June 1832 and three days later the Royal assent was read out to the empty benches opposite.*

Creevey was jubilant. He wrote the next day to Miss Ord: 'Thank God! I was in at the death of this Conservative plot, and the triumph of our Bill.' But Grey, writing to Princess Lieven, revealed that he was 'very unwell ever since the last debate in the House of Lords. . . . I was, at the time, so ill that I thought I should have dropped while I was speaking.'

During the protracted battle for Reform, Lord Grey lost his grandson, young Lambton, the son of Lord Durham. 'Why did the blow fall on this heavenly boy?' he wrote to Princess Lieven. 'I can think of nothing else, and am quite unnerved for the battle I have to fight.' While she cooed responsively to Grey's incessant letters of affection, the Princess had no liking whatsoever for his wife. She wrote to Lady Cooper: 'Do you know that Lady Grey is a very horrid woman, passionate, bitter, Jacobinical, anything you wish to say bad.'[102]

While the Parliamentary registers were being revised the Greys went to East Sheen; they had to move out of No. 10, as the house was once again in need of attention. The *Morning Herald* of 8th October 1832 stated: 'Earl Grey's house, in Downing Street, is undergoing an extensive repair and he will therefore reside at East Sheen until it shall be fit for his reception.' The builders were busy for a full three months and the Greys did not return until early in January. The cost of the repairs was £1,247. This did not, of course, include the new furniture and curtains Lady Grey now put in. For that the Prime Minister had to pay. Creevey, visiting the house on 12th January, wrote delightedly to Miss Ord: 'I might as well say a word of the new furniture in Downing Street at Earl Grey's, everything therein being all spick and span new. The two principal Drawing Rooms opening into each other are papered with a pattern of your Drawing Room *ground*, and a large *gold* rose or flower of some kind. . . . The curtains are yellow silk . . . as gay and handsome as possible.'

At the end of 1832, with the new registers ready, a fresh General Election was held, since the existing House of Commons was regarded

---

* The Reform Act specifically denied the vote to women, hitherto excluded by custom.

as no longer representative of the country. In fact only the worst of the rotten boroughs had been disfranchised; for one of those that still remained, namely Newark, William Ewart Gladstone, then aged twenty-four, was elected: he had ironically made a reputation, while President of the Oxford Union Society at the University only the year before, by a devastating attack on the Reform Bill. His eldest brother Thomas, in the previous Parliament for a rotten borough that had been abolished, had now to find another seat. Young William Gladstone, a Conservative at this stage (the old party label of Tory was by now beginning to be dropped), topped the poll with only 887 votes, which reveals how restricted the Parliamentary Reform was. There still remained nearly forty proprietary boroughs in England and Wales. Disraeli also stood for Parliament at this election: he stood as an Independent Radical for High Wycombe and was defeated. The two men were to switch their political allegiance later, Disraeli becoming a Conservative and Gladstone a Liberal.

The Conservatives suffered an overwhelming defeat. Their representation in the Commons was reduced to 149 as against 509 Whigs. But, despite this, most of the well-known faces were back on both sides of the House. About fifty Radicals were elected, determined to achieve an extension of the Reform which, they insisted, should include universal suffrage and vote by ballot. Greville describes the new House of Commons, which met in January 1833, in these memorable words: 'Formerly new members appeared with some modesty and diffidence, and with some appearance of respect for the assembly in which they were admitted: these fellows behave themselves as if they had taken it by storm, and might riot in all the insolence of victory. There exists no *party* but that of the Government; the Irish act in a body under O'Connell to the number of about forty; the Radicals are scattered up and down without a leader, numerous, restless, turbulent and bold – Hume, Cobbett, &c. – bent upon doing all the mischief they can and incessantly active; the Tories without a head, frightened, angry, and sulky; Peel without a party, prudent, cautious, and dexterous, playing a deep waiting game of scrutiny and observation.'

Grey's chief work was now done. But some further notable measures, of which he was not the principal architect, were passed during the eighteen months that remained of his premiership. Thus did the new reformed Parliament express itself. The total abolition of slavery throughout all the British colonies and possessions was at last achieved. Grey had supported Wilberforce a quarter of a century before when the first steps were taken to restrict this evil traffic. Young Gladstone, faced with recording his first vital vote, found himself in a dilemma, for his family owed its vast fortune to the slave trade, and for this he had been jeered at as a schoolboy at Eton. He had hedged in his election address, stating that he wanted to see the end of slavery, but considered that the ground should be well prepared first. 'I cannot forget that the English factory children are permitted to grow up in almost as great ignorance and deadness of heart as the West Indian negroes.' Now, in the House, hearing his father attacked by Lord Howick, the Prime Minister's heir, Gladstone rose to make his maiden speech. 'I do not admit that holding slaves necessarily involves sin,' he said. His speech, which lasted fifty minutes, made a great impression. But the Bill was passed and received royal assent in August 1833. Wilberforce, aged seventy-four and out of Parliament for some years, had died just a month before.

Then there was the Factory Act. Attempts had been made since the beginning of the nineteenth century to protect the children working in factories. The first of the Factory Acts was not, however, introduced until 1819, that is to say eleven years before the battle for Parliamentary Reform began. Lord Liverpool was Prime Minister then. The Act stipulated that no child under the age of nine (many indeed were only six) should be employed in the textile trade or work for more than twelve hours a day. It remained a dead letter, but it established the important principle that it was the duty of the State to protect from industrial exploitation those who could not protect themselves. In 1824 Pitt's wartime Combination Laws, making trade unions illegal and strikes criminal, were repealed. Further Acts in 1826 and 1831 provided some easing of the working conditions. The new Act, brought in by Althorp in 1833, widened the scope of the earlier legislation, which had been limited to workers in cotton mills, and was made to apply now to woollen, worsted, hemp, flax, tow, linen and silk mills. No one under the age of eighteen was allowed to work for more than sixty-nine hours a week. Inspectors were appointed to see that these regulations were observed and they had the right to enter factories at all times.

The Act was largely inspired by Lord Ashley (later Lord Shaftesbury), to commemorate whose further amelioration of the condition of factory workers the fountain in Piccadilly Circus was erected, showing in an awful pun Cupid burying the shaft of his arrow into the earth.

With the stimulus and strain of the Reform battle over, Grey began to weary of the political world. There were endless quarrels in the Cabinet and between Cabinet Ministers in private houses over matters that seemed to the Prime Minister to be of small consequence. He wrote tired, dejected letters from Downing Street to his 'dearest Princess' Lieven, complaining of little vexations, of being unwell, and expressing always his eagerness to see her again. 'I hate great dinners, and they are not suited to the present state of my health; but I find I must submit to several, and therefore I will not refuse yours on Tuesday. I hope to meet you also at Palmerston's on Monday. . . . Ever dearest, Princess, most entirely yours, Grey.' Was he, now in his seventieth year, in love with her as he had been in love with Georgina, Duchess of Devonshire, in his twenties? Lieven, in her forties, was attractive, vivacious and fascinating and many thought there was more to it than just friendship. 'I promised myself a kind note from you this morning', Grey wrote, 'and I have not been disappointed. . . . It did my heart good, and is the best compensation I could have; but, still, a very inadequate one for my not having the pleasure of seeing you.' And she, addressing him more circumspectly as 'My dear Lord,' made appointments for him to come and see her at three in the afternoon. 'If . . . you can only visit me late in the day, I shall put off my departure till Thursday. All this *pour vos beaux yeux*!'[95] They were constant visitors at each other's houses. The Princess came often to Downing Street, at times dining there with her husband, at others merely to leave a note for the Prime Minister.

All through this period and until the end of his stay at No. 10, Grey was beset by the greatly intensified troubles in Ireland. The peace achieved by the granting of Catholic emancipation was short-lived. A fresh discontent arose over the payment of tithes, which had always gone to the Protestant clergy. To this the Irish objected strongly and had recently stopped paying it. The Government's efforts to collect it had led to rioting, pillaging, cattle-houghing and murder. Edward Stanley (later Lord Derby), Chief Secretary for Ireland, suggested an extremely stringent Coercion Act, but many in the Cabinet disapproved angrily, declaring that the measures were far too harsh. Creevey, writing on the 14th March 1833, states: 'There has been most stormy work in the Cabinet for some time, and it has been with the greatest difficulty Grey and Althorp have submitted to Stanley's obstinacy about Irish tithes. The more violent Lambton* I dare say would *not* submit, and he retired with an earldom, to cure his headaches, of course. What pretty physic! How delighted his colleagues must be that he is gone, for there never was such a disagreeable, overbearing devil to bear with in a Cabinet.'

The Act gave the Lord-Lieutenant power to substitute martial law for the ordinary courts of justice, to suppress all meetings, search houses, suspend Habeas Corpus and punish all persons found out of doors after sunset. Surprisingly, in view of his subsequent sympathy with the Irish cause, this ruthlessly coercive measure was ardently supported by Gladstone, who indeed went further, insisting that all the privileges of the Anglican Church in that country should be fully maintained.

The disorders in Ireland were fanned by the distress brought on by a fresh famine. O'Connell and his followers, in great strength in the English Parliament since the removal of Catholic disabilities and the extension of the vote, never ceased to clamour and obstruct the normal business of the Government. Their cry was for the repeal of Pitt's Act of Union. They insisted on being untethered and left to manage their own affairs.

Grey had also a hand while at No. 10 in a far-reaching and long overdue change in India. The East India Company, a commercial enterprise which had by chance acquired control of a vast empire, was replaced by a Government department directly under the control of the Government in London. With Grey's support the independence of Belgium, disputed ever since the treaty of separation two years before, was now finally established. The King selected was Prince Leopold of Saxe-Coburg, who had been married to Princess Charlotte, daughter of the

---

* Should be Durham, Grey's son-in-law. He received his barony and became Lord Durham in 1828.

Prince Regent (George the Fourth), and who would have been Prince Consort had she succeeded to the throne. Now it was Prince Leopold's niece Princess Victoria who was the heir and he was later to play an important role as her adviser.

The people, however, did not seem to be particularly interested in any of this. Greville noted that they were 'getting tired' of the 'blunders and embarrassments' of the Government, and it was obvious that Grey was getting very tired too. The quarrels in the Cabinet continued. Some of the Ministers who had opposed the Coercion Act argued that it had merely worsened the relations between England and Ireland. Lord Stanley, loathed by the Irish, was removed from that post – Brougham had threatened to resign if he wasn't. Stanley became Colonial Secretary, and Edward Littleton, Lord Wellesley's son-in-law, succeeded Stanley as Chief Secretary for Ireland – 'which shows', wrote Greville, 'to what shifts they are put.' Wellesley was at the same time appointed Lord-Lieutenant of Ireland. When in the following year (1834) the Coercion Act came up for renewal, Littleton informed the Cabinet that he was in favour of allowing public meetings, as their suppression was 'mere personal spleen against O'Connell'.* He was imprudent enough to reveal this to O'Connell and told him that Lord Althorp, Leader of the House of Commons and Chancellor of the Exchequer, also supported it wholeheartedly. Lord John Russell, after a visit to Ireland, declared that the Irish ought not to be made to pay taxes for the maintenance of the Protestant Church, and that some at least of the money ought to be diverted to non-religious purposes, such as education. This horrified Stanley who, as an ardent Protestant, regarded it as an attack on the true religion. With these quarrels continuing in the Cabinet room, Grey's position as Prime Minister became impossible. He was unable to curb or control his Ministers. Creevey noted on 8th May: 'Our Government was in the gravest danger all yesterday' and added that these arguments had 'roused all the fire of those in the Cabinet.'

Brougham, irritated by the incessant quarrels, has recorded: 'I was obliged to declare that unless we had something like order, meaning only one speaking at a time, I should leave the room. We then called

* Brougham in a letter to Althorp.

230

out "Order" and stopped all who interrupted. . . . Things were continually told out of doors as having been said by members of the Cabinet and not only thus told but sent to newspapers. . . . All were traced
to *Cabinet dinners* – tales carried by the servants, who were in the habit,
no matter at what house we were dining, of seizing every pretence for
remaining in the room. Then some of our colleagues would go on
talking as if none but ourselves were in the room.'[80]

Clearly Grey could not carry on like this for long. The resignation
of the Duke of Richmond, then of Graham*, and finally of Goderich,
by now the Earl of Ripon, were followed by others. Princess Lieven
wrote to Grey: 'I feel so sick at heart. It is you who are principally in
my thoughts.'

At the end of May (1834) Grey began to reconstruct his Government. 'I dined yesterday,' writes Creevey on 29th May, 'at Stanley's,
with Johnny Russell by his side. All the offices were to be filled today.'
On 8th June the entire *corps diplomatique* was entertained at No. 10,
just as though nothing was happening.

On 8th July, Althorp resigned. As he was Chancellor of the Exchequer and Leader of the House of Commons it came as a great blow.
'Our poor Earl Grey was so deeply affected last night,' Creevey states
in a letter dated the 10th, 'as not to be able to utter for some time, and
was obliged to sit down to collect himself. When he did get under
weigh, however, he almost affected others as much as he had been
affected himself.'

Grey was now ready to go. Arrangements were being made at No. 10
for his departure. He wrote to the Princess: 'My life for the last
eight months has been one of such unhappiness as nobody can imagine.
. . . I feel, deeply feel, for the difficulties of the King and the country.'

A few days later, on 14th July, he assembled what remained of his
Cabinet. It was their last meeting. As the majority were against him,
it was decided that one of them should go and see the King at Windsor
and ask to be allowed to form a new Government.

The choice fell on Lord Melbourne. Though as Home Secretary he
was responsible for the direction of Irish Affairs and had himself been
Chief Secretary of Ireland in Canning's Government only a few years

---

* Sir James Graham, First Lord of the Admiralty.

before, he had adopted a lazy detachment towards what was going on in Ireland, and, if anything, had sympathized with Grey's attitude. Nevertheless, he was regarded by the others as a suitable successor to the Prime Minister. He hesitated a little. It would mean more work, there would be less time for his normal diversions. But he accepted and the next day set out for Windsor.

CHAPTER 23
Melbourne, then Peel

LORD MELBOURNE, well connected and extremely wealthy, was at fifty-five one of the younger men in the Cabinet. It was his colleagues' conviction that, with him as leader, they should the more easily jettison the repressive policy they had found distasteful, invite Althorp to rejoin the Government as Chancellor of the Exchequer and Leader of the House of Commons, and take steps to satisfy some at least of the demands of Daniel O'Connell and his irate Irish supporters.

The Melbourne family fortune had been amassed by his grandfather, Sir Matthew Lamb, a lawyer who was suspected of not always being scrupulous. The peerage had been acquired by Melbourne's father for being a consistent supporter of Lord North; but there was great doubt as to whether the first Lord Melbourne, Peniston Lamb, was in fact his father, for the lovely, flirtatious Lady Melbourne had numerous admirers, the Prince of Wales (later the Regent) among them. Of her Byron, whose love affair with the younger Lord Melbourne's wife, Lady Caroline Lamb, caused a scandal, said: 'If she had been a few years younger, what a fool she would have made of me.' He likened her morals to those of the notorious Athenian courtesan Aspasia. It was generally believed that Melbourne's actual father was George Wyndham, the third Earl of Egremont, whom he indeed strongly resembled. Wyndham was a member of one of the most distinguished families of the eighteenth century, closely related to the Grenvilles and through them to the Pitts.

Melbourne had many great qualities, but he seemed to be far more interested in the social round than in politics. His mother entertained lavishly. At Melbourne House in Whitehall, which is now Dover House, there were delightful distractions in the evenings, from which young William Lamb escaped only to find similar diversions at Devonshire House, Holland House, and Carlton House, where the Regent lived. Nevertheless, in 1806, having some months before become the heir on the death of his elder brother, he entered Parliament and attached himself to the Whig Prime Minister Lord Grenville. He had just married the tempestuous Lady Caroline, a disturbing alliance which he allowed to drag on for twenty years. It was not until after this ended that he was able to accept ministerial office, though it had been offered before. He served as Chief Secretary for Ireland in Canning's Government, retained the post during the brief Administration of Goderich and also after Wellington took over, but resigned together with the rest of the Canningites when it became clear that Wellington's policy was to be completely Tory.

The King did not like him, but agreed to accept him as Prime Minister only because he liked the others still less. He had thought of appointing Lord Lansdowne, but Lansdowne declined, and Melbourne embarked upon his duties convinced that he would find them 'a damned bore'.

When Grey moved out of Downing Street, Melbourne showed no disposition to move in. He preferred to remain on in his far more comfortable house in South Street. No. 10 was left untenanted, but Cabinet meetings, it is thought, continued to be held there because of the many offices where the Cabinet papers were kept and because of its nearness to the Houses of Parliament. The drawing-rooms may also have been used for political receptions, but of this there is no certainty, since Melbourne's tenure of office was short. It lasted barely four months. Melbourne indeed was surprised that it lasted so long. His interviews with the King were long and painful. Nor did he get on with the Queen. He found his colleagues in the Cabinet trying. One of them, Lord Lansdowne, was annoyed that two of his friends had not been given office; Lord John Russell wanted Daniel O'Connell in the Government in order to ease the Irish situation. And though Melbourne liked his Foreign Secretary Palmerston personally, he was uneasy about his eagerness to intervene in other nations' disputes and to take the side of the people against their autocratic rulers. Melbourne was an old-fashioned Whig and resented the way one wing of the Party kept on espousing reform. It was his conviction, born doubtless of his indolence, that natural and economic laws could, if given time, set everything right. Poverty, for example, he believed could only be solved by allowing the forces of supply and demand to take their course. For this reason he refused as Home Secretary to consider a scheme put before him in 1831 for relieving the distress of agricultural labourers by settling them on waste lands as smallholders. Steps of that kind he regarded as dangerous bureaucratic innovations. The Factory Acts fell into this category; but he felt sorry enough for the children working for long hours in trying conditions to stretch out a helping hand to them, and readily sponsored the alleviating Bill in the House of Lords. Similarly the rapid growth of trade unions disturbed him greatly. After the Reform Act of 1832 the working classes, finding that many of them were still without the vote and that their condition was really no better, turned to the unions, which seemed to Melbourne to be multiplying rapidly and spreading from the towns to the smallest country districts. A plan was even being furthered to unite them into one great organization, with political as well as economic aims. This frightened Melbourne. It smelt of revolution and he was old enough to remember the havoc that was caused in France. That was why he came down heavily against the new trade union at Tolpuddle in Dorset and imposed the severe penalty of seven years transportation upon its chief members. This led to fresh trouble with Lord John Russell, who was in sympathy with the Tolpuddle Martyrs. But by far the most troublesome of the Ministers was Lord Brougham, who had expected to be Prime Minister and never ceased to attack his Cabinet colleagues in his public speeches.

Outwardly Melbourne appeared to be unperturbed by all this. He went his amorous round, seeing a great deal of the beautiful Mrs. Caroline Norton,★ who still lived with her husband, and less frequently the virtuous Miss Emily Eden, the sister of Lord Auckland. But inwardly he was depressed. It added greatly to his despondency when on the night of 16th October 1834 he saw the Houses of Parliament in flames. For him the vast fire marked the passing of the age to which he belonged. The setting of Pitt's triumphs, of Fox's eloquence, of so many of England's dramatic debates and historic decisions perished in the conflagration. *The Times* described it with a complete lack of feeling and dwelt with delight on the new buildings, large and well ventilated, that would take their place. Nobody in fact seemed very concerned about the loss. The King arrived with the Queen to gaze at the ruins and, as has been recorded by Sir John Hobhouse (later Lord Broughton), 'looked gratified, as if at a show'. His Majesty suggested that Buckingham Palace should be the new meeting place of Parliament. His look of gratification, Hobhouse felt, may have been prompted 'by the prospect of getting rid of Buckingham Palace. Just before getting into his carriage he called the Speaker and me to him and said, "Mind, I mean Buckingham Palace as a permanent gift! Mind that." '[108]

The King had changed a great deal in the four years since his accession. Though still the breezy sailor, he no longer wandered about the streets followed by a large crowd who jostled and pushed him familiarly. The Queen had succeeded in restraining him to some extent, but she had been quite unable to stop him sticking his head out of the State Coach to spit while out on a royal occasion, with the Horse Guards bobbing in front and the crowds cheering from the pavements. He had also greatly modified his democratic outlook since the alarming disturbances, the rioting, the stones thrown at his carriage, before the Reform Act was finally passed. He became nervous and jumpy and was in a constant state of panic. By now suspicious of the Whigs, he began to bombard each of the Ministers with complaints and advice. He insisted that workmen should not be allowed to combine. Melbourne, irritated by all this, sent off-hand, facetious, often ironical replies and sometimes wondered if this wasn't the worst of his trials.

★ A granddaughter of Richard Brinsley Sheridan, the playwright and politician.

In the autumn Lord Althorp had to leave the House of Commons on the death of his father Earl Spencer and go to the Lords. The Government thus lost its brilliantly able Leader of the Lower House. Melbourne, in two minds about resigning, went down to Brighton to see the King. But the King anticipated him. After dinner in the Pavilion His Majesty said quite abruptly: 'By the way, Lord Spencer is dead, I hear. So is the Government, of course: where the head is dead the body cannot go on at all. Therefore there is no help for it, you must all resign. Here, my Lord, is a letter I have written to the Duke of Wellington, directing him to form a Government: be sure you give it to him, directly you arrive in town.'

Melbourne, despite his earlier thought that he might be better out of it, was taken aback by the King's autocratic manner. Feeling he owed it to his Party to avoid this ignominious dismissal, Melbourne suggested that Lord John Russell should succeed Althorp as Leader of the House of Commons. The King instantly flared up; he always did when the name of 'that young man' was mentioned. His dislike of Russell was so strong that he said of him: 'If you will answer for his death, I will answer for his damnation.'

Until late that night and all through the next day, the Prime Minister kept suggesting possible adjustments in the Government. But the King was not prepared to accept any of them. Melbourne returned to London late in the evening, his rule as First Lord of the Treasury at an end. It was the last time an English Sovereign exercised the prerogative of dismissing Ministers.

The Cabinet were surprised and indignant when they learned the news. His Majesty's high-handed manner merely confirmed Melbourne's view that the King 'had not the feelings of a gentleman'. But he put on his usual air of calm and expressed his complete indifference as to what had happened, and later wrote to Miss Eden: 'I have always considered complaints of ill usage contemptible, whether from a seduced, disappointed girl or a turned-out Prime Minister.'

The Duke of Wellington, meanwhile, was with the King. He told His Majesty that Peel should be asked to take over the chief office, but offered to hold the fort until Peel's return from Italy, where he was wintering with his wife and daughter. To Wellington, holding the fort meant taking over personally all the principal offices in the Government. Greville describes the meeting of the Privy Council at which the Duke kissed hands as First Lord of the Treasury. He was then sworn in as Secretary of State for the Home Department. His Grace 'came round, and after much fumbling for his spectacles, took the oath. . . .' The King then resumed: 'It is likewise necessary for me to dispose of the seals of the other two Secretaries of State and I therefore place them likewise for the present in the same hands.' When the swearing in was at an end Wellington instantly 'repaired to the Home Office and ordered the Irish papers to be brought to him, then to the Foreign Office, where he asked for the last dispatches from Spain and Portugal, and so on to the Colonial Office, where he required information as to the state of their department.'[79]

The outgoing Ministers, unaware of the wide powers conferred on the Duke, were startled to see him stride into their offices and take possession, as though the positions had just been captured from the enemy. Wellington brushed aside their protests. 'The complaint of incivility', he said, 'is a very good one *ad captandum*, but it is better to be uncivil than absurd. . . . Nobody is the worse off for what is doing except myself, who am worked as no post-horse at Hounslow ever was.'[106]

A messenger was at once dispatched to Peel, who returned from Rome with as much speed as he could. It nevertheless necessitated Wellington ruling the country as supreme panjandrum for a full three weeks. On surrendering his numerous seals he was persuaded by Peel to retain the office of Foreign Secretary.

Peel's authority as Prime Minister was weak and unenviable. His Party, Conservatives as they now called themselves, were a small minority in the House of Commons, greatly outnumbered by the Whigs, the Radicals and the Irish, who could together drive them out of office at any moment they chose. He had been placed in this unpleasant situation by the arbitrary action of the King, and admitted later: 'Had it been possible that I should have been consulted previously, I might have dissuaded the act of dismissal as premature and impolitic.'

He had to do the best he could. He tried to strengthen his position by inviting Stanley and Graham, both of whom had resigned from

238

The house at the back (the large building on the right) *circa* 1677, with Charles II and his courtiers walking in the Mall. To this house No. 10 Downing Street was joined later. From an oil painting ascribed to Thomas van Wyck.

No. 10 Downing Street, with its walled garden, seen from St. James's Park in 1827. From a water-colour by J. C. Buckler. *In the Cruse collection, British Museum.*

There was no access from Downing Street to St. James's Park when this water-colour sketch by J. C. Buckler was made in 1827. The cul-de-sac at this end was known as Downing Square. The first door on the right is the front door of No. 10. No. 12, at the end of the row, has now been restored, and once again has a doorway at the corner. But the other house, forming the square, and where Wellington and Nelson met for the only time, no longer exists.

The famous front door of what appears from Downing Street to be a small, unimpressive house, showing the lion's head knocker and the swirl of ironwork holding up a lantern surmounted by a crown.

The other side of the front door – the entrance hall. A long corridor links this hall with the Cabinet Room at the far end of the house.

Grey's recent Government and were far closer to his political outlook than Russell, for example. But they refused to be in the same Government as Wellington. 'In a querulous tone,' Croker records, Peel had accordingly to resign himself to the fact that it 'would only be the Duke's old Cabinet.' Nevertheless, he brought in some very young men, the eldest of them only twenty-five years old: these included Gladstone, Sidney Herbert, Edward Cardwell and Canning's young son, who was later Viceroy of India, all of whom were to make their mark later. But neither the House of Commons nor the country were impressed.

Like his predecessor, Peel declined to live at No. 10 Downing Street, but stayed on in his own house in Whitehall Gardens, which was just round the corner. He continued, however, to use the Cabinet room, where he had first sat as Secretary for Ireland under Liverpool nearly a quarter of a century before.

But the house did not remain untenanted, as it had been during the four months Melbourne was Prime Minister. Into it moved Sir Thomas Fremantle, one of the secretaries of the Treasury. He came of a distinguished naval family. His father, also Sir Thomas, had served with Nelson in a number of famous actions, was with him in *Seahorse* during the night landing at Santa Cruz when Nelson lost his arm, and had participated in the glorious victory at Trafalgar. The year before that battle he was married in Lady Hamilton's drawing-room in Naples. The son of that marriage was only thirty-seven when he moved into No. 10. He had been given a baronetcy at the remarkably early age of twenty-three and was by now a Conservative Member of Parliament. With him in the house were his wife, the daughter of Field-Marshal Sir George Nugent, and their nine children, the eldest of whom was not quite ten. Sir Thomas was small in stature like his father, and known as 'the pocket Apollo' because of his strikingly handsome appearance. Forty years later he was given a peerage by Disraeli and became Lord Cottesloe.

The family lived at No. 10 for only four months, for they had to move out when Peel's Government fell; but the brief stay supplies a loose link with the town of Fremantle in Western Australia, named after his uncle Admiral Sir Charles Fremantle, who, on arriving there with the first emigrant ships, took possession in the name of the

King in 1829, five years before the family moved into Downing Street.

With his position in the House so utterly hopeless, Peel decided to dissolve Parliament and appeal to the country. There was just the possibility that it might lead to an increase in the number of his supporters. Many were dubious of this and argued that it would have been wiser to face the House as Pitt had done when similarly situated: the country, disgusted by the persistent hostility of his opponents, gave Pitt an overwhelming majority. Peel declared that his own position was very different. His opponents had not discredited themselves as Fox and North had done in 1784.

Peel, in his appeal to the voters, broke away from the die-hard Toryism of the past and launched the policy of the new Conservative Party, with the promise of a moderate but slow reform. Some of his Ministers did not like it, but it roused the country. He almost doubled the number of his supporters, but did not obtain a majority, and so continued to be at the mercy of his opponents. Again and again the Government was defeated – six times indeed in six weeks. Lord John Russell, Leader of the Opposition in the Commons, waged an unremitting war, and had the full support of Daniel O'Connell and the Irish members. It seemed to Greville that the attitude of the Opposition was: 'The King exercised his prerogative in a most extraordinary and unjustifiable manner. We have the same right to reject his Government, that he had to turn out ours; if there is embarrassment, it is none of our creating, the King and the Tories must be responsible for it.'[79]

Among Peel's most hostile critics were many members of his own Party, particularly those ultra-Tories who had been ignored when offices were handed out. By March, Peel realized that he could not carry on much longer. Wellington urged him to go on fighting. But a succession of defeats – on 2nd April by 33 votes, on the 6th by 25 and on the 7th by 37 – led at last to Peel resigning on 8th April 1835.

For some days the King took no action whatsoever. On 13th April, five days after his resignation, Peel wrote to Croker: 'I received a note from the King about seven yesterday evening, requesting me to facilitate an adjournment until Thursday next, for the purpose of promoting the arrangements connected with the formation of a new Government. I understand that Lord Melbourne is to be at the head. . . . I presume the Government will be as nearly as possible that which was dismissed in November last.'[74]

The King was far from pleased at having his hand forced. Greville noted: 'He abhors all his ministers'; His Majesty, he added, was 'in dreadfully low spirits' and constantly in tears. His crown, he wailed, was 'tottering' on his head. A great constitutional principle had been 'at stake', and the Whigs, as the victims, won in the end.

The King sent for Melbourne again. This time, despite his reduced numbers in the House, Melbourne was to remain in office for more than six years. Again he preferred to live in his own house in South Street. He used to mount his horse and ride to Downing Street for Cabinet meetings at No. 10, and then ride on to the House of Commons, which now met in Westminster Hall, the only part of the old Parliament buildings still standing. The rebuilding of the two Houses was begun in 1840 by Sir Charles Barry and it took more than twenty years to complete.

But the residential quarters at No. 10 were not left unoccupied. Two of Melbourne's secretaries, working in offices alongside the Cabinet room, moved into the bedrooms and sitting-rooms above and made use of the kitchen. One of the two was married, the other a bachelor and they appear to have lived in perfect amity under the same roof. The bachelor was Melbourne's nephew, his sister Emily's younger son, the Hon. William Francis Cowper. He was twenty-three and had just been elected M.P. for Hertford. Through his father he was descended from a Lord High Chancellor, the first Earl Cowper. It is a little startling to discover that the Lord High Chancellor's brother, Spencer Cowper,* was tried for murder, and more surprising still that he later became a judge in the English courts. A further link of interest is that young Cowper's mother had for years been in love with Lord Palmerston, whom she later married, and Palmerston made this son his heir, whose name then became Cowper-Temple.

Though unmarried when he moved into No. 10, Cowper was not wholly unattached. He appears to have had the family's propensity for falling in love, but with it, unlike the rest of his family, he combined 'a fervent Victorian piety'.[110] His life must have been extremely

---

* Spencer Cowper's grandson was the poet William Cowper.

crowded, for in addition to his secretarial, parliamentary and amorous activities, interspersed as they must have been with many social diversions and religious observances, he had also as a member of the Royal Horse Guards to fulfil his military duties.

He enjoyed the full confidence of his uncle the Prime Minister, who, when King William the Fourth died in 1837, finding that he would have to spend a great deal of time with the young and inexperienced Queen Victoria, who was only eighteen, decided to be more circumspect in his private life, for only a few months before he had been involved in a divorce suit over Mrs. Caroline Norton. They had been seeing each other almost every day for five years, and were often alone for hours together either in her house or in his. However innocent the association may have been, it roused much censorious comment, partly because of his flirtatious reputation, but largely because of her licentious talk and outrageous behaviour. Lord Malmesbury records: 'Met Mrs. Norton at the French Ambassador's. She talked in a most extraordinary manner and kicked Lord Melbourne's hat over her head.' In April 1836 Mr. Norton turned his wife out of his house and sent his children to live with his relations. Melbourne, having earlier selected him to be a police court magistrate, now described him as 'a stupid brute'. Mrs. Norton he found not at all easy to manage now. He advised her to try and be calm, but she rounded on him with explosive fury, calling him cold and selfish. Melbourne was reminded unpleasantly of the other, equally excitable Caroline who had been his wife. When the case began he had but recently started his second term as Prime Minister. He thought of resigning, for he was aware of the damage the case would do to his Party – many indeed thought that the case had been maliciously inspired by the Tories to discredit the Government. As the date of the trial approached Melbourne became ill through worry. He need not have been anxious, for only three letters from him were produced in court and they were brief and noncommittal. One of them merely stated: 'How are you? I shall not be able to come today. I shall tomorrow.' Norton's counsel insisted that these words concealed far more than they revealed. His argument inspired the hilarious court scene in Dickens' famous Bardell v. Pickwick case in *The Pickwick Papers*. The jury acquitted Melbourne without leaving the box.

Relieved, he began imprudently to see Mrs. Norton again, but after the Queen's accession he felt he would have to be careful. So that Mrs. Norton should not feel neglected, he got his nephew William Cowper to keep in touch with her whenever he himself could not. In scolding letters she poured out her rage and her scorn and scarcely veiled her acute jealousy of the Queen. 'Your uncle has walked over from Storey's Gate to Buckingham Palace and pursues the same course with her as with me. . . . If he thinks I can be brought to bear tamely what the Royal Girl considers a fit punishment for me to being her predecessor in the long conversations which take place at her palace, I can't help it.'

Melbourne, with his much wider experience, tried to guide his nephew through his own romantic affairs. 'My dear William,' he wrote, 'I think you are quite right not to engage further in these affairs without the certainty of an adequate provision, and I am glad that you find a consolation in St. Paul's epistle to the Corinthians. But you must not run about flirting with girls and persuading them that you intend to marry, unless you have the intention. St. Paul would not approve of this. Indeed, would he like to think his epistles made the instruments of flirtation?'

Cowper stayed at No. 10 Downing Street until Melbourne, despite his reluctance to give up office, finally resigned in 1841. Two years later, his uncle's counsel bore fruit. Cowper, now in his early thirties, married the beautiful Harriet Gurney, but his happiness was short-lived: she died two months later. Not until five years afterwards did he marry again.

During his uncle's last months as Prime Minister, Cowper was given office as a junior Lord of the Treasury. Unencumbered by his uncle's lethargy, he plunged into his work with an industry that was unflagging. Later in life his interest in education and in the preservation of open spaces brought him immense responsibility and he was rewarded with a peerage; in his title of Lord Mount-Temple he enshrined Palmerston's family name.

The other secretary living at the same time at No. 10 was George Anson. He was a year or two younger and married, but Boyle's Court Guide does not list his wife as living in the house with him until the following year, 1839. Anson was a cousin of the Earl of Lichfield and so was connected with King Charles the Second's illegitimate daughter, Lady Charlotte Fitzroy who, it will be recalled, on her marriage to the first Earl came to live in the rear section of the house where the Cabinet room is. The Ansons moved out a year later, in 1840, on his appointment as private secretary to Prince Albert, Queen Victoria's fiancé. The Prince (seven years Anson's junior) was at the time only twenty, the Queen three months older. Though so very young, Her Majesty already had both a will and a temper. Her uncle, King Leopold of Belgium, who was also Albert's uncle, had sent the young Prince and his elder brother to England three years before in the hope that the Queen might marry one of them. But neither of the Princes made any impression on her. Albert came again two years later, alone this time, and the Queen fell passionately in love with him. She confided to her diary that he was 'beautiful', but was resolved, nevertheless, that he would have to submit to her, because she was Queen.

While the Prince was being groomed in England as her Consort, Melbourne suggested that Anson should be his secretary. Albert objected. He preferred to make his own choice, he said; besides Anson had already served Melbourne and his secretary, he insisted, should be completely free of any political alliance. The Queen, however, put her foot down and Anson was appointed. In fact the Queen chose the Prince's entire Household without even consulting him. He pleaded: 'Is it not even to be conceded to me that two or three persons, who are to have the charge of my private affairs, shall be persons who already command my confidence?' She refused to grant him this concession.

The Prince had seen Anson only once, dancing a quadrille. But the appointment proved to be a most fortunate one for Prince Albert. The Queen's resolve to exclude him from all political talks was firmly observed after their marriage. Melbourne cunningly contrived a way round it and kept the Prince fully informed through Anson. After a time, desiring to drop this circuitous procedure, Melbourne had a frank discussion with the Queen. He learned that Her Majesty's one fear was that political discussions might lead to disagreements and she wanted to avoid that in her home. Melbourne pointed out that disagreements were far less dangerous than secretiveness, since secretiveness led eventually to distrust. And so the position was adjusted.

Baron Stockmar, King Leopold of Belgium's confidential adviser,

wrote to the Prince: 'I have had much talk with Anson; he seems an
excellent fellow and sincerely devoted to you.' In the summer of 1841
Anson took on a fresh role as go-between. Melbourne's position in
Parliament had never been secure. His Party was virtually in a minority
in the Commons, where his own right wing was against him and he
dared not yield to them because of pressure from the left and the
Radicals. To remain in power he had to rely mainly on the Irish. In the
House of Lords the position was even worse. The House was solidly
against him, and Brougham, his former Lord Chancellor, but now left
out of the Government, never ceased to cause trouble. The Opposition,
fortunately, was similarly divided. Peel had to contend with the unyielding hostility of the 'ultras', as the reactionary Tories were called,
with Wellington the most vigorous of his critics: in the circumstances
Peel preferred to keep Melbourne in power until the wind changed. It
was only by trimming his policy, yielding a little to the right, then a
little to the left, that Melbourne was able to carry on for so long. He
tackled the Irish tithes question early. A large part of the money was
diverted from the established Anglican church and used for general
education. He also brought in the Municipal Corporations Bill, the
corollary of the Reform Act, for most of the older municipalities were
corrupt, self-elected and therefore not at all responsible to the towns-
people, while the new industrial towns such as Birmingham were
without any municipality. Both these measures were hotly contested
but they got through eventually. In April 1839, quite unexpectedly, the
Government was saved from defeat by merely five votes. Melbourne
decided to resign. When he called on the Queen to say goodbye, her
distress was so acute that neither could speak. She just held his hands in
hers and burst into sobs, saying 'You will not forsake me?' to which,
his own eyes brimming with tears, he replied 'Oh, no.' His devotion to
her made him stay on.

Two years later, in the summer of 1841, defeated this time on the
Budget, Melbourne decided to appeal to the country. The General
Election brought in the Conservatives with a comfortable majority,
and on 28th August, after a further defeat in the House of Commons,
he announced his resignation. The Queen was again distressed and shed
some tears, for she had come to rely on Melbourne, but she had no
alternative now except to let him go. He reassured her by saying that

she had Prince Albert to lean on. He 'understands everything so well, he has such a clear, able head. . . . When you married him you said that he was perfection, which I thought a little overrated, but I really think now that it is in some degree realized.' He liked teasing her about the Prince. When she confided during their engagement that Albert was not interested in other women, Melbourne replied with a twinkle: 'That will come later.' But the Queen was outraged and he withdrew the remark.

Saying goodbye now, she confessed that she was most reluctant to have Peel as her Prime Minister and she begged to be allowed to turn to Melbourne for advice. Melbourne, realizing that this would be quite unconstitutional, suggested that perhaps occasionally the Queen might talk over her problems with Prince Albert, who could then talk of them to Anson, who in his turn would ask Melbourne for his advice. But this the Queen firmly refused to accept. She must be in touch with Lord Melbourne direct, she said. She was only too conscious of the trouble she had with Peel when he so nearly succeeded Melbourne in 1839. He had demanded then that some of the ladies in the Royal Household should be dismissed because of their Whig connections, and had been backed up in this by the Duke of Wellington. She had, of course, refused angrily. 'The Queen maintains *all* her ladies,' she wrote to Melbourne.

But now she would have to put up with Peel. She had found him cold, stiff, awkward and ill at ease. 'Oh! How different, how dreadfully different to that frank, open, natural and most kind warm manner of Lord Melbourne.' In fact she had to put up with Peel for five years. But Melbourne, with his touching solicitude for her, told Anson to ask Peel to be patient and not too hasty with her.

As before Peel declined to live at No. 10 Downing Street, preferring his house in Whitehall Gardens. Both Cowper and Anson had already vacated No. 10, Anson only a few months before; and early in 1842 Peel's secretary, Edward Drummond, moved in. The son of a rich banker, Drummond had served as secretary to three earlier Prime Ministers – Goderich (now Ripon), Canning and Wellington. He was now fifty and still a bachelor. He had been sharing a house in Lower Grosvenor Street with his sister, and even after moving in he often spent a night or two there, possibly because he found it more companionable and comfortable. But his long association with No. 10, which went back to the eighteen-twenties, and the fact that he had his office there with the papers Peel would require for meetings of the Cabinet, made it certainly more convenient for him to live in Downing Street, a facility denied him when he served the three earlier Prime Ministers.

He did not, however, live there for long. Four months after moving in, while he was walking along Whitehall to No. 10 from Drummond's Bank at Charing Cross, of which his brother was the head, he was shot in the street. He died a few days later.

The assassin was Daniel Macnaghten, a young half-crazy Irishman who, it emerged, mistook Drummond for Peel. Macnaghten had been watching the official residence of the Prime Minister for more than two weeks and seeing Drummond, who was almost Peel's age, using it as his home, concluded that he was Peel. Indeed Drummond was often amused by the idea that he used to be mistaken for Peel. Greville records in his diary that Drummond frequently went about in Peel's carriage. 'I well remember his telling me this, and laughing at the idea of his having been taken for a great man.'[79]

All England was shocked by the news – 'one of the most unaccountable crimes that ever was committed', writes Greville. Drummond, he adds, 'was as good and inoffensive a man as ever lived, who could have had no enemy, and who was not conspicuous enough to have become the object of hatred or vengeance to any class of persons, being merely the officer of Sir Robert Peel, and never saying or doing anything but in his name.' It was later recalled that 'for many days before the murder', Macnaghten had been seen 'prowling about the purlieus of Downing Street, and the Duke of Buccleuch told me [Greville] that the day he [Peel] was expected in town, and when his servants were looking out for him, they observed this man, though it was a rainy day, loitering about near his gate, which is close to Peel's house. If, therefore, he saw, as he must have done, Drummond constantly passing between Peel's house and Downing Street, and recognizing in him the same person he had seen in the carriage in Scotland, and whom he believed to be Peel, he would think himself so sure of his man as to make it unnecessary to ask any questions, and the very consciousness of his own intentions might make him afraid to do so. This appears to afford a probable solution of the mystery.'[79]

Peel was hated by a large number of people, many of them members of his own Party. He had begun of late to flirt with the idea of adopting Free Trade, a policy beloved of his opponents the Whigs, and Lord Alvanley had exclaimed that Peel 'ought not to die a natural death'. It is not clear what Macnaghten's actual grievance was. All he mumbled as a policeman seized him after the murder was: 'He shall not disturb my mind any longer.' As an Irish Protestant, he was, of course, opposed to any further concessions being made to the Catholics and he was obsessed by the idea that the Pope and the Jesuits were also conspiring against him.

Queen Victoria wrote of the tragedy to her Uncle Leopold in Belgium: 'Poor Drummond is universally regretted. . . . People can hardly think of anything else.' And again a few days later: 'Poor Lady Peel has been very ill from this last terrible event, and no wonder.' Peel died seven years later after a fall from his horse. Thus was Lord Alvanley's cruel hope fulfilled.

At Macnaghten's trial in March that year, 1843, eight medical witnesses declared that, owing to his delusions, Macnaghten was deprived of all responsibility for his actions; and the judges, who included Lord Chief Justice Coleridge, endorsed this view, stating that 'if under the influence of his delusion he supposes another man to be in the act of attempting to take away his life, and he kills that man, as he supposes, in self-defence, he would be exempt from punishment.' Macnaghten was accordingly found 'not guilty by reason of insanity' and was sent to Bethlehem Hospital and later to Broadmoor Criminal Lunatic Asylum, where he died twenty-two years later.

This judicial approval of the doctrine of partial insanity was hotly debated in the House of Lords. Questions were put to the judges concerned and their answers have come to be known as 'The Rules in Macnaghten's case', which are still basically the law of England on the criminal responsibility of the insane.

To replace Drummond as his secretary, Peel appointed Mr. George Arbuthnot, the son of Lieutenant-General Sir Robert Arbuthnot, and in the following year he moved into No. 10. He shared the house with Mr. W. H. Stephenson, who had moved in not long after Drummond's death. Both remained there until Peel's resignation in 1846.

During his five-year ministry, his second and last as Prime Minister,

Peel had to direct his attention to dealing with the spreading distress in the country. There had been bad harvests for two years and a severe trade depression, leading once again to unemployment, hunger and general unrest. In 1839 the Anti-Corn Law League had been set up and at mass meetings, attended by the enlightened middle classes as well as the hungry workers, the cry was raised for the removal of duties that prevented the free import of corn, sugar and other food. The duty on corn, imposed immediately after the Napoleonic wars to protect the interest of landowners and farmers, came in for the sharpest attack. Huskisson, killed by a railway engine some years before, had favoured the idea of Free Trade, but the Whigs were not then prepared to adopt it. Melbourne, however, confronted by fresh disturbances in 1840, allowed his Chancellor of the Exchequer, Francis Baring, to reduce the duty on sugar and toyed with the idea of reducing the duty on corn, saying casually just as the Ministers were dispersing after a Cabinet meeting: 'By the by, there is one thing we haven't agreed upon, which is what we are to say. Is it to make corn dearer, or cheaper, or to make the price steady? I don't care which; but we had better all be in the same story.' But pressure from Lord John Russell and other colleagues eventually made Melbourne agree to reduce it. It was left to Peel, his successor, to deal with it. Further bad harvests had followed. 'The Hungry Forties' was the term applied to those lean years. Peel faced the crisis with decision and courage. Once again he had to withdraw from his earlier firm stand, for, as with Catholic emancipation, he had always insisted that the Corn Laws must be maintained.

There were many angry quarrels round the Cabinet table at No. 10 on this issue. To begin with, Peel merely lowered the duty on imported corn. The Duke of Buckingham resigned at once. Three years later, in 1845, when the potato crop failed in Ireland and there was still another bad harvest in England, the complete repeal of the Corn Laws was again discussed. Both Lord Stanley and the Duke of Buccleugh declined to support it. Peel instantly resigned, but was induced to carry on because no successor could be found. Stanley refused to remain any longer in his Government. In June of the following year (1846) after a long and fierce debate in the House, the 'repeal', as it has been called, was finally carried – but it was not either an immediate or even a total repeal: not until 1849 was the duty to be reduced to a shilling. The battle was won with Peel's support of his political opponents; from many of his former friends he had to suffer taunts and sneers. But the Duke of Wellington, changing his mind on this as he had on Catholic emancipation, steered the Bill carefully through the Lords, but on the very night it was carried there, Peel was defeated in the Commons on a measure that had nothing whatsoever to do with the Corn Laws.* The Protectionists in his own Party, led by Lord George Bentinck (son of the Duke of Portland) and by Benjamin Disraeli, in a show of their intense anger, joined forces with the Whigs and defeated Peel on an Irish Coercion Bill by a majority of 73. Disraeli, the architect of Peel's fall, has himself described the scene in the House: 'The flower of that great party which had been so proud to follow one who was so proud to lead them. . . . They trooped on. . . . Sir Robert looked very grave. . . . He began to comprehend his position, and that the Emperor was without an army.'

Peel walked from the House escorted by a large crowd, who respectfully took off their hats as he reached No. 10. Shortly afterwards he resigned.

His successor as Prime Minister was the Leader of the Opposition Lord John Russell, who had taken it over after Melbourne's decline in health. Russell preferred to stay on in his own house, 32 Chesham Place, but three of his secretaries now moved into No. 10; their names are given in Boyle's Court Guide for 1847 as 'Lieut.-Colonel the Hon. George Keppel, the Hon. Chas. S. Grey and the Hon. R. W. Grey.'

* 25th June 1846.

CHAPTER 24
Used only for Offices

THAT Peel had been using No. 10 Downing Street not only for Cabinet meetings but also for the official business of the Prime Minister is borne out by the letter he wrote to the Queen on that fateful night of 25th June from Downing Street. It was marked 'Two o'clock' – that is to say, two o'clock in the morning, for it was written after a prolonged discussion by the Cabinet, at which it was decided that Peel and the Government should give up the struggle and let the Whigs take it on. Four days later Peel went to Osborne in the Isle of Wight and tendered his resignation personally to the Queen.

Of Lord John Russell's secretaries the use of the prefix 'The Hon.' for both the Greys would suggest that they were the sons of Earl Grey, the former Prime Minister, but this is not so in either case. Ralph William Grey was in no way related, though it is possible that he was a kinsman because of his link with Northumberland where the Earl lived. He had served in Canada, where two armed rebellions had broken out shortly after Queen Victoria's accession in 1837. Melbourne had to deal with them and he sent out Lord Durham, Earl Grey's son-in-law, with whom the Earl had so much trouble while Prime Minister and with whom Melbourne could not get on either. Many said he chose Durham only to get him out of the way and thus end his consistent sniping against the Government, composed though it was of his own Party and included his brother-in-law, Grey's heir Lord Howick, as Secretary at War. It could not, however, be denied that Durham had outstanding ability and he dealt with the situation out there not only with firmness but with remarkable foresight. Canada, a colony at the time, had been divided by Pitt nearly fifty years before into two provinces – Upper Canada, which was populated mainly by English Protestants with mercantile interests, and Lower Canada which was almost wholly French, consisting of Catholics engaged chiefly in agriculture. Both rebelled against the ruling British officials appointed by Whitehall. It did not take long to put down the rebellion of the English settlers; the French were much more difficult to deal with as they wanted to break away and set up an independent French Republic. Durham, arriving as Governor-General after the first of the rebellions had been settled, turned his attention to the second. He banished some of the French ringleaders without trial, was censured severely by the authorities at home and resigned in a rage, after being in the country for only five months. But the recommendations in his Report, which advocated the grant of responsible self-government, laid the foundations of the British Commonwealth of Nations. He argued that, far from loosening the bonds of empire, this would preserve its unity. But it was not until 1867 that Canada was finally freed from the control of the Colonial Office and made an independent Dominion – the first of Britain's possessions to achieve this status.

Ralph William Grey, after serving as secretary to Durham's successor in Canada, Lord Sydenham, became Lord John Russell's secretary and later served Lord Palmerston in the same capacity. On his death in October 1869 he was praised in *The Times* for his quickness of perception, accuracy of judgement, knowledge of character, amiable disposition, refined taste and his deep interest in archæology.

The Hon. Charles Grey, one of the nine sons of Earl Grey, was in the Army and went to Canada as a member of the staff of his brother-in-law Lord Durham. Later, after he had attained the rank of General, he was appointed Secretary to the Prince Consort and was after that Secretary to Queen Victoria. It was not he, but his cousin Charles Samuel Grey who lived at No. 10 at this time. A nephew of the former Prime Minister, he is described correctly in *The Times* of 11th July 1846, as 'Mr.', not 'The Hon.' The newspaper states that he had been secretary to Mr. Francis Baring, who, as Melbourne's Chancellor of the Exchequer in 1839, had taken the bold step of reducing many import duties and, more adventurously, adopted Rowland Hill's penny post in 1840 against the angry opposition of Lord Lichfield, the Postmaster-General, who thought that post office buildings would collapse when the vast tide of letters began to pour in.

The third of Russell's secretaries, George Thomas Keppel, was in his late forties when he moved in to share the upper rooms at No. 10 with the two Greys. In his autobiography[114] he describes how at the age of nine he met Princess Charlotte, the daughter of the Prince Regent and eventual successor to the throne had she lived. She got her porter to give Keppel half a guinea from time to time and told him: 'If you use that well and give me an exact account of how you spend it, I will give you something more.'

Keppel joined the Army, fought at Waterloo when he was only sixteen, and entered Paris 'barefooted and in rags'. For a time he was a Member of Parliament. Doubtless he lived at No. 10 with his wife and son, though he says nothing of this in his book. Shortly after vacating the house he succeeded his brother as the Earl of Albemarle.

Lord John Russell, despite the overwhelming social changes wrought by the Industrial Revolution and the political changes he had himself initiated, surprisingly for the middle of the nineteenth century, adopted the practice of the eighteenth century in the selection of his Cabinet, for more than half the Ministers were hereditary peers and the rest, like himself, were closely connected with the peerage; the Dukes of Bedford, to whose family he belonged, had controlled a substantial section of the House of Commons through their wealth and influence in the boroughs which Russell was responsible for abolishing by the Reform Act of 1832.

His Party was in a minority in the House of Commons when he took over and even after the General Election, though his following was increased, he had not an absolute majority. His position was in consequence insecure. Yet he managed to remain Prime Minister for close on six years.

Short in stature, with broad shoulders and a massive head, Russell had been a sickly child like the younger Pitt. His health was never robust. He had a drawn look and a pallor that betrayed the physical discomfort he suffered all through life. He never allowed this, however, to restrain his activities in any way. He went, for example, to Portugal during the Peninsular War and rode with Wellington at Torres Vedras. He visited Napoleon at Elba and had a long talk with the exiled Emperor. He knew Charles James Fox well, was one of his most ardent supporters, breakfasted often with him and later wrote his biography. He was fifty-four when he became Prime Minister.

As a speaker Russell was not impressive: his voice was weak, his accent sounded affected, at times even mincing, his delivery was hesitant and occasionally he stammered. But in retort he was swift and effective. A dedicated reformer, he added to his initial achievement of political reform, fresh triumphs during the years he presided over the Cabinet in Downing Street. Part of the 'Hungry Forties' fell within his term of office. He applied the policy of Free Trade with vigour, extending the reduction of duties to other imported commodities and was supported by Peel, though the Protectionists raged against him as against Peel. The year after he became Prime Minister the famine in Ireland led, it was estimated, to a million people dying of hunger, while a million more left for America in that and the succeeding years. Russell arranged for vast quantities of seed to be distributed to the suffering people, land was acquired and sold, or let, to the people in small lots and on easy terms.

Despite these admirable endeavours Russell was not much liked. He was careless about conciliating his Radical supporters. His supercilious manner and his impatience made him unpopular in the House of Commons. His colleagues in the Cabinet were not wholly for him. But by far his gravest problem was his Foreign Secretary, Lord Palmerston, who acted without consulting either the Prime Minister or the Cabinet, and sent notes to foreign powers, some of them stern and disapproving notes, at other times congratulatory notes, as when Napoleon the Third seized power and proclaimed himself Emperor of France in 1851. Of these actions the Queen repeatedly expressed the strongest disapproval. Following angry quarrels in the Cabinet room at No. 10, Russell finally, on the Queen's insistence, dismissed Palmerston in December 1851. His ministry did not survive this for long. Palmerston got his 'tit for tat', as he called it, barely two months later when he and his friends voted against the Government and brought about its defeat. Russell resigned at once and the Queen sent for Lord Stanley, who had on Peel's death in 1850 succeeded as Leader of the Opposition and on his father's death the year after had become the Earl of Derby.

Like his three predecessors Melbourne, Peel and Russell, Derby did not regard No. 10 as a desirable residence. He already had a far more comfortable house in St. James's Square and did not relish the tedium of transferring his furniture and his pictures, his linen and his silver to Downing Street. Nor did his Chancellor of the Exchequer, Benjamin Disraeli, now in his first, important office, choose to move into the house, but used instead, though only as an office, No. 11 next door, part of which had been bought for Treasury needs in 1805 and had been enlarged as recently as 1846. The upper rooms at No. 10, therefore, were left empty, for George Keppel had by now moved out and the house remained untenanted as a residence for thirty years. The Cabinet room downstairs, however, was used, as were also the adjoining offices for the secretaries and the immense files of papers.

Derby's was one of the richest families in England. Brought up in the Whig tradition, he had served under Canning and under Grey, and had refused to join the Duke of Wellington's Government. While in Grey's ministry his brilliant and fiery speeches contributed to the successful passing of the Reform Bill, and as Colonial Secretary in the following year, he put through the Bill for the abolition of the slave trade. But he quarrelled with Russell, his close associate in the Cabinet, over the appropriation by the State of a part of the Irish tithes and its use for the purpose of education. Indeed Grey's entire Cabinet was divided on this, and the dissension drew from Stanley (as he was then) the memorable exclamation: 'I always upset the coach!' Stanley resigned, severed his connection with the Whigs and joined the more progressive section of the Tories under Peel, then becoming known as Conservatives. Under Peel he served again as Colonial Secretary, but refused to go all the way with him on Free Trade and resigned over the repeal of the Corn Laws. He was invited by the Queen to succeed Peel, but declined because he had not sufficient support in the House, and the Whigs came in under

Russell. Twice in 1851 the Queen asked Stanley to take the helm, but not until the following year, at the fourth time of asking did he finally accept. Surprisingly, one of the first things he did now was to ask Palmerston, his Whig colleague in Grey's ministry, to join his Government, although it was because of Palmerston that the previous Government fell. Palmerston refused and Derby, with no worthwhile talent to turn to, proudly proclaimed that his Government contained only untried men, 'not one' of whom 'had ever been in harness before'. They included Disraeli, who was Leader of the House of Commons as well as Chancellor of the Exchequer. By the end of the year, however, having failed to gain a majority in the General Election, Derby resigned after being in office for only ten months.

His successor was the Earl of Aberdeen, an old-fashioned but not ultra Tory, now in his sixty-ninth year. He had lost both his parents by the age of eleven and was brought up under the guardianship of William Pitt. With him at Harrow were Palmerston and Althorp (later Lord Spencer), both Whigs. He had served as ambassador in Vienna towards the end of the Napoleonic war and as Foreign Secretary under Wellington and under Peel. His policy was the exact opposite of Palmerston's: he refused to interfere abroad and was insistent that the country must at all costs maintain peace.

On becoming Prime Minister in 1852 he formed an impressive coalition of Whigs and Peelites: the former included Russell and Palmerston, the most notable among the latter was young Gladstone, who became Chancellor of the Exchequer. The Queen had parted from Lord Derby without regret and, resenting his advice that Lansdowne should be his successor, had turned instead to Aberdeen. She was delighted that 'our excellent Aberdeen' had formed 'so brilliant and strong a Cabinet'. Most of the members had been in conflict with each other in the past; what united them now was that they were all in favour of Free Trade and moderate reform. 'England will occupy her true position', Aberdeen said, 'as the constant advocate of moderation and peace.' But the vehemence of Palmerston (not now at the Foreign Office, but at the Home Office) overbore Aberdeen's pacific views, and by supporting the Turks in their quarrel with Russia the country drifted into war in the Crimea.

Early in 1854 Aberdeen wrote to Russell, who was President of the

Council: 'I wish I could feel as much at ease on the subject of the unhappy war in which we are about to be engaged. The abstract justice of the cause, although indisputable, is but a poor consolation for the inevitable calamities of all war, or for a decision which I am not without fear may prove to have been impolitic and unwise. My conscience upbraids me the more because seeing, as I did from the first, all that was to be apprehended, it is possible that by a little more energy and vigour, not on the Danube, but in Downing Street, it might have been prevented.'

Not only was Aberdeen without enthusiasm for the war, his Cabinet were at loggerheads over it. The military preparations were haphazard, and Britain suffered in consequence a series of early reverses. Palmerston's persistent pleas for more energy and Russell's continuous criticism were without avail. Russell resigned in January 1855. A week later Aberdeen went too. Disraeli wrote of his term in office: 'The country was governed for two years by all its ablest men, who by the end of that term had succeeded by their coalesced genius in reducing that country to a state of desolation and despair.'[115]

Aberdeen, a dark, pale ageing man, was, despite his many gifts and his wide interests, too timid and hesitant to be effective as Prime Minister. He was a dull and ungraceful speaker. Had he succeeded in preserving peace he might have remained in office longer, but with the country clamouring for a more vigorous waging of the Crimean War, he had to go. He did not live at No. 10, but remained in his own house at 7 Argyll Street.

He had been Prime Minister for just over two years and was succeeded, not surprisingly, by Palmerston, whom the need of the hour had brought to the supreme office at the age of nearly seventy-one.

CHAPTER 25
Palmerston's Finest Hours

PALMERSTON did not live at No. 10 either, but stayed on in his own large and comfortable house in Piccadilly which is now the Naval and Military Club. It soon became the centre of the social and political world in London.

At weekends Palmerston went down to Broadlands, the lovely family home in Hampshire where he was born.* Lavish parties were given there too, with his devoted wife Emily, Melbourne's sister, as the presiding genius. Palmerston's own gaiety contributed greatly to the rollicking success of these gatherings. His youthfulness of spirit he accentuated by dyeing his whiskers. His energy was unflagging, his interests varied. His zest for racing and his pride in his stables were rewarded when one of his horses won the Derby in 1860 while he was Prime Minister. Until the year before his death, although by then in his eighty-first year, he rode and shot and dined out regularly.

The drawing-rooms and bedrooms at No. 10 Downing Street were

---

* Now the residence of Earl Mountbatten. Queen Elizabeth the Second and Prince Philip spent their honeymoon there.

left empty. Only the Cabinet room and the offices of the secretaries and clerks were used.

As an Irish peer, Palmerston sat in the House of Commons to which, after three unsuccessful attempts, he had been elected at the age of twenty-two. Exceedingly rich, with fortunes inherited from his father and his mother, and blessed, moreover, with influential friends, he obtained his first political office even before his election to Parliament.

The Duke of Portland appointed him a junior Lord of the Admiralty and Spencer Perceval, Portland's successor, offered him the post of Chancellor of the Exchequer when Palmerston was only just twenty-five, but wisely he refused. He accepted instead the office of Secretary at War, which dealt merely with the finances of the Army and was therefore less important than the Secretaryship for War and the Colonies,* which carried a seat in the Cabinet. It was a shrewd choice: Palmerston became a Privy Councillor and, refusing all inducements to promotion, remained Secretary at War for no less than nineteen years.

When Canning became Prime Minister in 1827, Palmerston, after twenty consecutive years in office, at last agreed to become Chancellor of the Exchequer. But Canning, under pressure apparently, shortly afterwards withdrew his offer and suggested that Palmerston should be Viceroy of India instead, but he preferred to go back to his old office of Secretary at War. On Canning's death four months later, the new Prime Minister, Goderich, again offered Palmerston the Exchequer, but it emerged now that King George the Fourth disliked Palmerston and would not agree to it. Palmerston explains what happened. He says[116] that during a meeting of the Privy Council at Windsor 'Goderich then asked the King if he would not see me, and explain the matter to me.' The King saw Palmerston privately and indicated that he preferred Mr. Herries as being 'the fittest man in England for the office.' Palmerston refused to serve under Wellington after the other Canningites resigned, for he had been drifting towards the Whigs for some years and finally broke with the Tories in 1826. It was not until Grey went to Downing Street in 1830 that Palmerston became Foreign Secretary for the first time and retained that office for four years, returning to it for a further six under Melbourne in 1835, and five more when Russell became Prime Minister in 1846.

* These two Departments were separated in 1854.

Despite Queen Victoria's intense hostility to Palmerston, she had no choice on Aberdeen's resignation but to send for him. While he was in Aberdeen's Government, she firmly refused to invite him to Balmoral. Greville refers to this on 28th August 1853 and supplies a reason for her deep-seated antagonism: 'Her dislike of him is, in fact, of very long standing, and partly on moral and partly on political grounds. There are old offences, when he was at the Foreign Office, which sunk deep in her mind, and besides this the recollection of his conduct before her marriage when in her own palace he made an attempt on one of her ladies, which she very justly resented as an outrage to herself. Palmerston, always enterprising and audacious with women, took a fancy to Mrs. Brand (now Lady Dacre) and at Windsor Castle where she was in waiting and he was a guest, he marched into her room one night. His tender temerity met with an invincible resistance. The lady did not conceal the attempt, and it came to the Queen's ears. Her indignation was pacified by Melbourne, then all-powerful, and who on every account would have abhorred an *esclandre* in which his colleague and brother-in-law would have so discreditably figured. Palmerston got out of the scrape with his usual luck, but the Queen has never forgotten and will never forgive.'[79] The date of this incident is not given, but Palmerston was presumably unmarried then. He married Melbourne's sister towards the end of 1839; the Queen married Albert early in the following year. But Palmerston was certainly in love with Emily, Lord Cowper's widow, at the time. There had been other affairs during this period, one of them with the lovely Lady Jersey, which had been much talked about but which Emily decided to ignore.

On 31st January 1855, as the crisis around Aberdeen grew, Lord Derby informed Her Majesty 'that the whole country cried out for Lord Palmerston as the only man fit for carrying on the war with success.'

Palmerston had used Downing Street for more than forty years, for apart from the Cabinet meetings he attended at No. 10 while serving under ten Prime Ministers, the Foreign Office itself was only just across the road. It was in one of the four houses belonging to Sir Samuel Fuldyer stretching from Downing Street to Fuldyer Street at the back, and had for some time been used both as the office and residence of the Foreign Secretary. All four houses were bought by the Government in

1814 and later demolished, and on the site the present Foreign Office building was erected. In 1831 Downing Street was macadamized at a cost of £190 11s. 6d.

Palmerston found the Cabinet room much too dark to work in. He put up with it, however, for the first three years he was there, as the Treasury was not disposed to spend any money on putting in new windows; it was not until he returned in 1859, following Derby's second short spell in office, that Palmerston insisted on having larger windows put in. After much argument the Treasury finally gave way and the work was begun. But an Office of Works note of 3rd September 1859, addressed to Mr. H. Fitzroy at the Treasury, states: 'Lord Palmerston's private secretary came to see me to complain that the alteration in the Cabinet Room was being made with *Single* Windows: He says that the Ld. P. determined to have them *Double*: I find that they were to be single in consequence of your decision and I must therefore ask for your explanation.'

Fitzroy replied: 'There is nothing about double windows in the requisition, nor have I any means of knowing that they are requisite. I am writing by this night's mail to Lord Palmerston of the Subject.'

There came a firm broadside from his lordship in answer. It was scribbled on a quickly torn half sheet of notepaper and was dated 'Broadlands 7 Sept. 1859.' It read: 'My dear Fitzroy, the Cabinet Room is dark and in winter cold; by opening two windows it will be made light, but unless the windows are double, the Room will be much colder.'

That brought immediate action. Under 'Ordinary Grant of Parliament' an estimate was drawn up five days later 'To provide and hand folding glass Doore to the two new windows. £10 . 0 . 0.' – which was only a small additional sum since the single windows cost no more than £31 10s. od. A month earlier Parliament had voted £100,000 for the new Foreign Office building facing No. 10.

Palmerston's masterly handling of the Crimean War during his first term caused Queen Victoria to change her views about him and she rewarded him with the Garter. Sebastopol was captured by British troops in September 1855 and early in the following year peace was signed.

But the Prime Minister soon had another war in hand. During the winter of 1856–7, Persia seized Herat, regarded as the 'Gate of India'. Palmerston ordered an immediate withdrawal and on this being ignored, he joined India in an attack. It was all over in no time. Herat was evacuated. Palmerston, beaming with satisfaction, declared: 'We are beginning to repel the first opening trenches against India by Russia,' whose hand, he felt, was behind it.

Before this was settled there was trouble with China. A small coasting vessel on the Canton river, Chinese-owned but flying the British flag, had been seized by China on a charge of smuggling and piracy and twelve members of its crew had been imprisoned. Britain demanded an apology and redress. The vessel and the crew were released but there was no apology. Thereupon a squadron of the Royal Navy went in and bombarded Canton. Many Chinese were killed and the town was occupied by the British in December 1857. A special envoy was sent to Peking in 1859 to effect a settlement, but his ships were fired on and the following year a full-scale expedition was dispatched to Peking. The Emperor's Summer Palace was set on fire and the terms extorted were wounding to Chinese pride. Palmerston was severely criticized in the House of Commons for his 'high-handed action'; the condemnatory motion, supported by Russell and Gladstone, until recently his colleagues, as well as by Disraeli, was carried by a majority of sixteen votes.

Palmerston hit back instantly in a manner that was both effective and impressive. He dissolved Parliament and appealed to the country. The election brought him a tremendous triumph.

Meanwhile in May 1857 the Indian Mutiny had broken out. Palmerston seemed to regard it with a certain casualness, confident that all would come right. But the Queen, viewing it with far greater gravity, suffered the acutest mental distress. She wrote to the Prime Minister, as well as to the Secretary for War, and to the Viceroy in India, Lord Canning, son of the former Prime Minister who had been Palmerston's chief. Her Majesty informed Palmerston that 'the measures hitherto taken by the Government are not commensurate.' Jestingly he replied that it was 'fortunate for the Government that the Queen was not sitting on the Opposition benches in the House of Commons.' Her Majesty was not amused.

His colleagues in the Cabinet and in the House of Commons found

Palmerston increasingly brusque and dictatorial. They detested his abrupt jerky manner of speaking ('bow-wow', they called it) and his use of low ribaldry for reasoned argument and his often juvenile jokes. They decided it was time he went. In February 1858, on a relatively unimportant measure, the Conspiracy to Murder Bill, brought in to placate Napoleon the Third following his attempted assassination in Paris by Orsini with bombs manufactured in England, eighty-four members of Palmerston's own Party, now becoming known as Liberals, voted against him and the Government was defeated while the Mutiny was still raging. Derby came back, reluctantly because his Party was in a minority in the House – but it suited Palmerston. He waited. A year later on Derby's defeat Parliament was dissolved. The election gave the Liberals a diminished but adequate majority and Palmerston was sent for again by the Queen.

His second term as Prime Minister lasted until his death more than six years later. By that time he was eighty-one and had been Prime Minister, save for the brief Derby interruption, continuously since the age of seventy-one.

During all those years, during Derby's rule and his, No. 10 remained empty as a residence. It had been so ever since the two Greys and Colonel Keppel moved out in 1847 and was to remain untenanted until 1877. The ground floor, however, was continuously active. Secretaries sat at their desks in the rooms adjoining the Cabinet room, two and sometimes three to a room; clerks in ever-increasing number filled the smaller rooms beyond. Sheafs of paper were set out on the Cabinet table in front of each chair, and Ministers ambled down the long corridor and hung their coats on hooks by the Cabinet door before going in for their deliberations. Every morning, whether the Cabinet had been called or not, the Prime Minister arrived and, seated alone at the long table with his back to the fire, went through the documents and reports, while his groom waited outside with his horse. The stables were no longer by the Horse Guards but had been moved to College Mews, near the Jewel Tower by Westminster Abbey.

It was during these years, with the upper rooms shut off, that the inner courtyard began to be cluttered with shacks and lean-tos, and they remained a disfiguring blot for more than a century until the house was dismantled for alterations in 1960.

When Palmerston returned to office in 1859 his manner was markedly different. His startling defeat the year before had taught him to be conciliatory. The imperious tone in the House was dropped. He was pleasant even to his avowed opponents. He went out of his way to offer the Board of Trade to Richard Cobden, who had attacked him persistently and vehemently. But Cobden refused.

Towards Napoleon the Third his attitude had now changed. He had approved of the Emperor's invasion of Italy to liberate the people from the domination of Austria, but he nursed the suspicion that Napoleon 'had at the bottom of his heart a deep and unextinguishable desire to humble and punish England.' Accordingly he induced the House to vote nine million pounds for the strengthening of Britain's coastal defences, just as Pitt had once done against the other Napoleon.

On the outbreak of the American Civil War in 1861, Palmerston's sympathies were with the South. In this he was supported by his Chancellor of the Exchequer Gladstone and some other members of the Cabinet, but the majority, including Russell, who was Foreign Secretary, insisted that a strict neutrality should be observed.

Palmerston would not agree, however, to recognize the blockade imposed on the Southern States by Abraham Lincoln. The seceded Southern States, formed into a Confederation, established agencies in England for the purchase of arms: these were dispatched to the Bahamas and transhipped to fast steamers. Ships were also being built for the South in English shipyards at Liverpool. When two Confederate envoys, on their way to England in the British mail ship *Trent*, were taken off by force, Palmerston insisted on full and complete reparation and was backed in this by the whole country. It brought Britain and the United States once again to the brink of war. The situation was soon further aggravated. The United States Consul protested that one of the ships being built at Birkenhead by Laird's, the *Alabama*, was intended for use as a man-of-war and ought to be detained. Before the British could act the *Alabama* escaped, hoisted the colours of the South, and wrought havoc on the shipping of the North for more than two years. There were prolonged angry arguments which went on long after the Civil War had ended, and were not indeed settled until nearly six years after Palmerston's death.

He died in October 1865, while still Prime Minister. He had gone to stay at his wife's country house, Brocket Hall, in Hertfordshire, and had been out for a drive with her in their carriage. On returning, though feeling unwell, he insisted on taking a bath. A chill led to inflammation of the kidneys. His wife nursed him with loving solicitude all through that night and the next. On the 15th, a Sunday, the doctor suggested that Palmerston should go to church. He did, and three days later, while engaged in writing a letter, his pen fell out of his hand and he died. Beside him on the desk the official dispatch box lay open.

That he consistently used No. 10 as Prime Minister is supported by the large number of letters written by him from that address: the very first of these was to his brother, stating: 'Here am writing to you from Downing Street as First Lord of the Treasury.'[117]

CHAPTER 26
Disraeli and Gladstone

PALMERSTON was succeeded by his Foreign Secretary, Earl Russell,* who now became Prime Minister for the second time. Russell, who was nearly seventy-four, did not retain the office for long. In eight months he was out and Derby returned for a not much longer term. Neither of them lived at No. 10.

Though seven years younger than Palmerston, Russell had neither his vigour nor his health. Indeed his powers had already begun to decline. He seemed to spend his time diverting his friends with an endless flow of anecdotes, living in the past rather than facing up to the problems of the present. His handling of foreign affairs under Palmerston had come in for a severe and somewhat sweeping attack from Derby in the House of Lords. 'The foreign policy of the noble earl,' Derby said, 'as far as the principle of non-intervention is concerned, may be summed up in two truly expressive words – meddle and muddle. During the whole course of his diplomatic correspondence wherever

* An earldom was conferred on Lord John Russell in 1861.

he has interfered – and he has interfered everywhere – he has been lecturing, scolding, blustering, and – retreating.' The criticism was a little unfair because the interference had been begun earlier by Palmerston, who was never prepared to leave things entirely to his Foreign Minister.

Surprisingly, despite this, Russell tried to get Derby's son Lord Stanley to join his Government. But Stanley refused, just as he had refused to serve under Palmerston. Gladstone, quite definitely a Liberal now, took on the Leadership of the House of Commons, a task he had not undertaken before. It had been expected that Gladstone would be appointed Prime Minister and doubtless, had Russell refused, he would have been chosen; but, as King Leopold of Belgium wrote to his niece Queen Victoria: 'These politicians never refuse.'

Disraeli was certain that Russell's thoughts would go back to his Reform triumph of 1832. 'If Johnny is the man', he wrote, 'there will be a Reform Bill – very distasteful to the country.' Stanley was of the same opinion: 'The Reform crisis cannot now be delayed,' he wrote to Disraeli. 'There are at least fifty Conservatives on the Whig side; the question is, can we utilize them, and how?' These fifty Conservatives and the old Whigs were expected to resist a fresh Reform Bill – and it was on that that the Conservatives hoped to bring Russell down.

Gladstone was Russell's most ardent supporter in the project and worked night and day on preparing a new Reform Bill with a view to extending the vote. When the Bill was introduced on 12th March 1866, Gladstone explained that the property qualification in the boroughs was to be reduced from a rental of £10 a year to £7 and in the counties from £50 a year to £16. This, he calculated, would bring in about 400,000 additional voters – that is to say half as many again as the 800,000 the Act of 1832 had brought in.

It caused a political storm. Not only did the Conservatives oppose the measure, but a section of the Liberals too opposed it. One of the latter denounced the working classes as the ultimate repository of venality, ignorance and drunkenness. Disraeli begged the House to 'sanction no step that has a tendency to democracy' or 'you will have a horde of selfish and obscure mediocrities, incapable of anything but mischief, and that mischief devised and regulated by the raging demagogue of the hour.'

All this made Gladstone very angry. He hurled bitter taunts at the Opposition and gave great offence when he went so far as to describe Lord Grosvenor and Lord Stanley as a pair of selfish aristocrats who were conspiring to defeat an act of justice to the people. He was prepared, Gladstone added, to stake the existence of the Government on the passing of the Reform Bill and was backed in this by Russell, who regarded the Bill as 'a satisfactory close of my political life, whether carried or defeated.' Gladstone answered a fierce attack by Disraeli with a memorable peroration: 'You cannot fight against the future,' he said. 'Time is on our side. The great social forces which move onward in their might and majesty and which the tumult of your debates does not for a moment impede or disturb . . . are against you'; and he added that the banner of reform, however it might droop, would be borne in time by firm hands to a certain and not far-distant victory. He had spoken from one in the morning until half-past three.

The debate went on for weeks. It was not until the middle of June (1866) that an Opposition motion to substitute the rateable value for the rent of the house was carried by eleven votes. A week later, despite the Queen's pleas that the Government should ignore it and carry on, Russell resigned.

Derby, as the head of the Conservative party, succeeded Russell, although he had not a majority in the Commons. It was his third and last term as Prime Minister, each of them of short duration. In all he held the chief office for a total of less than four years. He put his son Stanley in charge of the Foreign Office – a not particularly effective choice. Lord Cranborne (later the third Marquess of Salisbury and three times Prime Minister) went to the India Office. Disraeli was once again Chancellor of the Exchequer and Leader of the House of Commons.

Indeed Disraeli was the effective head of the Government, for Derby, though not yet seventy, was old beyond his years and was frequently away, laid up with gout at his home at Knowsley. Disraeli presided over the Cabinet meetings at No. 10 and by a constant flow of confidential dispatches from Downing Street kept Derby informed of the many problems that beset the Government. As always there was trouble in Ireland. Then the great boom in railway shares during the preceding decades brought on a number of bankruptcies. There was also a preoccupation with the transfer of the telegraph services from the private companies operating them to the State – one of the earliest instances of nationalization, the first being the take-over of the main thoroughfares.

Though Disraeli's letters were headed 'Downing Street', they were not in fact from No. 10, but from the adjoining house No. 11, which had been acquired from Lord Eliot for the use of the Home Secretary. It was not, however, so used but was assigned to the Treasury and was often occupied by the Chancellor of the Exchequer. Disraeli first used it in 1852 when he took on that office, but he did not live there. But Gladstone, on succeeding him two years later, did move in – his son Herbert, later Viscount Gladstone, was born there.

It was Disraeli's practice to go back to his office at No. 11 after the House rose and send the Queen each night a long account of what had happened during the day. These private notes, normally written by the Prime Minister, helped to forge, from his earliest days at the Exchequer, the Queen's great attachment for Disraeli. She appreciated his thoughtfulness, was flattered by his courteous phrasing and, overcoming her initial dislike of him, began to think of him as 'dear Mr. Disraeli'.

Because of his immense ability and his brilliance, Disraeli was Derby's obvious successor as Prime Minister. But only grudgingly was this recognized, for the Tory Party still regarded him as something of a charlatan and treated him as a pariah.[118] To them he was the complete outsider – the son of a Jew, Isaac D'Israeli, and his wife Maria Baseri: an outlandish background, without much money in the family, for the father was a humble writer of books. At least the Pitts, though outside the aristocratic circle, were backed by the wealth of Chatham's grandfather, the East India interloper Thomas Pitt, and Peel, though the son of a cotton mill owner, belonged to the new industrial élite. Even after Disraeli had led them in the House of Commons for many years, a group of Tories, assessing his status as one would in cricket, said: 'Our team is the Gentlemen of England, with a Player given.' The Whigs, far more aristocratic in their attitude, also looked askance at him. Yet when in February 1868 continued ill health finally forced Derby to retire, it was to Disraeli, on Derby's recommendation, that the Queen turned.

Disraeli had always been confident that he would one day attain the chief office. More than thirty years before, when Melbourne, glancing disdainfully at his flamboyant satin trousers and his gleaming black ringlets, asked: 'Well now, tell me – what do you want to be?', Disraeli without hesitation replied: 'I want to be Prime Minister.' Melbourne was taken aback. It did not seem to him conceivable that this would ever be possible, and he warned the over-confident young man not to place his ambitions quite so high. But now, in his sixty-fourth year, Disraeli attained his goal. 'Yes,' he said, replying to the congratulations showered upon him, 'I have climbed to the top of the greasy pole.' It was a remarkable achievement when one considers the handicaps he had to overcome. It was fortunate for him that he became a Christian at the age of twelve, for the Jews were excluded from Parliament until 1858, only ten years before he attained the Premiership.

Even at this late date, with two-thirds of the nineteenth century over and the twentieth almost within sight, Disraeli conformed to the old pattern of having in his Cabinet three dukes, two earls and other peers or sons of peers. Derby's son Lord Stanley was kept on as Foreign Secretary. The Duke of Marlborough became Lord President of the Council, the Duke of Buckingham was Colonial Secretary, the Duke of Richmond was President of the Board of Trade and the Duke of Rutland's son, Lord John Manners, was First Commissioner of Works. But this formidable list was of little avail against the vast array of his Whig and Liberal★ opponents and their allies, the Radicals and the Irish, who together presented a powerful and united majority in Parliament against the Government. They too had had a change of leader, for Russell retired at the same time as Derby and was replaced by Gladstone. Like Disraeli, Gladstone had been Leader of his Party in the Commons for some years and the two came into frequent head-on collisions, just as Pitt and Fox had done. Both had changed parties, for Gladstone began as a Conservative and Disraeli as a Radical. But what enraged Gladstone was his opponent's brilliant skill in handling his most difficult followers: subtly and gradually Disraeli drew them closer to him. This Gladstone was never able to achieve. With his stiffness and obstinacy it was completely beyond him. He got heated, his gestures became violent: Disraeli reduced the House to laughter once by congratulating those on his own Front Bench on the security

★ The older aristocratic Whigs still adhered to the old name, the newer members of the Party, drawn from the industrial middle-classes, called themselves Liberals.

The main stone staircase, which rises from the basement to the first floor only. On the walls hang pictures of every Prime Minister since Walpole.

The ante-room, just outside the Cabinet Room. To the right of the grandfather clock are rows of pegs for the hats and coats of Cabinet Ministers, with tags stating 'Lord Chancellor', 'Lord President of the Council', etc.

The Cabinet Room. The table has been moved a little for the photograph. Normally the Prime Minister's leather upholstered chair, the only one with arms, stands immediately in front of the fireplace. All other chairs stand against the wall until required. Above the clock on the mantelpiece hangs van Loo's portrait of Walpole. The pillars mark the extension of the room by Taylor in 1783.

The picture shows the Prime Minister's section of the Cabinet table. Only he has a telephone and bell-buttons. His blotter is marked '1st Lord' because officially he is 'First Lord of the Treasury'. Every used sheet of blotting paper in this room is destroyed immediately after a Cabinet meeting.

The first of a row of three drawing-rooms on the first floor, all of which look out on to the Horse Guards Parade. This room was used as a bedroom by Sir Henry Campbell-Bannerman, who died there. Ramsay MacDonald used it as a study, so did Lady Churchill. Mrs. Neville Chamberlain, by opening the connecting doors, used the three rooms for her large parties.

The middle drawing-room. The large folding doors separate it from the small drawing-room in the upper picture.

The large State Drawing Room. It was extended by Taylor beyond the columns. A door on the left (not visible) leads to the small oak-panelled breakfast room built by Soane in 1825.

Soane's lovely State Dining Room. It is panelled in light oak and is nearly 42 feet long. The lofty vaulted ceiling rises right through the floor above.

they derived from the presence of 'a good piece of furniture' between them and the Leader of the Opposition.

Their fiercest rows were over the Reform Bill. Yet, on the change of Government and even before taking over from Derby, Disraeli introduced a similar Bill with minor modifications, most of which were abandoned in the committee stage. He had been induced to change his mind about Reform by the remarkable popular demonstrations in London and elsewhere on the defeat of Gladstone's Bill, when a large crowd marched from Trafalgar Square to Gladstone's house in Carlton House Terrace, shouting 'Gladstone and Liberty!' and mobs tore down the railings of Hyde Park in order to hold a protest meeting near Marble Arch. The disturbances there, so close to Disraeli's own home at No. 1 Grosvenor Gate, Park Lane, went on for three days, then spread to Birmingham, Manchester, Leeds and Glasgow. Like Wellington over the removal of Catholic disabilities and Peel over the repeal of the Corn Laws, Disraeli gave way on finding that the stand he had made was no longer tenable. Indeed, within four days of these demonstrations he was writing to Derby to suggest that they should take up the Reform Bill where Gladstone left off. 'It would cut the ground entirely from under Gladstone.'

Derby, who as a Whig had most enthusiastically supported Russell's Reform Bill in 1832 and when the Lords threw it out had jumped excitedly on to a table at Brooks's and shouted 'His Majesty can clap coronets on the heads of a whole company of Foot Guards', wrote now to express his complete agreement. 'If we should be beaten on some great leading principle, we should have a definite issue on which to go to the country,' he said, for there was no longer any doubt that the voters would support it. When it was discussed with the Queen, she insisted that it should be taken up without delay. Cranborne and Manners did not share this opinion; the latter felt that the Liberal Party had gone to pieces already, for the Whigs in that Party had not been in favour of any extension of the franchise.

Early in February 1867 Disraeli introduced his Reform Bill in the House of Commons. He indicated that household suffrage on a rating basis was to be adopted and that the electorate would be very substantially widened, with an addition of a million new voters as against Gladstone's 400,000. The Cabinet was by no means agreed on this.

There had been endless discussions at No. 10 and more than one Minister had threatened to resign – indeed three did resign before the Household Suffrage Bill was voted on, Cranborne among them.

The Bill was passed by the Commons without a division and became law on 15th August 1867. Derby, who had thought it a 'leap in the dark', was now jubilant and spoke with delight of having 'dished the Whigs'. Disraeli regarded it as one of his greater achievements because it introduced a tinge of democracy into the Tory Party and gave it a fresh vitality.

Disraeli's first term as Prime Minister did not last long – a mere ten months. His lack of a majority in the Commons, only temporarily adjusted over the Reform Bill, proved a serious handicap and Gladstone in consequence had things pretty much his own way. The newly formed Fenians, organized and sustained by angry Irish exiles in America to set up an Irish Republic, had begun a series of savage outrages, which spread from Ireland to England – in Manchester a dozen lives were lost. Gladstone advocated the abolition of the established Church in Ireland as a first step towards conciliation. Disraeli vehemently opposed this. It was carried nevertheless. Finding it impossible in these circumstances to continue in office, Disraeli dissolved Parliament as soon as the new electoral registers were ready.

The General Election was held in November 1868. With the vote given them by Disraeli the new electors came down heavily on the side of Gladstone: the Government suffered a crushing defeat.

Gladstone was busy cutting down trees in his park at Hawarden when the summons came from the Queen, inviting him to be Prime Minister for the first time. He read the telegram, then calmly picked up his axe and resumed his vigorous attacks on the tree. Some minutes later he said: 'My mission is to pacify Ireland.'

During his ten months as Prime Minister Disraeli merely moved his office from No. 11 to No. 10: the rest of the house, apart from the rooms occupied by his secretarial staff on the ground floor and the large anteroom for junior ministers in attendance, remained empty. He continued to live in his house at Grosvenor Gate, with his wife Mary Anne Wyndham Lewis, a very wealthy M.P.'s widow whom he had married thirty years earlier. She was nearly a dozen years his senior and was by now close on her eightieth year, but they remained deeply devoted throughout their long life together. On giving up the Premiership, he refused a peerage for himself, but his wife became Viscountess Beaconsfield, taking the title from the town near which Disraeli had bought the small manor of Hughenden with the money left him by his father.

Gladstone too declined to live at No. 10, but remained on at 11 Carlton House Terrace, where he had been residing for some years. But, like Disraeli, he used No. 10 Downing Street both for Cabinet meetings and his work. Such entertaining as he did, for he was not very sociable, was at his own home.

With his immense Parliamentary majority Gladstone was able to continue in office for more than five years. Disraeli withdrew to write a new novel, *Lothair*, emerging only occasionally to criticize and attack the Government. The new Cabinet was well chosen. Its leading figure was Lord Granville, not to be confused with Lord Grenville who was related to the Pitts and to Melbourne. Granville was the son of Granville Leveson-Gower, the first earl, who had been the lover of that great Whig hostess Lady Bessborough and the father of some of her children. The present earl, known as 'Puss', was a gay, social figure and his influence with Gladstone was such that he was able to induce the austere Prime Minister to accompany him once to the Derby. Their closeness led to their discussing many complex problems together before the Cabinet met, with the result that there was rarely anything but harmony at these meetings.

The new Prime Minister's endeavours were bent, initially, on pacifying Ireland. He was not liked in that country because of his extension of income tax to Ireland in 1853, a course Peel was careful to avoid when he re-introduced the tax.*

Gladstone began by disestablishing the Anglican church in Ireland. The lands laws were dealt with next. But the Fenians continued to be violently active and coercive measures had in the end to be adopted even by Gladstone. He wrote bluntly to the Queen to tell her of the part he expected her, as well as her heir, to play in public affairs, and especially in the promotion of better relations with Ireland. The Queen resented this strongly. Ever since the death of her beloved Albert in

---

* Pitt's wartime measure, introduced in 1798, ended in March 1816, a few months after Waterloo.

December 1861 she had withdrawn more and more from public life. She had never forgiven Gladstone for his persistent resistance to provide more money for the Albert Memorial in Kensington Gardens. Although he was always extremely respectful, his manner seemed to her to be too constrained, it contrasted badly with Disraeli's. She never asked him to sit down in her presence, he was kept standing throughout the lengthiest interviews while she herself remained seated. The letters she received from him now as Prime Minister caused her great irritation. They were always most involved, their meaning was never clear and she had to have a précis prepared so that she might find some lucidity through the fog of his words. It emerged at length that he wanted her to establish a home in Ireland, just as she had one at Balmoral in Scotland, and he told her that he had already obtained for this purpose the generous offer of a residence from a Dublin banker. He also proposed that the position of Lord-Lieutenant of Ireland should be abolished and that there should be a Viceroy instead, with the Prince of Wales (later King Edward the Seventh) as the first to hold that office. Both suggestions were unwelcome to Her Majesty. She replied cautiously to the first through her Secretary, General Grey, stating that nothing could ever take the place of Balmoral in her affections. It was at Balmoral that she and Albert had spent so many of their happiest hours and since his death the place had become hallowed in her memory.

A few days after Gladstone received General Grey's letter, Sir William Jenner, the Queen's doctor, called to say that Her Majesty did not intend to open Parliament in person. He added that her decision was not entirely due to her health. She was uneasy about the Irish question and especially about the disestablishment of the church and she preferred not to appear to be taking a personal part in these changes.

Gladstone was very angry. He had many talks about it with General Grey, who told him quite frankly: 'I am fairly persuaded that nothing will have any effect but a strong – even peremptory – tone. In spite of Sir William Jenner I believe that neither health nor strength are wanting, were inclination what it should be. It is simply the long, unchecked habit of self-indulgence that now makes it impossible for her, without some degree of nervous agitation, to give up, even for ten minutes, the gratification of a single inclination, or even whim.' He warned Gladstone that any 'postponement of the fight, which *must* come, will make it seem more painful and difficult'.[121]

It was an extraordinary way for the Queen's Private Secretary to talk of the Sovereign to the Prime Minister. One wonders what made General Grey open out to Gladstone in this manner. The General, as a son of Earl Grey, Whig Prime Minister at the time of the first Reform Bill of 1832, had a link with Gladstone's present political alignment. There was a further, somewhat intimate link between the two men, for Gladstone, when he was in his twenties, fell desperately in love with a young and very beautiful girl named Caroline Farquhar. He proposed to her, at first through her father, then through her mother and brother, who had been with him at Eton, but the girl, being gay and light-hearted, thought him much too austere and disapproving in his manner. Gladstone went through some agonizing months of pleading, but the girl remained adamant. She was already, it emerged later, interested in another man, whom she married – young Charles Grey,* now the Queen's Secretary: she was later appointed a Lady of the Bedchamber to the Queen. Gladstone took her refusal very badly and in his private diary resigned himself to the wisdom of God, who had thus seen fit to humble him.

Gladstone did not marry until three years later. In the interval he went through yet another shattering romance. He had fallen in love with Lady Frances Douglas, daughter of the Earl of Morton, and, without any hint to her of his feelings, quite suddenly he proposed to her. She was astonished and unresponsive. The Dean of Edinburgh and other friends were asked by Gladstone to plead with her, but it proved of no avail. Some months later she married Lord Milton. Then Gladstone met Catherine, sister of Sir Stephen Glynne, a Scottish baronet and M.P. The family was extremely wealthy: they had a house in Berkeley Square and owned Hawarden Castle, which eventually became Gladstone's home. He married Catherine in 1839.

Acting on General Grey's advice he kept on urging the Queen to come back to London and attend to her duties. All his colleagues in the Cabinet, he added, were of the same view. But despite his persistence he did not succeed. The Queen was obdurate. Her aloofness had already

---

* His cousin Charles Samuel Grey, who was secretary to Lord John Russell, lived for a time at No. 10 Downing Street.

made her extremely unpopular. For more than two generations the people had looked upon the monarchy neither with affection nor respect. The scandalous behaviour of most of George the Third's sons, and especially of the Prince Regent, whose immorality extended even into his declining years as King, had filled them with disgust. And now the Queen, on whom the enchantment of her extreme youth had cast such a promising glow, was fat and fifty and had withdrawn into a solitary widowhood to grieve over her Albert. Her heir, the Prince of Wales, lived as a profligate.

There were many public demonstrations against the Royal Family. There was even talk of abolishing the monarchy and setting up a republic. Fifty Republican clubs were formed in various parts of the country and Joseph Chamberlain, father of Neville Chamberlain, a future Conservative Prime Minister, was cheered by his constituents at Birmingham when he told them that the republic 'must come'.

General Grey died suddenly a few months after his talks with Gladstone and was succeeded as Private Secretary by Henry Ponsonby, also a confirmed Liberal and a great admirer of Gladstone. He fully shared his predecessor's views about the Queen's excuses and evasions, in which her 'feeble-minded' doctor, as Gladstone called him, encouraged her. Having made up his mind to solve this question finally and to make the Queen play her part more fully, Gladstone was too resolute and tenacious to be deflected. For his remaining years in office as Prime Minister this was the one obsession in his mind and it was repeatedly discussed at Cabinet meetings at No. 10. He made so bold as to tell the Queen bluntly of his doubts about her alleged headaches and her so-called nervous attacks. By August 1871, after Gladstone had been in office for two and a half years, the Queen could endure it no longer and wrote complaining that she was being 'driven and abused till her nerves and health give way with this worry and agitation and interference in her private life.' She even threatened to abdicate. 'She must solemnly repeat that unless the Ministers *support* her and state the truth she *cannot* go on, but must give her heavy burden up to younger hands.'[121] The doctor warned Gladstone that the Queen's grandfather George the Third had died mad.

Gladstone himself was getting tired of it. He wanted to give up his office and withdraw to live a more religious life, but he felt he must not shirk his duty, and his duty, as he saw it, was to get the Royal Family to play their part. He renewed his attack on the Prince of Wales, complained of his disastrous influence on society, his utterly purposeless existence, his love of frivolity, and drew up a schedule of public duties in order to keep the Prince fully occupied for the entire year 'with occasional fractions of time for other purposes'. This the Queen rejected outright. She said that the question was more properly one for herself to settle with members of her family.

The atmosphere got more and more vitiated, and as late as July 1873, after Gladstone had been Prime Minister for nearly five years, Lord Granville passed him a note across the Cabinet table, asking: 'Which do you and Mrs. Gladstone dislike the least – to dine with the Queen on Wednesday at Windsor, or to go down for a Saturday and Sunday to Osborne?' Gladstone chose Windsor as the lesser of two evils. It was Granville who by his timely intervention at all times helped to prevent the Prime Minister's relations with the Queen breaking down completely.

Gladstone did not, however, allow this obsession to deflect his attention from his plans for reform in other directions. The Irish Land Act was passed in 1870 to protect the tenant from eviction so long as he paid his rent and, in the event of a sale, to secure for him the full value of any improvements he had made. In the following session Religious Tests in the universities, which had excluded Catholics and Nonconformists from becoming undergraduates, were abolished. Secret voting at elections, for which the Chartists had fought more than twenty years earlier, was passed by the Commons but thrown out by the Lords. It became law a year later, in 1872.

He next turned to the purchase of commissions in the army, which had caused a scandal sixty years before when the mistress of the Duke of York was found to be profiting from this traffic. The sale, nevertheless, had continued. The attempt to put a stop to it now met with the most violent opposition. But Gladstone found he could deal with it without a vote in the House. As the purchase had been established by royal sanction, he was able to effect its abolition by getting the Queen to issue a royal warrant cancelling all regulations authorizing the purchase of commissions.

These were important and far-reaching reforms. He next set about establishing a university in Dublin for both Roman Catholics and Protestants. This did not meet with the approval of the House generally, or even of the Catholics in it, and it was defeated by three votes. Gladstone thereupon resigned.

The Queen sent for Disraeli, but he refused to take on the Premiership without having the support of the majority in the Commons. Nor did he want the Queen to dissolve Parliament yet, for he felt that if Gladstone remained in office for just a little longer, his unpopularity in the country could be assured. The Queen accordingly had to ask Gladstone to carry on, and this after much argument he agreed to do.

Disraeli's forecast proved to be correct. The Government lost one by-election after another. There was friction in the Cabinet. The work of many Government departments was badly mismanaged. The Postmaster-General was forced to resign and Gladstone replaced the Chancellor of the Exchequer by taking on the duties himself. The First Commissioner of Works, tactless and overbearing in his manner, provoked not only Gladstone but the Queen, with whom he came in frequent contact over the upkeep of the Royal palaces; yet, inexplicably, Gladstone kept him on.

After a very few months, Gladstone found it impossible to carry on and decided on a General Election. He dissolved Parliament in January 1874. To make sure that the votes would not go against him, he resorted to a course that one would not have expected from anyone so high-minded. His appeal to the electorate was entirely materialistic. The large surplus the Government had accumulated over the years he offered, if re-elected, to use for the total abolition of income tax. Since it would not, he found, be enough, he proposed slashing severely the naval and military estimates. This enraged the Service chiefs.

There were heated arguments about all this in the Cabinet room at No. 10, but Gladstone was confident it would bring him the support of the country. But since income tax at the time was only threepence in the pound, the pledge failed to interest the electorate.

Disraeli for his part, promised the voters a rest from the 'incessant and harassing legislation', a restoration of Britain's former great influence in Europe, and 'support by every means of her imperial sway'. He was returned with a majority of fifty over all other parties.

CHAPTER 27
'Jingoism'

THIS time, his second and last term as Prime Minister, Disraeli was in office for six triumphant years, as against his earlier spell of only ten months.

His life had been seriously affected in the interval by the death of his doting wife, Mary Anne, Viscountess Beaconsfield. She had been ill for some time and showed signs of severe strain in the spring of 1872, but continued to carry on bravely with her social duties. In December, after a week's acute illness, during which her husband scarcely left her side, she died. She was in her eighty-fourth year.

The Queen, whose telegrams and inquiries had been constant throughout her illness, wrote on the same day, hoping that her heart-felt sympathy would not be 'an intrusion in this his first hour of deso-lation and overwhelming grief.' Gladstone, writing from No. 10 Downing Street, said: 'You and I were, as I believe, married in the same year. It has been permitted to both of us to enjoy a priceless boon through a third of a century.'

It was fourteen months after this that Disraeli became Prime Minister.

He was now seventy. His wife's death had also made a great difference to his circumstances, for her income died with her. Disraeli thus lost £5,000 a year and the town house in Grosvenor Gate. He was in debt and for the time being moved into a nearby hotel off Hanover Square, where he found the loneliness overwhelming. Later he took a small house in Whitehall Gardens,* two doors from where Peel used to live. Downing Street was only just round the corner and there seemed no need for Disraeli to move in, though, as before, he used the Cabinet room both for Cabinet meetings and as his personal office.

He had led the Conservative Party for more than twenty-five years, the longest period of leadership in either Party, but there was still discernible a strong undercurrent against him. As recently as 1868 Lord Salisbury, bearer of the historic name of Cecil and a descendant of Lord Burleigh who had served Queen Elizabeth the First, was looked upon by many as the rightful leader of the Conservatives, the more so because he had always disapproved of Disraeli. An effort was made to appoint him Leader in the House of Lords, but this Disraeli would not countenance. Now in 1874, on Disraeli's return as Prime Minister, he generously offered Salisbury the India Office, where Salisbury had already served under Derby. He accepted. Derby's son Stanley, who had succeeded his father in 1869, went again to the Foreign Office, where Salisbury was to follow him presently and carve out an outstanding reputation for himself. Once again half the Cabinet of twelve consisted of peers.

Disraeli was regarded as the most arresting figure in politics since the death of Pitt. The Queen was, of course, delighted with the change, for she was heartily sick of Gladstone's constant nagging and did not disguise her pleasure at being rid of him. One aspect of the change though was not altogether pleasing to Her Majesty. Her normal antipathy towards High Churchmen, which had led to their complete exclusion from her Household, had become accentuated of late by the great spread of ritualism in the country. The presence of Lord Salisbury, a leading High Churchman, in Disraeli's new Cabinet presented a grave difficulty which had to be handled with the utmost delicacy. The Queen had to be mollified. Disraeli handled it with great tact. Focusing his

* This house later became the office of the Committee of Imperial Defence, and during the 1914–18 War Lloyd George's War Cabinet used to meet there.

attention on two others in the Government with similar leanings, Lord Beauchamp and Lord Bath, he wrote to Lord Salisbury and sought his co-operation in dealing with this thorny problem. 'Last night, the Queen, while accepting the appointment of Beauchamp as a favour to myself, requires that there shall be an undertaking from him, that he will take no prominent part in Ch. politics. It is very desirable, Her Majesty adds, that this condition should be clearly understood, as she looks upon the views of the Ch. party with wh. Ld. B. is connected, as detrimental to the interests of the Ch. of England, and Dangerous to the Protestant religion. . . . This morning comes another letter. She hears with regret that Lord Bath is as bad as Lord Beauchamp: consequently the same restrictions must be put upon him as on Lord Beau., etc., etc.' Gladstone would have handled it differently and doubtless clumsily. The Public Worship Act, brought in by the Archbishop of Canterbury to restrain ritualism, put it on a securer basis not long afterwards.

This was the greatest period of Disraeli's career. All he had ever dreamed of had at last been attained: he had a majority in both Houses, the Sovereign's enthusiastic support, recognition by the heads of the great aristocratic families, the Cecils, the Percies, the Lygons, the Bridgemans, the Lennoxes, the Stanleys, of course, and the Manners. But he felt it had come too late. If only he had been twenty years younger. His health, never robust, had begun to fail, and, though he seemed to be still fresh in spirit, he was not physically as energetic and robust as Palmerston was when he became Prime Minister at the age of seventy. Disraeli had to swallow pills and drink unpalatable mixtures in order to keep fit. He was troubled by gout and asthma, and the strain of the supreme office and having to spend long hours in the House of Commons greatly taxed his strength. After two years, in 1876, he decided, like Chatham, to go to the House of Lords and became the Earl of Beaconsfield.

But before he did this he was able to inform a wildly enthusiastic House of Commons that the British Government had acquired a large holding of Suez Canal shares from the bankrupt Khedive of Egypt. Disraeli wrote to the Queen to tell her of the scheme in brief outline: ' 'Tis an affair of millions; about four at least; but would give the possessor an immense, not to say preponderating influence in the management of the Canal. . . . Scarcely breathing time! But the thing must be done.'

The deal had to be completed with speed and secrecy in order to beat a French syndicate which was also after the shares; and the £4,000,000 had to be paid, and indeed was paid, without the sanction of Parliament, since the House was not sitting at the time.

There were excited but uneasy discussions for some days at No. 10 about this. The Chancellor of the Exchequer, agreeing eventually to apply direct to the Treasury for the money, said with some emphasis: 'I don't like it.' The money in fact was advanced by the Rothschilds. Disraeli had told his secretary, Montagu Corry (later Lord Rowton), to wait outside the Cabinet room. When Disraeli put his head through the door and said 'Yes', the secretary set off at once to see Rothschild. He found the great financier seated at his desk in the City eating grapes. Not until the last grape had been devoured did Rothschild speak: 'What is your security?' he asked. Corry replied: 'The British Government.' Rothschild nodded slowly. 'Then you shall have it,' he said.

The Queen wrote ecstatically to Disraeli. This 'gives us complete security for India . . . an immense thing!' India had been as much in her mind as in his. That winter the Prince of Wales went on a visit to India, and shortly afterwards, while opening Parliament in person (a rare event since her widowhood), the Queen announced the Government's intention of a 'formal addition to the style and titles of the Sovereign.' Her Majesty became 'Her Imperial Majesty, Empress of India.' It aroused the most furious opposition in Parliament and in the country. But that did not detract from the joy of either the Queen or Disraeli, who had said earlier: 'You can only act upon the opinion of Eastern nations through their imagination.' And indeed it was most enthusiastically welcomed by the Indian Princes.

Ireland, as always, remained an ever bleeding sore. The Fenians continued to be active there as well as in England. The problem demanded unremitting attention, but Disraeli had to direct his immediate thought to the disturbances that had broken out in the Balkans against Turkey, for he realized that Russia's inevitable intervention would be of the utmost disadvantage to Britain. Russia had to be contained; any expansion towards the Mediterranean would imperil Britain's access to the Suez Canal.

The situation was extremely tricky. The 'Three Emperors' (of Russia, Austria and Germany) insisted that the Turks should be compelled to grant better conditions to the vast number of Christians living under Turkish rule in the Balkans. But Disraeli refused to accept this: he declared it was merely a conspiracy on the part of Russia and Austria to divide Turkey's European possessions among themselves. To make it clear that he was not prepared to tolerate any such intervention, he at once dispatched British warships to the Dardanelles. This, unfortunately, encouraged the Turks to adopt an intransigent attitude. They treated the rebellious Bulgarians with savagery: 12,000 men, women and children, all of them Christians, were massacred. When this news reached England, the people, always against Russia, and enthusiastically behind Disraeli until now, were rudely shaken and wondered how they could possibly side with Turkey any longer.

Gladstone, who had given up the leadership of the Liberal Party in January 1875, now abandoned his resolve to retire from politics and re-entered the arena. Rising in great wrath in the House of Commons, he attacked the Government mercilessly, and insisted that Britain must support the Christian minorities against the Turks, on the grounds of humanity if nothing else. But Disraeli remained unshaken. He discounted the atrocities, he said. Besides, Britain's imperial and strategic interests were dependent upon the maintenance of Turkish integrity, and for this he was prepared to go to war. He was only deterred from adopting this course by dissensions in the Cabinet room and by the uneasiness in the country generally.

The public had been roused by a passionate pamphlet published by Gladstone, urging that the Turks should be bundled out of Europe 'bag and baggage'. This he followed up by a speech at an open-air meeting at Blackheath in the pouring rain at which he said: 'I, for one, for the purposes of justice, am ready as an individual to give the right hand of friendship to Russia when her objects are just and righteous, and to say, in the name of God, "Go on and prosper." '

The Queen was on the side of Disraeli and kept urging the Cabinet to go to war. She threatened to abdicate if they didn't.[121] By this time two of the Balkan countries, Servia and Montenegro, had declared war on Turkey, and Disraeli, in his speech at the Guildhall on 9th November 1876, threatened Russia with war if she did not stop the flow of so-called volunteers into those countries. It was this speech that prompted the music hall refrain: 'We don't want to fight, but by Jingo, if we do, We've got the ships, we've got the men, we've got the money too!' and added the word 'Jingoism' to the English language.

Both the Conservatives and the Liberals were divided on this issue. Disraeli informed the Queen that there were seven distinct shades of opinion in his Cabinet, ranging from those who wanted immediate war with Russia to those who were for peace at any price. Lords Salisbury, Derby and Carnarvon were on the side of the Christians. Her Majesty urged the Prime Minister to sack Derby and Carnarvon. 'Be very *firm*. A divided Cabinet is of NO *use*.' Among the Liberals, Gladstone's closest friend Lord Granville as well as Lord Hartington, heir to the Duke of Devonshire, were against him. Hartington told Granville that if Gladstone went any further 'nothing can prevent a break-up of the Party.'

On 24th April 1877 Russia declared war on Turkey and began her advance on Constantinople. Only the firm opposition of the Cabinet as a whole, who refused to go to war over this issue, held the Prime Minister and the Queen in leash. A policy of neutrality was finally adopted, but it was made clear that neutrality would only be maintained while there was no threat to vital British interests.

While the crisis mounted to its climax Disraeli, crippled with gout, found it impossible any longer to walk the short distance from Whitehall Gardens to No. 10 for the heated Cabinet discussions. 'I have been very ill and continue very ill,' he wrote to a friend, 'and am quite incapable of walking upstairs; gout and bronchitis have ended in asthma. . . . Sometimes I am obliged to sit up all night, and want of sleep at last breaks me down. . . . I have managed to attend every Cabinet, but I can't walk at present from Whitehall to Downing Street, but am obliged to brougham even that step, which I once could have repeated fifty times a day.' In November 1877 he decided to move to No. 10 and took up his residence there for the first time. The possibility of such a move had been obvious for some months. The upper rooms, empty for thirty years, had been opened and aired, and the decorators had been called in. Their estimate for doing just the large drawing-room, described as 'The Reception Room for Lord Beaconsfield', alarmed the Treasury. The cost for painting the ceiling in a plain colour, for decorating the walls and inserting handsome paper in the panels, and picking out the cornice in tints and gold came in all to £782 for the one room. The cost of a new grate and tiles alone was £40. An immediate letter from the Treasury, dated 21st November 1876, stated: 'My Lords trust that every effort will be made to confine the expenditure within narrow limits, as they should regret to see any greater outlay incurred than is absolutely essential for placing the room in a condition appropriate to the uses for which it is designed. Beyond this they could not consent to go, as it would be injudicious to spend any large amount upon so old a house and one in which the approaches and other arrangements are so decidedly defective. They should hope that the Estimate now submitted might yet be found susceptible for reduction.' Close on £200 was eventually lopped off.

Then there was the question of the furniture. Disraeli insisted that all the furniture required for the room should be paid for by the Treasury. He pointed out that this had been the practice next door at No. 11, the official residence of the Chancellor of the Exchequer, for a quarter of a century. Indeed it was a quarrel between Disraeli and Gladstone in January 1853 that had brought about this change at No. 11. Previously each new Chancellor of the Exchequer had bought the furniture from the outgoing tenant, but Gladstone, on taking over from Disraeli, declined to do this and asked the Board of Works to buy the furniture instead, at any rate for the rooms in official use. Disraeli indicated that the traditional agreement 'as between gentlemen' should be observed and that any new arrangement could only affect the next transfer. An acrimonious correspondence followed between the two. The furniture was eventually purchased by the State, and to prevent future disputes of this nature, a Treasury minute in 1853 clearly defined the degree of responsibility of each tenant. Now, on it being agreed that this practice should be extended to No. 10, a new Treasury minute, dated 30th May 1878, was issued. It laid down that at No. 10, as at No. 11 Downing Street, the entrance hall, staircase and first floor rooms should in future be regarded as used for public purposes and should be furnished at public expense, but that the use of all other contents of the residence should be debited to the occupant on the following basis: when he moved in a valuation was to be made of the furniture already there. To this would be added the cost of any new furniture supplied at his request. The cost of repairs to furniture carried out for him by the Office of Works during his occupancy of the house would also be added. On his leaving he would be credited with the value of the furniture at that time, which would be deducted from the initial total, and the outgoing Prime Minister would then have to pay for the depreciation in value – that is to say for wear and tear. This was adhered to until 18th November 1897. Since then the Office (later the Ministry) of Works has had to maintain and renew, as necessary and at public expense, all the existing furniture even in the residential rooms. But Prime Ministers, or others residing in the house in their stead, still had to bring their own linen, cutlery, crockery, vases, ornaments and so on.

The furniture, especially brought in for Disraeli's use in the redecorated main reception room, cost £1,042 10s. It included two large sofas covered with silk £106 10s.; four small easy chairs covered with silk £88; four high-backed chairs also covered with silk £9 each; eight small chairs covered with silk £7 each; a table £25; two octagon tables £40; an oblong table £18; partial parquet floor amounting to only three foot round the room £50; a fine Axminster Persian carpet twenty-three feet by twenty £140; another for the passages or stairs £38; and curtains of rich silk with cornices and valances £145. The house thus once more became the residence of the Prime Minister; and in the spring was brightened with bowls of primroses, his favourite flowers, sent to him by the Queen from the gardens at Windsor.

But Disraeli was not at all happy with the house. He found that much more needed to be done to it and by August of the following year (1878) he called the attention of H.M. Office of Works to the dilapidated condition of certain rooms and the want of proper accommodation in his private apartments. A supplementary estimate was drawn up and sent on notepaper headed 'Downing Street', stating: 'Lord Beaconsfield has approved the following estimate which it will now be necessary to send officially to the Treasury. New Drawing-room in all as arranged £1,000; First Lord's Official room, Bedroom, Dressing-room and ante-room, with Plate-glass for windows in Official rooms £400; all necessary painting, cleansing, whitewashing, i.e. in offices £600; Bath with hot and cold water in First Lord's Dressing room £150; Repair to staircase and take Down existing boxes for Messengers £200. Total £2,350.' A letter from the Treasury dated 28th August authorized this work to be started immediately as it was classed 'urgent'. The cost was, if possible to be 'defrayed . . . out of the savings which may be effected upon the votes for Public buildings and Furniture respectively'.

This was not all. An order for a brass candle chandelier for the drawing-room, to match one already there, was given to Mr. Richard Evens of 43 Baker Street in September. It cost £30.

Meanwhile more important affairs of State had to be attended to. The Russian armies reached Adrianople in January 1878. Telegrams and letters from the Queen immediately began to descend on the Ministers. Disraeli, who fully shared her view, promptly abandoned his policy of neutrality and ordered the British Mediterranean fleet to proceed through the Dardanelles right up to Constantinople, the Turkish capital.

Russia, anticipating trouble, immediately offered to make peace and dictated terms to the Turks in the Treaty of San Stefano. But Disraeli was not prepared to accept this. He insisted that the Treaty should be examined in its entirety by a European Congress. Two members of the Cabinet resigned – Lord Carnarvon in February, Lord Derby in March: Lord Salisbury took the latter's place at the Foreign Office, although the Queen did not want him there. Indian troops got ready to embark for Turkey, and in this agitated atmosphere a Congress was finally agreed to – it was to be held in Berlin in June (1878) under the presidency of the German Chancellor, Bismarck.

Disraeli was far from well, but he insisted on going. The Queen, greatly concerned as to how he would stand the strain of the long journey, tried to dissuade him. He was, she said, 'her great support and comfort' and his health and his life were of 'immense value' not only to her but to the country. He went nevertheless. Before leaving No. 10, he wrote to the Queen (in the third person as is customary) saying that 'in all his troubles and perplexities, he will think of his Sovereign Lady, and that thought will sustain and inspire him.'

As a result of the discussions some of the Turkish provinces were amputated, but Macedonia, which the Treaty of San Stefano tried to take from her, was returned to Turkey. Britain got Cyprus for her part in the negotiations and Turkey gave a pledge that in future all her peoples would be guaranteed better government.

Disraeli, or Beaconsfield as he should rightly be called, returned from Berlin triumphant. He had taken the country to the very brink of war and had won without having to fire a shot. He was received with tumultuous enthusiasm: the country was relieved that there was not to be a war after all. Beaconsfield described the settlement as 'Peace with Honour'. The words delighted the people. Britain had not fought, yet had got something out of it – Cyprus. The Queen urged him to accept a Dukedom, but Disraeli refused. The Gladstone family declared that he should have been made the Duke of Jericho and sent at once to administer the duchy.

Few would have been prepared to predict that, after such a widely acclaimed triumph, Disraeli and his Government would in eighteen months be turned out of office. Gladstone had won little more than derision for his wild onslaughts and certainly had no hope of winning the next election. Had it come immediately after Disraeli's return from Berlin, it is possible that the electorate would have given the Government its support. But Disraeli waited and the tide turned disastrously against him. One of the causes for this was that Russia, having been thwarted in her thrust towards the Mediterranean, suddenly struck eastwards towards India, and to check her, Britain was involved in a long and costly war with Afghanistan. A second war broke out in South Africa against the Zulus. At home the harvests failed and cheap corn from the prairies flooded the market, trade declined, many banks closed their doors, and the distress soon became widespread. Even so the by-elections during that autumn and winter went well for the Government.

Parliament was dissolved in March 1880. But Gladstone had got busy with his campaign long before this. He had been adopted as Liberal candidate for the Midlothian in the preceding year, and ever since November he had been in incessant eruption, determined to get the Conservatives out if he could. On his way by train from Liverpool to Edinburgh he was cheered at every station by large crowds of working people. No opportunity was lost for making speeches. He denounced the Government for its financial profligacy in the pursuit of false phantoms of glory. He denounced Disraeli's imperialism, pointing out that he had first annexed the Transvaal★; then he had annexed Cyprus; then together with France† he had established a protectorate over Egypt; next he had made war on the Zulus; and not satisfied with all this, he had by 'the most wanton invasion of Afghanistan broken that country into pieces.' Gladstone begged his audience 'not to suffer appeals to national pride to blind you to the dictates of justice.'[121] Disraeli, he said, had violated every canon of morality and had endangered world peace.

In this memorable campaign in the Midlothian, Gladstone's searing intensity and his denunciatory onslaughts, echoing the ardour of the Hebrew prophets of the Old Testament, did much to swing public opinion. All Scotland flocked to hear him and all England read what he had said.

The Liberals gained a decisive victory. Disraeli was out, but as Gladstone had given up the leadership of his Party, the Queen had to choose between Lord Granville, the Liberal leader in the Lords, and Lord Hartington, Devonshire's heir, who was the Liberal leader in the Commons.

Both stood down, however, and insisted that Gladstone should be entrusted with the government of the country. It was Gladstone's second term as Prime Minister and he held office for five years.

★ In 1877, when the Transvaal was facing financial collapse.
† Following the bankruptcy of the Khedive and his sale of the Suez Canal shares, control over the finances of Egypt was established by England and France.

CHAPTER 28
Gladstone's Unhappy Return

GLADSTONE, who had of late been living at No. 73 Harley Street, now followed Disraeli's example and moved into No. 10 Downing Street. Disraeli did not long survive his crushing defeat. He died in the following year, 1881.

It appears that Gladstone, who now combined with the Premiership the office of Chancellor of the Exchequer, took possession of both Nos. 10 and 11; the latter he allocated to his secretarial staff, which made it possible for him to use almost the whole of No. 10 as a private residence. He too wanted new furniture. A note from Wilson, First Commissioner of Works, dated 30th April 1880, only a few days after the Election, states: 'I beg to report that the cost of furniture supplied to Mr. Gladstone at Downing Street is £1,555 5s. As it was absolutely necessary that all the things should be provided at once, it was not possible to report the sum before the expenditure was incurred.'

Gladstone was now seventy-one and all his children were grown up. After a time his eldest son Herbert, in his late thirties and a Member of Parliament, moved into No. 10 and Gladstone appears to have used No. 12, the house beyond the Chancellor's, as his residence.

Queen Victoria, as may be imagined, was not at all happy about his return as Prime Minister. She still disliked Gladstone intensely. He was long-winded and, as she phrased it: 'He speaks to me as if I was a public meeting.' He had no small talk at all. His mind was wholly serious, his manner that of a hot-gospeller.

More than thirty years before, when Gladstone had just entered his forties, a contemporary in Parliament, Lord Macaulay, with astonishing discernment, said of him: 'Whatever Mr. Gladstone sees is refracted and distorted by a false medium of passion and prejudices. . . . His rhetoric, though often good of its kind, darkens and perplexes the logic which it should illustrate.' It was not always easy, even for those who worked closely with him, to understand what he meant: he was often, as Disraeli so aptly phrased it, 'inebriated by the exuberance of his own verbosity'.

It proved to be an unhappy five years of office. From the outset there were difficulties in the Cabinet. Gladstone had maintained the pattern by drawing almost half its members from the peerage: of the others two, John Bright and Joseph Chamberlain, were Radicals. Gladstone did not like Chamberlain and questioned his 'integrity', but found it impossible to exclude him, since Chamberlain's recently formed National Liberal Federation had contributed substantially to the victory by winning sixty seats in the election.

Many in the Cabinet did not approve of the inordinate amount of time Gladstone was giving to finance. It was unarguable, of course, that he had a brilliant understanding of figures and, to assist him in the task, he had taken on as Financial Secretary of the Treasury his nephew by marriage, Lord Frederick Cavendish, whom he regarded with doting affection. Lord Frederick was the brother of Lord Hartington, who was at the India Office.

Within six weeks of forming his Government, Gladstone presented his first Budget. He abolished the malt tax in order to help the farmers at a time of depression, and recouped the money by raising the income tax from fivepence to sixpence and also by slightly increasing the tax on beer. He was delighted with its success. But after some months he began to complain that he was finding the management of two offices an intolerable strain. Asked why he didn't give up the Exchequer, Gladstone replied: 'Because I have not sufficient confidence in the financial judgement of my colleagues.'

In foreign affairs Gladstone's resolve was to reverse Disraeli's policy. He began by organizing a naval demonstration off Albania because the Turks had not yet ceded the agreed sections of their territory to Montenegro and to Greece as stipulated in the Treaty of Berlin. He got the Concert of Europe to induce the French, the Germans and the Austrians to send warships in support of the British fleet, but these three countries gave strict orders that on no account were their warships to open fire.

Queen Victoria was furious and appealed to the Conservative ex-Ministers and, unconstitutional though it was, relays of members of the Opposition went up to Balmoral to soothe Her Majesty.

The naval demonstration, Gladstone soon saw, was no more than a farce. Determined on some effective action, he arranged for an expedition to be sent to seize the harbour of Smyrna, on the coast of Asia Minor, with a view to sequestrating the Turkish customs revenues. Russia and Italy were ready to co-operate, France and Austria were not. Bismarck, speaking for Germany, declared that all the support he was prepared to give Gladstone was with his prayers. The Turks, however, gave in. The Foreign Secretary, Lord Granville, hurried to No. 10 Downing Street with the news, which had just arrived by telegram from Constantinople. He found Gladstone at his desk, busy writing a letter. His son Herbert and his Secretary Arthur Godley, later Lord Kilbracken, were in the room with him. Gladstone did not look up even when Granville danced a *pas de joie* and waved the telegram with delight. But becoming aware after a time of what was going on, Gladstone looked up and was horrified to see Granville dancing with such abandon. He had the telegram read, then said 'God Almighty be praised! I can catch the 2.45 to Hawarden.'

Gladstone wanted to give Cyprus to Greece, but Granville told him that public opinion would not tolerate that. Kandahar, however, acquired from Afghanistan after Lord Roberts' brilliant victory in the recent war, was given back to Afghanistan. Transvaal, annexed by Disraeli after the Zulu war, was handed over to the Boers. Queen Victoria's fury knew no bounds.

Next Gladstone turned to Egypt. That country was still part of the vast Turkish Empire, but its importance to Britain after the opening of the Suez Canal was, of course, vital. Gladstone had strongly criticized Disraeli's acquisition of control of the canal, because he foresaw that political control of Egypt would inevitably follow, which it did. He had denounced it as one of Disraeli's 'mischievous and ruinous misdeeds'. But the joint control, set up by Britain and France, had gone too far for him to undo now. 'I affirm,' he said in the House of Commons, 'and I will show, that the situation in Egypt is not one which we made, but one that we found.'

A crisis was precipitated by a nationalist revolt in Egypt. Fifty foreigners were massacred during a riot in Alexandria in June 1882. The rebel leader mounted guns on the forts as a threat to the British and French fleets lying off Alexandria. The French fleet instantly sailed away, but Gladstone refused to withdraw. He was not prepared, he said, to tolerate the tyranny of the rebels, who were seeking to repudiate Egypt's debts to foreign bond holders. He was prepared to act alone against Egypt if necessary, he declared. The British Admiral, on instructions from home, ordered all work on the fortifications of Alexandria to cease within twelve hours. This was not done and on 11th July the British fleet opened fire. On 19th August British troops, under the command of Sir Garnet (later Lord) Wolseley, were landed at Port Said.

This brought the first resignation from the Cabinet. John Bright, who had served in the Governments of both Palmerston and Russell, denounced Gladstone's conduct as 'simply damnable – worse than anything ever perpetrated by Dizzy.' But Gladstone refused to depart from his policy. The Egyptian rebels were attacked and annihilated at Tel-el-Kebir in September, and the British became masters of Egypt.

Surprisingly, this put Gladstone in the highest of good spirits. He ordered a salute of guns to be fired in Hyde Park in honour of the victory. But his elation was soon followed by a profound depression. His staff had noticed that these black moods generally occurred when he was most excited.

Gladstone hoped that the occupation of Egypt would be short-lived, but finding it would not, he talked of retiring. He gave up the office of Chancellor of the Exchequer in December. His colleagues were worried about his health and had a word with his doctor, Sir Andrew Clark, who often visited him at No. 10. Clark stated that Gladstone was sound in head and limb and was built in the most admirable proportion he had ever seen in any human being – like some ancient Greek statue of the ideal man; and added that, with his careful habits, Gladstone of all his patients had the best chance of living to be a hundred. Gladstone died in fact in 1898, in his ninetieth year.

Trouble in the Sudan came on the heels of the victory in Egypt. After sixty years of oppression by their Egyptian rulers, the Sudanese rose under the leadership of the Mahdi, a self-appointed Messiah, who vowed that he would rid the country for ever of the cruel extortion they suffered and secure their complete freedom. His fanatical followers he called dervishes, or holy mendicants, to give the rising a religious significance. Gladstone approved of their aims and described their armed conflicts as 'a rightful struggle'. The first serious clash between the Egyptians and the Sudanese occurred in August 1881, but Britain was not involved until the following year. The Mahdi had gained considerable successes and the Egyptians sent a large army numbering 10,000 men under the command of an Englishman named Colonel Hicks, to quell them. The force was annihilated by the Sudanese.

By this time Britain was in military occupation of Egypt and the Queen regarded the reverse as a blow to Britain's prestige. She insisted that it should be avenged at once. Public opinion, she said, would never forgive Gladstone unless an end was put to the 'murder, and rapine, and utter confusion' caused by the Sudanese rebels.

Gladstone was not prepared to do anything, but after much pressure from his Cabinet, and especially from Lord Granville and Lord Hartington, he agreed eventually to send General Gordon to the Sudan, but only for the purpose of evacuating the Egyptian soldiers and civilians from various parts of the country in order to prevent their slaughter.

Gordon had been Governor of the Sudan some years earlier. He insisted now on being appointed Governor-General. This secured, Gordon publicly declared that his purpose was not only to withdraw the Egyptian garrisons, but to establish a new and stable Government in the country, apparently under British rule.

He reached Khartoum in February 1884 and a month later the

Mahdi's troops closed in on the town. Gordon telegraphed to Cairo for reinforcements, but Gladstone, furious at the way Gordon had been issuing proclamations of which he did not approve and which included the restoration of the Sudanese slave trade, insisted that his orders to Gordon were clearly for the withdrawal of the Egyptians. Before the end of May, Khartoum was isolated. Hartington, the Secretary for War, informed the Cabinet that it was impossible to say now whether Gordon would be able to leave Khartoum without the aid of an expeditionary force. But this Gladstone refused to dispatch.

The Queen became explosively angry. Public opinion was roused too, for the country realized that Gordon was in grave danger. It was not, however, until September that Gladstone at last asked the House for a grant of £300,000 for the rescue of General Gordon. A force of 10,000 men was assembled at Cairo under Lord Wolseley and set out on the 1,600 mile march up the Nile to Khartoum. It took Wolseley nearly four months to reach the town. Two days before the arrival of the expeditionary force Khartoum fell and General Gordon, facing the rebels as they stormed into the Palace, was killed on the stairs.

The Queen in her wrath sent an open, unciphered telegram to the Prime Minister, blaming him for the delay – 'all this might have been prevented and many precious lives saved by earlier action.' Then she took to her bed, ill with anger and distress.

The whole country was moved to grief and indignation. Gladstone thought of resigning. As he left Downing Street to go to the House a vast crowd in Whitehall greeted him with groans and hisses. The vote of censure against the Government in the House was defeated by only fourteen votes.

With Britain so preoccupied the Russians got busy again. For some years they had been extending their dominion over Central Asia. Now, early in 1885, shortly after the fall of Khartoum, their troops staged an incident near the Afghan frontier and marched into that country. It brought Russia to the gateway of India. A wave of anger swept through Britain. No one expected Gladstone to react vigorously. But he did. He denounced the Russians' wanton, high-handed oppression and announced that the forces of the Empire would be sent immediately to meet the threat. The Russians thereupon withdrew.

These were not Gladstone's only problems. All through these troubled years, ever present with him as with his predecessors, was the Irish crisis. A heavy fall in agricultural prices in that country had begun shortly before Gladstone took office in 1880, and in time most Irish tenant-farmers found it impossible to go on paying their rents. There were evictions and there were also retaliatory outrages against the landlords. With the population almost wholly dependent on the land, since there were scarcely any industries, and with much of the land held by absentee landlords living in England, the hostility against the English became increasingly acute. Hope for the solution of all their difficulties was raised by Charles Stewart Parnell, a young Irishman still in his early thirties, who was a member of the House of Commons, where he led the Irish Nationalist Party. He demanded Home Rule for Ireland and the transfer of all the land from the landlords to the actual farmers, and it did not seem odd to his followers that one who was not only a Protestant but a landlord himself, should be their leader. His loathing of the English seemed to outweigh all else in their eyes.

Gladstone's first step towards helping the tenants was a stop-gap measure to compel landlords to pay compensation to the tenants they evicted. This led to the immediate resignation of Lord Lansdowne from the Government. The Bill was eventually passed by the Commons, but it was rejected by the Lords. The Irish retaliated by applying what came to be known as a boycott, after Captain Boycott, the agent of Lord Erne. This method of retaliation spread rapidly and soon all landlords' agents throughout Ireland were boycotted.

The Lord-Lieutenant, Lord Cowper, advised Gladstone that law and order would have to be enforced if he wanted the new Land Bill he was preparing for the benefit of Irish tenants to be passed by Parliament. Gladstone was persuaded to bring in a new and severe Crimes Bill in 1882 for a period of three years. It was, of course, hotly contested by the Irish members. Powers of obstruction in the House were at that time unlimited. After a record sitting of nearly two full days, the Speaker at last, on his own responsibility, forced a vote and the Bill was passed. Gladstone then brought in his Land Bill, known as 'the three Fs', because it provided fair rents for tenants, fixity of tenure, and gave them the right to sell their holdings freely. This brought a further resignation from the Cabinet, that of the Duke of Argyll, who was Lord Privy Seal. He wrote to Gladstone: 'You think you have the Cabinet behind you. I wish you had heard the talk when you went off to see the Queen and left us mice without the cat.'

Despite these fresh concessions terrorist outrages in Ireland continued, and on 12th October 1881, after a further meeting of the Cabinet at No. 10, Parnell was arrested. Gladstone announced the news at the Guildhall, where he had gone to receive the Freedom of the City of London. It was received by the large audience with frenzied cheering. Parnell was released six months later following his promise to support the Land Bill and Gladstone, for his part, undertook to remit all arrears of rent due from the Irish tenants. This led to a still further resignation from the Cabinet – the third: this time it was the Chief Secretary for Ireland, W. E. Forster. He was replaced by Gladstone's nephew by marriage and Lord Hartington's brother, Lord Frederick Cavendish.

Lord Frederick crossed to Ireland the next day and was walking across Phoenix Park in Dublin with his Permanent Under-Secretary, T. H. Burke, when they were set upon by terrorists and both stabbed to death. When the news reached London late that evening and was taken to Gladstone, who had been dining with his wife at the Austrian Embassy, they had already left – Mrs. Gladstone to go on alone to a party at the Admiralty, while Gladstone set out on foot on his customary nightly errand of stopping prostitutes in the streets and urging them to go home and adopt a more moral way of life. Mrs. Gladstone, the moment she arrived at the Admiralty, was asked to return at once to No. 10 Downing Street. There, as she entered, she was informed of the tragedy by Gladstone's secretary. They were still standing in the inner hall of No. 10 when the front door opened and Gladstone walked in. He overheard what was being said and stood there stunned, trying to take it in; then seizing his wife's hand, he knelt with her by the front door and they prayed together. They then drove round to see Lady Frederick Cavendish in Carlton House Terrace.

It was by now one o'clock in the morning. Lord Hartington was already there. Lady Frederick has recorded in her journal that Gladstone

297

'came up and almost took me in his arms, and his first words were, "Father, forgive them, for they know not what they do." He then said to me, "Be assured it will not be in vain." . . . I said to him as he was leaving me, "Uncle William, you must never blame yourself for sending him." He said, "Oh no, there can be no question of that." ' The murderers were arrested and brought to justice in the following year 1883.

One further measure of importance introduced by Gladstone during this, his second term as Prime Minister, was the Representation of the People Bill. Its purpose was to extend the franchise by granting household suffrage to country dwellers, whereas Disraeli had granted it in 1867 to town dwellers only. The Bill was introduced in the House of Commons on 28th February 1884 and was expected to add a further two million voters. Gladstone said the strength of a country is increased in proportion to the number of capable citizens who enjoy the vote, because they 'had a direct and energetic interest in the well-being and the unity of the State'. He also promised to bring in as soon as possible a further Bill for the redistribution of the constituencies. Although it was obvious that the additional country voters would add greatly to the strength of the Conservatives, the Lords, overwhelmingly Tory though they were, insisted that the two Bills should be dealt with at the same time and not separately. Lord Salisbury, regarded by many as the leader of the Opposition since Disraeli's death, revealed that the real concern of the Tories was that the extension of the franchise, in Ireland at any rate, would make the most ignorant and disaffected class supreme at the polling booth. But Gladstone was not prepared to yield. He started an agitation to awaken the country once again to the obstructive powers of the Lords. A monster demonstration was held in London. Thousands of supporters of Gladstone's Bill marched through the streets. The issue would have to be fought out, Gladstone decided, at an election on the question whether the House of Lords should survive.

This brought the Queen into immediate action. Her Majesty informed the Prime Minister that the House of Lords reflected the 'true feeling of the country' better than the House of Commons. But Gladstone shrugged it off, saying it was useless to argue with 'Her Infallibility'. One member of the Cabinet, Lord Hartington, threatened to resign; another, Joseph Chamberlain, went about making violent speeches against the peers: this brought a further rebuke from the Queen on the Prime Minister's inability to control his colleagues. Gladstone ignored this too and set out on a series of 'whistle-stop' speeches in Scotland on the lines commonly adopted at a Presidential election in the United States. This was too much for the Queen. Her Majesty, in Balmoral at the time, complained to her secretary, General Ponsonby, of 'his *constant* speeches at every station. . . . The Queen is *utterly* disgusted with his *stump* oratory – so unworthy of his position – almost under her very nose.'

It was through her intervention, however, that a constitutional crisis was finally averted. She suggested that there should be secret negotiations between the two political parties with a view to reaching a compromise. Lord Salisbury and Sir Stafford Northcote, representing the Conservatives, came to No. 10 Downing Street to talk it over with Gladstone, Lord Hartington, and Sir Charles Dilke, who was President of the Local Government Board and one of the most advanced Radicals in the Government. Gladstone's daughter Mary records that she heard loud voices emerging from her father's room, the loudest being those of Salisbury and Dilke: 'But Papa was extremely cheerful when he emerged.' A compromise was eventually reached. Gladstone agreed to bring in his Redistribution Bill at once and Salisbury agreed to withdraw further opposition in the Lords. The Act was passed in 1885. Most of the two-member constituencies were split up and all the remaining rotten boroughs were abolished.

The Government had not much longer to live. When the Crimes Act came up for renewal in 1885 there were endless quarrels in the Cabinet. Lord Spencer, Lord-Lieutenant of Ireland, and Henry Campbell-Bannerman, the Chief Secretary, were insistent that it must be renewed. Chamberlain and Dilke, on the other hand, were for conciliation and suggested that Ireland should be given local self-government, but not a separate Parliament. The majority in the Cabinet was against this. Gladstone decided that in these circumstances some parts at least of the Coercion Act should be renewed. Chamberlain and Dilke instantly resigned.

When Gladstone's intentions were announced in the House the Irish M.P.s, to get their own back, voted with the Conservatives against the Budget and the Government was defeated by twelve votes.

Gladstone resigned the next day. He noted in his diary that it was a great relief to him, 'including in this sensation my painful relations with the Queen, who will have a like feeling.'

CHAPTER 29
The Home Rule Battle

THE Queen sent for Salisbury and asked him to form a new Government. This many regarded as irregular, since his position as Disraeli's successor had never been clearly established: in fact he shared the leadership of the Conservative Party with Sir Stafford Northcote, who led the Tories in the Commons.

Lord Randolph Churchill, who had formed the militant Fourth Party consisting of only four M.P.s (one of whom was Salisbury's nephew Arthur James Balfour) and had sniped ceaselessly at Northcote, declared that he would not serve in the new Government unless Northcote gave up the leadership. To this Northcote eventually agreed and went to the House of Lords as the first Earl of Iddesleigh. He was appointed First Lord of the Treasury, but was not Prime Minister. Salisbury took on that role, just as Chatham had done without being First Lord of the Treasury: with it Salisbury combined the office of Foreign Secretary. Lord Randolph Churchill went to the India Office.

The Cecils had attained distinction in the reign of Elizabeth the First when William Cecil, Lord Burleigh, was appointed her Chief

Secretary. Later his son Robert, who was Chief Secretary to her successor James the First, was made the Earl of Salisbury. But the family had been inactive and in obscurity for nearly two centuries. 'The general mediocrity of intelligence which the family displayed,' wrote their descendant Lady Gwendolen Cecil,[122] daughter of the Salisbury who now became Prime Minister, 'was only varied by instances of quite exceptional stupidity' – until now.

Gladstone's personal furniture and pictures were moved out of No. 10, but Salisbury did not move in. Instead Northcote took up his residence in the house. He arrived early: as he walked up the main stairway he saw Gladstone descending. They greeted each other warmly and paused to talk. More than thirty years before, Gladstone, at that time a Conservative, had Northcote as his private secretary at the Board of Trade. Before leaving Gladstone gave him 'three of his books on Homer' – it was one of Gladstone's chief diversions to translate Homer.

Northcote did not enter Parliament until 1855. His administrative skill had already led to his being selected by Prince Albert as one of the secretaries on the Commission in charge of the Great Exhibition of 1851. At the time of moving into No. 10 Northcote, or Iddesleigh as he was by now, was nearly sixty-seven. He had been married for over forty years and had ten children, seven of them sons. Though they were all grown up (his heir was just forty) some still lived with him. He was a gentle, quiet-tempered man, extremely efficient, but quite unequal to meeting the conspiracies against him by the more ardent spirits in his Party. His interest was largely centred on children, not only his own, but the children of the poor and underprivileged: he set up a home for them near his own country estate outside Exeter, where he used to go and read to them from Dickens' books, which he loved.

His stay at No. 10 was brief, for Salisbury was in office for only 227 days. His Party was in a minority in the House of Commons. In order to obtain the support of the Irish members the new Tory Government dropped Coercion. That at any rate was a step in the right direction. The possibility of improving their position by a General Election was next considered. The new register, it was felt, might benefit them. If only the greatly increased Irish electorate, of which Salisbury had been

The walled garden of No. 10 Downing Street. The flower beds edging the wall were planted by Neville Chamberlain. Beyond the wall is Horse Guards Parade. The door in the wall was used by Churchill during the war. The Cabinet Room opens on to the terrace from which a double flight of steps lead down to the garden.

This cartoon of John Wilkes was drawn from life by Hogarth in 1763 and was published at the time of the cry for 'Wilkes and Liberty'.

so openly critical, could be induced to come to their support – but the question was how? In order to achieve this Lord Randolph Churchill went to see Parnell. Churchill happened to be the only Englishman Parnell trusted, largely because Churchill had himself been a rebel. Parnell was ready to make a pact, but, with an eye to getting a better bid from the other side, asked Gladstone what terms he was prepared to offer. Gladstone was horrified and refused to counter-bid, although he had already made up his mind that Home Rule was the only solution for the Irish crisis. He had not, however, revealed this even to his closest colleagues (apart from Lord Granville) and he refused to make it an issue at the election.

Gladstone liked Salisbury and often stayed at Hatfield with him. He was drawn by Salisbury's high, conscientious principles, but there their closeness ended. Churchill, on the other hand, he wholly mistrusted. He felt that, like Disraeli, who had snatched the leadership of the Conservative Party from Peel, so now Churchill, having disposed of Northcote, was trying to take it away from Salisbury, by campaigning nebulously for a 'Tory democracy': this Gladstone described as 'demagogism not ennobled by love and appreciation of liberty, but applied in the worst way to put down the pacific, law-respecting, economic elements which ennobled the old Conservatism.' Salisbury, for his part, was determined not to give Churchill that chance. He showed patience and strove to smooth out his mutinous outbursts both inside and out of the Cabinet. The Queen, who seemed to be fully informed of what was going on, also took a hand in this. She wrote indignantly that 'the youngest member of the Cabinet must not be allowed to dictate to the others. It will *not* do and Lord Salisbury must really put his foot down.' After a time the mutiny was effectively crushed.

The General Election, held in November 1885, gave the Liberals a majority. But so long as the Tories were able to work with the Irish (who now numbered eighty-six), the two sides were equally balanced. The position in the House was thus a dead heat. Salisbury nevertheless decided to carry on.

In December, at a Cabinet meeting at No. 10, Lord Carnarvon, Lord-Lieutenant of Ireland, pleaded that Ireland should be given Home Rule. This startled the Conservatives and it was rejected – all the others voted against it.

Unaware of this, Gladstone decided on the very next day to approach Salisbury with precisely the same suggestion. Without consulting his colleagues, he set out for the Duke of Westminster's country house, where he had learned Salisbury was staying. There he found a large house party. He took Salisbury's nephew Arthur Balfour aside and told him that, unless Home Rule was given to Ireland at once, the violence and the assassinations would spread not only in Ireland but also in England. He offered to support Salisbury wholeheartedly if he brought in Home Rule: there should be no party conflict on this. It was discussed later by Salisbury's Cabinet and was once again rejected. They merely saw in it a plot by Gladstone to split the Conservative Party.

Gladstone was in fact faced with the eventual disruption of his own Party. So far it had only been whispered that he was in favour of Home Rule. When the facts emerged, through interviews given to the Press by Gladstone's son Herbert, the storm burst. Hartington publicly announced his opposition to Home Rule. Chamberlain and John Bright were also opposed to it. Soon there were still other objectors. When the House met and the Tory leader, Sir Michael Hicks-Beach, gave notice of Salisbury's intention to introduce a new Coercion Act, Gladstone rose and announced that he was going to turn the Government out at once. 'Are you prepared to go forward without Hartington and Chamberlain?' he was asked privately. 'Yes,' he replied. 'I am prepared to go forward without anybody.' He acted on it that same night and in the small hours the Government was defeated by 74 votes.

Salisbury resigned the next day, 28th January 1886, and Gladstone, now aged seventy-six, was asked by the Queen to form a new Government. Her Majesty had told her secretary Ponsonby: 'She does not in the least care, but rather wishes it should be known that she had the greatest possible disinclination to take this half crazy and really in many ways ridiculous old man – for the sake of the country.'

It was Gladstone's third term as Prime Minister and, as it turned out, it did not last any longer than Salisbury's first – a mere six months. The revolt in his Party had already begun. Eighteen Liberals, including Lord Hartington, voted with the Conservatives, and it was impossible to see how far this revolt would spread. With the selection of his Cabinet the schism became clearer. In addition to Hartingon and John

Bright, Lord Northbrook, Lord Selbourne, Lord Carlingford and the Duke of Argyll also refused to serve. This represented in effect the break away of the old Whig families who had once dominated the progressive political group. One by one they drifted now, into the Conservative camp. Lord Granville, however, remained loyal and Gladstone also had the support, a little reluctantly, of Lord Rosebery, Lord Spencer (whose name had once been associated with repression and coercion) and Lord Ripon, the son of a previous Prime Minister, Viscount Goderich, 'Prosperity Robinson'. Joseph Chamberlain agreed to take office, though he made it clear that he would have preferred 'a more limited scheme of local government' in Ireland. His friend Sir George Trevelyan joined the Cabinet with the same reservation. Sir Charles Dilke, who had just become involved in an unsavoury divorce case and had been advised by friends to flee the country because of the possibility of prosecution for perjury, was unable to serve.

But despite these recurrent stresses, the abuse and ridicule hurled at him publicly, the Queen's continuing displeasure, and his advanced age, Gladstone faced with resolve and in excellent spirits the adjustment he planned to put through. It was evident, of course, though possibly not to him, that even if he succeeded in getting the Commons to accept Home Rule for Ireland, the Lords would certainly reject it, and many of those still loyal to him in the Party dreaded forcing a constitutional crisis between the two Houses on an issue that was not likely to be popular. Gladstone was almost ostracized in society. Dighton Probyn, V.C., a member of the Prince of Wales's Household, wrote to the Queen's Secretary, General Ponsonby: 'Don't talk to me about Gladstone. I pray to God that he may be shut up as a lunatic at once, and thus save the Empire from the Destruction which he is leading her to. If he is not mad, he is a Traitor.'

Gladstone still clung to the hope of winning Salisbury's support on Home Rule for Ireland since it was a necessity that conscience must concede and Salisbury was a conscientious man. But this he did not get. Nor was he able to hold the Radicals under Joseph Chamberlain, despite the fact that Chamberlain had come into the Government. Obsessed as he was with Ireland, Gladstone ignored their persistent demand for social reforms at home. With these he was certainly in sympathy, but he disliked Chamberlain and when the latter resigned two months later, Gladstone told Lord Rosebery, his loyal Foreign Secretary, that nothing that had happened since the Government was formed had given him comparable satisfaction.[121] This resignation occurred when details of Gladstone's Home Rule plan were finally unfolded to the Cabinet. Chamberlain rose immediately from the table and, accompanied by his friend Trevelyan, 'stalked out of the Cabinet room'. Gladstone made no effort to call them back or even to question them.

A few days later, when Gladstone left No. 10 to drive to the Houses of Parliament, the rain was falling in torrents: nevertheless a large crowd, sodden but with their enthusiasm undamped, cheered him lustily as he went past. In the House itself the scene is described by contemporary observers as without parallel in living memory. Never before was it seen to be so crowded. Extra chairs and benches had been brought in and occupied every inch of floor space. Gladstone's daughter Mary, who sat with her mother and sisters in the gallery beside Lady Frederick Cavendish, wrote in her diary that 'the air tingled with excitement and emotion'. When Gladstone entered the Chamber at 4.30 his supporters rose and greeted him with tremendous applause. He spoke for three and a half hours. Home Rule, he pointed out, would not destroy the Empire, but would preserve and strengthen the bonds. Parliament in London, where Irish members would no longer be sitting, would still have control of foreign policy, defence, customs and excise, coinage, and so on. As far as Ulster was concerned, 'the Protestant minority should have its wishes considered to the utmost practicable extent.'

The debate went on for two months. The Bill was attacked by Chamberlain, Lord Hartington and others. Randolph Churchill declared bluntly that 'Ulster would fight'. Even the Irish did not like the Bill entirely.

Chamberlain, calling a meeting of those Liberals who were against their leader, mustered as many as fifty-five. John Bright, unable to come, sent a letter to say that he would vote against the Bill. It was surrender, he said – that word again: Gladstone had been accused of surrender in the Sudan, in the Transvaal and elsewhere.

When the vote was taken at one o'clock in the morning, ninety-three Liberals voted against it. But despite this enormous defection of his followers, there were 313 for and 343 against – an adverse majority of only thirty. At the Cabinet meeting next morning, though pale and bent, Gladstone remained undaunted. He dismissed abruptly the suggestion that he should resign. He had decided to appeal to the country, he said, and the Queen was asked to dissolve Parliament.

During the election Lord Randolph Churchill attacked him savagely. 'Mr. Gladstone has reserved for his closing days a conspiracy against the honour of Britain and the welfare of Ireland, more startlingly base than any of those other numerous designs and plots which, during the last quarter of a century, have occupied his imagination.' He called the design for the separation of Ireland from Britain 'this monstrous mixture of imbecility, extravagance, and political hysterics . . . the united genius of Bedlam and Colney Hatch would strive in vain to produce a more striking issue of absurdities.'

Gladstone suffered a shattering defeat. The Conservatives got 316 seats; with them were 78 Liberal Unionists under Chamberlain. The Gladstone Liberals numbered 191 and even with the 85 Irish Nationalists, they were in a minority of 118 in the House of Commons.

The Queen was delighted to receive his resignation and sent for Lord Salisbury, who asked Lord Hartington, the seceding Liberal, to take over the office of Prime Minister, but he declined. So Salisbury formed his second administration in July 1886, a wholly Conservative Government, and was to remain in office for just over six years. Lord Randolph Churchill was rewarded for his invective by being appointed Chancellor of the Exchequer and Leader of the House of Commons.

CHAPTER 30
W. H. Smith Moves in

Lord Iddesleigh (formerly Sir Stafford Northcote) was appointed Foreign Secretary in Salisbury's new Administration, a notable honour, for it was an office to which Salisbury himself had been very much attached and which he had retained during his previous term as Prime Minister.

Thus once more, as Gladstone vacated No. 10, Iddesleigh moved in, but he did not retain the office for long. He resigned in the following January, after only six months as Foreign Secretary, and at the same time gave up the house. He retired to his home in the country while Salisbury went back to the Foreign Office. Salisbury, though Prime Minister, was once again not First Lord of the Treasury.

Four days after retiring, Iddesleigh came up from Exeter to see Salisbury. He called at the Foreign Office first, then walked across Downing Street to No. 10. But he did not get as far as the Cabinet room, which, like his predecessors, Salisbury used as his office, but, feeling very ill as he reached the ante-room, he sank into a chair. They found him breathing with great difficulty. He never spoke again and died during the course of the afternoon.

The house was not left empty. Salisbury continued to live in his town house in Arlington Street, going to the famous family residence at Hatfield for the weekends. But in Iddesleigh's place on the other floors there was a new tenant, unlike, either by birth or background, any other who had ever lived there. The new tenant was W. H. Smith, whose name is seen today outside bookstalls throughout Britain. He was the son of a modest newsagent, who to begin with had just a small shop in the Strand above which Smith was born in 1825. He was thus sixty-one years old when he moved into No. 10.

Actually W. H. Smith got into No. 10 following a row with Lord Randolph Churchill. As Chancellor of the Exchequer, Churchill was resolved on imposing the most severe economies. He declared that the Army and Navy estimates were too high and insisted on drastic pruning, though in fact the combined estimates for the two Services were lower than they had been the year before. Smith, as Secretary for War, thought it imprudent to prune the Army estimates any further, and Churchill asked the Prime Minister for an interview. On 15th December 1886 Salisbury wrote to him: 'My dear Randolph – I will be in Downing Street at half past three. I have got to go to Windsor at a quarter to five. . . .

'The Cabinet, happily, not I, will have to decide the controversy between you and Smith. But it will be a serious responsibility to refuse the demands of a War Minister so little imaginative as Smith, especially at such a time. It was curious that, two days ago, I was listening here to the most indignant denunciations of Smith for his economy – from Wolseley★ – I am rather surprised at G. Hamilton† being able to reduce so much. I hope it is all right.'

Churchill, at the interview, insisted that Smith would have to give way and refused to allow the Cabinet to decide. Smith, who had been savagely attacked earlier by Churchill and his Fourth Party, took a strong line too. His comment to Salisbury was: 'It comes to this – is he to be *the* Government? If you are willing that he should be, I shall be delighted, but I could not go on on such conditions.'

A few days later Churchill resigned. His letter was brought by a special messenger, who arrived at Hatfield by the midnight train. A

★ Lord Wolseley, formerly Sir Garnet Wolseley.
† Lord George Hamilton, First Lord of the Admiralty.

ball was in progress. Lord Salisbury was seated beside Princess Mary the Duchess of Teck and her pretty daughter Princess May, later Queen Mary, the consort of King George the Fifth. Salisbury glanced at the letter and continued his conversation with his guests. Lord Randolph Churchill, who had felt that his resignation would bring down the Government, had already sent the news to *The Times*. He was only thirty-seven, but it was in effect the end of what might have been a remarkable political career. The quarrel with W. H. Smith was the culmination of a series of rows Churchill had with the Cabinet. His leaving led to a reconstruction of the Government. It was as a result of this that Iddesleigh went out and Salisbury took on the Foreign Office.

W. H. Smith profited greatly from Churchill's departure. Not only did he succeed him as Leader of the House of Commons, but he was also appointed First Lord of the Treasury, a position normally held by the Prime Minister, with Chatham and Salisbury as the only exceptions in the long history of that office.

Smith had entered politics rather late in life. He did not get into the House of Commons until he was forty-three. He was not an orator. Indeed no one could pretend that he had any discernible talent, save as a businessman. The acumen that had prompted his father to set up bookstalls in railway stations and expand his newsagency into the vast organization of W. H. Smith the son had inherited in ample measure, as well of course as the wealth that was derived from it. It opened many doors to him. Disraeli appointed him Secretary to the Treasury within six years of his entering the House. Three years later he was in the Cabinet as First Lord of the Admiralty: at that time Russia was at war with Turkey and Smith had to send the British fleet to Constantinople. He married a widow named Mrs. Benjamin Leach, who already had a growing family, and from her had a number of sons and daughters. His eldest son, not quite eighteen when they moved into No. 10, rowed for Oxford in the Varsity Boat Race during the period of their stay in this house.

W. H. Smith was a Methodist like his father. He had wanted to take holy orders, but his father, though deeply religious and so high-minded that he refused to allow any book or periodical to be sold at his bookstalls if he thought it coarse or corruptive, insisted that the boy, his only son, should go into the business. This he did, and when he came of age the 'Son' was added to the sign outside the bookstalls. It was not until after his father's death in 1865 that he entered the House of Commons. He had by now joined the Church of England and his entire political life was guided by his high principles. The Queen thought his character admirable, but others, both in his Party and in Gladstone's, referred to him as 'Old Morality' without, however, any hint of disrespect.

A year before he moved into Downing Street the Queen suggested to Lord Salisbury that he might be given the Grand Cross of the Order of the Bath, but with the greatest humility Smith declined it, saying, as Lord Salisbury informed Her Majesty, that 'in his peculiar position with respect to his extraction and the original avocation of his family', he would prefer not to accept it since such an honour was not normally given to 'men of his social standing'.

He wrote to the Queen every night from No. 10 when Parliament was in session, telling her of what went on during the day, of the attacks made upon him by the Irish Members, never omitting to work in vivid descriptions of Gladstone's violent gesticulations and excited harangues.

He worked unflaggingly and in less than two years was utterly worn out. Yet he refused to give in. 'I am very weary,' he wrote to his daughter, 'but I must go on doing my daily work as best I can, looking for guidance and wisdom where alone it can be had, until my rest comes. I hope it is not wrong to long for it.'[127] A year or so later he was given the coveted post of Warden of the Cinque Ports and went down from time to time during the recess to Walmer Castle for a brief respite. It was here that he died in October 1891 in the historic setting where Pitt and Wellington had once lived. His widow was given a Viscountcy and became Viscountess Hambledon: the title passed to her son after her death.

In all he and his family used No. 10 as their London home for four and a half years. He had been second-in-command for the whole of that period and had he lived might possibly have been Salisbury's successor, but that would not have occurred until 1902, by which time W. H. Smith would have been close on eighty years old. Salisbury spoke of him as a 'most lovable man' and used to say that Smith, more than any other man he knew, had shown that character was the most essential equipment for public life. Smith was succeeded as Leader of the Commons by Salisbury's nephew Arthur James Balfour, who in the course of time became Prime Minister. But, though he had to wait nearly eleven years for that, he was appointed First Lord of the Treasury at once and soon moved into No. 10 Downing Street. He took with him his grand piano on which he often played in his small study on the first floor when alone in the evenings. Two of his favourite pictures by Burne-Jones were hung in the State dining-room and a high desk was brought into the Cabinet room for his use and placed near the window.

Balfour was forty-three and still a bachelor, which indeed he remained throughout his life. Through the influence of his uncle he had come into politics at the age of twenty-six, and four years later, in 1878, he accompanied Disraeli and his uncle to the memorable Congress of Berlin as Lord Salisbury's private secretary. At this stage of his life his interest in politics appeared to be somewhat detached: it was no more than taking a hand in the running of a family estate. His main interests were scholarly and social. After Eton and Cambridge he entered the world of intellectuals with his book *Defence of Philosophic Doubt*, which displayed a subtlety of thought and a literary gift that won him the highest praise. In physique he was delicate, in manner languid: a refined indolence, coupled with an air of cynical superiority, led to his being regarded as a *flâneur*. He joined the select coterie of wits known as 'The Souls', displayed a passion for music, played tennis and golf, and plunged wholeheartedly into the diversions of his set. It is surprising that in politics nobody, apart from his uncle, took him at all seriously. That he should have joined Lord Randolph Churchill's Fourth Party caused a certain uneasiness, but he took no part in the wild sallies of the other three in the group and was generally regarded as the odd man out.

Until his uncle became Prime Minister in the summer of 1885 he was regarded in Parliament as a dilettante. Then quite suddenly, and unexpectedly, he was given office. Salisbury made him President of the Local Government Board. It will be recalled that Salisbury's first term of office lasted only six months, but on his return the following summer, Balfour was given a seat in the Cabinet as Secretary for Scotland;

and shortly afterwards he was given the trying and extremely difficult post of Chief Secretary for Ireland. The appointment was received by the Irish Nationalists with contemptuous ridicule, but Balfour, still in his thirties, soon proved himself to be an extremely able administrator. He showed strength and courage and handled Irish problems with remorseless vigour. He enforced coercion, but at the same time endeavoured to remedy some of the more glaring injustices, displaying a calm indifference to the carping both of the Irish and of the Gladstone group of Liberals. He was greatly helped by the downfall of Parnell in 1890 and the eventual disruption of his followers after the scandalous disclosures in the divorce case brought by Captain W. H. O'Shea, which established that Parnell, the Leader of his Party, had been carrying on an adulterous intrigue with Mrs. O'Shea for more than eight years and had had three children by her.

Balfour became Leader of the House of Commons in succession to W. H. Smith in 1891, and his prestige had risen sufficiently to command the respect of the House. Salisbury's six years in office were marked by an expansionist imperial policy, particularly in Africa, where Nigeria and the Gold Coast on one side of that continent and Kenya and Uganda as well as Northern and Southern Rhodesia, Nyasaland and Bechuanaland on the other, were added to the British Empire. This was Britain's share in the general scramble by European nations – particularly France, Germany and Belgium and in a lesser degree Portugal and Italy – for territory in Africa. Britain was first in the field, having acquired scattered settlements in the preceding century, but Salisbury realized: 'It was impossible that England should have the right to lock up the whole of Africa and say that nobody should be there except herself.' The German Kaiser, Wilhelm the Second, who was Queen Victoria's grandson and was to play a notable part in the outbreak of the First World War in 1914, looked askance at some of the recent annexations. In order to placate him and also to win his recognition of Zanzibar as a protectorate, Salisbury offered him the island of Heligoland at the mouth of the Kiel Canal. The Kaiser was delighted, but Queen Victoria was not. Angrily she wrote at once to Salisbury: 'It is a very bad precedent. The next thing will be to pro- pose to give up Gibraltar'; and again two days later: 'That any of my possessions should thus be bartered away causes me great uneasiness.'

The life of Parliament was still limited by the Septennial Act passed in 1716, 175 years before, and the seven years were by now running out. The immense majority with which Salisbury had taken office from Gladstone after the General Election of 1886 had been reduced in a succession of by-elections and Gladstone, though over eighty but still vigorously hacking down trees at Hawarden, was convinced that he would return to power when the next election was held. So certain was he of this that he lived only in rented houses or with friends in London, saying that he would soon be back at No. 10 Downing Street. Those who thought he was too old to take office again were laughed at scornfully by Gladstone's wife, who said her husband would be guilty of a breach of trust if he failed the country when the call came.

In the summer of 1892 Salisbury realized that the General Election could no longer be delayed. On 29th June Parliament was dissolved. The Queen was extremely pessimistic. She regarded the return of this 'deluded excited man of 82' as quite ludicrous. Gladstone's Party was in fact victorious. The results gave his Liberals 273 seats, and with him were 81 Irish Nationalists and one Labour member Keir Hardie, the Scottish miner, who shocked the House by arriving in a cloth cap, while the Liberal Unionists (the opponents of Home Rule) got only 46 seats and the Conservatives were reduced to 269. Gladstone's majority was thus 40, but for it he was dependent of course on the Irish vote.

When Parliament met on 11th August 1892, Mr. H. H. Asquith, a young Liberal M.P. elected for the first time six years before, moved a vote of no confidence in the Conservative Government. Salisbury was defeated and Gladstone became Prime Minister for the fourth time. Her Majesty's terse note to him ended with the words: 'The Queen need scarcely add that she trusts that Mr. Gladstone and his friends will continue to maintain and to promote the honour and welfare of her great Empire.'

Mr. Balfour wrote his last letter from No. 10 on the day the Government was defeated. When he moved out Gladstone moved in, bringing once again some of his own furniture and his piano. He was not, however, satisfied with the furniture already there. Only twelve years before, on his insistence, the State had spent as much as £1,555 on bringing in special furniture for him; an official note to the Treasury explains that it 'became necessary' on his return now in 1892 'to incur considerable expenditure for which no official provision had been made in the Vote for Public Buildings' and that it was done 'in anticipation of formal authority, because they were all more or less inevitable under the new conditions of occupation' which brought 'into use rooms previously not required' and for 'the making of sundry alterations which were needed to obviate inconvenience from the new distribution of the accommodation'. For these 'renovations' at No. 10 the cost was £356, for 'sanitary works' a further £84, for 'new works' £481 and for furniture £858 – a total of £1,779. This was eventually authorized and paid for by the State.

With one at any rate of Gladstone's new Cabinet appointments Her Majesty was pleased. Lord Rosebery, who had been Foreign Secretary for four months in Gladstone's previous Administration, was given that office again. Two others in the new Cabinet – Asquith and Campbell-Bannerman – were, like Rosebery, to be Prime Ministers and to live at No. 10. From then on in fact, save only for Salisbury's final term of office from 1895 to 1902, all Prime Ministers have resided at No. 10.

When Gladstone went to see the Queen she found it trying to have him sit close to her because he was so deaf. She noted that he had 'a weird look in his eyes, a feeble expression about the mouth'. She felt he was 'no longer fitted to be at the head of a Government'. Gladstone's analysis of her (the Queen was now seventy-four) was just as unfavourable. He found that 'her intellect' had 'grown sluggish and her judgement was impaired'. He got the impression, he said afterwards, that it was the sort of talk that Marie Antoinette might have had with her executioner at the guillotine.

Without any delay Gladstone set to work on the Irish Home Rule Bill. He knew the Queen was violently opposed to it, but he went ahead just the same. It occupied a great deal of his time: he spent hours every day on the draft and it was discussed again and again by the Cabinet committee set up for the purpose. By January it was ready. The full Cabinet, consisting now of seventeen members, then examined it and on 13th February 1893 it was presented to the House of Commons. Gladstone spoke for two and a half hours. Winston Churchill, then only eighteen, was in the Distinguished Strangers' Gallery when some days later Gladstone, speaking again, wound up the debate on the Second

Reading of the Bill. 'The Grand Old Man', Churchill has recorded, 'looked like a great white eagle, at once fierce and splendid. His sentences rolled forth majestically and everyone hung upon his lips and gestures, eager to cheer or deride. He was at the climax of a tremendous passage about how the Liberal Party had always carried every cause it had espoused to victory. He made a slip, "And there is no cause," he exclaimed "for which the Liberal Party have suffered so much or *descended so low*." How the Tories leapt and roared with delight! But Mr. Gladstone, shaking his right hand with fingers spread claw-like, quelled the tumult and resumed, "But we have risen again." '[128]

The Second Reading was carried by 347 votes to 304. Then the House went into committee and the Prime Minister, tireless as ever, took personal charge, making speeches on almost every amendment and hardly ever leaving the House. Apart from Lord Randolph Churchill, still his most vehement critic, Gladstone's truly formidable opponent was Joseph Chamberlain, who was joined now by his son Austen, only recently elected to Parliament. The debates got heated. There was often an uproar. Blows were exchanged between Members. But Gladstone went doggedly on. All through that summer Parliament was kept in session. Randolph Churchill confessed later his warm admiration for the old man. But for Home Rule, 'which I can never countenance,' he said, he would have been prepared gladly to give up the Conservative Party and Lord Salisbury to join Gladstone.

In September in the final vote, the Bill was passed by the House of Commons with a majority of 40. In the Upper House Lord Hartington, once a member of Gladstone's Government and now the Duke of Devonshire, moved the rejection of the Bill, with the ardent support of Lord Salisbury. The Lords threw it out by a crushing majority – 41 for, 419 against.

At a Cabinet meeting at No. 10 Gladstone announced that he was going to dissolve Parliament and have an immediate election on the issue 'Peers *versus* the People'. That was the conflict at the time of the Reform Bill sixty years earlier and it was to be fought out again in a dozen years or so. But his colleagues refused now to support him in this and Gladstone agreed finally to bide his time, aware that there would be a further clash with the Lords shortly.

A quarrel with his colleagues developed, however, shortly afterwards

- this time over the Naval estimates. In view of the continuous increase in armaments by foreign powers, public opinion was disturbed and so was the Queen. The Opposition called for an immediate expansion of the Navy. Gladstone thought the alarm was unnecessary. But his Cabinet took a different view. Gladstone refused firmly to give way. Day after day they argued. On one occasion he talked to the Cabinet for a full hour.

It was noticed by his friends that a great change had come over Gladstone. His private life at No. 10 was by now completely dominated by his wife and his family. They told him what he should or should not do. 'Mr. G.', his secretary Sir Algernon West wailed, 'was becoming more and more the mere tool in Mrs. G's hands, and she was less and less scrupulous about plans. If she wanted Mr. G. to go away, he went regardless of all public calls.' At times he acted strangely. He would suddenly and without any warning get down on his knees to say his prayers even when there were others in the room. On one occasion, after glancing about him, he sent Lord Ripon, who was a Roman Catholic, and John Morley, an agnostic, out of the room before beginning his prayers.

The following January (1894) he left for Biarritz with his wife and a party of friends. On his return a month later he gave a dinner at No. 10 for the Cabinet.* His colleagues expected him to announce his resignation, but he said nothing. When the dinner was over Rosebery asked if he would like the doors locked. Gladstone said: 'Certainly. If anyone has any topic to raise, it might be done now.' He glanced about him but no one spoke. It was not until a fortnight later that he wrote to the Queen to say that he was thinking of resigning. He saw her the next day and was grieved to find her 'at the highest point of her cheerfulness'. He left, however, without resigning.

On 1st March he assembled his Cabinet and at last informed them of his intention. They were prepared for it; indeed Sir William Harcourt, the Chancellor of the Exchequer, pulled out of his pocket the manuscript of his farewell speech and began to deliver it. Many dabbed their eyes. Gladstone, replying, spoke for only four minutes. Then he rose and saying 'God bless you all' went out of the room. The others trooped

---

* On 17th February 1894.

out through a different door, walked slowly down the long corridor and out into Downing Street. Gladstone spoke of it as 'a really moving scene' and of his colleagues as 'that blubbering Cabinet'.

His parting from the Queen at Windsor was so cold and cruel that it remained a smarting wound in his memory until he died. Not one word of appreciation was said by her of his many years of devoted and self-sacrificing service. She did not even consult him about his successor, but sent for Lord Rosebery, merely because she had always liked him and greatly preferred him to the others.

CHAPTER 31
The Boer War

ROSEBERY, the fifth earl, belonged to the old aristocracy. His mother, Lady Catherine Stanhope, was the daughter of the fourth Earl Stanhope and through her Rosebery was related to the Pitts and the Grenvilles. He did not distinguish himself at Eton (his tutor described him as 'one of those who seek the palm without the dust') and he was sent down from Christ Church at Oxford because he made his interest in racehorses a part of his official curriculum. As early as 1868, when he was twenty-one, he inherited the earldom and took his seat in the House of Lords. His marriage to Hannah, the daughter of Baron Meyer de Rothschild, brought him an immense fortune, which helped considerably in the furtherance of his political career.

As Lord-Lieutenant of Midlothian and responsible for Gladstone's adoption by the constituency, Lord Rosebery was in constant contact with the Leader of his Party and inevitably a close attachment followed. Gladstone appointed him Under-Secretary at the Home Office in 1880 and later Lord Privy Seal. He was Foreign Secretary in two of Gladstone's Administrations and was in that office at the time of Gladstone's resignation.

When the Queen appointed him Prime Minister he was comparatively young, only forty-seven. He did not move into No. 10 at once, but stayed on in his luxurious house in Berkeley Square, selecting, however, just one room on the first floor at No. 10 Downing Street, which was furnished as a bedroom and used occasionally. Some months later, in January 1895, while his own house was under repair, he moved in completely. But after five months he had to move out again, for his term as Prime Minister was brief – fifteen months in all. Friends consoled him with the reminder that Disraeli's first Premiership lasted only ten months. But Rosebery never returned.

From the outset, in fact before he had even formed his Government, Rosebery had trouble with some members of his Party. On the very first day after his appointment, he wrote to the Queen's Secretary, General Ponsonby: 'Things are not going very well. One or two of my colleagues in the Commons are endeavouring to impose conditions upon me – one of which is that the new Foreign Minister shall be in the House of Commons. I have refused to submit to any conditions not ordinarily imposed on a Prime Minister. I don't want to be Prime Minister at all, but if I am to be, I must be a real one.' On 4th March 1894 he wrote to Arthur Godley, who had been private secretary to Gladstone: 'I do not think I shall like any of the duties of my new position. Patronage is odious: ecclesiastical patronage distressing.'[129]

Much of the trouble was caused by the Queen's arbitrary action in selecting Rosebery. Sir William Harcourt felt that the succession should have been his because of his position as Leader of the House of Commons and Chancellor of the Exchequer. Had Gladstone been consulted his recommendation would have ignored both Rosebery and Harcourt and the dissensions might conceivably have been more acute.

At a Party meeting, held at the Foreign Office on 12th March, Rosebery made it clear that 'we stand where we did. There is no change in measures.' That meant that he was going on with Home Rule for Ireland. But the next day Campbell-Bannerman, the Secretary for War, rushed round to inform him that the Government had been defeated by eight votes in the Commons during a debate on the Queen's Speech when Labouchere, a Radical and a Republican, moved an amendment practically abolishing the House of Lords.

Rosebery had always been interested in the reform of the House of

Lords, but not its abolition. He wanted a small Upper House, consisting
of elected peers and life peers, together with representatives sent from
the Dominions. Time after time he had brought this up, but without
success. Now he decided to act. He sent the Queen, who was in
Florence, an elaborate memorandum on this and followed it up with a
speech at Bradford in which he foreshadowed a 'revision of the constitution'. The Queen was indignant and sent him a sharp rebuke. She
also wrote to the Leader of the Opposition, Lord Salisbury, to ask if his
Party was ready to face a General Election. Salisbury assured her that it
was and added that he was always ready to give her his opinions on any
questions she wished to ask him. It is interesting to recall that Melbourne
at the beginning of her reign, anxious though he was to help the young
and inexperienced Queen, thought it unconstitutional to advise her
after he had ceased to be Prime Minister. Discussing her anxieties about
the Lords with Rosebery later in the year, the Queen was bluntly
told that if Her Majesty would prefer it, he was quite prepared to
go, but Rosebery warned her that nearly half his Cabinet were in
favour of a single Chamber and were fully supported in this by
the more prominent members of his Party. The Queen thought it
more prudent not to force the issue.

The Cabinet too were anxious not to force the issue. They felt that
the Lords should be given every opportunity of showing the country
how obstructive they could be. With this in mind, a series of measures
were prepared that their lordships could be relied upon to reject. This
policy, called 'filling the cup', went on until June 1895. While the
Government's hopes rose at the approaching possibility of success, the
Opposition anticipated it by forcing a snap division on what seemed a
relatively trivial matter, namely the supply of cordite ammunition kept
in reserve in the country. The Government was defeated and Rosebery
resigned.

He was glad to go, for Harcourt had been a constant thorn in his
flesh – 'bitterly hostile' was how Rosebery described him to the Queen.
With Harcourt were other Cabinet colleagues ('a small but powerful
section' to whom he had to speak very strongly from time to
time for taking a different line from his in the House of Commons.
Their support was most noticeably lacking in foreign and colonial
affairs, for they regarded Rosebery as an imperialist. There was an early

divergence of opinion over France. Rosebery felt that the threat to India was as great from the French in the east as from the Russians in the north-west and he wanted Siam to form a substantial buffer between the British in Burma and the French possessions in Indo-China. He also viewed with concern the French encroachments in Africa – on the Niger and towards the Nile headwaters. Others in the Cabinet, however, felt that the British Empire was quite large enough and should not be extended any further. But Rosebery insisted that the time-honoured balance of power still had to be observed, only the balance had now to be maintained over a much wider area.

The strain of these heated arguments in the Cabinet room eventually wore him down. He was sleeping badly. He confided to John Morley, the Chief Secretary for Ireland, that he ought to have allowed Harcourt to try and form a Government when Gladstone resigned. A pleasing consolation came in June when his colt Sir Visto won the Derby – it was his second successive win, for Ladas had won it for him the year before.

The workmen were still in his house in Berkeley Square and it was not yet habitable when he had to leave No. 10. But his furniture was nevertheless taken there. He 'dressed in the caverns of Berkeley Square' he tells us; but the farewell dinner to his friends was given at the Reform Club.

In the House of Lords a few days later he fired a parting salvo. 'God forbid', he said, 'that such causes as Home Rule should be forgotten; but with the present Upper Chamber these could never be carried through.' He ended with a call for 'the annihilation of the House of Lords', which their lordships surprisingly greeted with frantic cheers.

The Queen sent for Salisbury, now in his sixty-sixth year. It was his third and last term as Prime Minister and it lasted for more than seven years, extending across the end of the century until July 1902. Once again he refused to be First Lord of the Treasury or to live at No. 10. Both the office and the house were taken over again by his nephew A. J. Balfour, who also took on the role of Leader of the House of Commons.

The General Election in July (1895) brought a great victory for the Conservatives and the Liberal Unionists, who now worked in close alliance; they were returned with a majority of 152. The new Cabinet accordingly included both Parties. The Duke of Devonshire (formerly Hartington) was Lord President of the Council, Joseph Chamberlain was given the Colonial Office, while Salisbury again took the Foreign Office himself. Lord Randolph Churchill had died earlier that year. Gladstone was to live for two years longer. Balfour paid a courtesy call on the Grand Old Man in 1896, travelling from the railway station to Hawarden on a bicycle. Gladstone was shocked. He thought it 'unbefitting' that the First Lord of the Treasury should use a 'bike'.[130]

In the brief span of two years Britain was very near to becoming involved in four separate wars, each of them with a major power. The supremely skilful handling of each of these sucessive crises stands to the great credit of Salisbury and to some extent also of Balfour.

The first of these nearly led to a fresh war with the United States of America – oddly over the demarcation of the frontier between Venezuela and British Guiana. Salisbury suggested that the dispute should go to arbitration. But quite unexpectedly President Cleveland of the United States asked Congress to appoint a boundary commission, whose findings, he declared, would be enforced by arms if necessary. War seemed extremely likely. Had it come, just as it nearly did during the American Civil War, it would have been the third war between the two countries, if one includes the War of Independence, in the course of little more than a century. Balfour, in a speech at Manchester in January 1896, said: 'The idea of war with the United States carries with it some of the unnatural horror of a civil war. . . . The time will come, the time must come, when someone, some statesman of authority . . . will lay down the doctrine that between English-speaking peoples war is impossible.' The crisis passed. The dispute was eventually settled by arbitration, as Salisbury had initially suggested.

The second of these narrowly averted wars would have been between Britain and Germany. Dr. Jameson, the British Administrator in Rhodesia, led six hundred men in a raid on the Boer territory of Transvaal. The force was captured by President Kruger's men and handed over to Britain for punishment. After a trial in London, Jameson was sentenced to fifteen months imprisonment in Holloway. The Kaiser sent a congratulatory telegram to Kruger and offered to send German troops to protect the Transvaal. The Queen, the newspapers and the British people were incensed at this astounding intervention by a foreign power. Her Majesty chided her grandson severely. It marked the beginning of anti-German feeling in Britain. Though war had been avoided, trouble with the Boers culminated three years later in the South African War.

There was the risk of war with Russia over Port Arthur, a Chinese naval base in Manchuria, which had been captured by the Japanese, but was taken over now by Russia on a long lease; and with France over Fashoda, on the Upper Nile, which had been seized by a French force from the Congo.

But while these major wars were avoided, fighting actually broke out in the Sudan in 1896. The Cabinet decided to reconquer that country, partly as a reprisal for Gordon's death eleven years earlier, but chiefly because of the strategic value of the Upper Nile to Britain in Egypt. The dervishes were now led by the Kalifa, who succeeded the Mahdi in 1885 and had ruled the Sudan ever since. His menacing moves against his neighbours gave Britain the opportunity of deposing him and sending in an army. Kitchener, who was in command, was expressly ordered not to advance beyond Dongola for the time being, largely because Salisbury felt the British Exchequer could not support a heavier financial burden. But Kitchener, as his brother Walter noted, was 'a real autocrat – he does just as he pleases'. By September of that year (1896), Balfour, acting as Prime Minister and presiding over the Cabinet of his uncle, who was ill and much more feeble than his years warranted, informed the Queen that the dervishes were in full retreat. The war went on for a further two years before final victory was won at the battle of Omdurman, in which Winston Churchill, then a young lieutenant, took part in a notable cavalry charge. Kitchener then marched on Foshada and ordered the French to withdraw. When news of this reached Paris there were angry exchanges with Whitehall and a threat of war. But the French eventually withdrew.

The South African War broke out in the following year, 1899. It was popularly regarded as a war on Krugerism. Britain had acquired Cape Colony from the Dutch in the Napoleonic wars and the Boers, to avoid being under the British, set out on their historic trek into the interior. The Orange Free State and the Transvaal, where they settled, found it difficult to survive, surrounded as they were by hostile native races. There were many clashes with the British, and Disraeli annexed the Transvaal in 1877. Two years later an army was sent to crush the Zulus, the fiercest of the local tribes. In 1881, however, Gladstone returned the Transvaal to the Boers. In the succeeding years a gigantic gold rush brought in a vast number of British prospectors. Kruger denied them all rights as citizens, and planned also to take over the British settlements of Cape Colony and Natal. Cecil Rhodes, with an immense fortune from diamonds found at Kimberley and by now Prime Minister of Cape Colony, was just as resolved to overthrow Kruger. War was inevitable. It came following an ultimatum from Kruger demanding the withdrawal of all British troops from the frontier.

The war started badly for the British. With astonishing speed the Boers besieged three important towns – Ladysmith, Mafeking and Kimberley, the diamond metropolis, where Cecil Rhodes happened to be then – and at the same time their commandos invaded Cape Colony. Attempts to recapture these towns brought further serious reverses. In the course of a single week in December, eight thousand British troops advancing to the relief of Kimberley were repulsed; the very next day four thousand men sent to drive the Boers out of Cape Colony were defeated; and a few days later General Buller, attempting to relieve Ladysmith with twenty thousand men, suffered a shattering defeat at Colenso. During that disastrous week Balfour set out every night from No. 10 Downing Street between eleven and twelve and walked over to the War Office in Whitehall, where he climbed 'all the stairs, for there weren't any lifts' and went through the late night telegrams. 'There never was any news except defeats,' he records.

When he called to see the Queen at Windsor, Her Majesty, then in her eighty-first year, said sharply: 'Please understand that there is no one depressed in this house. We are not interested in the possibilities of defeat; they do not exist.' On returning to Downing Street Balfour recorded how 'splendid' it was to go from 'the clamorous croakers in clubs and newspapers into the presence of this little old lady, alone with her women at Windsor, and hear her sweep all their vaticinations into nothingness with a nod.' Winston Churchill, in South Africa as a war correspondent for the *Morning Post*, was taken prisoner by the Boers in November, but escaped a day or so before this 'Black Week', as he called it. 'Mr. Balfour,' he records in *My Early Life*, 'deemed by his critics a ladylike dilettante dialectician, proved himself in this crisis the mainspring of the Imperial Government.' It was decided that General

Buller, in command of the British forces, was incompetent and would have to be replaced. Balfour sent him a telegram: 'If you cannot relieve Ladysmith, hand your command over ... and return home.'[128] Lord Roberts was appointed to take over, with Kitchener as his Chief-of-Staff. Before the end the British had nearly half a million men in khaki in South Africa, including Australians, New Zealanders and Canadians; the Boers never had more than 65,000.

The British Army at the time was governed by regulations 'generally dated about 1870 and intended for Aldershot manœuvres'.* The officers themselves regarded the war, Kitchener groaned, 'too much like a game of polo, with intervals for afternoon tea.' All this had to be adjusted and adjusted quickly. By the middle of February 1900 Kimberley was recaptured and Bloemfontein, the capital of the Orange Free State, was taken on 13th March. Mafeking was relieved in May; a fortnight later British troops took Johannesburg; and five days after that Roberts and Kitchener rode in triumph into Pretoria. Peace was expected 'in another fortnight or three weeks', Kitchener wrote. But it didn't come. The war dragged on. Kruger fled in September.

The following month, with the war still in progress, a General Election, known as the Khaki Election, was held. The Conservatives, expecting a great victory, increased their majority by only three. The election brought Winston Churchill, twenty-five and a Conservative, to the House of Commons for the first time. Salisbury, still Prime Minister in name, took little part now in public affairs. His big, heavy frame was a little bowed, his beard white, his hearing poor, his sight failing. It is recalled that while walking along Downing Street to a Cabinet meeting, he saw a colleague stop and respectfully take off his hat. 'Who is that man?' Salisbury asked his companion. He was informed that the man had been in the Cabinet for some years and was on his way to attend that morning's meeting.

In the summer of 1900 Balfour introduced the motor-car into Downing Street. Travelling up in it from the country with friends, he describes how it had 'a small break-down about every three miles' and adds that they had to finish the journey in hansom-cabs.

Sixteen months after the Queen's death in January 1901, the South

---

* Kitchener to his friend Pandeli Ralli.

326

African war finally ended. Two months later Salisbury retired, leaving to his nephew the title as well as the duties of Prime Minister.

Balfour stayed on at No. 10 for three further years. Although only in his early fifties, he was tired and talked often of retiring. His love for politics, never very great, had begun to be taxed by Joseph Chamberlain's campaign for Tariff Reform and Colonial Protection. Many members of the Conservative Party refused to accept it. There were arguments in the Cabinet and resignations from the Government.

In December 1905 Balfour resigned and King Edward the Seventh sent for Campbell-Bannerman, Leader of the Opposition, who was in his seventieth year. At the General Election that followed the Liberals, who adhered unswervingly to their doctrine of Free Trade, were elected with an immense majority.

CHAPTER 32
The Great Liberal Years

CAMPBELL-BANNERMAN, a Scot by birth, followed Balfour into No. 10 Downing Street. He was the son of Sir James Campbell, an extremely wealthy draper, and inherited a second fortune from his mother's uncle, which led to the addition of the suffix Bannerman. Despite a Conservative background, his admiration for Gladstone caused him to become an ardent Liberal quite early in life. On his entering the House of Commons at the age of thirty-two, he was found to be sufficiently brilliant to be appointed within three years Financial Secretary to the War Office, where he served under the great Army reformer Cardwell, who swept away the traditional practice of purchasing commissions. Campbell-Bannerman later became Secretary of State for War and after serving as Chief Secretary for Ireland was a staunch supporter of Home Rule. Sir William Harcourt said of him that there was 'no more able, more respected, or more popular Minister in the House.'

He had been married for forty-five years when he moved into No. 10. There were no children, but it was generally agreed that no marriage could have been more marked by such intense devotion on both sides. His wife meant much more to him than political success. No possible advancement or reward could be weighed against his life with her; and for her part she wanted nothing except to have him by her side, away from all the distractions that public service demanded. Yet she was unselfish enough not to deny him the leadership of the Party when it was pressed on him in 1898. Everybody knew at the time that the decision would rest with her and with her alone, for she was his final court of appeal in everything. For twenty years before they moved into No. 10, she had been continuously ill and often in great pain. Every moment he could snatch from his political career was spent in her sick room. For months at a time he never went to bed but dozed in a chair by her bedside. Their life was inevitably one of the utmost simplicity.

In 1902 she had a paralytic stroke and it was with the utmost reluctance that she moved from their large and comfortable house in Belgrave Square to No. 10 Downing Street. From the beginning she disliked the house. She found it dark and dingy and extremely inconvenient. 'It is a house of doom,' she said when they moved in. Yet she insisted on coming because the Cabinet room was there as well as the offices of his secretaries and the papers he required, and she wanted to be near him.

At the beginning of his term as Prime Minister she gave a large evening party at No. 10. It was a torture for her to dress and she found it impossible to stand up for more than a few minutes at a time to receive her guests. But she did her duty heroically as hostess in the magnificent State drawing-room on the first floor, propped up in a chair, concealing her pain.

They went to a hotel in Dover for Easter. On their return she was critically ill, and Campbell-Bannerman realized with a pang of despair that she might not recover. But by the end of June she got better. It was their practice to go every year to Marienbad in August, and because she expressed a desire not to depart from the routine, the doctors agreed that the journey could be undertaken, provided it was taken by easy stages. So they set out. She died there on 30th August. A service was held at the cemetery at Marienbad and was attended by King Edward the Seventh, who was there on a holiday; the body was brought back to No. 10 Downing Street and taken on to Scotland for burial.

Campbell-Bannerman was often found in his study at Belmont

Castle, his Scottish home, with his head in his hands, sobbing. Less than a month later he had the first of his heart attacks. He talked of resigning, but his health improved and he decided to carry on.

A very full legislative programme had been forecast in the pledges given to the electorate at the General Election, and of these one had already been fulfilled. This was the granting of self-government to South Africa by the setting up of the Union. This had been agreed to by a unanimous Cabinet as early as 8th February 1906. In the Cabinet Lloyd George, receiving office for the first time, sat as President of the Board of Trade, without having served at all as a junior Minister. He had been most violently opposed to the Boer War and had earned a great deal of unpopularity for his outspokenness. Asquith, who had been Home Secretary in Gladstone's last Cabinet (he was regarded as the best Home Secretary of the century – a considerable tribute when one remembers Peel), now became Chancellor of the Exchequer and moved into No. 11. The new Home Secretary was Gladstone's son, Herbert Gladstone. Sir Edward Grey was Foreign Secretary, an office he held at the outbreak of the First World War eight years later.

When the new Parliament met for the first time on 19th February 1906 there wasn't even standing room for the vast numbers on the Government side. The Liberals together with their Labour* and Irish supporters had 513 members of the total of 670. The Liberals alone numbered 377 and, even if their usual supporters chose to vote with the Opposition, they would have had a clear majority of 132. There was in the circumstances no Bill that the Government could not get through the House of Commons. But there remained, of course, the Lords, who had the right still to reject any or all the measures approved by the Commons.

One of the more contentious reforms which the Lords allowed to go through was the Trades Disputes Bill. It clarified beyond all doubt the right of the workers to strike, legalized peaceful picketing, and safeguarded trade union funds from being mulcted for damages by employers. Next came the Plural Voting Bill to prevent a voter from recording his vote in every constituency in which he happened to have qualifications. This was hotly contested by the Conservatives, who

* The Labour members, numbering 29, included J. Ramsay MacDonald, later the first Labour Prime Minister.

viewed it as a serious encroachment into the rights of property. It was passed by the Commons but rejected by the Lords. The Education Bill, brought in by Augustine Birrell, the Minister of Education, roused serious dissension in the Cabinet. The Government had pledged to put under State control all schools supported by public funds. The question of religious instruction in such schools raised serious problems. Lord Ripon, who had been born at No. 10 Downing Street when his father Viscount Goderich was Prime Minister nearly eighty years before, was a devout Roman Catholic; Lloyd George was an apostle of Non-conformity; others were supporters of the Church of England; Campbell-Bannerman, as a Scottish Presbyterian, stood somewhat aloof. The arguments grew heated. It was generally felt that public opinion was 'not ripe' for the abolition of religious instruction, and it was eventually decided that such instruction should be general and non-denomina-tional: it was set out in the 'Cowper-Temple clause' devised by the William Cowper who as Melbourne's secretary had lived at No. 10. In certain cases special denominational teaching was to be allowed on two mornings a week, but not by the regular teachers nor was it to be charged to the State.

There was furious opposition to this the moment the Bill was intro-duced in the House. Voices were raised in angry protest everywhere. Anglican Bishops held a mass meeting at the Albert Hall and the Roman Catholics supported their denunciation. Only the Nonconformists on the whole were for the Bill. Its fate in the House of Commons was of course never in doubt, but the Lords mauled it mercilessly and the Prime Minister felt it his duty to warn the King that if the Lords persisted in their attitude a most regrettable situation would arise. The quarrel between the two Houses was thus taken one stage further towards a decisive settlement. The Cabinet were quite determined to force it if necessary. Lloyd George summed up the situation in a speech at Oxford in December 1906. 'It is intolerable', he said, 'that every petition of right that comes from the people to their Sovereign should be waylaid and mutilated in this fashion. . . . If the House of Lords persists in its present policy, it will be a much larger measure than the Education Bill that will come up for consideration. It will come upon this issue, whether the country is to be governed by the King and the peers or by the King and the people.'

The King, Edward the Seventh, was angry at his 'name' being brought into this further 'violent tirade' as he called it, and asked the Prime Minister to prevent a repetition. The reply from No. 10 Downing Street pointed out that Lloyd George did not 'greatly err' when the 'exasperating conditions are considered' and explained that the phrase was used because it would have been disrespectful to speak of 'the peers' and 'the people', without a reference to the Head of the State: His Majesty was not, however, appeased. The Cabinet was exceedingly annoyed too, for a great part of the session had been spent in passing Bills only for the Lords to reject them.

In the following year the Government embarked on less controversial reforms. The only major measure was the reorganization of the Army by Haldane, the Secretary of State for War, who set up the Territorial Army and provided for an Expeditionary Force of 160,000 men, both of which rendered vital service in the First World War a few years later.

Many in the Cabinet, however, were not prepared to postpone indefinitely the inescapable fight with the Lords, and the opening shots were fired by the Prime Minister in Manchester in May, when he declared: 'We do not intend to be a Government on sufferance, or to act as caretakers in the House of a Party which the country has rejected'; and again the following month at Plymouth: 'The British people must be master in their own house.' These were merely generalities, but they kept the issue firmly before the electorate, while behind the scenes a plan was being worked out for adjusting the composition of the Upper House and its powers. It was eventually agreed that the powers of the Lords should be dealt with first, its composition later. When this was indicated to the House of Commons, the Prime Minister did not miss the opportunity of attacking Balfour personally for 'signalling' to the Lords to come to his rescue, not on great emergencies affecting national interests, but on measures which touched mainly the interests of the Conservative Party. In introducing a resolution as a forerunner to the Bill, he made clear the Government's intention to restrict the power of the Upper House so that the final decisions of the Commons should become law within a single Parliament; at the same time he accused Balfour of treachery against the Commons. 'I cannot conceive of Sir Robert Peel or Mr. Disraeli', he said, 'treating the House of Commons as the rt. hon. gentleman has treated it.' The resolution was carried by 432 votes to 147.

With his health already impaired, Campbell-Bannerman was finding the strain of office and these exhausting battles too much for him. He had a heart attack the day before he made his speech in the House attacking Balfour. His secretary sat just under the gallery with a dispatch box on his knees specially packed by the doctor in case first aid should be needed. Without his wife to make calls on his time, he had been accepting invitations and entertaining at No. 10 Downing Street as well as in his house in Scotland. His secretary Arthur Ponsonby moved into No. 10 to spare him as much of the strain as he could but many of the calls upon his time and his energy were unavoidable. He had to speak at the Lord Mayor's banquet at the Guildhall on the 9th November, go to Windsor two days later for the visit of the German Kaiser, return for a meeting of the Cabinet and go back to Windsor the next day for a State banquet. He returned to London the same night, attended a lunch to the Kaiser at the Guildhall, where he had to stand for an hour because the Kaiser arrived late, and immediately afterwards caught a train for Bristol where he spoke for an hour. That night he had a serious heart attack and was not expected to live. He was persuaded to take a short rest and then went to Biarritz. Not long after his return, seemingly restored to health, his illness recurred.

It was at this stage that the suffragettes became active in Downing Street. They had called to see Campbell-Bannerman about eighteen months earlier. Assembling by Boadicea's statue on the Embankment, they marched to Downing Street, led by Mrs. Pankhurst, Annie Kenny in her clogs and shawl and Mrs. Wolstenholme-Elmy in grey curls and a bonnet, with others in a forage lorry displaying a large red banner demanding votes for women. Campbell-Bannerman told them that he was in favour of giving them the vote but some members of his Cabinet were against it. It got about later that the fiercest opponent was Asquith.

Now in January 1908 as members of the Cabinet were arriving to discuss the programme for the ensuing session, suffragettes streamed into Downing Street and one of them began to address the group of sightseers. The police dashed across to stop her and found that she and a nurse had chained themselves to the area railings of No. 10. Files and hacksaws had to be fetched from Scotland Yard to free them.

Meanwhile they kept shouting raucously 'Votes for women'. Amid the confusion Mrs. Drummond, known as 'The General', arrived in a taxicab and, eluding the police, forced her way into No. 10, but was promptly ejected. On two subsequent occasions the suffragettes threw stones and broke the windows of the house, shouting: 'Next time it will be bombs'; later, for picketing the street, some were at last arrested.

On 12th February, after a busy day at the House of Commons, Campbell-Bannerman returned to No. 10 Downing Street and had still another heart attack. He never left the house again. On 4th March the King called to see him. His Majesty drove to the garden entrance in the Horse Guards so that his visit should not draw attention, climbed the steps to the terrace and went into the Cabinet room through the french window. He had not been in that room since his visit to Gladstone many years before.

Campbell-Bannerman, who had rallied a little that morning, had been brought down and was helped into an armchair. King and Prime Minister sat alone together in the room, with a nurse in attendance just outside the door. His Majesty urged him not to resign but to wait and see how he felt after Easter.

Queen Alexandra drove in her carriage to the front door of No. 10 from time to time to ask how he was and always brought a bunch of violets she had herself picked.

He resigned on 1st April and died three weeks later in the corner bedroom on the first floor, overlooking St. James's Park and the Horse Guards.

CHAPTER 33
Battle with the Lords

ASQUITH was appointed his successor. All through the last stages of Campbell-Bannerman's illness Herbert Henry Asquith, the Chancellor of the Exchequer, had been acting as Prime Minister. His wife Margot Asquith records in her diary: 'One evening he sent for Henry to go and see him at No. 10 Downing Street and, telling him that he was dying, thanked him for all he had done, particularly for his great work on the South African constitution. He turned to him and said: "Asquith, you are different from the others and I am glad to have known you. . . . God bless you!" C.B. died a few hours after this.'

Asquith and his family moved into No. 10 shortly afterwards. The new Prime Minister was fifty-six years old. He had married his first wife Helen Melland at the age of twenty-five and had by her four children, the eldest of whom Raymond was by now twenty-nine and already married. Of the others, two boys and one girl, Violet* was twenty. The first Mrs. Asquith died in 1891 and three years later

---

* Later Lady Violet Bonham Carter.

Asquith married Margot Tennant, the brilliantly witty daughter of a wealthy baronet. By her he had a daughter and a son Anthony, called 'Puffin', who was five now: with them at No. 10 lived Violet and his younger sons by his first marriage.

Asquith was by birth a Yorkshireman, of a middle-class family of Liberals and Nonconformists. After a distinguished career at Oxford, he went to the Bar and was made a Q.C. while still in his thirties. He had already taken up politics and been elected to Parliament. His vigour as a speaker led Gladstone to single him out to move the vote of no confidence which brought down Salisbury's Government in 1892, when Asquith was forty. Gladstone, on succeeding to the Premiership, appointed Asquith Home Secretary. One of the features that marks this period is that Asquith was responsible for allowing Trafalgar Square to be used by demonstrators. During the Boer War, while his Party was in Opposition, he sided with Lord Rosebery as a Liberal Imperialist and against Campbell-Bannerman, who, like Lloyd George, was pro-Boer. Of Free Trade, on the other hand, he was a staunch supporter and battled vigorously against Chamberlain's advocacy of Tariff Reform.

Shortly after taking over from Campbell-Bannerman in April 1908 and before handing over the office of Chancellor of the Exchequer to Lloyd George, Asquith presented his second Budget, notable for the inauguration of Old Age Pensions.

With the King still in Biarritz, Asquith took the unprecedented course of journeying there in order to kiss hands. Very few changes were made in the Cabinet. Winston Churchill (a Liberal now) succeeded Lloyd George as President of the Board of Trade, Reginald McKenna became First Lord of the Admiralty.

The first year passed uneventfully, save for the Licensing Bill, whereby the Government proposed to reduce the number of licensed public houses in the country as a curb on drunkenness. This roused the wrath of the brewers, some of whom were members of the Upper House, and they threatened to withdraw their support from the Tory Party if their lordships did not squash it. The peers accordingly mustered for battle and refused to give the Bill a second reading. The King, gravely concerned about the impending battle between the two Houses, tried to persuade Lord Lansdowne, the Tory leader in the Lords, to adopt a more conciliatory attitude, and was told that the peers had already had a 'bitter experience' in having to pass Asquith's Old Age Pensions Bill the year before. The pension was a mere five shillings a week payable at the age of seventy.

It was with the presentation of Lloyd George's Budget in 1909 that the continuing conflict with the House of Lords came at last to a head. This was achieved by the cunning device, evolved by Lloyd George and Winston Churchill, of tacking the more revolutionary reforms on to the Budget, since the Lords by tradition were not allowed to inter- fere in any way with a money Bill: they could only accept or reject it.

Lloyd George described it as a 'War Budget' against poverty, which he hoped would, as a result, become 'as remote to the people of the country as the wolves which once infested its forests.' He was resolved on 'robbing the hen roosts', as he termed it. There was a tax on motor- cars, an increase in income tax to one shilling in the pound, the intro- duction of surtax, a heavy increase in death duties and a tax on unearned increases in land values, as well as a tax on undeveloped land. The additional money thus raised was to be used in part to strengthen the Navy by building larger battleships, known as dreadnoughts, to meet any threat from Germany, also to pay the old age pensions, and to assist Lloyd George's novel scheme for social insurance against ill health and against unemployment.

He had the full support of Asquith, Churchill and Sir Edward Grey, the Foreign Secretary, but most of the others in the Cabinet were opposed to the tax on land values.

Lloyd George presented his 'People's Budget' in a four-hour speech on 29th April 1909. It startled many in the House and the country, for taxation was being used for the first time on an extensive scale for the purpose of social reform. It was debated in the Commons for months, often the arguments went on all through the night. On 4th November the House of Commons at last passed it by 379 votes to 149. It was thrown out by the House of Lords on 29th November by an over- whelming majority of Conservative peers, who insisted that it must first be 'submitted to the judgement of the country'. It was the first time for more than 250 years that the peers had rejected a Finance Bill.

Asquith immediately took up the challenge. Parliament was dis- solved and the election campaign was opened on 10th December in the City by Balfour, the Leader of the Conservative Party, and by Asquith at the Albert Hall where he had an audience of ten thousand. From this meeting all women were excluded because of the militant activities of the suffragettes, who had but a few weeks before dog-whipped Winston Churchill at Bristol.

Both Parties were optimistic of victory. The Liberals, who had been faring badly in by-elections, got back with a majority of only two, having 275 to 273 Conservatives. But with 82 Irish Nationalists and 40 Labour members, who could be relied on to vote with the Liberals on this issue, they could count on a majority of 124. It was nevertheless a considerable drop from the combined majority of 357 which they had in the previous Parliament.

It was generally believed that before the election Asquith had extracted a promise from the King that he would agree to a wholesale creation of peers if necessary. Such a promise was not in fact given. 'The King', Asquith's secretary reported after a talk with the King's secretary, 'had come to the conclusion that he would not be justified in creating new peers (say 300) until after a second General Election.'[135] Of this the Cabinet was no doubt informed at the time. On seeing the extremely close result of the election, the King was even more firm in his resolve not to give way. He told Haldane, a member of the Cabinet, that the result was inconclusive and he required 'a much more definite expression of opinion from the country'.[137]

While the Government were manœuvring for their next round, the King died* and Asquith, with his customary consideration, decided to suspend hostilities until the new King, George the Fifth, had a chance to settle down. Meanwhile work was begun on the preparation of the Parliament Bill to restrict the powers of the Upper House.

When the Asquiths moved into No. 10, the Lloyd Georges, who had been living in Chelsea, went into the official residence of the Chancellor of the Exchequer at No. 11. A door in the entrance hall connects the two houses and, though the garden belongs to No. 10, the Chancellor is not denied the use of it. Lloyd George was at that time forty-five years old. He had married Margaret Owen twenty years before and their four children, two boys and two girls, moved into the house with them. Of these the youngest, Megan, was of the same age as Anthony

* 6th May 1910.

Asquith and they soon became inseparable. The communicating door was in constant use. If Puffin did not run into No. 11, Megan would come in and the two children, both five, would divert themselves by going up and down in the lift installed at No. 10 for Campbell-Bannerman. It was a wheezy lift; its gates clattered as the children went in and out and the whine of their endless journeys distracted the Ministers, the secretaries, and even the messengers. But into the Cabinet room, secured by double doors so that the sound of the discussions, and dissensions, should not be overheard, the noise was unable to penetrate. It is among the pleasanter memories at No. 10 that on one of these diverting journeys the lift got stuck. At the time, however, it was not amusing either to the two trapped children or to their elders, who were completely unaware of what had happened. Even the cessation of the lift's whining did not appear to have roused any concern. Alarm came much later when it was discovered that the son of the Prime Minister and the daughter of the Chancellor of the Exchequer had vanished. They were called. The garden was searched. Both families went out into the street and into the Horse Guards Parade at the back. Fear of kidnapping in those disturbed days, with the suffragettes so active and the peers so angry, invaded the parental anxieties. Then suddenly someone pressed the button of the lift and found it was no longer working and the children were rescued, scolded and sent off to bed. Thereafter they took to playing in the garden. Puffin's fresh enthusiasm was for aeroplanes. They had to be launched by hand, preferably in the garden, and Megan was always there to assist. Their chortles of delight as each plane began its journey were not shared by the policemen on duty at the Horse Guards who had to bring the planes back. After their twentieth rescue a note of asperity seemed to creep into the phrase: 'I believe this is yours, sir.'

The warren of rooms at Nos. 10 and 11 were found by the children to be ideal for playing hide-and-seek. They ran in and out of the two houses until called for tea, and if Lloyd George happened to be at home, he came in and they sang hymns, always in Welsh, Puffin generally humming the tune as his knowledge of Welsh was inadequate.

However distracting these childish diversions may have been, the work on the Parliament Bill went on. It was suspended only after King George the Fifth advised the Prime Minister that the two Parties ought to get together and try to work out a compromise. This Asquith readily agreed to. Each side was represented by four members: Asquith and Lloyd George were the principals on the one side, Balfour and Lansdowne on the other. The Tories wanted to reform the Upper House by limiting the number of hereditary peers; Asquith insisted on limiting their power of veto first. Although the Prime Minister made it clear that there was 'no question of their indefinite continuance', the talks dragged on. No solution having been reached by 10th November, Asquith went to Sandringham to report the deadlock to the King. He asked that Parliament should be dissolved so that another General Election – the second that year – should enable them, if victorious, to bring the quarrel with the Lords to a final settlement. The King realized, of course, what that meant. He was as much opposed to the creation of hundreds of new peers as his father, and when a day or two later a promise was sought, His Majesty bluntly refused to give it.

The Cabinet were equally adamant and would not give way either. The King accordingly came up to London to see Asquith, who has been criticized for going to the interview with Lord Crewe, the Leader of the Lords, 'as though he needed a witness'. The King's record of the talk states: 'I agreed most reluctantly to give the Cabinet a secret understanding that in the event of the Government being returned with a majority at the General Election, I should use my prerogative to make peers if asked for. I disliked having to do this very much.'[138]

Parliament was dissolved twelve days later, on 28th November. The result of the election was very much as before – but the slight increase in the number of Irish and Labour members made the total working majority of the Government just a little better. It was the third Liberal win in succession and it was felt not only that the people still retained their confidence in the Government, but that the time had come for the King to comply with the Prime Minister's request.

The King said he wanted to have a word with Lord Lansdowne first. To this Asquith objected. It was clearly the duty of the Sovereign to act on the advice of his Ministers, he said, without consulting the Opposition. Nevertheless, under pressure, he did eventually agree and His Majesty saw Lansdowne at Windsor on 29th January. Parliament met on 6th February. The Parliament Bill was immediately placed before their lordships. Asquith insisted that it should be accepted without any amendment, but the peers mauled it mercilessly. About a hundred peers, who came to be known as 'Diehards', were prepared to 'die in the last ditch' rather than surrender. They were led by Lord Halsbury, Lord Chancellor in Balfour's Tory Government, and in-included Lord Salisbury, son of the famous Prime Minister and a cousin of Balfour.

In this embittered atmosphere the Coronation of the new King took place in June 1911, but the celebrations did not interrupt the discussions of their lordships for long. The mauling of the Parliament Bill went on and on 13th July their work was completed. The Bill was scarcely recognizable.

The time had come now, Asquith felt, to reveal to the peers the guarantee he had extracted from the King: it had been kept secret only out of consideration for His Majesty. He communicated it privately to the Tory leaders, then called on the King to honour his pledge. But His Majesty, still reluctant, insisted that the Bill should first be placed before the Commons in its altered form. Even to this Asquith agreed. When he rose in that House to explain it, there was an uproar. Insults were hurled at the Prime Minister. There were shouts of 'Traitor' and for half an hour he was unable to make himself heard. The rowdiness was led by F. E. Smith, later Lord Birkenhead, and by a brother of Lord Salisbury, Lord Hugh Cecil. Winston Churchill called it 'a squalid, frigid, organized attempt to insult the Prime Minister'. The uproar was so persistent that the Speaker had to suspend the sitting. Not for centuries had such a scene been witnessed in the Commons.

Behind the scenes the 'Diehards' held angry meetings over dinner and exchanged letters, in one at least of which violence was advocated if necessary.* But the more responsible of the Tory peers, following Lansdowne's lead, began to take a more conciliatory view and the Opposition was seriously split in consequence. In this changed atmos-phere, and because the King had urged it, it was decided at a Cabinet meeting at No. 10 that the immediate creation of extra peers should be suspended for the time being until the Parliament Bill, with the Commons' revision of the amendments, was sent back to the Lords.

On 9th August, the hottest for seventy years, Asquith, away in the

* Lord Willoughby de Broke to Lord Halsbury on 28th July 1911.

country with laryngitis, wrote to his secretary: 'If the vote goes wrong in the H. of L., the Cabinet should be summoned for 11.30 Downing Street tomorrow morning and the King asked to postpone his journey. . . . If I have satisfactory news this evening I shall come up for Cabinet 12.30. My voice is on the mend but still croaky.'

Lansdowne directed his arguments in the Lords chiefly against the 'Diehards' of his own party. The safeguards left to the Lords under the Bill, he said, while limiting their power of veto to two years, were worth something, which a wholesale creation of new peers would sweep completely away and, what is more, would present the next Tory Government with a hostile House of Lords, predominantly radical.

There were remarkable scenes in the Lords that day. The debate started at ten o'clock that morning. Peers who had never bothered to take the oath poured in and had to be sworn in before they could vote. Two of their lordships got very drunk and could no longer stand up, nevertheless, with assistance, they took part in the division.

The result was announced at eleven o'clock that night – 131 were for the Bill, 114 against: a majority for the Government of 17. It had scraped through. In addition to the 81 Liberal peers, 37 Tory peers and 13 bishops had given it their support. In the other lobby were seven dukes and many who bore historic names, such as Bute and Clarendon, Salisbury and Malmesbury. The King recorded in his diary: 'The Halsburyites were, thank God, beaten. It is indeed a great relief to me – I am spared any further humiliation by a creation of peers.'

CHAPTER 34
The Prime Minister's Lodgings

MRS. ASQUITH did not like No. 10 Downing Street, known at one time, she writes, as the Prime Minister's 'lodgings'. When she moved in on 5th May 1908, she had a feeling of sadness at leaving their home in Cavendish Square, where every curtain, every chair, table and rug had been chosen by her. That house was a home, whereas No. 10 was not, despite the endeavours of the Board of Works (as it was still called) to make the house comfortable, and the transfer of some of her own furniture, rugs and pictures. She records: 'It is an inconvenient house with three poor staircases, and after living there a few weeks I made up my mind that owing to the impossibility of circulation I could only entertain my Liberal friends at dinner or at garden parties.'[136] Telephones had been put in. There was the lift, but the house was too rambling and one almost needed a map to find one's way. 'Having no bump of locality,' she goes on, 'soon after our arrival I left the drawing-room by one of the five doors and found myself in the garden instead of the hall. By the help of mildly lit telephones and one of the many messengers, I retraced my steps through a long and sepulchral basement, but I began to regret the light and air of my deserted home in Cavendish Square.'

She noted in her diary on 10th November, after being in the house for six months: 'I never knew what prevented anyone coming into this house at any moment: some would say after lunching with us that nothing had. There was a hall porter who looked after our interests when visitors arrived, but he was over-anxious and appeared flurried when spoken to. Poor man, he was never alone; he sat in his hooded chair, snatching pieces of cold mutton at odd hours; tired chauffeurs shared his picture paper, and strange people – not important enough to be noticed by a secretary or a messenger – sat watching him on hard sills in the windows; or, if he were left for a moment, the baize doors would fly open and he would find himself faced by me, seeing a parson, a publican or a protectionist out of the house. But our porter was not a strong man, and any determined Baronet with hopes of favours to come about the time of the King's birthday could have penetrated into No. 10.'

Although she had visited four Prime Ministers at No. 10 – Gladstone, Rosebery, Balfour and Campbell-Bannerman – before moving in and was familiar with the main reception rooms, Mrs. Asquith never realized until she went to live there how ignorant many taxi-drivers were of its location: '10 Downing Street ought to be as well-known in London as the Marble Arch or the Albert Memorial but it is not. . . . I nearly always had to tell my driver the way. I was taken to Down Street, Piccadilly, when I was sleepy or unobservant; or there was a risk of the children and umbrellas being thrown into the streets by the taxi-driver opening the door suddenly from his seat and asking me where Downing Street was. The historic house is in a quiet cul-de-sac off Whitehall and of such diffident architecture that the most ardent tourist would scarcely recognize it again. Knowing as it did every Cabinet secret, and what was going on all over the world, I could not but admire the reserve with which No. 10 Downing Street treated the public. Even the Press while trying to penetrate the Prime Minister's heart was unable to divulge the secret of his home. Liver-coloured and squalid, the outside of No. 10 gives little idea to the man in the street of what it is really like.'

This is because the windows one sees from the street are of unimportant rooms. The big windows in the basement look only into the kitchen quarters. The two ground floor windows give a brief glimpse of the hall. On the first floor the only windows facing the street are those belonging to the room just above the front foor. When the Asquiths moved in that room was assigned to Violet Asquith as her bedroom. She had recently come out and went dancing night after night: 'We never left the dance floor until the band had actually packed up their instruments and gone. To draw it out we would try to persuade them to stay and go on playing. I never got back to No. 10 until the small hours. I remember going to the window very drowsily in the morning and seeing the young men I had danced with hanging up their bowler hats and umbrellas across the road at the Foreign Office.'*

Her room, facing west on to the narrow roadway, never got the sun and was the darkest room in the house. But it was reached by a separate staircase just past the messengers, so she could get to it without disturbing the rest of the house.

With such a large family living there, the place was extremely cramped. A further drawback was that the only bath in the house was off the Prime Minister's sitting-room, by his bedroom on the first floor. In order not to disturb him the family went in when they could. The sitting-room had in fact been partitioned to provide a separate bathroom. There were nevertheless compensations. Mrs. Asquith writes: 'The large garden was a joy to us, although a London garden is more delightful in theory than in practice. All my dresses were either torn or dirtied by disentangling Anthony's aeroplanes from the sooty shrubs; but the green trees and large spaces, after the traffic of our square, were infinitely restful. I amused King Edward by asking him one day if he would allow me to shoot some of his peacocks in St. James's Park as their spring screams disturbed my sleep. The ivied wall was also a danger, and several of our colleagues told me with what anxiety they had watched the athletic feats of my little son, which they could see from the windows of the Cabinet room.'

Throughout the long crisis over the House of Lords Mrs. Asquith could not but keep wondering when they would all have to pack up

* In a statement to the author.

and leave No. 10. Asquith was often away – either at Windsor with the King or dining with Lloyd George or one of the other Ministers. But whether he was at home or not she gave luncheon and dinner parties and had at her table Lord Kitchener, Lord Curzon, Lord Morley (the Leader of the Lords in succession to Crewe) and Arthur Balfour, an old friend, though the Leader of the Opposition.

Early in the battle with the Lords, which began with the rejection of Lloyd George's Budget in 1909, Margot Asquith wrote in her diary: 'Acceptance of the Budget would look like weakness, but in the end it would be better for them to give way: the Lords would hear no more of their veto.' The two year tussle was over now. The Budget had been accepted and Lloyd George was able to bring into operation his plan for national insurance, which laid the foundation of the Welfare State. He harnessed the existing Friendly Societies, which had been offering benefits of a similar kind to subscribers: they now became approved agents of the State scheme. The trade unions co-operated to the full and the forty-two Labour members in the House, led by J. Ramsay Mac-Donald, also gave it their support.

The most bitter opposition came from members of the medical profession, who with rare exceptions declined to work as panel doctors; and equally hostile were the *Daily Mail* and the other news-papers owned by Lord Northcliffe. An enormous demonstration of protest was held at the Albert Hall, at which titled women exhorted all parlourmaids to refuse to lick their national insurance stamps. In the House of Lords the arguments went on for six months. But after certain adjustments the Bill eventually went through.

The way was clear now for still further reforms, beginning with land reform, and going on to the setting of a minimum wage for all farm workers as well as security of tenure for farmers. But crises disrupted the programme of the Government. The first of these was the Marconi scandal.

At the Imperial Conference (as it was then called) held in London in the summer of 1911, it had been decided that to improve communica-tions a chain of wireless stations should be established across the Empire. Tenders were invited and the tender submitted by the English Marconi Company was accepted by the Postmaster-General, Herbert Samuel (later Viscount Samuel) in March of the following year (1912). This roused a surprising amount of gossip. It was not only whispered but affirmed that, since the managing director of the Marconi Company was Mr. Godfrey Isaacs, whose brother Sir Rufus Isaacs (later the Marquess of Reading) was Attorney-General in Asquith's Government, use was being made by certain Liberal Ministers to deal on the Stock Exchange in the shares of the Marconi Company, with considerable profit to themselves. It was stated scurrilously in one newspaper that it had been 'secretly arranged between Isaacs and Samuel that the British people shall give the Marconi Company a very large sum of money through the agency of the said Samuel and for the benefit of the said Isaacs.'[139] A second charge alleged that Rufus Isaacs, Lloyd George and the Master of Elibank, until recently the Liberal Chief Whip, acting on inside knowledge, had bought blocks of shares in the Marconi Company and had pocketed the profits.

Anxious discussions over all this took place in the Cabinet room. Asquith learned that 'there was not the slightest foundation in fact for either of the two sets of allegations'. Rufus Isaacs and Lloyd George had bought no shares at all in the English Marconi Company, which had been given the contract, but in the American Marconi Company, which had no interest whatsoever in the English company, but merely had the right to operate the Marconi patents in the United States. Asquith agreed that in these circumstances the shares they had bought, and still held incidentally, in no way conflicted with their duty as Ministers. 'On balance,' Asquith adds, 'they were substantial losers by the transaction.'[139]

In the House of Commons in October 1912 Asquith proposed the appointment of a Select Committee to investigate all the circumstances of the contract given to the Marconi Company. All the rumours against Samuel had been dropped by now, nor was anything made of the allegations against the Master of Elibank.

The Committee issued two reports in June 1913. Both acquitted the Ministers concerned of all the charges. 'Their honour, both their private and their public honour,' Asquith said in the House, 'is at this moment absolutely unstained. They have, as this Committee has shown by its unanimous verdict, abused no public trust. They retain, I can say this with full assurance, the complete confidence of their colleagues and of their political associates.'

The second, and far more serious crisis, was over Ireland. The Liberal Government was determined to fulfil the resolve made by Gladstone to grant that country Home Rule, a resolve that had to be suspended while the Tories held office. The Bill was introduced by the Government in April 1912 and had to be passed three times by the Commons (as a result of the Parliament Act) in order to force its way through the House of Lords. It reserved to the Parliament in Westminster all foreign policy, defence, taxation, customs duties, coinage and control of the police force, and was therefore not wholly acceptable to the Irish Nationalist Members in the House. To the Tories it was entirely distasteful, especially as regards the future of Ulster, which was largely Protestant and refused to be placed under the rule of the Roman Catholics of the South.

The leader of the Ulster rebels was Sir Edward Carson, a Southern Irishman. He arranged for a provisional Government to be formed in Ulster to take over that section of Ireland the moment Home Rule was granted. Volunteers, said to number 100,000, were enrolled, drilled and partially armed, in order to resist being absorbed by the South. The latter meanwhile began to raise their own army and it was obvious that a serious clash, resulting in civil war, would develop.

In Parliament the atmosphere became correspondingly heated. During one of the debates a Tory M.P. hurled a bound copy of the Standing Orders at Winston Churchill and cut open his forehead.

As the time approached for the Bill to become law there were accelerated preparations for the defiance of authority. There was gun-running into Ulster and the volunteers began to drill quite openly in the parks. In July 1913 Bonar Law, who had succeeded Balfour as Leader of the Conservatives in the Commons, sent a message to the Protestant Orangemen in Ulster, assuring them that whatever steps they might feel compelled to take 'whether they were constitutional or whether in the long run they were unconstitutional', they would have behind them the whole support of the anti-Home Rule or Unionist Party under his leadership. Asquith promptly moved troops from Curragh camp, near Dublin, into Ulster.

But before this crisis came to a head, another that had been gathering momentum for some time, loomed dangerously near. It was the threat of war with Germany. There had been clashes in the Cabinet between

Winston Churchill, now First Lord of the Admiralty, who having opposed the building of dreadnoughts to the number the Tories demanded, was insisting now on the further strengthening of the Navy, and Lloyd George, who was against diverting any money from his programme of reforms and regarded the Navy as being already 'at the height of its efficiency'. He took the opportunity of pointing out that Winston's father, Lord Randolph Churchill, had resigned his post as Chancellor of the Exchequer rather than accept increased estimates for the Army and the Navy.

The arguments across the Cabinet table raged for some days. Many of the Ministers supported Lloyd George, who did not believe there would be a war. Winston threatened to resign, but Asquith managed to patch up a peace by indicating that if the dispute continued it would only force a General Election, which he did not want for a further year.*

The murder of the Archduke of Austria at Sarajevo on 28th June 1914 meant war, but the war, it was felt, would be confined to one corner of Europe. As Lloyd George records in his *War Memoirs*, the Cabinet never discussed the possibility of Britain becoming involved until a week before war actually broke out. At their twice daily sessions at No. 10 Downing Street the Cabinet's discussions were centred on the gun-running in Ireland. Even as late as 24th July, eleven days before Britain was at war, the Foreign Secretary, Sir Edward Grey, after reading to the Cabinet the Austrian ultimatum to Servia, said he did not believe Britain would be involved; he then left for a fishing holiday in Hampshire and most of the other Ministers also left town. Only Churchill remained at his post. He had ordered a test mobilization of the First and Second Fleets and he kept them mobilized.

At a Cabinet meeting a week later, on 31st July, the possibility of war was discussed and more than half the Ministers, including Lloyd George, were against being drawn in. Churchill and Grey were for it and so was Asquith. For the next few days the Cabinet was in almost continuous session. The arguments were heated. Developments were watched closely with a map on the Cabinet table passed from one Minister to

---

* The seven year term for Parliament, established by the Septennial Act of 1715, was reduced to five years by the Parliament Act of 1911.

another. Winston Churchill insisted on immediate mobilization. Grey threatened to resign if Britain intended to remain neutral: after all, he said, there was an obligation to France, the *Entente*, and by it Britain would have to stand. Lord Rosebery had warned, when the *Entente* was signed in 1904: 'It will mean war with Germany in the end.' Lloyd George felt that no final decision should be taken yet. A few hours later Grey was instructed to inform the Germans that Britain would not stand aside and see the German fleet attack the Channel ports. John Burns resigned at once. The next day Lord Morley, Leader of the House of Lords, and Sir John Simon resigned too, but the latter withdrew his resignation when the Germans marched into Belgium, whose neutrality had been guaranteed by the British and the French as well as by the Germans.

On Saturday 1st August Germany declared war on Russia and two days later on France. It was Bank Holiday weekend and crowds assembled in Trafalgar Square to listen to protests against Britain becoming involved in the war. Other crowds swept into Downing Street. 'We could hear the hum of this surging mass from the Cabinet chamber,' Lloyd George wrote. By Monday the crowds, now singing *God Save the King* and the *Marseillaise*, had become so dense in Whitehall that it was impossible to get through and Ministers had to be helped by energetic policemen in order to reach the House of Commons after each Cabinet meeting. Britain's ultimatum to Germany to respect the neutrality of Belgium was sent on the morning of 4th August. It expired at midnight, unanswered, and Britain was at war – a war that was to last for four years and involve almost the entire world.

The atmosphere inside No. 10 during these tense days has been described by Margot Asquith, the Prime Minister's wife.[136] Only a few days before, on 25th July, her daughter Elizabeth,* then in her teens, had left to stay with friends in Holland. Four days later Mrs. Asquith wired to ask her to come home. When she mentioned this to the Archbishop of Canterbury and other guests at No. 10, they were surprised that she had done so: they did not share her apprehension. 'The strain of waiting for foreign telegrams with the fear of war haunting my brain had taken away all my vitality,' she wrote on the 29th. 'I went

_____
* Later Princess Elizabeth Bibesco.

to rest before dinner earlier than usual; but I could not sleep. I lay awake listening to the hooting of the horns, screams of trains, the cries of street traffic, as if they had been muffled drums heard through thick muslin. At 7.30 p.m. the door opened and Henry [Asquith] came into my bedroom. I saw at once by the gravity of his face that something had happened: he generally walks up and down when talking, but he stood quite still. I sat up and we looked at each other. "I have sent the precautionary telegram to every part of the Empire," he said.' At a dinner two nights later, messengers kept arriving 'with piles of Foreign Office boxes' for Sir Edward Grey, who was one of the guests. 'He jumped up and left the room.' Asquith had already gone down to the Cabinet room.

On the night war was declared, Mrs. Asquith states: 'I looked at the children asleep after dinner before joining Henry in the Cabinet room. Lord Crewe and Sir Edward Grey were already there and we sat smoking cigarettes in silence; some went out, others came in; nothing was said. The clock on the mantelpiece hammered out the hour and when the last beat of midnight struck it was as silent as dawn. We were at War. I left to go to bed, and, as I was pausing at the foot of the staircase, I saw Winston Churchill with a happy face striding towards the double doors of the Cabinet room.'

CHAPTER 35
Lloyd George and the First World War

It was at first thought that the war would not last more than three months. This was being said quite blatantly by many in high places, but Lord Kitchener, the new Secretary of State for War, foresaw 'a long' and unremitting struggle. Searchlights and guns were set up on Admiralty Arch, in Hyde Park and elsewhere, for, although aeroplanes were far from numerous, there were Zeppelins and precautions had to be taken. A fear of invasion was prevalent and there were scares about spies. In the garden of No. 10 huts were put up for the use of military and other additional staff – huts indeed began to go up everywhere in London. And special protection was provided for the Prime Minister and other Ministers. War budgets had to be framed. Income tax was doubled to two-and-eightpence in the pound, super tax was also doubled, the duty on beer was trebled, on tea doubled. War loans were floated and were immediately over-subscribed.

As the German troops drove back the Russians and thrust deep into France until they were bogged down there by trench warfare, an expedition was dispatched to Antwerp, in October 1914, at Churchill's suggestion – indeed he wanted to lead it. It failed. Another was dispatched to the Dardanelles in the spring of 1915, also at Churchill's suggestion, and had eventually to be withdrawn.

Lloyd George, pouring money into the factories, was gravely concerned at the inadequate output of munitions. He urged that the State should take over all the necessary resources of the country in order to ensure supplies. But it was not until news of the serious shell shortage on the Western Front reached the Cabinet in May 1915 that the Ministry of Munitions was set up and Lloyd George was moved from the Exchequer to take charge of it. At the same time Asquith formed a Coalition Government, which included the Conservative leaders Bonar Law, Austen Chamberlain, Balfour, Lord Curzon and Sir Edward Carson. The Irish Home Rule Bill had received Royal assent in September 1914, but it was left in abeyance until after the war and the old quarrels were buried. Labour was also brought into the Coalition with three representatives, only one of whom, Arthur Henderson, had a seat in the Cabinet.

All three Parties were united in their resolve to defeat the enemy. But the means to be employed roused many dissensions in the Cabinet room. Within a very few months the new Cabinet was split over conscription, which the Conservative Ministers, backed by Lloyd George and Churchill, insisted should be adopted, while Sir Edward Grey, Sir John Simon and other Liberals as ardently opposed it. After many angry scenes across the green table it was eventually agreed to and was introduced by the Prime Minister in January 1916.

The threat that it would be extended to Ireland, made by recruiting agents in that country, is said to have caused the rising in Dublin on Easter Sunday. Both the Lord-Lieutenant of Ireland and the Chief Secretary resigned from the Government and Lloyd George was asked by Asquith to evolve a solution. He suggested that Ireland should be granted Home Rule at once, but that Ulster should be excluded. This was accepted by both Redmond, the Irish Nationalist leader, and by Carson; but the Diehards in the Lords, with the aged Lord Halsbury at their head, exercised their veto – it was thus deferred for some years.

At about the same time, June 1916, Kitchener, on his way to Russia, lost his life in H.M.S. *Hampshire*, sunk by a mine off the Orkneys. He had already lost the confidence of his colleagues in the Cabinet and

Lloyd George was moved from the Ministry of Munitions to the War Office to succeed him. Lloyd George had hesitated for some time before accepting it. His energies, he felt, might be far better employed in a role of greater authority, and many Conservatives were of that view too, for they were dissatisfied with Asquith's direction of the war. His move to the War Office also displeased the generals, who did not like a soldier being replaced by a civilian. Mrs. Asquith was uneasy too. She noted in her diary: 'We are out, it is only a question of time when we shall have to leave Downing Street.' Her forecast proved to be correct: in five months Asquith was out and Lloyd George became Prime Minister. Lord Beaverbrook, at that time Mr. Max Aitken, played a vital part in this adjustment by manipulating the strings effectively from behind the scenes. First he brought Lloyd George and Bonar Law together to discuss a more vigorous prosecution of the war. An ultimatum was then sent to Asquith and he resigned. Mrs. Asquith records: 'We had to leave Downing Street without a roof over our heads in 1916 – as our house in Cavendish Square was let to Lady Cunard – she put her own bedroom and sitting room at my disposal and insisted upon living on an upper storey herself.'

Lloyd George and his family moved into No. 10 from No. 11, where they had stayed on even after he gave up the office of Chancellor of the Exchequer the year before. Bonar Law, the new Chancellor of the Exchequer, now moved in next door.

All the Liberal members of the Cabinet remained loyal to Asquith and refused to serve under Lloyd George, with the single exception of Dr. Christopher Addison, who had formed the Ministry of Munitions for Lloyd George, had served under him there and had taken charge of that office as Minister when Lloyd George went to the War Office. But of the Liberal Party as many as 120 M.P.s, almost half, came over to Lloyd George. The Tories stipulated that they would only serve if Winston Churchill was not included in the new Government. Churchill had been driven from the Admiralty and was dropped from the Government later in 1915, since when he had been serving at the Front. A War Cabinet of only four members was then formed. In addition to Lloyd George, there were Lord Curzon, Sir Edward Carson, and Arthur Henderson, representing the Labour Party, all three without portfolio. Balfour, who had succeeded Churchill at the

Admiralty and was now nearly seventy, was appointed Foreign Secretary. The rest of the Government consisted chiefly of Tories, with a few businessmen and a sprinkling of Labour members. Beaverbrook (then Sir Max Aitken) had expected to be made President of the Board of Trade. He did not get it and was offered a peerage instead. He refused this at first, but was pressed to take it because Bonar Law wanted his seat in the House for the man who, ironically, actually was appointed President of the Board of Trade.

These dramatic developments in December 1916 were followed by a most anxious year, for 1917 was marked by an intensification of submarine warfare: the U-boat havoc on merchant shipping caused a grave shortage of rations in Britain. The Russian Revolution in March led to the withdrawal of that country from the fight, but the entry of the United States in the following month, April 1917, more than counterbalanced this, once American resources were employed. It was also the year of some of the bloodiest battles of the war, including Passchendaele, with its appalling toll of lives. Just before the battle was launched, the Commander-in-Chief, Field-Marshal Haig, had come home from the Front and had spread out his map on the long table in the Cabinet room, his hands indicating the course the offensive would take. He did not, however, reveal that the French High Command were strongly opposed to it.

In the months that followed a succession of fierce clashes occurred between the Prime Minister and the generals, some of them by letter and ciphered telegrams, many face to face at No. 10. Since becoming Prime Minister Lloyd George spent most of his time in the house. He said at the outset: 'One man cannot possibly run Parliament *and* run the war.' So he left Parliament to the care of Bonar Law and worked at No. 10, receiving here the great military and naval commanders, all the Allied emissaries, and eventually the President of the United States, Woodrow Wilson. With his activities centred here, there was inevitably a considerable increase in his secretariat. Hut after hut went up in the garden as offices. The Cabinet no longer looked out upon a pleasing expanse of green during their deliberations, but on what came to be known as 'The Garden Suburb'.

Lloyd George was an early riser and a great deal of his entertaining (though it could hardly be called that) was done at breakfast. In the small panelled breakfast room on the first floor, Cabinet Ministers and others would assemble and talk. Yet it remained a family meal, for his wife and his two daughters breakfasted with them, as well as his two sons when they were home on leave from the Front. Top secrets were frankly discussed and the Prime Minister never felt it necessary to warn his family not to repeat anything they overheard. Megan, fourteen when her father moved into No. 10, was alarmed one afternoon to see in an evening paper something that had been discussed at breakfast. She went to her father and said: 'I hope you don't think I talked.' He put his arm round her shoulders. 'Of course not,' he said, 'I would trust you with my life and, what is much more important, I would trust you with the future of our country.'*

Megan had lost her companion Anthony Asquith when his family moved out, but had found a new friend in Kitty, Bonar Law's younger daughter, who was three years her junior. In order to avoid using the main staircase and the communicating door between Nos. 10 and 11, Kitty Law used to climb on to the roof of the Chancellor's house and walk along the narrow and not very secure ledge between the two houses, then scramble over the glass roof of the corridor in No. 10, to talk to Megan before breakfast and again at night. Megan, fearful that she would fall through the glass and hurt herself, remembered her own escapades when she was only six or seven and had herself climbed on to the ledge from No. 11. Lloyd George was in the garden at the time, talking to a group of distinguished French Ministers. Without a word he left his guests and raced up the stairs two at a time, leaned out of a top window and, snatching her in his arms, said sharply: 'Don't you ever do that again.' Now she was away at a boarding school all term, and when she was due back at No. 10 her small black pug Zulu would be adorned with a red ribbon and would prance excitedly in the front hall. Missing him on one home-coming, she was told he was ill, but he had died and lay in a grave in the garden, a fact not revealed to her until much later.

In June 1917 her sister Olwen, older than Megan by ten years, was married from No. 10 to Dr. Thomas Carey Evans. It was the second wartime wedding from that house, for two years earlier, in 1915,

---

* In a statement to the author by Lady Megan Lloyd George, M.P.

Asquith's daughter Violet was married from here to his secretary Maurice Bonham Carter. Olwen says: 'My fiancé was in Mesopotamia and we did not know when he would be able to get home. One day when Carson, who was First Lord of the Admiralty, was over to lunch, he informed me that Thomas would be home "very shortly" and the wedding had to be arranged at very short notice. We had a very small reception and an enormous wedding cake – but it was almost all cardboard, because we had hardly any sugar.'*

The domestic staff at No. 10 was entirely Welsh. Mrs. Lloyd George brought in a Welsh cook, all the maids were Welsh, even their old Welsh nannie Lollie was there. The endless rows of copper pots and pans in that enormous basement kitchen made them gasp. 'Good God! What am I to do with all that!' the cook exclaimed, only she said it in Welsh, for that was what was spoken all the time below stairs and quite a lot of the time above stairs too. 'Our friends from the chapels in Wales when they came to London, used to drift in,' Olwen says, 'and often some of them spent the night at No. 10. We always had visitors, for one meal or another. Mother somehow managed to cope with those who turned up at the last minute. I remember Harry Lauder coming to breakfast, General Smuts came several times, so did Sir James Barrie, the author, and Ramsay Macdonald. Churchill was constantly there, but never for breakfast – it was too early for him, he was always a late riser.

'I remember,' Olwen went on, 'M. Thomas, the French Minister of Munitions, coming to breakfast. I was asked to translate. I'm afraid such words as "barbed wire entanglements" were beyond me. Lord Reading came to the rescue, but my father stopped him. "Let her do it. She's been to Paris," he said.'

Megan's Zulu was not the only dog in the house. Lloyd George had a Welsh terrier called Cymru, but felt he would be happier at Walton Heath and had him moved there, but two or three days later he somehow found his way back to No. 10. A third dog was Olwen's peke Ching. Just as the Cabinet was about to meet one morning Lloyd George saw Ching seated in one of the ministerial chairs, with his chin resting on the blotting pad. 'I see,' said the Prime Minister, 'we have

---

* In a statement to the author.

357

a new member of the Cabinet,' and led him gently out of the room.

During 1917 the Prime Minister had to solve a number of inter-departmental squabbles. The most serious of these rows was between the War Office and the Admiralty over the merging of their separate air services into the unified Royal Air Force, which Lloyd George described as 'the cavalry of the clouds'. The fusion was achieved before the end of the year. By now Churchill had been brought back into the Government, despite the pledge given to the Conservatives, and the production of all aircraft was put under his control as Minister of Munitions.

The tide of war turned in the spring of 1918 after the failure of the Germans' mighty thrust towards Paris. American troops had begun to arrive in increasing numbers. When an American mission, led by Colonel House, reached London, it was received by the Prime Minister in the Cabinet room at No. 10, the very room, Lloyd George pointed out, where nearly a century and a half before, Lord North had decided on the policies of taxation and control that had driven the American colonies to their War of Independence.

The certainty of victory was apparent in September. News of the Armistice was brought to No. 10 very early in the small hours of the morning of 11th November. Lloyd George and his wife were in bed. The messenger hurried up the stairs to the corner bedroom on the first floor overlooking St. James's Park. The Prime Minister was roused. The entire household was informed. Soon a crowd began to gather in Downing Street and in time it filled not only the street but the great courtyard of the Foreign Office opposite. Men and women with children in their arms were pressed tight against the walls. It was impossible for any of them to move. They called for 'L.G.' and presently he appeared at one of the only windows, other than those in the attic, that overlook Downing Street – a window of the room that had once been Violet Bonham Carter's bedroom. The Prime Minister's face was flushed. He was overcome with emotion and hardly able to speak. It was the only time in his life when words failed him.

That night Lloyd George and Churchill dined together in Soane's panelled State dining-room on the first floor. Churchill records: 'We were alone in the large room from whose walls the portraits of Pitt and Fox, of Nelson and Wellington and – perhaps somewhat incongruously – of Washington – then looked down.'[145]

Some weeks before an admirer had sent the Prime Minister an Egyptian scarab for luck. Sarah, the housekeeper, was horrified when she saw it and begged Mrs. Lloyd George not to keep it in the house: she was sure it would bring the most awful calamities. Quite suddenly it disappeared. It was searched for everywhere and Sarah finally admitted that she had buried it in the garden. Where it was buried she could not, or would not, remember. It is there to this day and no doubt when it is unearthed in the course of some future excavations the theory is likely to be advanced that at some time the Egyptians must have been in occupation of London.

CHAPTER 36
The Fall of Lloyd George

THREE days after the Armistice, amid the wild excitement and rejoicing, it was announced that there was to be an immediate General Election. Bonar Law, as Leader of the House, informed the Members that Polling Day would be in a month's time and that the votes would be counted on 28th December. The preparations had in fact been made months before when the Representation of the People's Act was passed, granting votes to women at the age of thirty and to all men at the age of twenty-one. The electorate, as a result, had been doubled.

The purpose of the election was to ensure the continuation of the Coalition Government. But the Labour members in it resigned the moment the election was announced. It was fought on a coupon basis – all candidates prepared to support Lloyd George were supplied with a certificate and the electors were asked to vote only for them. He promised the prosecution of the Kaiser, the punishment of all Germans responsible for atrocities, the rehabilitation of those who had suffered in the war, the extraction of an indemnity from Germany to the full capacity of that country to pay, and a wide range of fresh domestic reforms. Reduced to slogans it guaranteed to 'Hang the Kaiser', to 'Squeeze the German lemon till the pips squeaked' and to 'Provide Homes for Heroes'. It resulted in the personal triumph of Lloyd George and though the Conservatives (334 in number) predominated in the new House, they were for the time being at any rate his staunch supporters. Asquith was defeated and his followers were reduced to only 33; the Labour Party, on the other hand, had 59 members in the new House. Arthur Henderson, however, was defeated and Ramsay MacDonald became the new Labour leader.

Having secured the authority from the country, Lloyd George set out for the Peace Conference in Paris. President Wilson had already arrived in London and, following a banquet at Buckingham Palace, was entertained at No. 10 Downing Street on 28th December by the Imperial War Cabinet before going on to Paris. Together he and Lloyd George set up the League of Nations, Wilson's pet project, and carved up Europe, forming each nationality into a separate State, with the intention of eliminating the risk of future war. H. G. Wells, however, proved to be right when he prophesied that the Polish Corridor, cut across Germany to give the new State of Poland access to the sea, would be the cause of the next world war, and forecast the date of its outbreak almost to the month.

The Peace Treaty was signed on 28th June 1919 in the Hall of Mirrors at Versailles and Lloyd George returned to No. 10 Downing Street to cope with the many problems of peace. Among the first of these was demobilization. Churchill, appointed Secretary of State for War in the new Government, had urged before even taking up his office, that the Allies should deal with the Communist (or Bolshevik as it was then called) menace which Russia presented to the world. He was convinced that only a very little resolute action would be required to eliminate Lenin and his followers, and was even prepared to use troops for this purpose. But Lloyd George would not hear of it. The fighting forces, restive already, would have to be demobilized, he said, and there was no other available man-power, nor for that matter was there any money with which to conduct a campaign such as Churchill envisaged. Moreover, unless its result was decisive, the Communists would win far greater support from the Russian people in their endeavour to repel the foreign invaders.

But Churchill was not to be discouraged. There was already a British Expeditionary Force in North Russia: it had been sent during the war to assist those Russians who were prepared to go on fighting against the Germans. Introducing his Army Estimates in March, he blandly told the House that the British Expeditionary Force could not leave Russia until the late summer because of 'that ice-bound shore', and that they could be used meanwhile to ease the problem of the Allies who would otherwise have to evacuate 30,000 or more people who had helped us in the war. Disaster, however, overtook the project. In July the White Russian troops in the North revolted and murdered their officers. Criticized in the House for getting British troops embroiled, Churchill pointed out with aplomb that had the Red forces not been thus engaged they would have fallen upon the border States the Peace Conference in Paris had been busy setting up, and dismembered them.

Next Lloyd George had to deal with Ireland. At the General Election the Sinn Feiners, with 73 M.P.s, had secured a sweeping victory over the Irish Nationalist Party, who had only seven elected to the House. Flushed with their triumph, the Sinn Feiners proclaimed Ireland a Republic, and called a meeting of their own independent Parliament, the Dail, at which they announced that at last, after seven hundred years under foreign domination, they had achieved their freedom. Of the Sinn Feiners elected to Westminster, one was a woman, Countess Markievicz, the first woman ever elected to the British House of Commons. Like the others, she did not take her seat, but was in an English prison, together with De Valera who had been elected the first Prime Minister of the Irish Republic. From this moment the alternation of coercion and conciliation, which had been a feature of British rule through the centuries, developed into a continuing guerilla warfare between the Irish Republican Army and the Royal Irish Constabulary, expanded by recruitment in England and called the 'Black and Tans' because of their black caps and khaki uniforms. The fighting, marked by ambush and murder by gunmen, went on for two years.

In December 1920 Lloyd George set up two separate Parliaments for Ireland, one for the South, the other for Ulster, but it did not placate the Republicans. The final settlement was not achieved until the latter part of 1921. Lloyd George had four talks in July with De Valera, all of them at No. 10 Downing Street. Dominion status was offered to Ireland but rejected. The Sinn Feiners insisted on the inclusion of Ulster, but by masterly handling Lloyd George, on 6th December 1921, got them to sign a treaty of independence, which included participation with the Commonwealth and the exclusion of Ulster. It was one of Lloyd George's greater achievements.

The end of his long Premiership was now drawing near. Many of the Conservatives regarded the Irish Treaty as a betrayal. It was inevitable that Lloyd George's radical policies, regarded as undiluted Socialism, would sooner or later lead to a head-on collision. With their enormous number in the House, the Conservatives were restive to have their own Prime Minister. It was only the loyalty of the chief Tory leaders to Lloyd George that had delayed the impending break.

Following a brief period of boom, a deep depression had set in. There was acute unrest, as after Waterloo. Strikes followed, then came unemployment. During 1921 the number wholly or partially unemployed rose to over two millions. By the end of February 1922 Lloyd George thought of resigning. He wrote to Austen Chamberlain, who on Bonar Law's retirement through illness had succeeded him as Leader of the Conservative Party as well as Chancellor of the Exchequer, to suggest that he should take over the Premiership. But Chamberlain declined, saying that Lloyd George's resignation would be a disaster. A few in the Tory Party shared this view, but others, though eager to get rid of Lloyd George, thought it would be more advantageous to wait.

Lloyd George's continued absences from the House of Commons now caused a great deal of uneasiness and resentment: the war was over, he should be there, it was said. But he liked working at No. 10 Downing Street. The huts had been removed from the garden and in the mornings he would take his two granddaughters – Olwen's and his son Richard's children – for a walk and a romp along the Horse Guards Parade. If there was to be a Cabinet meeting he always lifted them on to the long table so that they might step from one freshly filled blotter to another, walking always on the squares, as A. A. Milne's poem puts it. This delighted Lloyd George immensely. At weekends he liked to get away to the country. He often played golf at Walton Heath, but after October 1917 there was Chequers to go to – a magnificent Tudor mansion in Buckinghamshire, which Sir Arthur Lee (later Lord Lee of Fareham) presented as the official country residence for Prime Ministers – a counterpart to No. 10, away from the bustle of Whitehall, though inevitably it often became a hive of activity at weekends.

It was trouble in Turkey that finally brought Lloyd George down. The Turks, allies of Germany in the war, had their Empire dismembered by the Treaty of Sèvres. Many of the Western Allies still had detachments of troops in occupation of certain parts of what remained of that country. Fighting had recently broken out between the Turks and the Greek army, which had landed in Asia Minor with the knowledge and encouragement of Lloyd George. There was an outcry against this and when Mustapha Kemal, the newly elected President of Turkey, routed the invaders in the summer of 1922 and came face to face with the slender British forces at Chanak, Churchill, now Secretary for the Dominions and Colonies, with the approval of Lloyd George urged the Dominions as well as the French and Italians to assist in repelling Kemal by force of arms. The prospect of a new war against their co-religionists roused the Moslems in India. The situation soon became grave.

This, the Tories decided, was their moment. A dramatic meeting was held at the Carlton Club in London on 19th October 1922. Bonar Law, a Member of Parliament still, emerged from his retirement to address the assembled Conservative M.P.s. He said the time had come for the Tories to leave the Coalition. Stanley Baldwin, President of the Board of Trade in the Government, warned the Party in a short but effective speech that, just as the Liberals had been smashed by Lloyd George, so would the Tories be disrupted if they did not break away. By 187 votes to 87 the Tories decided to adopt this course. Austen Chamberlain, their leader, voted with the minority.

In the Cabinet room at No. 10 four days later Lloyd George bade farewell to his secretaries. He was playful. He walked up and down the room and said it was the last time he would ever be in it unless he came as a visitor. He was right. The end had come after six years as Prime Minister, two as a forceful and brilliant leader in war, the remaining four during the harassments of peace.

CHAPTER 37
First Labour Government

LLOYD GEORGE had in fact resigned immediately after the Carlton Club meeting. As soon as he left Buckingham Palace the King's secretary, Lord Stamfordham, set out for Bonar Law's home in Onslow Square, Kensington, and summoned him to an audience.

Bonar Law was reluctant to form a Government. He was not any longer, he said, the official leader of his Party, nor would his health be equal to the strain of office.

Many of the ablest Conservatives in the Coalition Government stood loyally by Lloyd George. These included Austen Chamberlain, the actual Leader of the Party, who but for his loyalty would now have become Prime Minister. Balfour, a former Prime Minister, Lord Birkenhead, and Lord Lee of Fareham also stood by Lloyd George. The others rallied round Bonar Law and an immediate General Election was decided on. It was held on 15th November 1922. A tape machine was installed in the long red-carpeted corridor at No. 10 just outside the Cabinet room and those candidates who were not in their constituencies gathered round it for the results. The Tories were returned with a majority of 77 over all the other Parties put together. The Labour Party increased its strength in the House to 138, which was double their previous number, and thus became the official Opposition. Of the divided Liberals, the Asquith group mustered 60 M.P.s, the Lloyd George Liberals numbered only 55. Winston Churchill, a Lloyd George Liberal, was defeated at Dundee, and before long joined the Tory Party.

In the new Government, Stanley Baldwin became Chancellor of the Exchequer and moved into No. 11 Downing Street; Neville Chamberlain, younger brother of Austen, and a future Prime Minister, was Postmaster-General; Lord Curzon remained at the Foreign Office.

When Bonar Law moved into No. 10 Downing Street he was sixty-four. His wife had died some years before and the desolation caused by that loss never really left him. The war had taken a toll of two of his four sons (both were killed in 1917) and he moved in now with his sister, Miss Mary Law, his surviving sons and his younger daughter Kitty, who was seventeen and went to a day school. The elder girl, Isabel, had married Major-General Sir Frederick Sykes in 1920 from No. 11. For official dinners and receptions she came to No. 10 to act as hostess and in December there was a christening party at No. 10 for her baby.

Bonar Law lived in the house for less than seven months. His illness was far more serious than had been supposed – he was suffering from cancer of the throat – but he carried on bravely, without betraying the pain he had to endure.

It was not long after he had moved into No. 10 that Mussolini, by now Fascist dictator of Italy, came to London and dined with Bonar Law in the State dining-room of this historic house. Richard Law, the Prime Minister's younger son (later Lord Coleraine), was an undergraduate at Oxford at the time and had come to stay at No. 10 for the vacation. He was not invited to the dinner, but peering through the curtains, he saw the small party of men assemble. Mussolini was not dressed in his black shirt, but wore a white tie and tails, looking like a cross between a head waiter and an opera singer. The occasion of the visit was a conference of European Prime Ministers in December 1922, which was also held at No. 10 in the State drawing-room on the first floor.

Bonar Law was by temperament the exact opposite of Lloyd George. He had not the flamboyant exuberance of his predecessor, nor had he the wizardry which had held the world spellbound for so long. He was always calm, his arguments were always carefully reasoned. He had promised the country 'Tranquillity' at the General Election ('There are times when it is good to sit still and go slowly') and he strove to fulfil this promise. In the glamour of high office he was not interested. He had a duty to the people and to that he applied himself. His experience was considerable, for during Lloyd George's consistent absence from the Commons, it fell to Bonar Law, the Leader of the House and in effect acting Prime Minister, to shoulder the full Parliamentary burden. Lloyd George had described him as 'honest to the verge of simplicity', and Bonar Law's comment on this was that he could wish for no better epitaph.

The jibes that met his efforts to form a Government without the tried leaders of his Party, he parried with skill. To Lloyd George's sneer that he had to descend to the kitchen to replace the brilliant Ministers who refused to serve under him, he retorted that Lloyd George had himself been taken out of the cellar by Campbell-Bannerman. 'My desire', said Bonar Law, 'is to be the family solicitor, standing firm on the hearth-rug among the harsh realities of the office furniture, while he prefers to fly round on one wing.'

The intrusions Lloyd George had constantly made into the various ministries were abandoned: to each Minister Bonar Law restored the fullest authority. Thus when a deputation of unemployed asked to see him, they were told to see the Minister of Labour, and he refused to alter his decision despite their persistence.

It was during his brief reign at No. 10 that two outstanding settlements were achieved. One of these was the Treaty with the Irish Free State, which came up for endorsement within a few days of his becoming Prime Minister. Despite the earlier opposition to it by the bulk of the Tory Party, they agreed that Bonar Law should honour the settlement. The other concerned the immense loan advanced to Britain by the United States during the war. Baldwin, as Chancellor of the Exchequer, went to Washington early in 1923 to negotiate the terms of settlement and, although they were hard and not altogether to Bonar Law's liking, they were accepted as the best that could have been obtained in an extremely difficult atmosphere, exacerbated by the renewal of the Anglo-Japanese alliance.

Bonar Law's health got progressively worse and by April 1923 he was unable to speak. He sat voiceless on the Front Bench with Baldwin beside him, leaving it to the latter to make all the pronouncements. But he remained at his post until after the wedding of the Duke of York* at the end of April, when, on medical advice, he set out on a Mediterranean cruise. He appeared to be no better at the end of it and broke the journey in Paris on the way home. There his doctor joined him and advised him to resign. This he did on 20th May within a few hours of arriving in England.

Bonar Law died on 30th October and was buried in Westminster Abbey. The Prince of Wales (later the Duke of Windsor) together with four Prime Ministers, past, present and future – Balfour, Asquith, Baldwin and Ramsay MacDonald – were among the pall bearers.

During Bonar Law's absence on the cruise Lord Curzon acted as Prime Minister, while Baldwin led the House of Commons. It was the prerogative of the King to choose which of the two should succeed as Prime Minister. Queen Victoria was faced with a similar choice on Gladstone's resignation in 1894 – Lord Rosebery was Leader of the Lords and Sir William Harcourt of the Commons: she chose the former. King George the Fifth chose Baldwin, despite his short and so far uneventful political career. His Majesty held, and the majority of the Privy Councillors he consulted endorsed the view, that with Labour as the official Opposition it was essential that the Prime Minister should be in the House of Commons. It was a bitter blow to Curzon: he is said to have cried all night in his palatial home in Carlton House Terrace.† But in public he conducted himself with his customary dignity and grace, for it fell to him to propose that Baldwin should be elected Leader of the Conservative Party and later he welcomed him into the Cabinet room as the new Prime Minister. Outside a swarm of newspaper men waited. Baldwin went shyly to the front door of No. 10 and said he needed their prayers rather than their congratulations.[151]

Baldwin moved into No. 10 shortly afterwards. He was fifty-six, married and had five children, two of them sons: the eldest of these,

---

* Later King George the Sixth.
† Later the Savage Club.

Oliver, now twenty-four, had just returned after fighting in Turkey, where he had been a prisoner of the Bolsheviks and the Turks. He was unmarried and spent much of his time at No. 10 together with his younger brother, Wyndham, who was then nineteen, and Betty, the youngest of his sisters, the other two having already married. Even so they found the house crowded. The entire ground floor was given up to offices. On the floor above, Mrs. Baldwin used the inner room with the bathroom as her bedroom, while Baldwin slept in the ante-room outside and had to curtain it off so that he should not be seen lying in bed indulging his passion for detective stories by the office-keeper, who had a flat in the house which overlooked the ante-room. This flat was in the attic above Violet Bonham Carter's old bedroom over the front door. The youngest of the Baldwin children, Wyndham and Betty, used two of the attic bedrooms on the top floor; they were originally maids' rooms and could only be reached by the back stairs.

Baldwin was to be in this house for only six months – a shorter time even than Bonar Law. To the country he was comparatively unknown, but the cartoonists soon made his stocky farmer figure and his pipe immediately recognizable. A slow, cautious man, he brushed aside many of the problems that beset him and concentrated only on a few, which he handled with considerable skill, as will emerge. But his seeming indifference to the rest led to his being regarded as lazy, which to a large extent he was.

The overriding problem confronting him was unemployment. The figures were still alarmingly high and Baldwin resolved to apply to its solution the protective tariff so dear to the heart of his Party. He felt, however, he was barred from adopting this course because of a pledge given by Bonar Law that no change of such a kind would be made in the present Parliament. At the Cabinet table many of his colleagues insisted that the remedy was required and must be applied: the electors, they said, had already given them an overwhelming vote of confidence and it was unnecessary to appeal to them again.

But Baldwin refused to see it in that light. The honest course was to hold another election and he accordingly asked the King on 12th November 1923 to dissolve Parliament so that he might seek from the people their verdict on tariff reform.

369

The result was disastrous for the Conservatives. They lost 88 seats and while with 258 elected members they were still the largest party in the House, Labour's representation had risen to 191 and the Liberals (reunited to fight for Free Trade) had 158. Baldwin no longer had a clear majority and could only govern with the backing of the Liberals, and that he was certainly not going to get for his policy of Tariff Reform.

Realizing the situation when the results were declared on 8th December, Baldwin's intention was to resign at once, but the King dissuaded him, saying that as the head of the largest elected Party he had the right to rule until he was defeated in the House.

The new Parliament met on the 15th January 1924 and later that week, on the day the vote of no confidence was to be taken, Mrs. Baldwin telephoned to the Hampstead home of Ramsay MacDonald, Leader of the Opposition. He was away in the House and she invited his eldest daughter Ishbel, then aged twenty, to come and see her at No. 10 Downing Street.

When Ishbel arrived it was clear at once to the large number of pressmen and photographers waiting in Downing Street that the country was to have its first Labour Government. Shy and a little embarrassed by the flashing camera bulbs, Ishbel, looking straight ahead of her, walked to the front door with Miss Byvoets, the daughter of a Dutch architect, who was housekeeper in the motherless Mac-Donald home. Mrs. Baldwin explained the position and showed them round the house that was to be theirs. Both were appalled by its vastness, unsuspected from the street, by its rambling passages and the large number of rooms. Apart from the offices on the ground floor, there were no fewer than forty rooms for them to take over and look after. After their small residence, where they lived frugally, for Ramsay MacDonald had never earned much money as a clerk or a schoolteacher, the prospect seemed frightening. They were told that they would have to bring in some of their own furniture and provide all the linen, crockery and cutlery. Just as they were leaving Baldwin returned. Defeated in the House of Commons by 72 votes, he had already been to the Palace and resigned. The Press gathered round the new tenant. 'What do you think of the house?' they asked Ishbel, and ignoring the fact that she had been brought up entirely in England, they added, because of her Scottish background, a touch of heather to her accent in their printed version. 'It's awfu' complicated,' the newspapers made her say and it was picked up by George Robey and others in the music halls and laughed at by delighted audiences.

On the day following his daughter's visit to No. 10, Ramsay MacDonald was invited to Buckingham Palace to see the King. The new Prime Minister was not even a member of the Privy Council and members of the Council had been especially assembled so that he should be sworn in at once and then kiss hands on taking office. 'I had an hour's talk with him,' the King noted in his diary on 22nd January 1924, 'he impressed me very much; he wishes to do the right thing. Today 23 years ago dear Grandmamma* died. I wonder what she would have thought of a Labour Government!'[138]

The King himself was far from uneasy at the prospect of Labour taking over. He realized that the Prime Minister and his colleagues were inexperienced and assured them that they might count upon his assistance in every way.†

MacDonald chose his team with care. J. H. Thomas, who had been an engine-driver, was made Secretary of State for the Colonies. J. R. Clynes, formerly a mill hand, was appointed Lord Privy Seal and Deputy Leader of the House. Ramsay MacDonald himself kept the office of Foreign Secretary because there was no one else he could offer it to. Philip Snowden, a factory worker who had lost the use of both his legs, was selected to be the new Chancellor of the Exchequer. The Labour Party was not represented in the House of Lords. Three existing peers agreed to join the Labour Government – Lord Haldane, the great Liberal Secretary of State for War in Campbell-Bannerman's Government eighteen years before (he was nearly seventy), Lord Parmoor and Lord Chelmsford; to these the Prime Minister added by creating three new peers. Arthur Henderson, who had obtained some experience during the war by serving in two Coalition Governments, was the new Home Secretary; Major C. R. Attlee, a future Prime Minister, was given junior office as Under-Secretary of State for War. Lord Beaverbrook noted: 'Heretofore no British Government for a hundred years had been without considerable newspaper backing. The

* Queen Victoria.
† Memorandum by Lord Stamfordham, the King's Secretary.

Socialists could only claim one organ with a small circulation,* and this newspaper could not be depended on by the new Prime Minister, for it really represented the extreme Left of his own supporters.'[153]

The Labour Party had been formed a little over twenty years before and to have attained the right to rule in so short a span of time was regarded as a considerable achievement. The working classes, which it was organized to represent politically, with the Trade Unions as the industrial wing, and the support also of the Co-operative movement, had given their votes in the previous century to the Liberals, the only radical group with which they had any kinship, and the Liberals had indeed fought for many of their causes – in Gladstone's day and more recently in the reforms of Asquith and Lloyd George. Keir Hardie, the first Labour member in the House, formerly stood for Parliament as a Liberal. But they had their own organization now and were in office, though still dependent on Liberal help if they were to continue as the Government of the country.

Ramsay MacDonald was fifty-seven years old when he moved into No. 10. All his life had been a struggle. He had known poverty and unemployment in his earliest years, when he left the small fishing village of Lossiemouth at the age of twenty in quest of work: no employer seemed interested in making use of the abilities of a future Prime Minister and he had to take such temporary makeshift jobs as he could get. He had married at the age of thirty Margaret Gladstone, the daughter of a prominent scientist. Her family, remotely connected with the great Gladstone but more directly with Lord Kelvin, was well-to-do and lived in a large house in Pembridge Square. But Margaret was drawn to Socialism and through it to MacDonald. After fifteen intensely happy years together, she died in 1911 and it was as a widower that MacDonald moved in with his young children, three of them girls, and one son Malcolm, the other, Alister, being already married.

Furniture for No. 10 presented some problems. Until 1853 the entire house had to be furnished by the incoming tenant. In that year, following the departure of the three secretaries who lived at No. 10 while Lord John Russell was Prime Minister, it was decided that the

---

* *The Daily Herald* in its earlier very attenuated form before it was taken over by Lord Southwood and built up into a widely read newspaper.

Treasury should in future be responsible for the furnishing, carpeting and curtaining of the entrance hall and all the rooms on the first floor that were used for official purposes. The rest of the house remained unfurnished and untenanted for thirty years until Disraeli moved in in November 1877. Even then only some of the furniture was supplied for the upper rooms by the Board of Works. Twenty years later, in 1897, when Salisbury was Prime Minister and his nephew A. J. Balfour lived at No. 10, almost all the furniture was provided and renewed at public expense. But the rooms were by no means fully furnished. The Asquiths brought in some of their own furniture, so did the Lloyd Georges. Ramsay Macdonald was unable to do this and the State accordingly supplied the rest. But all the linen, cutlery and crockery had to be brought in by him and MacDonald's modest home was unable to meet the requirements of official entertaining. He appealed to his wife's stepsister, Miss Florence Gladstone, and she came nobly to his rescue. She went to the sales (it was January), bought bed-sheets and table-linen, cups and saucers, a large quantity of plates, for she realized that entertaining by the Prime Minister would have to be on an extensive scale, and even bought a certain amount of silver. At the end of the second day Ramsay MacDonald asked her how much she had spent. When she told him he was startled. 'My salary as Prime Minister for these two days,' he said, 'is much less than you have so far spent. We'll have to be extremely careful. I'm here on suffrance. I could be defeated in the House tomorrow and there won't be enough money then to pay for all this.'*

The furniture in the house was shoddy. It had been brought in from store-rooms instead of museums. Ramsay MacDonald got some of it changed and also arranged for a few pictures to be lent by the National Gallery so that the house should have again some of the dignity and elegance it displayed in the days of Walpole and Pitt. Though lost without his library, MacDonald decided, in view of the uncertain length of his stay, that it would be wiser not to bring his own books from Hampstead. There ought to be, he felt, a library at No. 10, a collection of books apart from the Hansards in the Cabinet room; and he started one. It is known as 'The Prime Minister's Library' and is

* As stated to the author by Ishbel MacDonald.

373

an essential feature of the house. A special bookplate was designed and the collection has since been added to by other Prime Ministers. Fresh bookshelves were put up in the Cabinet room, on the wall facing the fireplace. Later, Winston Churchill presented his books on his father and on his ancestor Marlborough, and even got earlier Prime Ministers who were still living to add at least a volume to the shelves. Harold Macmillan brought in a complete set of the works of Kipling.

The room above the front door was taken over as a study by Ishbel. One of the rooms built round the well separating the house in front from the one at the back, was used by Ishbel as her bedroom: just under the office-keeper's flat, she heard him drop his boots when he took them off every night. Campbell-Bannerman's old bedroom at the corner, used by Mrs. Baldwin as her boudoir and filled with family photographs, became Ramsay MacDonald's study, with his bedroom and partitioned bathroom alongside.

A fresh domestic staff was engaged: their wages were the Prime Minister's liability. The butler, a feature of the house through the centuries, was replaced for the first time by a parlourmaid. A cook, a pantrymaid and two chambermaids were also taken on by Miss Byvoets, the MacDonalds' housekeeper. Messengers, provided at public expense, were on duty all day and far into the night, under the care of Berry, the office-keeper, whose flat was reached by a private staircase, which was also used by MacDonald's family as it had been by Lloyd George's daughters and by Violet Bonham Carter.

The charwomen for cleaning the offices and main reception rooms were paid by the State. The cost of the coal was carefully divided, such of it as was used for domestic purposes had to be paid for by the Prime Minister. For official entertaining the meals were as a rule supplied by caterers, who prepared the dishes and warmed them up in the large kitchen in the basement.

'There were no ornaments and no vases anywhere in the house. They never are provided,' says Ishbel.* 'You just have to get your own. I inherited £50 from an aunt at about this time and I spent the money on Venetian glass, light green in colour, and some large vases for the State drawing-room. I also bought some candlesticks and menu card

---

* In a statement to the author.

holders. I felt I had to do something about it, as the entertaining was a great strain on Papa's finances. He found he had to pay for quite a lot of it, and often there were as many as eighteen to dinner. Not much entertaining was done at lunch because Papa had to get to the House of Commons early.

'At this time my two younger sisters Joan and Sheila were in school. They were fifteen and thirteen years old and used to travel by bus every day to Camden Town. They had two of the attic rooms as their bedrooms, alongside the rooms in which the cook and the five maids slept. There were by this time three bathrooms in the house – one for Papa, an Edwardian bath with a frame of mahogany, one not far from my bedroom and the third in the basement near the kitchen, rather dark and dank with a stone floor, not at all nice. It was used mostly by the resident staff.

'I found that as hostess at No. 10, I had to have a secretary. She lived in and Papa had a private secretary, Rose Rosenberg, apart from his official ones – he had of course to pay her salary himself. She worked in a pokey little room just by the gent's lavatory on the way to the Cabinet room and found it very noisy with the flush going almost ceaselessly.'

The King kept a watchful eye on events. A great change had occurred in the history of the country and, to help and guide the new Prime Minister, he drew up a memorandum on procedure. He pointed out that the Leader of the House of Commons normally sends a letter each evening to the Sovereign, describing the day's proceedings, that all important Foreign Office dispatches are always submitted to the King, and he urged that a firm hand should be kept on the distribution of honours, since these had been bestowed rather extravagantly in recent years. He was thoughtful enough to realize that the cost of the uniform usually worn by Ministers at a Levée, approximately £73, would be beyond the means of most of the members of the Government, and stated: 'In no case do I expect anyone to get more than the Levée coat; full dress is not necessary on account of the expense.' A hint was even dropped by the King's Secretary that Moss Bros., the dress hire firm, might be approached.

Having undertaken the dual role of Foreign Secretary and Prime Minister, Ramsay MacDonald found that he had to answer as many as sixty questions in Parliament in a single afternoon. The strain after a time became oppressive, but he achieved some notable successes in foreign affairs. There had been disagreements between Britain and France over Germany. French forces were occupying Germany's vital industrial region in the Ruhr and had met with passive resistance. MacDonald felt that the exchange of stern diplomatic notes could be replaced by a more conciliatory approach. He invited both sides to a conference at St. James's Palace in London and the French eventually agreed to evacuate the Ruhr. The King sent his warmest congratulations to MacDonald on this signal triumph. The Soviet Union was recognized as the *de jure* government of Russia and MacDonald held a conference in London for the resumption of trade between the two countries. This was not at all to the liking of the Conservatives and before long it brought down the Labour Government.

The dominating task at home was, of course, to seek a solution for the seemingly insoluble problem of unemployment. In addition to the nearly two million who were out of work, there were vast numbers who, though in employment, had had their wages cut severely. There was widespread unrest and a succession of strikes – by the railwaymen, by the miners, and others. London was without street transport for ten days and very short of necessary supplies. The public were irritated and grumbled that Labour was unable to control its own people. There was also trouble within the Labour Party, many members of which felt that the moment for the millennium had arrived but Mac-Donald was taking no steps to attain it. Driven from behind, confronted by the massive brick wall of Conservatism in front, and dependent wholly on Liberal support to remain in power, MacDonald was fully aware that the situation could not be sustained for long.

The quarrels in the Labour Party became vocal publicly. Backbenchers criticized the Government and the Prime Minister had on occasion to rebuke his undisciplined followers. There was conflict, and confusion, even in the Cabinet. The Civil Lord of the Admiralty, the First Lord being in the Upper House, rose in the Commons one day and announced that the Government planned to build five cruisers in order to ease the unemployment in the shipbuilding trade. A great many Labour members were startled: their pacifist fervour blinded them to the duty, imperative and inalienable, of every Government

376

to ensure the fullest possible protection of the people from attack by sea, land or air. Yielding a little to the critics, MacDonald explained that the cruisers would be laid down but would not be built without the consent of Parliament and that in any case these were replacements and would not be an addition to the total strength of the Fleet.

Two further concessions, or what appeared to be concessions to his extremist backbenchers, finally brought him down. One of these was the sudden abandonment of the case against J. R. Campbell, the acting editor of the Communist newspaper *The Workers' Weekly*, who was charged with inciting the armed forces to mutiny. The other was the Prime Minister's complete reversal of his assurance to the House that on no account would a loan to Russia be guaranteed by the Government. When it was revealed that he had gone back on this, he was denounced for giving way 'to forces outside the Cabinet'. The Liberals and the Tories voted together and MacDonald's Government was defeated in the House on 8th October 1924 by 384 votes to 198.

An immediate election was held. The voters' verdict was influenced by the publication, just before polling day, of the 'Zinovieff letter', the authenticity of which was later challenged and has never been clearly established. It indicated an attempt by Russia to interfere in Britain's domestic affairs and to establish Communist cells among the unemployed, the armed forces and the munition workers. Labour lost as a result 41 seats and the Conservatives came back 413 strong – a clear majority of 211 over all the other parties combined, for the Liberals were reduced by now to only 40 – a mere 'busload', as the Press described it.

Shortly before the election, the MacDonalds had the Glasgow Orpheus Choir to sing in the State drawing-room on the first floor. The Duke and Duchess of York were present. A day or two later the floor was found to be giving way: there had been too many people in the room, but the singing of the choir was jestingly blamed. Cracks appeared in the ceiling of the room below, used by three of the secretaries as their office. The cracks were covered over with stamp-paper and it was said, playfully no doubt, that when the stamp-paper split something would have to be done.

CHAPTER 38
The Return of Baldwin

MACDONALD moved out of No. 10 after a stay of barely ten months and Stanley Baldwin moved in again with his wife, his youngest daughter and his younger son, Wyndham. Safe with their enormous majority, the Baldwins were able to stay here for nearly five years.

The Conservative Party had by now closed its ranks. Austen Chamberlain and Lord Birkenhead, who had loyally stood by Lloyd George when the Coalition broke up, returned to the fold; and Winston Churchill, after being defeated in a by-election earlier in the year as an Independent Conservative, had been admitted to full membership of the Party and was back in Parliament after an absence of two years.

In constructing his Government, Baldwin surprised many by giving the important office of Chancellor of the Exchequer to Churchill, who had only just joined the Party. Chamberlain became Foreign Secretary; his half-brother Neville became Minister of Health; Birkenhead went to the India Office. The most disappointed was Curzon, who having missed the Premiership the year before, was now moved out of the Foreign Office and became Lord President of the Council.

Most of Baldwin's Ministers found him an easy man to work with. Foreign affairs he left completely to the Foreign Secretary, and in the solving of crises he relied chiefly on his common sense and his instinct to guide him to a solution. Both served him well. Essentially he was a moderate. He tried to steer a middle course between the Conservatism of his followers and the Socialism which he sensed the country wanted. Clearly the Liberal Party was no longer an effective force and the only alternative Government was Labour.

The deep unrest caused by unemployment, still alarmingly high, would, he foresaw, require most sympathetic understanding if serious conflict was to be avoided. That was why when the Cabinet discussed a Private Member's Bill, which sought to prevent trade unionists being made to contribute to the Labour Party funds, Baldwin said he would not support the Bill, though the majority of his colleagues were in favour of it. Birkenhead passed him a note across the table at No. 10 saying: 'I think your action shows enormous courage and for that reason will succeed.' The others eventually gave in. When the Bill was introduced, the Prime Minister said: 'We have our majority; we believe in the justice of this Bill . . . but we are going to withdraw our hand, we are not going to push our political advantage home. . . . Suspicion, which has prevented stability in Europe, is the one poison that is preventing stability at home. . . . We, at any rate, are not going to fire the first shot.' The speech, and the gesture it conveyed, won Baldwin world-wide tributes. Curzon, in almost the last letter he ever wrote, congratulated Baldwin on 'Your wonderful speech'. Indeed it ranks among the great speeches made in Parliament.

But while Baldwin strove to woo the workers he grew more and more impatient with the unyielding attitude of the employers. Conditions were unhappily greatly worsened for the country by the return to the gold standard, announced by Churchill in his first Budget. It was done to enable London to retain its position as the banking centre of the world, but in fact its effect on Britain's exports was most damaging. Coal was seriously affected. One after another the mines were shut down, and the mine-owners found that the wages they had agreed in the preceding year could no longer be maintained. An attempt

379

to terminate all existing agreements was rejected by the miners. Other trade unions instantly rallied to their support. The situation became critical and a meeting of the Cabinet was hurriedly called at No. 10 for 6.30 in the evening on 31st July 1925. The faces of the Ministers as they came along Downing Street reflected their anxiety and their gloom. After much argument, and angry disagreement, Baldwin got his colleagues to agree that the Government should pay the difference between the wages fixed in 1924 and the lower sum the mine-owners were now offering. This costly subsidy seriously affected the Budget, but it enabled the mines to keep going until the spring. It bought time. It was described by some as a bribe to the owners not to serve their lock-out notices. But, as Baldwin admitted afterwards, it was done because he was not yet ready to face a General Strike.

That came early in the following year and throughout the intervening winter the Government proceeded quietly with their plans to meet the threat.[150] A Royal Commission was also appointed to inquire into the mining situation. Its report, issued in March, advised that the mine-owners should be bought out by the State; that a great many technical improvements would have to be introduced; that the underground working hours should be kept to seven hours and not increased as suggested by the owners; and that the cut in wages should be small and not as large as proposed by the owners.

The miners were not prepared to accept the Report as a whole and expressed their opposition in the phrase – 'Not a minute on the day, not a penny off the pay' – which by constant repetition became inflammatory. The owners, on the other hand, were ready to negotiate on wages provided the hours of work were increased. Baldwin hoped that some compromise would be reached. Talks were arranged with both sides, but preparations to meet a General Strike went on. For the purpose of combating it, the country was divided into eleven areas, each under a Civil Commissioner. Troops were to be placed in certain industrial centres, and further battalions were to be held in reserve, to be moved as required.

On 27th April 1926 the Cabinet, in the absence of Baldwin who was engaged at the time in negotiations with the miners, advised that a State of Emergency should be declared. Three days later the General Council of the Trades Union Congress, indicating that the miners had the full backing of the other unions, decided to call a General Strike. They informed the Cabinet that the unions would be responsible for the distribution of food throughout the country so that there should be no shortage and no hardship.

The Cabinet met on the night of Saturday 1st May and continued its discussions until 1.15 on Sunday morning. Baldwin felt that trouble could be averted and a little extra time could be bought by continuing the subsidy for a further three months, by which time the reorganization of the mining industry could be begun. But the Cabinet, meeting again at noon that Sunday, regarded this as a surrender under threat. By five o'clock that afternoon it was announced that, unless there was an unconditional withdrawal of the threat of a General Strike, negotiations could not be resumed. The Cabinet then adjourned and met again at 9.30 that evening. Two hours later they were joined by Baldwin and two other Ministers, who had been engaged in discussions with the T.U.C. delegates; they reported that no irrevocable step had been taken with regard to a General Strike and that the T.U.C. were prepared to withdraw all instructions at once if negotiations were resumed.

At this point a message was brought to the Cabinet, which was sitting at the time at No. 11 because of other discussions that had been going on at No. 10. The message stated that the printers of the *Daily Mail* had refused to print a leading article dealing with the case of the miners and the supporting unions. This changed the situation. Baldwin drew up a Note for the waiting T.U.C. committee, indicating that 'overt acts have already taken place, including gross interference with the freedom of the Press' and asked for a repudiation of such action. The Note was handed by the Prime Minister to the waiting delegates and he then went up to bed. It was too late by now to stop the Strike.

The Government was ready for the fight that followed; the unions were not. The General Strike began in the early hours of 4th May 1926 and lasted for eight days. Everything was brought to a standstill; but, following a broadcast appeal, large numbers of the public, being no longer at work, offered to continue all the essential services, including transport. As the newspapers were not appearing, a Government sheet, called the *British Gazette*, under the editorship of Winston Churchill, was issued daily. The strikers brought out their own paper, the *Daily Worker*. The Government insisted on 'unconditional surrender'.

Mr. Justice Astbury pronounced the strike to be illegal, and Sir John Simon charged the leaders of the strike as lawbreakers. Many eminent legal authorities questioned the soundness of these pronouncements. The strikers, however, seized the opportunity of sending representatives to No. 10 for further talks, and the strike was over.

Baldwin, in a broadcast to the nation, asked that there should be no recriminations, no allocation of blame: look forward, not backward, he said. But among his followers there was a desire to be severe with the vanquished. The Prime Minister, weary from the strain, gave in to the extremists in his Party, just as Ramsay MacDonald was accused of doing less than two years before. First the Seven Hours Act, limiting the hours worked underground by the miners, was suspended. Next came a new Trades Disputes Act, making all sympathetic large-scale strikes illegal and imposing heavy penalties on those who assisted or took part in them. It also curtailed picketing and compelled Civil Service trade unions to withdraw from their affiliation to the Trades Union Congress. These measures caused great resentment and left a deep-seated bitterness. The Tories, though they had succeeded in imposing their will on him, regarded Baldwin as being closer to the trade unionists than to them: his elder son, Oliver Baldwin, was already a member of the Labour Party, and they remembered moreover that Baldwin had not hesitated to reprimand his own followers for what he regarded as a breach of courtesy towards their opponents.

But much more than this was responsible for the gradual erosion of his popularity with his Party and especially with his Cabinet. He avoided action. He evaded decisions. He appeared to have adopted Walpole's golden precept 'Let sleeping dogs lie'; but, whereas Walpole's desire was merely to avoid trouble (he was indeed extremely active in furthering his economic and international schemes), with Baldwin the deterrent was indolence. His interests were narrow, his knowledge superficial. But his love for England and his instinctive understanding of the people was considerable. He could be called upon to speak on a wide range of subjects at an assortment of assemblies and is said to have delivered more speeches than any other Prime Minister. The tasks of government were left largely to the departments. In foreign

Gillray's cartoon, showing Britannia in 1804, menaced from one side by Napoleon, as Death; and from the other by Addington (in doorway) and Fox, whose lethal inter-ferences the Younger Pitt disposes of briskly.

John Doyle's cartoon, entitled 'Reading The Times' (1829). King George the Fourth (left) asks: 'Well, Arthur: what's the news?', to which Wellington replies: 'We announce on unquestionable authority that a serious difference has arisen between a great Personage and his Prime Minister.'

A contemporary cartoon from *The Gladstone ABC* (Blackwood) showing Gladstone
invading Egypt in 1882.

THE WOLF AT THE DOOR

Sir David Low's cartoon in the London *Star* of 27th October 1932, showing Ramsay Macdonald at No. 10 with the Wolf of Unemployment at the door and Neville Chamberlain, Winston Churchill and others waiting their opportunity to take over.

CLEM. "I DO WISH THAT OLD CHAMP WOULD DO HIS TRAINING SOMEWHERE ELSE!"

Strube's cartoon in *Everybody's* of 29th September 1951, during the closing days of Clement Attlee's term as Prime Minister. Aneurin Bevan stands outside No. 10 while Churchill, Leader of the Opposition, and Lord Woolton, Chairman of the Conservative Party, prepare for the October general election.

'Labour troubles!' Vicky's cartoon in the London *Evening Standard* of 11th May 1962, showing Harold Macmillan as the anxious Prime Minister and Iain Macleod as Chairman of the Tory Party. While reconstruction of No. 10 was delayed by strikes, the Labour and Liberal parties showed a number of gains in local elections as well as by-elections.

affairs Austen Chamberlain achieved a remarkable triumph through his persistent endeavour for a general appeasement in Europe. The Locarno treaties marked the acceptance by Germany of some of the most vital provisions of the Peace Treaty of 1919 and led to her admission into the League of Nations. Chamberlain was rewarded with the Garter.

But at home unemployment still eluded solution. A slight improvement had been achieved by the building of nearly a million new houses (for which Neville Chamberlain as Minister of Health and Housing was chiefly responsible), and hundreds of new schools. But the dole paid to the workless tore into Churchill's Budgets. Tariff Reform, still dear to the heart of the Tories and regarded by many as an infallible cure, Baldwin refused to consider because of the pledge given to the voters at the General Election. In 1928 he was responsible for the extension of the franchise to all women on precisely the same terms as men. Limited hitherto to women over thirty, it now brought in every woman at the age of twenty-one and came to be known as 'The Flapper Vote'. It is believed that this vote brought his Government down in the General Election of the following year. The election was fought under the uninspiring slogan of 'Safety First'. Labour came in with greatly increased forces in the House, numbering 288 as against 260 Conservatives. The Liberals improved their position a little to 59.

Baldwin handed in his resignation on 4th June 1929. He had been four and a half years at No. 10 Downing Street and was doubtless glad to get away, for he and his wife both loved the country. They liked going for long walks, stopping to look at pigs over a stile, and spending the hours watching a game of cricket, which both played. When he was younger Baldwin used to be a sprinter. His son tells us that even in maturity his zest for leaping over obstacles had not left him and he would 'spring over . . . sofas and arm-chairs, low windows, flights of stairs. . . . I cannot recall ever seeing him climbing upstairs one at a time at Downing Street; always at the double.'[151] He had an antipathy to social gatherings and could never wholly conceal, his son adds, 'his misery when penned in by a fence of small talk' and by the banquets and assemblies that were an inescapable part of his life at Downing Street – the White Russian Cossack choir in the garden, using the Cabinet room as their dressing-room, the display of the traditional quilting work of the South Wales miners' wives in the drawing-rooms to raise funds, and other of Mrs. Baldwin's activities for the care of mothers in childbirth. His compensatory refuge was to withdraw to the small room above the front door of No. 10 and read. Shelves had been built round the room to hold his books and whenever he could he spent hours here each evening with his wife seated beside him.

CHAPTER 39
The National Government

WITH Labour the largest Party in the House, the King sent for Ramsay MacDonald. But once again Labour was at the mercy of the Liberals. By joining forces with the Tories in the lobbies they could at any time get him out. Nevertheless with fortitude and hope he took on the task and became Prime Minister for the second time. Baldwin moved out of No. 10 and MacDonald returned, with his daughter Ishbel once more as his hostess.

This time MacDonald did not combine the duties of Foreign Secretary with those of Prime Minister, but handed that office over to Arthur Henderson. A woman was admitted to the Cabinet for the first time and took her place at the famous long table. She was Miss Margaret Bondfield, Minister of Labour in the new Government. Herbert Morrison became Minister of Transport; Attlee, the future Prime Minister, who had been a junior Minister in the previous Labour Government, was left out. Philip Snowden was once again Chancellor of the Exchequer and went back to No. 11 next door.

Changes were made in the furniture of the main rooms. Ishbel

385

insisted that the chairs in the State dining-room, in the panelled break-fast-room alongside, and in the two State drawing-rooms could and should be improved – and they were. The Office of Works brought along drawings and samples of what could be supplied and from these Ishbel made her choice. To add to the pictures already in these rooms, others were brought in from the cellars of the National Gallery. A cheerful air was provided by arranging flower boxes in the windows, especially those round the central well, and tubs of plants were also set out on the roof.

Ishbel wanted to do much more. She wanted to remove the clutter of partitions and add more bathrooms, but with an economic crisis looming this was not possible.

Their favourite among the State rooms was the large dining-room designed by Soane: it is an attractive room with its old panelling, its pictures – a large one of Pitt over the fireplace, an equally large one of Nelson over the sideboard, with smaller pictures of Burke over the door to the pantry and of Fox in the panel beside it. Two other pictures are of the Duke of Wellington and the Marquess of Salisbury. While the MacDonalds were at No. 10 a picture of Gladstone was hung in this room, just by the entrance: it caused a young grandson of the Prime Minister's to remark: 'I know why you've got him here. It's to remind us to chew each mouthful thirty times before swallowing it.' Ishbel says: 'We liked this room so much that even if only one of us was in for a meal, we had it alone there rather than in the small breakfast-room alongside.'*

Of the younger girls, Joan was a medical student in London, Sheila was at Oxford. Malcolm, who had just been elected to Parliament, took over Baldwin's small study above the front door, but boarded up the bookshelves and hung his Japanese prints on them. 'For us,' Ishbel continues, 'No. 10 was just a colony of bed-sitting rooms with a large communal dining-room where we met for breakfast at eight o'clock. We didn't use either of the State drawing-rooms ourselves. Prime Ministers don't have any home life because of the demands made by the House of Commons and by political and other meetings in the evenings. I was lucky in having two comfortable rooms furnished to

* In a statement to the author.

my liking, instead of just a bed-sitter, although these were inner rooms with the windows looking out on to an ugly yard. The main drawing-rooms were used for official entertaining of course – when Dominion Prime Ministers were in London and when delegates came to attend various conferences – scientific, economic, naval, that sort of thing.'

It was a crowded life for the young hostess, for, in addition to these official evenings, there were personal occasions when Sir James Barrie or Mackenzie King from Canada dined and the maids went round in their black dresses and white aprons. Ishbel also organized charity appeals, some with sales of work, others musical: usually these were predominantly Scottish. Then there were meetings at which she had to take the chair: one of these was addressed by the Prince of Wales*, another by the Duke of York.†

'The only thing I disliked about being at No. 10,' she says, 'was the unceasing publicity. Everything you did was in the news. There was no escape, no privacy whatsoever. I got a key to the garden gate and used to let myself out into the Horse Guards Parade in order to avoid the cameras and get away from the clusters of sightseers in Downing Street.

'The nights I loved, especially when it was late. One had an eerie feeling about the rooms downstairs – empty, dark and silent.'

Ramsay MacDonald had once again to be extremely careful about the legislation he tried to put through Parliament. He managed to get the Coal Mines Bill through, which reduced the working hours underground from eight to seven and a half; but his other measures were either thrown out or amended beyond recognition. He failed in his endeavour to repeal the Trades Disputes Act. American relations were excluded from the control of the Foreign Secretary, Arthur Henderson, and kept in his own hands; and it was to his tact and patience that an agreement was reached in London between Britain, the United States and Japan, establishing an accepted ratio of naval construction. This saved Britain £60 million and the United States 500 million dollars. The agreement was later extended to include Italy and France.

There were minor irritants in foreign affairs. The Prime Minister did not like Philip Snowden's sharp rejoinder at a conference on

---

* Later King Edward the Eighth and then the Duke of Windsor.
† Later King George the Sixth.

German reparations in Holland, when he referred to the French representative's remarks as 'grotesque and ridiculous'. Snowden threatened to resign if MacDonald did not publicly accord him his fullest support. Trouble also occurred with Arthur Henderson over the terms of a settlement in Egypt, at that time still under British occupation. This brought another Minister to the verge of resignation. But both incidents were smoothed out. Over the handling of the unemployment problem, however, there was a resignation. The number of workless rose steeply during 1930 and the trend continued in 1931. It had become by now a world problem, affected in a great measure by the widespread economic slump in the United States. MacDonald appointed a committee to deal with it, headed by J. H. Thomas, the Lord Privy Seal, and including the First Commissioner of Works, George Lansbury, and Sir Oswald Mosley, who was Chancellor of the Duchy of Lancaster. Mosley insisted that only State-aided public works could effect a cure. As not very much could be done without immense financial resources, he resigned in despair in May 1930 and C. R. Attlee was appointed to take his place.

The Labour Party, disgusted and angry that unemployment should still be rising, attacked the Prime Minister at the Party Conference in October 1930. MacDonald, in a fighting reply, said: 'My friends, *we* are not on trial; it is the system under which we live. It has broken down, not only in this little island, it has broken down in Europe, in Asia, in America; it has broken down everywhere, as it was bound to break down.' The Conference stood by MacDonald.

But the economic depression swelled and threatened the economy of Britain, as of other countries, with collapse. The Prime Minister was advised that sacrifices would have to be faced, including a cut in the dole paid to the unemployed. The Cabinet was stunned when it was told of this. If work could not be provided, the dole at least saved the workless from some of the worst pangs of hunger. How could it be reduced? That the total of such payments had risen alarmingly no one could deny. The crisis, some began to feel, could only be courageously met by a Coalition Government, drawn from all Parties.

In June 1931, an Austrian bank closed its doors, and panic set in. It spread to Berlin. The German mark tottered. Foreign investors next began to withdraw the money they had deposited in London banks.

The Bank of England found it impossible to save the pound without large credits from America and France, both of which countries had been accumulating gold. Such credits, it soon became clear, would not be provided unless the British Government had a balanced budget, which was impossible without drastic economies. Credits were in fact obtained from both those countries in July 1931 but not sufficient to surmount the crisis. It now became essential for the Government to act.

August being a holiday month, most members of the Cabinet and of the Opposition were away. Ramsay MacDonald returned to London from Lossiemouth on the morning of 11th August and immediately had a talk at No. 10 with officials from the Bank of England. Baldwin, on his way to Aix-les-Bains where he and his wife went annually for August and September, was advised to return. Lloyd George being ill, Sir Herbert Samuel was acting as Leader of the Liberals.

The Cabinet Economy Committee of five, of which MacDonald and Snowden were members, met at No. 10 on 12th August and sat all through that day and the next. It was a sad and anguished deliberation, but they agreed at last that economies, including cuts in the dole, would have to be made. Their report was discussed at a meeting of the full Cabinet at No. 10 on 19th August. Many insisted that no cuts in unemployment relief could humanely be imposed and suggested that additional revenue should be raised by an all-round tariff of ten per cent. The T.U.C. General Council expressed the same opposition when the Prime Minister went to see them the next day. He returned to Downing Street in a mood of despair. The Cabinet met again the following morning, Friday 21st August, and could come to no agreement. That afternoon MacDonald saw the Tory and Liberal leaders. They made it clear that much more would have to be done than the Cabinet was prepared to agree to.

The Cabinet met again on the morning of Saturday the 22nd and was informed of the Opposition leaders' views. The King, at Sandringham since 11th August, had kept in constant touch with the Prime Minister by telephone. On Friday he left for Balmoral, but the moment he got there he was told that he would be required in London and travelled back by the night train, arriving at eight on the morning of Sunday 23rd August. Two hours later he saw MacDonald at Buckingham Palace.

Later that day His Majesty, 'convinced of the necessity for a National Government'* saw Baldwin and Samuel separately, then he saw MacDonald again, and the Prime Minister handed in his resignation. His Majesty asked him to reconsider his decision, and the next morning, at MacDonald's request, called together the three Party leaders. Within a few hours a Coalition Government of all three Parties was formed, with MacDonald as Prime Minister.

When he returned to No. 10 he found his colleagues waiting in the Cabinet room. Informing them of what had occurred, he asked if they were prepared to join him. He looked at each in turn; all refused, except Snowden, J. H. Thomas and Lord Sankey, the Lord Chancellor. The meeting lasted twenty minutes. Later the others elected Arthur Henderson as their new Leader and became the official Opposition. MacDonald, deeply grieved by their decision, felt it was no more than a temporary rift, and that the Party would be reunited after the crisis; but the bitterness, and the denunciation heaped upon him by his former followers, made this quite impossible. He felt this acutely for the rest of his life.

Snowden retained the office of Chancellor of the Exchequer and one of the first things he did was to go off the gold standard, which it was felt had contributed largely to the accentuation of Britain's economic difficulties. Severe economies were imposed, and in time confidence was restored and foreign capital began once again to pour into London.

In October 1931 a General Election was held. The voters were asked for a 'Doctor's Mandate' – an overall authority for treatment, as required, to cure the ills of the country. Baldwin in his appeal to the country defined his position in these words: 'Here am I,' he said, 'the Leader of the Conservative Party, who took my political life in my hands nine years ago to escape from a Coalition, asking you to support a Government, led by a Socialist Prime Minister, and to enter myself under him in another Coalition.' The public's response brought overwhelming victory. The Coalition – or National Government, as it was called – won all seats except 59: to that attenuated number was the opposition Labour Party now reduced.

---

* Recorded by Sir Clive Wigram (Later Lord Wigram), Private Secretary to the King.

Ramsay MacDonald retained the Government almost as constituted when the Coalition was formed two months before. Baldwin served under him as Lord President of the Council; Herbert Samuel was Home Secretary; Lord Sankey remained Lord Chancellor. Philip Snowden, who had been ill, went to the Lords as Viscount Snowden and his place at the Exchequer was taken by Neville Chamberlain. Among the junior Ministers was Anthony Eden, a future Prime Minister: he was appointed Parliamentary Under-Secretary to the Foreign Office.

CHAPTER 40
Baldwin and the Abdication

THE National Government, not fully national since almost the entire Labour Party had refused to join it and the handful who were in bore the label 'National Labour', soon lost the main Liberal group too, and the remnant of that Party, adopting MacDonald's precedent, became known as 'National Liberals'. This breach, threatened by Samuel in January 1932, was postponed until the Ottawa Conference in the summer: the introduction of preferential tariffs in favour of the Empire was regarded as having disposed finally of Free Trade, brought in nearly a century before with the repeal of the Corn Laws. Samuel resigned from the Government and Snowden, who was Lord Privy Seal, resigned too as a staunch Free Trader. Sir John Simon, now Foreign Secretary, became the Leader of the National Liberals. But in complexion the Government was almost wholly Conservative.

Churchill was not included in the National Government and on many issues was its severest critic. His earliest attack was on the plans drawn up for the future of India. Following on the India Reform Act of 1919, pledges had been given that India would be granted full

Dominion status, and this was assured by the Labour Government in a pronouncement made by the Viceroy* on 30th October 1929. Sir John Simon had already been sent out by Baldwin with a Commission of Inquiry (of which Attlee was a member): its report was published in June 1930 and the First Round Table Conference met in London in November of that year. Gandhi, the leader of the Indian nationalists (whose weapon was not terrorism but civil disobedience, though outrages were recurrent), attended the second of these conferences in September 1931. The little wizened man with no front teeth, his sharp eyes glittering behind glasses, arrived at No. 10 Downing Street dressed in a *dhoti* displaying his spindly legs.

The Conferences failed because the proposal to make India a federation of self-governing provinces and Native States, with a central federal assembly, was rejected by the Indian Princes. But a new Government of India Bill was presented and passed, and received the Royal Assent in August 1935. Every step in this planned progression towards independence was subjected to the most persistent attacks by the diehard section of the Tory Party, with Winston Churchill louder in his denunciation than the rest. Ever since his freedom from office he had become attached to Lord Beaverbrook and Lord Rothermere, the Press peers whose morning, evening and Sunday newspapers maintained a strenuous and unremitting criticism of Baldwin. It weakened but did not destroy Baldwin's authority as Leader of the Conservative Party; it disclosed, however, that the influence of the popular Press was by no means as wide and effective as had been imagined. After suffering it in silence for some years, Baldwin finally turned on his assailants: 'What the proprietorship of these papers is aiming at is power, and power without responsibility: the prerogative of the harlot throughout the ages.'

Churchill also used his considerable powers of scathing denunciation to expose the weakness of Britain's defences and their inadequacy to meet the growing Hitler menace. Britain was burdened by a dual handicap. In the first place, since the war her policy had been based on collective security through the League of Nations, which each successive Government had most ardently supported; secondly, the acute

---

* Lord Irwin, later Lord Halifax.

financial crisis of 1931 made it difficult for her to enter into an arms race on an effective scale without making further drastic economies in other directions. There was moreover a great wave of pacifist feeling in the country, emphatically expressed at by-elections as early as 1933. Nevertheless by July 1934 Baldwin, as Lord President of the Council, announced that the expansion of the Air Force was to begin. A five-year programme had been drawn up, providing 41 new squadrons and raising the total to 75 for home defence. A few months later, on 23rd November 1934, speaking at Glasgow, he revealed that in his mind the collective system was no longer practicable, as both Japan and Germany had by now left the League, but it was not until early in 1937 that a detailed plan for rearming the country was drawn up, allocating the expenditure of £1,500 million over a period of five years.[183]

MacDonald, who had an operation for glaucoma in each eye and was tired and ailing, exchanged offices with Baldwin in the summer of 1935, and Baldwin became Prime Minister for the third time. At the General Election in November 1935 the Government lost 79 seats but still had a majority of 245. Labour's strength in the House was now increased to 154.

Baldwin, who had faced two grave crises, had still another to deal with in the year ahead. King George the Fifth died in January 1936 and before the end of the year the Abdication of the new King confronted the Prime Minister. There was no hint of such a possibility when the reign began. Edward the Eighth was extremely popular – indeed no Prince of Wales had ever enjoyed such overwhelming popularity. He had been most carefully trained for his responsibilities and had conscientiously carried out his duties both at home and on his many tours in the Dominions and Colonies. But, though by now forty-two, he had never married. He had been seen about of late, even before his father's death, with Mrs. Wallis Simpson, an American, who had already divorced one husband and was shortly to divorce her second. The British Press were reticent about their association, but the newspapers abroad and especially in America, featured it prominently and even went so far as to say that the King was thinking of marrying her. The fact that she was an American did not at all affect the attitude of Baldwin and the other Ministers. That she had been through the divorce courts did: they did not consider it suitable in the circumstances that she should be Queen of England, particularly as the King was by title Defender of the Faith.

Baldwin had been away during the summer: it was a more extended absence because of his illness earlier in the year following Hitler's occupation of the Rhineland in March, the campaign of murder in Palestine, and the outbreak of civil war in Spain. He returned to No. 10 on 12th October and had his first interview with the King on this subject a few days later. It became clear to the Prime Minister not only that marriage was in the King's thoughts, but that his mind had in fact been irrevocably made up.

The Cabinet was greatly exercised about this. Plans for the Coronation were already in hand. The problem was debated at many sessions at No. 10, for the King's marriage was not a private matter, but concerned the people of England, among whom there were a great many Nonconformists; it concerned also the Calvinists in Scotland, and the Roman Catholics in both countries. Nor could the feelings of the people in the Dominions be ignored. Baldwin was convinced that the King's immense popularity would not be able to withstand the shock of his marriage to Mrs. Simpson.

After further talks, the King asked the Prime Minister on 25th November to consider the possibility of a morganatic marriage. Baldwin said he was quite prepared to consult the Cabinet, but was confident that Parliament would not pass the necessary legislation. This was discussed by the Cabinet on Friday 27th November and it was decided that the Prime Ministers of the Dominions should be consulted too. Attlee, by now the Leader of the Opposition, was also consulted and stated that the Labour Party was unanimously opposed to such a marriage. Soon from the Dominions came the same answer.

On 2nd December the Press broke its silence. The whole country now knew of the King's dilemma. On the next evening the Prime Minister went to the Palace on the King's invitation. His Majesty stated that he wanted to put his case to the country in a personal broadcast. Baldwin pointed out that this would only serve to divide the country.

After further discussions with his colleagues at No. 10 he informed the King that so long as he remained King he could only broadcast in words approved by his Ministers. In Parliament a King's Party began to emerge with Winston Churchill at its head. Some wondered if the

King would defy his Ministers, ignore the opinion of the Dominions, cause the Cabinet to resign and force a General Election on the issue. It was a possibility until Monday 7th December, when Churchill was shouted down in the House as he rose to speak.

The discussions had by now been going on for more than six weeks. They could not be much further prolonged. Very few of the newspapers were on the side of the King: among these were the papers of Lord Beaverbrook and the second Lord Rothermere. It was still hoped by the Prime Minister that the King might be induced to reconsider his intention of marrying Mrs. Simpson.

During a Cabinet meeting on the afternoon of Wednesday 9th December a message from Queen Mary, the King's mother, was brought to the Prime Minister, asking if he would go and see her. He rose from the Cabinet table and set out at once, accompanied by the Home Secretary Sir John Simon. It is said that Queen Mary, apart from her own personal grief about her son, was gravely concerned about the future of the monarchy. It had already suffered a most damaging blow through the publicity about the King's association with Mrs. Simpson, which daily filled many columns of the Press; if the monarchy was to continue to play its important part in the continuity of Great Britain and the Empire, then it was inevitable, she felt, that someone else should take over the succession.★

Further talks then took place with the King. Although Mrs. Simpson, by now on the Continent, offered to 'withdraw from the situation' in order to spare the throne any damage, the King was still resolved to go on with the marriage, and abdicated on 11th December 1936. His brother Albert, next in line, succeeded as King George the Sixth.

For those living at No. 10 these crises caused a stir and traffic that made rest impossible. Messengers kept arriving. Ministers came and went. There were hurrying footsteps down the long corridor through most of the night, with raised voices at intervals. MacDonald's daughter Ishbel, during the economic crises of 1931, had found such bustle and whirr wearing on the nerves. 'Otherwise the place was always so very quiet at night,' she says, 'save for the clatter of dustbins, which woke one up very early in the morning.'

★ In a statement to the author by Mr. A. Duff Cooper, later Viscount Norwich.

Baldwin did not remain in office much longer. After the Coronation of the new King in May of the following year 1937, he resigned and went to the House of Lords as Earl Baldwin of Bewdley. The Chancellor of the Exchequer, Neville Chamberlain, took over the chief office on 28th May 1937.

397

CHAPTER 41
Second World War and Churchill

NEVILLE CHAMBERLAIN, tall, extremely thin, and wearing a permanently harassed air, was sixty-eight years old when he became Prime Minister. The younger son of Joe Chamberlain, who had served under Gladstone as a Liberal and broke away over Home Rule for Ireland, and the half-brother of Austen Chamberlain, he was the least likely member of his family one would have expected to be Prime Minister. Austen had been groomed for it and would indeed have attained it had he not stood loyally by Lloyd George at the time of the critical Carlton Club meeting, as a result of which Bonar Law went to No. 10. Austen died just three months before his brother attained the supreme office.

Neville Chamberlain did not take up politics until well into his mature life. He had been trained for business. His father had bought 20,000 acres of land in the Bahamas to grow sisal and sent Neville out to manage the estate. He was out there for seven vital years. The venture was not a success. On his return to England, Neville settled in Birmingham and was elected to the local Council, which he served well, and was later made Lord Mayor. In December 1916, when Lloyd George became Prime Minister, he sent for Neville and appointed him Director-General of National Service, but after seven frustrating months, Chamberlain resigned and went back to Birmingham, grumbling that he had been given neither instructions nor powers. Lloyd George's comments were much more scathing about Chamberlain's incapacity for the task. The only thing that was clear was that each had developed an obsessive dislike for the other.

Chamberlain did not get into Parliament until after the First World War. By that time he was in his fiftieth year. There is no other instance in English history of a Prime Minister entering Parliament so late in life. He was offered office in the Coalition Government by the Tory leader Bonar Law, but refused to serve under Lloyd George. In 1923, when Baldwin took over, he became Chancellor of the Exchequer, but the Tariff Reform election later that year prevented him from presenting a Budget.

The Chamberlains did not move into No. 10 when the Baldwins vacated the house in 1937. The new Prime Minister's wife found it far from pleasant to live in or easy to run. She found the offices, the State rooms and the living quarters too interwoven and decided to separate them. So she moved the residential section one floor up – to the second floor from the first. The main staircase did not go up so far; it could only be reached by the back stairs, as that floor had always been used by the servants, though the two younger MacDonald girls had had their bedrooms there. A new staircase was accordingly built, near the main staircase but not so handsome. The whole of that servants' floor was taken over, leaving seven small attic rooms above for staff use. It is from this time that the second floor has been mainly used as the residential section of No. 10 by Prime Ministers and their families. The old attic windows were removed and larger ones were put in, the ceilings were raised, the slope of the walls was in a measure straightened. The room at the north-western corner overlooking St. James's Park and the Horse Guards Parade, was converted into a comfortable bedroom for the Prime Minister, Mrs. Chamberlain took the room facing it across the passage, while the room beside it was made into a spacious bathroom. The bedrooms on the floor below, alongside the State reception rooms, were now used as additional offices. Many of the floors had sagged and the walls of one of these bedrooms was found to be four inches out of line and had to be put right. It took ten months for these alterations to be completed. Until then the Prime Minister and his wife continued to live at No. 11, into which they had moved when he was appointed Chancellor of the Exchequer. They had one son and one daughter, both grown up, and neither lived with them.

At No. 10 their residence was confined entirely to that upper floor. Of the two main bedrooms on the first floor, the one at the corner facing the Horse Guards and the Park was made into an extra drawing-room, thus forming a line of three reception rooms, including the small drawing-room and the State drawing-room at the other corner. The inner bedroom became the Prime Minister's private study. It was here that he worked late in the evenings.

The big kitchen in the basement was also modernized so that it should be easier to work in, and a small service lift was put in to take the food up to the passage just outside the State dining-room. The total cost of these alterations was £25,000.

Mrs. Chamberlain, with her artistic sensitivity and flair for decoration, strove to provide No. 10 with the elegance and grace it once had. She had many talks with Sir Philip Sassoon, the Minister of Works, a man of great taste himself, whose sister the Marchioness of Cholmondeley had married into the family of Sir Robert Walpole and lived at his old house at Houghton. With his help the three main drawing-rooms were transformed. Painted white, the large State drawing-room was supplied with fresh furniture, including some eighteenth century settees and Regency sofas; the middle drawing-room, with its pink walls and recently acquired suite of red upholstered furniture which had once belonged to Clive of India, came to be known as the Red drawing-room; the room at the Park end was decorated in yellow. Many additional pictures were lent by the National Gallery for use in these rooms: some came from the cellars, but she was lucky enough to secure a few that were of interest – Dutch interiors, a large landscape by Turner and another by Claude Loraine. The staircase walls were painted a greeny yellow and a deep red carpet was put down on the stairs. When Mrs. Chamberlain talked of curtains, she was told that these she would have to provide herself. She used country chintzes for the new bedrooms facing the Park – a happy and admired choice.

Her pride in the house was great and, having absorbed much of its history, she derived a joy from showing visitors round: among these was Sir Hugh Walpole, the novelist, distantly connected with Sir Robert Walpole, and the relatives and friends of past Prime Ministers. One evening an extremely well-informed address was delivered by her at No. 10 to the Empire Parliamentary Association, after which they were shown the State dining-room and main reception rooms. The Prime Minister was too busy to attend, for by this time the many crises with which he was faced during his short stay of less than three years in the house had already begun.

Chamberlain retained Anthony Eden as Foreign Secretary. Sir John Simon was appointed Chancellor of the Exchequer, Hore-Belisha, Minister of Transport in the previous Government, was made Secretary of State for War, with the specific instruction that the Army, so long regarded as the poor relation of the Services, should be strengthened and modernized. The other two Service Ministers were Sir Kingsley Wood for Air and Alfred Duff Cooper at the Admiralty. That war was likely was not overlooked, but Chamberlain was resolved to avoid it if he possibly could. Churchill, not in the Government and with a critical eye still on the inadequacy of the country's defences, said of him: 'Chamberlain has an absolute lust for peace.'*

The chief crises indeed sprang from this pursuit. The first of these involved the resignation of the Foreign Secretary Eden. Italy's unscrupulous war on Abyssinia, launched in defiance of the League of Nations in October 1935, had led to an endeavour by Eden's predecessor Samuel Hoare and the French Foreign Minister Pierre Laval, to essay a settlement by offering Mussolini large tracts of Abyssinian territory. The suggestion shocked the world, since the aggressor was to be compensated with land extorted from the unfortunate victim. Hoare resigned and was then succeeded by Eden. Abyssinia was conquered and occupied by the Italians. Mussolini, triumphant in his aggression, was enthusiastically acclaimed by Hitler as a worthy colleague and the Rome–Berlin Axis was formed. Both countries then plunged into the Spanish civil war with 'volunteers' supporting Franco. It was Chamberlain's resolve to separate the two dictators and

---

* Quoted to the author by Sir A. Beverley Baxter, M.P.

thus confine the war for which Hitler was so avidly arming. Feeling that Eden was out of sympathy with Mussolini, the Prime Minister conducted the negotiations himself. Eden promptly resigned* and was replaced by Lord Halifax. The detachment of Mussolini, though for a time it appeared to be hopeful, failed completely.

Hitler seized Austria less than three weeks later, on 11th March 1938. His endeavours to deal in the same way with Czechoslovakia became apparent in July, and throughout that summer critical meetings of the Cabinet were held at No. 10 in an attempt to prevent this. Ministers met daily, sometimes twice a day, and talked often far into the night. On the 14th September the Prime Minister informed his colleagues of his sudden decision to go and see Hitler. It came as a bombshell.[158] The meeting took place at Berchtesgaden: the interview was stormy. When he returned the French Prime Minister, M. Daladier, and the French Foreign Secretary flew to London to discuss Hitler's demands at No. 10. A week later Chamberlain went again to see Hitler, this time at Godesberg. The next evening the Cabinet was informed of Hitler's fresh demands, and the French Ministers came again for talks. Chamberlain's third and final meeting with Hitler took place at Munich on 29th September. Before setting out, he prepared for the possibility of war. A State of Emergency was declared. The Fleet was mobilized. Fifty thousand officers and men of the Territorial Army were called up: changing from lounge suits to khaki, they set out to man the coastal defences and anti-aircraft guns and took their places at isolated searchlight stations.

On Chamberlain's return, waving an agreement of Anglo–German friendship and speaking of 'Peace with Honour', the crowds gathered in Downing Street and cheered wildly, relieved that war had been averted. But it had not. Chamberlain knew, and the call-up revealed, that the country was not yet ready for war. Having acquired time, he accelerated the rearmament of all the services. Whether it would have been more advantageous to fight has been argued unceasingly ever since. Many were suffused by shame at the sacrifice imposed on Czechoslovakia in the cause of appeasement. Dissatisfaction, and even anger, were expressed in the House of Commons by Churchill, by

* On 20th February 1938.

Duff Cooper, who instantly resigned from the Government, by Conservative members and by the Labour Opposition. Only a small section of the Press was critical, but the uneasiness spread and it began to be said openly that Churchill should take over the helm as the only leader capable of rousing the country to the inevitable danger of war. One of the first of such calls was made some months before Munich in the *Sunday Referee*: as early in fact as May 1938. Churchill's reply to it was despondent.* Endeavours were made to induce the Prime Minister to bring Churchill into the Government, but Chamberlain refused. 'I won't have anyone who will rock the boat,' he said.[158] The Tory Party as a whole was also against Churchill: they were not prepared to serve under him, only Labour and the Liberals were.†

Mrs. Chamberlain did a great deal of entertaining. She usually gave three parties on consecutive evenings during each Parliamentary session – on Tuesday, Wednesday and Thursday: arranged in this way the flowers lasted and they could use the same hired china. Members of Parliament were invited with their wives and each Member was asked to bring two of his constituents. Her memory for names and faces was quite astonishing: she always knew the Member and could say at once which constituency he represented. Mingled with them were Ambassadors and High Commissioners (the American Ambassador, Joe Kennedy, was often among the guests) as well as the Archbishop of Canterbury, and Cardinal Hinsley in his scarlet robes. The Prime Minister was rarely there: he looked in for a few minutes when he could spare the time. Several hundred guests were invited over the three days, and were given tea, hot or cold coffee and cakes. A great many waitresses had to be hired and Mrs. Chamberlain's secretary, Miss Marjorie Leaf, and personal friends were placed at the doors of the three drawing-rooms to keep the guests moving, as the floors were unsafe and could not hold more than a limited number in any one room. Smaller sherry parties were held at other times for distinguished visitors such as President Le Brun of France, the Governor-General of Canada, Lord Bessborough, and his wife when they were home on leave, Mr. Lyons, the Australian Prime Minister and later his successor Mr. Menzies, and, a departure from precedent, the various General

---

* In a letter to the author.
† In statements to the author.

Officers Commanding-in-Chief, Admirals and Air Marshals, not normally entertained at No. 10. There were also small luncheon parties, generally on Thursday – a short quick meal because the Prime Minister had to go on to the House. Princess Mary and Lord Harewood came to one of these lunches.

The King and Queen came to dinner one night in March 1939 and sat with twenty other guests in the State dining-room. The catering was done by Mrs. Chamberlain's cook. Only twice before in this century had the Sovereign and his consort dined in the house: the first time when King George the Fifth and Queen Mary came to dinner with the Asquiths in 1911, the second when George the Sixth and Queen Elizabeth dined with the Baldwins just before he retired from the Premiership.

The favourite diversion of the Chamberlains was to walk in St. James's Park every morning as far as the bridge and back, followed at a discreet distance by a detective. The Prime Minister took a keen interest in the garden at No. 10 and had a herbaceous border laid out along the Horse Guards wall. There had not been many flowers there before, only a lawn with two or three trees, one of them an evergreen oak.

When Hitler, in a breach of his guarantee, seized the rest of Czecho-slovakia on 15th March 1939, it was clear that war could no longer be averted. Conscription was introduced a fortnight later: it was the first time such a course had been adopted while the country was still at peace. The preparations for war were furthered with increasing speed and a clear warning was given to Hitler that Britain would fight for the independence of Poland, Greece and Rumania. It did not deter Hitler. He secured his flank by coming to terms with Russia and immediately began his pressure on Poland along the familiar pattern of allegations about Polish aggressions on the frontier.

It was August when this news reached London and the Ministers were scattered, as is customary in that month. The Prime Minister hurried down from Scotland and called an urgent meeting of the Cabinet on 23rd August. From the South of France and elsewhere the Cabinet gathered. They were informed of the movements of German troops and tanks and planes, and expressed their determination to stand by Poland even if it meant war. Parliament, in recess for the holiday, was summoned to return at once and met the next day. The Emergency Powers Bill was passed rapidly through both Houses and received the Royal assent that same evening at 10.15.

The next day, 25th August, the British Ambassador returned by plane from Berlin and saw the Prime Minister at No. 10; Hitler at the same time ordered all Germans in Britain to return home. The Cabinet met again the next day, Saturday, and twice on Sunday. Hitler had announced that he was not going to be deterred by Britain's attitude, and the Cabinet deliberated their reply. As soon as it was dispatched, the evacuation of children and of women and invalids from London was arranged and four days later, on 31st August, the Army reserve, consisting of 140,000 men, were called up. Very early the next morning, 1st September, the Germans invaded Poland.

From that moment the Cabinet was in almost continuous session at No. 10, breaking off only to go to the House of Commons where the insistent question was why Britain had not already declared war. The delay was caused by the endeavour to provide coincident action by the French. An ultimatum was sent to Hitler late on the evening of 2nd September. It expired at 11 a.m. the next day and the Second World War had begun.

From No. 10 Downing Street at 11.15 a.m. the Prime Minister broadcast to the nation. 'You can imagine what a bitter blow it is to me that all my long struggle to win peace has failed.' A War Cabinet, as in the preceding war, was immediately formed: it was large and included Ministers with departmental responsibility, which Lloyd George had been careful to avoid. Into this Cabinet, which met each morning at No. 10, Winston Churchill was brought as First Lord of the Admiralty, the post he held on the outbreak of the First World War. Before long he began to dominate the discussions and intervened in the plans of every Service department. Disagreements with the Secretary for War Hore-Belisha occurred more than once and in January, after complaints by the Commander-in-Chief and the Chief of the Imperial General Staff to the Prime Minister, private talks in the Cabinet room with Hore-Belisha led to the latter's resignation.

Poland, crushed in less than a month, was divided between Germany and Russia and the war settled down to what became known as the 'phoney' period. There were scares galore, almost all of them brought to the notice of the Cabinet by Churchill: after much inquiry they proved to be without foundation. Stalin's war on Finland was launched in November 1939, but before Britain and France could intervene actively, that country made peace.

It was not until the German attack on Norway on 9th April 1940 that Churchill got his chance. The Cabinet met at 8.30 that morning. Expeditious moves were made to send detachments of the British fleet to various Norwegian ports and to land troops, but despite the most valiant and heroic struggles at Narvik and Trondheim, the British were repulsed, and following critical meetings of the House of Commons on 7th and 8th May, in which Churchill was challenged for the inadequate part played by the fleet, the attack turned on the Prime Minister. Though he secured a majority of 81 when the vote was taken, the uneasiness in the House caused Chamberlain to decide that the Government must be reconstructed.

On the afternoon of the next day, 9th May, Churchill was summoned to No. 10. He found Halifax, the Foreign Secretary, with the Prime Minister, and in a few minutes the Leader of the Opposition, Mr. Attlee, together with his deputy Mr. Arthur Greenwood joined them. They had refused earlier to serve in a National Government under Chamberlain and they refused again now. Churchill notes[161]: 'It was a bright, sunny afternoon, and Lord Halifax and I sat for a while on a seat in the garden of No. 10 and talked about nothing in particular.' Early the next morning all hell broke loose in Holland and Belgium. Tanks crossed the frontiers and German troops were dropped by parachute at many points. 'At eleven o'clock,' states Churchill, 'I was again summoned to Downing Street by the Prime Minister. There once more I found Lord Halifax. We took our seats at the table opposite Mr. Chamberlain. He told us that he was satisfied that it was beyond his power to form a National Government.' He was wondering, he revealed, whom to suggest as his successor and seemed to favour Lord Halifax. But since it was essential that the Prime Minister should be in the House of Commons, the choice finally fell on Churchill. He had achieved at sixty-five what his father, for all his ardent striving, realized at thirty-seven he would never attain.

At six that evening Churchill went to see the King. By ten that night he had formed his Government. It was a coalition. The War

Cabinet was reduced to five, of whom two were members of the Labour Party. Attlee became Deputy Prime Minister, Chamberlain served as Lord President of the Council and Leader of the House of Commons. Churchill took on the additional duty of Minister of Defence, a role he was straining at the leash to undertake ever since the outbreak of war. Halifax was retained as Foreign Secretary; he was the only one in the War Cabinet with a department to manage. Churchill thus reverted to Lloyd George's plan for the conduct of war.

The Chamberlains did not leave No. 10 at once. Churchill insisted, as Chamberlain was far from well: 'On no account must you move from here until you are better.' Four weeks later the Churchills moved in. Their son Randolph was in the services. The two elder daughters, Diana and Sarah, were already married. But Mary, the youngest, moved into the house with them.

The Chamberlain floor – the second floor – was favoured by the Churchills. There the new Prime Minister had the bedroom with a bathroom opening off it. Mrs. Churchill had the room opposite overlooking the Horse Guards and the Park and Mary occupied two rooms at the other end of the corridor. Alongside, Major John Churchill, the Prime Minister's brother, had a room: he was a widower and was the father of Clarissa Churchill, who later married Anthony Eden.

Throughout the early fighting – the fall of Holland and Belgium, the miracle of Dunkirk and then the fall of France – Churchill, using No. 10 as his headquarters, went on his recurrent rounds of naval, military and air inspection, attended the House of Commons regularly and roused the country with his exhilarating speeches, many of them broadcast direct to the people. Working through most of the night it was not his practice to rise early – usually it was after eight in the morning – but his principal personal secretary, Mrs. Kathleen Hill, and her two assistants slept at No. 10, for one of them was wanted at 11.30 at night to take down minutes for the Service chiefs and the heads of departments – this went on till 2.30 a.m. if not later; and another had to be ready to come in the morning with her pad and spare pencils to his bedroom, where, propped up against the pillows, his breakfast done and his first cigar lit, the Prime Minister began his day's work. They could tell by the condition of the morning's newspapers what sort of mood he was in. If the papers lay neatly folded by the bedside, all was well, but if they had been crumpled into balls and hurled to various corners of the room, then it was obvious that the day was going to start badly.

Usually it was from his bed that he dictated his speeches. At that early hour his words were scarcely audible or articulate and one dared not ask him to repeat what had been said: one had to guess and hope it was right or he would glower over his glasses and roar. It was in this room at No. 10, with Mrs. Hill seated by his bed, that he dictated at the end of the Battle of Britain the historic words: 'Never in the field of human conflict was so much owed by so many to so few.' It was round these words, dictated in isolation at the outset, that the speech was built. 'I am speaking in the House today,' he said and Mrs. Hill knew that the normal speed and urgency with which everything had to be done for the Prime Minister would have to be redoubled. The typewriter kept clicking, the sheets were taken in to him in relays, corrections were made in illegible squiggles in red ink, and then it had to be typed out in speech form, four or five words to a line. A watch was kept in the passage. 'He's just gone for his bath' – and all would have to be ready, the pages tagged together through a hole punched in them, to be handed to him as he emerged from the bathroom with only a towel wrapped round his waist and quite often without even that.

There were distinguished guests at lunch almost every day, with often a Duke among them: Churchill's sense of fitness must have made him feel that No. 10 required that. Last minute invitations issued over the telephone or in personal conversation had to be listened for by the secretaries and quickly passed on to Mrs. Churchill, who had to adjust with the cook arrangements already made. As with everything else throughout the day, these lunches and indeed all the entertaining, despite the social note introduced into them, were devoted to discussions and planning for the further prosecution of the war, for some members of the Cabinet were always there, as well as scientific and military advisers like Lord Cherwell and Lord Ismay, and representatives of the American President Roosevelt, like Averell Harriman and Harry Hopkins, and, after the fall of France, occasionally the leader of the Free French, General de Gaulle.

The afternoons, when not in the House or on one of his missions, Churchill spent in the Cabinet room, using it as his office as all Prime Ministers have done. Here one of his personal secretaries, seated opposite him at the table with her noiseless typewriter, would wait while he, rising suddenly, paced the room in his boiler-suit, cigar in mouth, and gesticulated as he mouthed his phrases, selecting the words carefully before dictating them. It was hard to hear every word when he walked up and down: on the lawn outside, the secretary followed with a notebook and was able to see the tears come to his eyes with the emotion of his words. His capacity for going on hour after hour was wearing to the secretaries but not apparently to him, though he would snatch an hour or so for sleep, often as late as six or even seven o'clock in the evening.

When the bombing started in September he was urged to leave No. 10, because it was unsafe. A flat had already been prepared for him at Storey's Gate, on the first floor of a more solid building just across the Foreign Office courtyard and facing St. James's Park: it came to be known as 'The Annexe'. It was not easy to overcome his reluctance to go there and, even after he moved, so great was his affection for No. 10 that he would come back from time to time to dine in the house and sleep there. In the garden-room, under the Cabinet room, used normally by the clerical staff, meals were now served in the evenings about once a week. A series of dinners were expressly given here so that the King should spend an evening with small groups of his Ministers.

Churchill was dining here with some friends on the evening two bombs fell.* A shelter had been constructed near the kitchen and under the Treasury building alongside, with about thirty bunks and, though Churchill never used it himself, he always insisted that his staff should when the bombing got bad. He records[162]: 'We were dining in the garden-room of No. 10 when the usual night raid began. . . . The steel shutters had been closed. Several loud explosions occurred around us at no great distance, and presently a bomb fell, perhaps a hundred yards away, on the Horse Guards Parade, making a great deal of noise. Suddenly I had a providential impulse. The kitchen at No. 10 Downing Street is lofty and spacious, and looks out through a large plate-glass

* 14th October 1940.

window about twenty-five feet high. The butler and parlourmaid continued to serve the dinner with complete detachment, but I became acutely aware of this big window, behind which Mrs. Landemare, the cook, and the kitchen maid, never turning a hair, were at work. I got up abruptly, went into the kitchen, told the butler to put the dinner on the hot plate in the dining-room, and ordered the cook and the kitchen-maid into the shelter, such as it was.'

Mrs. Landemare elaborates on this.* 'He said sharply: "Why aren't you in the shelter?" I replied: "If you'd been in time for dinner I should have been." He was never in time for any meal.'

Churchill goes on: 'I had been seated again at table only about three minutes when a really very loud crash, close at hand, and a violent shock showed that the house had been struck. My detective came into the room and said much damage had been done. The kitchen, the pantry, and the offices on the Treasury side were shattered. We went into the kitchen to view the scene. The devastation was complete. The bomb had fallen fifty yards away on the Treasury, and the blast had smitten the large, tidy kitchen, with all its bright saucepans and crockery, into a heap of black dust and rubble. The big plate-glass window had been hurled in fragments and splinters across the room, and would, of course, have cut its occupants, if there had been any, to pieces. But my fortunate inspiration, which I might so easily have neglected, had come in the nick of time. . . . As the raid continued and seemed to grow in intensity we put on our tin hats and went out to view the scene from the top of the Annexe buildings. Before doing so, however, I could not resist taking Mrs. Landemare and the others from the shelter to see their kitchen. They were upset at the sight of the wreck, but principally on account of the general untidiness!'

At this period, when Churchill spent a night at No. 10, he slept in the room alongside the garden-room and used the staff bathroom, a dark, dismal place, in the basement. Mrs. Landemare prepared his breakfast, which he always had in bed. 'He liked a cooked breakfast,' she says, 'something hot and something cold – an omelette or a poached egg, a cold lamb cutlet or cold ham. But he never ate much of it.'

* In a statement to the author.

It was in the Annexe, in the deep underground shelter, that the Cabinet occasionally met and many Ministers and Service chiefs had their offices and bunks to sleep in at night: it was so deep down that large notices were displayed to indicate what the weather was outside. Churchill hated being there. His flat, one floor above ground, was only tolerated. On Fridays he escaped as a rule to Chequers for the weekend, but it was a weekend of discussions and planning, never of relaxation and rest. On Monday mornings he would set out in one of the large official Humber cars on the return journey to No. 10. He always had Mrs. Hill beside him, for he dictated while they travelled and the glass between him and the driver was always kept lowered so that he could urge him on to greater speed. 'Come on, Steve,' he would call, thinking doubtless of Steve Donoghue, the famous jockey. As the car swung its way through the narrow, winding roads, flinging Mrs. Hill at one moment into Churchill's lap and at the next him into hers, she tried with difficulty to take down what he said. The compartment was heavy with cigar smoke and Churchill had a gesture for almost every word he uttered, often endangering Mrs. Hill's sight by a sudden dramatic move of his arm.

The journey completed, as they alighted at the garden door of No. 10, Churchill would say: 'Now where are you going? I want you in the Cabinet room. They are waiting.' Entering, she would see Beaverbrook, Bracken and the other Ministers. 'Now sit down and read out the notes to the Cabinet.' They were almost impossible to read and made all the more difficult because her head ached badly. It was an ordeal she dreaded, but it had to be faced.

The blitz was followed after an interval of three years by the flying bombs, or V1s, which came unpiloted and caused much havoc. These were followed later by the more devastating V2 rockets. But by that time the worst phase of the war was over. The tide had turned – at Alamein in Africa, at Stalingrad in Russia, and in due course the Allied armies were landing on the beaches in Normandy. Just before this General Eisenhower was a constant visitor at No. 10. The house was by now badly scarred. The woodwork of the windows was studded with shrapnel. There were cracks in almost every wall and in many places portions of the ceiling had come down and lay in dusty debris on the carpets.

At intervals all through the war Churchill was away – in America on a visit to the President, to various fronts and conferences in Africa, Marrakesh, Egypt, Teheran, and Yalta. After one of his trips to Russia the State dining-room at No. 10 was filled with presents: bottles of vodka, caviare (which Churchill liked), glass bowls, inkstands, massive blotting pads, leatherwork, illustrated books, all gifts from various cities and organizations, and a few personal presents from Stalin. The visitors now included Molotov, Field-Marshals Alexander, Wavell and Montgomery, Queen Juliana of Holland, King Peter of Yugoslavia, the heads of other exiled Governments, and General Smuts. An unexpected visitor was one of the mallards from St. James's Park, who used the terrace outside the Cabinet room as a maternity ward and was later photographed escorting her young down the steps into the garden.

Churchill was with Montgomery at the crossing of the Rhine by the British forces and a few weeks later on 4th May 1945, the German forces surrendered unconditionally at Luneberg Heath. The war against Nazi Germany ended three days after that.

The national rejoicing in Britain was followed by Party strife, for Churchill had committed himself to holding a General Election at the end of the German war. The Coalition broke up accordingly and both the Labour Party and the Conservatives began to prepare for the decision of the nation as to which of them should govern. No election had been held since the autumn of 1935, when the Conservatives and their associates in the National Government led by Baldwin won a substantial victory with 420 members against Labour's 154. The country had thus been governed by an essentially Tory Government for a period of ten years. Few expected the dramatic reversal of this position which the poll showed on 26th July 1945. Labour's triumph was overwhelming. For the first time since the formation of the Party it had a clear majority to rule. Churchill, as the architect of victory, was both surprised and stunned at being 'immediately dismissed by the British electorate from all further conduct of their affairs'. He resigned the same evening and, leaving No. 10 Downing Street at once, moved into a suite of rooms at Claridge's Hotel.

CHAPTER 42
Attlee's Six Years

ATTLEE, small in stature, now sixty-two and almost bald, was quiet, uncommunicative, but resolute. He did not move into No. 10 Downing Street at once. A lot had to be done there. Apart from the war damage which had of course to be attended to, the Attlees introduced a still further change into the house. It was suggested indeed by Mrs. Churchill. Having lived on the second, or servants' floor, herself, but unable because of the war to add to Mrs. Chamberlain's adaptations, she indicated to the Attlees the great advantage of converting a part of that floor into a self-contained flat, with its own drawing-room, dining-room, kitchen, pantry and additional bathrooms. It took three months to complete this and until then the Attlees lived in the Annexe in the first floor flat the Churchills had occupied during the worst phase of the bombing.

As all the furniture was now provided by the State, the Attlees did not need to bring very much in with them, except certain pieces of their own for which they had a preference. They had been married for twenty-three years and had a family of four: a son and three daughters

– Martin was at sea, the youngest girl was at school, but they all lived at No. 10 from time to time. They confined themselves completely to the flat and did all their personal entertaining and catering there, using the first floor only for State occasions and the ground floor as offices.

The pledges given to the country by the Labour Party, as set out in their Election pamphlet 'Let us Face the Future', were considerable. Only the nationalization of land, an early aspiration, had been excluded, otherwise all the other aims had been set down – as dreams, without any plans for fulfilment. It was Attlee's resolve that not an iota of any pledge given to the electors should be neglected. Every dream had to become a reality. He chose his team well. Herbert Morrison, who had served under Ramsay MacDonald in 1929 as Minister of Transport and under Churchill, first as Minister of Supply, then as Home Secretary, was appointed Deputy Prime Minister and Leader of the House of Commons. Ernest Bevin, who had worked on a farm as a boy at six-pence a week plus his keep, became Foreign Secretary – a sturdy John Bull of the working classes, as Churchill called him. For the second time a woman was admitted to the Cabinet – Ellen Wilkinson, who became Minister of Education. They had all served in the Coalition Government during the war and had therefore been in office for five continuous years and, though exhilarated by the opportunities offered, were actually on the verge of exhaustion through the strain of the war. Aneurin Bevan, appointed Minister of Health and Housing, was among the newcomers who had not had office before.

They were faced with almost insuperable difficulties. Most serious of these was the bankruptcy to which the country had been reduced by the war. An immediate loan of £1,000 million was advanced by the United States Government, but the austerity enforced during the war as well as the rationing had to be maintained and were the targets of the taunts of the Tories. The legislation required to fulfil the Government's pledges was put through the House of Commons with Labour's immense majority. It fell to Lord Addison, as Leader of the Lords, to get it through the Upper House. With his tact and charm and the co-opera-tion of the Opposition leader there, Lord Salisbury, he achieved this despite angry protests. The coal mines were nationalized (it had been recommended by the Samuel commission twenty years before), so were electricity and gas, the railways, and all the motor transport services, compensation being paid in every instance to the owners. A full Health Service for all, including visitors, was brought in at great cost and against fierce opposition. An extensive National Insurance scheme was introduced with family allowances and increased pensions for the aged. India and Pakistan, Ceylon and Burma were granted independence and all except Burma elected to remain within the Commonwealth. Only the nationalization of steel encountered the most vigorous resistance, not only in the Commons, where it was easily overcome, but in the Lords, where the resolution not to yield was adamant. The old battle between the two Houses was once again opened. The Government dealt with it skilfully. A Bill was introduced to amend Asquith's Parliament Act of 1911, which limited the veto of the Lords to two years, and imposed a veto of one year only. The Conservatives were extremely angry at this, but, as Attlee records: 'The best shots in our oratorical locker were provided by extracts from the speeches of their own leader* when he was a Liberal.' The Bill was rejected by the Lords but under the old two-year rule it was passed 'over the heads of the peers'.[168]

The strain of this ceaseless legislation was oppressive. It killed four members of the Cabinet – Ellen Wilkinson, George Tomlinson, who succeeded Ellen Wilkinson, Ernest Bevin, and Sir Stafford Cripps, who by that time had become Chancellor of the Exchequer; and both Attlee and Morrison were ill on more than one occasion.

There was not much time for entertaining, nevertheless official lunches and dinners had to be given and Soane's panelled State dining-room, always admired by visitors and loved by those who lived in the house, was used on these occasions. Attlee says: 'When we were entertaining members of the French Government I had to pause and think for a moment. "No, don't sit there, take this chair," I said, for I felt it would be embarrassing for them to face the portrait of either Wellington or Nelson. With the Danes only Nelson was involved because he had bombarded Copenhagen. But they smiled as I placed them with their backs to the picture, and one of them said: "We don't mind. It happened a long time ago." When we entertained the Russians

---

* Winston Churchill, who vehemently denounced the Lords in 1911.

it was so much easier. I told them to sit anywhere they liked as they were not likely to find a Crimean General in that room.'*

Just before the present Queen's marriage to the Duke of Edinburgh they dined with the Prime Minister and Mrs. Attlee at No. 10. But a number of smaller dinners and lunches were given in the breakfast-room where eight people at a time were entertained. Charity fêtes were held in the garden in summer and the Commonwealth Prime Ministers were also entertained there.

Attlee loved the house and, after steeping himself in its history, acquired a dislike for Downing and 'the horrible picture in the hall of Downing with his thick, sensual lips'. All the way up the stairs are pictures of the Prime Ministers, the earlier ones in engravings, the more recent in photographs. A painting of Robert Walpole hangs above the fireplace in the Cabinet room – it is the only picture in the room.

The privacy of his flat greatly appealed to Attlee. It was away from the rest of the house. Nobody could intrude there. The offices were kept apart. The old cottage on the Whitehall side which Walpole had acquired from Mr. Chicken in 1735, had been equipped with a large bow window and was used as a Public Relations office by Attlee's Press officer Francis Williams. It is still used for that purpose. Attlee loved also the stillness of the Park at night and the bird song in the early morning. Like so many other Prime Ministers he used to walk round the Park with his wife and his dog before beginning the day's work. His is the second dog to be buried in the garden at No. 10. A Welsh terrier named Megan, she died while he was Prime Minister and lies not far from Lady Megan Lloyd George's black pug Zulu.

The wide range of reforms, building on the foundations laid more than a generation before by Asquith and Lloyd George, ushered in the Welfare State. It ensured the care of the sick and needy, provided full employment for men and women and raised the standard of living for millions of workers. On their new social level many were drawn closer to the Conservatives and chafed against the inevitable irritations caused by austerity and rationing, which kept firmly shut the desirable outlet for their larger incomes. That supplies were not available to ease these restraints was never fully accepted. At the same time the Tory Party's

---

* In a statement to the author.

fury at the socialization of the country was given ample expression at public meetings and in the columns of the Press, which with rare exceptions were organs of Conservative opinion.

It was unfortunate for the Government, with the atmosphere so explosively charged, that a senior member of the Cabinet, Aneurin Bevan, brilliant and outspoken, should have been provoked by these denunciations to liken the Tories to 'vermin' which, although he qualified its application in the very next sentence to those who were harsh and immoderate as employers, provided the opponents of the Government with a war cry they were to use most effectively in the General Election that was approaching.

The Labour Party was not split but disaffection was certainly apparent. A section, not very large, felt that the speed of alteration and adjustment in the economy and life of the country was too fast – a halt should be called to allow for digestion. Two members of the House of Commons and one of the Lords left the Labour Party over the nationalization of steel. A much larger section, more vocal, did not think the reforms cut deep enough; they sharply criticized Attlee and Herbert Morrison. This division was not noticeable in the Cabinet, but some of the Ministers did not like Attlee's quiet tongue-tied manner, of listening but saying nothing.

After one of their meetings at No. 10, as they trooped out of the Cabinet room and stretched for their coats and hats, hanging from pegs in the red carpeted lobby outside, they grumbled about this until someone pointed out that Attlee's silence was in fact his greatest strength. 'Now Nye Bevan is just the reverse – and in consequence he is his own worst enemy.' At which Ernest Bevin observed: 'Not while I'm alive he isn't.'

The General Election, anticipating the completion of the five-year term, was held in February 1950. Labour lost a number of seats, but was still the largest Party in the House with 315 members to the Conservatives 297. There were, however, also nine Liberals and some Independents, and Labour had the infinitesimal majority of only seven over all other parties.

This made the position of the Government extremely difficult. The Tories kept harassing them with all-night sessions whenever possible and, in order to avoid defeat, the Whips had to muster every Labour

Member: even the sick and bedridden were brought from their beds and waited many hours for the divisions. After a time the strain became unendurable. Most of the senior Ministers had been in office continuously for close on eleven years. Ernest Bevin was dying, so before long was Lord Addison. Attlee had two serious bouts of illness and was in hospital when a crisis developed in the Cabinet. The outbreak of the Korean war in June 1950 had repercussions on the Budget, and the imposition of certain charges in the free Health Service in the following year led to the resignation of two Cabinet Ministers, Aneurin Bevan and Harold Wilson.

It was impossible to go on, and Attlee, after twenty months of it, decided on a second General Election. It was held in October 1951 and brought defeat. The Tories were returned with a clear though small majority. Together with their associates they had a total of 321 members in the House, whereas Labour's representation fell to 295. With an overall majority of 17 the Tories were better placed to govern. Attlee resigned and the King sent for Winston Churchill.

CHAPTER 43
Eden and Suez

CHURCHILL was not far short of seventy-seven when he became Prime Minister for the second time – his third if one counts the brief existence of the 'Caretaker Government' formed on the break-up of the Coalition in 1945. He and Mrs. Churchill moved in almost at once and were to live at No. 10 for nearly four years. Their youngest daughter Mary, who had been living there with them through a large part of his previous term of office, for even after she joined the A.T.S., as the women's Auxiliary Territorial Service was called, and was attached to an anti-aircraft unit in Hyde Park, she occasionally came and spent the night at No. 10, but she had married in 1948 and by now had a home of her own.

The Attlee flat was used chiefly by Churchill and his personal staff of secretaries. Mrs. Churchill moved down to the first floor. The corner room, in which Campbell-Bannerman had died, became her private study: here she dealt with her letters and attended to the domestic arrangements. The room alongside it, once Ramsay MacDonald's bedroom, was Mrs. Churchill's bedroom now. At the front of the house, near the State dining-room, two rooms were converted into kitchen and pantry units.

In appointing his Cabinet Churchill once again chose Anthony Eden as Foreign Secretary and gave him in addition the title of Deputy Prime Minister. This title was first introduced by Churchill in 1940 when Attlee joined the Coalition Government and it was later conferred by Attlee on Herbert Morrison in 1945. It has, however, been objected to on constitutional grounds since it implies a line of succession and thus deprives the Sovereign of his prerogative of choice.[175] Lord Salisbury, grandson of the former Prime Minister, was appointed Lord Privy Seal and Harold Macmillan, a future Prime Minister, was made Minister of Housing.

The King, ill through most of the summer, was barely convalescent when the Election was held and died early in the morning of 6th February 1952. The heir to the throne, his elder daughter Princess Elizabeth, had left for East Africa with her husband the Duke of Edinburgh less than a week before. She hurried home and was proclaimed Queen Elizabeth the Second on her return.

Churchill's aim was to undo as far as possible the socialization brought in by Attlee's Government and to rid the country of the controls and austerity required by the war and imposed then by Churchill himself. The controls were easiest to dispose of: indeed Attlee had begun to shed them before his Government fell. Bit by bit now the rest were removed and in February 1952 the Identity Cards introduced in 1939 were also abolished. The Health Service, Churchill realized, would have to remain, despite the stern criticism to which it was subjected by the Conservatives. He saw also that it would not be of advantage to denationalize the mines and railways, or even gas and electricity. These were accordingly left under State control. But steel was in part returned to private enterprise, so was road haulage. A promise had been made to extend and accelerate the building of new houses, and this was achieved by Harold Macmillan.

The practice adopted during the war of flying to America and elsewhere for discussions was maintained – it was introduced in fact by Ramsay MacDonald, who was the first Prime Minister to fly. Churchill greatly extended it and during these years of peace his visits to Canada and the West Indies as well as the United States were in a sense tours of the great war leader whom the world was eager to welcome with their rapturous thanks.

Early in 1953 he was awarded the Garter by the Queen, and after the Coronation in June his health began to decline. He was by now entering his eightieth year and the strain of the war had taken a heavy toll of his system. The possibility of his retirement was constantly in the public mind, but not in his. Rumours persisted throughout 1954, but he dismissed them with a laugh even as late as the spring of 1955.

It was during a newspaper strike, which began at the close of March and lasted for four weeks, that Churchill finally retired. He left in consequence without a fanfare from the Press to mark his exit. On 4th April 1955 the Queen and Prince Philip dined with him and Lady Churchill at No. 10 Downing Street. With them in the State dining-room were members of his family and some of his wartime colleagues. Rising to give a toast to Her Majesty, Sir Winston remarked that he had enjoyed drinking the same toast as a cavalry subaltern 'in the reign of Your Majesty's great-great-grandmother'. It is interesting to recall that at a similar distance from Queen Victoria was her own great-great-grandfather George the Second, in whose reign No. 10 became the home of the Prime Minister. On the next day, 5th April 1955, Churchill resigned and the Queen invited Sir Anthony Eden to succeed him.*

Eden arranged for an immediate General Election. The announcement was made on the radio, since there were still no newspapers. The result, announced on 27th May, gave the Conservatives and their associates a more comfortable majority – they had 345 as against 319 in 1952, while Labour dropped to 277 from 293, a loss of sixteen seats. Towards the close of the year Attlee retired too and Hugh Gaitskell was elected Leader of the Opposition in his place.

The Churchills moved out of No. 10 soon after Sir Winston's resignation and the Edens moved in. Both Sir Anthony and Lady Eden knew the house well. Indeed Lady Eden, as the daughter of Churchill's brother, Major John Churchill, who had lived in the house during the war, had herself stayed there from time to time and was married from there in 1952: Sir Winston arranged for his niece's wedding reception to be held at No. 10 Downing Street. They had no family. Of Sir

---

* Eden was awarded the Garter in 1954.

Anthony Eden's two sons by his first marriage, one was killed in Burma during the war and the other, Nicholas, by now twenty-four, had his own home.

It was Lady Eden's intention to restore No. 10, in so far as the decoration of the main reception rooms was concerned, to the style introduced by Kent when he adapted the house for Sir Robert Walpole more than two centuries before. She went to Houghton, Walpole's country house in Norfolk, which had also been decorated by Kent, and was shown some of the old brocades and damasks Kent had used there. Lady Cholmondeley readily agreed to these being copied for No. 10 Downing Street, but when Lady Eden discussed it with the Ministry of Works, normally most co-operative in trying to meet the wishes of each new Prime Minister, it was pointed out that the credit squeeze imposed by the Government would make it impossible for the Treasury to sanction the cost involved. That ruled out also her plan to bring in furniture of the Kent period. The furniture already in the drawing-rooms was a strange mixture: there were some attractive Regency pieces, later than the date of the house but admirably suitable, and an assortment of chairs and tables that did not blend at all. So she brought in some of her own furniture for the large green drawing-room at the Treasury end of the house. Lady Churchill had already put in a splendid Persian carpet in her study, and by a neat arrangement of what was available, together with some fresh pictures from the National Gallery (out of the cellars again) the rooms were agreeably transformed. Sir Anthony introduced a change in the lighting of the Cabinet room. It had been lit by three inverted bowls hanging from the ceiling. Churchill had found them not bright enough and had a desk lamp for himself. Eden replaced the light bowls by chandeliers – two large ones and a small one for the section between the Corinthian pillars and the door.

The Churchills had left behind three or four cats. Sir Winston was very fond of cats and had one favourite in particular, Nelson, which he took with him: but their number had been added to during the war because the bombing caused No. 10 to be overrun with rats of enormous size. For months the cats were found wandering about the house. But Lady Eden eventually had them taken to Sir Winston's home in Hyde Park Gate.

The Edens lived at No. 10 for just over twenty months. Quite a lot of entertaining was done, mostly in the small breakfast-room, which they found much pleasanter than the large Soane dining-room, with its heavy panelling and vaulted ceiling. The panels of the breakfast-room, also by Soane, were now painted cream: this gave the wood a slightly gayer air. Here and in the smaller drawing-room they entertained their personal friends, Dr. Albert Schweitzer and Greta Garbo among others. Bulganin and Krushchev, travelling in that order of precedence, visited No. 10 in April 1956, but did not stay to a meal. The State dining-room was used only for large dinners and banquets, attended by Eisenhower, Foster Dulles, Adenauer, Mollet the French Prime Minister, King Hussein of Jordan, King Feisal of Iraq and his Prime Minister Nuri es-Said, the Prime Minister of Thailand, and other distinguished foreign guests. The seven servants employed by the Edens had to be supplemented for such occasions and the catering was done by one of the outside firms normally used for Government hospitality. Sir Anthony had laid down some wine when he was Foreign Secretary and he drew on the small stock that remained for official entertaining.

During his brief term as Prime Minister, Eden was confronted by many testing problems. Just before taking over the office he had been to Bangkok for a conference and on his way home in February 1955, had stopped at Cairo, where he was entertained by Nasser. There was trouble in Cyprus, which began its struggle for independence in that year, and a general uneasiness over the situation in the Middle East, where the threat of war between Israel and her Arab neighbours was a constant and disturbing possibility. In his Guildhall speech on 9th November 1955, Eden appealed to both Israel and her neighbours to abate their territorial claims for the sake of peace.

The Suez crisis developed in the summer of 1956. British troops had left the Canal zone on 13th June and six weeks later, on 26th July, Nasser seized the Canal. The Prime Minister and Lady Eden were entertaining King Feisal of Iraq and his Prime Minister Nuri es-Said* at No. 10 that night and just as they were going in to dinner the telegram informing him of Nasser's action was handed to Eden.

---

* King Feisal and Nuri es-Said were murdered in Baghdad on 14th July 1958.

Nasser had already indicated his intention to take over the Canal, legally and by negotiation, in 1968 when the existing concession under the Convention of 1888 expired. It was thought that his high-handed anticipation of this date was in retaliation for the withdrawal, first by the United States and a day later by Britain, of an expected loan for the building of the Aswan dam. He proposed now to use the Canal's revenues for financing the project.

The anger not only in Britain but throughout the Commonwealth and the Western world generally, was intense, for the Canal was an international waterway on which most countries were dependent. Eden tried to bring financial pressure to bear on Egypt, and the Admiralty and the War office took precautionary measures to strengthen Britain's position in the Eastern Mediterranean.

Dulles hurried across the Atlantic for discussions with Eden, who put off his holiday to deal with the emergency. On 2nd August the American, French and British Foreign Ministers met in London and agreed to call an immediate conference of users of the Canal for the purpose of setting up an international company to control the Canal, with both Russia and Egypt as members.

On that same day, 2nd August, the position was debated in the House of Commons. Gaitskell, who had denounced Nasser, said he did not object to the precautionary military measures, but warned the Government that 'we must not allow ourselves to get into a position where we would be denounced as aggressors'.

The feeling in the country had already begun to divide over the possibility of getting the Canal back by force. On the one side were those who were opposed to any attempt at appeasement, on the other those who felt that the United Nations should seek a solution.

Meanwhile the international conference had met, Russia attending, Egypt abstaining. Menzies, the Australian Prime Minister, was authorized to see Nasser on the setting up of international control. The talks failed.

Parliament was by this time in recess. From 13th August Gaitskell had been demanding its recall. On 31st August a statement issued from No. 10 Downing Street declared that the date of recall could not yet be fixed. Eventually both Houses met on 12th September for a two-day debate. On the day before its reassembly the British and French Prime

Ministers conferred at No. 10 and were said to be 'in complete agreement as to the next step to be taken'.

On 29th October it was announced in Tel Aviv that Israeli forces were advancing across the desert between the Egyptian frontier and the Suez Canal because of continuous military attacks on Israel's land and sea connections. The next day Eden informed the House of Commons that the British and French Governments had asked Egypt and Israel to stop fighting within twelve hours and withdraw their forces to a distance of ten miles from the Canal. Egypt had also been asked to agree to British and French forces occupying temporarily certain key positions on the Canal. If one or both Governments had not undertaken to comply, Eden said, then both France and Britain would move in 'in whatever strength may be necessary to secure compliance'.

Israel accepted the ultimatum, Egypt rejected it and French and British bombers began their attack on military targets in Egypt on 31st October. President Eisenhower immediately protested that the attack could not be reconciled with the principles of the United Nations, a view that was at once endorsed by India. On the same afternoon Gaitskell attacked the Prime Minister in the House, vociferously supported by his own followers and the Liberals. A rowdy scene developed, with reiterated cries of 'Resign'. The scene was renewed the next day when Gaitskell moved a vote of censure, and the Speaker had to suspend the sitting for half an hour. Great indignation was expressed in the American press and on American television and radio, accusing Britain of trickery and deceit.

Within forty-eight hours, on 2nd November, the Israeli forces won a decisive victory over the Egyptians in Sinai, and British and French bombers practically destroyed the Russian-supplied air force of Egypt.

The House of Commons met again on Saturday, 3rd November. Two Conservative Ministers resigned from the Government – Anthony Nutting, Minister of State for Foreign Affairs, and Sir Edward Boyle, Economic Secretary to the Treasury; from the Labour Party there was one resignation – Stanley Evans, M.P. When the House was informed by the Foreign Secretary, Selwyn Lloyd, that British troops were about to be landed in Egypt there was an uproar. Gaitskell called for the resignation of the Prime Minister.

That evening Eden broadcast to the nation to explain that his object was to separate the armies and stop the fighting. Until the United Nations were ready to take over, the British and French forces must go on with the job till it was done.

The next day Canada called on the United Nations to send an international force to put a stop to hostilities.

British and French troops were dropped by air near Port Said on 5th November, but the next day Eden announced that British forces were to cease-fire at midnight and that an international force would be taking over. Speaking in the House he said: 'As the dust settles it may well be that out of this anxiety . . . a better opportunity will come than has ever been available before for the United Nations to prove itself a really effective international organization.'

Thus in the Cabinet room where seventy years before by the astuteness of Disraeli and the co-operation of the Rothschilds control of the Suez Canal was acquired by Britain, so now its loss was accepted.

Eden remained in office only a few weeks longer. On 9th January 1957, after returning from a brief stay in Jamaica, he had an audience of the Queen and handed in his resignation. The reason given was his health and, though some doubt was cast on this at the time, his health had in fact made it impossible to carry on. He had been ill off and on since before his marriage and actually returned from his honeymoon on a stretcher. The four doctors who issued a bulletin at the time of his resignation stated specifically: 'The Prime Minister's health gives cause for anxiety' – and he has been in need of treatment and has had to undergo a series of operations since.

The question of his successor caused much speculation. R. A. Butler, Lord Privy Seal and Leader of the House of Commons, had acted as Prime Minister during Eden's absence in Jamaica and it was certain that he would be chosen. But after consulting Sir Winston Churchill and Lord Salisbury, Lord President of the Council and Leader of the Lords, the Queen's choice was Harold Macmillan, the Chancellor of the Exchequer.

Macmillan was sixty-three. He had married Lady Dorothy Cavendish, the daughter of the ninth Duke of Devonshire, in 1920, and had four children – one son, Maurice, who was a Member of Parliament, and three daughters, all of them married. The Edens vacated No. 10 almost at once, taking the furniture they had brought, and Macmillan and Lady Dorothy moved in. No redecoration was asked for; Lady Dorothy was quite content to accept the house just as it was. She brought none of her own furniture, but the furniture removed by the Edens was of course replaced by the Ministry of Works.

Not many changes were made in the Government. Butler retained his position as Leader of the House of Commons and Selwyn Lloyd was kept on as Foreign Secretary. Macmillan won plaudits both in the House and outside it by reducing taxes and announcing that there would be no further call-up for national military service after the end of 1960. But in successive by-elections fought shortly afterwards the Conservative majority was alarmingly reduced. The Tories had won two elections in a row and these results pointed ominously to their not achieving the hat trick when the next General Election was fought. But that was not to be for another two years.

Much had to be done in the interval. His first endeavour was to repair the damage done to the Tory Party by the Suez disaster and to restore the warm understanding that had existed with America. This he achieved.

The granting of independence to colonial countries, begun by Attlee, was continued. In that year, 1957, Ghana, Malaya and Singapore became self-governing. The Federation of Rhodesia and Nyasaland had already been set up in 1953 and of the West Indies followed in 1958. Two years later Nigeria was granted independence, and Cyprus and Tanganyika were added to the lengthening list shortly after that.

An early blow descended in 1958 when the new Chancellor of the Exchequer, Peter Thorneycroft, and both his Treasury colleagues, Enoch Powell and Nigel Birch, resigned suddenly after a disagreement in the Cabinet on pruning the expenditure for the coming year. Macmillan was about to set out on a Commonwealth tour and many expected him to postpone it. But, with an air of imperturbability, which afterwards came to be recognized as his characteristic, he dismissed the crisis as 'a little local difficulty'.

In the Budget, presented by the new Chancellor Heathcoat Amory, purchase tax was reduced, the entertainment tax for cinemas was cut by just over a half, and there were still further, though slight, concessions in income tax.

An important first step towards reforming the House of Lords was taken when the Life Peerages Act was passed in April. The initial list of creations, published in July, comprised ten men and four women. This brought women for the first time into the Upper House.

Macmillan's visit to Moscow in February 1959 was followed by visits to Paris, Bonn, Ottawa and Washington. The General Election was held in October and was won by the Conservatives, who thus successfully achieved their hat-trick and actually increased their majority in the House by twenty-one.

Not a great deal of entertaining was done at No. 10 Downing Street. The inescapable official dinners were held there. Prince Philip attended a dinner that was entirely for men; the King of Nepal was a guest on another occasion; President Eisenhower dined there too; and African rulers on a visit to London were also invited. But the house was considered unsafe. For some years each Prime Minister in turn had been asked not to have more than a strictly limited number of guests in any of the upper rooms. The staircase was known to have sunk a few inches. A committee under the chairmanship of the Earl of Crawford and Balcarres* had been appointed to report on the condition of the house. Its recommendations, made in July 1958, were against demolition and replacement by an entirely new building; but suggested that, provided the work was undertaken before the structure suffered further deterioration, the house could be underpinned and strengthened, the roofs renovated or renewed, the dried-wood replaced, and that the existing building could thus be substantially retained.

This was agreed to. The Prime Minister and Lady Dorothy Macmillan moved out on 1st August 1960. The last thing Macmillan did at No. 10 before leaving was to sit for his portrait to Sir James Gunn, the artist. The next day workmen began to remove the furniture, carpets and curtains. They were taken to Admiralty House in Whitehall which became the temporary residence of the Prime Minister.

---

* Lord Crawford, an eminent figure in the world of art, has been a trustee of the National Gallery and the British Museum for many years, Chairman of the Royal Fine Art Commission, the National Trust, and the National Art-Collections Fund.

CHAPTER 44
The New No. 10

THE work of reconstruction began on 13th August 1960 and was expected to take two years, but a succession of strikes caused a delay of almost a whole year. The two houses adjoining, Nos. 11 and 12 (of the latter only the basement and ground floor were still standing, the rest had been gutted by fire in 1879), were dealt with at the same time and the total cost was estimated at half a million pounds. To the distinguished architect Raymond Erith, with his sensitive understanding of eighteenth-century buildings, the elaborate work of reconstruction was entrusted.

Sections of the walls and roof coverings at No. 10 were stripped so that the nature and extent of the work required should be judged. It was found that the timber in the floors and roofs was old and in a bad state: there was evidence of both dry rot and beetle decay. The house had no damp-proof courses. Many of the walls were out of alignment because of the sinking of the shallow foundations, which were composed of timber sills laid on the silt subsoil and the overlying gravel: the sills were found to be 'in an advanced stage of decay'. Repeatedly through the centuries the house had to be underpinned and strengthened and, just before the 1939 war, when the air-raid shelter was built, the Cabinet room floor beams were strutted from below and some of the roof beams were stiffened with steel framing. But the floors generally were still 'out of level and of low loading capacity', and very substantial reconstruction had at last become necessary.

'The sanitation and water supply', the report added, 'were originally intended for a very limited use and have been constantly added to; the whole system is a complicated and make-shift arrangement. . . . The pipe runs are faulty and the wiring needs renewal. When the Prime Minister is in residence a maintenance engineer has to be kept constantly available to attend to the lift in case of breakdown. A new lift was kept in store for several years but was not installed pending the main decision on reconstruction, because it could not be placed in the existing lift shaft.' The fire risk was described as 'abnormally high'.

Mr. Erith's plan was to preserve so far as possible the historical appearance and atmosphere of the important rooms, and this he has succeeded in doing. Despite very substantial reconstruction, the ground floor and the first floor appear to be almost unchanged. The entrance hall is as it was before, the corridor leading to the Cabinet room, first inserted for Walpole in 1735 and rebuilt by Taylor for the younger Pitt, has been almost completely reconstructed, but the eye will detect no difference; nor has the appearance of the Cabinet room been altered in any way. The main State drawing-rooms on the first floor and the panelled dining- and breakfast-rooms also remain unchanged. The attractive ornamental cornices in these rooms were guarded with the utmost care during the reconstruction and have been repaired where necessary. Even in the basement, where the alterations were many, the famous kitchen with its enormous window and solid oak table, may still be seen.

The house, a large part of it used for offices manned twenty-four hours a day for seven days a week, had to be greatly enlarged. Rooms were needed for a permanent day staff of about fifty, with sleeping accommodation for those who may be required to stay overnight in times of stress. The day staff had already overflowed into the Treasury building alongside and the files into the kitchen in the basement. Mr. Erith has made use of the single-storied wing with the bow window on the east side (originally Mr. Chicken's cottage) by providing it with additional floors to the height of the rest of the house. He extended No. 10 further on the other side by taking in a slice of No. 10a (the section behind the disused door) and inserting another staircase. Feeling that this may not be enough, he has given to No. 10 the whole of the top floor, running above the entire length of Nos. 10, 10a, 11 and 12 Downing Street, in order to provide living accommodation for some of the staff. A part of the new roof is supported by a vast beam of Douglas fir, forty-nine feet long and nearly two feet square, specially imported from British Columbia. He has also, by removing certain basement walls, given No. 10 the entire basement space save for two or three rooms under No. 12. The foundations, completely new, have been sunk to a depth varying from six to eighteen feet and have been substantially constructed in concrete.

The accommodation on the second floor, which Mrs. Neville Chamberlain adopted as the residential floor, has been extensively redesigned. The old attic windows have been pulled back; this enabled the straightening of the walls and the use of larger windows, and the size of the main bedrooms was maintained by the removal of some of the corridors and unnecessary ante-rooms. Many more bathrooms have also been added. Throughout the house the old wooden floors have been replaced by a double flooring of concrete, carrying in the intervening space pipes for water, sanitation and heating, as well as electric and telephone wiring. A new lift shaft has been constructed near the front door for an entirely new and efficient lift. The central courtyard between the two original houses joined together by Walpole has been completely cleared of the clutter of sheds and the old glass-roofed passages that skirted it, and has been made an attractive feature of No. 10.

Mr. Erith's aim throughout has been to improve the building within its established framework, to let in more light and to tidy up the piecemeal additions made in the course of the preceding centuries. 'It was not a ramshackle house, as some people seem to think,' he says.* 'It was substantially built, but the original foundations were not strong enough and they have shrunk. My purpose has been to make No. 10 and the adjoining houses strong and solid enough to last for many years, and I

---

* In a statement to the author.

have allowed in my reconstruction room for further alterations and adjustments for future occupants. The old rambling appearance of the house has been removed, and I have made the residential floors more comfortable and have supplied them with all modern services – bathrooms, sanitation, heating, telephones, and so on. I am painting the lofty vaulted ceiling of the dining-room – it was a stark white and will look the better for a little colour. I am also dealing with the furniture, some of which is good; I am re-covering, for example, the Clive of India suite.'

To give it something of its original outer shape the row of houses has been turned at the corner and taken up to the steps leading down to St. James's Park. The heating of all these houses is supplied by the Whitehall district heating system, which has a boiler house under the new Government buildings in Whitehall Gardens, where both Peel and Disraeli once lived.

During the excavations under No. 10 some important pieces of Tudor pottery were found, as well as pieces belonging to the period of the Roman occupation, at which time the site was nearer a much wider River Thames; the finds indicate that it has been in constant use for nearly two thousand years. As the excavations did not extend to the garden, the Egyptian scarab buried by Lloyd George's housekeeper Sarah during the First World War was left undisturbed.

The work completed, back into their original places will go the porter's black leather hooded chair, the marble busts of Pitt and Melbourne and Wellington, Walpole's portrait in the Cabinet room, the clock beneath it on the mantelpiece, and engravings and photographs of former Prime Ministers all the way up the staircase wall.

It will be asked again, as it was asked nearly two centuries ago*: 'So much has this extraordinary edifice cost the country – for one moiety of which sum a much better dwelling might have been purchased.'

Ruskin provides an answer. 'Watch an old building with anxious care,' he wrote; 'guard it as best you may, and, at any cost, from any influence of dilapidation. Count its stones as you would jewels of a crown. Set watchers about it, as if at the gate of a besieged city; bind it together with irons when it loosens; stay it with timber when it

---

* *Morning Herald*, 21st June 1783.

declines. . . . Do this tenderly and reverently and continually and many a generation will still be born and pass away beneath its shadow.'

Thus may it be said of No. 10 that it was here, not on this site but in this house, that Walpole, Pitt, Wellington, Disraeli, Gladstone, Lloyd George and Winston Churchill lived and worked for the greatness of the country and the happiness of the people.

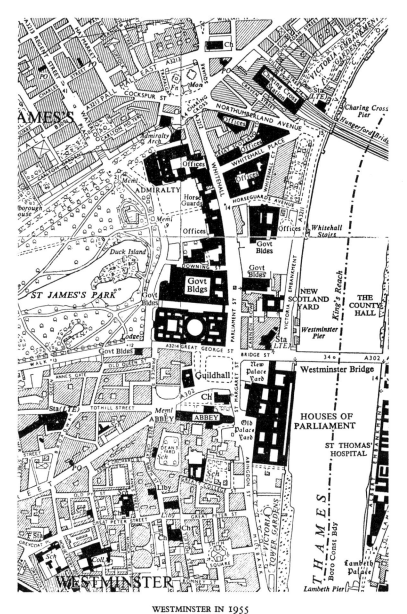

WESTMINSTER IN 1955

From the six inches to the mile Ordnance Survey, sheets TQ27NE, TQ28SE,
TQ37NW, TQ38SW.

(See also page xviii)

No. 10 Downing Street

FLOOR PLANS BEFORE THE 1960
RECONSTRUCTION

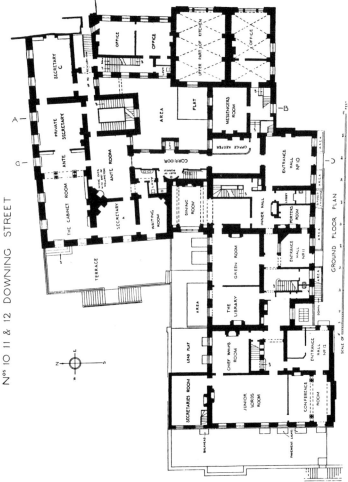

Nos 10 11 & 12 DOWNING STREET

GROUND FLOOR PLAN

In this ground floor plan, No. 11 begins in the Lobby, behind the 'disused entrance' to the left of the Entrance Hall of No. 10. The whole of this front section of No. 10A, as it may be called, has been transferred to No. 10 during the reconstruction. Otherwise, despite a very thorough strengthening and even rebuilding of the walls, the adjustments made on this floor of No. 10 have been few. All the main features – the corridor to the ante-room of the Cabinet room, the stone staircase and the secretaries' rooms, are exactly as they were. A new lift has been installed, a little nearer the entrance.

Nᵒˢ 10 11 & 12 DOWNING STREET

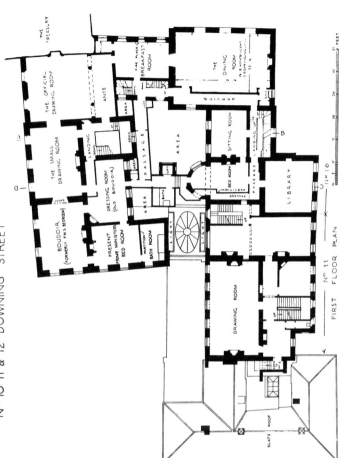

FIRST FLOOR PLAN Nᵒ 11

The first floor of No. 10 has also been very little changed. The three drawing-rooms facing Horse Guards Parade are just as they always were. The bedrooms have been removed to the floor above and a new staircase to that floor has been built a little nearer the main staircase, which ends on this floor.

N° 10 & 11 DOWNING STREET

The second floor has been substantially altered. All the bedrooms and bathrooms are on this floor and extend for the entire length above Nos. 10, 10a, 11 and 12 Downing Street. The third floor, shown in the inset, has been removed completely.

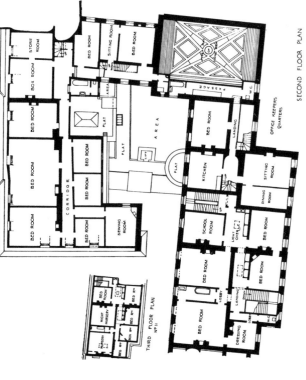

SECOND FLOOR PLAN

THIRD FLOOR PLAN
N° 11

SCALE OF

Prime Ministers and Others who have lived at No. 10 Downing Street

The following is a list of the residents at No. 10 Downing Street and the house at the back. Chancellors of the Exchequer are shown in italics and First Lords of the Treasury are indicated by*.

THE HOUSE AT THE BACK

c. 1673–c. 1676	Duke of Buckingham
1677–90	Earl and Countess of Lichfield
1690–1708	Lord Overkirk
1708–20	Lady Overkirk
1720–32	Count Bothmar

No. 10 DOWNING STREET

1735–42	*Sir Robert Walpole*★
1742–43	*Samuel Sandys*
1743–44	Lord Sandys
1745–53	Earl of Lincoln
1753–54	Lewis Watson
1754–61	*Henry Bilson-Legge*
1762	Thomas Pelham
1762–63	*Sir Francis Dashwood*
1763–65	*George Grenville*★
1765–66	*William Dowdeswell*
1766–67	*Charles Townshend*
1767–70	*Lord North*
1770–82	*Lord North*★
1782	*Lord John Cavendish* (doubtful)
1782–83	*William Pitt*
1783	Duke of Portland
1783–1801	*William Pitt*★
1801–04	*Henry Addington*★
1804–06	*William Pitt*★
1806–07	Lord Grenville★
1807	Duke of Portland★
1807–09	*Spencer Perceval*
1809–12	*Spencer Perceval*★
1810	Chas. Arbuthnot

441

1812–23	*Nicholas Vansittart*
1823–27	*F. J. Robinson*
1827	*George Canning*★
1827–28	Lord Goderich★
1828–30	Duke of Wellington★
1830	Earl Bathurst
1830–34	Earl Grey★
1835	Sir Thomas Freemantle, Peel's secretary
1838	The Hon.William Cowper and G. E. Anson
1839–40	G. E. Anson and the Hon. Mrs. Anson
1842	Edward Drummond
1843	Edward Drummond and W. H. Stephenson
1844–46	W. H. Stephenson and George Arbuthnot
1847	Col. the Hon. George Keppel
	Charles S. Grey
	R. W. Grey

(The residential part of No. 10 was untenanted for thirty years)

1877–80	Benjamin Disraeli★
1880–85	*W. E. Gladstone*★
1885–86	Sir Stafford Northcote★
1886 (Feb. to July)	W. E. Gladstone★
1886–91	W. H. Smith★
1891–92	Arthur James Balfour
1892–94	W. E. Gladstone★
1894 (March)	Earl of Rosebery★
1895–1905	Arthur James Balfour★

(Mr. Balfour became Prime Minister in August 1902. From that date onwards all Prime Ministers have lived at No. 10 Downing Street. None of them has combined with it the office of Chancellor of the Exchequer.)

1905–07	Sir Henry Campbell-Bannerman
1907–16	Herbet Henry Asquith
1916–22	David Lloyd George
1922–23	Andrew Bonar Law
1923–24	Stanley Baldwin
1924 (Jan.)	James Ramsay MacDonald
1924 (Nov.)–1929	Stanley Baldwin

1929–35	James Ramsay MacDonald
1935–37	Stanley Baldwin
1937–40	Neville Chamberlain
1940–45	Winston S. Churchill
1945–51	Clement R. Attlee
1951–55	Sir Winston S. Churchill
1955–56	Sir Anthony Eden
1957–60†	Harold Macmillan

† The house was vacated on 1st August 1960 for extensive repairs and rebuilding.

BIBLIOGRAPHY AND SOURCES

1. *Survey of London.* Vol. XIV (Being Part III of the Parish of St. Margaret, Westminster). By Montague H. Cox, LL.B. (Lond), Clerk of the Council, and G. Topham Forrest, F.R.I.B.A., F.R.S.E., F.G.S., Architect to the Council. (London County Council 1931).

2. *London Past and Present* by H. B. Wheatley, based on book by P. Cunningham (Murray, 1891).

3. *Pepys' Diary*, edited by Henry B. Wheatley (G. Bell & Son, 1928).

4. *Samuel Pepys: The Man in the Making* by Arthur Bryant (Collins, 1933).

5. *The Life of Cardinal Wolsey* by George Cavendish (Harding, 1827).

6. *Survey of London* by John Stow (Strype's edition, 1720).

7. *Life and Letters of John Winthrop*, edited by R. C. Winthrop, 2 vols. (Ticknor & Fields, 1864–7).

8. *Jean de Witt* by Antonin Lefèvre-Pontalis (trans. S. E and A. Stephenson), 2 vols. (Longmans, Green, 1885).

9. *The Greatness of Oliver Cromwell* by Maurice Ashley (Hodder & Stoughton, 1957).

10. *Oliver Cromwell* by John Buchan (Hodder & Stoughton, 1934).

11. *Oliver Cromwell and the Rule of the Puritans* by Charles Firth (Putnam, 1924).

12. *The Regimental History of Cromwell's Army* by Charles Firth, 2 vols. (Oxford University Press, 1940).

13. *Memorials of the Great Civil War in England, 1646–52* by Henry Cary, 2 vols. (Henry Colburn, 1842).

14. *Diary of Burton, Member in the Parls., 1656–9* by Thomas Burton, 4 vols. (Henry Colburn, 1828).

15. *State Papers, collected by Clarendon, commencing from 1621*, 3 vols. (1767–86).

16. *State Papers of John Thurloe, Secretary to the Council of State, and to the Two Protectors*, 7 vols. (1742).

17. *The Egerton Papers* (Camden Society, 1840).

18. *The Speeches, Discourses and Prayers of Col. John Barkstead, Col. John Okey, and Mr. Miles Corbet, etc. . . . .* (1662). (A copy of this pamphlet is in the British Museum.)

19. *Calendar of State Papers, Domestic Series.*

20. *The Godfather of Downing Street: Sir George Downing* by John Beresford (Cobden-Sanderson, 1923).

21. *No. 10 Downing Street* by Charles Eyre Pascoe (Duckworth, 1908).

22. *No. 10 Downing Street* by Basil Fuller and John Cornes (Stanley Paul, 1936).

23. *Memoirs of the Reign of George II* by John, Lord Hervey. Edited by J. W. Croker, 2 vols. (Bickers, 1884).

24. *No. 10 Downing Street 1660–1900* by Hector Bolitho (Hutchinson, 1957).

25. *A New View of London* by Edward Hatton, 2 vols. (John Nicholson, 1708).

26. *Political History of England 1702–60* by J. S. Leadam (Longmans, Green, 1909).

27. *Sir Robert Walpole: The Making of a Statesman* by J. H. Plumb (Cresset Press, 1956).

28. *Sir Robert Walpole: The King's Minister* by J. H. Plumb (Cresset Press, 1960).

29. *Walpole* by John Morley (Macmillan, 1890).

30. *Robert Walpole and His Age* by J. R. Stirling Taylor (Jonathan Cape, 1931).

31. *Memoirs of Life &c. of Sir Robert Walpole* by William Coxe, 3 vols. (Longman, Hurst, etc., 1798).

32. *The Letters of Horace Walpole*, edited by Peter Cunningham, 9 vols. (Grant, 1906).

33. *The Prime Ministers of Britain 1721–1921* by the Hon. Clive Bingham (John Murray, 1922).

34. *Memoirs of the Reign of King George II* by Horace Walpole, 3 vols. (Henry Colburn, 1846).

35. *Memoirs of the Reign of King George III* by Horace Walpole, 4 vols. (Richard Bentley, 1845).

36. *Journals of the Reign of King George III* by Horace Walpole, 2 vols. (Richard Bentley, 1859).

37. *History of England from the Accession of Anne to the Death of George II* by J. S. Leadam (Longmans, 1909).

38. *The Historical and the Posthumous Memoirs of Sir Nathaniel Wraxall 1772–1784*, edited by Henry B. Wheatley (Bickers & Son, 1884).

39. *Hell-Fire Francis* by Ronald Fuller (Chatto & Windus, 1939).

40. *The History of England in the Eighteenth Century* by William Lecky, 8 vols. (Longmans, 1882).

41. *The History of England* by Lord Macaulay, 5 vols. (Longman, Brown, Green, etc., 1849–61).

42. *Critical and Historical Essays* by Lord Macaulay, 3 vols. (Longmans, Green, etc., 1860).

43. *Chatham* by J. H. Plumb (Cains, 1953).

44. *Chatham* by Lord Rosebery (Humphreys, 1910).

45. *Lord North* by W. Baring Pemberton (Longmans, 1867).

46. *The Correspondence of King George III with Lord North, 1768–1783* (Murray, 1867).

47. *William Pitt* by Lord Rosebery (Macmillan, 1919).

48. *William Pitt and National Revival* by J. Holland Rose (G. Bell & Sons, 1911).

49. *Boswell's Life of Johnson*, 2 vols. (Henry Frowde, 1904).

50. *Boswell's London Journal, 1762–63*, edited by Frederick A. Pottle (Heinemann, 1950).

51. *Life of the Rt. Hon. William Pitt* by Earl Stanhope, 4 vols. (Murray, 1862).

52. *The War Speeches of William Pitt*, selected by R. Coupland, with a Foreword by Winston S. Churchill (Clarendon Press, 1940).

53. *Letters Relating to the Love Episode of William Pitt*, with an Introduction by Lord Rosebery (Privately printed, 1900).

54. *William Pitt, the Younger* by P. W. Wilson (Stanley Paul, 1930).

55. *Memoirs of Lady Hester Stanhope*, edited by C. L. Meryon (Henry Colburn, 1845).

56. *Charles Napier* by Rosamund Lawrence (Murray, 1952).

57. *History of The Times (The Thunderer in the Making), 1785–1841* (The Times, 1935).

58. *Grand Whiggery* by Marjorie Villiers (Murray, 1939).

59. *The Whig Supremacy: 1714–1760* by Basil Williams (Clarendon Press, 1939).

60. *Works of the Rt. Hon. Edmund Burke*, 8 vols. (Francis & John Rivington, 1852).

61. *Edmund Burke* by Sir Philip Magnus (Murray, 1939).

62. *The Origins of Commerce* by Adam Anderson, 4 vols. (J. White and others, 1801).

63. *Historical Sketches of Statesmen in the Time of George III* by Lord Brougham, 3 vols. (Charles Knight, 1839–43).

64. *History of the British Army* by J. W. Fortescue, 13 vols. (Macmillan, 1899–1930).

65. The Barrington MSS.

66. *Memorials and Correspondence of Charles James Fox*, edited by Lord John Russell, 4 vols. (Richard Bentley, 1853–7).

67. *Silver Tongues*, edited by John Hayward (Michael Joseph, 1937).

68. *Anecdotal History of the British Parliament* by G. H. Jennings (Horace Cox, 1880).

69. *The Years of Endurance, 1793–1802* by Arthur Bryant (Collins, 1942).

70. *Years of Victory, 1802–1812* by Arthur Bryant (Collins, 1944).

71. *The Age of Elegance, 1812–1822* by Arthur Bryant (Collins, 1950).

72. *Life and Correspondence of Henry Addington, 1st Viscount Sidmouth* by the Hon. G. Pellew (John Murray, 1847).

73. *The Life of the Rt. Hon. Spencer Perceval* by Spencer Walpole (Hurst & Blackett, 1874).

74. *The Croker Papers: Correspondence & diaries of the Rt. Hon. John Wilson Croker*, edited by Louis J. Jennings, 3 vols. (John Murray, 1884).

75. *The Creevey Papers*, edited by Sir Herbert Maxwell, 2 vols. (Murray, 1904).

76. *Lord Liverpool and Liberal Toryism* by W. R. Brock (Cambridge University Press, 1941).

77. *The Life and Administration of Robert Bankes, 2nd Earl of Liverpool* by C. D. Yonge, 3 vols. (Macmillan, 1868).

78. *Lord Liverpool and His Times* by Sir Charles Petrie (Barrie, 1954).

79. *The Greville Diary*, edited by P. W. Wilson, 2 vols. (Heinemann, 1927).

80. *Henry Brougham* by Francis Hawes (Cape, 1957).

81. *Life of Canning* by H. W. V. Temperley (Finch, 1905).

82. *Some Official Correspondence of George Canning*, edited by E. J. Stapleton (Longmans, 1887).

83. *George Canning and His Friends*, edited by Capt. Josceline Bagot (Murray, 1909).

84. *Castlereagh, the Political Life of Robert, Second Marquess of Londonderry* by Sir J. A. R. Marriott (Methuen, 1936).

85. *Memoirs of the Life of Sir Samuel Romilly*, edited by his sons, 3 vols. (Murray, 1840).

86. *The Life of the First Marquess of Ripon* by Lucien Wolf, 2 vols. (Murray, 1921).

87. *The Duke* by Philip Guedalla (Hodder & Stoughton, 1937).

88. *Despatches of the Duke of Wellington*, 36 vols. (Murray, various editions).

89. *Wellington in Civil Life* by Muriel Wellesley (Constable, 1939).

90. *Royal Dukes* by Roger Fulford (Duckworth, 1933).

91. *The Life and Times of William IV* by Percy Fitzgerald (Tinsley, 1884).

92. *Memoirs* by the Rt. Hon. Sir Robert Peel, 2 vols. (Murray, 1856).

93. *Some Account of the Life and Opinions of the 2nd Earl Grey* by Lt.-General the Hon. C. Grey (Bentley, 1861).

94. *Princess Lieven* by H. Montgomery Hyde (Harrap, 1938).

95. *Unpublished Diary and Political Sketches of Princess Lieven*, edited by H. W. V. Temperley (Cape, 1925).

96. *Lord Grey and the Reform Bill* by G. M. Trevelyan (Longmans, 1952).

97. *Correspondence of Princess Lieven and Earl Grey*, edited by Guy de Strange (Bentley, 1890).

98. *The Age of Grey and Peel* by H. W. Carless Davis (Clarendon Press, 1929).

99. *The Young Melbourne* by Lord David Cecil (Constable, 1939).

100. *Queen Victoria and Her Ministers* by Sir J. A. R. Marriott (Murray, 1933).

101. *Palmerston* by Philip Guedalla (Benn, 1926).

448

102. *Lady Palmerston and Her Times* by Mabell, Countess of Airlie (Hodder & Stoughton, 1922).

103. *Sir Robert Peel* by A. A. W. Ramsay (Constable, 1928).

104. *A Political Diary 1828–30* by the Earl of Ellenborough, edited by Lord Colchester (Richard Bentley & Son, 1881).

105. *Sir Robert Peel from his Private Papers*, edited by C. S. Parker, 3 vols. (Murray, 1891–9).

106. *Personal Reminiscences of the Duke of Wellington, 1831–51* by the first Earl of Ellesmere (Murray, 1903).

107. *The Life and Letters of Lord Macaulay* by Sir George Otto Trevelyan, 2 vols. (Longmans, Green, 1908).

108. *Recollections of a Long Life* by Lord Broughton, with additional extracts from his private Diaries, edited by Lady Dorchester, 6 vols. (Murray, 1909–11).

109. *Lord John Russell* by A. Wyatt Tilby (Cobden-Sanderson, 1932).

110. *Lord M.* by Lord David Cecil (Constable, 1954).

111. *Queen Victoria* by Lytton Strachey (Chatto & Windus, 1921).

112. *The Letters of Queen Victoria 1837–1861*, edited by A. C. Benson and Viscount Esher, 3 vols. (Murray, 1930–32).

113. *The Prince Consort* by Roger Fulford (Macmillan, 1949).

114. *Fifty Years of My Life* by George Thomas, Earl of Albemarle (Macmillan 1877).

115. *Endymion* by Benjamin Disraeli, 3 vols. (Longmans, Green, 1880).

116. *The Life of H. J. Temple, Viscount Palmerston* by Sir Henry Bulwer (Lord Dalling), 3 vols. (Richard Bentley & Son, 1871–4).

117. *The Life and Correspondence of H. J. Temple, Viscount Palmerston* by the Rt. Hon. A. Evelyn Ashley, 2 vols. (Richard Bentley & Son, 1879).

118. *Life of Benjamin Disraeli, Earl of Beaconsfield* by W. F. Monypenny and G. E. Buckle, 6 vols. (Murray, 1929).

119. *Gladstone* by John Morley (Edward Lloyd, 1908).

120. *Gladstone* by Francis Birrell (Duckworth, 1933).

121. *Gladstone* by Sir Philip Magnus (Murray, 1954).

122. *Life of Robert, Marquess of Salisbury* by Lady Gwendolen Cecil, 2 vols. (Hodder & Stoughton, 1921).

123. *The Queen and Mr. Gladstone*, edited by Philip Guedalla, 2 vols. (Hodder & Stoughton, 1933).

124. *Diary of Lady Frederick Cavendish*, edited by J. Bailey, 2 vols. (Murray, 1927).

125. *Henry Ponsonby – His Life and Letters* by Arthur (Lord) Ponsonby (Macmillan, 1942).

126. *Life, Letters and Diaries of Sir Stafford Northcote, 1st Earl of Iddesleigh* by Andrew Lang (Blackwood, 1891).

127. *Life and Times of William Henry Smith, M.P.* by Sir Herbert Maxwell (Blackwood, 1893).

128. *My Early Life: A Roving Commission* by Winston S. Churchill (Macmillan, 1941).

129. *Lord Rosebery* by the Marquess of Crewe (Murray, 1931).

130. *Arthur James Balfour* by Blanche E. C. Dugdale (Hutchinson, 1936).

131. *Prime Ministers and Some Others* by the Rt. Hon. G. W. E. Russell (Unwin, 1918).

132. *Life of Joseph Chamberlain* by J. L. Garvin, 3 vols. (Macmillan, 1932–4), 4th volume by Julian Amery (Macmillan, 1951).

133. *Sir Henry Campbell-Bannerman* by J. A. Spender (Hodder & Stoughton, 1923).

134. *Lord Randolph Churchill* by Winston S. Churchill (Macmillan, 1906).

135. *Herbert Henry Asquith* by H. Spender and Cyril Asquith, 2 vols. (Hutchinson, 1932).

136. *Autobiography of Margot Asquith*, edited by Mark Bonham Carter, one volume edition (Eyre & Spottiswoode, 1962); (and *More Memories* by Margot Asquith: Cassell, 1933).

137. *Haldane, 1856–1928. The Life of Viscount Haldane of Cloan* by Sir Frederick Maurice, 2 vols. (Faber & Faber, 1937–9).

138. *King George V* by Sir Harold Nicolson (Constable, 1952).

139. *Memoirs and Reflections 1852–1927* by H. H. Asquith the Earl of Oxford and Asquith, 2 vols. (Cassell, 1928).

140. *The Prime Minister – David Lloyd George* by H. Spender (Hodder & Stoughton, 1920).

141. *Lloyd George* by Tom Jones (Oxford University Press, 1951).

142. *Tempestuous Journey: Lloyd George, His Life and Times* by Frank Owen (Hutchinson, 1954).

143. *War Memoirs* by David Lloyd George, 6 vols. (Nicholson & Watson, 1934).

144. *Mr. Balfour's Poodle* by Roy Jenkins (Heinemann, 1954).

145. *The World Crisis* by Winston S. Churchill, 6 vols. (Butterworth, 1931).

146. *The Unknown Prime Minister: The Life and Times of Andrew Bonar Law* by Robert Blake (Eyre & Spottiswoode, 1955).

147. *The General Strike* by Julian Symons (Cresset Press, 1957).

148. *The Modern British Monarchy* by Sir Charles Petrie (Eyre & Spottiswoode, 1961).

149. *Stanley Baldwin* by G. M. Young (Hart & Davis, 1952).

150. *Stanley Baldwin* by Arthur Bryant (Hamish Hamilton, 1937).

151. *My Father: The True Story* by A. W. Baldwin (Allen & Unwin, 1955).

152. *The Life of James Ramsay MacDonald: 1866–1919* by Lord Elton (Collins, 1939).

153. *Politicians and the Press* by Lord Beaverbrook (Hutchinson, 1926).

154. *Men and Power: 1917–1918* by Lord Beaverbrook (Hutchinson, 1956).

155. *Votes for Women* by Roger Fulford (Faber, 1957).

156. *The Life of Neville Chamberlain* by Keith Feiling (Macmillan, 1946).

157. *Neville Chamberlain* by Iain Macleod (Muller, 1961).

158. *The Private Papers of Hore-Belisha* by R. J. Minney (Collins, 1960).

159. *Thoughts and Adventures* by Winston S. Churchill (Thornton Butterworth, 1932).

160. *Great Contemporaries* by Winston S. Churchill (Thornton Butterworth, 1937).

161–166. *The Second World War* by Winston S. Churchill, 6 vols. (Cassell, 1948–54).
   161. *The Gathering Storm.*
   162. *Their Finest Hour.*
   163. *The Grand Alliance*
   164. *The Hinge of Fate.*
   165. *Closing the Ring.*
   166. *Triumph and Tragedy.*

167. *Mr. Churchill's Secretary* by Elizabeth Nel (Hodder & Stoughton, 1958).

168. *As It Happened* by C. R. Attlee (Odhams, 1954).

169. *A Prime Minister Remembers. War and Post-War Memories of Earl Attlee* by Francis Williams (Heinemann, 1961).

170. *Herbert Morrison: Autobiography* (Odhams, 1960).

171. *Government and Parliament* by Herbert Morrison (Oxford, 1954).

172. *Call Back Yesterday* by Hugh Dalton (Muller, 1953).

173. *The Fateful Years* by Hugh Dalton (Muller, 1957).

174. *High Tide and Afterwards* by Lord Dalton (Muller, 1962).

175. *King George VI* by John Wheeler-Bennett (Macmillan, 1958).

176. *The Eden Memoirs: Full Circle* by Sir Anthony Eden (Cassell, 1960).

177. *The Dictionary of National Biography.*

178. *The Encyclopædia Britannica.*

179. *Seven Gardens and a Palace* by Richard Burlington, Earl of Boyle. Edited by E.V.B. (John Lane, The Bodley Head, 1900).

180. *Memoirs of Pitt* by Henry Cleland (Cundee, 1807).

181. *Wilkes and Liberty* by George Rudé (Oxford University Press, 1962).

182. *Crossroads of Power* by Sir Lewis Namier (Hamish Hamilton, 1962).

183. *The Eden Memoirs: Facing the Dictators* by the Earl of Avon (Cassell, 1962).

184. *The Marconi Scandal* by Frances Donaldson (Hart-Davis, 1962).

185. *The Great Hunger* by Cecil Woodham-Smith (Hamish Hamilton, 1962).

INDEX

Aberdeen, 4th Earl of, 210, 256-7, 260

Abyssinia, Italian attack on, 401

Addington, Henry (later Viscount Sidmouth), sees Pitt's duel, 135-6; Ministry of, 140-6, 165, 172-3; Canning's quips on, 142, 187-8; makes peace with France, 143; made peer, 150; resigns, 151; in Ministry of All the Talents, 156-7; in Home Office, 174; angered at prorogation of Parliament, 220; mentioned, 148, 153, 190, 224

Addington, John Hiley, 144-5, 173

Addison, Dr. Christopher (later Lord Addison), 354, 414, 418

Addison, Joseph, 54

Adelaide, Queen of William IV, 217, 224, 235-6

Adenauer, President, 423

Adrianople, 287

Afghan Wars, 288-9, 292, 295

Africa, European annexation of land in, 313

Alabama, the, 264

Albania, naval demonstration off, 292

Albemarle, Duke of (General Monk), 16, 25, 31

Albemarle, George Thomas Keppel, 6th Earl of, 250, 253, 255

Albert, Prince Consort, 244-5; Queen's mourning for, 273-6

Albert Memorial, 274

Alexander I, Tsar of Russia, 188

Alexander, Field-Marshal Earl, 412

Alexandra, Queen, 334

Alexandria, attack on, 293

Aliens Act, 133

Althorp, Lord (later Earl Spencer), Liberal leader, 211; Chancellor of Exchequer, 215; Factory Act of, 227-8; and Irish question, 229-30;

resigns, 231; in Melbourne's Ministry, 233; succeeds father, 235; mentioned, 222, 256

Alvanley, Lord, 248

Alvard, Thomas, 23

Amelia, Princess, 168

American Civil War, 264

American colonies, Puritan, 8-10; Britain loses, 73, 88, 109-11; taxing of, 74-6, 82, 103; Walpole's concessions to, 75; Congress assembles in, 76, 107; import duties levied on, 86, 91; repealing of duties except on tea, 91-2; resent presence of British army, 103; Irish immigrants in, 138; William IV in, as prince, 217

American War of Independence, 104-5, 107-11; starting point of, 75; negotiations to end, 115-16; mentioned, 138, 217

Amherst, Lord, 91

Amiens, Peace of, 133, 143-4, 173

Amory, D. Heathcoat, Budget of, 427

Anglo-Japanese Alliance, 368

Anne, Queen, 32-3, 39-41

'Annexe, The', 409, 411, 413

Anson, George, 243-6

Anti-Corn Law League, 249

Antwerp, expedition to (1914), 352-3

Apsley House, 198, 207; King and Queen at, 209; attacked by mob, 212-13

Arab struggle with Israel, 423

Arbuthnot, Charles, 174, 200, 207

Arbuthnot, George, 248

Arbuthnot, Harriet, 198, 205, 207

Argyll, 8th Duke of, 297, 305

Armistead, Mrs., 121

Army, British, Pitt's reduction of, 133; purchase of commissions in,

Army – *cont.*

167, 277, 328; in South African War, 326; Haldane's reorganization of, 332; strengthening of (1937), 401; reserves called up, 405

Ashley, Lord (later 7th Earl of Shaftesbury), 228

Asquith, Raymond, 335

Asquith, Violet – *see* Bonham-Carter, Lady Violet

Asquith, Anthony ('Puffin'), 336, 338–9, 345

Asquith, Elizabeth (later Princess Elizabeth Bibesco), 350

Asquith, H. H. (later Lord Oxford and Asquith), 335–6; moves vote of no confidence on Salisbury, 314, 336; Chancellor of Exchequer, 330; and votes for women, 333; Campbell-Bannerman thanks, 335; Ministry of, 335–42, 343–51, 352–4; starts Old Age Pensions, 336; opens election on People's Budget, 337–8; and reform of Lords, 338–42; and Marconi scandal, 347; and outbreak of war, 349; wartime Coalition Government of, 353; resigns, 354; defeated at election, 361; entertains King and Queen, 404; mentioned, 315, 368

Asquith, Margot (later Lady Oxford and Asquith), 335–6; on No. 10, 343–5; on outbreak of war (1914), 350–1; and end of Asquith's Ministry, 354

Astbury, Mr. Justice, 382

Aswan dam, withdrawal of loan for building, 424

Attlee, Clement (later Earl), 385; Under-Secretary of State for War, 371; on Committee to consider unemployment, 338; and Edward VIII's marriage, 395; refuses to serve under Chamberlain, 406; Deputy Prime Minister under Churchill, 407, 420; Ministry of, 413–18; on amendment of Parliament Act, 415; ill-health of, 415,

418; on entertaining at No. 10, 415–16; quietness of, 417; resigns, 418; retires, 421; mentioned, 393, 427

Auckland, 1st Lord, 136, 142

Austerlitz, Battle of, 154

Austria seeks to acquire Bavaria, 127; at war with French, 131–2, 152, 178; British subsidy for, 134; freeing Italy from, 264; anti-Turkish attitude of, 283; economic crisis in, 388; Hitler seizes, 402

Axe, the (brewhouse), 2, 25–6

Baldwin, Betty, 369, 378

Baldwin, Mrs. 369–70, 374, 383

Baldwin, Oliver, 369, 382

Baldwin, Stanley (later 1st Earl), 369, 379, 382–4; demands end of Coalition, 364; Chancellor of Exchequer, 366–8; in Washington, 367; first Ministry of, 368–70; resigns, 370, 383; second Ministry of, 378–84; woos the workers, 379; and General Strike, 380–2; loses popularity with Party, 382; and National Government, 389–91; Lord President of Council, 391; Press criticism of, 393; and re-arming of Britain, 394; third Ministry of, 394; and Abdication crisis, 394–6; resigns and goes to Lords, 397; entertains King and Queen, 404

Baldwin, Wyndham, 369, 378

Balfour, Arthur James (later 1st Earl), 312–13; in Fourth Party, 301, 312; Gladstone approaches on Home Rule, 304; in No. 10, 312, 314, 322; Leader of Commons, 312–14, 322; visits Gladstone on bicycle, 323; on idea of war with U.S., 323; acting Prime Minister, 324–5; and Boer War, 325–6; motor-car of, 326; Prime Minister, 327; Campbell-Bannerman attacks, 332–3; opens election campaign on 'People's Budget', 337; and reform

of Lords, 340; visits Asquiths, 346; in Coalition Government, 353; Foreign Secretary, 354-5; loyal to Lloyd George, 365; mentioned, 348, 368
Balkans, at war with Turkey, 282-3
Balmoral, 274, 292
Bank of England, encourages speculation, 183; planned run on, 224; cannot save pound, 389
Banks, panic run on, 183
Barbay, Louis, 48
Baring, Francis, 249, 253
Barkstead (regicide), 20
Barré, Colonel Isaac, 75, 105
Barrie, Sir James, 357, 387
Barrington, 2nd Viscount, 107
Barry, Sir Charles, 241
Bastille, storming of, 172
Bath, 4th Marquess of, 281
Bathurst, 3rd Earl, 207-8
Bavaria, 127, 132
Beaconsfield, Benjamin Disraeli, 1st Earl of, hears Canning, 192; changes Party, 226; opposes Peel, 250; Chancellor of Exchequer, 255-6; Leader of House, 256; on Aberdeen's Ministry, 257; criticizes Palmerston, 262; on Russell and Reform Bill, 267; effective head of Government, 268-9; Queen's attachment to, 269, 280-1, 286-7; regarded as outsider by both parties, 269-70, 280; first Ministry of, 269-72; rivalry with Gladstone, 270; Reform Bill of, 271-2; opposes abolition of established Church of Ireland, 272; wife of, 272-3; novels of, 273; refuses Premiership, 278; second Ministry of, 278, 279-89; loses wife, 279-80; failing health of, 281, 284; accepts peerage, 281; buys Suez Canal shares, 281-2; supports Turkey against Russia, 283-4, 287; n oves into No. 10, 284-7, 373; quarrel with Gladstone over furniture for No. 11, 285; primroses for, 286; at Congress of Berlin, 287-8; death of, 289; annexes Transvaal, 289, 324; mentioned, 303, 310, 332
Beaconsfield, Mary Anne, Viscountess, 272-3, 279-80
Beauchamp, 6th Earl, 281
Beaverbrook, Max Aitken, Baron, and Lloyd George Ministry, 354-5; on Labour Government, 371-2; papers of, criticize Baldwin, 393; supports Edward VIII, 396; in Cabinet, 411
Bechuanaland, 313
Bedford, 4th Duke of, 95
Beer, duty on, 291, 352
Belgium, French designs on, 127; French occupation of, 143; separates from Holland, 210; independence of, 229; Germany invades, 350, 406
Bell inn, 2
Bellingham, John, 170
Bentinck, Lord George, 250
Berlin, Congress of, 287-8, 312
Berlin, Treaty of, 287-8, 292
Bessborough, 9th Earl and Countess of, 403
Bessborough, Lady, 273
Bevan, Aneurin, 414, 417-18
Bevin, Ernest, 414-15, 417-18
Bibesco, Princess Elizabeth (née Asquith), 350
Bilson-Legge, Henry, 64-5, 95
Birch, Nigel, 427
Birkenhead, Lord (F. E. Smith), 341, 365, 378-9
Birmingham, representation of, 200; Political Union forms in, 210; without municipality, 245; demonstrations in, on defeat of Reform Bill, 271; republicanism in, 276
Birrell, Augustine, 331
Bismarck, Prince, 287, 292
'Black and Tans', 362
Blake, William, 133
Bloemfontein, 326
Boer War, 324-7, 336
Boers, 292, 324-5

Bolingbroke, Henry St. John, Viscount, 39, 54, 55
Bondfield, Margaret, Minister of Labour, 385
Bonham Carter, Lady Violet (née Asquith), 335–6, 357; room of, in No. 10, 345
Boston, mob violence in, 76; 'Massacre', 92; 'Tea Party', 103–4; closure of port of, 104
Boswell, James, 48, 70–1
Bothmar, Count, 33, 42, 46
'Boy Patriots', 73
Boycott, Captain, 296
Boyle, Sir Edward, 425
Bracken, Brendan, 411
Brazil, Portuguese Royal family in, 161
Bright, John, 291, 293; opposed to Home Rule, 304–6
Bristol, rioting in, on Reform Bill, 222
Bristol, Earl of, 101
Britain, weakness of (1784), 121, 126; prosperity of, under Pitt, 121; French declare war on (1793), 132; threatened by invasion, 134, 144, 147, 149, 152; post-war hardship in, 178; later periods of great hardship in, 183, 210–12, 249; violence in, at rejection of Reform Bill, 222, 224, 271; 'Hungry Forties' in, 249, 254; strengthening coastal defences of, 264; and American Civil War, 264; narrowly escapes war, 264, 323–4; at war with Germany, 348–52; depression of, in 1920s, 363, 379–81; U.S. loan to, during war, 367; economic depression in (1930–1), 388–90; inadequate defences of, against Hitler menace, 393–4; prepares for war, 402, 404; near bankruptcy after war, 414; and Suez crisis, 424–6
British Empire, expansion of, under Salisbury, 313; Rosebery and, 322
British Gazette, 381

British Museum, 182
Broadlands, Romsey (Hants), 258
Brougham, Lord, supports Parliamentary Reform, 211, 222; in Grey's Ministry, 215, 218–20; suggests creation of peers, 221, 223; on quarrels in Cabinet, 230–1; and Melbourne, 235, 244; mentioned, 177
Brunswick, Duke of, 131–2
Buccleuch, 5th Duke of, 247, 249
Buckingham, George Grenville, 1st Marquess of, 74, 158–9
Buckingham, George Villiers, 2nd Duke of, 25, 28, 30–1
Buckingham and Chandos, Richard Grenville, 2nd Duke of, 249
Buckingham and Chandos, Richard Grenville, 3rd Duke of, 270
Buckingham House, 79
Buckingham Palace, 5; King offers as new House of Parliament, 236
Buckinghamshire, Countess of (née Eleanor Eden), 136, 150, 180
Buckinghamshire, 4th Earl of, 136, 150–1, 180
Bulganin, M., 423
Bulgarian atrocities, 283
Buller, General Sir Redvers, 325–6
Burgoyne, John, 102
Burke, Edmund, 81–2; on Grenville, 74; attacks North's American policy, 105; in Rockingham's Government, 113–14; on Pitt, 115; votes against reform, 119; and impeachment of Hastings, 122–3; opposes French Revolution, 130–1, 142, 187; mentioned, 84, 120, 124, 186
Burke, T. H., 297
Burleigh, William Cecil, Lord, 301
Burma, 415
Burns, John, 350
Bute, 3rd Earl of, 67; persecutes Whigs, 68, 80; resigns, 72; suggests Grenville's appointment, 72; failure of design of, 73; bribery by, 74; North and, 96; mentioned, 70, 85

Butler, R. A., 426–7
Byron, Lord, 233
Byvoets, Miss, 370, 374

Cabinet Economy Committee, 389
Campbell, General Sir Colin, 196
Campbell, J. R., 377
Campbell-Bannerman, Sir Henry, 328; supports renewal of Crimes Bill, 299; Ministry of, 327, 329–34; marriage of, 328–30; heart attacks of, 330, 333–4; and Lords' power of rejection, 331–2; approves votes for women, 333; death of, 334, 335; mentioned, 315, 320, 336, 367, 374
Canada, British gains in, from Seven Years War, 65, 68, 74; rebellion in (1837), 251–2; granted independence, 252; and Suez crisis, 426
Canning, 1st Earl (Charles), 191, 239, 262
Canning, George, 186–93; Under-Secretary for Foreign Affairs, 137; on Pitt and Addington, 142, 144–5, 187; Foreign Secretary under Portland, 159–61, 188; duel of, with Castlereagh, 161–2; refuses to serve under Liverpool, 174; resigns, 179; Foreign Secretary under Liverpool, 184, 189–90; Prime Minister, 184–5, 190–3; quips of, 187–8; illness of, 191, 193; appearance and speech of, 192; death of, 193; Palmerston and, 259; mentioned, 149n, 151, 182, 209, 234, 246, 255
Canning, Harriet, 191
Canning, Joan (née Scott), 187, 191–3
Canning, Stratford, 186
Canning, William Pitt, 191
Canton, bombardment of, 262
Cape Colony, 324–5
Cape of Good Hope, 134, 143
Cardwell, Edward, 239, 328
Carlingford, Lord, 305
Carlton Club meeting, 364, 398
Carmarthen, Lord – see Leeds, Duke of
Carnarvon, 4th Earl of, 284, 287, 303
Caroline, Queen of George II, and

Walpole, 44, 50–1, 54, 61; death of, 56; question of allowance for, 61
Caroline, Queen of George IV (Princess of Wales), 165, 179, 188, 215
Carson, Sir Edward, 348, 353, 354, 357
Castilain, John Baptist, 26
Castlereagh, Viscount (later 2nd Marquess of Londonderry), refuses to serve under Addington, 141; serves under Pitt, 149, 151; refuses Premiership, 149n, 156; Secretary for War, 160–1; duel with Canning, 161–2; Leader of Commons, 174; at Congress of Vienna, 177–8; suicide of, 184, 189; foreign policy of, 189; Wellington and Nelson meet in waiting-room of, 198–9; mentioned, 180, 188
Catherine the Great, of Russia, 128
Catholics – see Roman Catholics
Cave, Edward, 97–8
Cavendish, Lady Frederick, 297–8, 306
Cavendish, Lord Frederick, 291, 297–8
Cavendish, Lord John, 113–14
Cecil, Lady Gwendolin, 302
Cecil, Lord Hugh, 341
Ceylon, 143, 415
Chamberlain, Sir Austen, 316; in Asquith's Coalition Government, 353; his loyalty to Lloyd George, 363–4, 365, 398; Foreign Secretary, 378, 383; death of, 398
Chamberlain, Joseph, republicanism of, 276; serves under Gladstone, 291, 299; opposed to Home Rule, 304–6, 316, 398; Liberal Unionists of, 307; serves under Salisbury, 322–3; campaigns for Tariff Reform, 327
Chamberlain, Neville, 398–9; Postmaster-General, 366; Minister of Health and Housing, 378, 383; Chancellor of Exchequer, 391, 399; Prime Minister, 397, 401–6; in No. 10, 399–401, 403–4, 407; pursuit of peace by, 401–2; meets Hitler, 402;

Chamberlain, Neville – *cont.*
and Churchill, 403; and outbreak
of war, 404–5; fails to form National
Government, 406; serves under
Churchill, 407
Chamberlain, Mrs. Neville, 399–401,
403–4
Chambers, Sir William, 117
Charles I, King, 6; in Civil War, 10–
11; children of, housed on site of
No. 10, 24; and Buckingham, 30;
mentioned, 7, 26
Charles II, King, Downing works
against return of, 13–14; Downing
approaches, 15–17; restoration of,
17, 18–19, 25; employs Downing,
19, 21, 27; daughters of, 31–2;
Parliament under, 37–8; descend-
ants of, 83, 96, 244
Charlotte, Princess, daughter of
George IV, 168; death of, 179, 230;
husband of, 229; protégé of, 253
Chartists, 277
Chatham, Countess of, 148
Chatham, William Pitt (the Elder),
1st Earl of, 53–4; attacks Walpole,
55–6; family of, 65; and Seven
Years War, 65, 68; resigns, 68;
relations with Grenville, 73, 80;
George III approaches, 79; upholds
resistance of colonies to taxation,
82; last Ministry of, 83–6, 91; ac-
cepts peerage, 83, 281; illness of,
86; fortune left to, 90, 114; de-
nounces policy against America,
93, 105, 108; demands reversal of
decision on Wilkes, 94; opposes
North, 95–6; challenges rights of
East India Company, 101; death of,
109; means of, 114; interested in
Parliamentary reform, 118–19, 211;
aggressive attitude of, 127–8; mentioned, 63–4, 81, 157, 180
Chatham, 2nd Earl of, 134, 141
Chelmsford, Lord, 371
Chequers, 364, 411
Cherwell, Lord, 408
Chesterfield, 4th Earl of, 54, 100

Chicken, Mr., cottage of, 34, 416,
430–1
China, war with, 262
Cholmondeley, Marchioness of, 400,
422
Churchill, Charles, 70
Churchill, Major John, 407, 421
Churchill, Mary (*née* Walpole), 52
Churchill, Mary, 407, 419
Churchill, Mrs. (later Lady), 408, 413,
419, 421
Churchill, Lord Randolph, in Salis-
bury's first Ministry, 301; Fourth
Party of, 301, 309, 312; approaches
Parnell, 303; Gladstone's mistrust
of, 303; on Gladstone's Home Rule
Bill, 306–7, 316; Chancellor of
Exchequer and Leader of Commons, 307; resignation of, 309–10,
349; death of, 323
Churchill, Randolph, 407
Churchill, Winston (later Sir Winston), hears Gladstone on Home
Rule, 315–16; at Omdurman, 324;
taken prisoner by Boers, 325;
elected to Parliament, 326; President of Board of Trade, 336;
and conflict between Houses, 337,
341; attacked by suffragettes, 338;
hurt in debate on Home Rule, 348;
prepares for war, 349–51; expeditions suggested by, in First World
War, 352–3; dropped from Government (1915), 354; visits Lloyd
George, 357–9; Minister of Munitions, 358; on North Russian expedition 361–2; urges war against
Turkey, 364; joins Conservatives,
366, 378; presents books to library
at No. 10, 374; Chancellor of
Exchequer, 378–9, 383; edits *British
Gazette*, 381; critic of National
Government, 392–3; head of King's
Party in Parliament, 395–6; on
Chamberlain, 401; and Munich
crisis, 402–3; in War Cabinet
(1939), 405–6; Prime Minister and
Minister of Defence, 406–7; in No.

10, 407–12, 419; wartime working day of, 407–9; in bombing of No. 10, 410; difficulties of working for, 411; defeated at election, 412; attacks Lords, 415n; second Ministry of, 418, 419; seeks to undo the socialization of Attlee's Government, 420; visits abroad of, 420–1; receives Garter, 421; retires, 421; cats of, 422; consulted by Queen, 426; mentioned, 422

Cider tax, 80, 90

Cinque Ports, Wardens of, Pitt, 134, 147; Liverpool, 173; Wellington, 207; W. H. Smith, 311

Civil War, 9–12, 30

Clanricarde, 1st Marquess of, 191

Clarendon, Lord Chancellor, 19, 21

Clark, Sir Andrew, 294

Clarke, Mrs. Mary Anne, 167

Cleveland, President, of United States, 323

Clive, Lord, of Plassey, 101–2, 122, 173

Clynes, J. R., 371

Coal industry, depression in, 379–81; subsidy to, 380–1; nationalization of, 380, 414

Coal Mines Bill, 387

Cobbett, William, 226

Cobden, Richard, 192, 264

Cobham, Lord, 157

Cockpit, the, 4–6, 22, 23; theatre, 6, 25; lodgings, 23–5, 27, 46

Colenso, Battle of, 325

Coleraine, Richard Law, Lord, 366

Coleridge, Lord Chief Justice, 248

College Mews, 263

Colonial Preference, 327

Combination Laws, repeal of, 227

Commissions, purchase of, 167, 277

Commons, House of, meets in St. Stephen's Chapel, 3; Whig control of, 38, 44; Walpole adds to power of, 45; orders prosecution of Wilkes, 78–9; expels Wilkes, 94; Opposition facing Pitt in, 120, 149;

Pitt seeks freedom for entry of Catholics into, 139; O'Donnell elected to, 201; new, after passing of Reform Bill, 226; Gladstone introduces Home Rule Bill in, 306, 315–16; conflict with Lords brought to head, 337; scene in, on reading of mauled Parliament Bill, 341; violence in, during debate on Home Rule, 348; uproar in, on Suez attacks, 425 – see also Lords, House of; Parliament

Communists, Churchill wants expedition against, 361–2; 'Zinovieff letter' and, 377

Compton, Sir Spencer (later Lord Wilmington), 61–2

Conscription (1916), 353; (1939), 404; end of, 427

Conservative Party, Tory Party becomes known as, 226; minority Government of, under Peel, 238, 240; in power (1841), 245–6; Derby joins, 255; opposes Russell's Reform Bill, 267; Disraeli leads, 280; divided on war with Russia, 284; make pact with Parnell, 303; and Home Rule, 303–4; Whig families drift into, 305; Liberal Unionists work with, 322; on Tariff Reform, 327, 370; House of Lords supports, 332; ideas of, on reform of Lords, 340; splits on Lords reform, 341; opposes Home Rule Bill, 348; supports conscription, 353; in wartime Coalition, 353–5, 361, 363–4; restive under Lloyd George, 363–4; loyalty to Lloyd George in, 363–4, 365; returned in 1922, 366; Baldwin loses popularity with, 382; and Churchill, 403; loses election in 1945, 412; propaganda by, during Labour Government, 414, 416–17; returned to power (1951), 418; loses by-elections, 427; wins three elections running, 428 – see also Tory Party

Conspiracy to Murder Bill, 263

Constantinople, Russian advance on, 284; British fleet ordered to, 287; 310

Co-operative movement and Labour Party, 372

Copenhagen, bombardment of, 188

Corbet (regicide), 20

Corn Amendment Bill, 192

Corn Law (1815), 181, 192; demonstrations against and repeal of, 249–50, 255; Free Trade and repeal of, 392

Cornwallis, Marquess, 111, 141

Corry, Montagu (later Lord Rowton), 282

Corunna, Battle of, 161

Corsica, 95

Coupon election (1918), 360–1

Courts of Law, Westminster, 3–4

Couse, Kenton, 84

Cowper, 5th Earl, widow of, 260

Cowper, 7th Earl, 296

Cowper, Spencer, 241

Cowper, Hon. William Francis (later Cowper-Temple, Baron Mount-Temple), 241–3; lines of religious instruction, 331

Cranborne, Lord - see Salisbury, 3rd Marquess of

Crawford and Balcarres, Earl of, 428

Credit squeeze, 422

Creevey, Thomas, on Pitt, 144, 150; on retention of Tories by Regent, 168–9; Grey writes to, on Wellington, 196; Sefton writes to, 210; on Wellington, 212; Treasurer of Ordnance, 215–16; on Grey's Reform Bill, 216–20, 223, 225; further quotations from, 145, 229–31

Crewe, 1st Marquess of, 340, 346, 351

Crimean War, 256–7, 261

Cripps, Sir Stafford, 415

Croker, John Wilson, on Canning-Castlereagh duel, 161; on 'Prosperity Robinson', 181; on Peel's Ministry, 239; Peel's letter to, 240–1; mentioned, 167, 203

Cromwell, Oliver, Downing and, 11–13; death of, 14–15; lives on site of No. 10, 24–5; imprisons Buckingham, 31; Parliamentary reform of, 38; mentioned, 26, 137

Cromwell, Richard, 15

Crosby, Brass, Lord Mayor of London, 98–9

Cumberland, Duke of, visits No. 10, 177; and Catholic Emancipation, 202–3; and Reform Bill, 223

Currency Act, 75

Curzon, 1st Marquess, visits No. 10, 346; in wartime Coalition, 353; in War Cabinet, 354; Foreign Minister, 366; disappointed of Premiership, 368; Lord President of Council, 379; on speech of Baldwin, 379

Cyprus, Britain acquires, 288–9; Gladstone wants to give, to Greece, 292; struggle for independence in, 423; granted independence, 427

Czechoslovakia, 402–3

Dacre, Lady (Mrs. Brand), 260

Daily Herald, 372

Daily Mail, printers of, trigger General Strike, 381

Daily Worker, 382

Daladier, M., 402

Danish fleet, capture of, 188

Dardanelles, Disraeli sends troops to, 283; British fleet proceeds through, 287; expedition to (1915), 353

Dashwood, Sir Francis (Lord Le Despencer), 68–71, 78, 80, 174

D'Auverquerque, Mr. – see Overkirk, Lord

De Valera, Eamon, 362–3

De Witt, Jan, 19–20

Declaration of Independence, 109–10

Deputy Prime Minister, 420

Derby, Reform Bill riots in, 222

Derby, 13th Earl of (Edward Stanley), 219, 255; Chief Secretary for Ireland, 229–30; refuses to serve with Wellington, 238–9, 255; refuses to serve under Peel, 249;

Ministries of, 255–6, 263, 266, 268–9; on country's need for Palmerston, 260; on Russell's foreign policy, 266–7; supports Reform, 271–2

Derby, 14th Earl of (Lord Stanley), 267; Foreign Secretary, 268, 270, 280; against war with Russia, 284; resigns, 287

Derwentwater, Earl of, 42

Devonshire, 4th Duke of, 65, 80–1, 160

Devonshire, 6th Duke of, 193

Devonshire, 7th Duke of (Lord Hartington), opposed to Gladstone's policy on Turkey, 284; offered Government, 289, 307; presses for action in Sudan, 294–5; and murder of Cavendish, 297–8; threatens to resign, 298–9; at inter-party negotiations, 299; opposed to Home Rule, 304, 306, 316; Lord President of Council under Salisbury, 322; mentioned, 291

Devonshire, Georgina, Duchess of, 215, 228

Devonshire House, 186

Dilke, Sir Charles, 299, 305

Dino, Duchess de, 217–18

Disraeli, Benjamin – see Beaconsfield, Earl of

Divan Club, 69

'Doctor's Mandate', 390

Dominions, opposed to King's morganatic marriage, 395

Dorchester, 1st Baron, 95

Douglas, Lady Frances (later Lady Milton), 275

Dover Volunteer Corps, 134, 147

Dowdeswell, William, 81–2, 84, 86, 102

Downing, Charles, 34–5

Downing, Emmanuel, 7–9, 11, 27, 35

Downing, Sir George, 7–17; education of, 9; early career of, 10; works for Cromwell, 11–14; marriage of, 12; approaches Charles II, 15–17, 18–19; knighted, 17; acquires site of Downing Street, 18, 21, 26; captures regicides, 19–21; baronetcy for, 21; builds Downing Street, 26, 28–9, 31, 34, 47; wealth of, 27; family of, 34–5; portrait of, 416

Downing, Sir George, 2nd Bt., 34

Downing, Sir George, 3rd Bt., 35

Downing, James, 8

Downing, Lucy (née Winthrop), 7–9, 11, 27, 35

Downing College, Cambridge, 35

Downing Square, 34

Downing Street, site and environs of, 1–6, 25; Downing acquires site, 18, 21, 26; building of, 26, 28–9, 31, 34; in 1720, 34; in 1735, 48; Boswell in, 70–1; rioting in, 99, 110–11; Colonial Office in, 198–9; Foreign Office in, 260–1; macadamized, 261; Treasury in, 269; motorcar brought to, 326; Suffragettes in, 333–4; crowds in, at outbreak of war, 350; crowds in, on Armistice Day, 1918, 358; crowds in, after Munich agreement, 402

No. 10, houses on site of, 23–9; early residents of houses later forming, 30–5; combined into one house, 33–4, 46; Walpole's alterations to, 46–8, 54; garden of, 46–7, 345, 404; Cabinet Room in, 47, 117–18, 261, 263, 430; foundations of, 47, 429–31; Walpole in, 49–60; Horace Walpole on, 59–60, 62; Chancellors of Exchequer in, 62, 64–5, 68–71, 81, 83, 86–7, 89, 173; furnishing of, 62–3, 225, 285–6, 290, 314, 372–3, 385–6, 413, 422, 432; in use as Prime Minister's residence, 72–3, 286, 315, 421; restricted living space in, 81, 165–6, 345, 369; repairs and reconstruction of (1766), 82–3, 117; attacked by rioters, 99, 110–11; visitors to, in Lord North's day, 100–2; Pitt in, 113–14, 117–18, 142, 146, 147–9, 152–4; Portland in, 116, 159–60; repairs and alterations to (1783), 116–18; alteration to Horse Guards front, 118; cost of

Downing Street – *cont.*

repairs and alterations to, 118, 157, 183, 225, 285–7, 315, 400, 429; Addington in, 142, 146; Lady Hester Stanhope in, 147–9; dinner in honour of Queen's birthday at, 154; repairs to (1806), 157; Grenville in, 157, 159; Percevals in, 160, 162, 165–6, 170, 173; Regent dined by Perceval at, 168; Vansittart in, 173–4; visitors to Vansittart in, 177–8; Robinson (Goderich) in, 181–3, 194; Soane's alterations to, 182–3, 423; dining-room of, 182, 358–9, 386, 415, 423, 430; breakfast-room of, 183, 356, 386, 423, 430; Canning in, 190–3; Wellington in, 198–9, 202–3, 207; Bathurst in, 207–8; Grey in, 216, 225, 228; visitors to Grey in, 217–20; repairs to (1832), 225; drawing-rooms of, 225, 284–5, 377, 386–7, 400, 422–3, 430; unoccupied during Melbourne's Ministry, 234; Fremantle in, 239; Prime Minister's secretaries lodged in, 241, 243–4, 246–8, 250, 251–3, 255; used only for offices, 255–7, 258–9, 263, 272–3, 280; larger windows in Cabinet Room, 261; Palmerston works in, 261, 265; stables of, 263; shacks in courtyard of, 263, 431; Disraeli moves into, 284–7; cost of furniture for Disraeli and Gladstone, 286, 290; decorations and repairs to (1877–8), 285–7; Gladstone in, 290, 302, 314–15; Herbert Gladstone in, 290–1; secret negotiations between Parties in (1884), 299; Northcote in, 302, 308; question of Home Rule discussed at, 303–4, 306; Iddesleigh collapses in, 308; W. H. Smith in, 309, 311; Balfour in, 312, 314, 322, 373; alterations to (1892), 314–15; Gladstone announces resignation to Cabinet in, 317–18; Rosebery in, 320, 322; Campbell-Bannerman in, 328–9,

333–4, 419; Ponsonby moves into, 333; suffragettes in, 334; Edward VII in, 334; Asquiths in, 335–6, 338–9, 343–6, 354; lift in, 339, 431; Mrs. Asquith on, 343–5, 373; hall porter in, 344; room above front door, 345, 358, 374, 384, 386; bathrooms of, 345, 375, 431; visitors of Asquiths in, 346, 404; huts in garden of, 352, 355, 363; Lloyd Georges in, 354–9, 363–4, 373; President Wilson visits, 355, 361; dogs buried in garden of, 356, 416; weddings from, 356–7, 421; Welsh housekeeper in, 357, 359; pictures and portraits in, 358–9, 373, 386, 415–16, 422, 432; talks with De Valera in, 363; tape machine installed in, 365; Bonar Law in, 366; Mussolini dines at, 366; Baldwin in, 368–70, 378, 383–4, 464; office-keeper's flat in, 369, 374; attic bedrooms of, 369, 375, 399; Ishbel MacDonald shown over, 370–1; MacDonalds in, 371–5, 377, 378, 385–7, 397, 419; Library at, 373–4; floors giving way in, 377, 400, 403; 'a colony of bed-sitting rooms', 386; Gandhi at, 393; living in, during national crises, 396; Chamberlain in, 399–401, 403–4, 407; alterations to (1937), 399–400; staircases of, 399, 428; second floor becomes residential section, 399, 407; kitchen in, 400, 409–10, 420, 430; new decorations and furnishing of (1937), 400–1; Kings and Queens entertained at, 404, 421; Churchills in, 407–12, 419–21; garden-room in, 409; war damage to, 409–11, 413; air-raid shelter at, 409, 430; wartime visitors to, 411–12; Attlees in, 413–16; self-contained flat in, 413–14, 416, 419; Attlee's love for, 416; Public Relations Office in, 416; first floor bedroom used, 419; Edens in, 421–3, 426; credit squeeze prevents period furniture for, 422; altered lighting to Cabinet Room, 422; visitors to Edens in, 423; decisions on Suez crisis in, 424–6; Macmillans in, 427–8; found to be unsafe, 428; reconstruction of (1960–), 428, 429–33; sanitation and water supply of, 430–1; enlargement of, 430–1; heating of, 432; objects found during excavations under, 432

No. 11, Disraeli works in, 269, 272; Gladstone occupies, 269, 290; furnishing of, 285; Asquith in, 330; Lloyd Georges in, 338–9, 356; communications between No. 10 and, 338–9, 356; Bonar Law in, 354; Baldwin in, 366; Cabinet meeting in, 381; Snowden in, 385; Chamberlain in, 400; reconstruction of, 429, 431

No. 12, 32; Gladstone in, 291; reconstruction of, 429, 431

Drummond, Edward, 246–8

Drummond, Mrs. ('The General'), 334

Dublin, university for, 278; Phoenix Park murders in, 297; troops moved to Ulster from, 348; Easter Rising in, 353

Dudley, 4th Viscount, 200

Duff Cooper, Alfred, 401, 403

Dulles, Foster, 423–4

Dundas, Henry – see Viscount Melville

Dunkirk, 407

Durham, Lady, 218

Durham, Lord, 218n; son of, 218, 225; difficulties with, in Parliament, 229, 252; Governor-General of Canada, 251–2; mentioned, 222

East India Company, question of Government taking over lands of, 101; nearly bankrupt, 102; and Boston Tea Party, 104; payment by, to Hastings, 123; replaced by Government department, 229; mentioned, 65

Easter Rising, Dublin, 353

Eden, Sir Anthony (later Earl of Avon), Parliamentary Under-Secretary to Foreign Office, 391; Foreign Secretary, 401–2, 420; resignation of, 402; Deputy Prime Minister, 420; Ministry of, 421, 423–6; alters lighting of Cabinet room, 422; and Suez crisis, 423–6; resignation of, 426

Eden, Hon. Eleanor (later Countess of Buckinghamshire), 136, 150

Eden, Emily, 236

Eden, Hon. Isabelle (later Mrs. Vansittart), 173

Eden, Lady (née Clarissa Churchill), 407, 421

Eden, Nicholas, 422

Eden, William, 168

Edinburgh, Prince Philip, Duke of, 258n, 416, 420–1, 428

Education Bill, Birrell's, 331–2

Edward VII, King (Prince of Wales), Gladstone's plans regarding, 274, 277; profligacy of, 276; visits India, 282; sends for Campbell-Bannerman, 327; angry at Lloyd George's speech, 332; in Biarritz at change of government, 336; concerned at battle between Houses, 336; on creation of new peers, 338; death of, 338; mentioned, 329, 345

Edward VIII, King – see Windsor, Duke of

Egmont, Lord, 52

Egypt, Napoleon bottled up in, 134; given back to Turkey, 143; Anglo-French protectorate over, 289, 293; British occupation of, 293–4; Sudan rises against, 294; settlement of (1930), 388; takes over Canal, 423–4; Israel attacks, 425–6

Eisenhower, General Dwight, visits No. 10, 411, 423, 428; and Suez crisis, 425

Elba, France seizes, 144; Napoleon in, 175, 254; escape from, 176–7

Eldon, 1st Earl of, Lord Chancellor, 174, 184; resigns, 190; opposes Wellington, 196
Elibank, Master of, allegations against, 347
Eliot, Edward, 125n, 136
Eliot, Harriet (née Pitt), 125n, 136, 148
Eliot, Lord, 269
Elizabeth I, Queen, 6, 26, 137; 'prime' Minister of, 58, 301
Elizabeth II, Queen, 258n; entertained at No. 10, 416, 421; accession of, 420-1; sends for Macmillan, 426
Elizabeth, Queen of George VI (Duchess of York), 377, 404
Elizabeth, Princess (daughter of James I), 24, 33
Ellenborough, Earl of, 200
Ellis, Charles, 161
Emergency Powers Bill, 405
Empire Parliamentary Association, 401
Entente with France, 350
Erith, Raymond, 429-31
Europe, Pitt's balancing of power in, 127
Evans, Lady Olwen Carey (née Lloyd George), 356-7
Evans, Stanley, 425
Evans, Dr. Thomas Carey, 356-7
Evelyn, John, 20-1
Everard, Everard, 26
Expeditionary Force, Haldane's provision for, 332

Factory Acts, 227-8, 235
Fairfax, Lord, 10-11, 31
Falkland Islands, 96
Falmouth, Lord, 204-5
Farquhar, Caroline (later Mrs. Grey), 275
Fashoda, 324
Fawkes, Guy, 24
Fenians, 272-3, 282
Feisal, King of Iraq, 423
Finland, Stalin's war on, 406
Fitzgerald, Sir Maurice, 201
Fitzgerald, Lord William Vesey, 200

Fitzherbert, Mrs., 122, 165, 215
Fitzpatrick, Colonel, 187
Fitzroy, Lady Charlotte (later Countess of Lichfield), 28-9, 31-2, 244
Fitzroy, H., 261
Florida, 144
Foreign Office building, 260-1
Forster, W. E., 297
Fort George, 76
Fourth Party, 301, 309, 312
Fox, Charles James, North wins over, 96; gaming by, 100-1; attacks North over American policy, 105, 111; attacks Germain, 108; in Rockingham's Government, 113-14; on Pitt, 115, 119, 144, 155; in coalition with North, 115-16, 120; Secretary of State, 116; votes against Reform, 119; and attack on Pitt, 121; and Prince of Wales, 121-3; supports French Revolution, 130-1, 133; on Addington Ministry, 142; joins with Grenville, 145; George III excludes from Government, 146, 149, 151; in Ministry of all the Talents, 156-8; death of, 159, 193; Russell and, 254; mentioned, 124, 149, 164-5, 186, 214
France, in alliance with Spain, 56; loses American colonies, 74; seizes Corsica, 95; joins America against Britain, 108-10, 115; peace negotiations with, 115-16; designs of, on Holland and Belgium, 127; Revolutionary war in, 131-4; reign of terror in, 132; Paine in, 133; threatens invasion of England, 134, 144, 147, 149, 152; loses remaining colonies, 134; Pitt ready to negotiate with, 136-7; Addington makes peace with, 143-4; occupies Spain and Portugal, 161; British invasion of, 175; fresh revolution in, 209-11; threat to India from, 322; African encroachments of, 322, 324; British treaty with, 350; Germany declares war on (1914), 350; evacuates

Ruhr, 376; Britain needing credits from, 389; at war with Germany (1939), 405; fall of, 407; and Suez crisis, 424–6. *See* French Revolution

Francis, Sir Philip, 93, 122

Franciscans, Brotherhood of, 69, 174–5

Frederick, Prince of Wales, 56, 66–7, 69, 89

Frederick the Great, King of Prussia, 64–5, 68

Frederick William, King of Prussia, 127, 131

Free Trade, Peel turns to, 248–9, 254; Russell works for, 254; Aberdeen's Ministry in favour of, 256; Liberal adherence to, 327; Asquith supports, 336; Liberals resign from National Government on loss of, 392

Fremantle, Admiral Sir Charles, 239–40

Fremantle, Sir Thomas (later Lord Cottesloe), 239

French Revolution, 129; side effects of, 121; sympathy for, in England, 130–1; wars provoked by, 131–4

Fuldyer, Sir Samuel, 260

Gage, General, 104

Gaitskell, Hugh, 421, 424–5

Gandhi, Mahatma, 393

Garbo, Greta, 423

Gaulle, General de, 408

General Strike, 380–2

Gentleman's Magazine, Parliamentary reports in, 97–8

George I, King, 33, 38, 41–3

George II, King, Parliamentary influence of, 38; succeeds father, 43–4; leaves country in care of Whigs, 45; offers No. 10 to Walpole, 46; and Walpole, 57, 60; death of, 66; on North, 89; mentioned, 33, 61, 64–5, 421

George III, King, control of Parliament by, 38, 88–9, 95, 119; accession of, 66–8; his dislike of Grenville, 79–80; madness of, 80, 123–4, 141, 168; appoints Rockingham, 80–1; selects own Ministers, 88–9, 114; North and, 89, 94–5, 106–7, 109–12; on expulsion of Wilkes, 93; his attitude to American colonies, 103–4; son's quarrel with, 122; creates new peers, 124; and French Revolution, 131–2; anti-Catholic feeling of, 139, 141, 159; chooses successor to Pitt, 140; and return of Pitt, 145–6; refuses to have Fox in Government, 146, 149, 151–2; forms Coalition, 156; and Lord Grenville, 157, 159; death of, 179; creates son Duke of Clarence, 217; scandalous behaviour of sons of, 276

George IV, King (Prince of Wales, Prince Regent), Fox and, 121–2; restrictions on Regency of, 123–4, 141; Perceval incurs enmity of, 165; and investigation of Duke of York's conduct, 167; becomes Regent, 168; retains Perceval, 168–9; stoned by crowd, 178; Coronation of, 179; on Goderich, 181; appoints Canning, 184–5, 189–91; divorce proceedings of, 188; Canning visits, 193; appoints Goderich, 194–5; and Wellington, 195–6, 202–3, 207; and Catholic Emancipation, 202–3, 206; declining health of, 207; death of, 209; his dislike of Grey, 215; and Lady Melbourne, 233; his dislike of Palmerston, 259; scandalous behaviour of, 276

George V, King, 338; and conflict between Houses, 339–42; agrees to make new peers, 340–1; Coronation of, 341; summons Bonar Law, 365; and Baldwin, 368, 370; and Labour Prime Minister, 371, 375–6, 389; and National Government, 390; death of, 394; entertained at No. 10, 404

George VI, King (Duke of York), wedding of, 368; at concert at No. 10, 377; accession of, 396–7; entertained at No. 10, 404; wartime dinners at No. 10, 409; death of, 420; mentioned, 387

George, Lloyd – see Lloyd George

Germain, Lord George (formerly Sackville), 105, 108, 111

Germany, Britain near war with, over Jameson Raid, 323; strengthening Navy to meet threat from, 337; threat of war with, 348–50; and outbreak of First World War, 350–1; invades Belgium, 350; indemnity from, 360; Polish Corridor across, 361; joins League, 383; economic crisis in, 388; threat from Nazis, 393–4; leaves League, 394; Britain again at war with, 404–5; invades Norway, Holland and Belgium, 406

Ghana, 427

Gibbon, Edward, on Lord North, 90

Gladstone, Catherine (née Glynne), 275, 277, 297, 314; influence of, over husband, 317

Gladstone, Florence, 373

Gladstone, Herbert, 292, 304; in No. 10, 290–1; Home Secretary, 330

Gladstone, Mary, 299, 306

Gladstone, Thomas, 226

Gladstone, William Ewart, elected for rotten borough, 226; maiden speech of, 227; supports Coercion Act, 229; in Peel's Ministry, 239; Chancellor of Exchequer, 256, 290–3; criticizes Palmerston, 262; sympathizes with South, in American Civil War, 264; Leader of Commons, 267; prepares and upholds Reform Bill, 267–8; oratory of, 268; leader of Liberals, 270; in rivalry with Disraeli, 270; Irish policy of, 272–4, 296–7, 299; first Ministry of, 272–8; his relations with Queen, 273–7, 280, 291, 298–300, 315; obscurity of style

and diction of, 274, 291; romances of, 275; letter of sympathy of, to Disraeli, 279; anti-Turkish speeches of, 283–4, 288; quarrels with Disraeli over furniture for No. 11, 285; Midlothian campaign of, 288–9; second Ministry of, 289, 290–300; foreign policy of, 292–6, 324–5; health of, 293–4; and Mahdi's rising, 294–5; vote of censure on, 295; and murder of Cavendish, 297–8; 'whistle-stop' speeches of, 299; resigns, 300, 317–18; and Northcote, 302; determines on Home Rule, 303–7; third Ministry of, 304–7; Queen Victoria on, 304, 314–15; fourth Ministry, 314–18; on Queen, 315; introduces Home Rule Bill, 306, 315–16; Churchill's praise for, 316; wants 'Peers versus People' election, 316; dominated by family, 317; his farewell to Victoria, 317–18; and Rosebery, 319; Balfour visits on bicycle, 323; mentioned, 328

Glasgow, demonstrations in, on defeat of Reform Bill, 271

Glasgow Orpheus Choir, 377

Glynne, Catherine – see Gladstone, Catherine

Goderich, Frederick Robinson, Viscount (later Earl of Ripon), 149n, 180–1; Chancellor of Exchequer, 179, 181–4; loses daughter, 183; unable to deal in Lords with Grey and Wellington, 191–2, 194; Ministry of, 194–5, 234; resigns from Grey's Ministry, 231; offers Exchequer to Palmerston, 259; mentioned, 190, 246, 305, 331

Goderich, Viscountess (née Lady Sarah Hobart), 180, 183–4

Godley, Arthur (later Lord Kilbracken), 292, 320

Godolphin, Lord, 39–40

Gold Coast, 313

Gold standard, return to, 379; Britain goes off, 390

Gordon, General Charles George, 294-5
Gordon, Lord George, 110
Goring House, 5
Government of India Bill, 393
Grafton, Duke of, 83; and Townshend, 85-6; Ministry of, 91-4; Junius attacks, 92-3; and Wilkes, 93-4
Graham, Sir James, 231, 238
Grant, Charles, 200
Grantham, Thomas Robinson, 1st Baron, 57, 180
Grantham, 2nd Baron, 180
Grantham, Earl of, 34, 51
Granville, 1st Earl, 273
Granville, 2nd Earl, 273, 277; opposed to Gladstone's Turkish policy, 284; offered Government, 289; announces submission of Turkey, 292; presses for action in Sudan, 294; and Home Rule, 303, 305
Gray, Thomas, 53
Greece, liberation of, 189; Turkey's concessions to, 292; army of, in Turkey (1922), 364; Britain prepared to fight for independence of, 404
Greenwood, Arthur, 406
Grenville, George, 72-4; angers American colonists, 73-6; prosecutes Wilkes, 76-9; relations with George III, 79-80, 157; Pitt ridicules, 80, 90; defends taxation of colonies, 82-3; cuts down land tax, 86; North's defence against, 91
Grenville, Lady (née Anne Pitt), 157-9
Grenville, Lord, Foreign Secretary, 137; opposed to Addington, 141-2; on terms of Peace of Amiens, 143; urges Pitt to unite against Addington, 145; refuses to join Pitt's Ministry, 149, 151; and death of Pitt, 154; Ministry of, 156-9, 214; Canning and, 186-7; Melbourne and, 234
Grenville, William, 74

Greville, Charles, 209; on Bathurst, 208; on 1833 Parliament, 226, 230; on Wellington taking over for Peel, 238; on opposition to Peel, 240; on William IV, 241; on assassination of Drummond, 247; on Queen's dislike of Palmerston, 260
Grey, General the Hon. Charles, 252-3, 274-6
Grey, Charles Samuel, 250, 253
Grey, Countess (née Elizabeth Ponsonby), 216, 218, 220; Princess Lieven on, 225
Grey, 1st Earl, 214
Grey, 2nd Earl, 214-16; attacks Canning, 190-2; on Wellington's Ministry, 196; Wellington and, 209; and Parliamentary Reform, 211, 215-17, 219-26; Ministry of, 214-16, 217-31, 255; decides on dissolution of Parliament, 219-20; resigns, 223; King gives in to, 224; measures passed during Ministry of, 226-8; relations of, with Princess Lieven, 228; and Irish question, 228-9; unable to control Cabinet and resigns, 230-1; difficulties with son-in-law of, 252; sons of, 252-3, 275; mentioned, 255, 259
Grey, 3rd Earl (Lord Howick), 227, 252
Grey, Sir Edward (later Viscount Grey of Fallodon), 330, 349-51, 353
Grey, Ralph William, 250, 251-2
Grosvenor, Lord, 268
Guilford, Earl of, 89-90, 95
Gunn, Sir James, 428
Gunpowder Plot, 24, 40
Gurney, Harriet, 243

Haig, Field-Marshal Earl, 355
Haldane, Viscount, 332, 338, 371
Halifax, 2nd Earl of, 54, 95, 99
Halifax, Earl of (Lord Irwin), 393, 402, 406-7
Halsbury, Earl of, 341-2, 353

Hambledon, Viscountess (Mrs. W. H. Smith), 310-11
Hamilton, Lord George, 309
Hampden, John, 26
Hampden, Richard, 26
Hampden House, 23, 26, 28-9
Hanover, defence of, 64-5, 68
Hansard, 'Journals of the House of Commons' and 'Parliamentary Debates' of, 100
Harcourt, Sir William, 317, 320-2, 328, 368
Hardie, Keir, 314
Hardinge, General Sir Henry, 200, 204-5, 224
Hardwicke, 1st Earl of, 55
Harewood, 6th Earl of, 404
Harley, Robert (later Earl of Oxford and Mortimer), 39-40, 42
Harriman, Averell, 408
Harrington, Lord, 55
Harrowby, 1st Earl of, 152, 154
Hartington, Lord – see Devonshire, 7th Duke of
Harvard College, 9
Haselrig, Sir Arthur, 10-11
Hastings, Warren, Governor-General of India, 102; impeachment of, 122-3, 164
Hawkesbury, Lord – see Liverpool, 2nd Earl of
Health insurance scheme, 337
Heligoland, 313
Hell Fire Club, 69-70, 77, 174
Henderson, Arthur, in Cabinet, 353; in War Cabinet, 354; defeated, 361; Home Secretary, 371; Foreign Secretary, 385; American relations excluded from control of, 387; and terms of settlement in Egypt, 388; leader of Opposition to National Government, 390
Henry VIII, King, 2-6
Herbert, Sidney, 239
Herries, John, 178, 182; Chancellor of Exchequer, 195, 259
Hervey, Lord, 57; on Horatio Walpole, 53; on Lord Wilmington, 62

Hill, Mrs. Kathleen, 407-8, 411
Hill, Rowland, penny post of, 253
Hinsley, Cardinal, 403
Hitler, Adolph, menace of, 393; and Mussolini, 401; Chamberlain's efforts to appease, 402-3; seizes Czechoslovakia, 404; launches out on war, 404-5
Hoare, Sir Samuel, 401
Hobart, Sir John, 26
Hobhouse, Sir John (later Lord Broughton), 236
Holbein Gate, 5
Holland, Downing in, 12-17, 19-20, 27; joins America in war against Britain, 109, 115; French designs on, 127; French occupation of, 132, 134, 143; Belgium separates from, 210; German invasion of, 406
Holland, 1st Baron, 96
Holland, 3rd Baron, 211
Home Rule, Parnell demands, 296; Gladstone and, 303-7; Carnarvon suggests, 303; Bills introduced into Commons, 306-7, 315-16, 348; thrown out by Lords, 316; Rosebery upholds, 320; becomes law under Asquith, 348, 353; civil war threatening over, 348
Hopkins, Harry, 408
Hicks-Beach, Sir Michael, 304
Hood, Admiral, 134
Hore-Belisha, Leslie, 401, 405
Horse Guards, 4
Houghton, 33 45-6 400, 422
House, Colonel, 358
Household Suffrage, 271-2, 298
Howard, Tom, 14-16
Howard, Sir William, 12
Howe, Admiral Lord, 126-7, 134
Howick, Lord (later 3rd Earl Grey), 227, 252
Hume, Dr., on Wellington's duel, 204
Hume, Joseph, 227
'Hungry Forties', 249, 254
Huskisson, William, works on Robinson's Budgets, 182; in Wellington's

Ministry, 199–200; resigns, 200, 206; death of, 212; and Free Trade, 249; mentioned, 193, 195, 209

Hussein, King, of Jordan, 423

Iddesleigh, Stafford Northcote, 1st Earl of, 299, 301–2, 308, 310

Imperial Conference (1911), 346

Imperial War Cabinet, 361

Income tax, introduction of, 134–5; extension to Ireland, 273; Gladstone promises abolition of, 278; raising of, 291, 337; doubled in First World War, 352; reduction of (1958), 427

India, British gains in, from Seven Years War, 65, 68; East India Company and, 101–2; Government department takes over, 229; Palmerston repels threat to, 262; Queen becomes Empress of, 282; Russia strikes towards, 288, 295–6; and Greco-Turkish War, 364; Dominion status for, 392–3; granted independence, 415; and Suez crisis, 425

Indian Mutiny, 262

Indo-China, French, 322

Industrial Revolution, 121, 178

Ireland, problem of, 137–8, 268, 282; Pitt's attempt to solve, 138–9; united to England, 138–9; Catholic Emancipation and, 201, 228; trouble in, on paying of tithes, 228–9, 245; famine in, 229, 254; quarrels in Cabinet over, 230; potato crop fails in, 249; Fenian outrages in, 272, 282; abolition of Established Church in, 272–3; Gladstone's attempts to solve problem of, 272–4, 296–7; extension of income tax to, 273; question of Queen's home in, 274; terrorist outrages in, against landlords, 296–7; local self-government for, 299; Salisbury's Ministry discusses question of, 302–4; Balfour Chief Secretary for, 313;

civil war threatening in, 348–9; 1916 troubles in, 353; granted Home Rule, 353; independence for, 362–3, 367 – see also Home Rule; Ulster

Irish Coercion Bills and Acts, 229–30, 250, 299, 304

Irish Crimes Bill and Act, 296, 299

Irish Free State, 362–3, 367

Irish Land Act (1870), 277

Irish Land Bill (1881–2), 296–7

Irish Nationalist Party, 296, 313, 338, 348, 362

Irish Party, in 1833, 226; demands repeal of Act of Union, 229; supports Russell, 240; supports Melbourne, 245; supports Gladstone, 270; helps defeat Gladstone, 299–300; Conservative pact with, 303; and Home Rule, 306–7; supports Liberals, 330

Irish Republican Army, 362

Isaacs, Godfrey, 347

Isaacs, Sir Rufus (later Marquess of Reading), 347

Ismay, Lord, 408

Israel, 423, 425

Italy, Napoleon III invades, 264; ready to co-operate with Gladstone, 292; attacks Abyssinia, 401

James I, King, 6, 26, 137

James II, King (Duke of York), 13, 32, 37

Jameson, Dr., 323

Japan, captures Port Arthur, 324; agreement with, on naval construction, 387; leaves League of Nations, 394

Jemappes, Battle of, 132

Jenkins, Captain, 56

Jenner, Sir William, 274, 276

Jersey, Lady, 260

Jervis (later Earl of St. Vincent), Admiral, 134

Jews' Relief Bill, 206, 270

'Jingoism', 284

Johannesburg, 326

Johnson, Samuel, 54; Parliamentary reporting of, 98, 100; Wilkes's 'Letter' to, 99
Jones, Inigo, 6
Jordan, Mrs. Dorothy, 217
Joseph II, Emperor of Austria, 127
Joseph Bonaparte, King of Spain, 175, 188
Juliana, Queen of Holland, 412
Junius, Letters of, 93, 99
Junot, General, 161

Kalifa, the, 324
Kandahar, 292
Kendal, Duchess of, 42
Kennedy, Joseph, U.S. Ambassador, 403
Kenny, Annie, 333
Kent, William, work of, in construction of No. 10, 33, 37n, 46–7, 182; work of, at Houghton, 45–6, 422
Kenya, 313
Keppel, Lieut.-Colonel George Thomas (later Earl of Albemarle), 250, 253, 255
Khaki Election, 326
Khartoum, fall of, 294–5
Kilbracken, Arthur Godley, Lord, 292
Kimberley, 325–6
King, Mackenzie, 387
King Street, 5, 21, 25
Kitchener, Lord, 324, 326, 346, 352–3
Knevett (Knyvet), Sir Thomas, 21, 23–4, 26
Korean War, 418
Kruger, President, 323, 325–6
Krushchev, N., 423

Labouchere, Henry, 320
Labour Party, 372; first Member, 314; in 1905 Parliament, 330; supports 'People's Budget', 338; supports national insurance scheme, 346; in wartime Coalition Government, 353–5; resigns from Coalition, 360; becomes Opposition, 366, 379; increase in Commons of,

370; first Government of, 370–2, 375–7; conflict in, 376; depends on Liberal support, 376, 385; defeated in 1924, 377; second Government of, 383, 387–90, 393; bitterness of, at MacDonald, 390; refuses to join National Government, 390, 392; gains strength, 394; opposed to morganatic marriage, 395; prepared to serve under Churchill, 403; majority for, in 1945, 412; pledges of, 414; austerity under Government of, 414, 416; disaffection in, 417; returned with minute majority (1950), 417–18
Ladysmith, 325–6
Lamb, Lady Caroline, 233–4
Lamb, Sir Matthew, 233
Lambton, Charles, 218n, 225
Land reform, 346
Land taxes, 86, 96, 337
Landemare, Mrs., 410
Lansbury, George, 388
Lansdowne, 20th Baron, 34
Lansdowne, 1st Marquess of – see Shelburne, Earl of
Lansdowne, 2nd Marquess of, 191, 211; mentioned, 256
Lansdowne, 3rd Marquess of, 211
Lansdowne, 4th Marquess of, 234–5
Lansdowne, 5th Marquess of, 296, 336, 340–2
Lauder, Harry, 357
Laval, Pierre, 401
Law, Andrew Bonar, and Home Rule, 348; in Coalition Government, 353, 355; Chancellor of Exchequer, 354; runs Parliament for Lloyd George, 355, 360, 367; successor to, 363; urges end of Coalition, 364; Ministry of, 365–8, 398; death of, 368; pledge of, on tariff reform, 369; mentioned, 399
Law, Kitty, 356, 366
Law, Mary, 366
Law, Richard (later Lord Coleraine), 366
Le Brun, President, of France, 403

Leaf, Marjorie, 403
League of Nations, 361, 383, 393-4
Lecky, William, on Dashwood's Budget, 70
Lee of Fareham, Lord (Sir Arthur Lee), 364, 365
Leeds, demonstrations in, on defeat of Reform Bill, 271
Leeds, Duke of, 128
Legg, Henry–seeBilson-Legge, Henry
Leopold, Emperor of Austria, 131
Leopold I, King of the Belgians, 229-30, 244, 248, 267
Leveson-Gower, Granville (later 1st Earl Granville), 273
Lexington, Battle of, 104-5
Liberal Party, Whigs become, 263, 270n; divided on Russell's Reform Bill, 267; divided on war against Russia, 284; opposition to Gladstone's Irish policy in, 296-7, 299; splits on Home Rule, 304-7; returned to power (1905), 327, 330; loses large majority, 338; and reform of Lords, 338-42; in Coalition, 353-5, 361; opposed to conscription, 353; division in, on resignation of Asquith, 354, 366; reunite for Free Trade, 370; and Co-operative movement, 372; Labour dependent on support of, 376, 385; no longer effective force, 377, 379; improve position, 383; and National Government, 392; prepared to serve under Churchill, 403
Liberal Unionists, 307, 314, 322
Licensing Bill, 336
Lichfield, Earl and Countess of, 28-9, 31-2, 244
Lichfield, Lord, Postmaster-General, 253
Lieven, Princess, 213, 223, 225, 228, 231
Life Peerages Act, 428
Lincoln, Abraham, 264
Lincoln, Earl and Countess of, 63
Littleton, Edward, 230

Liverpool, 1st Earl of, 139, 160, 172-3
Liverpool, 2nd Earl of (Lord Hawkesbury), 172-3; refuses Premiership, 156, 173; at War Office, 162; Ministry of, 172-4, 177-9, 183-4, 198, 227; death of, 184; mentioned, 141, 149n, 186, 190, 193, 208
Lloyd, Selwyn, 425, 427
Lloyd George, David (later Earl Lloyd George), in Campbell-Bannerman's Ministry, 330-1; and House of Lords, 331, 340; 'People's Budget' of, 337, 346; and Marconi scandal, 347; opposes further strengthening of Navy, 349; War Memories of, 349; opposes war, 349; at Ministry of Munitions, 353; at War Office, 354; Prime Minister, 354-5, 358-9, 360-4; in No. 10, 354-9; divides Liberals, 354, 364, 365; scarab given to, 359, 432; at Peace Conference, 36; achieves settlement in Ireland, 362-3; end of Premiership, 363-4; grandchildren of, 363; resigns, 365; supporters of, 366; Bonar Law 367; and Neville Chamberlain, 399; mentioned, 336, 339, 389
Lloyd George, Megan (later Lady), 338-9; her memories of No. 10, 356-7
Lloyd George, Mrs. David, 356-7, 359
Locarno Treaties, 383
Lockhart, Sir William, 153
London, mob carries Walpole's effigy, 60; City of, in 1770, 96-7; rioting in, on imprisonment of Crosby and Oliver, 98-9; Gordon riots in, 110-11; supports Pitt, 120, 123; rioting in, after Napoleonic War, 178-9; rioting in, on Robinson's Corn Act, 181; violence in, on delay in Parliamentary Reform, 224, 271; strikes in, 376; evacuation of women and children from, 405
Londonderry, 138
Londonderry, 3rd Marquess of, 190

Lords, House of, in 15th and 16th centuries, 3; orders prosecution of Wilkes, 79; members of, in Pitt's Cabinet, 120, 149; creation of new peers for political purposes, 124, 222-4, 338, 340-2; and Catholic Emancipation, 203-4, 206; rejects Reform Bill, 219-25; conquered by threat to create new peers, 224; question of survival of, 298-9, 320-1; rejects Home Rule Bill, 316, 322; Rosebery's plan for reform of, 320-1; 'filling the cup' of, 321; Rosebery calls for annihilation of, 322; powers of rejection of, 330; rejects Education Bill, 331; rejects Liberal Bills, 331-2; restriction of powers of, 332-3, 338; rejects Licensing Bill, 336; rejects 1909 Finance Bill, 337; mauls Parliament Bill, 340-1; 'Diehards' of, 341-2, 353; passes Finance Bill of 1909, 346; vetoes granting of Home Rule (1916), 353; and Labour's post-war legislation, 414-15; veto of, limited to one year, 415; step towards reforming, 427-8
Loughborough, Lord, 139
Louis XIV, King of France, 41
Louis XVI, King of France, 132
Louis XVIII, King of France, 177
Louis Philippe, King of France, 219
Louisiana, 74, 144
Luttrell, Colonel, 94, 96
Lyndhurst, Lord, 203, 223
Lyons, J. A., Australian Prime Minister, 403

Macaulay, Lord, 219, 291
MacDonald, Alister, 372
MacDonald, Ishbel, shown round No. 10, 370; in No. 10, 374-5, 385; her memories of life in No. 10, 386-7, 396
MacDonald, J. Ramsay, 372; leader of Labour Party, 346, 361; visitor to No. 10, 357; pall-bearer to

Bonar Law, 368; first Ministry of, 370-2, 375-7; Foreign Secretary, 371, 375-6; his difficulties in furnishing No. 10, 372-4; King's help and advice to, 375; second Ministry of, 385, 387-90; makes international agreement on ratio of naval construction, 387; resigns, 390; leads National Government, 390-1; passes leadership to Baldwin, 394; mentioned 330n 382, 420
MacDonald, Joan, 386
MacDonald, Malcolm, 372, 386
MacDonald, Margaret (née Gladstone), 372
MacDonald, Sheila, 386
Macedonia, 287-8
McKenna, Reginald, 336
Macmillan, Harold, 426; presents books to No. 10 library, 374; Minister of Housing, 420; Prime Minister, 426-8; visits abroad, 427-8; moves to Admiralty House, 428
Macmillan, Lady Dorothy (née Cavendish), 426-7
Macmillan, Maurice, 426
Macnaghten, Daniel, 247-8
Macnaghten Rules, 248
Macpherson, Sir John, 110-11
Mafeking, 325-6
Mahdi risings, 294-5
Mahon, Lord (later Earl Stanhope), 109, 147-8
Malaya, 427
Malmesbury, 1st Earl of, 140, 142, 152, 180
Malmesbury, 2nd Earl of, 242
Malt tax, abolition of, 291
Malta, 143
Manchester, demonstrations in, over defeat of Reform Bill, 271; Fenian outrages in, 272
Manchuria, 324
Manners, Lord John, 270-1
Marconi scandal, 346-7
Marie Antoinette, Queen of France, 131-2
Markievicz, Countess, 362

Marlborough, 1st Duke of, 39–41
Marlborough, 7th Duke of, 270
Marlow, Sir John, 14
Martin, Admiral Byam, 126
Mary, Queen of George V (Princess May), 310, 404; and Abdication crisis, 396
Mary, Princess-Royal, Countess of Harewood, 404
Massachusetts, 76, 103; revision of Charter of, 104
Mazarin, Cardinal, 12
Medmenham, 69–70, 77, 174
Melbourne, 1st Viscount, 233
Melbourne, William Lamb, 2nd Viscount, 233–4; refuses office under Wellington, 209; in Grey's Ministry, 215, 219n, 222; goes to see King, 231–2; first Ministry of, 234–7; dismissed by King, 237; second Ministry of, 241, 245, 253; involved in divorce suit, 242; advises nephew, 243; keeps Prince Consort politically informed, 244; Queen's dependence on, 245–6, 321; resigns, 245; reduces duties, 249; failing health of, 250; sends Durham to Canada, 251–2; and Palmerston's indiscretion, 260; and Disraeli, 269–70; mentioned, 219
Melbourne, Viscountess, 233–4
Melville, Henry Dundas, Viscount, 123, 145n; impeachment of, 150–1
Menzies, R. G., 403, 424
Metternich, Prince, 177
Mexico, 189
Middleton, Sir Charles, 126
Midlothian Campaign, 288–9
'Ministry of all the Talents', 156–9
Minto, Lord, 141
Mollet, M., 423
Molotov, V. M., 412
Monk, General (later Duke of Albemarle), 16
Montagu, Admiral Sir Edward (later Earl of Sandwich), 17
Montagu, Lady Mary Wortley, 51
Montenegro, 283, 292

Montgomery, Field-Marshal Viscount, 412
Moore, Sir John, 161; on Nelson, 199
Morice, Sir William, 21
Morley, John (later Lord), 317, 322, 346, 350
Mornington, Earl of, 197
Morpeth, Lord, 35
Morrison, Herbert (later Lord), 385, 414–15, 417, 420
Moscow, retreat from, 175
Mosley, Sir Oswald, 388
Mote, the, 2, 4
Mount-Temple, Baron, 243
Mulgrave, Lord, 152
Munich, 402
Municipal Corporations Bill, 245
Munitions, Ministry of, 353–4
Murray, General Sir George, 200, 224
Mussolini, Benito, 366, 401–2
Mustapha Kemal, 364

Napier, General Sir Charles, 196
Napoleon I, Emperor of France (Bonaparte), 133; temporary peace with, 143; invasion preparations of, 144, 147, 149, 152; proclaimed Emperor, 149; victories of, against Third Coalition, 152, 154; places embargo on British goods, 167, 169, 188; marches to and from Moscow, 174–5; defeat and abdication of, 175; escapes from Elba, 176; places brother on Spanish throne, 188; Bathurst and, 208; at St. Helena, 208; Russell visits, 254
Napoleon III, Emperor of France, 254, 263–4
Napoleonic War, 131–3, 160; temporary end to, 133, 143–4; Third Coalition to fight, 152, 154; in Portugal and Spain, 161–2, 166, 169, 175; paying for, 166–7, 175–8
Narvik, 406
Nasser, Colonel, 423–4
Natal, 325
National Gallery, 182; pictures from, in No. 10, 373, 386, 400, 422

National Government, 388–91; election victory for, 390; under MacDonald, 391, 392–4; Conservative complexion of, 392; under Baldwin, 394–7; Chamberlain fails to form, 406

National Health Service, 415, 420; imposition of charges, 418

National Insurance, Lloyd George's scheme for, 337, 346; Labour's post-war scheme for, 415

National Labour Party, 392

National Liberal Federation, 291

National Liberal Party, 392

Nationalization, of telegraph services, 268–9; Labour's post-war legislation on, 414–15, 420

Navy, Royal, in 1770, 96; reconstruction of, by Pitt, 126–8, 132–3; victories of, in war with France, 133–4; mutinies in, 134; need to strengthen, 144, 337, 349; Gladstone opposes expansion of, 317; in Norwegian expeditions, 406; Churchill mobilizes, 349–50; new cruisers for, as cure for unemployment, 376–7

Nelson, Horatio, Admiral Lord, victories of, 134, 143, 152, 239; Wellington meets, 199; and William IV, 217

Nepal, King of, 428

New England, colonization of, 8

New Gate, 5, 21, 25–6

New York, Congress in, 76; suspension of functions of assembly, 86; William IV in (as prince), 217

Newcastle, Thomas Pelham Holles, Duke of, Parliamentary control of, 38, 44; his clashes with Walpole, 55–6; quarrels with Pelham, 63; Prime Minister, 64–5, 66–7; senility of, 81; mentioned, 54, 160, 180

Newspaper strike, 421

Nigeria, 313, 427

Nile, Battle of the, 134

Nootka Sound, ships seized in, 128

North, Lady (née Anne Speke), 90, 105

North, Lord, 89–91; in No. 10, 84, 89, 112, 113–14; Chancellor of Exchequer, 88, 91; similarity of, to King, 89; subservient attitude of, 89, 95, 105; daughter of, 90, 181; repeals American duties except tea, 91–2; and Wilkes, 94, 98–9; Ministry of, 94–5, 105; attacks on, in Commons, 96, 105, 111–12; attacked by mob, 98–9, 110–11; and Johnson, 99–100; Ranger of Bushey Park, 100; and Clive, 101–2; anti-American measures of, 104–5; decline in appearance and demeanour of, 105, 110; tries to resign, 106, 109; debts of, 106–7, 125n; resigns, 111–12; in coalition with Fox, 115–16, 122; Secretary of State, 116; and repairs to No. 10, 117; votes against reform, 119; mentioned, 120

North Briton, 71, 77–8

Northbrook, Lord, 305

Northcliffe, Lord, 346

Northcote, Sir Stafford (later Earl of Iddesleigh), 299, 301–2, 308

Norton, Mrs. Caroline, 236, 242–3

Norway, British expeditions to, 406

Nottingham Castle, burning of, 222

Nugent, Lord, 101

Nuri es-Said, 423

Nutting, Anthony, 425

Nyasaland, 313

O'Connell, Daniel, election of, 201, 206, 211; arrest of, 216; leads Irish Party, 226; demands repeal of Act of Union, 229; and Coercion Act, 230; supports Russell, 240; mentioned, 235

Oczakoff, 128

Okey, Colonel, 10, 19–20

Old Age Pensions, 336–7

Oliver, Alderman, 98–9

Omdurman, Battle of, 324

Orange Free State, 324

Orangemen, 348

Ord, Elizabeth, Creevey's letters to, 216, 225
Orford, Earl of – see Walpole, Sir Robert
Ormonde, Marquis, 16
O'Shea, Captain and Mrs., 313
Ottawa Conference (1932), 392
Overkirk, Lord and Lady, 32

Paine, Tom, 133, 164; *Rights of Man* of, 131
Pakistan, 415
Palmerston, 3rd Viscount, 258-9; Secretary at War, 184, 190, 259; in Wellington's Ministry, 200; in Grey's Ministry, 215, 219, 222; Foreign Secretary, 235, 254, 259; marriage of, 241, 260; dismissed, 255; asked to join Derby's Ministry, 256; Home Secretary under Aberdeen, 256; Ministries of, 257, 260-4; becomes Whig, 259; Queen's hostility to, 260; love affairs of, 260; offensive manner of, 263-4; defeated, 263; death of, 264-5; mentioned, 252, 266-7, 281
Palmerston, Viscountess (*née* Emily Lamb later Lady Cowper), 241, 258, 260
Pankhurst, Mrs., 333
Parliament, King's control of, 38, 88-9, 95, 119; distribution of seats in Stuart and Hanoverian, 38-9; expulsion of Walpole from, 40, 94*n*; abolition of three-year, 44; expulsion of Wilkes from, 94; publication of debates of, 97-100; Pitt's attempts at reform of, 118-19; burning of Houses of, 236; rebuilding of Houses of, 241; Victoria refuses to open, 274; five-yearly, 349*n*; first woman elected to, 362; first woman Cabinet Minister, 385; King's Party in (1936), 395-6. *See also* Commons, House of; Lords, House of
Parliament Bill and Act (1911), 340-2; Asquith prepares, 338-9; passed by Lords, 342; results of, 348, 349*n*; amendment to, 415
Parliamentary Reform, public demand for, 210-12, 219, 222, 224; Radical aims regarding, 226; secret ballot at elections, 277; Gladstone's Bills for, 298-9. *See also* Reform Bills
Parmoor, Lord, 371
Parnell, Charles Stewart, 296-7, 313
Passchendaele, Battle of, 355
Peacock, the, 21-2
Peel, Sir Robert, 190; Home Secretary, 183-4, 196; opposed to Catholic Emancipation, 184; resigns, 190; opposed to Parliamentary Reform, 200, 224; agrees to support Catholic Emancipation, 201-2, 224; police force of, 210; Wellington on, 221; in 1833 Parliament, 226; Wellington 'holds the fort' for, 237-8, Ministries of, 238-40, 246, 248; 'ultras' hostile to, 245; wishes to dismiss Queen's ladies, 246; family of, 269; Drummond killed in mistake for, 247-8; death of, 248; repeals Corn Law, 249-50; defeat and resignation of, 250, 251; re-introduces income tax, 273; mentioned, 220, 256, 303, 332
Peking, expedition to, 262
Pelham, Henry, 63-4
Pembroke, Earl of, 24
Peninsular War, 161-2, 166, 254
Penny post, 253
Pepys, Samuel, 15-17; quotations from Diary of, 20
'People's Budget', 337, 346
Perceval, Mrs. (*née* Wilson), 163-6, 173
Perceval, Spencer, 163-5; Under-Secretary for Foreign Affairs, 137; on Pitt and Addington, 142, 144-5; Foreign Secretary in Portland's Ministry, 159-61; in No. 10, 160, 165-6, 168; Prime Minister, 162, 166-70, 259; Regency Bill of, 168;

Perceval, Spencer – *cont.*
initiates searching of neutral ships, 169–70; murder of, 170–1; mentioned, 149*n*, 190, 193, 208
Persia, seizes Harat, 262
Peter, King of Yugoslavia, 412
Peters, Hugh, 11
Pheasant Court, 21
Philadelphia, 107–8
Phoenix Park murders, 297–8
Pickering, Sir Henry, 35
Pitt, Lady Harriet (later Eliot), 125, 136, 147
Pitt, Thomas, 269
Pitt, William (the Elder) – *see* Chatham, Earl of
Pitt, William (the Younger), 114–15; in No. 10, 113–14, 117–18, 142, 146; Chancellor of Exchequer, 114–16; refuses Premiership, 116; Reform Bills of, 119, 124; first Ministry of, 119–20; successful economic policy of, 121; attacked by roughs, 121; and Hastings, 122–3; and restrictions on power of Regent, 123; uses creation of new peers, 124; debts of, 125–6, 134, 155; character of, 125; country house of, 126; foreign policy of, 126–9; attitude of, to French Revolution, 129, 130–3, 142; assured position of, 130; raises money for war against France, 134–5, 150; Warden of Cinque Ports, 134; duel of, 135–6, 164; love affair of, 136; always ready to negotiate with France, 136–7; on object of war, 137; Irish policy of, 138–9; and Catholic Emancipation, 139, 141; resigns, 139, 143; loyalty of, to Addington Ministry, 141–2, 144; oratory of, 144; second Ministry of, 146, 149–53; failing health of, 146, 151; niece makes home with, 147–9; war policy of, 151–2; forms European alliance against Napoleon, 152; daily life of, 152–3; last speech of, 153; death of, 154–5; Grenville and,

157; on need for war of patriotism, 161; and Perceval, 164–5; and Vansittart, 172–3; and Canning, 187; and Aberdeen, 256; mentioned, 109, 158, 193, 198, 208, 214
Plural Voting Bill, 330–1
Poland, plea for reunification of, 177; German attack on, 404–5
Polish Corridor, 361
Political State, The, 97
Ponsonby, Arthur, 333
Ponsonby, General, Secretary to Queen Victoria, 299, 304–5, 320
Pope, Alexander, 55
Port Arthur, 324
Port Said, 293
Portland, Duchess of (*née* Lady Dorothy Cavendish), 160
Portland, 3rd Duke of, 159–60; in Rockingham's Government, 81, 160; first Ministry of, 116, 119; in No. 10, 116–17; brings Old Whigs over to Pitt, 133; against concessions to Catholics, 139; in Addington's Ministry, 141, 160; second Ministry of, 159–62, 165, 259; political influence of, 160; death of, 162; Perceval and, 166; mentioned, 193, 208–9
Portland, 4th Duke of, 190
Portugal, campaign in, 161; Napoleon and, 188; defence of, against Spain, 189. *See also* Peninsular War
Potter, Thomas, 77
Powell, Enoch, 427
Press, the, demand for liberty of, 79; Labour a Government without backing of, 371–2; Baldwin and, 393; and Abdication crisis, 395–6; and Munich crisis, 403; supports Conservatives, 417
Press gangs, 135
Pretenders: Old, 40–1; Young, 67–8, Pretoria, 326
Privy Garden, 4
Privy Steps, 2
Probyn, Dighton, 305

Proctor, William, 18
Property tax, 176
Prussia, Pitt forms alliance with, 127; and war with France, 131, 152, 178; subsidy for, 134
Public Worship Act, 281
Publick Advertiser, 93
Pulteney, William, 97
Puritans, restrictions on, 7
Pye, Sir Robert, 26
Pynsent, Sir William, 90, 114

Radical Party, 226, 270; members in Cabinet, 291, 299; opposed to Home Rule, 305
Railway, opening of Manchester–Liverpool, 212
Reading, Rufus Isaacs, Marquess of, 347, 357
Redistribution Bill, 298-9
Redmond, John, 253
Reform Act (1832), 225-6; (1867), 272
Reform Bills, Pitt's, 118-19, 124; Russell's, 200, 219; Grey's, 215, 219-26; Lords reject, 221-4; passed, 224-5; Gladstone's, 267-8, 271; Disraeli's, 271-2. *See also* Parliamentary Reform
Regency, arrangements for, 80, 123-4, 141, 168; Bill, 168
Religious tests, abolition of, in universities, 277
Representation of the People Act and Bill (1884), 298; (1918), 360
Rhodes, Cecil, 325
Rhodesia, North and South, 313
Rhodesia and Nyasaland, Federation of, 427
Richmond, 5th Duke of, 231
Richmond, 6th Duke of, 270
Rigby, Richard, 105
Rights of Man (Paine), 131, 133
Ripon, 1st Earl of – *see* Goderich, Viscount
Ripon, 1st Marquess of, 184, 305, 317, 331
Ritualism, control of, 280-1

Roberts, Field-Marshal Earl, 292, 326
Robinson, Frederick – *see* Goderich, Viscount
Robinson, John ('Prosperity'), 106, 110
Robinson, Mrs. Mary (Perdita), 122
Robinson, Sir Thomas (later Lord Grantham), 51
Rochester, Lord – *see* Somerset, Earl of
Rockingham, 1st Marquess of, 80
Rockingham, 2nd Marquess of, 80-1, first Ministry of, 81, 85, 160; refuses to serve under Pitt, 83; in Opposition, 95; second Ministry of, 113-15
Roman Catholics, excluded from Parliament, 55n, 200-1; easing of restrictions against, 110; Pitt's concessions to Irish, 138-9; feeling in England against, 139; question of emancipation of, 139, 141, 156, 159, 165, 184, 189, 201-4; emancipation of, 206; in universities, 277-8
Rome–Berlin Axis, 401
Romilly, Sir Samuel, 163
Rose, George, 143, 145
Rose and Crown, the, 48
Rose inn, 2
Rosebery, Countess of (*née* Hannah de Rothschild), 319
Rosebery, 5th Earl of, 319; on Wilmington, 62; on Pitt, 125, 151; supports Gladstone, 305-6; Foreign Secretary, 315; expects Gladstone's resignation, 317; Ministry of, 318, 319-22, 368; foreign policy of, 321-2; on Entente Cordiale, 350; mentioned 336
Rosenberg, Rose, 375
Rothermere, 1st Viscount, 393
Rothermere, 2nd Viscount, 396
Rothschild, Lionel, 282
Rothschild, Baron Mayer de, 319
Rothschild, James, 177-8
Rothschild, Nathan, 177-8, 182
Round Table Conference, First, 393
Rowton, Montagu Corry, Lord, 282

Royal Air Force, 358
Royal Irish Constabulary, 362
Ruhr, French evacuation of, 376
Rumania, 404
Russell, Lord John (later Earl Russell), 219, 254; Reform Bills of, 200, 211, 267–8; in charge of Parliamentary reform under Grey, 215, 219, 253; and Ireland, 230, 235, 255; and Tolpuddle Martyrs, 235; William IV's dislike of, 237; opposes Peel, 240; presses for reduction of corn tax, 249; Ministries of, 250, 251–5, 266–8; secretaries of, 250, 251–3, 372; family of, 253; in Aberdeen's Ministry, 256–7; criticizes Palmerston, 262; demands neutrality in American Civil War, 264; Foreign Minister, 266–7; retires, 270; mentioned, 190, 231
Russia, seizes Turkish Black Sea port, 128; in alliance against France, 152; at war with France, 178; at war with Turkey, 282–4, 287, 310; India threatened by, 288, 295–6, 322; ready to collaborate with Gladstone, 292; leases Port Arthur, 324; Germany declares war on, 350; Revolution in, 355; Communist menace in 361; British Expeditionary Force in N., 362; recognition of Soviet, and resumption of Trade, 376; question of loan to, 377; Hitler comes to terms with, 404; presents for Churchill from, 412

Sacheverell, Dr. Henry, 40
Sackville, Lord George – see Germain, Lord George.
St. George's Fields, Massacre of, 93
St. James's Palace, 5–6
St. James's Park, 28; fields on site of, 3; making of, 5; buildings abutting on, 23, 25, 34; peacocks in, 345; Prime Ministers walk in, 404, 416
St. John, Henry – see Bolingbroke, Viscount

St. Margaret's Westminster, 3, 5
St. Stephen's Chapel, 3
Salisbury, Robert Cecil, 1st Earl of, 302
Salisbury, 3rd Marquess of (Lord Cranborne), at Indian Office, 268, 280; opposes Reform, 271–2, 298–9; Disraeli's letter to, on High Church Ministers, 281; opposed to war on Russia, 284; Foreign Minister, 287, 323; first Ministry of, 301–4, 312; family of, 301–2; Gladstone offers to support, on Home Rule, 304–5; second Ministry of, 307, 308–14; on W. H. Smith, 311–12; expansionist imperial policy of, 311; Queen seeks advice of, 321; third Ministry of, 322–7; failing health of, 324, 326
Salisbury, 4th Marquess of, 341, 414, 420
Salisbury, 5th Marquess of, 426
Samuel, Sir Herbert (later Viscount), 346–7, 389–92
San Stefano, Treaty of, 287–8
Sandwich, 1st Earl of, 17
Sandwich, 4th Earl of, 70, 78–9, 101
Sandys, Samuel, 57, 62–3
Sankey, Lord, 390–1
Saratoga, Battle of, 107–8
Sassoon, Sir Philip, 400
Saxony, Elector of, 131
Scarlett, Sir James, 220
Schools, religious instruction in, 331
Schweitzer, Dr. Albert, 423
Scotland, Gladstone's speeches in, 288–9, 299
Scotland Yard, 2
Scott, Sir Walter, 192, 201
Scroop, John, 34
Sebastopol, capture of, 261
Sefton, Earl of, 210, 218
Selbourne, Lord, 305
Septennial Act, 44, 314, 349
Servia, 283; Austrian ultimatum to, 349
Seven Hours Act, 382
Seven Years War, 65, 67–8, 70, 74

Sèvres, Treaty of, 364
Seymour, Minnie, 165
Shaftesbury, 7th Earl of, 228
Shelburne, Earl of (later Marquess of Lansdowne), 81, 91, 113; Ministry of, 114-15, 180, 191n
Sheridan, Richard Brinsley, in Rockingham's Government, 113-14; opposes Pitt, 120, 135; and Hastings' impeachment, 122; on Grenville, 158; on retention of Perceval, 168; mentioned, 186
Siam, 322
Simon, Sir John, and German invasion of Belgium, 350; against conscription, 353; and General Strike, 382; Leader of National Liberals, 392; on Commission of Enquiry on Indian question, 393; Home Secretary, 396; Chancellor of Exchequer, 401
Simpson, Mrs. Wallis (later Duchess of Windsor), 394-6
Singapore, 427
Sinn Feiners, 362-3
Slavery and slave trade, limitation of, 124, 158, 169; abolition of, 227, 255
Smith, F. E. (later Lord Birkenhead), 341
Smith, W. H., 309-12
Smollet, Tobias, 48
Smuts, General Jan, 357, 412
Smyrna, 292
Snowden, Philip (later Viscount), Chancellor of Exchequer, 371, 385, 390; threatens to resign, 387-8; supports National Government, 390; goes to Lords, 391; resigns, 392
Soane, Sir John, 182, 386
Sons of Liberty, 76
'Souls, The', 312
South Africa, Union of, 330
South African War, 324-7, 336
South America, rebels against Spanish rule, 183, 189
South Sea Company, 42-3
Southey, Robert, 192
Spain, War with (1739), 56-7; in

Seven Years War, 68; seizes Falkland Islands, 96; joins America in war against Britain, 109-10, 115; claims Pacific coast of America, 128; given back colonies, 143; enters war against Britain (1804), 150; French troops take possession of, 161, 188; revolt of colonies of, 183, 189. See also Peninsular War
Spanish Civil War, 401
Spencer, 5th Earl, 299, 305
Stamfordham, Lord, 365, 371
Stamp Act, 75-6, 92, 103; repeal of, 82, 86
Stanhope, General James, 52
Stanhope, 3rd Earl (Lord Mahon), 109, 147-8
Stanhope, James, 154
Stanhope, Lady Catherine, 319
Stanhope, Lady Hester, 147-9, 154; on daily life of Pitt, 152-3; on Grenville, 157
Stanley, Edward – see Derby, 13th Earl of
Stanley, Lord – see Derby, 14th Earl of
Stapleton, Augustus, 192
Steel, nationalization of, 415, 420
Steele, Sir Richard, 54
Stephenson, W. H., 248
Stockmar, Baron, 244
Sudan, Mahdi rising in, 294-5; Kitchener's campaign in, 324
Suez Canal, Disraeli buys shares in, 281-2, 289n, 293; Nasser seizes, 423-4; fighting near, 425; lost to Britain, 426
Suffragette movement, 333-4, 338, 360
Sugar Act, 75-6
Sunday Referee, 403
Surrey, Earl of, 112
Sussex, Earl and Countess of, 31-2, 34
Suvarov, General, 133
Sweden, joins Napoleon, 188
Switzerland, France occupies, 144
Sydenham, Lord, 252
Sykes, Major-General Sir Frederick, 366
Sykes, Lady (née Isabel Law), 366

Talleyrand, Prince, 119, 177; at No. 10, 217-18

Tanganyika, 427

Tariff Reform, 327; Conservative answer to unemployment, 369, 383; result of election on, 370

Taylor, Sir Robert, 118

Tel-el-Kebir, Battle of, 293

Temple, Richard Grenville, Earl, and Wilkes, 77-8; wager of, 101; refuses office under Pitt, 120; mentioned, 157

Territorial Army, 332, 402

Thomas, J. H., 371, 388, 390

Thomas, M., French Minister of Munitions, 357

Thorneycroft, Peter, 427

Thrope, Robert, 18

Thurloe, John, 12-17

Thurlow, Edward (later Lord), Lord Chancellor, 90

Tierney, George, attacks Pitt, 135, 137; Pitt's duel with, 135-6, 164; opposes Vansittart, 176; in Canning's Ministry, 191

Times, The, attacks on Pitt in, 144-5; urges people to revolt, 224; on burning of Houses of Parliament 236; Lord Randolph Churchill announces resignation to, 310

Tolpuddle Martyrs, 235

Tomlinson, George, 415

'Tory democracy' of Churchill, 303

Tory Party, start of, 37-8; supports Old Pretender, 41-2, 67; comes into power with George III, 66-7; ends Seven Years War, 68; in 1782, 115; break up of, on appointment of Canning, 189-90; name Conservative being applied to, 226; overwhelming defeat of, 226; divided, 245; regards Disraeli as outsider, 269; opposed to extension of franchise, 298. See also Conservative Party

Townshend, Charles, 83-7, 88, 91, 102

Townshend, 2nd Viscount, 41, 83

Trades Disputes Bill and Act, 330, 382, 387

Trade Unions, Perceval and 169; formation of, 210; made illegal by Pitt, 227; rapid growth of, 235; safeguards to funds of, 330; co-operate in national insurance scheme, 346; contribute to Labour funds, 379

Trades Union Congress, and General Strike, 380-1; Civil Service trade unions to withdraw from, 382; opposes cuts in dole, 389

Trafalgar, Battle of, 151-2, 188, 239

Trafalgar Square, use by demonstrators, 336

Transvaal, annexation of, 289, 324; returned to Boers, 292, 325; Jameson Raid into, 323; Kruger's policy in, 325

Treasury Passage, 34

Trent, British mail ship, 264

Trevelyan, Sir George, 305-6

Trevor, Sir John, 26

Trinidad, 143

Trondheim, 406

Turkey, Russian designs on, 128; Egypt returned to, 143; Balkans rebel against, 282-3; Russia at war with, 284, 287; terms of Berlin Treaty regarding, 287-8, 292; dangers of war in (1922), 364

Uganda, 313

Ulm, Austrian defeat at, 152

Ulster, colonization of, 137-8; and Home Rule, 306, 348; rebellion threatening in, 348; excluded from Home Rule, 353; separation from rest of Ireland, 362-3

Ultra-Tories, 240, 245

Unemployment: in 1765, 76; due to American trade boycott, 91; due to War of Independence, 110; after Napoleonic War, 178; in 1820s, 183; in 1840s, 249; insurance scheme, 337; in 1920s, 363, 369,

376, 379, 383, 388; a world problem, 288; reductions in relief of, 388-9
United Nations, and Suez crisis, 424-6
United States, buys Louisiana from France, 144n; Britain at war with (1812), 169-70, 174-6; Britain on brink of war with, 264, 323; in First World War, 355, 358; loan to Britain from, during war, 367-8; agreement with, on naval construction, 387; economic slump in 388; Britain needing credits from 389; post-war loan of, 414; and Suez crisis, 424-5. *See also* American colonies
Universities, abolition of religious tests in, 277

Vanbrugh, John, 45
Vancouver, 128
Vansittart, Henry, 173, 175
Vansittart, Nicholas (later Lord Bexley), 173-9, 190; Budgets of, 175-6, 181
Vansittart, Robert, 174-5
Venezuelan Boundary question, 323
Versailles Peace Treaty, 361, 383
Victoria, Queen, Leopold and, 230; Melbourne and, 242-3, 244-6; appoints Albert's secretary, 244; admiration of, for Albert, 246; on death of Drummond, 248; Peel tenders resignation to, 251; disapproves of Palmerston, 254-5, 260; awards Garter to Palmerston, 261; worries about Indian Mutiny, 262; her attachment to Disraeli, 269, 280-1, 286-7; Gladstone's relations with, 273-7, 280, 291, 298-300, 304-5, 307, 314; her continued mourning for Albert, 273-6; secretaries of, 274-6; refuses to open Parliament, 274; unpopularity of, 276; letter of sympathy of, to Disraeli, 279; antipathy of, to High Churchmen, 280-1; Empress

of India, 282; urges war against Russia, 283-4, 287; anger of, against Gladstone, 292, 295; urges action in Sudan, 294; and Churchill's 'Tory democracy', 303; on Gladstone, 304, 314-15; W. H. Smith and, 311; angry at giving Heligoland to Kaiser, 313; Gladstone describes, 315; Gladstone's farewell to, 317-18; makes choice of Rosebery, 318, 320, 368; Rosebery suggests Lords reform to, 321; on South African War, 325; death of, 326, 371; mentioned, 421
Vienna, Congress of, 176-7

Waldegrave, Lady, 160
Walpole, Edward (grandfather), 36
Walpole, Edward (son), 51
Walpole, Horace, parentage of, 49; stepmother of, 51; at No. 10, 53; on end of father's office and leaving No. 10, 58-60, 62; on Bilson-Legge, 64; on Lady Dashwood, 70; on Grenville, 73-4; on Dowdeswell, 81; on Townshend, 85, 87; on George III and North, 89; on Portland, 160
Walpole, Horatio, 51-3
Walpole, Sir Hugh, 401
Walpole, Lady (*née* Catherine Shorter), 36, 49-51
Walpole, Lady (*née* Maria Skerrett), 51-2
Walpole, Lord, 51, 59
Walpole, Robert, 36
Walpole, Sir Robert (later Earl of Orford), 36-48, 49-60; enlarges No. 10, 33-4, 46-7, 118; first wife of, 36, 49-51; enters Parliament, 37; early career of, 37, 39-40; sent to Tower and expelled from Parliament, 40, 94n; Chancellor of Exchequer, 41-3; Ministry of, 43-5, 57-8; uses bribery, 44; lavish expenditure of, 45-7; daughters of, 51-2, 60; second wife of, 51-2; maintains peace, 54-5; battles with

Walpole, Sir Robert – *cont.*
Commons and Cabinet, 55–60, 73; forced into war, 56–8; accepts peerage, 60; gains support of Queen, 61–2; and Bilson-Legge, 64; concessions of, to American colonies, 75; on 1st Marquess of Rockingham, 80; week-ends of, at Richmond, 100; portrait of, 416; mentioned, 400–1
War Cabinet (1916), 354; (1939), 405–6; (1940), 406–7
Wardle, Colonel, 167
Warrant, general, 77–8, 99
Washington, British fire White House in, 176
Washington, George, 107, 217
Waterloo, Battle of, 176, 178
Watson, Mr. and Mrs. Lewis, 63–4
Watson-Wentworth, Thomas (later 1st Marquess of Rockingham), 80
Wavell, Field-Marshal Earl, 412
Wedderburn, Alexander, Solicitor-General, 90
Welfare State, 416
Wellesley, Marquess (Lord Mornington), friend of Pitt, 154, 198; on Grenville's marriage, 158; Foreign Secretary, 162, 169; Lord Lieutenant of Ireland, 184, 230; on Wellington's 'bold act of cowardice', 213
Wellesley, Sir Arthur – *see* Wellington, Duke of
Wellington, Duchess of (*née* Catherine Pakenham), 197, 207
Wellington, Arthur Wellesley, Duke of, 197–8; Chief Secretary for Ireland, 160–1; in Peninsular War, 161–2, 166, 169, 175; at Congress of Vienna, 178; Master-General of Ordnance, 184, 198; and Catholic emancipation, 184, 189, 201–6; opposed to Canning, 189, 191–3, 195; resigns on Canning's appointment, 190, 195; Prime Minister, 195–203, 206–9, 211–13, 234; mistress of, 198, 205, 207; in No. 10,

198–9; meets Nelson, 199; brooks no opposition, 200, 203; his manner with George IV, 202, 207; duel of, 204–5; appearance and personality of, 206–7; Lord Warden of the Cinque Ports, 207; seeks to strengthen his Ministry, 209; opposed to Parliamentary Reform, 211–13, 221–2; unpopularity of, 212–13; resignation of, 213; on Russell, 219; fails to form Ministry, 223–4; 'holds the fort' for Peel, 237–8; Foreign Secretary, 238; critical of Peel, 245; supports repeal of Corn Law, 250; mentioned, 240, 246, 255–6, 259
Wells, H. G., 361
Wesley, John, 107, 197
West, Sir Algernon, 317
West Indies, Federation of, 427
Westminster, Palace of, 3–4
Westminster Abbey, 2–3
Westminster Hall, 3–4, 40, 241
Westmorland, 10th Earl of, 139
Whalley, Colonel Edward, 26
Whig Party, start of, 37–8; controls Parliamentary boroughs, 38, 44; unpopularity of, 40; supports Hanoverian succession, 41; break in long period of influence, 67; persecuted by Bute, 68, 80; divided, 81, 115; split by French Revolution, 131, 133; Perceval's opposition to, 165; hopes to profit by Regency, 168; coalition between progressive Tories and, 190; call for Parliamentary Reform, 211; returns to power under Grey, 214; returned to power after passing of Reform Bill, 226; turned out by William IV, 239–40; Protectionists combine with, 250; attitude to Disraeli, 269; Liberals and, 270*n*
White Russian Cossack Choir, 383
Whitehall, Palace of, 4–6
Whitehall Gardens, 239, 280, 432
Wigram, Sir Clive (later Lord), 390*n*
Wilberforce, William, friend of Pitt,

119, 123, 126; works for abolition of slave trade, 124, 169, 227; estranged from Pitt, 133; joins in censure of Melville, 151

Wilhelm II, Kaiser, Heligoland offered to, 313; congratulates Kruger, 323; visits England, 333; demand for prosecution of, 360

Wilkes, John, member of Hell Fire Club, 70; attacks Bute, 71, 77; prosecution of, 77-9, 94; Townshend and, 84; elected to Parliament, 93-4, 100; takes himself to jail, 93; elected City alderman, 96-7; and publishing of Parliamentary reports, 98-9; enters Parliament, 100

Wilkinson, Ellen, 414-15

William, Prince of Orange, 13

William III, King, in house preceding No. 10, 31-2; Whig support for, 37, 39; mentioned, 40, 137

William IV, King, 209, 213; and Parliamentary Reform, 216-17; 222-4; life of, before accession, 217; prorogues Parliament in hurry, 219-20; asked to create new peers, 221-4; sends for Wellington, 223-4; attack on carriage of, 224, 236; and Melbourne, 234; offers Buckingham Palace as House of Parliament, 236; changes in, 236; dismisses his Ministers, 237-8; sends for Melbourne, 240-1; death of, 242

Williams, Francis (later Lord Francis-Williams), 416

Williams, John, 170

Willoughby de Broke, Lord, 341n

Wilmington, Earl of (Sir Spencer Compton), 61-2, 163

Wilson, Harold, 418

Wilson, Sir James, 163

Wilson, President Woodrow, 355, 361

Winchilsea, 10th Earl of, 203-6, 221

Windham, William, 140-1

Window tax, 28, 181

Windsor, Duke of (Prince of Wales, Edward VIII), 368, 387; abdication of, 394-6

Windsor Castle, 260

Winthrop, John, 7-9, 92

Winthrop, John (the younger), 9-10

Wolseley, Lord (Sir Garnet), 293, 295, 309

Wolsey, Cardinal, 2, 4

Women, agitation for votes for, 333-4; excluded from Albert Hall meeting, 338; given vote, 360, 383; first elected to Parliament, 362; first in Cabinet, 385; in Lords, 428

Wood, Sir Kingsley, 401

Wordsworth, William, 192

Workers' Weekly, The, 377

World War, First, 352-8; Haldane's reorganization of Army and, 332; outbreak of, 348-52; end of, 358-9

World War, Second, outbreak of, 404-5; 'phoney', 405; No. 10 in, 407-12; end of, 412

Wostenholme-Elmy, Mrs., 333

Wraxall, Sir Nathaniel, on Pitt, 125

Wren, Sir Christopher, 28

Wyndham, George (later 3rd Earl of Egremont), 234

Yarmouth, Countess of, 34

Yarmouth, Earl of, 161

York, Duke of, 145, 167, 184

York Place, 1-2

Yorktown, surrender at, 111

Zanzibar, 313

Zeppelins, 352

'Zinovieff letter', 377

Zulu War, 288-9, 324

UC